*In Joy
Still Felt*

IN JOY
STILL FELT

The Autobiography
of Isaac Asimov

1954–1978

Doubleday & Company, Inc., Garden City, New York
1980

The lyrics from "Fight Fiercely, Harvard," copyright © 1953 by Tom Lehrer, and "The Subway Song" by Tom Lehrer are reprinted by permission of the author.

ISBN: 0-385-15544-1
Library of Congress Catalog Card Number 79–3685

Contents

Introduction

I suppose it is quite unlikely that you will be buying this book unless you have already bought and read the autobiographical book that preceded it, *In Memory Yet Green* (Doubleday, 1979). Presumably, having read it, you found yourself interested and are curious to see what happens next, so that you now have this volume, *In Joy Still Felt*.

There is, however, no law of nature to this effect. You may not have read the first volume; you may not be able to get it on short notice; and you may wish, nevertheless, to read this second volume.

To take account of this possibility, I would like to supply a short synopsis of the first volume so that you don't have to start absolutely cold. (If you have indeed read the first volume, you can, of course, skip this introduction.)

I was born in Russia on January 2, 1920, the oldest child of two middle-class Jews. My father was Judah Asimov; my mother Anna Rachel Asimov, née Berman.

Considering that Russia had just gone through a world war and a revolution, my parents did not suffer unduly, but horror tales reached the outside world. My mother had an older half brother, Joseph Berman, in the United States. He wrote to find out how we were doing and offered to sponsor our emigration to the United States.

My parents decided to take advantage of the offer and in February 1923 they arrived in New York with myself and my younger sister. They found a small apartment in Brooklyn and settled down to an attempt to make a living.

I flourished in the new environment, taught myself to read at the age of five, entered the first grade before I was six, and was quickly pushed ahead by teachers who discovered I was unusually bright.

My father, meanwhile, unable to do much at ordinary jobs for which he lacked both experience and English, bought a candy store in 1926, and from that moment on, my life revolved about that candy store. It was open seven days a week and eighteen hours a day, so my father and mother had to take turns running it, and I had to pitch in, too.

Nevertheless, life progressed. My father became an American citizen in September 1928, and I became one automatically in consequence. I even gained a new sibling when my brother Stanley was born on July 25, 1929. By that time we had sold the candy store and bought a second, better one, but the stock market crashed that fall and like everyone else we found ourselves hanging on precariously. We never went hungry, but life was an adventure of counting pennies.

My schooling continued apace. I entered junior high school in 1930, high school in 1932, and Seth Low Junior College (a division of Columbia University) in September 1935.

Meanwhile, something new had entered my life. In 1929, I had discovered science-fiction magazines and, despite my father's general refusal to allow me to read magazines, I persuaded him to make those an exception. I became an ardent science-fiction fan and by 1931, I was beginning my first experimental scribblings.

In 1935, my writing efforts stepped up a notch when I persuaded my father to get me an old, secondhand typewriter. For some years, though, my writing continued to be a private matter between myself and that typewriter.

On January 1, 1938, I began to keep a diary and have kept it up ever since. A lucky thing, too, for 1938 turned out to be a particularly eventful year.

For one thing, I joined a science-fiction fan group called the "Futurians." One of its other members was Frederik Pohl.

Then, too, I finally managed to finish a story and on June 21, 1938, I actually took it in personally to *Astounding Science Fiction*, the leading magazine in the field. It was then that I met its editor, John W. Campbell, Jr., who was to have a greater influence on me than anyone but my father.

He rejected the story, but from then on I wrote regularly, taking in each story I wrote and accepting the rejections gladly since they were always accompanied by the most helpful discussions and letters. Finally, on October 21, 1938, I sold one of Campbell's rejections to *Amazing Stories*. It was published in the March 1939 issue of that magazine.

In 1939, I obtained my Bachelor of Science degree and entered Columbia University Graduate School, majoring in chemistry. Although I continued to do well at school, and continued to work in my father's candy store (by now he was in his fourth), I also continued to write furiously.

In 1940, I wrote the first of my positronic robots stories. Campbell rejected it, but Fred Pohl, who was now editor of two science-fiction magazines, accepted it.

In 1941, I published "Nightfall," which brought me at once into the magic circle of top-ranking science-fiction writers, and in 1942, I published the first of my Foundation stories.

By then, though, things in the outside world were changing rapidly. World War II had started in Europe soon after I entered graduate school, and the attack on Pearl Harbor brought the United States into the war on December 7, 1941.

I had just attained my M.A. when Pearl Harbor was bombed and was continuing toward my doctorate under the guidance of Professor Charles R. Dawson. It could not last long, though. The war emergency had its demands and in May 1942 I suspended my studies in order to take a position as a chemist with the U. S. Navy Yard at Philadelphia. Also working there were two other science-fiction writers and friends of mine, Robert A. Heinlein and L. Sprague de Camp.

It was the first time I had ever left home but the trauma was eased by the fact that I was deeply in love and was planning to get married. I had met Gertrude Blugerman on February 14, 1942, and we were married on July 26 of that year.

I spent the duration of the war at the Navy Yard, but immediately after V-J Day I was drafted. I entered the Army on November 1, 1945, but didn't stay long. Though for a few months I was as far afield as Hawaii, I was back in civilian life on July 26, 1946.

I went back to my research, obtained my Ph.D. in 1948, and accepted a post-doctorate assignment at Columbia under Robert C. Elderfield.

That only lasted a year. Then, through the influence of Professor William C. Boyd of Boston University School of Medicine (whose acquaintance I had made when he wrote me a fan letter while I was in the Army) I got a post as instructor in biochemistry at that institution. The head of the department was Professor Burnham S. Walker and I did research work on a grant administered by Professor Henry M. Lemon.

I had been writing science fiction all through the 1940s, even while I was in the Army. All my stories had sold except for one rather long one written in 1947 for *Startling Stories*. It had been rejected and I had retired it.

Fred Pohl persuaded me to submit it to Doubleday & Company, Inc., as the basis of a possible book. Walter I. Bradbury of that publishing firm agreed to use it after satisfactory revision. It was published on January 19, 1950, under the title of *Pebble in the Sky*, and it was my first book.

Later that year, my robot stories were collected under the title of *I, Robot* and plans were made for the collection of my Foundation stories in three books. I began writing additional novels.

Nor did I confine myself to fiction. William Boyd had spent some months in Egypt and when he returned he cast about for an interesting project and suggested I join him in writing a biochemistry textbook. Burnham Walker joined also and as we got to work I discovered that it was even more fun writing nonfiction than fiction.

While the textbook was in progress, Gertrude and I became the parents of a son, David, born on August 20, 1951.

Toward the end of 1951, I attained professorial rank, becoming assistant professor of biochemistry, and the next year the textbook, *Biochemistry and Human Metabolism*, was published.

The textbook was not entirely satisfactory to me since I had to be continually adjusting my style to suit those of Walker and Boyd. I ached to do a bit of non-fiction on my own and after considerable difficulty managed to publish a small book for teen-agers called *The Chemicals of Life* in 1954.

It was at this point that the first volume of my autobiography ended. I had reached mid-life, for I was approaching my thirty-fifth birthday, halfway to threescore and ten. I had reached what seemed to be the peak of the possible—and it wasn't enough.

In my professional career as a chemist, I had finally achieved professorial status, but my position was very low-paying and I didn't see that I could possibly advance either in remuneration or reputation very much beyond the point I had reached.

In my professional career as a writer, I had become a first-rank science-fiction writer as early as 1941, but even after more than a decade of constant success both in magazine short stories and in hard-cover novels, my earnings as a writer were very moderate, and I didn't see any possibility of increasing them further, or of gaining any reputation outside the constricted boundaries of science fiction.

I had, in short, reached a blank wall; a dead end.

And yet I managed to overleap the blank wall and burrow through the dead end and to reach both an income and a reputation which to me, in 1954, would have been inconceivable. The story of how I did this is contained in this second volume, which, if you wish, you may now begin.

In memory yet green, in joy still felt,
The scenes of life rise sharply into view.
We triumph, Time's disasters are undealt,
And while all else is old, the world is new.

ANON.

PART
I

Collision—and Out

1

Pregnancy Again

1

On July 1, 1954, my salary was still six thousand dollars per year, but it was entirely out of the school budget now and there was no obligation to teach student nurses. This was what I wanted and I was, for the time, satisfied.

My next ambition, though, was to be promoted to associate professor. It was only at the associate professor level, according to a book of university regulations that someone had given me, that tenure was obtained. With tenure, one could be fired only for cause—and cause was not easy to get. With associate professorship, therefore, I would finally have job security.

It might seem strange that I should want job security or attach any importance to it when I already made considerably more money through my writing than at my job—but it made sense. I could write with greater ease and peace if my rear were secure; if I didn't have to spend time and nervous energy justifying my actions; if I could fulfill my teaching duties and spend all the rest of the time (some 80 per cent of the whole) doing exactly as I pleased, protected by tenure.

Then, too, what if my writing sagged, diminished, dwindled? It didn't seem likely, but what if it did? It would be nice to have a school salary, a secure one, to fall back on.

And this struck me as important since, that July, my wife, Gertrude, was wondering if she were pregnant again. She had thought she might be in 1952 but that had proved a false alarm. Now the question arose once more.

It was conceivable, of course. After the birth of David, we had taken no particular precautions against conception. It had seemed to me that since it had taken us years to have one child, we were not likely to find lightning striking twice.

Yet Gertrude, having been through the process once, could recognize the symptoms and was finally sufficiently suspicious to undergo a test. On July 30, we had the results—positive! Another child was on the way.

It meant we were faced with a housing problem again. The coming of my son David had made the Somerville attic apartment untenable, and the coming of a new child would make the Waltham apartment untenable. That was regrettable. We had been living at 265 Lowell Street in fair contentment even longer than we had lived in Wingate Hall, and our search for a house had dwindled and faded. Even our party-line telephone, a perennial irritant, had finally been changed into a private line on April 29, 1954. Now even I, who hated change, had to admit it wouldn't do, and our search for a house was reluctantly reactivated.

2

Copies of the second edition of *Biochemistry and Human Metabolism* arrived on July 6, 1954. It had taken almost as long to do the second as the first. Revising and adding was a meticulous job and the proofing and indexing had to be done all over again, as though for a brand-new book.

I was under no illusions that it would do better than the first edition, but it certainly looked better and *was* better, and I was already collecting references for the third edition.

3

For some months, I had been hearing occasionally from David White, a professor at the main campus of the university, that Al Capp, the famous originator of the comic strip "Li'l Abner," had read my books and would like to meet me. I said I would be delighted to meet him, but for a while nothing happened.

Then, on July 10, 1954, Al Capp called me and invited us to dinner and to a showing of Arthur Miller's *The Crucible* at an open-air theater in Wellesley.

We were flattered out of our skulls and accepted very readily. It was all perfect, too. Excellent meal and excellent company. We found Al just as pleasant and as witty as we expected he would be, and Mrs. Capp was sweet and friendly. We even enjoyed the play.

What I remember most clearly about the evening, however, was that I fell prey to the vile temptation of haughtiness. As I was heading up the stairs at play intermission to visit the men's room, someone who was a technician at the med school and who knew me, stopped me and said, "Say, isn't that Al Capp with you?"

"That's right," I said.

The technician then said, "What's he doing with *you?*"

I thought that the stress on the final word indicated that a science-fiction writer represented a stratum too far below that of cartoonist to make the association anything but a *mésalliance*, so I said, haughtily, "He's a fan of mine, so I thought I'd give him a chance to enjoy my company," and went off.

It was a terrible thing to say, even though it was true, after a fashion.

<h2 style="text-align:center">4</h2>

On July 11, I drove to New York myself and the next day picked up my royalty check at Doubleday. It came to forty-four hundred dollars, the largest single royalty check I had ever received (or check of any kind). Every one of my six Doubleday books was selling reasonably well, and Brad seemed very pleased with me. And I was delighted to be pleasing him.

I also visited Horace Gold, editor of *Galaxy*, who had been writing to me and urging me to send him stories. I was growing increasingly reluctant to submit stories knowing it would mean I would also have to submit to a rough-tongued rejection, but I tried.

I gave him a story I had written that I called "A Hundred Million Dreams at Once," and which was not in my usual style at all. It was about a day in the life of an old movie-producer, who, in the story, was a producer of "dreamies"—reveries transmitted directly from the dreamer's brain to the listener's. And it ended with some sad words about the life of a dreamer, which could be applied without alteration to the life of any artist, certainly any writer.

While I was there, Horace showed me an advance copy of a science-fiction magazine called *Imagination*, in which I had never appeared and to which I had never submitted, even though some thirty issues had already been published.

Imagination had a reviewer named Henry Bott, whom I had never met and of whom I knew nothing except for his reviews. Bott didn't like my books. In fact, he *hated* them, and he seemed at a loss for words to explain how much he hated them and how little he thought of me as a writer.

Some months before he had reviewed *Second Foundation* and had done it with sufficient snide cruelty to infuriate me. I do not, at any time, accept criticism of my stories with noticeable grace; but had I been a saint, his snottiness would have broken through the barriers.

Nevertheless, I managed to suppress my anger. It seemed to me that what Bott disliked about *Second Foundation* was its Galactic Empire vistas, which were to be found in all my books up to that time except for *I, Robot*.

Well, this was a legitimate dislike and there were others who disliked it, too, although others expressed themselves with far greater decency. Anthony Boucher, editor of *Fantasy and Science Fiction*, didn't like the Foundation series, for instance, and the science-fiction writer George O. Smith, in his review of *The Currents of Space*, said, in urging me to adopt a narrower background, "Come back, Isaac, all is forgiven."

That was one reason I had written *The Caves of Steel* as I did. In *The Caves of Steel* I did not wander all over the Galaxy or across the generations. *The Caves of Steel* had only one arena of action, New York City, and that action covered a period of exactly sixty hours. It was an excellent example of a near-approach to the Aristotelian unities.

It seemed to me that even Bott would like *The Caves of Steel*. That seemed all the more likely because ever since publication of the book the comments and reviews had been uniformly favorable.

Well, then, when Horace handed me the new *Imagination*, it was to show me Bott's review of *The Caves of Steel*. I could scarcely believe my eyes. It was even more violently and unnecessarily insulting than his review of *Second Foundation* had been. It was, in fact, a deliberate baiting of me. He even remarked that I had once again wandered all over the Galaxy, and that made it clear to me that he hadn't bothered to waste his time reading the book—or even the flap copy.

I was almost out of my mind with fury and for nights afterward I stayed awake writing letters in my mind to this Bott. It was all I could do to hold onto enough sanity to realize that it would be useless and even counterproductive to do so. The only sensible action was to ignore him as beneath contempt.

As for Gold, he rejected "A Hundred Million Dreams at Once" the next day.

5

I had dinner with the Ballantines that next day, too. They were very kind to me, as they always were, but I got the impression they weren't doing as well as they had hoped to be doing. I listened with sympathy, but couldn't help think of the time, three years before, when Fred Pohl had tried to persuade me to ditch Doubleday for Ballantine.

6

I had by now published five articles in the *Journal of Chemical Education*. All were trivial, but amusing. The fifth was entitled "Potentialities of Protein Isomerism," and it appeared in the March 1954 issue of the magazine. It dealt with the number of possible ways in which the amino acids in various protein molecules could be lined up. The possibilities were absolutely flabbergasting, since the 539 amino acids in the horse hemoglobin molecule could be arranged in a number of different ways equal to a 4 followed by 619 zeroes.

It occurred to me that this was amazing enough to be of science-fictional interest, and, after all, the *JCE* did not pay for an article, while *Astounding* would.

I therefore wrote up my protein isomerism article in an entirely different style and shape, made it 5,000 words long, entitled it "Hemoglobin and the Universe," and sent it off to Campbell on July 19, 1954. He accepted it and paid me $150 for it.

My thiotimoline articles were fiction pieces written in nonfiction style. "Hemoglobin and the Universe" was the first true nonfiction article I had ever sold to a science-fiction magazine.

It excited me enormously. Writing nonfiction for the science-fiction audience meant I did not have to keep either my science or my vocabulary to the early teen-age level, as in *The Chemicals of Life*, nor did I have to adopt the stylized turgidity of a textbook. In "Hemoglobin and the Universe" I wrote about science in a friendly, bouncy way, and I could tell at once I had come home. That was the way I *wanted* to write nonfiction, and from then on I sought out every possible opportunity to do so. Not only friendly and bouncy but, even more so, *personal*.

7

Bott wasn't the only source of overwhelming irritation for me at this time. On July 27, 1954, I picked up the August 1954 *Popular Science* because a neighbor had called it to my attention. It contained an article on science fiction by the well-known science writer John Lear.

I read it with a certain amount of amused contempt, since Lear was apparently a holdover from the Gernsback era and wanted science-fiction stories to contain more didactic science.

My amusement came to a sudden end when, to show how poor contemporary science-fiction stories were, he quoted a recent one-paragraph review of a science-fiction novel in the New York *Times* and said, "What can the author of this novel possibly know of the scientific method?"[1]

Only a fool would judge the quality of a novel on the basis of a one-paragraph review, and I was quite ready to dismiss Lear as a fool and would have, except for the fact that the review happened to be of *The Caves of Steel* and it was *me* whom he was accusing of an ignorance of the scientific method.

I was too fresh from my anger over Bott to be willing to take this lying down. I went home and wrote a letter to Lear in care of *Popular Science*. It was angry and insulting and, after I read it, I tore it up. I often do this when I am impelled by emotion to write an angry and insulting letter. I write it to get it out of my system, place it in an envelope, and put a stamp on it to show that I am seriously intending to mail it. I then tear it up and write a far milder and more reasonable letter.

This time, in the case of Lear, it didn't work. Having written the letter and torn it up, I found that when I wrote the second it was even angrier and more insulting than the first. I therefore gave up and mailed the second letter.

I did not get an answer.

I eventually visited the offices of *Popular Science* during a New York visit in order to find out if the letter had indeed been forwarded, and I told the editor, Volta Torrey, exactly what I thought of the article. I did it very eloquently, too. Mr. Torrey was conciliatory and assured me he had forwarded the letter.

But I never got an answer.

To this day I have never met John Lear. I have read his science writing on occasion and always admire it. He knows science and he can write about science (what's true is true), but I still long to tell him to his face that he is a jackass.

8

Since "The Evitable Conflict," I had not written a positronic robot short story, just as since "—And Now You Don't" I had not written a Foundation story. It was as though the publication of *I, Robot* and the Foundation books had frozen both series and had brought them to an end.

[1] I don't have the article before me, since it was torn into a thousand pieces shortly after I read it, so I can't guarantee that the quote is letter perfect, but that is what he said.

In the case of the Foundation series, that was so, but not in the case of the positronic robots. There, the logjam broke on July 18, 1954, after a five-year hiatus, and I began "Risk," a positronic robot story that was the sequel of "Little Lost Robot." "Risk" dealt with the discovery of a method of interstellar travel and was the only robot story I ever wrote in which no robot has a speaking part.

I mailed it to Campbell on August 3, and he wanted a fairly extensive revision, with which request I complied, so that I eventually sold it to him on September 13.

Since then I have continued to write robot stories now and then. In fact, of all my science-fiction shorts, I enjoy my robot stories most. I almost feel as though I have the patent on the robots. When other writers produce robot stories in which the robots follow the Three Laws (though no one is allowed to quote them except myself), I feel benign about it. When, however, some other writer dares have his robots defy and disobey the Three Laws, I can't help but feel it is a case of patent infringement.

9

At just about this time, I wrote my most important scientific paper, one that, all by itself, justifies my scientific career.

Despite my sale of "Hemoglobin and the Universe," I did not totally abandon the *JCE*, for which I wrote another small paper, entitled "The Radioactivity of the Human Body."

In it, I discussed the radioactive atoms that occurred naturally in the human body and pointed out that by far the most important of these and the one that was absolutely bound to have crucial effects upon the body was carbon-14.

As far as I knew at the time, this was the first occasion on which anyone had pointed out the importance of carbon-14 in this respect. It was an original idea of mine, although I believe Willard Libby, the Nobel Prize-winning specialist in carbon-14, may have had the idea at the same time.

I sent off the article on August 13, 1954, and it was published in the February 1955 issue of the *Journal of Chemical Education*.

Nearly four years later, Linus Pauling published a paper in the November 14, 1958, *Science* that discussed the dangers of carbon-14 in a careful and systematic way.

I'm sure Pauling's article played its part in the eventual agreement on the part of the three chief nuclear powers to suspend atmospheric testing, for Pauling was one of the most prominent and influential critics of such tests, and he used the production of carbon-14 in such tests as one of its chief long-term dangers.

I do not in any way want to dispute priorities with Pauling. I merely had an idea, which I did not develop. Pauling developed it thoroughly on the basis of the work done by Libby.

Still, I did work up the courage to send Pauling a reprint of my *JCE* article by way of a mutual friend, carefully stating that I was not disputing priorities.

Pauling was kind enough to send me the following letter, dated February 11, 1959:

> Dear Professor Asimov:
>
> I am pleased that Mr. William Kaufmann should have sent on to me the copy of your carbon-14 paper that appeared in the *Journal of Chemical Education* four years ago. I now remember that I had read that paper when it appeared (I always read the *Journal of Chemical Education*) but I had forgotten about it, except that without doubt the principal argument remained in my mind. I am sorry that I did not mention it in the carbon-14 paper that I published recently, a copy of which is enclosed.
>
> Sincerely yours,
> s/ Linus Pauling /s

I don't want to arrogate to myself too much importance, of course, but I think it is fair to say that I may indeed have influenced Professor Pauling, and that through him I therefore played a very small part in bringing about the nuclear-test ban—and I'm delighted.

10

In August, I received an invitation to write an article for *Peon*, a fan magazine. I receive invitations of this sort often; so does every other science-fiction writer. Fan magazines are produced by eager fans and exist, literally, in the hundreds. All but a very few are evanescent and exist only a few issues before the time and the costs become insupportable.

I have no theoretical objection to writing an occasional piece for love, but I have always steered clear of the fan magazines. There are so many that to write for one will mark you down as a target for the others and you will be nibbled to death.

On this occasion, though, the offer came when I was still experiencing mental agonies over Bott's review of *The Caves of Steel*. I realized I could not write an angry letter to a reviewer without being marked as a sorehead, but *Peon*, it seemed to me, would be just the so-lution. It had a circulation that was surely less than a hundred, so only a handful of people would see what I would write, and yet I would safely get the poison out of my system.

I therefore wrote an article on Bott, without naming him. It was a very reasonable article in my opinion (I have just this moment reread it to make sure), and I did not answer in kind. I merely asked for fair re-viewing that did not involve personal invective, unfair statements, and clear evidence that the critic had not read the book. In particular, I ob-jected to Bott's statement that I "was neither a writer nor a story-teller"; that was ridiculous.

Yet it proved to be a terrible mistake, for which my ignorance was responsible.

Though I had been an almost lifelong reader of science fiction, though I had written letters to magazines, though I had even involved myself with the Futurians, I had never really immersed myself in what was called "fandom."

I had no experience whatever with the ferocious single-mindedness with which that handful of people lived their science fiction. They in-terpreted literally the catch phrase among us that "Fandom is a way of life."

Whatever such enthusiasts could earn in their work they invested in their collections, or in their fan magazines. Their time was entirely devoted to their correspondence and to their meetings. Often, in fact, their fan activities crowded out the basis on which it was all founded—for they were so busy being fans of science fiction, they lacked the time to read science fiction.

Fans knew each other, loved each other, hated each other, quar-reled with each other, formed cliques and threatened lawsuits, and, in short, formed a small subculture to which everything else in the world seemed alien and of no account.

News spread through the world of fandom at the speed of light, even though it might never so much as touch the world outside. Any controversy involving science fiction or the fan world elicited a joyful response at once as a vast number of fans (well, dozens anyway) plunged into the fray—on either side, it didn't matter which.

And there I was, foolishly unaware of what I was doing in writing my article. *Peon* might be only a fan magazine, but it was, at the time, one of the more important ones, and its readership included many ac-tive fans and writers. No one had any trouble in understanding who it was I was talking about, even though I called him only "The Nameless One." *Imagination* got a copy of the fan magazine, of course, and I imagine a number of readers sent theirs along, for fear the editor, William Hamling, would not see it, and out of a sheer pleasure in making mischief.

So while I sat at home, pleased with what I had written, pleased I had gotten rid of my bile in a gentlemanly way and that I was no longer staying up part of each night fuming, editorial artillery was being cranked up and trained on me.

11

On August 20, 1954, David was three years old and it looked as though that would be his last birthday as an only child. He was playing outdoors on his own, could ride a tricycle with skill, and had a fairly large vocabulary beginning with a firm, loud, "No!"

12

As far as my writing was concerned at this time, I was deep in the novel version of "The End of Eternity" (which, in its original novelette form, had been rejected everywhere).

Lillian McClintock of Abelard-Schuman proved she was indeed interested in my books by going back to Henry Schuman's original idea of a popular version of William Boyd's *Genetics and the Races of Man*. She suggested that I write it but that it appear as a Boyd and Asimov collaboration. I agreed, got Bill's permission, and, on August 17, 1954, began it.

I called it *Genes and Races* at first, a clear shortening of Boyd's title, but eventually Lyle Boyd, Bill's wife, suggested *Races and People*, and that proved the title finally adopted.

On August 28, I received the October 1954 *F & SF* containing "The Foundation of S.F. Success."[2]

13

Gertrude's pregnancy was continuing, but was occupying our attention far less than it did the first time. Not only was the second pregnancy automatically less suspenseful than the first, but the real agony came in house-hunting. We were getting nowhere. We had an upper limit that we were willing to spend on a house, and for that money we couldn't get anything that would suit us.

[2] See *Earth Is Room Enough*.

I wanted to raise our financial sights based on the notion that my writing earnings would continue high, but Gertrude was generally more cautious than I (or less grandiose), and for a while we continued to hope we could find what we wanted at eighteen thousand dollars.

On August 31, Gertrude awoke with cramps, and while we were worrying about a possible miscarriage, Hurricane Carol hit. Those were the days before weather satellites, and the weather bureau never had anything but the most general notions as to the existence and whereabouts of hurricanes, depending largely on reports from ships that were caught in them (and ships did their best not to be caught in them).

As a result, no one was prepared, and if they had been, it would have made very little difference.

Down went the trees, taking the power lines with them, and our electricity went off at noon. Under the stress of the emergency, Gertrude's cramps ceased at once.

The loss of power was exciting at first, simply because it was so different. In some ways it wasn't bad. It was still late summer, so we required no heat. David was no longer a baby and could do with makeshift meals, and the new baby was still safely in the womb.

However, we lived in an all-electric house and without power, there were no lights, no cooking facilities, and no hot water—and the power stayed off for five days!

The whole thing quickly lost the charm of novelty when I found I had to take cold sponge baths in the morning, that I could not watch television, that I had to play cards by candlelight, that I had to either eat out in restaurants that had gas stoves, or eat cold food at home. Fortunately, my typewriter was not electrified, so that I could still work on *The End of Eternity* in the daytime hours at least.

The power went on at 9:20 A.M. on September 5.

On September 11, however, a second storm, Hurricane Edna, hit. There was less wind this time, but more rain, and at 4:15 P.M., off went the power again. Gertrude was just putting spareribs in the oven when it went dead.

It was much harder to take this time (like being reinducted into the Army), and we spent a sixth night with candles. The next morning, even the phone went dead, and in absolute despair, we packed up our spareribs, took them over to the Boyds (who had a gas stove), and cooked them there. They turned out to be the best spareribs I ever ate.

When we came back we found the power on again. It had been off only twenty hours this time. The phone stayed off for two more days, however.

14

On September 27, 1954, I received a check for $332.50 from Campbell in payment for "Risk," and the importance of that was that it brought my year's writing earnings to past the $10,000 mark. It was unprecedented. It was awesome. I was thunderstruck.

However, I did not think I was very likely ever to do it again. I wrote in my diary, "I just said to Gertrude that 1954 will probably be my peak year of all time. The s.f. bust is bound to catch up with me next year."

By the "s.f. bust" I meant that the proliferation of science-fiction magazines that had begun in 1949 was petering out, with many failures. It would clearly become harder to sell stories, and payment rates might decline.

But at present things were going well. In fact, I had just received a signal honor. The thirteenth annual World Science Fiction convention was to be held in Cleveland over the Labor Day weekend in 1955, and on October 2, 1954, I received a bid to be the guest of honor there.

It was the highest accolade in science fiction, and I accepted. I believe I was the youngest guest of honor up to that point (one last gasp of child-prodigyism).

Two days later, advance copies of *The Chemicals of Life* arrived. It was the first of my nonfiction books for the general public, and after three years of trying, I finally had my popular biochemistry book in my hand.

And on October 8, Tony Boucher bought "A Hundred Million Dreams at Once."

15

I maintained my friendship with Bill Boyd's assistant, Bernie Pitt, even after he was fired, of course, and one day at his place, he put a record on just as I was supposed to go home, and I listened in puzzlement as someone sang something called "Fight Fiercely, Harvard." It began:

> *Fight fiercely, Harvard, fight, fight, fight,*
> *Demonstrate to them our skill.*
> *Albeit they possess the might,*
> *Nonetheless, we have the will.*

Halfway through I gathered that it was not meant seriously and I begged Bernie to start all over. He did and I listened to the whole record, both sides, and got home an hour late.

The singer was the clever satirist Tom Lehrer, and I have been an ardent Lehrer fan ever since.

On October 9, 1954, I took the Boyds to a nightclub in Boston where Tom Lehrer was performing and I saw him in real life, toothy, wavy-haired, and very charming. He sang all the songs I knew and a number I didn't yet know, including two that I have never heard at any other time but that one occasion.

In one, he sang very cleverly about Jim getting it from Louise and Sally from Jim; and after a while you gathered the "it" to be venereal disease. Suddenly, as the combinations grew more grotesque, you realized he was satirizing every perversion known to mankind without using a single naughty phrase. It was clearly unsingable (in those days) outside a nightclub.

The other one was useless for general distribution because it dealt with the Boston subway system. He made use of the subway stations leading into town from Harvard. They were Harvard, Central Square, Kendall, Charles, Park Street, and Washington. The song, heard only that once, burned itself into my mind, and here it is, to the tune of the famous Mother's Day song.

> *H is for my alma mater, Harvard.*
> *C is Central, next stop on the line,*
> *K is for the cozy Kendall Station, and*
> *C is Charles that overlooks the brine.*
> *P is Park Street, busy Boston center,*
> *W is Washington, you see,*
> *Put them all together, they spell HCKC-PW*
> *Which is just about what Boston means to me.*

And what killed me was that when he came to HCKC-PW, he pronounced it quite well enough by clearing his throat and pretending to spit.

I haven't gone to nightclubs often, but of all the times I have gone, it was on this occasion that I had by far the best time.

16

On October 22, I drove to New York to attend a local convention. I met Tony Boucher for the first time, round-faced and with sharp, dark eyes. I also attended a Mystery Writers of America cocktail party

and felt at home. After all, *The Caves of Steel* was a real mystery even
if it was science fiction.

17

On November 2, I voted in the congressional elections; straight
Democratic, of course. I discovered that one could watch even a com-
puterized election night on television with pleasure—provided your
own side won. The Democrats took over both houses of Congress.

18

I was learning that to a writer, all is useful raw material. I had
gone through a student-nurse textbook of chemistry, and two editions
of a medical-student textbook of biochemistry, and was working desul-
torily on a third edition of the latter. The experience, looking back on
it, had been a dreary one, but it had its comic parts, and it could be
made interesting to a science-fiction audience. I began an article for
Campbell, therefore, that I called "The Sound of Panting." (That was
the sound that resulted from trying to keep up with the literature.)

Meanwhile, the January 1955 issue of *F & SF* arrived with "The
Singing Bell"[3] in it, and I received a paperback edition of *The Stars,
Like Dust—*, published by Ace.

Ace had changed the title of *The Stars, Like Dust—* to *The Rebellious Stars*, which I felt was sharp practice. I couldn't help but think
it was an attempt to lure readers into buying it under the impression
they had not read it before. That struck me as doubly bad, since not
only would the reader be cheated, but I felt that his resentment would
be aimed not at the publisher but at the author. I therefore began reading it in a bad humor.[4]

My bad humor quickly intensified. There were places where I simply didn't follow my own novel! I checked with the hard-cover and
found, to my annoyance, that whole paragraphs had been omitted here
and there. I knew what had happened. At the last minute they found
the novel was too long and they cut it. Only instead of cutting it carefully by words and sentences, they hastily amputated chunks.

Well, you can't do that to my stories. Whatever faults my novels

---

[3] See *Asimov's Mysteries* (Doubleday, 1968).
[4] I always read my stories after they appear in print, even today. In the early days,
when less of my material was flooding the market, I even reread my books when
they appeared in paperback.

may have, they are not spongy. Every paragraph contributes to the plot, and if you cut out any, you reduce the story to gibberish.

Worse yet, the cover said, "Complete and Unabridged," so that readers would think the gibberish was my fault.

I called Brad in high dudgeon, complained about the title change and the idiot amputation. I asked Brad to face the Ace people with this and to be less ready to give them reprint rights. Brad *did* complain to them and in no uncertain terms, and for many years Ace was last on the list in the bidding.[5]

In those days, Don Wollheim was science-fiction editor for Ace, and I finally got a letter of apology from him. Well, it was not exactly a letter of apology, for Don didn't apologize. It was more a letter of complaint. He said rather bitterly that it was the first case he had ever heard of where an author read his own novels in paperback reprint.

I suppose he meant that it showed an unlovely conceit on my part, a rather disgusting self-absorption. I replied that if more authors read their Ace reprints, Ace might go out of business.

19

On December 12, I drove to New York and spent the next day passing out manuscripts. I handed *The End of Eternity* to Brad and to Horace; "The Sound of Panting" to Campbell; and *Chemistry and Human Health* to McGraw-Hill.

Trouble started at once with *The End of Eternity*. It turned out that even if Gold approved and didn't throw my schedule into an uproar by demanding revisions, he couldn't publish for a year. The pages in *Galaxy* had been cut from 160 to 144, and that meant his story backlog filled that many more issues. Brad didn't want to delay publication of the novel version that long, and neither did I. Since it turned out that Campbell was overstocked on novels as well, we had to face the possibility of publishing *The End of Eternity* without prior serialization.

It meant the loss of a couple of thousand dollars, not something to take with a light laugh, but I consoled myself with the thought that the book version might sell more if it weren't already familiar through serialization.

[5] Eventually we made up. Nowadays, Ace does a number of my books, and I am very satisfied with them. You can bet they don't fool around with either titles or contents.

20

On December 14, I drove back to Boston, although the weather bureau was sounding notes of doom. It would have been sensible to wait another day, but I had a luncheon appointment with a number of faculty members, including Lemon and Walker, for that day, and I felt I had to make it.

So I got up at 4:45 A.M. and left at 5:45 A.M. It was dark and it was raining hard, the highways were crowded even at that hour, and the weather bureau kept interrupting the programs on the car radio to warn sepulchrally of death and destruction.

By the time I got into Connecticut, the rain was very cold; and by the time I got into Massachusetts, it was an ice storm. My windshield wipers froze and wouldn't work; I had to move along slowly and carefully, and forty miles from home I was held up for half an hour by someone else's accident.

I had planned to get home early enough to wash, shave, change clothes, and arrive at school in fine fettle. After all, there were three people from the main campus due to be there, and, on top of that, Dr. Charles Keefer from the Department of Medicine.

I had seen Keefer now and then but had never spoken to him. He had a close-cropped mass of curly gray hair, a round, unsmiling countenance, and a soft voice. He was considered the med school's most distinguished faculty member.

Boyd disliked him. According to Bill, Keefer was overbearing, tyrannical, and sadistic. Also according to Bill, Walker didn't like him either, but Walker was not much of a talker, and he never went into detail.

What with the ice storm and the delays, I didn't get home till 11:30 A.M., and after the sketchiest of preparations, I dashed right off to school. I didn't even stop to shave.

I didn't manage to get to the luncheon conference in time, but I was only fifteen minutes late, after an enormously difficult trip from New York. I didn't feel particularly disgraced.

Everyone else was there when I burst in. It was either bore everyone with explanations or carry it off with a flair. I decided to attempt the latter.

"All right, everyone," I said, "you can begin now. I'm here."

I was grinning and unshaven, and it didn't go over at all. There was a dead silence, and I caught Keefer's eye. He looked icy. That may have been his first clear impression of me. If so, it was a rotten one.

21

The Winter 1955 issue of *Thrilling Wonder* reached me on December 20, 1954, and it contained "The Portable Star."

I reread it, and now that my initial enthusiasm of writing had died down, I was forced, with chagrin, to agree with Fred Pohl's unfavorable assessment of the story. I thought it was awful.

I am frequently asked which is my favorite story, but no one ever asks me which is my least favorite story. If you stop to think of it, you might suppose it was "Black Friar of the Flame" or some other one of my very early stories. Well, that's not so, I may have turned out some stinkers to begin with, but that doesn't bother me—they were the best I could do.

It is "The Portable Star" that I like the least and that I am even ashamed of. I wasn't aware of what I was doing when I wrote it, but on reading it after it was published it seemed to me that I was deliberately trying to put sex into it to try to keep up with a new trend.

In the August 1952 *Startling*, you see, Phil Farmer had published "The Lovers," which overnight catapulted him into science-fiction stardom. It had treated sex more openly than was customary in science fiction, and everyone started getting into the act. In "The Portable Star," I did, too, and I did it sleazily.

For that reason, I have never put the story into any of my collections, and I never will. Nor have I ever allowed anyone to anthologize it. In fact, the only time it ever appeared, except in that issue of *Thrilling Wonder*, was when, ten years later, Standard Magazines, the publishers, exercised their right to reprint it, and did so in a one-shot magazine called *A Treasury of Great Science Fiction Stories*. Needless to say, they didn't consult me or ask my permission.

22

The Christmas season was very active, with one excellent turkey dinner at the Whipples' on the twenty-fourth, and a second elsewhere on the twenty-fifth.

Add to that the fact that my father called on December 24 to tell us that Marcia was engaged to a man named Nicholas Repanes. My father was a little worried because Nick was not Jewish but was Greek Orthodox (though nonobservant). He suggested the possibility of forbidding the marriage.

I was rarely disrespectful to my father, but I was this time. At least I was, if you consider an explosive, "Are you crazy, Pappa?" disrespectful.

I said, "Marcia has a right to live her own life. Don't you dare interfere."

So he didn't, and thank goodness for that. Nick, a tall, rather slow-moving and soft-spoken person, turned out to be patient, gentle, affectionate, and exactly what Marcia needed.

23

On December 28, 1954, the affair of Bott and his review of *The Caves of Steel* suddenly sprang to life. I had totally forgotten my article in *Peon*. It had served its purpose in lancing the boil, and that was that as far as I was concerned.

But Bill Hamling was now counterattacking. He sent me a copy of the editorial he was going to run in the March 1955 *Imagination*, in which he took me to task as a sorehead and as someone who was trying to limit Bott's freedom of speech. Having raked me over the coals unmercifully, he wrote to ask me politely if I wanted to answer the editorial. He would give me the space for it.

I was more furious than ever now, but heavy-hearted. I saw that I had foolishly stepped into a trap. It was clear to me now that Bott's stupid reviews had been deliberately designed to elicit just such a response as I had made. I was all the more chagrined because I imagined Bott and Hamling must have gone over a list of authors to see which one would be stupid enough to take the bait. They must have decided on me, and I had not disappointed them. Now Hamling was pushing for a continuing feud that would titillate the fans and boost the sales of his magazine.

It seemed therefore that the only thing I could do was to come back with a "No comment." My rational article in a magazine with a circulation of one hundred was going to be answered by invective before an audience of fifty thousand, but I had no recourse. Anything I did would make it worse. I had to let it go.

It took a while before I could make myself swallow the humiliation, and while I tried to nerve myself to the task I came across the February 1955 *Imagination* on December 30. I bought it out of sheer curiosity to see what Bott was doing now. To my utter astonishment the review that month was of *Lucky Starr and the Oceans of Venus* by Paul French.

It was quite an amiable review. To be sure, Bott explained, French didn't turn out juveniles as good as Heinlein's, but it was quite good just the same. Considerably above average, one gathered.

Apparently, Isaac Asimov might be neither a writer nor a story-teller, but Paul French was both—and thus the Lord delivered Bott and Hamling into my hands.

I whipped off a letter at once, in which I apologized for my unkind thoughts concerning Bott. He was quite obviously a gentle soul who liked authors and was willing to help them. He might not like Asimov's writing, but he did like French's, and that showed his discrimination, for clearly one writer was bound to be better than another.

I went on and on as long as I thought I could carry the game and then ended with the final comment that, by the way, Paul French *was* Isaac Asimov, and Bott liked Asimov stories after all if he didn't know Asimov wrote them.

It was absolutely devastating, and Hamling was forced to run it along with his editorial. He tried to say that Bott *did* know French and Asimov were the same but that space considerations had forced the excision of that sentence. That excuse was so lame that I'm sure it increased the laughter at Bott's expense.

In any case, the feud died at once and I got out of it with a whole skin and a learned lesson.

24

I had three books published in 1954.[6] They were:

11. *The Caves of Steel* (Doubleday)
12. *Lucky Starr and the Oceans of Venus* (Doubleday)
13. *The Chemicals of Life* (Abelard-Schuman)

By all rights, I should have included the second edition of *Biochemistry and Human Metabolism*. It took more work and more time than *The Chemicals of Life*, for instance.

In 1954, of course, I had, as yet, no inkling that the time was to come when what was most interesting about me as a writer was the number of books I had done. In later years, I kept that in mind and listed every book that I could honestly manage to. I didn't list trifling revisions or updatings of this book or that. Nor did I list old books in which the only changes were a new book-jacket or a new title. However, whenever a revision was sufficiently thoroughgoing to compare in time and effort to the writing of a new book, I included it in the list.

[6] In *In Memory Yet Green*, I listed my published books each year including all ten that had been published between 1950 and 1953 inclusive. For the record, I am continuing the practice in this volume beginning with 1954 and Book ⌗11.

I was tempted for a while to begin a new numbering in this autobiography and to include the second edition of the text so that I would have four books in 1954 and fourteen altogether by the end of the year. However, the numbering system has already been fixed in print in a number of places and I can't upset it now without confusion—so let it go.

My school earnings in 1954 reached a record high of $6,000, but my writing earnings also reached a record high of $11,500. I was making almost twice as much writing as teaching, and my total income was $17,500. It seemed more than ever important to me to raise our financial sights in our house-hunting and to be prepared to shell out more money, and I persuaded Gertrude to consider houses that were being offered for sale at as much as $30,000.

25

On January 2, 1955, I was thirty-five years old, and that was a rather sad birthday for me. I woke to realize that I was now old enough to qualify for the presidency (were I but native-born). If three score and ten is considered the traditional stretch of the human lifespan, then my life was half over.

Gertrude had insisted we invite Ted and Marilyn Kalin for dinner that night, and I had agreed. They had been friends of ours for years. Ted was a handsome young man, quick-witted and good-humored, and Marilyn was a little on the silent side but very good-looking. We both liked them both.

However, they were not as timebound as I was, and when they called at 8 P.M. to tell us their car wouldn't start and for me to come over and get them, I was a little annoyed.

I said to Gertrude, with my hand over the mouthpiece, "Let's call it off. I hate that sort of slipshoddery."

Gertrude, however, insisted quite firmly that I go get them. I was surprised because it was very cold and the streets were not in good condition and she wasn't the kind to send me out in bad weather. Sure enough, when I tried to start the car, it wouldn't, so I came up and said, "Oh, the hell with it."

But Gertrude, still oddly insistent, asked our landlord (who sold second-hand cars, as I recall) to start it and he managed to succeed in doing so. Off I went to the Kalins' with poor grace. When I got there, the Kalins weren't ready and I grew sarcastic in my comments. Ted got annoyed in his turn, but kept insisting there were things they had to do. Then there was a phone call they had to make and *then* they were ready to go.

By the time I brought them back I was in good humor again, and as we walked up the back stairs, I was telling them in a loud voice about *l'affaire Bott.* Then I opened the door and fell silent, for the apartment was full of people.

Gertrude had arranged a surprise birthday party.

Many people believed that I wasn't really surprised.

"Oh, yes, he was," said Ted. "He was all ready to knock me down when I kept delaying things in order to make sure all the guests arrived before he came back."

"And he never had an inkling?"

"Of course not," said Gertrude. "I sent him out to do the shopping for this party and he came back with three of everything and never suspected."

"Didn't he say anything?"

"Sure," said Gertrude. "He said, 'What are you doing? Buying up stuff for a party?' "

"Then he had to suspect."

"No, he didn't," said Gertrude. "I said, 'No, there's no party,' and he just looked confused and went off to write something."

"Even though his birthday was coming?"

"Oh, well," said Gertrude, "that would mean he would have to put two and two together, and unless he's at his typewriter, he never can."

I listened to this whole conversation, which was carried on as though I weren't there. Everyone was quite convinced I was stupid, and there was a gallon or two of condescending laughter from all sides.

I would have liked to protest, but everything Gertrude said was absolutely true, and what the heck, I never pretended to worldly wisdom. Besides, it's more fun to be surprised, so who needs worldly wisdom? I just shut up, sat back, and enjoyed the party.

26

It was about this time that, through the good offices of Abe Burack, editor of *The Writer,* I met Ben Benson. He was about ten years older than I was and had been badly wounded in World War II. While he was recovering (he had never entirely recovered and was still somewhat disabled), Abe Burack encouraged him to try his hand at writing, and he had done very well.

He wrote murder mysteries—police procedurals, to be exact—in-

volving the Massachusetts State Police. I took to reading his books after
I had met him and I enjoyed them.

We got along well. He teased me good-naturedly about the steadi-
ness of my output. He also urged me to get an agent. He pushed pretty
hard, but I was impervious.

He (like Heinlein) was particularly pleased with his own agent
and pushed him particularly. The only hard-and-fast example, however,
of what his agent could do was the fact that he got twenty-four free
copies of his novels for distribution, instead of the twelve I got.

I couldn't see very much advantage in twelve extra copies that I
could buy at author's discount if I simply had to have them, and I was
also unshaken by his point that agents could squeeze publishers harder
and more effectively than authors could. My point was that I suspected
publishers to be like cats: They purred when they were stroked and
scratched when they were squeezed.

I intended to continue stroking, and I did, and I think I was right.

Certainly, my writing continued to move smoothly. I managed to
sell "The Last Trump," after six rejections, to a relatively new magazine, *Fantastic Universe* (edited by my old friend Hans Santesson) on
January 10, 1955, and on January 18, I got the February 1955 *Astounding* with "Hemoglobin and the Universe"[7] in it.

27

Now that *The End of Eternity* was in press, I rather regretted that
the day of easy books seemed to be over. After all, the four Gnome
Press books *I, Robot* and the three Foundation books, did not have to
be written; they had been written years before. They only had to be
put together and smoothed out a little.

Was there any way I could put together more?

Not in the same way. *I, Robot* consisted of nine connected stories;
and the Foundation books consisted of nine connected stories. I had no
more connected stories.

I could, of course, put together unconnected stories; simply have a
book of short pieces. Such collections, I had been told, were death at
the box office, and didn't sell. Still, there was no charge for asking, so I
asked Brad on January 16.

Rather to my surprise, Brad agreed to take the chance. I had pro-
posed that I put together my stories "The Martian Way," "The Deep,"
"Youth," and "Sucker Bait" in a book to be called *The Martian
Way and Other Stories*, and Brad was willing to have that done.

My Doubleday books were obviously continuing to sell well

---

[7] See *Only a Trillion* (Abelard-Schuman, 1957).

enough to make even a collection of unconnected short stories look palatable if my name were on them.

It made me regret that I had not held back on my robot stories and Foundation stories until now, because it was clear to me that if I had asked in 1955 instead of in 1950, Brad would have been delighted to do *I, Robot* and the three Foundation books. Then I would not have to be waiting while Marty Greenberg slowly dribbled out money in twenty-five-dollar amounts.

But then, one has no chart to the future. You must make your decisions on the spot as best you can.

28

There was an administrative blow at the medical school. Dean Faulkner resigned as of the end of the school year. Walker was dourly depressed over it, predicting that either Keefer or some Keefer satellite would be the new dean.

I had no cause for delight, either. My few contacts with Dean Faulkner had been happy ones. He knew my peculiarities and didn't seem to mind much. I was wary of Keefer, and if it turned out to be someone from the outside, who could tell how palatable (or unpalatable) I might be to him.

And yet I didn't see that a new dean could do me much harm. I felt I could depend on Walker to stand between me and the storm, if only to protect the third edition of the textbook.

2

Robyn

During the early morning hours of February 17, 1955, Gertrude decided she might be going into labor soon. There was no point in taking chances, so I had her in Beth Israel Hospital by 1 P.M., where her obstetrician this time was a Dr. Factor.

Mary Blugerman, my mother-in-law, got the news and took the 1 P.M. train, arriving at our apartment at 6 P.M.

I visited Gertrude during the evening visiting hours and found time hanging heavily on her hands. I wasn't exactly relaxed either, but I had always wanted to have a daughter, and since we already had a son, the need for a daughter seemed desperate. I said, "It's got to be a girl. If it isn't a girl, don't come home."

She smiled wanly.

I visited her again on the eighteenth, but there was no sign of labor. Then, at 5 A.M. on the morning of February 19, 1955, Factor called me. When the labor did come, it was hard but quick, and the result *was* a girl. I rushed in with Mary, and later in the evening, Henry arrived, and I took him in, too.

When I finally saw Gertrude, she was not exactly happy. The labor had come so fast that there had been no time to anesthetize her.

The new baby weighed only four pounds fourteen ounces, but she was perfectly shaped.

The question was what to name her. I had suggested Amy or Alice because I liked both names, but Gertrude and Mary voted them down.

Gertrude spent some time going through a book of names and came up with Robin. I pointed out that it was an epicene name, used for boys as well as girls, so Gertrude suggested spelling it differently.

"Robinne?" I said, and spelled it. Gertrude shook her head. That would invariably be accented on the second syllable, and I agreed.

"Robyn?" I asked. "With a 'y'?"

And Robyn it was. It did occur to us that she might not like the name Robyn if she turned out to be an unrobinlike girl, so we decided to give her as plain a middle name as possible so that she might always turn to that. Her name therefore became Robyn Joan Asimov—but it turned out all right. She loved Robyn and has used it all her life.

I call her Robbie, and some people suggest that I named her after the robot in the first of my positronic robot stories, but no such thing! That is simply a coincidence. Her friends, I believe, call her Rob.

2

Gertrude had a semiprivate room at the hospital, and in the other bed was a pleasant woman who had also had a daughter on February 19. Hers had been by Caesarian birth, and Gertrude warned me not to make her laugh, because laughing would contract the muscles of her abdomen and cause her pain.

I did my best, but I'm only human. I said to her, "Do you know why they call it a Caesarian birth?"

She said innocently, "No?" (Actually, it's so called because Julius Caesar was supposed to have been born in that fashion.)

And I said, making cutting gestures with my fingers, "Because they cut you with seezairs."

And she said, "Ha, ha—ouch—ha, ha—ouch—ha, ha—ouch—"

3

As Robyn was born, *Thrilling Wonder Stories* died. The two are not comparable, of course, but I felt a twinge when I got the news from my friend Sprague de Camp on February 23 that the last issue of the magazine was on the stands.

Thrilling Wonder was the descendant of *Wonder Stories*, which was, in turn, the descendant of *Science Wonder Stories*, which, twenty-six years before, was the magazine that my father gave me permission to read—and that started me on my science-fiction career.

4

Gertrude came home on the twenty-fourth, but Robyn, who had still not reached the five-pound mark, remained at the hospital till March 5. On that day, we went to the hospital, got her, and drove her home through a sleet storm, safely.

Before I brought her home, I rearranged my writing office. David's room was what I had originally used as my office on moving into the Waltham apartment. After it had been turned over to David, I had used the bedroom, but now Robyn would be moving into that. I there-

fore moved my desk and filing cabinet into the central hall that surrounded the staircase.

It was a tight fit and totally inadequate, but it would have to do.
The trouble was that despite the fact that we had looked for a house
pretty steadily for some eight months, we had not found one, and now,
with a brand-new baby, we weren't going to have a chance to look for
one in the immediate future. We were stuck with the apartment for a
while and we were going to be crowded.

Once Robyn came back to the house, it was once again formula
time and diaper time and night-feeding time. The second time around
lacked the excitement of novelty.

Mary left on March 6, and my mother arrived on the seventh.
What with the help of the mothers and our own greater experience, we
needed no nurse this time. On the eleventh, my mother left and we
were finally on our own.

5

On March 6, 1955, the New York *Post* reprinted my story "Flies."
It was the first time a piece of fiction of mine had appeared in a newspaper.

In a newspaper, it was more accessible to the general public than
in a magazine, and some people who had only heard that I was a writer
received their first actual evidence of the matter on this occasion.

An elderly neighbor of Gertrude's mother greeted the event with
great excitement. "I saw your story in the New York *Post*," she said to
me when she saw me on one of my visits to New York. "What an
achievement! How much did you get for it?"

"Twenty-five dollars," I said.

"Twenty-five dollars! That's peanuts!" she said, and turned away in
contempt.

It is easy, apparently, to find out the precise value of an achievement: You just determine how much money it has brought in.

6

On March 20, 1955, Robyn was a month old. She weighed over
seven pounds now and we were no longer afraid she would break if we
lifted her. She was a more eager feeder than David had been, but also
threw up more readily. She would give us no warning, nor show any
sign of distress; she just opened her mouth and gave it back.

David was as interested in his little sister as you would expect, and seemed delighted with her. He showed no signs of jealousy then or ever. He could speak fluently now (though it had seemed to us for a while he was slow in starting). On April 10, I took him for a long walk and finally he said, "I am very tired."

I picked him up and he said, "This is much easier. God bless you."

As for myself, I was *so* pleased to have a girl, and yet unexpected complications showed up. Whereas I had always been ready to un-diaper, clean, and rediaper David, I found myself oddly hesitant in Robyn's case and would find ways of wishing the job on Gertrude whenever I could.

Robyn had a birthmark, a strawberry mark on one buttock. When we took her from the hospital, a nurse pointed it out and assured us it would be neither dangerous nor troublesome and would probably respond to treatment.

"Don't worry," I said. "In its location, no one will ever see it but we three and her numerous boyfriends."

The nurse was shocked and said I shouldn't talk about the poor little thing that way.

We kept watching the mark and it grew larger as she did, but eventually, on her pediatrician's advice (Dr. Joseph Lewis), we had it subjected to X-ray treatment on May 23. One treatment was enough. The strawberry mark faded steadily and was finally merely a slightly raised bit of surface that was completely unnoticeable.

7

The June 1955 *Fantastic Universe* arrived on April 6, with "The Last Trump."[1]

More important was my progress in nonfiction. The success of "Hemoglobin and the Universe" and "The Sound of Panting" had made it seem logical to me to write nonfiction articles for *Astounding* periodically. I did one, for instance, on paper chromatography, which was not an easy subject to handle for a general audience (though the *Astounding* audience was by no means entirely general).

I called the article "Victory on Paper," and on April 6, Campbell took it and paid four cents a word, just as he would have for a story.

To be sure, the time spent on writing a nonfiction article could not be spent on writing a story, so that my nonfiction had to appear at the expense of my fiction. This did not bother me, however. In the first place, nonfiction pieces went much faster than fiction, so that not as much time was lost as one might think. Another and much more im-

[1] See *Earth Is Room Enough*.

portant justification for my switch in emphasis was that I wanted to. I simply loved writing articles and books on science.

In fact, having completed *Races and People*, I was now working on another book for the same young audience. It was on nuclear physics this time and I called it *Inside the Atom.*

The May 1955 *Astounding* contained my story "Risk,"[2] and the June 1955 *Astounding* contained my article "The Sound of Panting."[3]

8

On April 16, after having made a routine visit to New York, I brought back both Henry and my father. It was my father's first chance to see Robyn, and the grandparents took turns in holding her. My father was fifty-eight years old and Henry fifty-nine, and in each case Robyn was the second grandchild and the first granddaughter.

Robyn cried more than David used to at an equivalent age, but on the other hand, she slept through the night at an earlier stage, and that was very welcome to us. What's more, Robyn showed no signs of the milk allergy that had plagued David when he was two months old, and we were thankful for that also.

9

Advance copies of *The Martian Way and Other Stories* reached me on May 12. On the spine of the book, my name was spelled Isaac Azimov.

My name is often misspelled. The first name comes out Issac a considerable fraction of the time, and that "z" in my last name is as frequent. More exotic misspellings also occur sometimes.

I make it my business to complain each time. I have a strong sense of personal identity, and my name is me. Besides, once I became a writer, I realized that literary and financial success depended, at least in part, on the recognition level of my name, and any misspelling would tend to diffuse that.

This was the only time that my name was misspelled on one of my own books. It was misspelled only on the spine, though, for it was correctly spelled on the book jacket and on the title page. Nevertheless, I wrote to Doubleday at once to make sure that the mistake was corrected on all future printings and editions. This was done.

I was pleased with the result, aside from the misspelling, by the

[2] See *The Rest of the Robots.*
[3] See *Only a Trillion.*

way. It had been very easy to do a short-story collection, and it appeared quickly, too. It appeared before *The End of Eternity* did, even though the latter had been contracted for over a year earlier.

10

On the day *The Martian Way and Other Stories* appeared, something else took place that pleased me even more. Walker's secretary handed me an envelope without comment, and when I opened it, I found a notice that I was promoted to associate professor of biochemistry as of July 1, 1955.

I was delighted. I had not pushed for it, and Walker hadn't said anything about it, but now that I had it I felt that a turning point in my career had come. An associate professorship gave me tenure, and my position and salary at the school were now assured.

That was enormously different from what my situation had been when I had arrived at the med school six years before, when either Lemon or Walker could have fired me out of hand, or when any failure of renewal of the grant would have left me without a job, as with Elderfield.

Looking back on it now, I feel quite sure that Walker had pushed through the promotion while Dean Faulkner was still in office. Walker must have felt that no such promotion would be approved after Faulkner was gone, and he was right, for on June 3 it was announced that Chester Keefer would be the new dean.

11

On May 14, 1955, I received a card from my old college friend Sidney Cohen. He had an office on upper Park Avenue now, and he was married!

And on May 21, 1955, Marcia also was married and became Mrs. Nicholas Repanes. It was a very quiet wedding day, and with a three-month-old baby on our hands we could not make the trip to New York to attend.

12

Robyn was a much quieter baby than David had been. David had laughed and gurgled and made random sounds from an early age, but Robyn, when she wasn't crying, lay there quietly and at peace—which was fine except that we would have welcomed some indication she was making contact with the universe.

It was welcome news, therefore, when, on May 16, she produced a feeble little laugh, her first, when I was tickling her ribs. It was Gertrude's birthday, too, so that it was a sort of birthday present.

13

On June 3, we went to New York, trying this time to drive in the evening to avoid the heat of the day. The experiment was a flop. It was indeed cooler and the children gave no trouble, but we arrived at 1:15 A.M. and I was fatigued to death.

On June 5, Gertrude, her brother John, and I made our ritualistic walk along the boardwalk at Coney Island, and the next two days I made my rounds. I took in the manuscript of the fourth juvenile, *Lucky Starr and the Big Sun of Mercury,* to Margaret Loesser.

14

Gertrude seemed annoyed with me in the course of this visit. Two small children and the matter of house-hunting had got her down, and when I left for Boston alone on June 8, she wouldn't say good-bye to me.

I drove home, thinking the unthinkable for the first time. Our thirteenth anniversary was coming up and I was thinking that our marriage was a failure.

In all those years I had not made her happy and I didn't see how I could make her happy in the future. I could see my faults.[4] I was self-centered and wrapped up in my writing. I didn't like to travel or do those things most people consider "having a good time." I wasn't handy around the house. I lacked the worldly-wise knack of knowing how to find the perfect house, how to make clever investments, how to finance things on expense accounts, and so on.

But what was the use of seeing those faults? There was no way I could change them. I could not make a silk purse out of the sow's ear of my character. So I thought, for the first time, of separation and even of divorce. But how could that be? Even if I could bring myself to leave Gertrude (which was doubtful), could I leave the children?

I could feel myself beginning to drop into the life of "quiet desper-

---

[4] There were faults on both sides, to be sure, but I am not an impartial witness, and it would not be fair to Gertrude to have me discuss her faults when she has no soapbox on which to stage a rebuttal. Her good points were numerous and she was, in many ways, an excellent wife. I'll discuss my own faults only, those that I can see—and there may be many I stubbornly refuse to see.

ation" that Henry Thoreau spoke of, and saw a vicious cycle intensifying. Clearly, the more I found myself unable to make Gertrude happy, and unable to live with her unhappiness, the more I would seek my writing as a refuge, and the more I would intensify the situation that helped create her unhappiness.

The next weekend I drove to New York again, stayed a couple of days, and drove back with the family this time. Gertrude seemed more cheerful, so I was relieved and my own spirits rebounded. On the other hand, Gertrude also kept thinking of divorce now and then, for she occasionally mentioned it as a possibly desirable way out. (I noted one such case in my diary entry for August 7, 1955.)

We drifted along. There were good times and happy times, but the thought of separation and divorce would recur, now and then, to one or the other of us.

15

Between these two visits to New York, the August 1955 *If* appeared with "Franchise."[5] Coming up in the near future was the September 1955 *Astounding*, with "Victory on Paper,"[6] and the October 1955 *F & SF*, with "The Talking Stone,"[7] the second of my Wendell Urth mysteries.

16

On June 27, 1955, David, now nearly four years old, went off to spend his first day at a summer day camp, Meadowbrook. It was not, on the whole, a successful experiment.

David was always self-willed and could never bend or compromise to suit others. And if he could not have his way, he grew angry and would not co-operate. Nor would he engage in rough-and-tumble. To put it briefly, he had trouble getting along with his peers.

I could sympathize, for as nearly as I could remember my own childhood at that age (and older) I, too, had difficulty getting along with my peers.

17

On July 1, 1955, I was officially Dr. Isaac Asimov, associate professor of biochemistry. On that same day, Chester Keefer was officially

[5] See *Earth Is Room Enough.*
[6] See *Only a Trillion.*
[7] See *Asimov's Mysteries.*

dean or, rather, director, which was the higher title. Under him was Lamar Soutter, who fulfilled the narrower duties of deanship. Soutter was a pleasant person with old-fashioned eyeglasses and an unassuming air. I liked him from the start.

As for Keefer, I couldn't forget Bill Boyd's dislike of him, and Walker's forebodings concerning him—and the icy glance Keefer had given me that time I walked in late to the luncheon meeting.

What's more, Keefer had been head of the Department of Medicine, and Lemon was a member of that department. Lemon was therefore a close associate of Keefer and had, I believe, influence over him. I was quite aware that Lemon did not have a particularly warm regard for me, especially since I was no longer connected with him in any way, and he knew that that had come about through my wish. I did not expect his influence, therefore, to be exerted in my favor.

Fortunately, Walker had been farsighted enough to get me my associate professorship in time. I had tenure, and what could anyone do to me? At least, that was my feeling at the time.

I was aware, of course, that I didn't fit in to the close-knit and highly specialized academic community. I had never fit in from my earliest days in graduate school. I was never single-minded enough about my chemistry, and I was never sufficiently aware of the subtle nuances of the do's and don'ts of academic life.

I was too loud, too boisterous, too indifferent, too nondeferential, too self-satisfied. Just as I never remembered the names of my parents' customers or thought to greet them pleasantly when I met them on the street, so I never remembered the names of most of the faculty or remembered my place in the pecking order.

All this is not said as a kind of self-praise for my independence. I recognize it now (indeed, I recognized it at the time) as a source of trouble and annoyance for everyone around me. My not fitting in made me a piece of grit in the smoothly oiled functioning of a watch mechanism.

I was a danger to no one, to be sure. I was not pushing for promotion, or salary, or power, but even the fact that I wasn't was an annoyance, since it implied an indifference to that which others found important, and an indication that I found importance lying elsewhere—which meant in my writing. I didn't flaunt my growing success there, but neither did I hide it.

All in all, I expected trouble and, in my more soberly self-evaluative moments, even felt I probably deserved some. I just didn't care. My attitude was a semicontemptuous, "What can they do to me?"

3

House-hunting

1

We took advantage of David's absence during much of the day-light hours to begin house-hunting again, and we spent all the summer at it.

It was, however, once again, one of those really hot summers that would come to plague us at particularly crucial periods. July 1955 was the hottest in the Boston Weather Bureau's records. Tempers were short, discomforts great. Furthermore, though David was out of the way, we had to take Robyn with us wherever we went, and she was generally just as uncomfortable in the hot weather as we were, and she kept telling us about it in the only way a baby can.

One house was a near-miss. It was put on the block by a couple who were getting a divorce, and it seemed to be almost good enough and almost cheap enough. Gertrude held back, partly because it was a fearful decision to make, and partly because Robyn was crying badly. We left, discussed the matter, convinced ourselves that we ought to (maybe) buy it, came back timorously—and found it had been snapped up by someone else.

That resolved our doubts about the house. We were sure we should have bought it, and were chagrined and unhappy over our failure to do so.

2

On July 22, I received a letter from Stanley telling me that he was virtually engaged to a divorcee with an eight-year-old son. On the thirty-first, Stanley was passing through Boston on his way to Annisquam and he stopped at our place. With him was Ruth, the young woman with whom he was in love.

She was a pleasant girl, with a ready smile, dark hair, and an unaffected way of talking. She had a slight stammer.

Apparently she was a science-fiction fan, and on first meeting Stanley, and having been introduced to him, she asked him what, in

our family, we call The Question. That is: "Pardon me, but are you related in any way to Isaac Asimov?"

Stanley, who is the most patient and good-natured fellow in the
world, takes the question with enormous goodwill (much more so than
I would, were the situation reversed), but he had to admit that having
it asked by a pretty girl in whom he took an instant interest was hard to
take. Fortunately, he survived the shock and decided fairly quickly that
this was the girl for him.

The most interesting occurrence of The Question, by the way,
took place about now in New York. (I don't know the exact date because I learned of the incident only long afterward from my mother,
and she didn't remember the statistics.)

After my parents sold the candy store, my mother decided to go to
night school and learn how to write. She knew, of course, how to write
Yiddish perfectly and Russian just as perfectly, but neither used the
Latin script. She had to learn that to write English.

She learned quickly and in a very short time was able to send me
short letters in painstakingly formed English writing. One of the
teachers at the night school finally nerved himself to ask The Question.

"Pardon me, Mrs. Asimov," he said, stopping her in the hall, "are
you by any chance a relation of Isaac Asimov?"

My mother, who was four feet, ten inches tall, drew herself up to
her full height and said, proudly, "Yes. He is my dear son."

"Aha," said the teacher, "no wonder you are such a good writer."

"I beg your pardon," said my mother, freezingly, "no wonder *he* is
such a good writer."

3

The heat continued into August without letup. We were driven to
even small expedients. As I said in my diary for August 2, "I just got
David a real short haircut. Gertrude sent me out saying, 'Short' and
greeted me when I came back with 'Not that short.'"

The heat was accompanied by a very severe polio epidemic in the
Boston area—the last such epidemic to take place, as it happened, for
the Salk vaccine had just been developed—and that kept us in a state
of terror, too.

4

On August 3, I received my advance copy of *The End of Eternity*.
The first thing I did was to check the spine. My name was correctly
spelled.

A few days later I received the news that *Planet Stories* had ceased publication. That induced a nostalgic sigh. I had not dealt much with it; my only published story with them was "Black Friar of the Flame," but they took that when no one else would. Now it was gone.

On August 10, I did some calculating from my records and found that in 17 years of writing, I had sold about 1,250,000 words of fiction. This was roughly 75,000 words a year, which wasn't bad, considering that in those years I had to work in the candy store, in the Navy Yard, in med school, get my degrees, serve in the Army, and have a wife and two children.

5

When John Campbell accepted an item, he did so with a check. When he rejected one, however, he would (if the author were an important and regular contributor) do so with a long letter. Sometimes it was an unclear letter as he talked endlessly of whatever pet notions he was pushing at the time. This habit of his intensified in the postdianetics years.

Thus I had written an article entitled "The Abnormality of Being Normal" on the vast variety of genes and the virtual certainty that we were all quite different from each other. I mailed it to him on August 11, 1955, and on August 18 received a long letter from him with the returned manuscript, which he was rejecting (as nearly as I could make out) for the crime of being too important a subject for *Astounding*.

I shrugged and, in September, sent it to *F & SF*. Boucher rejected it, too, on September 23 and I retired the article till something else might turn up.

Then, on the twenty-fifth, I happened to be visiting Campbell's house in New Jersey, and he said to me, "What's happening to your article on genes?"

I said, dispiritedly, "I tried *F & SF*, but they turned it down."

He said, with obvious astonishment, "Why did you send it to them?"

"It seemed a possibility."

"But why not to me?"

It was my turn to be astonished. "I *did* send it to you. You turned it down."

He said, "I did *not* turn it down. I asked for a revision." And he told me what kind of revision.

When I got home, I reread his letter. For the life of me I could find no revision request in it. However, I revised the article according to his verbal instructions and, on October 12, I received a check for it.

6

Robyn was half a year old on August 19, 1955, and David was four the day after. The unprecedented summer heat had been broken by hurricanes which, fortunately, did not produce extensive power failures (the worst losses of power lasted only twenty minutes). Hurricane Diane, however, dropped over a foot of rain on the Boston area on August 18 and 19, and large parts of New England were badly flooded.

This was inconvenient. The World Science Fiction convention was about to come up in Cleveland over the Labor Day weekend of September 2 to 5, and some of the key highways from Boston to New York were flooded and closed.

My original plan had been to drive the family to New York and leave them there with the Blugermans, going to Cleveland by myself (or with Gertrude, if she felt like going).

As it was I would have to go to New York by train, and taking two children plus the necessary luggage on the train seemed too severe a task. So I went to New York by myself, and Mary Blugerman traveled in the other direction to keep her daughter and grandchildren company.

I left for New York by train on Monday, August 29, and went on my rounds on the thirtieth. I saw Lillian McClintock of Abelard-Schuman and got her to agree to my doing a book on the chemical elements as my fourth juvenile science book (though my second and third were not yet published).

I visited Leo Margulies and his wife, Cylvia, in the evening. Leo and I were good friends, now, something I wouldn't have believed possible when he drove Sam Merwin to reject "Grow Old With Me" eight years before. I also met Fred Dannay ("Ellery Queen") for the first time that day.

On August 31, I met Marcia as a married woman, and was very pleased indeed with her husband, Nick.

On September 1, 1955, Marty Greenberg picked me up in Manhattan, just two blocks from the old apartment in Stuyvesant Town, and we drove to Cleveland through mostly cloudy weather, without incident. It took us twelve hours—which Marty took in stride. I can't think of anyone who drives more smoothly and effortlessly.

That night I met André Norton who, writing excellent science-fiction juveniles under that name, was actually a woman. The masculine character of science fiction at that time made that sort of thing seem sensible then.

As guest of honor, I had a two-room suite (at the convention's expense), and I had parties in my room, as the guest of honor was supposed to do. It meant messing up the place with cigarette butts and liquor glasses and not being able to have any privacy or go to sleep till everyone decided to leave (and they never decided to leave). It seemed fun at the time but I never again gave parties at conventions.

A very pretty twenty-five-year-old girl named Ruth Landis attended that convention. It was her first. She looked, to my dazzled eyes, exactly like Grace Kelly. Dave Kyle saw her first and, like a fool, told her to wait at the elevator while he ran an errand somewhere. When he came back, she was gone, for I had seen her waiting there and had spirited her off. Thereafter, Randall Garrett, Forrest Ackerman, and I (and, I imagine others, when we weren't looking) kept squiring her here and there. On the night of Saturday, September 3, Randy and I found an all-night diner and we sat up all night with Ruth between us, talking all sorts of gibberish and loving it.

Dave Kyle had the last laugh, however. Though he was completely helpless during the convention, he managed to grab Ruth after the convention and eventually he married her.

On the whole, the Cleveland convention may have been small (only three hundred attended as compared with one thousand at some earlier conventions and four thousand at some later ones), but it overflowed with *Gemütlichkeit*. Randy and I saw to that single-handedly. Wherever we went, a comet tail of noise and laughter followed us, much of which we created ourselves.

At one point (I think it was at this convention, though it may just possibly have been at another) the program was delayed in the morning, and the audience was restless. Randall suggested he and I get up on the platform and engage in some snappy patter. We did and for a while we stood there (of approximately equal height and girth) and did well, I thought—until Harlan Ellison appeared at the back of the hall and called out, "There they are—Tweedledum and Tweedledee."

And I called out, "Come up here, Harlan; stand between us and be the hyphen." (That got the bigger laugh, I'm glad to say.)

The most characteristic joke (if you can call it that) of the convention arose accidentally. Judy Merril was there, glooming over an unhappy break in her relationship with a certain writer, and I did a lot of the arm-on-the-shoulder-buck-up-old-girl routine.

Then came the awarding of the Hugos—and I'll have to explain about those.

The annual award of the movie Oscars has inspired annual awards of all kinds of named figurines for all kinds of activities, and science fiction did not lag behind.

The idea first occurred to a gentleman by the name of Hal Lynch, who passed on the idea to the fans who were organizing the eleventh convention, in Philadelphia in 1953. Several awards were manufactured by Jack McKnight of Lansdale, Pennsylvania. They were small stainless-steel rocket ships, finned at base and center and set on a cylindrical wooden base on which an appropriately inscribed plaque was set.

There was no feeling at the time that such an award ought to be repeated; it was just a feature of the eleventh convention. At the twelfth convention, held in San Francisco in 1954, there were no awards. At the thirteenth, though, the awards were presented again, and this time a new design was worked out by Ben Jason of Cleveland. It was larger than the earlier one, lacked the central fins, and was set on a cubical base. It could be mass-produced.

These awards were, very naturally, named Hugos (for Hugo Gernsback), and from the thirteenth convention on, they have been a feature of every World Science Fiction convention. The banquet at which they were awarded has always been the convention's high point.

At Cleveland, it was Tony Boucher who was toastmaster, and it was Tony who handed out the Hugos in his own gentle way. The room was not air conditioned, and it was warm; Tony therefore began by suggesting that those gentlemen who felt that the warmth was excessive might feel free to dispense with the usual formality and—

About halfway through his hesitant suggestion, I got the drift, stood up, and took off my jacket. Since, as guest of honor, I was at the dais and conspicuous, everyone else did, too, but, as I recall, Tony didn't.

One of the Hugos was awarded to the very same science-fiction writer over whom Judy Merril was mooning, and he was not present to accept the award. Tony noted that and said, "In his absence, the award will be accepted by Judy Merril, by whom he has been so often anthologized." No one could have thought of a more graceful way of putting it.

However, I turned to the person next to me and said, jokingly, "Anthologized?—Always euphemisms."

It was a bit of mockery I need not have voiced, but I *did* whisper it. I *did* mean it to be just a quick, private joke. What I *didn't* know was that the microphone in front of me was live. The statement boomed out, and the entire banquet audience burst out into laughter. Judy Merril walked up as the waves of merriment parted before her and accepted the award—while I sat stricken on the dais. I think I was the only person in the room not laughing.

It wasn't just that I was horrified at having perpetrated so heartless a joke. It was that I was certain that as soon as Judy could get her hands on me, she would kill me.

She didn't. The next time I saw her, I noted that she looked sweet and gentle. I therefore sidled up to her (making sure my line of retreat was clear) and began a kind of incoherent apology. She thrust the whole thing aside. "It's okay, Isaac," she said. "It was a good thing. When I heard everyone laughing, I thought: What's the use of carrying a torch when no one else can possibly take it seriously? So I quit. I feel much better now."

She apparently meant it. Even though everyone in the place was shouting "Anthologize you!" and "Go anthologize yourself," Judy returned good for evil. On Monday the fifth, when I felt low because the convention was coming to an end, Judy dragged me off, fed me coffee, patted my shoulder, and made like a mother hen until I brightened up again.

I took the train back on the evening of the fifth and got home Wednesday afternoon.

It had been a hundred very unusual hours. I had never spent so long a time being idolized and lionized and made much of. When I got on the train and walked its length with nobody looking at me or whispering, "There's Asimov," I felt as though I couldn't bear the workaday world again.

7

The November 1955 *F & SF* contained my story "Dreamworld."[1] It wasn't much of a story, only five hundred words ending in a terrible pun, but it marked my mastery of one more science-fiction variety. I had tried to do it with "Shah Guido G." four years before, but it wasn't till this time that I did it right.

I was hitting *F & SF* regularly now. The December 1955 issue contained "A Hundred Million Dreams at Once," which Tony had retitled "Dreaming Is a Private Thing."[2] I was proud of that story, and because it ended with a poignant few paragraphs that could easily be applied by writers to themselves, several of my writer friends wrote to me at once to praise the story. Heinlein, more jokingly, wrote to tell me that I was clearly making money out of my neuroses.

[1] See *Opus 100* (Houghton Mifflin, 1969).
[2] See *Earth Is Room Enough.*

The February 1956 *F & SF* had "The Message,"[3] another short-short story that was all ending.

8

Dr. J. Franklin Yeager of the National Heart Institute in Washington arrived at the med school on September 29, 1955. He had read my science fiction and my science writing, particularly "The Sound of Panting," and he was anxious to have me do a book on cardiovascular research, one that would serve to publicize the kind of work in which the National Heart Institute was interested. It was not, however, to be a propaganda piece. I would write whatever I wanted and could publish it commercially as another one of my books.

I told Yeager that I didn't really know anything about cardiovascular research, and he said I could learn. When I said that that would take time and that I had my duties, he spoke of sabbaticals, fellowships, grants, and of visits and stays in Washington.

It was all very exciting for me and I was delighted that this was happening in full view of the department, for Yeager also spoke to Walker, for instance. I had no objection whatever to being made to seem important to them.

On October 4, I traveled to Washington for the first time (as opposed to passing through when I was in the Army just ten years before), and I did so at government expense. I took the overnight sleeper.

I was shown around the National Heart Institute and I spent the evening and night at the home of Dr. and Mrs. Yeager, where I was, according to my diary, "treated like a king. Room and private bath, good meal, books and music."

I stayed three days altogether, and when I got back to school, I discussed the matter with Walker. He approved but thought I could easily do it without abandoning any school duties. At his advice, I saw Robert W. Wilkins of the school's Department of Medicine. He was a pleasant gentleman who impressed me favorably (he was also the first to introduce the use of tranquilizers into the United States). He advised me to write a memo on the subject to Keefer, and I did. Eventually, on October 25, Keefer approved.

I had touched all bases and all seemed well.

[3] See *Earth Is Room Enough.*

9

On October 11, 1955, Stanley called to say he was getting married about Thanksgiving and he had already bought a house.

I was a little nervous about it. Ruth was seven years older than Stan, and she had an eight-year-old son who was as headstrong as David. Did Stan know what he was doing? I didn't discuss the thing with him, of course, since I had no right to interfere—and if I had, I'm sure Stanley would have shut me up in half a second—but I worried.

But at least the news inspired Gertrude and myself to get to house-hunting with renewed vigor. If Stanley could find a house, surely we could.

10

Lloyd Roth of my prewar days at Columbia was passing through Boston, and on October 19 we had lunch together. I hadn't seen him for seven years. He had an M.D. now as well as a Ph.D.

11

On October 19, Robyn was eight months old. She could sit if you sat her up and stand if you stood her up, but she didn't enjoy either position.

As for myself, I had started *The Naked Sun*, a new novel that was to be a sequel to *The Caves of Steel*. I had also started *Building Blocks of the Universe*, the new science juvenile on chemical elements for Abelard-Schuman.

12

Past events are not easily forgotten when you keep a diary. On November 1, 1955, I carefully noted that ten years ago that day I was inducted into the Army.

And on that tenth-anniversary day I was doing my best to induct myself into something else—Yeager's project. I called him and suggested that I receive a grant that would include fifteen hundred dollars to the school (as overhead, something that usually accompanied all grants, to the school's great satisfaction), two thousand dollars to me, fifteen hundred dollars for a secretary (Walker's suggestion), and two thousand dollars travel expenses. The next day I wrote a letter adding five hundred dollars for an electric typewriter, making the payment to me twenty-five hundred dollars in all.

13

On November 18, Dr. Yeager visited me. We discussed the details of the grant application, and over the next few days I worked it out in full, got the necessary signatures and covering letters, and took the whole thing over to Keefer's office on the twenty-first.

On November 23, I got a letter from Keefer, and for the first time I was subjected to what I had heard described as "Keefer's sneer."

Keefer wrote that he wouldn't approve the book deal if I got royalties for it. So far, so good. He then added a final and entirely unnecessary sneer to the effect that many faculty members would be willing to write books if they were paid to do so and could collect royalties in addition.

My impulse, of course, was to answer at once, but I knew that I might as well wait and let the first slam-bang fury die down. I had a good excuse to do so since we were all about to attend Stanley's wedding in New York, which was scheduled for the twenty-sixth.

We did attend. Marcia and Nick were there, too, and we drove them back to their place in Queens afterward. Marcia was pregnant.

Naturally, I had plenty of time in the course of the trip to New York and back to write imaginary letters in my head, and I had no trouble batting one out once I got back to the med school. The fury, however, hadn't settled, and if Keefer's letter was a sneer, mine was haughty.

I pointed out that I didn't need a grant to write a book; that I had been a professional writer for seventeen years; that I had published sixteen books in six years; that my writing earnings were higher than my school salary, and that no other faculty member could match this—nor could they do so merely by getting a grant.

Furthermore, I went on, growing more angry as I wrote, unless I could collect royalties, I would certainly not apply for the grant, but would write the book on my own. And if I did so, I would get my royalties just the same, but the school would not collect its overhead.

I checked the letter with Walker, who approved it, glad, no doubt, to have someone talk tough to Keefer. I took it in to Keefer's office on November 29, and the next day, Keefer's reply came. He backed down; I could have royalties.

The first round was to me. What I didn't quite see was that it was only the first round. Keefer hadn't given up; he was merely preparing to shift the ground of battle.

14

I had three books published in 1955:

14. *The Martian Way and Other Stories* (Doubleday)
15. *The End of Eternity* (Doubleday)
16. *Races and People* (Abelard-Schuman)

Races and People, which had appeared in November, was a collaboration. It was "by William C. Boyd and Isaac Asimov." However, I had done every bit of the writing, using, to be sure, Bill's book on the subject as my reference.

I was already establishing my book career as something that was to be characterized by both quantity and variety. My books had now been appearing for six years, and in no year had there been fewer than two. In one year, 1952, there had been four.

What's more, among these sixteen books were science-fiction novels for adults, science-fiction novels for youngsters, collections of science-fiction short stories, textbooks at the professional level, and science for the general public.

I was pleased. I felt that the increasing number of nonfiction books dealing with science at various levels, combined with my associate professorship, had made my position at school unassailable. And since the director of the institution was clearly my enemy, I needed unassailability.

My earnings were disappointing. My school income was six thousand dollars, but my writing income had shrunk to less than eighty-nine hundred dollars, only three quarters what it had been the year before. It was not unexpected. The science-fiction magazine field was fading, as I had known it would, from its peak in the early 1950s, and I had failed to make a magazine sale for *The End of Eternity*, which had cost me nearly three thousand right there.

My total income was still nudging fifteen thousand dollars, and it was the fourth year in a row where it was either that or more than that, so really, there was nothing to worry about. Besides which, I had three books in press and three more in preparation, so *surely* there was nothing to worry about—I hoped.

15

With the end of 1955, I had been keeping a diary for 18 years—half my life.

On January 2, 1956, I was 36, and David, now nearly 4½, could sing "Happy Birthday" to me. There was no surprise party for me this year, but there was a devil's-food cake and a box of bow ties (for some years I had been wearing clip-on bow ties on all but the most stately occasions). All of us but Robyn had some of the cake and milk and were cheerful.

A week later, a more prosaic birthday present came. My Doubleday statement appeared on January 9, quite early, and totaled thirty-eight hundred dollars. It was much better than the year before, got me off to a flying start, and represented as much as I had made for the first five months of the previous year.

Money isn't the primary reason I write, of course (I write for the love of it), but it is a strong secondary reason. Besides, if I were going to have showdowns with Keefer now and then, I preferred to do my arguing with money in my pocket.

16

For some months, Gertrude had been taking driving lessons once more, picking up where she had left off nearly six years before. She didn't take them in solid, concentrated fashion, unfortunately, so she had trouble gaining the kind of confidence that comes with driving a car every day, but by Friday, January 13, 1956, she felt she could take the test.

Friday the thirteenth lived up to its stereotype this time, however. I had remained home, taking care of the children, but when the door was unlocked downstairs and I heard Gertrude sobbing, I knew what had happened. I got her into bed, and disregarding her statement that she would give up, I called the driving teacher and arranged for additional lessons for her. I told her, quite firmly, that if I could learn to drive a car, *anyone* could. Then I took David out to a local restaurant and kept him there for quite a while, giving Gertrude a chance to recover.

By evening, her confidence had returned.

17

On January 15, 1956, David and I drove to New York, and on the next day I made my rounds.

I visited Abelard-Schuman and handed in the manuscript of *Building Blocks of the Universe.*

I also visited Larry Shaw, an old-time fan, who was now editor of a new science-fiction magazine that was bucking the tide of failure among other magazines. The new magazine was *Infinity Science Fiction.* Larry, a short fellow with thick glasses, a big pipe, and a very quiet voice, wanted stories from me and I submitted one called "Someday" about a little mistreated story-telling machine. He read it and accepted it on the spot.

I saw Campbell and Margulies during the day and then spent the evening with Gerard Pick and his wife, Helena, a plump and pretty blonde.

Gerard had got in touch with me some time before because he wanted one of my stories for an anthology. I called him when I was in New York on one of the previous occasions, and when the phone was picked up at the other end, a woman's voice in my ear said, "Drop dead!"

I flinched a little and then said, "Could I speak to Gerard Pick *before* I drop dead?"

It was Mrs. Pick, of course, who had been expecting a call from someone to whom her remark would have been fittingly humorous. She was overwhelmed with embarrassment and by the time she was through apologizing, we were good friends and nothing would do but that next time I was in New York, I must have dinner with them.

January 16 was the time, but the meal, although very good from the culinary standpoint (for Helena was, as promised, a good cook), proved to be a hectic one. Shortly before arriving, I had called the Blugermans to inquire about David. He was all right but they told me that Gertrude had called to say that she thought she had found a suitable house but that they wouldn't take a deposit from her unless I approved also.

There was nothing to do but drive home the next day and go over with her to see the house.

It was in West Newton, about two miles south of our Waltham apartment. It was at 45 Greenough Street. On the main floor, it had a large living-room/dining-room combination, an adequate kitchen, and three rather small bedrooms, so that we could have one and assign another to each of the children.

There was a basement with two large rooms semifinished, one of which was a playroom, the other a laundry. There was a two-car, heated garage under the bedroom portion of the house so that never again, if we took the house, would I be unable to start the car because of the cold, or have to sweep snow off a car before I could use it.

The living room faced the back of the house, where there was a porch (without a roof, which had blown off in the recent hurricanes) and a pleasant quarter-acre backyard (with a barbecue pit) in which the kids could play. The bedrooms faced the front. There were two bathrooms, and the one attached to the master bathroom had a stall shower. There was also a hopper in the basement.

Most interesting of all was the fact that there were two finished rooms in the attic (but no plumbing), which I could use as an office.

Add to that the fact that there were adequate closets, that Newton was known nationwide for the excellence of its school system, and that the price was no more than twenty-four thousand dollars, and what more could we ask? I put down a check for one thousand dollars at once as a deposit. On January 20, I signed a full agreement, and we settled down to wait for a title clearance.

As though to celebrate, Robbie, who was now eleven months old, produced the first sign of two incisors peeping through her gums.

There were other reasons to celebrate, too. Writing was going well! I was ready to start the final copy of *The Naked Sun*, and I had persuaded Brad into letting me do another book of unconnected short stories, this one to contain a larger number of shorter stories than in *The Martian Way and Other Stories*. I was collecting the manuscripts of stories to appear in that new book, and I was selling additional short stories to the magazines as rapidly as I could write them.

With books showing every sign of pouring out in a steady stream, and with the thought of the large Doubleday statement that month, I favored buying the house outright—just putting down an additional check for twenty-three thousand dollars.

We could do it. Living with our accustomed prudence, we had accumulated—despite the expense of two babies—a bank account of thirty-five thousand dollars by then.

Gertrude, however, thought it unwise to cut our savings by two thirds at one stroke, and she said a mortgage would be a good way of establishing credit. Therefore I applied at my local bank for a fifteen-thousand-dollar mortgage, to stretch over twenty years at whatever the going rate of interest was. I arranged, however, for permission to pay larger installments than called for if I could do so—saving on interest, of course. The bank readily agreed, judging from my appearance, I suppose, that they were in no danger of losing interest. (To ordinary people, I look stupid; to banks, I look poor.)

Buoyed up by the house situation, Gertrude was taking the additional driving lessons I had arranged for her. On February 2, she took another test, and in the worst possible weather, for a sleet storm hit the city. Despite that, she *passed,* and had her license.

By February 15, the title was cleared and the old owners had moved out. Our painter moved in, with his paraphernalia.

18

Robbie was one year old on February 19, 1956. She weighed eighteen pounds and had two teeth. She still didn't like standing and she showed no signs of walking.

On that day I picked out science-fiction wallpaper for what was to be my office and writing room. It had spaceships on it, planets with rings, and so on.

When Gertrude passed on my choice to the painter, he looked at it in disbelief and said, "Does the doctor know that this is children's wallpaper?"

"The doctor is in his second childhood," said Gertrude, and that settled it.

On February 22, we celebrated Washington's birthday by driving to the new house—with Gertrude at the wheel.

On March 3, I drove my car into the garage of the new house, enjoying the feeling of having a car in my own garage for the first time in my life.

I raced to finish *The Naked Sun* before everything became a shambles. I managed. On March 10, 1956, *The Naked Sun* was complete, and on March 12 we moved—and left the Waltham apartment after having lived in it for nearly five years, and having had both our children there.

The next day, we had a phone—one on the wall in the kitchen and an extension in my office upstairs. Heavens! the luxury in which we were living.

4

West Newton

1

We were now landed gentry, but we found out almost at once that houses have their disadvantages.

We had a nice wide driveway on the street side of the house, and on Friday, March 16, 1956, four days after we had moved in, it started snowing about noon. It kept on snowing. That in itself was not surprising. It had been a bitterly cold winter, following the bitterly hot, dry summer, and there had been much snow.

But *this* snowstorm kept on snowing and storming and turned out to be the worst of the season. The wind blew it into the driveway and the retaining walls on either side kept it there, so that when I woke on Saturday morning, there were three feet of snow in the driveway. I am not exaggerating or being dramatic. I *measured* the snow depth.

There had been times, as it happened, when I shoveled snow for my father to make a path in front of the candy store. That had always been a minor job. Since I had left the candy store, fourteen years before, I had not shoveled one snowflake.

At 7:15 A.M. on Saturday, I started shoveling with one of the snow shovels I had bought as part of the normal paraphernalia of a New England house. All Saturday, I chipped away at the snow mountain in front of the house, and finally in the evening, two men and a Jeep came around and for eight dollars bulldozed away most of the snow, leaving it to me to do the work around the edges and along the walkways on either side of the house.

Whereupon on Monday, March 19, *another* blizzard hit, and this time we ended with *four* feet of snow in the driveway. It was the worst one-two snowstorm in the history of the Boston Weather Bureau, nor has anything like it been repeated since—and it came in the first week that I moved into the new house.

We were too inexperienced to shovel the snow away from the immediate contact it made with the walls of the house. Inside the porch in back of the house the snow piled up against the house halfway to the roof, well above the copper flashing that kept the house impervious to water from outside. When the warmth of the house started melting that snow, the water trickled down the inside of the flashing and into the cellar. I had to race home from school to try to deal with it.

And the hot-water heater, with the discrimination for which such objects are noted, chose this time to go on the fritz, so that we had to call the appliance people, who already had more than they could handle.

It all worked out in the end and never again did we have such a ten-day period in the house—but that was the *first* ten-day period. It hit us hard. We lost all our euphoria concerning the house, and it never really returned.

2

There were other problems that seemed to be inseparable from the design of the house. When the snow on the roof melted, it would drip down, forming huge icicles and making puddles on the paths on either side of the house. These would freeze at night and make the paths and steps extremely dangerous in the morning. Had the paths been placed three feet away from the actual walls and eaves of the house, this would not have happened.

And in the fall, as we discovered half a year later, the trees shed their leaves, and raking proved even more time-consuming than shoveling. And for eight months a year there was lawn-mowing.

I hated doing *anything* about the house and grounds. In the first place, I had no aptitude for it; and in the second, I had better things to do.

It made me look bad because all around us there were husbands mowing and hedge-clipping and planting and weeding and doing all kinds of things. Why not? If they weren't actually working, there was nothing else to do. For myself, I was always working. I didn't keep *hours*, for goodness sake; so I had to hire people when I could to do these things. That looked bad.

3

In the short space of time between the two storms, I received the April 1956 *Astounding* with "The Dead Past"[1] in it. The story, one of my favorites, is most memorable to me for what I put in it accidentally.

What I was planning was a story that inverted the usual assump-

[1] See *Earth Is Room Enough.*

tions that government planning is tyrannical and that freedom of scientific inquiry is good. In the course of the story, however, I threw in, almost at random, a reference to Carthage that somehow took on a life of its own and quite unexpectedly introduced a subplot that provided the whole course of the story with excellent motivation. Any critic reading the story is bound to conclude I planned that subplot from the beginning, though I swear I didn't. It made me wonder if I did some planning that I didn't recognize as such, as my old philosopher-friend Gotthard Guenther had once implied.

The May 1956 *Science Fiction* contained my story "Living Space."[2] At that time, *Science Fiction* was being edited by that old Futurian, Robert W. Lowndes. He worked on a tight budget and had very little money to spend. When he asked me for a story now and then, however, I let him have it, but on my conditions.

I would not send him a story from the bottom of the barrel. I would write one for him, just as though I were writing it for *Astounding*. In return, if he liked it, I would expect him to pay the *Astounding* rate of four cents a word. If he didn't like it (or if he wanted to take a chance), he could send it back to me. I would then send it on to *Astounding* and *Galaxy*, and if they rejected it I would recognize the story as not first-rate Asimov and I would send it back to Lowndes, who might then have it (if he wished) at whatever his usual rates were.

I tried this same device on other ordinarily low-paying markets and it worked perfectly. Never once was one of my stories sent back to me on the gamble. As a result, some of my best stories of the period, including my all-time best (in *my* opinion), appeared in minor science-fiction magazines—which paid me top rates for them.

4

On March 28, I drove to New York, where I submitted *The Naked Sun* to both Doubleday and Campbell.

On this occasion, Campbell, to whose house in Mountainside, New Jersey, I had driven to make the submission, proudly showed me his newest toy. It was called the "Hieronymus machine" after its inventor, and it was a device of surpassing idiocy. It contained a meaningless electric circuit inside, one that could (Campbell seriously claimed) even be replaced by a paper diagram of the circuit without impairing its efficiency.[3]

To work the machine, you turned a dial while stroking a plastic

[2] See *Earth Is Room Enough.*
[3] Which is true, I suppose, since you can't impair zero efficiency.

surface, and at some reading of the dial there would be a change in the feel of the surface. It would become stickier. From the dial reading at this point one could diagnose diseases and so on.

Campbell insisted I try the machine. Ordinarily, I would have refused, since I lack any desire at all to lend myself to such folly. On this occasion, though, I was delivering a manuscript on which thousands of dollars would rest on Campbell's decision and, frankly, since the dianetics thing, I no longer trusted the rigidity and integrity of his judgment.

So I agreed to play. Naturally, no matter how I turned the dial I felt no change in the feel of the plate; there was no onset of stickiness and I certainly wasn't going to lie to Campbell and say there was so that he could then use me as evidence of the working of the Hieronymus machine.

So I twisted and stroked, and stroked and twisted, while my fingers grew sweaty with anxiety and began to slip more easily along the plate.

"Mr. Campbell," I said, hesitantly, but truthfully, "the plate feels slippery."

"Aha," said Campbell, triumphantly, as he carefully took the reading. "Negative stickiness!"

And that's how great nonsense discoveries are made.

Yet I might have saved myself the trouble if I were trying to use my compliance to sell him the novel, for he read through it that day and when I returned the next, he rejected it. I was quite dismayed, but after we talked it over, ways of revising it to meet Campbell's objections were devised.

That was a relief, for I wanted it in *Astounding*, even though it was the sequel to *The Caves of Steel*, which had appeared in *Galaxy*. It seemed to me that I ought to alternate serials between Gold and Campbell.

I also gave Campbell another gag article, "Paté de Foie Gras," a mock-serious study of a goose that laid golden eggs, which I thought was much cleverer than my thiotimoline articles. Campbell took the new article without trouble.

On that occasion, too, I picked up an unusually large check from Marty Greenberg: one for $750.

5

I attended the student-faculty show on April 7, 1956. I did that every year and I routinely gave a talk as part of the festivities—a funny talk, naturally.

I had become quite used to doing this, since I always talked at any science-fiction gatherings I attended—not just the national conventions, but small local gatherings, too.

Generally, I had no trouble. Once in a rare while, though, I did poorly, and this was one of those rare whiles. According to my diary, "My own bit at the show, by the way, was a flop, but total. Hostile audience."

I don't remember why they were hostile or how it showed itself, but I never took part in a student-faculty show again. In fact, I never attended one again.

I do remember, though, that I made some humorous comments about Dean Soutter's secretary, who wore skin-tight clothes and had the figure to make the procedure worthwhile. The secretary complained to Soutter, and Soutter called me in to his office and asked me to apologize in writing.

I pointed out the generally licentious tone of the show (and my comments were as nothing compared to the tastelessness of some of the proceedings). Soutter said that the standards of behavior for faculty were tighter than for students.

I thought about it, decided I was in the wrong, and typed the required apology. I also typed a letter of resignation, showed it to Soutter, and asked if he wished me to put it through channels.

"No," he said, "I asked for an apology. Nothing more."

That was a relief. It had occurred to me that I might be hounded over little things just to force my resignation through petty humiliations. (Such things have been known to take place.) What I had done was a risky test of that.

Had he asked me to put my resignation through channels, I would have counted on Walker to stop it. Had Soutter himself accepted my resignation then and there, I'd have been in trouble indeed, but I didn't feel he would choose to go over the department head. As it was, I felt Soutter was being honest and that I might be able to rely on him in future crises.

6

I sent in the revised *The Naked Sun* on April 10, and, thank goodness, Campbell took it, as I found out when I called him on the sixteenth. It meant nearly three thousand dollars, and this time I didn't even have to hand over 10 per cent to Fred.

But then, the next day, Brad called and told me that *The Naked Sun* needed a lot of work. He complained of my inaccurate use of words. As an example, he questioned the phrase "knife-edge sudden-ness." How sudden, he wanted to know, is a knife edge?

I chafed at this and found myself wishing that editors wouldn't try to be writers. I still hadn't reached the stage where I felt I could cross him, but I longed to tell him that "knife-edge suddenness" meant that something had changed in a period of time no greater than the width of a knife's edge, and that it was a colorful metaphor that no reader would fail to understand. I kept my mouth shut, though.

I drove to New York and on the nineteenth went over *The Naked Sun* with him. Things weren't too bad. No more work was involved in Brad's case than there had been in Campbell's. By April 29, I had completed the revision, incorporating Campbell's changes (at least, those I wanted to make permanent), and with this Brad was satisfied.

<h1 style="text-align:center">7</h1>

I got what seemed to me the brilliant idea of writing an article on the names of the elements. What did the names mean and why were they given to the individual elements?

I wrote to Campbell to suggest the notion, and when I didn't hear from him at once, I found I could not wait, but began the article on April 29, 1956. It was the longest article I had yet written—seventy-five hundred words—and I didn't finish till the evening of May 6. I still had not heard from Campbell, so I mailed it to him on the morning of the seventh, and when the mail arrived later in the day, there was a letter from him, vetoing the idea.

That was embarrassing. There was nothing to do but write a special-delivery letter to him, explaining that I had sent the article prematurely and asking him to return it without even opening the envelope. I then put it out of my mind as an example of just one more of those fiascos with which a free-lancer's life is filled.

On May 17, I was off being interviewed on a daytime talk show on radio, and called Gertrude afterward for her opinion on how I sounded. She dutifully told me I sounded fine and then said, "There's a $225 check that's arrived."

I was puzzled. There was no check of that size due. "For what?" I said.

"For you," she said.

"I mean, what have I sold?" I said pettishly.

"Something called 'Names! Names! Names!' ", she said.

That was what I called my article on the names of elements. "It's from Campbell?" I asked, thunderstruck.

"Yes," she said.

I called him up at once to ask what had happened.

He said he had gotten my letter before the manuscript arrived, but when it did, he couldn't resist taking a look at it and it turned out much better than he had imagined it would be, so he bought it.

Listening to that, I decided I had reached the stage where it was useless to consult editors in advance. More and more, I simply wrote what I pleased and then put it up to them.

8

I had been gathering references and making changes in the copy of the second edition of the textbook that had been sent me—one with the intervening blank pages. Then in early spring, Dick Hoover of Williams and Wilkins had written to say he would want the manuscript for the third edition by November.

On May 2, Walker, Boyd, and I sat down for the first of our triple conferences over the third edition. It went pretty quickly. We had the book well organized now and had only to update. The big job would be the index, of course, for even minor changes threw the pagination out so that the index would have to be done from scratch.

Walker and Boyd didn't worry about that, though. They knew that I would take care of the index—and all of the other routine details.

9

Meanwhile, the final official confirmation of the cardiovascular research project had arrived on May 8.

My excitement over it had died down considerably. Now that I had had months to think of it, the glamor had faded. I didn't want to spend inordinate amounts of time and effort traveling about the country learning all there was to know about cardiovascular research. The twenty-five hundred dollars of the grant plus the royalties of the book could not possibly replace the money lost through my not being able to do science fiction in the interval.

The trouble was that it was becoming apparent to me that time was the most valuable property I had, and that I could not afford to sell it cheaply. And it was becoming rapidly more valuable too. My writing earnings in 1956, thanks to the large Doubleday royalty and my sale of The Naked Sun to Campbell, had already reached the nine-thousand-dollar mark, and it was only early May.

Yet I could not refuse to do the book. I had pushed for it hard enough, and to abandon it might make it seem that I was knuckling under to Keefer. It eventually occurred to me, therefore, that I ought to write two books. The first one would be a book on blood and all its ramifications, which I would call *The Living River*. That book I could do in my usual fashion, working from reference material.

Then, for a *sequel*, so to speak, I could write the book on cardiovascular research. That, however, would require another grant, and I simply wouldn't apply for another one.

This was a little underhanded, but I rationalized that the first book would be valuable to the National Heart Institute and that I would write it as well as I could. But even so, I felt guilty, and I let a long time pass without starting the book or, indeed, doing anything at all on the grant. And, as the months passed, the whole thing weighed more and more heavily on my mind and conscience.

10

We had some minor snowfalls after the double whammo in March, one as late as April 8, giving us a White Passover, but by May, summer was on its way and no mistake. On May 17, I mowed the lawn, and that was the first time in my life I had ever used a lawnmower.

There had been some hot days already by then, but the house remained quite cool. The main floor was not directly exposed to the sun after all, and there was complete four-way ventilation.

The attic, however, which was my workroom, was the duplicate, as far as temperature was concerned, of the Somerville attic. This time it was bearable, since I could always set my typewriter up in the basement during heat waves and since I knew I would eventually purchase an air conditioner.

11

On May 20, 1956, Gertrude and I went out to dinner for a slightly belated birthday celebration for her. With us were the Soodaks, Morris and Edith. We had met Edith at Chester's Zunbarg in 1948, and she could tell jokes in Yiddish very well. She was an intelligent and vivacious girl, and she married Morris not long after we had come to Boston. When they came to Boston as well, we became friends. Morris was a short fellow, who, like Edith, could tell jokes well. He was sometimes frenetic and overexcited, but then so was I.

Edith's birthday was also within a few days of this period, as was

that of another woman present. It was therefore a triple birthday celebration for the four couples present altogether.

It was Gertrude's first birthday as a house owner (the house was in
both our names, of course), and the feeling that the trauma of house-
hunting had been lifted from our shoulders for a long time, perhaps forever, was a good one, and contributed to the feeling of festivity.

In fact, so overwhelmed was I with the end-of-sorrow illusion, that
when one of the other women (not Gertrude) said pessimistically that
she felt "a mood" coming on I said, "For heaven's sake, avoid that.
Remember, 'mood' spelled backward is *'doom.'*" It snapped her right
out of the mood.

What I remember most about that meal is this: I had ordered
Lobster Diavolo, and Gertrude, who had been studying the menu in-
decisively, said, "That sounds good. Bring me one, too."

Eventually, the waiter arrived with an enormous platter on which
both orders for Lobster Diavolo rested in succulent and widespread
glory. He put it proudly down in front of me, for it was a dinner fit for
royalty, and the two of us, redoubted trenchermen though we were,
would have trouble finishing it.

And I said, calmly, "Well, that looks good. And where is my wife's
platter?"

12

I hadn't wanted a mortgage in the first place, but since I got one
to establish a credit rating, it seemed to me the credit rating would be
even higher if I paid it off quickly. What I did, then, was to pay it out
of current income, in installments as frequent and as large as I could
manage. I was careful, however, not to touch our savings past the slash
caused by the necessity of making the down payment on the house to
begin with.

Thus, on March 21, I used part of Campbell's check for *The
Naked Sun* to present a payment of twenty-seven hundred dollars to
the bank.

13

Of course, we all have our little superstitions, and I tend to feel
that any change in venue might affect my writing. Every time I move,
it is always a relief to me to find that I can still write, even though my
surroundings have changed.

I shouldn't have worried this time, though. By May 22, we had been there ten weeks and I had sold two articles and a poem parody, to say nothing of having revised a novel successfully for both Campbell and Brad. I had not, however, written and sold a complete work of fiction since I had moved into the house, and that made me a little uneasy.

On May 22, then, I was delighted to get word from Larry Shaw that he was taking "Jokester," which I had written earlier that month.

"Jokester" had arisen out of a lunch I had had with Larry. I was telling him a number of jokes (I'm a good jokester), and he said, "Who makes up these jokes, Isaac?"

"Who can say?" I said.

Larry said, "Why don't you write a science-fiction story about it?"

So I did, and included six of my favorite short jokes as part of the story.

And if that wasn't enough, I went on to write what was (in my opinion) the best science-fiction story I ever wrote and (if you want my *secret* opinion) the best science-fiction story *anyone* ever wrote—much better than "Nightfall"—and I wrote it right there in the house in West Newton.

It came about this way:

On June 1, 1956, I received a request from Bob Lowndes for another story. I was already thinking about writing another story about Multivac ("Franchise," which had been the first, had been written as a direct consequence of my introduction to Univac in the 1952 election).

I had worked out ever greater developments of Multivac, and eventually I was bound to consider how far I could go; how far the human mind (or, anyway, *my* human mind) could reach.

So as soon as I got Bob's letter I sat down to write "The Last Question," which was only forty-seven hundred words long, but in which I detailed the history of ten trillion years with respect to human beings, computers, and the universe. And, in the end—but no, you'll have to read the story, if you haven't already.

I wrote the whole thing in two sittings, without a sentence's hesitation. On June 4 I sent it off, and on June 11 I got the check from Lowndes—at four cents a word.

I knew at the instant of writing it that I had become involved in something special. When I finished it, I said, in my diary, that it was "the computer story to end all computer stories, or, who knows, the science-fiction story to end all science-fiction stories." Of course, it may well be that no one else agrees with me, but it was my opinion at the time, and it still is today.

While I was writing and selling these stories, previously sold stories appeared. In the June 1956 *Saint Detective Magazine,* there appeared my story "What's in a Name?"[4] The magazine had altered the name of the story to the utterly undistinguished "Death of a Honey-Blonde," but I changed it back when it appeared in one of my collections. It was the first piece of fiction I had published that was not science fiction. It was a "straight" mystery, although its characters were chemists, its setting a chemistry department, and its solution depended upon a chemical gimmick. It was therefore borderline science fiction.

The May 1956 *Astounding* contained "The Abnormality of Being Normal";[5] the July 1956, *F & SF* contained "The Dying Night,"[6] another Wendell Urth story, and the August 1956 *Infinity* contained "Someday."[7]

14

As of July 1, 1956, my salary was raised again, to sixty-five hundred dollars a year. I had not asked for the raise.

15

Fletcher Pratt died on June 10, 1956, at the age of fifty-nine. He had organized the war games I attended in the years just before I went to Philadelphia. He had also supervised my interview by the students at the Breadloaf Conference.

I remember walking along a New York street with him some time in 1955, while he was telling me of a book he was planning on the history of cooking. The Chinese, he said, always suffered a shortage of fuel but never suffered a shortage of hands, so they chopped all their food and quick-fried. The medieval Europeans, however, with a shortage of labor but endless supplies of fuel, developed stews and casseroles that could be heated for hours without attention.

Then we said good-bye, and I remember his smile as he waved his hand and turned away—and I never saw him again.

16

Robyn was a year and a quarter now and would still neither stand nor walk spontaneously, though she would do both if allowed to hold on and if urged forward.

[4] See *Asimov's Mysteries.*
[5] See *Only a Trillion.*
[6] See *Asimov's Mysteries.*
[7] See *Earth Is Room Enough.*

Then, on June 14, 1956, when Gertrude and I were in the kitchen, talking, Robyn walked in. She was a tiny little creature, with her long blond hair in a pageboy, and Gertrude said, "Hello, Robyn!"

It took a couple of seconds for us to do the double-take and say, simultaneously, "You're *walking!*"

And so she was. She had finally decided it was time on that day, and she never went back to crawling. From then on, somehow, she wasn't a baby anymore, but a little girl—blond-haired, blue-eyed, and beautiful.

17

June saw the temperature hit the high nineties for several days in a row, and I was forced to move my typewriter into the basement where, on June 15, I began another story for Lowndes called "Each an Explorer." I finished it in three days.

On June 17, I drove to New York with David, after some fear that I might not be able to do so because a small group of special technicians threatened a strike that would tie up the New York subway system. Fortunately, the danger passed.

In the course of the trip, I submitted "Each an Explorer" to Lowndes, which he eventually took, and found that Campbell had accepted another article, "The Sea-Urchin and We," on comparative biochemistry. I also discovered that I had sold "First Law" (which I had written fifteen years before for "Probability Zero") to *Fantastic Universe.*

On June 24, I started still a third story for Lowndes. This one, inspired by the near-miss subway strike, was called "Strikebreaker" and dealt with a situation where the strike of *one* man completely stops a world and threatens it with destruction. It was another one that went very quickly, and on the twenty-seventh I sent it to Lowndes. He took that one, too.

I was also about to begin the fifth of my Paul French juveniles, *Lucky Starr and the Moons of Jupiter.* The whole rationale for the Paul French pseudonym had disappeared, since there wasn't going to be any TV series. I made no effort to hide my identity, therefore, and in *Lucky Starr and the Moons of Jupiter* I even introduced the three laws of robotics, which was a dead giveaway to Paul French's identity for even the most casual reader.

I also dropped the "space ranger" bit, with the corny futuristic space shield Lucky Starr was supposed to wear. It never appeared after the second book in the series.

Copies of the fourth book of the series, *Lucky Starr and the Big Sun of Mercury*, had reached me on March 16, 1956.

The student-nurse textbook, *Chemistry and Human Health*, had come out even earlier in the year. Of all the books on my list, it is the one I least regard. There was no second edition, no second printing, virtually no sales. You couldn't even say it dropped dead; it was stillborn.

Copies of *Inside the Atom* reached me on March 14, 1956. It proved the most successful of the juvenile science books I wrote for Abelard-Schuman.

In July, I wrote a series of three interrelated articles for Campbell, all on biochemistry: "Planets Have an Air About Them," "The Unblind Workings of Chance," and "The Trapping of the Sun." Campbell took all three.

I was distinctly growing even more interested in writing articles than in writing stories, and an idea came to me that I began putting into practice when Lillian McClintock and her husband visited Boston on July 21. I took them to lunch at Locke-Ober's and there tried to talk them into doing a collection of my science articles in *Astounding*. I brought her my manuscripts to read.

18

Gertrude and I celebrated our fourteenth wedding anniversary on July 26, 1956, by going to a good restaurant with our neighbors, Mr. and Mrs. Harvey Pofcher.

And for once our anniversary (usually celebrated in a sweatbath) came on a pleasant day. In fact, the summer of 1956, except for the mid-June heat wave, was extraordinarily pleasant. It was as though the weather gods knew we were no longer living in a top-floor apartment.

The pleasant weather made it possible for me to continue writing stories at top speed. One of them was "Let's Get Together," which I based on a suggestion by Howard Bensusan, a graduate student at the medical school. He was a handsome and good-natured fellow who had fallen prey to polio and was on crutches permanently, though this did not affect his sunny disposition.

19

For the first time since David was born, Gertrude and I made plans to have a summer vacation together. This meant leaving the children with Mary and John Blugerman. They got in at 8:30 P.M. on the night of August 7, 1956, and we left the next day for "Timberland" in the Adirondacks.

It was not an extremely exuberant vacation, but the surroundings were pleasant and there were some good points. The entertainer-in-chief was a young man named Martin Charnin, who did a creditable imitation of Jerry Lewis.

The first night in our cabin I was disturbed by the low talking, tittering, and laughing of a group of young people just near enough to be bothersome and just far enough away to be undistinguishable. About 2 A.M. I wearily put on my pants and slippers and walked out the door toward them.

They fell silent as they watched me approach and I said nothing. Neither did I particularly hasten my steps. Finally, when I was virtually on top of them, I peered at each one in an exaggeratedly myopic fashion and said, mildly, "I *thought* there was someone there."

They burst into relieved laughter (I suppose they had expected yelling, outraged screaming, followed by complaints to the management) and in great good humor broke up and went their separate ways. It was an example that more could be accomplished by a smile than by a frown, but I have the greatest difficulty in remembering that in moments of crisis and outrage.

In any case, Martin Charnin was one of the group, and we were friends thereafter.

I was sitting on the lawn one day at Timberland when a group of young men nearby began to talk about science fiction. I called out to them, "What authors do you like?"

One of them said at once, "Asimov!"

I said, suspiciously, "Do you know my name?"

They didn't. As always we were all on a first-name basis only. I revealed myself and after that I was made much of (which I enjoy). One young woman asked me how many books I had written. I said "Nineteen," and she said, "Wow!"

It was the first time, as far as I can remember, that I was asked the question. I have been asked it continually ever since. Eventually, as the number became the most important thing about my professional activities, the question was altered into a sophisticated, world-weary, "What's the number now, Isaac?"

20

We called Mary every night, and every night she assured us she was living in paradise. On the sixth night, however, the paradise she described didn't match the shakiness of her voice, and early on August 15 we drove home as fast as we could.

We got home to find that Robyn had an abscess on her chest and David had a fever of 102. Mary held out till we had put down the suitcases and then went into hysterics.

For two days I scurried till the children got well and we were back in the swing.

21

Robyn was a year and a half old on the nineteenth. She could walk, run, and climb stairs; and amid her voluble gibberish were two words: "hi" and "cookie." She had seven teeth.

David was five years old the next day, and we had a delayed birthday party for him on the twenty-fourth, one that he decided not to enjoy but in which Robyn found great delight.

It was our first clear indication of the basic difference between the two. Whereas David seemed never at ease with other children and preferred always to go his own way, Robyn was a social animal and melted easily into any group.

22

On the morning of the twenty-fourth, I found I had little cause for celebration myself. I felt the familiar abdominal stab that meant I had a kidney stone, the first of consequence in four years. I promptly drank two quarts of water and the pain abated, at least for a while.

It came at a particularly bad time, since the World Science Fiction convention was to be held in New York that year and I was planning to go. I did *not* want to be immobilized by a kidney stone.

23

Kidney stone or not, my stories were appearing in the magazines in a virtual flood. The November 1956 *Science Fiction Quarterly* (one of Lowndes' magazines) contained "The Last Question,"[8] and the September 1956 *Astounding* contained "Paté de Foie Gras,"[9] my gag article. I had "First Law"[10] in the October 1956 *Fantastic Universe*, and

[8] See *Nine Tomorrows* (Doubleday, 1959).
[9] See *Only a Trillion*.
[10] See *Rest of the Robots*.

another short-short, "The Watery Place,"[11] in *Satellite Science Fiction*, the first issue of a new magazine put out by Leo Margulies. Lowndes published "Each an Explorer"[12] in an undated issue of *Future* (No. 30), and my Gilbert parody, "How to Succeed at Science Fiction Without Really Trying" (never placed in one of my collections), in the November 1956 *Science Fiction*.

Finally, in the October 1956 *Astounding*, the first of the three parts of *The Naked Sun* appeared.

24

All this, however, was secondary to my plans for the convention. I was going alone, by train, and I had made arrangements to room with Harry Stubbs. Harry made the ideal roommate (if one overlooks the fact that he is male). He didn't drink or smoke or carouse; he slept quietly without the trace of a snore; he was gentle and agreeable at all times.

Rather it was I who was the pest, involuntarily. I, too, didn't drink or smoke or carouse. I am told I snore, but Harry slept too soundly to be bothered by it. No, my problem was my kidney stone. It didn't have me in agony, but there was a dull pain associated with it that made it very hard for me to be pleasant, vivacious, and effervescent. Worse yet, the stone managed to get itself into a position where it activated the "I have to urinate" button, and I was up all night long trying to urinate, and failing. No amount of intellectual awareness of the fact that the bladder was empty kept me from the bathroom. What's more, the function rooms were not air conditioned, and therefore we had a very hot and humid weekend (don't tell me there's no connection), which didn't raise the level of my spirits.

Nevertheless, I did what I could. I met science-fiction writers Walter Miller and Mildred Clingerman for the first time. Randall Garrett and I shrieked it up in fashion reminiscent of Cleveland, whenever I could forget my kidney stone long enough to allow it.

Sunday, September 2, 1956, was my worst day. During the afternoon, I stood in the ballroom, signing books with a scowl on my face, for I was in agonizing discomfort.

Attending the convention (for that day only so that she and her brother could attend the banquet that night) was a young woman named Janet Opal Jeppson, who had just turned thirty.[13]

[11] See *Earth Is Room Enough.*
[12] See *Buy Jupiter and Other Stories.*
[13] I have this story from her, for I don't remember it at all.

She had been introduced to science fiction by her brother, John (who was going to turn twenty-one later that month). Janet fell in love with science fiction as a result of reading Arthur C. Clarke's *Childhood's End*—and he was guest of honor, which accounted for her interest in the banquet. She then went on to my books and loved them as well.[14]

Seeing me signing books, Janet rushed to the huckster room to get something for me to sign. (Every convention has a huckster room where small dealers sell their secondhand magazines and books, and science-fiction-related paraphernalia.) She obtained a copy of *Foundation and Empire* and waited in line.

Finally, she reached me, rather put off by the fact that I was scowling and looking angry. She had no way of knowing I wasn't angry, but suffering torture.

I took the book from her, without looking up at her, and said, "What's your name?" so I could inscribe it properly.

"Janet Jeppson," she said, spelling it.

I signed appropriately, and said, making conversation, "And what do you do?"

"I'm a psychiatrist," she said.

"Good," I said, quite automatically, for, believe me, I was in no mood for dalliance, "let's get on the couch together."

Janet stalked off, furious, deciding that while my books were great, I was, personally, a "pill" (her most extreme derogatory term for anyone) and someone whom she never wanted to see again, lest repeated exposure to my nastiness spoil her pleasure in my books.

That was my first meeting with Janet.

25

The banquet that night was long and elaborate. Al Capp was a special guest and delivered a very funny speech that was excellently well received. Randall Garrett got up to sing the patter song from *The Gondoliers* ("Rising early in the morning/We proceed to light the fire") but was a little high, I suppose, and didn't remember the words. So, since I was sitting at the dais and was supposed to give a talk of my own, I whispered across to Robert Bloch, who was toastmaster, "Quick, Bob, introduce me."

He did, in two sentences, and I was up and grabbed Randall and made him sing it along with me. I didn't know all the words either, but

[14] Clarke and I are remarkably similar in our appeal. Anyone who likes his books seems sure to like mine, and vice versa.

I knew enough to put them into his mind, we interspersed it with our own brand of lunacy, and it went better than singing it straight would have.

Then I vanished momentarily to visit the nearest men's room. I had warned the people who were organizing the convention that I would be periodically leaving the dais and explained why, and they said that it would be perfectly all right.

But when Arthur Clarke got up to speak, I was determined *not* to leave the dais until he was through, lest the audience assume that I was demonstrating my disapproval of what he was saying. I turned slightly green, therefore, when he rose with something like thirty sheets of typing paper, which he proceeded to read slowly. I can't remember ever spending a more agonizing hour.

There was no use trying to sleep that night. I spent the early part in Dick Wilson's room, and the later part in a cafeteria with A. J. Budrys and Jim Blish, and at 5 A.M. of September 3, I visited the men's room, and out came the kidney stone. It was not a very large one at all, but it had a crystalline outgrowth like a tiny sword.

Why the devil couldn't I have passed it three days sooner?

The next day, Al Capp drove back to Boston and took me and Harry Stubbs with him. Al and I alternated jokes all the way back (with Harry an appreciative audience), so that the ride was like an extension of the convention.

26

On September 10, 1956, David began kindergarten sessions at Peirce Grammar School, and I had by then paid off half the mortgage. But if I was settling down into fatherhood and house ownership and becoming an old hand at each, the past did not vanish. On September 19, I received a letter from Bernie Zitin of the old Navy Yard days.

What had inspired it was an article I had written—"The By-product of Science Fiction,"[15] which had appeared in the August 13, 1956, issue of *Chemical & Engineering News*, the news organ of the American Chemical Society. It was my first effort, but certainly not my last, to explain the importance of science fiction to the great world outside. (Tony Boucher referred to me once as "the apostle to the Gentiles.")

[15] See *Is Anyone There?* (Doubleday, 1967).

27

Another intrusion of the past came when I discovered that living across the street was Gerry Cohen of the days in Camp Lee. He was Gerry Conrad now, and was married to a pleasant Danish woman. Our friendship was renewed at once, though Gerry sounded more cynical and world-weary than I remembered him.

28

And still my appearances in the magazines continued unabated. The November 1956 *F & SF* contained "Gimmicks Three,"[16] which combined the three well-worn gimmicks of pact with the devil, locked-room mystery, and time travel. (Tony Boucher changed the name of the story to "The Brazen Locked Room," but I changed it back when I put it in a collection.) The December 1956 *Infinity* contained "Jokester,"[17] and the December 1956, *Astounding* contained my article "Names! Names! Names!". The January 1957 issue of *Science Fiction* contained "Strikebreaker,"[18] which, for some reason known only to Satan, Lowndes had retitled "Male Strikebreaker."

Bob Mills was editing a magazine called *Venture Science Fiction,* a sister magazine to *F & SF*, and its first issue was dated January 1957. It was going to feature daring stories with more sex in them than one expected to find in ordinary science fiction. In that first issue, my story "The Dust of Death"[19] appeared. It had no sex at all. It was originally a Wendell Urth story, but Tony Boucher hadn't liked it and neither had Bob Mills. Mills, however, needed stories desperately for that first issue and I offered to remove the Urth motif. For some reason, he agreed.

And in the February 1957 *Infinity*, "Let's Get Together"[20] appeared. In no year yet, had I published as many science-fiction stories as in 1956.

[16] See *Earth Is Room Enough.*
[17] See *Earth Is Room Enough.*
[18] See *Nightfall and Other Stories.*
[19] See *Asimov's Mysteries.*
[20] See *The Rest of the Robots.*

5

Hiatus at School

Dr. Walker's troubles were obviously growing worse. Added to his commuting difficulties and his depression over Keefer's position as his superior, there came the fact that in September 1956, Mrs. Walker was seriously ill and required surgery.

It was too much for him and, on October 2, 1956, he told me he had resigned as of November 1. He had been my boss for 7½ years, and although we had had our differences, he had, on the whole, been friendly and understanding, and I was dreadfully upset at his departure.

It was not just the matter of losing him. It was a question of who was to succeed him. Who would be standing between myself and Keefer? Surely I would need some buffer, since it was quite obvious to everyone at the school that I was Keefer's pet abomination on the faculty.

For the moment, Bill Boyd was going to be acting head of the department on the basis of seniority, but Bill was no administrator, nor was he a fighter in any way. He was a good friend and I loved him, but if it came to a fight between myself and Keefer, there was no chance in the world that I could expect effectual support from Bill. In fact, I wouldn't want him to get in between; he was too likely to get hurt.

A silver lining was that the third edition of the textbook was almost done, so that I would not be compelled to make frequent trips to Ashby to work on it. (I had made some and had visited Mrs. Walker in the hospital on September 21, for instance.)

A more distant silver lining was that I was certain, now, that there would never be a fourth edition with Walker gone. I was heartily sick of the textbook. It was a failure, from beginning to end.

The manuscript of the third edition, almost complete, was mailed off to Williams & Wilkins on October 16.

I then settled down to live through the hiatus caused by Walker's resignation—to see who his successor might be and what the upshot would be.

2

Though my various novels had been put into paperback, *Pebble in the Sky* remained an exception. Ever since the first offer had fallen through, nothing further had happened. Then Pyramid Books, one of the smaller paperback concerns, offered to do it, with a one-thousand-dollar advance, provided I cut the book to fifty-five thousand words. I agreed with the greatest reluctance and explained carefully that they would have to get Doubleday's permission and that I could in no way guarantee that they would get it.

I went to considerable trouble cutting *Pebble in the Sky* and sent it in to Pyramid on October 1. Pyramid then took up the matter with Doubleday, and Brad's secretary, Betty Shapian, called me at once. Bantam was offering twenty-five hundred dollars with no suggestion of a cut at all.

It was almost a repeat of what had happened in connection with *The Currents of Space* four years before, but the situation was changed. I had carefully warned Pyramid and had disclaimed personal responsibility.

I explained this to Betty and said, "Give it to Bantam!" And that's the way it was.

3

It was another presidential year. Dwight Eisenhower and Richard Nixon were running for re-election, and opposing for the Democrats was Adlai Stevenson again, and this time his running mate was Estes Kefauver. I had precious little doubt that Eisenhower would be re-elected, even though he had had a heart attack the year before. If there was any chance of an upset, it vanished on October 30 when Great Britain and France tried to take over the Suez Canal with the help of Israel, which sent its armor cutting through the Sinai Desert.

The United States stepped in to prevent this so that the whole affair ended in a fiasco. Eisenhower was able to take up the role of world statesman, and the election took place in an atmosphere of world emergency. On November 6, I gloomily voted for Stevenson, then conceded the election to Eisenhower at 7:25 P.M. I didn't need Univac.

The Democrats, however, retained both houses of Congress. The country might trust Eisenhower as a person, but it had a great deal of difficulty in trusting the Republicans as a party.

4

I was turning out my books regularly. On November 11, I completed *Lucky Starr and the Moons of Jupiter*, and I was already working on a new science book for Abelard-Schuman, one on organic chemistry, which I called *The World of Carbon*.

What's more, I was putting together a collection of the stories that had been flooding the magazines, for Brad had agreed to publish one. I was still thinking of the remarks of reviewers such as George O. Smith and the unspeakable Bott concerning my penchant for wandering over the Galaxy. I therefore picked stories that took place on Earth and called the book *Earth Is Room Enough.*

I drove down to New York with David and submitted both *Lucky Starr and the Moons of Jupiter* and *Earth Is Room Enough* to Doubleday on November 14, 1956.

At Abelard-Schuman, there seemed to be a willingness to do my collections of essays, but "Names! Names! Names!" was definitely rejected. That set me back, since it was my favorite among the articles to be included and the longest. Without it, I didn't have a book's worth and I would have to write three articles simply to replace it. I agreed gloomily to do that and went away, hugging poor "Names! Names! Names!" to my bosom.

I had the three additional articles done by the end of the month. To do this, I merely expanded and popularized several of the articles that had appeared in *The Journal of Chemical Education*. (I try to waste nothing.)

5

For over six years, I had been speaking here and there and getting better and better at it. Unfortunately, there was never any chance of being paid for these talks. Some were to science-fiction groups, some to schools; none were to any organizations that had money.

Besides, I just spoke off the cuff, and it never occurred to me that one charged for talks that one didn't prepare. I chalked it all up to publicity and hoped they helped sell my books.

One of my faculty colleagues was Herbert Wotiz, Viennese-born and with a slight accent. He was of moderate height and he was bright and a little aggressive, but I got along well with him. He threw himself into community affairs, and in Milton, the southern suburb in which he then lived (Harry Stubbs also lived there), Wotiz was an active member of the PTA.

He asked me to address them and it seemed to me I couldn't let a friend down, so I agreed. On November 28, 1956, I made my way down to Milton and spoke to the PTA meeting. According to my diary, I "made a big hit."

Wotiz, over my weak protests, paid me ten dollars of the PTA's money for the talk. I believe this was my first *paid* talk.

6

By the end of 1956, I had been using typewriters for some twenty-one years. First had been the old Underwood No. 5 my father had bought me secondhand. Then there had been two successive Smith-Corona portables.

The grant from the National Heart Institute included five hundred dollars for an electric typewriter, but it took me several months to nerve myself to the task. It was an awfully large purchase—that much money just for a typewriter.

I overcame the hesitation. I ordered one and paid for it with my own money, for I couldn't bring myself to use public money for a typewriter that I would use for my own needs almost all the time. I bought a special typewriter stand, and on December 8, 1956, the typewriter, an IBM Electric, arrived.

It was a nice, whopping standard-size model, and for the first time in eighteen years, I did not have a portable. It had a wide carriage so that I could insert my typewriter sheets the broad way and prepare tables if I had to.

It took a while to get used to the feel of an electric typewriter. I had to learn to stroke the keys more easily and to avoid fiddling with them while thinking. Once I got the hang of it, though, I found I could —quite literally—type all day without getting tired.

Of course, I kept my manual typewriter as a backup, but that proved a useless precaution. I hadn't been using an electric typewriter long before I was completely spoiled. When I tried to return to the manual temporarily, I found I could not bear to push at the keys or to return the carriage by hand.

Nevertheless, the manual remained. Gertrude could use it if she wished, and someday the children might learn to type on it.

I celebrated the arrival of the electric typewriter by beginning a story called "Profession" on the very next day, December 9; the story dealt with the mechanized education of the future and its consequences.

7

By this time Robyn was twenty-two months old and she was speaking very clearly. On December 18, when Gertrude was about to diaper her, Robyn avoided her and said, quite definitely, "I want Daddy to do this."

I had little time to congratulate myself, however, for on December 23, we had a terrible fright. We were giving her a bath in the tub and she, not feeling she needed one, I suppose, was crying desperately. We noticed that when she forced her breath out in a wail, a swelling the size of a golf ball appeared under her left ear.

We called Lewis, the pediatrician, and he said it was an enlarged vein, which might require treatment, but which was not dangerous. On the twenty-seventh, we went to Children's Hospital, where we were told it was a pulmonary hernia and that the tip of Robyn's lung poked up past the shoulder into the neck region. He advised us to do nothing, that such a condition always corrected itself—so we let it go.[1]

Between the twenty-third and the twenty-seventh, between discovering the condition and being soothed, we were absolutely afraid to do anything to cross Robyn in any way, for we didn't want her to cry and, perhaps, pop the vein and die. Robyn, sensing the situation with the unerring instinct of the 2-year-old, behaved with unusual naughtiness, and poor David couldn't understand why she was getting away with it. His experience as a 5½-year-old had long convinced him that we *never* let either kid get away with *anything*.

Of course, that interval included Christmas, and we fixed up a rather small tree gloomily.[2] On Christmas Eve, Robyn casually pulled the tree over and David was overjoyed. Now (I knew he was thinking) this rotten kid is going to be bounced off the wall.

He walked into the kitchen and reported gleefully, "Robyn has just knocked over the tree."

But there was nothing I could do to Robyn, and I was sufficiently beside myself with worry and tension to explode on any safe target. "So

[1] Actually, as the years passed, it did *not* correct itself and we discovered that Lewis's original diagnosis was correct. Nevertheless, we are still told that it can be treated but is not dangerous.

[2] We never had a tree, or celebrated Christmas—or Chanukah, for that matter—in any way before David was about two. Then we had a tree to amuse him. After the children were old enough to be sufficiently worldly wise to find Christmas presents to be just as good without any frills, we discontinued the tree.

what are *you* so happy about?" I said, and gave him a juicy one on his behind.

Poor kid! I apologized later and tried to make it up to him, but it took him a long time to get over his self-righteous sense of undeserved victimization.

8

But if the year ended with this terrible scare, there was nothing to complain of as far as my writing was concerned. In 1956, I had published three books:

17. *Lucky Starr and the Big Sun of Mercury* (Doubleday)
18. *Chemistry and Human Health* (McGraw-Hill)
19. *Inside the Atom* (Abelard-Schuman)

Already I had a multiplicity of publishers. Of the nineteen books, ten had been published by Doubleday, four by Gnome, three by Abelard-Schuman, one by Williams & Wilkins, and one by McGraw-Hill.

This was not my doing. I would cheerfully have published everything with Doubleday, which paid far more copiously and far more promptly than anyone else. Brad had, however, specifically rejected the Gnome Press books before I turned to Marty and had also disclaimed interest in my nonfiction.

As for my literary earnings, they came, for 1956, to the unbelievable sum of just over $16,600, nearly twice what I had made the year before and half again as much as my previous record, in 1954. By now I realized why $10,000 wasn't necessarily the maximum. As my backlist of books grew, each continued to earn something both in sales and in subsidiary rights, and this was added to the earnings of my current writings.

Under those conditions, I didn't dare estimate what a reasonable maximum earning power might be, but each time the figure expanded I felt that surely I would never be able to do that again. In 1956 (as in 1954) I felt that I might perhaps have hit my best year and be looking back upon it as a receding peak forever after.

My school earnings were $6,250, so that my writing was now bringing me in nearly three times as much as my teaching was, and this was important, for it strengthened my will and prepared me for any struggle that lay ahead with Keefer.

My total income for 1956 came to nearly $23,000.

9

There was every sign that my literary prosperity would continue into the new year of 1957. *The Naked Sun* came out very early in the new year. In fact, I received an advance copy on December 20, 1956.

More satisfying, somehow, was that I had gotten a letter from Horace Gold, pleading once more for stories. He enclosed two letters from fans who specifically asked for more stories by me, and one of them berated poor Horace for letting *The Naked Sun* go to Campbell.

Gertrude advised against sending anything to Horace because of his penchant for insulting demands for revision, but I am not immune to flattery. I had finished "Profession" on January 6, 1957, and I sent it to Horace.

Gertrude was right. On January 15, 1957, the story came back with, by all odds, the most insulting rejection letter I ever got—quite needlessly insulting. An editor can say a story is bad without implying that the author is so used to selling his stories without any effort that he is too lazy to make them good anymore. The best way to get across the flavor of his letter is to quote a piece of verse I wrote nearly a year later, entitled "Rejection Slips."[3]

The poem—a satire, of course—gave three sample rejection slips. The first, subtitled "Learned," was a pastiche of the kind of letters I got from Campbell, which often couldn't be easily understood. (I was thinking of his request for a revision of "The Abnormality of Being Normal," which I had taken for a flat rejection.) The third was subtitled "Kindly" and was the kind of letter Tony Boucher wrote, that was so full of praise and sweetness you hardly noticed that the manuscript had been returned. The second one, however, was subtitled "Gruff" and I wrote it with Horace's letter on "Profession" in mind. It went:

> *Dear Ike, I was prepared*
> *(And, boy, I really cared)*
> *To swallow almost anything you wrote.*
> *But, Ike, you're just plain shot,*
> *Your writing's gone to pot,*
> *There's nothing left but hack and mental bloat.*
> *Take back this piece of junk;*
> *It smelled; it reeked; it stunk;*
> *Just glancing through it once was deadly rough.*

[3] See *Nine Tomorrows.*

But Ike, boy, by and by,
Just try another try.
I need some yarns and, kid, I love your stuff.

As you see, I was capable of making fun of the rejection a year later, but when I received it I was furious and my instant decision was the natural one that any writer would make under the circumstances. I was determined never to submit anything more to Horace.

It wasn't as though "Profession" was that bad. I *knew* it was a good story. In fact, I mailed it to Campbell at once, and before the end of the month, I had his check for $840 in hand—21,000 words at $.04 a word.

By January 17, 1957, we had had seven snowstorms and cold snaps in which the temperature went as low as —12° F in Boston and very likely lower by a few degrees in Newton. (On the coldest day, when the milkman showed up, he looked so darned cold that I got out of the house, walked down to the curb, and took the milk from him to save him the trip. As it happened, I was in my shirt sleeves. Actually, this wasn't too quixotic, for there was no wind at all and I was only out for a minute or so, not long enough for the natural heat of my clothing to vanish altogether. The milkman stared and said, "Are you crazy?" I grinned and said, "No, Russian.")

The walks on either side of the house iced up. Water leaked around the main door, froze, and warped the wood, so that for the rest of the winter we could not open it and had to use the back door.

Then, on January 17, I got my first set of snow tires ever. My comment in my diary for January 17 was, "I got my snow tires on finally, first I ever owned. I dare say there will be no more snow now."

I was *right*. The snowstorms stopped as though chopped off with an ax. I'm not paranoid; I don't really think the universe is run entirely in order to spite me. But sometimes I waver.

10

My eighth teaching semester began on January 21, 1957, and three days later I received a copy of the March 1939 *Amazing* from Forrie Ackerman. It was the one that contained my first story, "Marooned off Vesta." It was eighteen years since that magazine had first appeared, alive, on the stands. I had been a professional writer, now, for nearly half my life.

Also on the twenty-fourth, I received a request to lecture to the Carbon Club at Harvard. (It was the undergraduate chemistry club.) It wasn't so long before that I would have agreed without thought. Now, Wotiz's ten dollars had spoiled me. Therefore, I asked a fee. Nor was I such a fool as to ask for a mere ten dollars; I asked for fifteen.

The Carbon Club accepted that gleefully and I gave the talk, most successfully, on February 25. I felt very guilty about pocketing the fifteen dollars.

11

On January 30, 1957, I began the cardiovascular book at last, or, at least, the preliminary book on blood, which I was calling *The Living River*.

Less pleasant was the fact that Gertrude had been suffering from aches in her shoulders. As I recall, she felt them first after she had been pottering about the lawn the previous summer, trying to dig up dandelions. On February 8, the pains were diagnosed as rheumatoid arthritis. Mary Blugerman had long been arthritic, and apparently the tendency to it was inherited.

12

I continued to be on the lookout for misspellings of my name and made every attempt to get after the misspellers. Since the most frequent misspelling was to place a "z" in my last name, my plaintive request was often "Spell my name with an 's.'"

Larry Shaw, being the recipient of one such letter, replied (perhaps with a touch of waspishness) that I ought to write a story entitled "Spell my Name with an 'S.'"

Why not? When, on February 11, 1957, Fred Pohl asked me, by mail, to write a story for him, I began one with just such a title. It was a semifantasy in which the history of the world was changed simply because a physicist by the name of Zebatinsky was induced to change his name to Sebatinsky.

Meanwhile, the March 1957 *Astounding* appeared with my article "Planets Have an Air About Them," and others followed in rapid succession. The April, May, and July issues of *Astounding* each contained a science article by me.[4]

As these articles appeared, I could feel the desire to undertake a monthly science column in *Astounding*, rather similar to the one Willy Ley was doing for *Galaxy*. I never broached this possibility to Campbell

[4] For all of them, see *Only a Trillion*.

who, I knew, preferred to have various writers compete for a place in the magazine.

The thought remained in my mind, however.

13

I had discovered, as surely almost everyone discovers, in the course of my life that few things told confidentially remain confidential. For that reason, I have tried never to say anything confidentially that might rebound upon me uncomfortably if it were not kept confidential. That is not always possible, and in one case I lost a friend.

At some time in 1956, on one of his periodic visits to MIT, John Campbell told me that Randall Garrett was engaged to his step-daughter. Randall was writing regularly for Campbell now and his stories suited the Campbell philosophy right down the middle. Campbell was delighted at the prospective marriage.

We were in an automobile at the time; it was nighttime; it was dark; he couldn't see my face.

My silence didn't seem appropriate, however, and Campbell said, "What's the matter, Isaac? Don't you approve?"

I was in a quandary. Randall and I had had wild and essentially innocent fun at several conventions and I greatly admired his somewhat erratic brilliance. To mention just one of its aspects, his ability to write comic-verse parodies far exceeded mine. On the other hand, the fact was that I owed everything in my writing career to Campbell, so how could I remain silent?

Finally, I said, "I don't think I approve, actually. Randall is a brilliant fellow, generous and kind to a fault, but I don't know if he would be right for your daughter."

I wouldn't have said that if Campbell hadn't asked me flatly, and if I hadn't found myself unable to deliver the lie direct.

Eventually, the engagement broke up, but, I rather think, not because of what I had said.

Campbell had many pseudopsychiatric ideas, and one of them was that quarrels ought to be tape-recorded and listened to in cold blood afterward so that each side could hear exactly what was said on both sides and, what was more important, the exact tone in which everything was said.

I think there may be something to be said for that idea, but Campbell went rather too far, I think. He recorded many arguments and played them back not only to the people involved but to others, too, I think. I know that once, when I visited his home, he played one such tape, to my intense embarrassment. He wanted to use the tape to point out exactly at which moment Randall had proved the engagement to be an undesirable one. He overbore my suggestion that it was not really any of my business, because there was a psychological point he wanted to make that he considered important. I could do nothing but maintain a frozen silence.

On February 21, 1957, Campbell called me to say that Randall had "guessed" (Campbell's word) that I had said some uncomplimentary things about him, and he felt he ought to warn me about that. I didn't see how Randall could *guess* it, and I could only suppose that in the heat of debate, Campbell had *told* him that I had given my friend an unfavorable reference.

I regretted that now, but it was too late to do so. Some years passed in which Randall and I were estranged, and I always felt it was my fault.

14

But if old friendships break, new friendships arise.

I received a letter, dated January 21, 1957, from Austin Olney, head of the Juvenile Division of Houghton Mifflin Company, a publishing firm based in Boston. He had read my science fiction and knew of my interest, science fictionally at least, in computers. (In fact, the handwritten postscript to the letter was, "I am a long-term Asimov fan, myself.")

Houghton Mifflin was planning to put out an American edition of a book on computers called *Thinking by Machine*, written by Pierre de Latil. Olney sent me a copy of the British edition and asked my opinion of it.

On February 27, I visited Houghton Mifflin for the first time, met Olney, and had lunch with him at Locke-Ober's. We discussed *Thinking by Machine*, and the next day I received a letter from him asking me to write an Introduction to it.

I did, and that was the beginning of a close friendship.

15

Robyn's second birthday came on February 19, 1957, and March 12 was the first anniversary of our move into the West Newton house.

. Both passed quietly, and in the case of the house we were in no mood to celebrate. Even its advantages seemed to have their disadvantageous side effects. We were quite close to excellent schools, which was good—and bad.

Our street, you see, was a funnel leading from the Warren Junior High School out to the various places where the students lived, and much of the student body walked along it when school was let out. They yelled and shouted (and also smoked and screamed obscenities to prove their adulthood) and tended to gather on our lawn. It was almost as bad in the morning, when they were going to school.

We were uneasy over collections of teen-age children, and neither of us knew quite how to handle them. We wished that our house was located about ten miles away from any school.

16

We were told by the kindergarten nurse, on March 28, that David was nearsighted and would need glasses. It did not come as any shock to me. Everyone in my family was nearsighted and wore glasses. In fact, my sister's eyes and my brother's were worse than mine.

As it turned out David's eyes were more astigmatic than nearsighted, but that's only a detail. The fact is that he had to begin wearing glasses at the age of six.

The real surprise is that Robyn has never developed a need for glasses. I doubt that she can see a straight 20/20, but she has always seen well enough without glasses, and could pass the driver's eyesight test without them.

17

I received a rather humble letter from Horace in mid-March, which I decided was a sufficient apology for his offensive one rejecting "Profession." He asked for more stories, implying that he would either accept or reject and, if the latter, he would do it without any insulting embroidery.

I wrote "Ideas Die Hard," therefore, in which I explained the uselessness of trying to reach the Moon, pointing out that when astronauts did get there they would find it a false front on some sort of movie set, designed to fool human beings for some reason. It was not meant seriously, of course, but in early 1957 there was already talk of launching satellites and of making serious efforts to reach the Moon—so I took the upside-down view, as in the case with "Everest."[5]

[5] Once again, of course, human advance would make nonsense out of my story, but in this case, at least, not till a couple of years *after* publication.

I sent it off to Horace on April 1, and he was as good as his word. A postcard reached me on April 9, with the news of an acceptance.

18

In those days, I was also writing a series of short science articles for *Science World*, a Street & Smith publication that served as a science magazine for distribution to high schools. Campbell was involved as a consultant and it was through him that I came to the attention of Patricia Lauber, its pleasant and pretty editor.

Some of the articles I wrote were simplified and shortened versions of those I wrote for *Analog*; some were new. They were very easy to write, and in doing them I learned one thing about nonfiction as compared to fiction:

In fiction, every story has to be different, no matter what. Not so in nonfiction. I could write an article for the *Journal of Chemical Education*, expand and popularize it for *Analog*, shorten and simplify it for *Science World*. Though it remained essentially the same article, the changes were useful and did not represent "cheating," since each article was aimed at a different audience and had to be tailored to suit.

It also became apparent that I could write all these different nonfiction articles much more rapidly and with less mental turmoil than I could write fiction. Then, too, although a nonfiction article could be rejected, it simply *was* rejected. Never did I have the long, complicated arguments for revision that I received from Campbell, or the short, brutal ones that I received from Horace Gold. As a matter of fact, the percentage of rejections was less in the case of nonfiction.

Insensibly, I found myself increasingly drawn to nonfiction.

19

I was working madly on the galleys of the third edition of *Biochemistry and Human Metabolism*. Bill Boyd was always lackluster about such things and now had the duties of acting headship of the department to fill his time. Walker was away in Ashby and confined himself to remaining in touch by way of the mails.

The lion's share of the work of proofreading and indexing fell on me, which was another reason I knew that the third edition would be the last. I simply would do it no more.

The galleys were finally mailed off on April 17, 1957.

20

On April 11, Horace Gold called me. Again, he needed a story. He *had* to have one. I explained that I could not write another story just now, for I was busy with galleys, and he said, rather impatiently, "Have someone else do the galleys."

"Impossible," I said, with horror. "I wouldn't trust anyone else."

That ended the conversation, and I walked to my desk to resume reading the galleys—and thought: What about a *robot* to read the galleys?

The idea developed rapidly and I dropped a line to Horace, telling him I would do the story after all. The next day I started it, giving it the rather felicitous title (I thought) of "Galley Slave."

It turned out to be thirteen thousand words long, the longest positronic robot story I had done up to that time (excluding novels), and, in my opinion, the best up to that time. I mailed it to Horace on the eighteenth and he accepted it without trouble.

21

My office upstairs was beginning to look more like an office.

We ordered bookcases, simple wooden ones 2½ feet high and 3 feet wide. They were unpainted, but we had them sanded, stained, and varnished, and the man we hired for the purpose did an excellent job.[6]

I then lined my attic wall with them and had a place for my reference books, for my collection of my own books, and for the bound volumes of magazine pieces and paperbacks which, by mid-1957, already numbered twenty-seven.[7]

I had a large filing cabinet at the head of the stairs leading to the two rooms in the attic and eventually I got a large desk with a smooth white top, plus a small filing cabinet with twenty drawers capable of holding typewriter-size paper, and there I could store manuscripts in progress.

My office therefore gained as its core a U-shaped structure. My desk and my small filing cabinet made up the two arms of the U, and my typewriter on its special stand (with its two folding leaves in an

[6] In later years, when we bought additional bookcases, Gertrude sanded, stained, and varnished them herself, doing just as excellent a job.
[7] I made the mistake of binding foreign soft-cover editions of my novels, too, which caused a great proliferation of volumes that I couldn't read. Eventually, I stopped that and restricted my bound volumes to material in the English language only—but even so I remained insufficiently selective and they overproliferated.

outstretched position) formed the crossbar. My stenographer's swivel chair, with me on it, sat within the U, facing the typewriter. On the walls around me was my library.

This arrangement, which took its shape in the attic room in West Newton, has been with me ever since, surviving all later moves.

I also found a way of avoiding the inevitable loss of time that comes with waiting for the mail. I discovered that if I drove down to the branch post office they would be glad to give me my mail. I could get it when the windows opened at 8:00 A.M., sort it quickly, discard the junk, and have the live material back at home and be at work on it by 8:30 A.M.

At first I did it only occasionally, but soon it was a regular thing with me, and my car was on the road at five minutes to eight regardless of the weather. Once when the snow was so deep that there was no question of even getting the car out of the garage, I donned rubber boots and slogged to the post office.

22

On April 7, 1957, I became an uncle for the first time, when Marcia gave birth to a son, whom she named Larry.

23

On April 24, 1957, I made one of my periodic trips to New York, and I planned to stay in a hotel room. Staying at the Blugermans', which I usually did even when I was in New York alone, saved money, but it was hard on Mary Blugerman, and it involved a tedious subway ride to Manhattan each morning and back to Brighton Beach each evening. And I had reached the point where I could easily afford a hotel room.

When the train pulled in to Grand Central, I happily walked to the Hotel Biltmore, just across the street, where the Fourteenth World Science Fiction convention had been held a half year before, and blithely asked for a room. I was told there were no rooms available, and I could hardly believe it. It had never occurred to me that hotels might be filled. I thought hotels had an endless supply of rooms, the way drugstores had endless supplies of toothpaste.

Feeling foolish and most unwilling to drag out to Brighton Beach, I had a brilliant idea. I lugged my suitcase to Doubleday, walked in, and said I needed a hotel room and could they find me one?

By heaven, they did. They got me a very pleasant room at the Hotel Westbury, on Sixty-ninth Street and Madison Avenue.

From then on, I frequently (and, finally, always) got a hotel room when I came to New York alone. After this, however, I knew enough to make a reservation in advance.

My first task after getting my room at the Westbury was to visit Marty Greenberg who gave me, as usual, a check for fifty dollars, with instructions to wait a week before cashing it. He then took me out to Hempstead to look at the new house he was having built for himself and his family. I couldn't help but contrast the exuberant descriptions of the luxury he was planning, with his request that I not cash his rotten fifty-dollar check. I will not deny I felt resentful—yet what was there to be done?

At *Infinity*, Larry Shaw showed me an advance copy of a review by Damon Knight of *The Naked Sun*. Damon said, "As science fiction it is thin, as a murder mystery it is farfetched, but as a love story it is wonderful." He further went on to ask rhetorically, why, if I could write like this, I bothered to write science fiction.

I wrote a letter to *Infinity* to the effect that I loved science fiction and would always write science fiction out of that love, regardless of how well my talents might suit me for other media.

Yet it was during this trip that I undertook, for the first time, to do a piece of major fiction that was not science fiction.

So far, I had written science-fiction mysteries, and I had also written one short story, "What's in a Name?," that was a "straight" mystery, but only minimally removed from science fiction.

Now Isabelle Taylor of the Crime Club, Doubleday's mystery-fiction outlet, asked me to do a mystery novel. I was tempted and agreed. Bradbury said I could do it in place of another Lucky Starr book, and I set about writing the first couple of chapters for Isabelle. She could then judge from that whether to give me a contract or not.

24

I had finished *The World of Carbon*, but Lillian McClintock thought it was far too long and could not be published at any price that was suitable for a juvenile.

I was ready for her, since I knew for myself that it was too long. I pointed out that the first half could be printed as *The World of Carbon* and the second half as *The World of Nitrogen*. Very little would be required to heal over the split by writing an ending for the first book and a beginning for the second.

Lillian agreed, and I was satisfied. Already I was rather proud of the number of my books, and any legitimate device that would fairly increase the number pleased me. To have two books in place of one seemed great.

25

We continued to fix up my attic office.

On May 11, 1957, we ordered an air conditioner, a large one fit to do a heavy job, and it was installed on the twenty-third. It meant that from now on my attic would be suitable for work in the summer. It worked well and I never again had to hide in the basement to do my work.

A purchase of lesser moment was that of a record player and the beginning of a collection of records. I imagined I could type and play records as "background music." Though I stubbornly refused to admit it, it never worked. If I typed, I didn't hear the music. If I wanted to hear the music, I would have to stop typing. Usually I typed.

And on May 13, fifteen months after I had moved into the house, I paid the last installment on the mortgage and owned the house free and clear. Our savings at the time stood at about thirty thousand dollars, or five thousand dollars less than before we had bought the house, but it was clear that the value of the house much more than made up the difference.

26

On May 14, *Super-Science Fiction*, a new magazine, accepted my story "The Gentle Vultures," which, at their request, I had written for them the week before at my usual fee of four cents a word.

I began my murder mystery, too. My first title was *Sit with Death*. After I had written two chapters, I sent it off to Isabelle Taylor and began a new science-fiction story, whose genesis was as follows:

During the course of the science-fiction convention the year before, I had been regaling a group of people at lunch with various funny stories of things that had happened to me in the course of my visits to New York in recent years, and I would say, to account for the fact that I wasn't my usual sober and steady self, "Of course, I was in New York without Gertrude."

Bob Mills, who was at the table, said, "Why don't you write a story called 'I'm in New York Without Gertrude'?"

"Gertrude wouldn't consider that funny," I said.

Mills gestured impatiently. "Don't be so literal. Entitle it "I'm in Marsport Without Hilda.'"

I laughed and forgot it as a trivial joke.

On April 25, 1957, I was lunching with Larry Shaw and mentioned, apropos of whatever the conversational topic was, that I had written every kind of science-fiction story imaginable.

Larry said, "You've never written a science-fiction sex story."

I said, testily, "That's because I choose not to, that's all."

Larry said, "Some people think you don't know how."

I have always been a sitting duck for statements like that. I made up my mind to write a science-fiction sex story, and Mills' old title "I'm in Marsport Without Hilda" occurred to me.

I started it on May 20, and it was my intention either to give it to Ted Sturgeon for any revision he cared to make in it and subsequent publication under *his* name (he had written some very skillful science-fiction sex stories), or I would publish it under a pseudonym. I was determined to keep my own name free of unnecessarily sex-riddled material.

When I finished it and reread it, however, I found I liked it so much, and thought the sex to be so clever and, essentially, inoffensive, that I sent it in to Mills under my own name on June 5, and he bought it at once.

27

Isabelle Taylor agreed, on May 29, to a contract on the basis of the sample chapters I had sent her, asking for certain changes that I agreed to make, and we were in business.

28

On June 2, 1957, I walked into David's room and said, "Goodness, David, you must be gaining weight. Your face looks wider."

Actually, it was his jaws that seemed wider. I touched one of the swellings curiously, and he said, "Ouch."

I tumbled back against the wall and said, "Oh, boy, you've got mumps." And so he had.

I woke up Gertrude and said, "Gertrude, you're going to have to take care of David. He's got the mumps and I've never had it."

I knew what happened to male adults who contracted mumps. The result is, frequently, infected, inflamed, and swollen testicles, and that is no joke indeed. Sometimes the result was sterility. Sprague de Camp had had mumps as an adult, and his story was horrifying.

Of course, I didn't worry about being left sterile, since I had all the children I intended ever to have—but that doesn't matter. I wanted my testicles left in pristine condition.

I called my mother to check with her, and she agreed that while Stanley had had the mumps, when he was seven or eight years old, I myself had never had it.

So Gertrude loyally took charge of David and I maintained myself at the opposite end of the house as much as I could. By June 10, David was well enough to go to school, but on that day, Gertrude herself came down with the mumps. She hadn't told me that she had never had it either. And on June 11, Robyn decided it was lonely out there in Healthyland, and she displayed swollen jaws as well.

I was now the sole survivor, so to speak, and I could avoid my fate no longer. I had to bid my testicles a fond farewell and get to work. While I fed and cared for the two women, I kept surreptitiously feeling my cheeks for the first signs of telltale pain, but nothing ever happened.

It occurred to me, then, that when Stanley got the mumps as a little boy, we were sleeping in the same room. I hadn't gotten the mumps then, at least visibly, but I must have caught a subclinical case that was not intense enough to bother me but was enough to give me immunity.

Robyn improved quickly, but on June 13, Gertrude's mumps passed through a serious stage. In fact, she had mumps encephalitis, which made her delirious, and I had to set up a cot in the living room, keep her there, and sit by her side. The worst of it didn't last long, and mumps encephalitis is benign and never does damage (measles encephalitis, on the other hand, is dangerous and can kill), but it was all very frightening. By June 15 she was clearly improving, and in a few more days we were all well again, with myself the only one to have escaped entirely.

6

New Department Head

1

While the mumps was ravaging our household, a crucial change was taking place at school. A new head of the department had been appointed.

It wasn't Bill Boyd. Bill had applied for the post and was eager to have it as a climax to his distinguished career. His hopes were low because he was convinced Keefer wouldn't consider it for a moment, but Bill gave it the old college try just the same. He went to see Lemon, who was the head of the committee in charge of finding a new head.

According to the story Bill told me later, Lemon advanced some trivial reasons arguing against Bill's candidacy; then Lemon paused and said, "And then there's Asimov!"

Bill understood him to mean that since Bill Boyd was a friend of Isaac Asimov, he would not, as head of the department, consent to the firing of said Isaac Asimov. What Lemon wanted was some head of the department who would be indifferent to my fate and who would cooperate in the extermination; at least that was how Bill judged the situation.

Bill didn't say anything, however, till he was certain he had been rejected. On June 7, 1957, he was called into Keefer's office and was told that one F. Marrott Sinex was to be the new department head.

Bill came out very depressed, and now he told me that he expected me to be fired once the new head took over. I laughed scornfully and said that I didn't think so. I wasn't sure that Bill's assessment of the situation was accurate. It might just be his own gloom over his failure speaking. But even if he were correct, that made no difference. I was quite determined not to be fired.

I neither needed, nor even particularly wanted, the job, but I did enjoy the professorial title, and I certainly wasn't going to allow myself to be pushed out in a disgraceful way.

On June 18, Sinex visited the department for the first time, and I was on hand. I received calls, not only from Bill Boyd, but from many others as well, warning me he would be in. Apparently the whole school was aware that there was going to be a move to fire me, and the whole school was waiting to see my reaction. If they thought I was going to avoid the encounter, they were quite wrong. I made sure I was there.

I met Sinex. He was a young man, only thirty-three at the time, so that he was four years younger than I was. He had a nervous smile, a loud voice, expressed himself rather disjointedly, and broke out into stentorian laughter at odd moments.[1]

He seemed amiable enough at the moment. In my diary I said, "I suspend judgment." I didn't have to suspend it for long.

2

But work went on. The page proofs of the third edition of the textbook came in, and I was busy indexing.

On June 21, I received a letter from the University of Maryland medical school. They wanted me to lecture there the next February 8, and they offered me, as payment, one hundred dollars plus expenses.

That was an awesome fee. It was the first time I had ever been offered a fee in three figures just to talk for an hour. I accepted at once.

3

A young man named Robert Rubin passed his Ph.D. examination on June 25. Rubin was the only doctoral student I ever had working under me.

On that same day, I got a fan letter from television actress Polly Bergen. She had read *The End of Eternity* and loved it. I was delighted. Not only was it flattering to have among my readers someone so beautiful and prominent, but also I had always been taken with her when I saw her on television. She was beautiful *and* intelligent.

4

It was time to go to another Midwescon. I went to New York on the twenty-sixth, and early in the morning the next day, Marty Greenberg picked me up and drove me to Cincinnati. We got there at 11 P.M. after sixteen hours of fairly solid driving. The last fifteen miles was through the tail end of a hurricane that had penetrated far inland, and the rain was torrential.

[1] After Sinex had taken over his duties, a member of the department—not I—was asked if Sinex were in. The person questioned listened for a moment, then said, "He's not anywhere in the building. I'd hear him if he were."

The 2½ days of the convention were pleasant and rather low-key. I met Robert Silverberg there for the first time. He had not been writing science fiction long, but he was establishing a record of prolificity that put even me in the shade. He was a young man with dark, satanic eyes, and a generally lowering expression. He was one of the brightest people I have ever met, but somehow an unhappy one. With him was his wife, Barbara, very good-looking, intelligent, and lighthearted.

I was home in West Newton on the evening of July 1.

5

My science-fiction stories kept appearing. The June 1957 *Infinity* had my short story "Blank!,"[2] which had been written in Larry Shaw's office on a dare, from the title only. Two other writers, Randall Garrett and Harlan Ellison, also wrote stories with the same title, and all three appeared in that issue.

"Does a Bee Care?"[3] appeared in the June 1957 *If*, and "A Woman's Heart" appeared in the June 1957 *Satellite*. This last one was so entirely trivial that I never included it in any of my collections.

The July 1957 *Astounding* included "Profession"[4] as the cover and also my article "The Sea-Urchin and We."[5] It was particularly gratifying to me to see "Profession" in print, and to have it well received after Horace's savage rejection.

The August 1957 *F & SF* published my five-hundred-word "A Loint of Paw,"[6] which, of all my gag stories, pleased me the most. The end point was a Spoonerism: "A niche in time saves Stein."

I wrote additional stories, too. On July 17, I began a new computer story, "All the Troubles in the World," describing the sad lot of a computer that had too many of humanity's problems loaded on its shoulders.

And on July 30, I began a short story called "The Feeling of Power," which dealt with a world in which computers were so ubiquitous that people had forgotten the techniques of pen-and-ink computation.

That story had its origin in the fact that Bill Boyd dared me to think up the plot of a science-fiction story on the spot. Since he had a desk calculator on his desk (one of the old mechanical ones), I used

---

[2] See *Buy Jupiter and Other Stories.*
[3] See *Buy Jupiter and Other Stories.*
[4] See *Nine Tomorrows.*
[5] See *Only a Trillion.*
[6] See *Asimov's Mysteries.*

that as the basis. He liked the plot and I said, magnanimously, "You can have it."

Driving home that evening, however, the story so developed itself in my mind that I couldn't bear to let him have it after all. I called Bill the instant I got home, took back the story, and wrote it as quickly as I could.

And meanwhile, on July 8, I mailed off the index to the third edition of *Biochemistry and Human Metabolism*. The galleys of the index arrived on July 29; I checked them and mailed them back on July 30, 1957. After six years, my work on that ill-fated and useless venture was over forever.

6

Stanley called on the morning of July 17, 1957, to tell me he was a father. Ruth had borne a son, who was named Eric. That meant I had two nephews. In fact, I had three, for Stanley eventually adopted Ruth's son, Danny, too. And a week later, Stanley turned twenty-eight. My kid brother was no kid anymore.

7

On July 22, 1957, Catherine de Camp was at MIT with her two sons. She was checking out colleges for her son Rusty (it was over twelve years since we had baby-sat with him as a preschool youngster). I hadn't seen her for five years and she was forty-nine now, and I felt I would be distressed at seeing her beauty fade.

How wrong I was! I saw her coming down the long corridor at MIT and she looked almost as though it were still 1941, when I had first met her. I took her and the children to lunch and then drove them past our house. Since David was down with a throat infection, I didn't want them coming in and subjecting her children to the contagion. The rest of us congregated in the driveway, and David waved from the window.

8

I was on television for the first time on July 23, 1957. I shared the program (a talk show on Boston's educational channel) with Norbert Wiener, who took me to MIT afterward and told me, in some detail, of a novel he was writing.

9

On August 3, 1957, I drove to Washington from Boston, covering 450 miles in 9½ hours. While there, I gave a series of lectures on biochemical subjects to a summer class for high-school teachers of science.

On my way home, I stopped in New York for a couple of days and picked up an advance copy of *Lucky Starr and the Moons of Jupiter.*

I also called Abelard-Schuman to get the latest news on my books. I wasn't entirely happy with Abelard-Schuman. In the first place, Lillian McClintock's husband, who copy edited my books, copy edited them heavily, leaving scarcely a sentence untouched, and I hated that. For another, publications were often delayed, I was charged for diagrams, and so on. I felt restive and was ready to move on to another publisher if one offered itself.

10

I finally got home on August 8, and at 4 P.M. I said to Gertrude, "Where's Robyn?"

"Out playing," said Gertrude, who was busy preparing dinner.

I went out to call her. She didn't answer. No one had seen her. She was only 2½. I ordered David to find her but he failed and I felt he should have been watching her and told him so angrily. The poor kid was only 6; how responsible could he be?

I took out the car and drove slowly about the neighborhood calling for Robyn. There was no answer. At our wits' end, we called the police.

It was the first time we had ever lost a child. David had a perfect sense of direction and never got lost. He always knew exactly where he was and how to get home.

Now there was nothing to do but wait for the police, and this we did with mounting terror. Finally, a police car came driving slowly down the street and we waved to it frantically, out of our minds with eagerness to tell the story and get them looking.

We didn't have to. They had Robyn with them.

"Is this the child?" they asked.

"Yes," I said, seizing her and holding her so tightly I nearly collapsed her rib cage. "How did you find her?"

"Well," one of them said, "after we got your call, we got another call from a woman two blocks away saying there was a lost child wandering about, and we thought there wouldn't be two children lost in this neighborhood, so we went there first."

They drove off after refusing the five-dollar bill I tried to press upon them.

11

Williams & Wilkins put out a small in-house periodical called *Kalends*. Since we were Williams & Wilkins authors we got copies. I always found them of surpassing dullness to anyone outside the shop and would dump them without reading them.

In one issue, however, a puzzle was introduced, and some sort of minor prize was offered the first to solve it. The editor of the periodical said he didn't know the answer himself, but the contributor had assured him there was one. (It was rather foolish not to know the answer before publishing.)

The puzzle went as follows:

> *To five and five and fifty-five*
> *The first of letters add.*
> *It was a thing that pleased a king*
> *And made a wise man sad.*

I had thrown away my copy without opening it, but one of Boyd's assistants arrived with it. With touching faith in my cleverness she said, "Please solve it for me, Dr. Asimov, so I can send it in and win the prize."

I looked at it and immediately I thought of Bathsheba. She had pleased King David, who took her from her husband and arranged to have the inconvenient gentleman killed in battle. That wicked deed saddened the wise prophet Nathan.

Well, then, "five and five and fifty-five" expressed in Roman numerals was V and V and LV, and if we add "the first of letters" or A, we get VVLVA, and, remembering that in Latin, inscriptions V and U are identical, we get the answer "vulva," which is the female genital organ—and certainly that pleased David and saddened Nathan.

I said to the girl, "I don't think you want to send this in," and explained the reason. She agreed that I should write a letter and I did, gently telling the editor he was an ass for buying a pig in a poke.

It turned out that my analysis was correct, of course, and in a future issue of *Kalends* the editor begged off from announcing the solution and listed some of those in the firm who had solved the puzzle. My name was not listed, nor was my letter answered. The editor, apparently, felt his asshood should not have been mentioned.

12

The October 1957 *Galaxy* contained "Ideas Die Hard." It was the first time I had had anything in *Galaxy* since "The Caves of Steel" almost four years before. "Ideas Die Hard," with its gag suggestion that the Moon was only a false front, became foolish once the Soviets photographed the far side of the Moon. The idea of the story became too silly for me to tolerate, in fact. It was anthologized a few times, but I never put it into one of my collections.

13

On August 13, the whole family, children included, went to Moodus, Connecticut, to spend a vacation at "Holiday House." It was the first time we had ever taken the children with us.

On the whole, it was not a success. They had a kind of nursery school at which the children could stay, but we were never at ease with that arrangement. Furthermore, David could not bring himself to eat the resort-hotel food, breakfast in particular.[7] His breakfast those days consisted invariably of toast broken up into two soft-boiled eggs and the whole mixed together. I had to come down every morning and prepare that for him.

What's more, all four of us, one at a time, got "red throat," which was, apparently, endemic in the hotel. Nothing serious; it just meant that each one of us was out of things a day or so and, in the course of the week, no one day saw all of us out and about.

I spent part of my time working on a robot story for *Infinity*, one I called "What's the Use?" It was about a robot that had accidentally come off the assembly line as the equivalent of a human idiot and the problem of finding a use for it. I had brought my manual typewriter and it was my first idea to work indoors.

Gertrude, however, urged me to take advantage of the beautiful weather and work outdoors. I saw her point and went outdoors.

It had its disadvantages. In the first place, it was sufficiently windy so that I had to use stones to keep my paper in place. In the second place, people kept coming up curiously to see what I was typing and, after they had watched a while, they would say, "What are you doing?"

"Typing a story," I would say.

"What for?" they would want to know.

"So I can sell it. I'm a writer."

"You mean you're working?" they would say, horrified. The fact

---

[7] I was sympathetic. I could well remember my own stays at resorts when I was a little older than David was then and my own objections to resort-hotel food.

that I was working spread throughout the camp and created some ill will. It was un-American, apparently, to want to work and to prefer work to vacation.

I finished the story, however, and mailed it off to Larry Shaw from Moodus, at the same time I was buying penicillin for the red throat. Larry took it at once.

We got back on August 20, just in time to celebrate David's sixth birthday.

14

On August 21, I did my second television appearance, again on the educational channel. This time it was with David O. Woodbury and John Hansen, two science writers. We were to discuss the art of writing on scientific and technical matters for the public, and in a preliminary lunch with them at the MIT faculty club, I got the impression they would ask me to write a science-fiction story right there on the air.

So, just in case they did, I quietly invented a very short one. On the air, sure enough, the task was sprung on me, as a challenge, and I agreed. With the lights blazing and the camera rolling, I wrote away, answering questions that the others put to me as a deliberate distraction.

I managed to finish (the story was only 350 words) and read it out before the half-hour program was over.

Once I got home, I typed it up, entitled it "Insert Knob A in Hole B," and sent it off to *F & SF*, with an explanation as to how it came to be. Tony Boucher accepted it at once.

That month, the Abelard-Schuman book *Building Blocks of the Universe* finally came, as well as my Doubleday collection of short stories, *Earth Is Room Enough*.

Some of my science-fiction stories appeared at about this time, too. The November 1957 *Venture* arrived with "I'm in Marsport Without Hilda."[8] the December 1957 *Super-Science* had "The Gentle Vultures,"[9] and the October 1957 *Astounding* had my science article "Overflowing the Periodic Table."[10]

15

On September 4, 1957, I got a phone call from Dr. Yeager of the

[8] See *Asimov's Mysteries.*
[9] See *Nine Tomorrows.*
[10] See *Science Past—Science Future* (Doubleday, 1975).

National Heart Institute concerning my request for a year's extension of the grant without additional funds.

I was glad to be able to explain to him that *The Living River* was finally under way but that I wouldn't be able to finish it till the second year of the grant.

"However," I said, "I haven't drawn the twenty-five hundred dollars assigned me in the grant. I won't touch a penny of that until the book is finished."

"No, no," said Yeager, sounding quite alarmed. "You mustn't do that. You will upset our bookkeeping. That money must be drawn before the expiration of the grant year."

"I'm sorry," I said, "I didn't know. I'll draw it at once—but I'll pay it back if I don't finish the book. And don't worry, I *will* finish it."

After I got off the phone, I went down to the school office and asked them to set the wheels in motion to make out a check for twenty-five hundred dollars against my grant.

16

On September 6, 1957, we decided we no longer needed diapers for Robyn and cut our relations with the diaper supply company. After six solid years, we no longer saved old diapers to give back and receive clean diapers in their place. It was better than paying off the mortgage.

And on September 9, David entered the first grade. It wasn't a cut-and-dried affair. The school wasn't at all sure he was ready for it, emotionally, and we weren't either. However, we had a talk with the principal, a Miss Caldwell, and we decided to chance it.

17

Sinex was now at school regularly, using Walker's old office, and I was slowly becoming accustomed to his loud voice and abrupt manner. He continued to seem amiable.

I was having a little trouble with that twenty-five-hundred-dollar stipend, however, and that I found irritating. I had thought that since the grant was mine (I was the "principal investigator") I had only to ask for a check to be made out and it would be made out. I found, though, after a few days had passed and I had inquired about the matter, that it was necessary for me to get Keefer's signature.

When I registered instant indignation, they assured me it was only a formality and I trundled down the hall to Keefer's office, in a bad mood, and handed over my application to his secretary.

7

Keefer

1

On September 18, 1957, I was called into Keefer's office.

"Well, Asimov," he said with a catlike smile, "what's all this about you wanting twenty-five hundred dollars from the school?"

I said, "I don't want a penny from the school, sir. I want twenty-five hundred dollars from my grant, money that was assigned to me."

"No," he said, "the grant is to the school, and it rests entirely with us as to whether you get that money."

"It does not," I said hotly. "That money has been assigned to me. The school took its overhead and that's all it gets. My money *I* get."

"We'll see about that," he said. "You know we object to your writing books on school time, and your case will have to be reviewed at the end of the year."

"Go ahead and review it all you want," I said, "but meanwhile I want my money and I mean to get it."

And I stalked out of his office. Actually, I didn't want the twenty-five hundred dollars at all. It could go to hell, for all I cared, but I wasn't going to let *him* have it.

I went straight to Sinex and told him what had happened and demanded to know where he stood. Sinex seemed disturbed, not so much at the confrontation but at its having taken place so soon. He said he would back me up, but with such a lack of enthusiasm that I recognized at once that here was an ally I had better do without.

I therefore said, "I intend to get that twenty-five hundred dollars as a matter of principle, Dr. Sinex, but I don't need any help from you. You've just come here and you may find yourself in trouble if you engage in a controversy on my side. So stay out of it and I'll handle this myself."

I then stalked out of *his* office.

It was clear to me that I'd been neatly mousetrapped. When, in our first round, I had told Keefer that if I were forced to do the book without a grant, I would still get my royalties but that the school would not get its overhead; Keefer had outmaneuvered me. He let the grant go through and collected the overhead and then intended to keep my part of the grant as well.

Had I applied for my twenty-five hundred dollars the instant the grant had become official, as anyone else would have done, it might have gone through, for Bill Boyd would have been department head and Keefer might have felt he couldn't rely on Bill's co-operation. Because I had allowed my conscience to hold me back from trying to get the money until I had earned it, I had played into Keefer's hands. With Sinex in place, Keefer expected no trouble.

On the other hand, Keefer had, to some extent, outsmarted himself as well. Had he resisted the temptation to win the small stake, and let me have the money, he could have kept me quiet till the end of the school year, when he could have faced me with a *fait accompli* in the form of a piece of paper telling me that my position had been terminated.

As it was, there was now going to be a very loud and noisy fight—something I don't think he had expected.

2

Compared to the beginning of the confrontation at school, there came much better news at home. Bob Mills called me and suggested a monthly science column for *Venture*. I agreed enthusiastically, for this was just the sort of thing I wanted. I was to make each column twelve hundred words long and I was to be paid fifty dollars for each column. What's more, I was to have an absolutely free hand on subject matter.

I sat down immediately and wrote "Fecundity Limited," my first article on the population problem. I sent it in on September 19, and it was taken at once.

3

On September 19, Bill Boyd finally told me that Lemon had told him, "Asimov, although a brilliant man, has done a great deal of harm to the school's reputation, and *he must go!*" Bill was anxious to warn me that more was at stake than the twenty-five hundred dollars. There was "the Asimov problem," as Lemon had called it.

I knew that, and my comment in my diary was: "The simple bastards think they can solve it [the Asimov problem] easily, I suppose." Not for a minute did I think they would win out over me.

On the twentieth, Sinex told me he had talked to Keefer and had suggested trying to get me onto the graduate school payroll and therefore, in theory, out of the med school.

To me this seemed to be an attempt by Sinex to set up a compromise that would keep me from exploding, as I threatened to do. I was certain, however, that Keefer would not allow this compromise and, for that matter, that I would not accept it if he did.

I said, "If I were you, Dr. Sinex, I'd just bow out and stay out of trouble." That indeed was what I wanted him to do. I knew that if he weren't neutral he would have to be on Keefer's side. There was no way in which he could risk his newly gotten job by coming out on my side.

4

I received copies of the third edition of *Biochemistry and Human Metabolism* on September 23, but it meant nothing to me. I put it on my shelves without even looking inside. Its arrival was symbolic of the final passing of the Walker years, that's all.

Meanwhile, all that month I had been racing to finish *Sit with Death*, my mystery novel. It was done on September 22, and I liked it a great deal. On Wednesday, September 25, I drove to New York to take it in personally. It had, not entirely coincidentally, a subplot in which the professorial hero struggled to obtain tenure.[1]

I visited Horace Gold on the twenty-sixth for the first time in two years. He and Evelyn were divorced now.

On the twenty-eighth, I drove into Long Island to see Stanley and Ruth at their house, which I saw for the first time—and I saw my nephew Eric for the first time, too.

Then I drove home to West Newton. I was feeling quite ill, my muscles were aching, and I was coughing constantly. I was coming down with a bad siege of bronchitis. The next day was Sunday, and I spent most of it in bed in a semistupor.

The next day I pulled myself together and went to school to hear Sinex lecture for the first time. He talked on protein structure to a class on "Special Topics." He clearly knew his subject, but his lecturing was as disjointed as his ordinary speech, and I was quite certain the students were having difficulty following him.

[1] As in "What's in a Name?," the new novel had a chemistry department as the scene and chemists as characters.

5

On October 1, I checked at Keefer's office to see if a decision had been reached on my twenty-five hundred dollars. It hadn't, so I began my counterattack.

I went to see Vice President McLaren of Boston University, who was in charge of administrative matters concerning grants, and stated my case as strongly as possible. I was in no mood to be diplomatic, so I told him what I thought of Keefer in straightforward terms and warned McLaren that if I did not get my twenty-five hundred dollars I would take the matter up with Washington and, if necessary, with the courts, and that I would not rest till I got the money.

He urged me to wait before doing anything drastic, and I said that unless Keefer let me have the money, I would do whatever was necessary to get it, however drastic.

6

On the next day, October 2, I asked for an appointment to see Lamar Soutter, the dean who worked directly under Keefer. Soutter said he would come up and see me—and he did, almost at once.

I closed and locked the door and said,[2] "I have something to say, Dr. Soutter. I should say it to Dr. Keefer, but I will not speak to him, and I am going to have to depend on you to tell him this.

"You may remember that a year and a half ago, you confronted me with a demand that I apologize in writing to a young lady. I did so, and then offered to resign, an offer you refused. I gave in at that time because, on reflection, I felt I was in the wrong; and I do not fight blindly when I am in the wrong.

"This time, however, I am in the *right*, and nothing will budge me from my demand for justice."

I then went through the background of the conflict, stressing the fact that Dr. Yeager had come to *me*, had offered *me* the grant, had badgered *me* into taking it, and that Keefer had approved it. I explained that I was doing the book and that I had not touched one penny of the money till Yeager virtually ordered me to take it, and that now it had become a matter of principle.

---

[2] I did not record the conversations I had in connection with my quarrels with Keefer, but I have an excellent memory, and while I can't say my quotations are word for word, they are essentially accurate even in fine detail.

I said, "I have been out there in the harsh world of business, Dean Soutter. For nearly twenty years, I have been dealing with editors and publishers, and, on occasion, a mere handshake has closed a business deal involving far more money than this twenty-five hundred dollars. And not once in all that time have I been cheated and robbed; not once. There have been times when someone didn't have the money to give me at once, but they never denied my right to have it, and they always paid me in the end.

"Do you think that I will now sit still here in the cloistered halls of ivy and let myself be cheated out of money that a written and signed contract says is mine? Never!

"You can be certain, Dean Soutter, that I will take this up with Washington, and I will not rest, nor give in, no matter how high up I have to go. Nor need you think that fear of losing my salary will deter me. I make far more money through my writing than I do at school, and I can afford to fight, however long it will take me. The publicity that it will entail will help sell my books, and I will make a profit out of it, but that same publicity can only hurt the medical school."

I was warming to the topic now, driven by the heat of my anger, and there was no pause in my eloquence—after all, I had been a professional writer for nineteen years and a public speaker for seven years, and words were my business.

"And speaking of publicity, just consider what will happen if, by some chance, Keefer does take my money, and then succeeds in taking my job. What reason is there for doing so? Certainly, it isn't because of any flaw in my teaching, since any student will tell you I am the best teacher in the school. You are welcome to attend my lectures if you doubt this. Keefer says it is because I write science books.

"Well, when I came here to the medical school eight years ago, I had not yet published a single book, and was known to only a few thousand science-fiction readers. In the eight years I have been at the school, I have become internationally known and have published twenty-three books."

I emphasized the number and caught him. Dean Soutter had clearly not known the number. "Twenty-three?" he asked.

"Twenty-three! And of those twenty-three, six are books on science that have been highly regarded. I am already considered an important and skillful science writer. I am one of the best science-fiction writers in the world, of course, but that is not what I am talking about. I am now an important and skillful *science* writer, and I don't intend to stop. In the next eight years, I will have twenty-three more books,[3] and I will be recognized as the *best* science writer in the world.[4] I have fulfilled my ambitions to this point, Dean Soutter, and I assure you I will fulfill this one.

"And when I am recognized as the *best* science writer in the world, I will be frequently asked by ordinary people, by newspaper reporters, by television hosts—and I am already frequently interviewed in newspapers and on radio and television—why on Earth I gave up my position at Boston University School of Medicine, and I will answer that I did not give it up, but that I was kicked out. And when they ask why, I will say that the school felt that my science writing would disgrace them. And they will *laugh*, Dean Soutter. They will laugh at the school, not at me.

"Now you tell all this to Keefer, Dean Soutter, and tell him it will be better for him to give me my money."

Dean Soutter, who had said almost nothing through all this, nodded and left. What he told Keefer, I don't know, but I got the twenty-five hundred dollars and had won the second round.

7

This time I knew it was only the second round and that Keefer would now be more than ever ready to fire me. So did everyone else, and I suddenly found that people at the school stopped seeing me. I had become a nonperson.

It was each person's obvious notion that by becoming too closely associated with me, he or she would be viewed as part of some "Asimov clique" and would be marked down for destruction as well. I didn't blame them.

One exception was Elizabeth Moyer, a professor in the Anatomy Department. Elizabeth was a tall, large woman who was, herself, an odd character. She was an excellent teacher, very popular with the students, and not entirely popular with the administration. She was a single woman who led a lonely life, and, as is natural under the circumstances, she filled her world with office politics and office gossip.

She was delighted at seeing me tackle the administration, and I could always go down to her office when I felt the pressures mount, and there relax for an hour or so, while she told me what this person said and what that person said. I never depended entirely on what she told me, but it fulfilled a need for companionship that I wasn't getting else-

[3] This proved a gross underestimate.
[4] Perhaps an overestimate, but I had no intention of pulling punches.

where. Even Bill Boyd, though his position was secure and he therefore did not have to avoid me, was doubtful solace, since his feeling—freely expressed to me—was that there was no way in which I could win.

8

On October 2, 1957, I had begun a new science-fiction story called "The Ugly Little Boy." It dealt with a Neanderthal boy brought into the present by a time machine of sorts, and of a nurse who gradually came to love him.

Merely writing the story, however, did not soothe me. My restlessness over the quarrel with Keefer required something more. I had boasted to Soutter concerning the number of my books, and I wanted some evidence that there were more to come. I had not yet heard about *Sit with Death* from Isabelle Taylor, so on October 4 I called her up.

Isabelle hesitated and at first I thought she was going to ask for a revision. She wasn't. She didn't like the book at all. It was a flat rejection. It was the first time any book of mine, written for Doubleday, had been rejected outright by that firm.

I was staggered. After I hung up the phone, I closed and locked my office door, went to my desk, and simply put my head down on my arms. Perhaps everything was changing. Perhaps my wild boast to Soutter had been too much and from now on everything would go downhill.

Then I thought: No, I can't let myself slide into despair. I may lose, but I won't surrender.

So, with the door still locked, I began to write a piece of comic verse. Before I got up from that desk, I had prepared a poem called "I Just Make Them Up, See!," which, for multiplicity of rhyme and jocularity of meter, I have never surpassed. It was the funniest poem I had ever written, and I can't resist quoting it now that I've explained the circumstances under which it was written. Here's how it goes:

I Just Make Them Up, See!

Oh Dr. A.—
Oh Dr. A.—
There is something (don't go 'way)
That I'd like to hear you say.
Though I'd rather die
Than try
To pry,
The fact, you'll find,

Is that my mind
Has evolved the jackpot question for today.

I intend no cheap derision.
So please answer with decision,
And, discarding all your petty cautious fears,
Tell the secret of your vision!
How on earth
Do you give birth
To those crazy and impossible ideas?
Is it indigestion
And a question
Of the nightmare that results?
Of your eyeballs whirling,
Twirling,
Fingers curling
And unfurling,
While your blood beats maddened chimes
As it keeps impassioned times
With your thick, uneven pulse?

Is it that, you think, or liquor
That brings on the wildness quicker?
For a teeny
Weeny
Dry martini
May be just your private genie;
Or perhaps those Tom and Jerries
You will find the very
Berries
For inducing
And unloosing
That weird gimmick or that kicker;
Or an awful
Combination
Of unlawful
Stimulation,
Marijuana plus tequila,
That will give you just that feel o'
Things a-clicking
And unsticking
As you start your cerebration

To the crazy syncopation
Of a brain a-tocking-ticking.

Surely something, Dr. A.,
Makes you fey
And quite outré.

Since I read you with devotion,
Won't you give me just a notion
Of that shrewdly pepped-up potion
Out of which emerge your plots?
That wild secret bubbly mixture
That has made you such a fixture
In most favored s.f. spots—

Now Dr. A.,
Don't go away—
Oh, Dr. A.—
Oh Dr. A.—

9

I sent the poem off to Tony Boucher the next day, and he took it with delight. The poem only earned me thirty dollars, but it was a very important thirty dollars. I took it as an indication that even when I seemed to hit bottom I could still write.

And, after all, my science-fiction stories were still appearing. The December 1957 *Galaxy* contained "Galley Slave."[5] The December 1957 *F & SF* contained "I Feel It in My Bones," a science article on fallout and strontium-90 that was then much in the news, but that rapidly became outdated so that I never included it in any of my collections, and "Insert Knob A in Hole B."[6] The December 1957 *Astounding* included "The Whenabouts of Radioactivity" (which, again, appears in no collection of mine).

The January 1958 issue of Fred Pohl's new magazine *Star Science Fiction* (its first and only issue) contained "Spell My Name with an 'S,' "[7] which Fred, with incredible obtuseness, retitled "S as in Zebatinsky." You can be sure I changed the title back in my collection.

Most important of all, the January 1958 issue of *Venture* con-

[5] See *The Rest of the Robots.*
[6] See *Nightfall and Other Stories.*
[7] See *Nine Tomorrows.*

tained "Fecundity Limited,"[8] which I hoped would be the first of an open-ended series of such articles.

10

Yet this was the final explosion of science fiction. That portion of my writing career in which I dealt chiefly with science fiction was coming to an end, and "The Ugly Little Boy," which I was in the process of writing, was to be the last of a series of perhaps 150 stories (including a few articles) that I had placed in science-fiction magazines in a steady stream over the past twenty years.

What happened was that on October 4, 1957, the day I called Isabelle, discovered the rejection of *Sit with Death*, and wrote, "I Just Make Them Up, See!," the Soviet Union sent up the first artificial satellite, Sputnik I.

The United States went into a dreadful crisis of confidence over the fact that the Soviet Union had gotten there first and berated itself for not being interested enough in science. And I berated myself for spending too much time on science fiction when I had the talent to be a great science writer.

From that time onward, it was science that chiefly interested me, and though I continued to write science fiction now and then, it was only now and then. Never again, after the fall of 1957, was science fiction to form the main portion of my output.[9]

Sputnik also served to increase the importance of any known public speaker who could talk on science and, particularly, on space, and that meant me. I was hunted down, for this reason, by a lecture agent named Harry Walker.

I had lunch with him on October 15, and he told me he could get me a lecture a week at $100 each. Of course, Harry was going to take 30 per cent of each check for his services, but $70 a week meant $3,640 a year, better than half my school salary, and Harry assured me that with time my fees would go up. I agreed to consider the matter and called Willy Ley to make sure that the 30 per cent fee was legitimate. Willy assured me it was.

On October 17, Harry called me and talked me into agreeing to give a talk at Fall River, Massachusetts, on November 4 for $100. Actually, this wasn't bad, for on October 19 I had to fulfill an engagement I

[8] See *Is Anyone There?* (Doubleday, 1967).
[9] Till now, I have listed the appearance of all my magazine fiction, and I shall continue to do so. I will *not*, however, bother to list all my magazine nonfiction—there are too many. I will mention only those that come up naturally in the narration.

had made to speak at Swampscott, Massachusetts, and they only paid me $25. Even with Harry's cut, Fall River would pay me $70.

On November 4, I went to Fall River and gave my talk to the Adams Club, a group of bankers, lawyers, and industrialists. I talked on the significance of Sputnik and it went over very well, all the more so since on the day before, the Soviets had put up Sputnik II.

The club prided itself on its universalism, by the way. One of its officers told me proudly, "We include all religions in our membership—Methodists, Baptists, Episcopalians. We even have a few Presbyterians."

And I kept on working. The break with science fiction was neither completely sudden nor entirely complete. I wrote an outline for a sixth Lucky Starr book, *Lucky Starr and the Rings of Saturn*, which I sent to Doubleday for its approval.

11

Occasionally, a ghost out of the past rises before you. On November 4, 1957, Morris Samberg visited unexpectedly just before lunch. He had been my best friend in junior high school, and I hadn't seen him in twenty-two years. He was short, he looked old, his hair was graying and thinning. I thought uncomfortably that I must look old, too—and fat.

12

On November 10, 1957, I quickly dashed off a Gilbert and Sullivan parody called "The Up-to-date Sorcerer," which was intended to be humorous. It was, in fact, my first *successful* humorous story (in my opinion). After some revision, I placed it with *F & SF*.

Merely writing and selling the story was a relief to me. It was the first completed and sold piece of fiction since the rejection of *Sit with Death* ("The Ugly Little Boy" had been started earlier but I was still working on it), and this was another indication that, somehow, the heavens had not fallen.

On November 12, as though to reinforce the turn of the tide, I received my regular paycheck with one seventh of the twenty-five hundred dollars added. Obviously, I was going to be given the money in seven equal installments through May. Keefer apparently expected me to stay that long but not (I was willing to bet) any longer.

13

I went by train to New York on November 13. When I visited Doubleday, Margaret Loesser agreed to send a contract for *Lucky Starr and the Rings of Saturn*.

Brad was going to try an experiment. Since he did not expect *Earth Is Room Enough* to do well (collections of unrelated short stories don't), he thought he would risk putting it out as a trade edition and as a Science Fiction Book Club selection simultaneously.

Doubleday had been running the Science Fiction Book Club since 1952, and their own science-fiction books were often chosen as selections (though not invariably, for the book club was an independent unit). Its first selection had, in fact, been *The Currents of Space*.

Generally, there was a wait of some time for the selection, since the book-club editions were lower priced and there was no use killing the sales of the higher-priced trade edition. There was no way of telling how much damage was really done, however, unless one took the chance of experimenting with some particular book and seeing how much the regular sales fell off with simultaneous book-club selection.

The experiment was conducted on *Earth Is Room Enough* with, of course, my permission, for I was curious, too.

To my surprise, and even more to Brad's, *Earth Is Room Enough* sold as well in trade editions as my other books did, despite the simultaneous availability of the book-club edition.

This led to a small difference of opinion at a meeting of writers soon after. Cyril Kornbluth attacked Doubleday bitterly, charging them with damaging authors' sales by throwing books into the book-club hopper too soon. I never like to hear Doubleday criticized in my presence, so I rose to say that that could not be so, for *Earth Is Room Enough* was put into *simultaneous* book-club edition and sold the usual amount in trade. My statement was not persuasive; I was simply tabbed a company man.

14

Anticipating Keefer's next move, I was still consulting various high officials in Boston University. Some of them seemed to think I didn't have tenure. I was shown a book representing the constitution, so to speak, of the university, and it demonstrated that, indeed, I did not fulfill the requirements.

I pointed out that the book was a 1957 edition. I pointed out that there was a 1955 edition that stated associate professorship to be sufficient for tenure if I had been on the faculty a certain length of time, and that under that rule I qualified for tenure. I said I would not allow any *ex post facto* ruling to stand.

It turned out, however, to be impossible to get a copy of that 1955 edition—which alone convinced me that I was right. Had I been wrong, I was sure they would have produced it without trouble in order to prove I was.

15

We had been in the house for nearly two years, and the living room was still largely empty and lacked even a rug. Neither Gertrude nor I could decide on the furnishings, and we finally obtained a decorator who worked on the matter for months, and with whom we spent endless hours of uncertainty deciding on wallpaper, drapes, slipcovers, carpeting, and furniture.

Eventually, it was done—though at considerable expense. I always thought that the interior decorator was more worn out over the whole thing than we were.

16

I finished "The Ugly Little Boy" on December 2, 1957, and sent it to Larry Shaw, who accepted it promptly. Unfortunately, what I didn't know was that *Infinity*, which had been coming out for two years now, was on its last legs. They might accept a story, but they could not pay for it. I kept waiting uselessly; the check never came.

I had even less luck with *Sit with Death*, which I had now renamed *A Whiff of Death*. I sent it to several publishers of mystery novels, such as Harper and William Morrow, and it kept coming back. Apparently, Doubleday's decision as to its unworthiness was part of a general notion.

That bothered me, for I was convinced the murder mystery was a good one. Of course, the setting of a graduate chemistry department was an esoteric one,[10] but that should have been a point in the book's favor.

[10] In order to make certain that no one detect any similarities in the book to anyone at the medical school, I set the scene firmly in my memory of the Columbia graduate chemistry department and wrote the characters with specific Columbia faculty members in mind—at least as far as appearance was concerned, *not* personality or character.

I discovered, eventually, that the chief flaw in the book from the standpoint of the publishers was the inadequacy of the motive for the murder. It involved a Ph.D. student faking results, and that seemed a tiny sin to most editorial readers.

When I gave fellow professors an inkling of the plot, however, they shuddered and turned away from me, obviously suspecting some deep-seated perverse element in my nature even to imagine so heinous a crime. Too little for one group of people, too much for another!

Oh well, the February 1958 *If* appeared with "The Feeling of Power,"[11] and the February 1958 *F & SF* had my poem "I Just Make Them Up, See!,"[12] which they had rushed into print quickly. The February 1958 *Future* had a short cautionary tale of mine called "Silly Asses,"[13] and the March 1958 *Venture* had my second science column.

On December 14, 1957, I began *Lucky Starr and the Rings of Saturn*.

[11] See *Nine Tomorrows*.
[12] See *Nine Tomorrows*.
[13] See *Buy Jupiter and Other Stories*.

8

Job at Stake

1

What I was waiting for was another confrontation with Keefer—the third round. He had asked to see me. On December 18 I went to his office, and Sinex was there.

I did not make a record of the proceedings. In my diary I merely say, "I spoke fluently, forcibly, and eloquently," but it has only been a matter of decades since then. There's no danger of my having forgotten the details. Essentially, here's how it went:

Keefer said that the school was dissatisfied (meaning *he* was dissatisfied, of course, and even more so, I suspect, that Lemon was dissatisfied) with the fact that I had given up my research to turn to science writing, and that I seemed unwilling to alter this phase of my activities.

I said, "Dr. Keefer, I was hired to teach, and I do teach, and I think that teaching is the most important, and the primary task of a professor at a School of Medicine. I had this out with Dean Faulkner two years ago and he ended by agreeing with me. This is the ninth year in which I have carried a full teaching load. I have told Dr. Soutter and I am telling you now that I am the best teacher in the school, and I do not shirk my duties in that respect at all.

"As for what I do when I do not teach, that is entirely my business. The school has a right to ask that what I do be scholarly in nature and that it redound to the credit of the school. I would fulfill these requirements by doing research, and I would fulfill them equally well by science writing, providing my talent in other directions were equal.

"However," I went on, "as a researcher, I can do a creditable job, but I am merely adequate—no more. As a science writer, on the other hand, I am one of the best in the world, and I intend to become *the* best. I am perhaps B— as a researcher, but I am A+ as a science writer.

"The school can well afford to have on its faculty the best science writer in the world. Much publicity will accrue to the school, and all of it will be good. And" (but here I had a hard job to control my anger and speak distinctly) "if there is one thing that Boston University

School of Medicine does *not* need, it is *one more* merely adequate researcher."

Both Keefer and Sinex stirred at this. They knew that what I was saying was true—that Boston University School of Medicine did not exactly shine like a beacon in the research heavens. Still, to have me say so, however indirectly, was a clear stab in the rear end for them. I didn't expect to endear myself to them with that statement, but I didn't intend to win out through endearment. I intended to win out by force of being in the right.

Keefer said, after a pause, speaking as softly and icily as ever, "Nevertheless, the school cannot afford to pay a science writer."

"Then don't pay me," I said promptly. "You don't think I need your sixty-five hundred dollars a year, do you? However, if I don't get paid, I don't teach, and you lose your best teacher. There are others here who get two or three times what I do and don't teach one half or one third as well. If you feel you can afford them and not me, you will have to live with that as an example of the worth of your administrative judgment."

"Very well," he said, "I think I can live with it. I will arrange to have your appointment ended as of June 30."

"No, sir," I said, hotly, "you will not. I said you needn't pay me, and I won't take any money from you after June 30. However, my appointment I keep, because I have tenure."

"That is a mistake. You do not have tenure."

"You are mistaken, I do. By the rules in force in 1955, when I was promoted to associate professor, that rank automatically entailed tenure. Show me the book of rules for that year and I'll show you the paragraph. And I assure you that if you try to fire me, I will carry it to higher and higher authorities endlessly."

That was where we stood when I left.

I was more isolated than ever now, for the news was out that I was fired and was going to make a fuss over it, and everyone was anxious to stand out of the line of the cannonade. Sinex went out of his way to cajole Boyd, who let himself be cajoled, and I had only Elizabeth Moyer to depend on. I took to finding occasion to visit her office nearly every day.

There was now nothing to do but wait. I knew that I could not save my salary, but I didn't particularly want to. Losing the salary meant being relieved of all school duties and that, in turn, meant writing more and earning more so that my financial situation would actually be improved by the loss (or so I told myself).

The question was: Would my appointment be renewed without

salary? If it was, I remained an associate professor, perhaps indefinitely, and I would have won. If it wasn't—well, I didn't like to think of what I would then be forced to do. I had made threats in the heat of anger that I couldn't walk away from without humiliation.

2

The year 1957, ending in a blaze of unprecedented fireworks for me, was nevertheless a highly satisfactory one from the literary standpoint. In that year I had published *five* books, a record number. They were:

20. *The Naked Sun* (Doubleday)
21. *Lucky Starr and the Moons of Jupiter* (Doubleday)
22. *Building Blocks of the Universe* (Abelard-Schuman)
23. *Earth Is Room Enough* (Doubleday)
24. *Only a Trillion* (Abelard-Schuman)

Only a Trillion was my collection of nonfiction essays, taken mostly from *Astounding*.

Actually, I ought to have included the third edition of *Biochemistry and Human Metabolism* as a sixth book, but I did not, and that's the way it stands.

As to my writing earnings (counting the portion of the money paid me out of my grant for the writing I was doing on *The Living River*), those came to just a hair over sixteen thousand dollars. That was some six hundred dollars less than the previous year's record mark, but in 1957 I had made no magazine sale comparable to that of *The Naked Sun*. That I could manage to hold nearly even despite that absence was a remarkably good sign and it bolstered my self-confidence for the fight ahead with Keefer.

My school earnings of sixty-five hundred dollars were far less in amount, for the *sixth* successive year, than my writing earnings were, and that, too, was a source of self-confidence. My total income in 1957, as in 1956, came to over twenty-three thousand dollars.

3

My thirty-eighth birthday, on January 2, 1958, passed almost unnoticed. What I did notice was that, literarily, things continued to look well as the new year opened—and that was important to me at this time.

On December 26, 1957, I had had lunch at Locke-Ober's with Austin Olney of Houghton Mifflin. Austin asked me to do a juvenile science book on mathematics, and I agreed at once. I had no contract with Abelard-Schuman that forbade me to publish science books for other firms and, as I explained before, I was disenchanted with Abelard-Schuman.

However, I still remembered my article "Names! Names! Names!," which Abelard-Schuman had rejected for use in *Only a Trillion.* They could scarcely object if I used the article they rejected as the basis for a book with another firm. Serve them right, in fact.

I therefore pointed out to Austin that while I would do the book on math, I would also like to do a book on the derivation of scientific words, including the names of the elements, and he agreed. Now I had two new books in prospect, for a new publisher—and one in Boston, too, whom I could see with no trouble any time I wanted to, and with a new editor, who impressed me as one of the nicest persons I had ever met.

I started work on the derivation book, which I called *Words of Science* at once, and by year's end I had a sample batch of ten derivations, which I sent to Austin for consideration.

By January 24, 1958, it was official. I called Austin and he told me that a contract for *Words of Science* was in the works and would be reaching me soon.

Meanwhile, on January 12, 1958, I had driven to New York and the next day delivered what I had done of *The Living River* to Abelard-Schuman.

I also delivered nine stories to Brad, with the idea of preparing another collection, to be called *Nine Tomorrows.* In view of how well I had done with *Earth Is Room Enough,* he was amenable—another book in view and one that cost me no trouble.

And on January 23, 1958, my first Doubleday statement of the year had come in, and it was for forty-eight hundred dollars, a new record for a single check—three quarters as large, in itself, as my entire annual salary from the school.

It all bucked me up tremendously, and my air at school was one of complete calm and self-confidence.

In fact, I began to be told by those of my fellow faculty members who stopped to talk to me if they thought there was no one around to see them, that they admired me greatly for the fight I was putting up. Some of them actually said that if Keefer got away with it in my case, none of the rest of them would be safe, so that it was important for me to make the fight on their behalf as well as on my own.

I might have asked them, then, why they did not back me up

openly and noisily in that case. I knew the answer, though. They had wives, they had children—

So when one of them made some whispered comment on how brave I was, I said,

"Brave? I'm not brave. There's just nothing they can do to me no matter how I fight them. I've got academic freedom. Do you know what the proper definition of academic freedom is?"

"No."

"It's two words long. Academic freedom is 'outside income.' When a professor has an adequate outside income, he can tell the administration to go to hell, and that's what I'm doing. But there's no bravery to it."

Despite that, my reputation for "guts" grew, and I began to be conscious of admiration, from a distance.

I was satisfied. Public opinion was building up in my favor, and I felt that Keefer would have trouble handling it, even if it showed itself only cautiously.

4

In the course of my January visit to New York, by the way, I did something I had been dreaming of for sixteen years. The Encyclopaedia Britannica, which my father had bought just before I left for Philadelphia, was still in the parental apartment, and of course he never had occasion to use it.

I said, "Well then, Pappa, I have a house now and I have room for it. Let me have it and I'll pay you for it."

My father would not accept money. I piled the books and the bookcase into the car and took them back with me. At last I had a copy of the encylopaedia and could find out how it came out. It was a most useful addition to my reference library.

5

My ninth teaching semester (my first under Sinex) began toward the end of January, and I knew it would be my last as a full member of the department.

In this last of my teaching classes was one John R. Jeppson. I wasn't particularly aware of it; I didn't notice. He, however, was the brother of Janet Jeppson, the young psychiatrist whom I had casually offended at the New York science-fiction convention over a year before.

(Of course, I didn't remember that. I didn't even know I had offended her at the time.)

John, as I discovered later, discussed his course work with Janet (they were the children of a successful ophthalmologist in New Rochelle, New York, so medicine was a not-unnatural career for both of them) and apparently had much good to say of me. This helped change Janet's mind about me so that when the time came, she was willing to forget the unfortunate occurrence at the convention and give me another chance.

6

On January 31, 1958, I learned that the Thomas Alva Edison Foundation was awarding me a scroll plus $250 for *Building Blocks of the Universe*. The money was nice but the scroll was nicer.

After all, I had rather vauntingly announced at the top of my voice to the med school powers that I intended to be the best science writer in the world, and I couldn't very well become that without winning a few awards on the way. This was my first.

7

Brad called on February 4 to tell me that even though Doubleday was going to do *Nine Tomorrows* he wanted me to clean up "I'm in Marsport Without Hilda." The story dealt with three men who were apparently drugged and completely out of touch with the real world—but one of them was faking. The question was which one. The hero finally solved the problem by describing a session he had had with a woman and then seizing the one who understood him sufficiently well to develop an erection. I very carefully did not detail the hero's sexual description, nor did I specifically state there was an erection. Brad sternly said that the implication was clear enough, however, and I was to *clean it up*.

I did so, but felt rather humiliated, for I was, and am, proud of the decency of my stories.

In fact, when I wrote *The End of Eternity* and let the hero go to bed with the heroine, Brad wrote in the margin: "At last. A bedroom scene in Asimov." When Gertrude saw that, she insisted on reading the chapter. She read and read and then said, "Well, where's the bedroom scene?" and I said, rather annoyed, "You just passed it."

Some time later, I read one of Sprague de Camp's wonderful historical novels, *The Dragon of the Ishtar Gate*, and read his description of an orgy, which included details far worse than anything in "I'm in Marsport Without Hilda." Yet Sprague's book was published by Doubleday.

I called up Brad indignantly and asked why Sprague could do so much and I couldn't even do a little. And Brad, utterly unrepentant, said, "Isaac, your books are so proper that librarians are confident enough to buy them without reading them, and we don't want to do anything to upset them."

Nevertheless, years later, when another collection of mine was to appear and there was some desire to include "I'm in Marsport Without Hilda," I balked and said, "I don't want to use the bowdlerized version."

By then, the progress of explicit sex in literature had reached the point where even the "unexpurgated" version read like decency itself—and in it went.[1] The tampered-with version in *Nine Tomorrows* will never appear anywhere else, if I have any say about it.

But the day after Brad had confirmed the sale of *Nine Tomorrows*, Larry Shaw admitted he didn't have the money to buy "The Ugly Little Boy" after all, and that was the last and anchor piece in *Nine Tomorrows*. It was a disappointment.

There were some minor disappointments, too. The April 1958 *Super-Science* came out with "All the Troubles of the World,"[2] and on the cover my first name was spelled "Issac." I protested, of course.

And Lillian McClintock had left her editorial position with Abelard-Schuman. I didn't like the intensity of her editing but I am always upset when I lose an editor. Abelard-Schuman offered a high rate of editorial replacement, and that was another source of discomfort there.

8

On February 7, 1958, I took the train to Baltimore in order to give a talk the next morning at the University of Maryland School of Medicine. There the inviting professor made me comfortable with an excellent chicken dinner at his home, and then took me to the Lord Baltimore Hotel, where I was to spend the night. I must admit that the pampering I get when I am a guest lecturer is as pleasant as the fee.

I was reading the New York *Times* at breakfast the next morning (just before my talk, which was scheduled for 9 A.M. on the eighth), and when I got to the obituary page, I noted, with wry amusement,

[1] See *Asimov's Mysteries*.
[2] See *Nine Tomorrows*.

that some fellow with the look-alike name of Henry Kuttner had died. My first thought was that I would write a letter to Hank and pretend I thought *he* had died—except that when I read the obituary I found he had. It did not occur to me till then that science-fiction writers of my own generation were mortal—or that if they were, they rated space in the New York *Times*. Hank had died of a heart attack, and he was only forty-three.

Fortunately, I had finished breakfast or I wouldn't have been able to eat any more.

But the show must go on. I had to leave for my morning talk, a walking distance away. I was reasonably dressed for midwinter, but when I came to the door of the hotel I could see passersby walking in coats, scarves, and gloves, and with heads bent low.

I said in alarm to the doorman, "Cold day?"

"Bitter," he said, eying my coat. "Better warm up."

I didn't want to freeze, so I buttoned every button I could find, upended my collar, sank my head down as far as it would go, buried my hands deep in my pockets, then signaled the doorman to open the door.

I stepped out into springlike weather. I doubt that the temperature was lower than twenty-nine, and we don't call that cold in Boston. Indignantly, I yanked my hands out of my pockets, turned down my collar, unbuttoned every coat button I could find, and walked leisurely to the University of Maryland School of Medicine, enjoying the balmy weather. More than one Baltimorean must have thought me crazy.

9

When it came time to parcel out the lectures for the teaching semester, Sinex asked me which lectures I wanted.

I said, with conscious haughtiness, that if everyone else would select the lectures they thought they would shine in, I would take whatever was left over. If I thought that the rest of the department would chivalrously refuse to take advantage of me, I was wrong. They all grabbed vigorously and I was left with the sickest collection of no-chance lectures I had ever seen. Served me right!

My first lecture was on February 11, 1958, and the subject was heme—the iron-containing compound that was the cutting edge, so to speak, of hemoglobin. It was the heme that picked up the oxygen in the lungs and gave it up in the cells.

It was straight chemistry and therefore bound to be unpopular with medical students, who never believe that chemistry has anything to do with medicine and always think of it, impatiently, as a college course that, by rights, should be over and done with.

I did pretty well, but Sinex did not attend that lecture.

The next day, February 12, I was to lecture again, this time on abnormal hemoglobins, a subject with medical applications that could be made highly dramatic, if skillfully developed—and Sinex walked in to attend.

I had a clear alternative. I could deliver a perfectly competent, perfectly ordinary lecture, and let things go at that. *Or* I could put on a show, tear passions to tatters, and demonstrate that I was indeed the best lecturer (or, at any rate, the most spectacular) in the school. That would demonstrate me to be no liar, but I knew well it might not endear me to Sinex. You get no points for being better than the boss.

So was I going to play it safe and not outshine the chairman? Would Hotspur? Would D'Artagnan? Would Cyrano?

I wasn't aiming low for anybody, that's all. I took a deep breath and delivered the best class lecture of my life, and when I finished at a dramatic peak as the bell sounded (I always kept my eye on the clock and paced myself carefully), the class rose joyfully out of their seats as one student and gave me a wild standing ovation.

It was customary for students to applaud each instructor on the occasion of his last lecture of the semester, but this was only my second lecture. And it wasn't the customary polite applause that wavered into silence halfway on its trip to the podium. It all but broke the windows, and I stood there grinning and bowing like an actor—which, in my way, I am, of course.

It was a silly piece of braggadocio and lost me any sympathy Sinex might have felt for me, but I didn't care (feeling he had very little sympathy for me anyway) because the whole thing felt *good*.

10

Life, however, is in a conspiracy to keep me from going too far off my head with triumph. Things tend to balance.

That same evening, I drove out to North Leominster, Massachusetts, to give a talk to a group who gathered at a Catholic church. Like a good boy, I arrived half an hour early, as Harry Walker (who had arranged the talk) told me always to do, so that those responsible for the talk should not get heart attacks waiting.

The trouble was that I was *not* treated royally, as I had been in Baltimore. I was put in one of the parish rooms, with no human being for company, and nothing to read but devotional literature.

When they came to get me, then, I was in no lighthearted mood. The topic I was to discuss was the recent satellites (the United States had put up its first successful satellite two weeks before, on January 31) and their importance to us. What I didn't know was that Harry Walker had sold me to the fellow who organized the group on the basis of my being the world's funniest person. He had never heard of me otherwise.

The audience settled down to listen to Bob Hope, and I began a sober lecture on the significance of space exploration. After I had talked about twenty minutes, the chairman of the program walked up to the desk and deposited a slip of paper on it. For one panicky moment I thought it was a message of catastrophe from home—but there were only two words on it: "Be funny."

I stopped dead and said, "I'm afraid we've got our wires crossed here. I was under the impression I was to deliver a serious speech. I have just been ordered to be funny. I will stop now. I will not collect any fee." And I began to walk off the stage.

The audience shouted, "Go on. Go on."

The chairman, looking sick, also waved me back.

I resumed my talk, finished it, collected a check for a hundred dollars to mail to Harry Walker, and along with it that night I wrote a letter explaining that I would do the talks I had agreed to do, but that aside from that I had rather not use an agent.

I wanted to be invited to talk only by those groups who knew of me and knew what to expect. I didn't want to be "sold" to strangers.

11

Williams & Wilkins, which published our textbook, also put out Stedman's Medical Dictionary. This was not the standard in the field, but it was a respectable second best. The publishers were planning a new edition and wanted to give it a complete overhaul. For that purpose they wanted a number of authorities to look over every definition and change it, if necessary—to say nothing of adding new definitions and dropping outdated ones.

They asked me to be their authority on biochemistry. It was an offer that tickled my vanity, but I knew that the level of work would never be compensated for by any payment they could make me. Therefore, I vacillated. I told them there was a good chance that by the end of the semester I might be without academic affiliation, and what credibility would I have as an authority if I did not have a medical school connection?

On February 15, 1958, I received a letter from Eleanor Cochrane, who was in charge of the project, saying that she would be glad to have me on the editorial board *with or without* academic affiliation.

That was so flattering, so clear an indication that I was loved for myself alone, that I accepted. The result was several years of hard, nit-picking work to put first the nineteenth and then the twentieth edition of the dictionary into shape.

It was a terrible punishment for being so easily flattered, but I did get one small satisfaction out of it, aside from the payments and the free copies of each edition I worked on. The editorial board was listed on the title page in alphabetical order, and my name was therefore first. In many reviews, the book was listed as having been written "by Isaac Asimov et al." It was a credit I didn't deserve, but I enjoyed it anyway.

12

We had a little party for Robyn on her third birthday on February 19, 1958. When David was her age, Gertrude was pregnant, but there was no pregnancy this time. We had all the children we wanted, and there would be no more.

13

On February 26, 1958, I sent off the manuscript of *Lucky Starr and the Rings of Saturn* to Doubleday. I had been working on the adventures of Lucky Starr for seven years now and had done six books for a total of nearly a quarter-million words. The Lucky Starr opus was about the length of the Foundation series.

It was not my thought to end it. I liked Lucky Starr and his shrimp sidekick, Bigman Jones, and the books were, on the whole, easy to write. I even knew what the seventh book in the series was going to be. It was going to be *Lucky Starr and the Snows of Pluto*.

It was, however, never written. My shift to nonfiction was well under way, and I was to write no more Lucky Starr novels. There were to be six and no more.

14

I did a bit of ghostwriting. One bit. The only one of my life.

Fred Whipple had been asked to contribute to a series called "Adventures of the Mind," which was being run by *The Saturday Evening Post*. He asked me, on March 5, to write an article from notes he had prepared, in return for five hundred dollars, explaining that it would have to appear under his name only.

I would have refused, but for two reasons. First, I was very fond of Fred, and second, I did have a sneaking desire to have my words appear in *The Saturday Evening Post*, even if no one knew they were mine. So I wrote the article "Eyes on Space," about telescopes and their importance, and eventually it appeared in the August 16, 1958, issue of *The Saturday Evening Post* under the title of "The Exploration of Space."

I had little daydreams of people writing letters to the magazine to say how well it was written, or of people praising it in my hearing, or of Fred winning some sort of prize with it. Nothing of the sort happened, however. As far as I know, the article sank without even producing a ripple.

15

Dr. Sinex, after a visit to Washington, informed me on March 10 that he thought my salary could be picked up by the government in some way, and said he would speak to Keefer about it.

I shrugged. It was pleasant that Sinex was trying to find some viable compromise, but I wasn't interested in government money and had no intention of going back to the yearly-renewal rat race. Nevertheless, I let it go. I didn't think that Keefer would agree, and I wanted the onus of inflexibility to be on him.

I was right. On the twelfth, Sinex informed me that Keefer was "totally against everything" (that is, everything that meant Asimov's survival as a member of the medical school) and that a written notification of termination of appointment was in the works.

It looked bad for me. It looked as though I would have my bluff called and that I would have to institute legal proceedings. (I didn't even have a lawyer—or know one.)

16

On March 18, 1958, I had to drive to Hazelton, Pennsylvania, to fulfill a talk commitment that had been arranged by Harry Walker before the North Leominster disaster. I followed the route recommended by the AAA, but their maps are two-dimensional and they didn't tell me that the last twenty-five miles would be over twisting mountain roads.

My pronounced acrophobia spoiled the pleasure of looking over the left side of my car at pretty countryside stretching out half a mile below. I dropped the car's speed to a cautious walk and watched with wonder and envy the natives of the region zoom past me with one hand on the wheel and the other stifling a yawn as they wiggled along the road.

Fortunately, I made a description of my drive the introductory section of my talk at Hazelton and got the audience into a very good humor as they laughed at the tale of the unsophisticated coastal native caught in the mountains.

The next day, I drove to Swarthmore through a light snowstorm that was irritating but not serious, since it melted as it touched the ground. On the way I visited my old fan-friend, Milton Rothman, and his wife, and by the time I parked in the Swarthmore College parking lot (outside Philadelphia) the snow was just beginning to remain on the ground.

I still wasn't worried. The local weather forecast was for an accumulation of but one or two inches, with temperatures reaching forty-five later in the day. And the next day would be the vernal equinox besides—the first day of spring.

I woke on that vernal equinox to find the forecast was a bitter lie. There was something like one or two *feet* of snow on the ground, rather than inches, and it was very wet, very heavy snow, the sloppiest weather imaginable. It was, indeed, the worst late-winter snowstorm in Philadelphia's recent history.

I was to speak at a 9 A.M. convocation, which all students were *compelled* to attend. I was warned by the vice president that many students resented compulsory attendance at this quasireligious function (Swarthmore was a Quaker school) and ostentatiously read newspapers during the speaker's talk. It wasn't intended as a personal insult, I was assured.

I had said, with my usual braggadocio, "Any student who can bear to read a newspaper while I'm talking is welcome to do so."

But then as I watched the students walking to the convocation hall in boots and other wet-weather gear, my heart sank. Being compelled to attend in weather like *this* must surely be several notches beyond student endurance.

I got to the hall with considerable difficulty myself and was amazed to find it filled. Facing an audience that might be unrelievedly hostile, I began with a stirring encomium on spring, the rebirth of nature, the season green and perfumed, the epitome of hope, the welcome release from winter's icy grip—making the whole thing more and more lyrical until I greeted the coming of the vernal equinox that day in a veritable Everest of floral gush.

The audience caught what I was doing, went on with me to the peak in happy irony, and I was home safe. I could do anything I wanted for the remainder of the speech.

After it was over, I despairingly tried to drive home though mountains of standing slush. I had to maneuver through streets that were flooded in some places, nearly barred by fallen branches in others.

I managed to make it to the New Jersey Turnpike and may have been among the last cars to be allowed on, for I hadn't traveled on it long before the radio informed me that the turnpike was closed. I drove through what seemed a double row of stalled cars, with hapless families standing by each. I thought gloomily that if my car stalled, I wouldn't even have the dubious comfort of having someone with whom to share my misery.

The gas stations were closed; the restaurants were closed. When I stopped to urinate, there was no place to do so.

A woman, noting the uncertainty with which I surveyed the sad panorama, said to me, "The men have gone behind the building."

I went behind the building and there they were, lined up. Necessity makes a joke of civilization. I took my place in line.

When I came back, I said to the woman who had directed me, "What do the women do?" She gestured an I-don't-know very unhappily.

It took me six hours to get to New York, a trip that ought to have taken me two hours.

17

I spent the night at the Blugermans', and the next day, March 21, I made my rounds.

Almost the first thing I discovered was that the snowstorm that had given me such trouble on the New Jersey Turnpike had been fatal to my Futurian friend Cyril Kornbluth. He had shoveled snow, then gone to the station to catch a train, had a heart attack there, and died. He was only thirty-four.

I delivered my manuscript of *The World of Nitrogen* to Abelard-Schuman, and visited Horace to pick up my manuscript of "The Ugly Little Boy."

"The Ugly Little Boy" was giving me a great deal of trouble. After *Infinity* had sent it back, Campbell rejected it, and now Horace, inevitably, wanted changes. On principle, I objected, for I had already included the story in *Nine Tomorrows*, and Brad had praised it highly.

Horace, however, pointed out that the ending was ridiculously high-pitched. I had my ugly little boy, the Neanderthal child, taken out of time and then not properly returned, and it turned out that he had been the discoverer of fire. Human history was delayed about twenty-five centuries and all of modern Earth was suddenly converted into a parallel time-track in which it was still in the Paleolithic Period. Horace said that this was like solving the crisis set up by Edward VIII's love for Wallie Simpson by having the British Isles slide into the ocean.

Unwilling to make me angry (he was having enormous troubles with authors by now), Gold stressed that I would have to make only minor changes—but I shook my head.

I said, "No, you're right. I'll rewrite the whole damned thing!"

I spent the last week of March rewriting, and the rewritten version (with some additional minor changes) was taken by Horace with great delight. And I was delighted, too, for the ending had now become very touching and underwritten, one I like a great deal. Brad, too, admitted that the story was improved.

Years later, when the Science Fiction Writers of America published the letters of some writers recalling their troubles with Horace and the difficulty of enduring his nasty letters, I wrote in order to agree that he was troublesome and wrote nasty letters. *But*, I said, he was, nevertheless, a good editor, whose requests for revision were sometimes justified. And I gave the case of "The Ugly Little Boy," which, ever since, has been one of my favorite stories.

18

On April 4, I received the official note telling me that my salary would end as of June 30.

And then, as I was girding myself despairingly to continue the battle at all costs, Soutter asked to see me. When I went to his office, he told me that Keefer was willing to let me keep my title.

I couldn't imagine what had made him change his mind, since only three weeks before, Sinex had reported him to be totally intransigent. Had Soutter argued in my favor? Had there been the feeling of a faculty revolt?

I didn't know, and I decided not to ask. I told Soutter that retention of my title alone was acceptable. Of course, it was to be understood that without a salary I would fulfill no duties except those that I chose to fulfill, and Soutter nodded.

I told Sinex that I was keeping my title and he, rather to my surprise, grew furious. Up to that point, I had felt he was only allowing himself to be used as a cat's paw, but now he seemed more eager even than Keefer to get rid of me. Perhaps Sinex had not been informed of this sudden turnabout and he felt his position as department head had been compromised. In any case, he incautiously warned me that he had an appointment to see Keefer on Tuesday, April 8.

On Monday, April 7, I anticipated this by seeing Soutter and asking that the satisfactory settlement of the dispute not be upset now. Soutter spoke to Sinex at once, and Sinex rather grumblingly accepted my continuing hold on my title. I had won the third round.

On April 10, I visited the main campus and was part of a panel on communication and death headed by Karl Menninger of the Menninger Clinic. I did well, and afterward attended a tea hosted by President Case of Boston University.

To my astonishment, he asked me how I was coming along in my fight with Keefer.

With my usual lack of aplomb, I said, "How do you know about that, President Case?"

He said, "I'm president. I've got to know these things."

I said, "My salary will be stopped on June 30, but that doesn't matter. I agreed to that long ago. I will keep my title, and that was what I was fighting for."

"Good!" he said. "If Keefer had managed to take away your title, I assure you I would have replaced it."

"Really?" I said, again astonished. "I'm glad I didn't know that. It would have spoiled my fun."

So it may have been subtle pressure from above that forced Keefer to back down.

9

Full-time Writer

1

I had not forgotten my poor mystery. It had been rejected by five publishing houses, the fifth being Random House, which handed it back to me on April 21, 1958.

I passed it on to Avon Books, the soft-cover publishing firm. They were interested in having science fiction from me, but there was no way in which I could write science fiction without showing it first to Brad. Nevertheless, I didn't stress that fact as hard as I might have and, without actually telling a lie, I managed to let Avon believe they might get science-fiction originals from me.

Avon then accepted the mystery on June 4, but I found I got no pleasure out of the sale. It seemed to me they took the book not for its own sake but as an earnest of my future patronage, so to speak, which I couldn't really deliver. I felt like a crook.

2

The May 1958 *Venture* contained a little story of mine called "Buy Jupiter."[1] The title was Bob Mills', and was one of those with which I wholeheartedly agreed, and I was sorry I hadn't thought of it myself. I had called the story "It Pays" originally, a much poorer title. All things being equal, I'll go for the play on words every time. The issue also contained my third article, "The Big Bang."

Unfortunately, *Venture* was not a success. The next issue, July 1958, was its tenth and last. That last issue contained my fourth science column, "The Clash of Cymbals," which was about colliding galaxies, and then I was out of a job, at least as far as my science column was concerned.

I was very disappointed. I was, at that time, doing numerous articles for the various magazines Bob Lowndes was editing, but those magazines were very shaky ones as well, and each article was a one-shot to be accepted or rejected.

What I wanted was a column, and that had vanished.

[1] See *Buy Jupiter and Other Stories*.

On May 9, something else vanished. I gave my last lecture to the freshman class at Boston University School of Medicine as a fully salaried member of the department, just about nine years after I had arrived in Boston. In round numbers, I think I had given a hundred lectures.

3

The fact that I was going to be a full-time writer after June 30 was not something I could view with complete indifference. For twenty years I had written in my spare time only—twenty hours a week at most.

Could I do more than that?

I could, of course, stay physically at the typewriter for forty hours a week or for seventy hours, for that matter, but would I be producing?

There was no way I could tell, of course, without actually trying, and it was the thought of possible "empty time" that had been one of the factors impelling me to take on long-term jobs. My work on derivations for the Stedman Medical Dictionary was one such job. Another was a physical-science survey I undertook to write for Macmillan earlier in the year. Still another was a column of book reviews of science books for children, which I agreed that spring to write for the magazine *Hornbook* (it being understood I would review only those books I could write of favorably).

The work on the derivations was limited, of course; there were only so many to do. The physical-science survey fell through. It was too much like a textbook, and I talked Macmillan into letting me go. The science-book review column, however, continued for years, though I found it a steadily increasing burden.

4

On May 27, I sat through the grading session on the biochemistry class, and my last regularly paid teaching duty was over.

5

With my teaching duties over, I threw myself into project after project:

First, I finished my book of derivations for Houghton Mifflin (*Words of Science*), and that meant I would have to start on the children's mathematics book for them next (*Realm of Numbers*).

Second, I planned a new book for Abelard-Schuman on timekeeping, which I planned to call *The Clock We Live On.*

Third, unaware as yet of the extent to which my interests were shifting, I obtained a contract from Doubleday for the third book in the trilogy involving Lije Baley and R. Daneel, who had so far starred in *The Caves of Steel* and *The Naked Sun*. This third book was to be *The Bounds of Infinity* (a deliberate balance in title to *The End of Eternity*).

Fourth, I agreed to do a series of sixteen short biographies of scientists for *Scholastic,* a magazine that was distributed to high-school students.

I was determined to keep myself busy and to fill that "full time" I was now to have.

(It would be nice if circumstances co-operated fully, but they never do. On May 31, just as I was squaring myself into mounting my literary horse and riding off in all directions, David came down with the chicken pox, and I knew that Robyn would follow down the path, loyally, within a few days.)

6

I had lunch with Austin Olney on June 2 and handed in the manuscript of *Words of Science*. Within a few days, he called me to tell me how much he enjoyed it.

I knew at once that I could have the kind of faith in Houghton Mifflin that I had in Doubleday. Austin, even more than Brad, had become a personal friend of mine, always kind and even loving, for such was his nature.

Times had changed. Even if every science-fiction magazine ceased publication (which I did not expect to happen), I felt certain I could keep going very well with Doubleday and Houghton Mifflin alone. It was no longer the way it had been a decade before in 1948, when the thought of the suspension of *Astounding* seemed to herald the end of my writing career.

7

David was back in school on June 6, 1958, having recovered from the chicken pox, but was flat on his back on June 8, having come down with the measles. And as soon as his fever and other symptoms vanished on June 15, Robyn came down with the chicken pox. On June

25, she showed signs of measles but got away (I hope) with a subclinical case.

Naturally, the children came through all this fine, but it was a near squeak as to whether Gertrude and I would survive.

8

In the midst of the siege of sicknesses, I had to take the train to New York, because I had agreed to speak at the Brooklyn Public Library on June 12, 1958. This was the first time I was able to play my role as celebrity with my mother and father watching. It was almost twenty years to the day after I had taken in my first story to Campbell.

My mother and father were already there when I arrived, and the librarians were making much of them—something my parents already accepted as their due. They were given seats in the front row and sat there, haughtily, as I gave my talk on science fiction.

It was quite an adequate talk but would undoubtedly have been better if I could have made myself unaware of my mother's eyes fixed proudly on me. Then, when I was through and was trying to acknowledge the applause, my mother came up and threw her arms around me. Applause changed to laughter and I turned pink—partly from the viselike grip around my ribs.

"Mamma, sit down—sit down—thank you, thank you—if you don't sit down, Mamma—thank you, all—I'll hit you."

She finally sat down. Thank goodness, I didn't have to hit her.

9

At home, I found the July 1958 *F & SF* with "The Up-to-date Sorcerer"[2] in it.

On June 16, I began my mathematics book for Houghton Mifflin. No book I had ever written proved as easy to write as *Realm of Numbers*. I had all the facts in my head and in the right order, and I had only to put them down. The whole thing—first draft, final copy, and all —took me thirteen days. By June 28, I was finished and I had a thirty-three-thousand-word book all done.

Gertrude warned me it might be a mistake to submit it at once. A book that had obviously been written so quickly might not seem very good. It was good advice, but I was simply unable to follow it. It would have burned a hole in my soul if I had left it sitting around.

[2] See *Nightfall and Other Stories*.

On June 30, I took it to Austin. He looked astonished, but he didn't dislike the book because it had been written overquickly. In fact, he liked it.[3]

10

On June 30, my medical school salary came to an end after nine years and one month.

Ever since I was five years old, I had been either in school, in the Army, or on a job. Not one day had been spent otherwise. Now it all came to an end—and I wasn't worried. The end of a steady paycheck meant *nothing*.

My school earnings for the first half of 1958 were $3,250. My writing and lecturing earnings for that same half year, including five sevenths of the $2,500 for my book *The Living River*, were just under $17,500. It was the best half year I had ever had. In fact, I had earned more money though writing and lecturing in the first half of 1958 than I had ever earned in any previous full year.

As I ended my school career, I was making five times as much money in my writing as in my teaching. What's more, I had now reached the stage of mass production that has characterized my literary life ever since. As of the time the med school cut me loose, I had six books in press with three different publications and six in various stages of preparation.

In fact, it was quite obvious that Sinex, Lemon, and Keefer had, by their action, done me the most enormous favor. Had they been willing to let things be as they were, I would have had to quit on my own within the space of a year or so, or watch my literary career be aborted.

Indeed, my freedom from the bonds of my teaching position seemed to be joined by a freedom from the bonds of chemistry as the subject of my nonfiction.

As of June 30, I had written articles for a variety of learned journals and science-fiction magazines—but every one of them had been on chemistry or biochemistry or nuclear chemistry. The same was true of the nonfiction books I had written. All were well within the expertise one would expect of my specialized education.

But then, entirely by coincidence (but perhaps highly symbolic just the same), on July 1, 1958, the very first day of my new jobless status, I began *The Clock We Live On*, which was to be entirely on as-

[3] That same June 30, I had dinner with a woman named Lillian Asimow from the West Coast. She and her husband, Morris, could trace his ancestry back to Petrovichi. Despite the difference in spelling, he had to be a distant cousin of mine.

tronomy and chronometry. These were subjects in which I had never taken a single course at any stage in my school career.

You might say that, having cut free, I could now afford to take my chances. I had no formal academic standing to endanger, no colleagues to offend.

However, I was not being foolhardy either. I was not blithely launching myself onto a sea of ignorance. The fact is that I had now been reading science fiction for nearly thirty years and had been writing it for twenty. One cannot be a *serious* reader and writer of science fiction without getting a broad smattering of many aspects of science and a surprisingly deep understanding of some. And astronomy is, pre-eminently, *the* science most clearly associated with science fiction.

The fact, therefore, that I had never taken any courses in astronomy merely meant that I was weak on some of the mathematical aspects of celestial mechanics and on the nuts and bolts of telescopes and other instrumentation.

On the descriptive and conceptual aspects of astronomy and even on some of the celestial mechanics, I had an iron-bound grip, so that I began work on *The Clock We Live On* with absolute assurance.[4]

And, as I went on to discover, each time I wrote a book on some subject outside my immediate field it gave me courage and incentive to do another one that was perhaps even farther outside the narrow range of my training. Beginning with July 1, 1958, then, I advanced from chemical writer to science writer, and, eventually, I took all of learning for my subject (or at least all that I could cram into my head—which, alas, had a sharply limited capacity despite all I could do).

As I did so, of course, I found I had to educate myself. I had to read books on physics to reverse my unhappy experiences in school on the subject and to learn at home what I had failed to learn in the classroom—at least up to the point where my limited knowledge of mathematics prevented me from going farther.

When the time came, I also read biology, medicine, and geology. I collected commentaries on the Bible and on Shakespeare. I read history books. Everything led to something else. I became a generalist by encouraging myself to be generally interested in all matters.

Fortunately, I didn't have to approach anything (or almost anything) completely fresh. My avid and generalized reading as a youngster came to my aid, for as the years passed, I discovered (with a great deal of pleasure) that I simply never forgot the trivia I had read. It was

---

[4] Indeed, the time was to come when I would write a good book (I think) on telescopes.

all there in my head and required only the slightest jog to spring to the surface.

This is not to say I wasn't capable of making mistakes through carelessness or through writing overhurriedly or through being misled by my sources—but none of those mistakes (as far as I know) ever betrayed ignorance of the subject. I grew more casually confident of my polymath abilities with each year, and it was that, even more than my prolificity, that has impressed people and led to my gaining a rather unusual reputation for "knowing everything."

As I look back on it, it seems quite possible that none of this would have happened if I had stayed at school and had continued to think of myself as, primarily, a biochemist.

For that reason, it has been hard for me to think of myself as having been ill used in 1957 and 1958. Rather, I was forced along the path I ought to have taken of my own accord if I had had the necessary insight into my own character and abilities.

While I cannot believe that Lemon and Keefer had my welfare in mind, it all worked out for my benefit whatever they had in mind, and I feel no resentment against them.

11

In the summer of 1958, we decided to try a new experiment in summer vacations. We rented a cottage on the beach in Marshfield, Massachusetts, for three weeks. On July 12, 1958, we drove there and settled in.

It was a quiet vacation. To show you how unexciting a time it was, my chief memory of the period is that Robyn went to sleep while chewing gum.[5] During her sleep, the chewing gum transferred itself into her hair and we spent what seemed like several weeks trying to tease it out, bit by bit. In the end, we had to simply cut a hank of hair off with the scissors to everyone's grief, for she had, and has, beautiful blond tresses.

I did make occasional trips back to Newton to pick up my mail. In this way, I got a copy of the September 1958 *Galaxy*, which contained "The Ugly Little Boy."[6] Horace had, for some reason, decided that that title wouldn't sell magazines. Maybe he thought people would find it unpleasant. So he changed the title to the terrible one of "Last-born." I changed it back for every other appearance of the story.

---

[5] She is still, even today, rarely without a slab of gum in her mouth, but she very rightly says that this is better than a cigarette.
[6] See *Nine Tomorrows*.

I also got the galleys to *The World of Nitrogen*, which gave me something to do.

The Bounds of Infinity, however, which I had hoped to advance mightily in the course of the vacation, simply didn't catch on. I moved more and more slowly and with greater and greater effort. It did occur to me that perhaps the loss of my job was destroying my ability to work. Therefore when Leo Margulies asked me for a story for *Satellite*, I thought up a short piece that I called "Benefactor of Humanity" and dashed it off at a feverish pace, more to convince myself I could do it than for any other reason. Margulies took it without much trouble.[7]

On August 2, thank goodness, we were home.

12

On August 4, I received official notification that my job as associate professor of biochemistry was renewed for another year. I took great satisfaction in that, and from then on, for a decade or more, I made a point of showing up at school periodically to pick up my mail. I would not allow it to be forwarded to my home, for it was important to me to show my face at the school and make it quite plain I belonged there as much as ever.

13

On August 12, when I visited Bob Mills in New York, he asked me if I would continue my *Venture* science column, but for *F & SF*.

I agreed very happily and instantly passed over a short science column on meteoric dust on Earth and on the Moon, which I called "Dust of Ages" and which I had intended as the fifth column in *Venture*.

It appeared in the November 1958 issue of *F & SF*, and finally I had the column I wanted.

The first column in *F & SF* was only twelve hundred words long, and the notion was that each was going to be of that length. Bob, however, experimented with a four-thousand-word length for the second and third column, went back to a twelve-hundred-word length for the fourth, but then with the fifth, it was four thousand words again and

[7] And in the outside world there was a brief war scare over a civil war in Lebanon. President Eisenhower sent in troops, and the situation quickly quieted down. The United States could still play policeman of the world—but not for much longer.

has remained that ever since. I was to get one hundred dollars per column, and they were to continue indefinitely.

At the very beginning, Bob made some suggestions, but that stopped very quickly, and it came to be understood that I was to write what I wanted, exactly how I wanted, and that I was to get galleys of each column so that I could see to it that it was set in print just as I wanted it to be.

It was an ideal arrangement. Bob Mills was the first to call me "The Good Doctor" in blurbing my articles. Eventually, the articles settled down in the form in which they now exist, with each one being introduced by some personal anecdote or reminiscence (usually funny, always true).

It was in these articles, in fact, that I first developed my leisurely and personal style of talking to the readers directly.

14

My parents were now spending part of the summers in the Catskills, at the Paramount Hotel. The first time they went there, my father was so inexperienced that he had only city clothes with him. By the next time, though, my parents were old-timers who went rowing and indulged in other activities as well.

My father, in particular (I gathered from what I was told) made the surroundings hideous by talking about nothing but me. He always had books of mine with him and he would eagerly show them to people but would not allow them to touch the book. No fingerprints but his own must be upon them. How he managed to survive an onslaught from an infuriated mob, I don't know.

He used to call me up in those days to ask me how I was doing. I had de-emphasized my misadventures at school, but let him know, carefully and truthfully, that my earnings were steadily rising. He was doubtful about this. It seemed that one of his habits on passing a bookstore was to walk in and demand to see any books they had by Isaac Asimov. They generally didn't have any.

"How can you make a living, Isaac? Are you sure you're telling me the truth?" he would ask.

"Pappa," I would say, "most of my sales are library sales, and I get money through book clubs and paperbacks. I *assure* you I am making plenty of money."

"Why don't you tell Doubleday to advertise you more?"

"That's their business, Pappa. I don't interfere."

As a matter of fact, I have constantly been asked by relatives, friends, even strangers, why my publishers don't advertise me more. I pay no attention to that; I have never urged promotion on my publishers; I get uneasy on those few occasions when they *do* invest in publicity. My feeling is that my books support each other and my talks support them all and that that is the best promotion.

Of course, none of my books has ever been a best seller in the sense that none has sold a great many copies in any one year. On the other hand, many of them sell a respectable number year after year indefinitely—and that is better. Furthermore, if you consider all my books to be a single book entitled *Isaac Asimov* each with a different subtitle, then I have a best seller every year.

15

Robyn celebrated David's seventh birthday on August 20, 1958, by running a fever. David joined her a few days later, and to my horror, on August 25, I had a fever of 101.8°.

In the course of my adult life I have had the usual incidence of colds and intestinal upsets, but I am almost never feverish. This was the first fever I had had in twenty-one years, and I took it as a personal insult.

Actually, it was the start of another bout of bronchitis, such as the one I had had the previous fall. This was a worse one, for I continued to cough for three months.

It occurred to me this time that the fault lay in the air conditioning of my workroom during the summer. I kept the air conditioner on maximum and I worked in my underwear (my general costume at the typewriter). I also kept the door closed and walked freely in and out of the room from cold to heat and back to cold.

I took thereafter to wearing a shirt and pants when the air conditioner was on, and to keeping the door to my attic room open to lower the temperature difference in and out. Thereafter, I had bad attacks of bronchitis no more.

16

On August 22, we bought a parakeet. It was the first pet the children had ever had, and the first I had ever had that wasn't a cat. David was fascinated by the little bird and somehow trained it to perch on his shoulder. It wouldn't perch on anyone else's.

It was rather a shame he couldn't get along with other children as he could with the parakeet. We decided it was wise to follow the recommendation of the school and let him repeat the first grade in order to give him another year to adjust himself to classmates before progressing.

17

At this time, the quiz shows were in their heyday on television. There was "The $64,000 Question" and all its imitations. In such shows people answered questions of the type that required short answers based on memory alone. No judgment was required. ("On what day was Abraham Lincoln assassinated?" "On April 15, 1865." "You are *right*. Give that man $100,000.")

I didn't like the shows and rarely watched. I saw no value in that sort of question-and-answer setup and, in fact, I felt it cheapened the whole matter of intelligence down to the parlor-trick level.

On August 26, 1958, the matter came around to me. A new quiz show, "Brain and Brawn," was beginning, and I was asked to be on, along with Willy Ley.

I was tempted, but a little thought changed my mind. Why lend myself to such nonsense? If I answered questions correctly, what did I prove but what everyone knew to begin with—that I had a trick memory and instant recall. On the other hand, one simple question, answered incorrectly, would be incredibly humiliating.

I thought of spelling "weigh" W-I-E-G-H. I thought of Sprague de Camp who had managed to get on "The $64,000 Question," and who (for reasons known only to himself and God) chose motion pictures as his category, then muffed the very first question.

So I refused, using my bronchitis as a handy excuse.

Later on, when the newspapers erupted with scandals concerning these shows—to the effect that they were rigged, that contestants were coached in their answers—I was delighted I had resisted. I honestly believe that I would never have consented to let myself be coached and would never have knowingly been involved in any fraud—but would I have been believed?

18

The November 1958 *Astounding* had my article "Our Lonely Planet,"[8] and I began a new book for Abelard-Schuman, *The Kingdom of the Sun*, which dealt with the solar system.

[8] See *Fact and Fancy* (Doubleday, 1962).

My novel, on the other hand, continued to languish. There was no way in which I could force myself to work on it. All I wanted to do was nonfiction. On October 20, 1958, I abandoned *The Bounds of Infinity* and never returned to it.

Yet that didn't mean I abandoned science fiction *entirely*. I had lunch with Bob Mills in New York on October 23, and he asked me to write a story for him. He said that that morning he had seen the name Lefkowitz two or three times, each time spelled differently, and he thought there was a story there.

"What kind of a story?" I asked blankly.

"I don't know," he said, pettishly. "A *story!* You're the writer."

So on the twenty-ninth, I began a story about a man who is haunted by Lefkowitzes in different spellings and called it "Unto the Fourth Generation." I had it done in a day, sent it off, and it was accepted. A very nice little story, I thought. (Bob Mills was now editor of *F & SF*, by the way, Tony Boucher having left the post.)

"Unto the Fourth Generation" is the only even faintly Jewish story I have ever written, in the sense of its dealing with what might be considered a Jewish theme.

As soon as "Unto the Fourth Generation" was concluded, I wrote a slight piece called "Rain, Rain, Go Away." Mills had suggested that one, too, but he rejected it when he saw it.

19

Robyn was going to a nursery school three days a week, and on October 31 she joined David for the first time in Halloween trick-or-treating. David wore a leopard costume and Robyn went as Little Red Riding Hood.

Robyn was already showing signs of the absolute fearlessness that was to characterize her in her relations with "bullies." She was as fierce as David was gentle. When other children would pick on David, three-year-old Robyn would charge forward with a "You let David alone" and would loose an ineffectual shower of blows on the other child.

I feared for both in later life—for David, who was sure to be scapegoated, and for Robyn, who was sure to join every fight on the weaker side.

20

My straight-Democratic vote on November 6, 1958, was more or less the mood of the nation, and I stayed up till 2 A.M. to enjoy the spectacle of another Democratic Congress despite furious compaigning on the part of Vice President Nixon. My comment in my diary was, "A terrible licking for Nixon, in particular, that dirty bastard."

21

The death of Cyril Kornbluth, nine months before had had a peculiar effect on me. I didn't say so in the diary, but it seems to me that I remember his death having made the first page of the New York *Times* in a box in the lower left-hand corner—though perhaps it was only on the obituary page.

A queer kind of envy overcame me, a feeling that I might not get equal billing when it came my time to die, and a frustration at never knowing whether I had or not.

I recognized the feeling to be a silly one and I decided to exorcise it by writing a story about it. After a false start, I tried a second time on November 4 and carried it through.

I called the story "Obituary," and actually it was more a thriller than a science-fiction story, but it was a thriller in which the villain used time travel to see his own obituary. I think it is the only story I ever wrote that was in the first person with a woman as the narrator, and I think the story was a *good* one. I think it's one story of mine that has unjustly been passed over in anthologies. Bob Mills did buy it, however.

22

On November 14, I got a letter from Norman Lobsenz, the new editor of *Amazing*. He asked for stories.

I pointed out that the March 1959 issue would be the twentieth anniversary of the issue that contained my first published story, "Marooned off Vesta." Should I not write another story for that issue? He agreed at once and promised to reprint "Marooned off Vesta" in that same issue.

I decided to have the three characters of "Marooned off Vesta" come back for a twenty-year reunion, so I pulled out my copy of "Marooned off Vesta" and read it carefully, looking for something I could hang a peg on. I found some lines that read, "He did manage, however, to pick up a small field-glass and fountain pen. These he placed in his pocket. They were valueless under present conditions—"

I did nothing more with those objects in the story. They were only mentioned to give an air of verisimilitude to a nightmare journey across the remnants of a wrecked spaceship. I now picked them up, however, and built my story "Anniversary" about them.

I began it on November 21, finished it the next day, and sent it off to *Amazing*, which accepted it at once. I also wrote another biographical sketch to bring that first, embarrassing one up to date.

23

The Massachusetts School of Art was inducting a new president. Protocol called for other college presidents to attend and greet their fellow. Under such circumstances, most sent proxies. President Kirk of Columbia, finding that a Boston professor (me) was a Columbia alumnus, asked me to be his proxy and, of course, I was flattered enough to agree.

What I didn't know then, but found out shortly thereafter, was that I would have to take part in an academic procession wearing academic robes. I had avoided that nonsense throughout my own college career, but on November 20, 1958, thanks to my vanity, I found myself swathed in medieval gown and mortarboard—for the first time in my life—taking part in a ceremony that lasted forever.

24

John Campbell had a new project. He was going to form an "Interplanetary Exploration Society," which was going to become a power in the land. Taking care of the details was an elderly gentleman who, John said, had organized the Diners Club, so that he knew all about organizing successful societies.

The first meeting was slated to be held at the Museum of Natural History on December 10, 1958, and Campbell rather put the pressure on me to attend. I was going to go into New York a week earlier, but Campbell *did* have a claim on me and I adjusted my schedule.

On December 10, I went to New York by train and handed in the manuscript of *The Kingdom of the Sun* to Abelard-Schuman. I also met a new editor, Hal Cantor.

In the evening I went to the museum. The meeting was held in a hall that had a capacity of 440, but only 52 people attended. I was deputed, on five minutes' notice, to introduce Campbell, which I did. That meant I was stuck on the platform along with the elderly gentleman of Diners Club fame and, of course, Campbell himself.

Campbell then gave the scientific talk of the evening. It was long and, with all my love for Campbell, I cannot say it was interesting. I lis-

tened gravely, however, as did everyone in the audience, *except* the elderly gentleman who, it seemed, was rather hard of hearing.

He sat through some fifteen minutes of Campbell's speech with an
increasingly unhappy look on his lined face and then began making
comments to me, who sat next to him, in what I imagined he felt to be
a low and scarce-heard whisper. It wasn't. His voice was louder than
Campbell's. He kept saying, "What's all this? He's killing the club.
This isn't what we're here for."

I tried gently to shush him, but he wouldn't have any of that. I got
pinker and pinker and managed not to laugh. In fact, nobody laughed,
and Campbell, pretending he heard nothing, continued his talk, flat-
footedly, to the very end.

As far as I know there was never a second meeting of the Interplanetary Exploration Society, at least not in New York, although a
couple of issues of a periodical with that name managed to struggle
into existence.

A Boston branch continued for some time, and I dutifully attended meetings. Campbell maintained that the Boston branch remained alive because of the peculiarly academic nature of Boston, but
that wasn't it at all. It remained alive because of a very puzzling and
peculiar woman named Alma Hill, who spoke perfect English words,
but rarely put them together into a sentence I could understand. She
insisted on running the society and singlehandedly kept it alive despite
the torpor of everyone else.

What I remember best about Alma Hill is that once when I
pleaded the press of business as an excuse for not doing something she
wanted done, she called me a "humbug." Assuming that a "humbug"
meant a phony, I allowed my feelings to be hurt and said so. Alma
promptly wrote a long letter explaining exactly what she meant by
"humbug," and since I couldn't make head or tail of what she said, I
let it drop.

25

On that December 10 trip to New York, I picked up an advance
copy of the Avon paperback edition of my mystery. They called it *The
Death Dealers*, a totally inappropriate name. What's more, there was
on the cover a beautiful woman holding a gun—which was fine except
that there was no beautiful woman in the story and no gun. I complained, but the Avon editor told me the cover was simply a device to
label the book as a mystery and it didn't necessarily have to have anything to do with the story.

I read the book on the train on my way back to Boston and decided it was no good after all—and felt very depressed. (Nor did I feel compensated by the fact that the February 1959 *Satellite* arrived containing "Benefactor of Humanity," which Margulies had retitled "A Statue for Father."[9])

One important fact about *The Death Dealers*, however, I recognized only in retrospect—and only long after, too.

My detective in the book was named Jack Doheny. He was lower-class in origins and in speech, and was terribly impressed and overawed by all the scientists among whom he found himself.

He was polite, he asked elementary questions about chemistry, was abashed, apologized—and, in the end, he solved the crime and you realized that at no time had he really been abashed, or had he apologized for anything more than effect.

I liked him, and I planned to use him in future stories, but the poor reception that *The Death Dealers* received, both in manuscript and in print, deterred me.

Years later I realized that I could never use him again, for the television program "Colombo" had arrived, and Colombo was Jack Doheny to the life.

I don't for one minute suggest that anyone got the idea for Colombo from my book—the notion of a lower-class detective pitted against the upper crust is not so startling an idea that it can't arise independently. Besides, "Colombo" does it much better and it was, in its time, just about my favorite noncomedy program.

What I do regret is that if I were ever to try to use Jack Doheny again, everyone will be sure I am copying "Colombo," even though I was there first by over a decade.

26

I ended 1958 with four books for the year:

25. *The World of Carbon* (Abelard-Schuman)
26. *Lucky Starr and the Rings of Saturn* (Doubleday)
27. *The World of Nitrogen* (Abelard-Schuman)
28. *The Death Dealers* (Avon)

The Death Dealers was my first paperback original.

As for my writing earnings, the year kept to the high level of the first six months. I ended up with a literary income of $31,100, counting the remainder of my $2,500 stipend for *The Living River*.

[9] See *Buy Jupiter and Other Stories*.

If the last of my school earnings are included, my annual income was nearly $34,300. I felt fine.

27

January 2, 1959, was my "Jack Benny birthday," my thirty-ninth, and the Soviets celebrated by sending up the first successful Moon probe. It skimmed around the Moon and took the first photographs of the far side that, till then, no human being had ever seen. And it was that which made nonsense of my story "Ideas Die Hard," which I had written and published nearly two years before.

28

On January 10, I received copies of my short-story collection *Nine Tomorrows* (the best short-story collection, in my opinion, I have ever published). It was my fifteenth Doubleday book and now, for the first time in nine years, I did not have a single book in press with Doubleday.

It was not that I lacked for publishers. My remaining books were distributed among five other publishers, and I had two in press with still another one, Houghton Mifflin. And yet another one, Random House, showed up on January 30, when Janet Finney of that publishing house first asked me to do a children's book on rockets and I agreed. Nevertheless, none of them did, or could ever, replace Doubleday.

29

On January 29, Marcia had a second son, named Richard. I now had four nephews; Larry and Richard through Marcia and Nick; and Danny and Eric through Ruth and Stanley. Ruth was pregnant at this time and eventually gave birth to Nanette, my first niece, and that ended child-bearing for all three of us. My parents ended with seven grandchildren: five boys and two girls.

30

On February 5, 1959, one of David's milk teeth fell out; it was the first to do so. I followed the American cliché: I told him that if he put it under his pillow, the tooth fairy would leave a dime in its place. And so she did.

I followed the practice for both children in years to come, and if they learned, eventually (or guessed) that the tooth fairy was in reality a stout, middle-aged male, they didn't let on, for they didn't want to spoil a good thing.

I remember once, after this had been going on for a few years, we were having dinner at a restaurant when Robyn remarked that one of her teeth was about to come out.

"Fine," I said. "The tooth fairy will surely leave a dime."

"What?" said the waitress. "Does your tooth fairy still leave dimes? Ours leaves a quarter."

"Really?" I said, indignantly. "Well, wait and see what the tip fairy leaves *you*."

She scurried away, but I left her the usual tip anyway. I didn't have the heart to punish her.

31

The March 1959 issue of *Amazing* arrived, with the reprint of "Marooned off Vesta," followed by the new story, "Anniversary."[10] It did occur to me that I had laid myself open to any number of letters that would go, "Well, Asimov, I read the two stories and you've surely gone downhill a great deal in twenty years." It seemed the obvious thing to do even if the writer didn't believe it.

Fortunately, no such letters arrived. I guess the fans didn't want to spoil the anniversary.

An anniversary of another sort, Robyn's fourth birthday, came at almost the same time, on February 19, 1959. We had the usual little party.

32

On March 7, 1959, I became aware of the new financial situation I found myself in. A gentleman arrived from an aerospace firm in Los Angeles and offered me a job at a salary of fifteen thousand dollars, and I turned it down out of hand. I couldn't afford to take it since my income as a full-time writer was twice as high.

I had, it appeared to me, priced myself out of the job market. Thus, when well-meaning friends would tell me that if I played my cards right, Keefer would relent and the medical school would put me back on salary, I would have to say, "I don't want Keefer to relent and don't want to be back on a salary."

I couldn't exactly tell them my earnings, which were higher than

10 See *Asimov's Mysteries*.

any professorial salary at the school, lest I seemed to be vaunting my-self. And on their own, they didn't seem to guess, but just thought me obdurate and foolish. Apparently, it didn't occur to them that writing something as trivial as science fiction and nonfiction books for young people could bring in such an income.

33

After Bob Mills had rejected "Rain, Rain, Go Away," it was rejected in turn by Scholastic, by *Amazing,* and even by *Satellite.* Rejec-tions of this sort were becoming terribly embarrassing. I had reached the point where my name alone made it worth buying a science-fiction story; so to have it rejected under such conditions meant that the story was very bad indeed.

Fortunately, Hans Santesson took it for *Fantastic Universe* on March 19, and I was saved the ultimate shame of having an un-publishable piece of science fiction on my hands.

The April 1959 *F & SF* came out with that much better story "Unto the Fourth Generation."[11]

11 See *Nightfall and Other Stories.*

10

One More Battle

1

I went to New York on March 23, 1959, and, during the next day, made my rounds. Doubleday and I, for one thing, agreed to cancel the contract for *The Bounds of Infinity*, and I felt an enormous relief. For the first time I realized, *consciously*, that I was drifting away from science fiction.

I saw Mac Talley of NAL the same day and he wanted an adult nonfiction book on nucleic acids, viruses, and, in general, the basic components of living tissue. He even had a title for it: *The Wellsprings of Life*.

That was an excellent suggestion. When I wrote *The Chemicals of Life* five years before, I had never even mentioned nucleic acids. At the time I was writing it, the importance of nucleic acids had just been made plain by James Watson and Francis Crick with their double helix theory, but it had passed me by.

If I now wrote *The Wellsprings of Life*, however, I could include the nucleic acids and give them the importance they deserved. What's more, it would be for adults and I wanted that, too, if only as a change in pace. What I did not want, however, was a soft-cover original, as had been the case with *The Death Dealers*. It seemed to me that through that route lay oblivion. I wanted a hard-cover.

Mac was agreeable. "Sure," he said, "do a hard-cover with Abelard-Schuman and we'll buy the soft-cover rights."

That evening I went to Park Avenue and Ninety-fourth Street and visited my old friend Sidney Cohen from the days of Seth Low Junior College. For the first time, I met his wife, Lea, an Israeli woman with a delightful accent (though her English was fluent) and with an equally delightful beauty. I also met Sidney's three small children.

We went out for dinner and discussed Israel and the Jewish heritage. As usual, I found myself in the odd position of not being a Zionist and of not particularly valuing my Jewish heritage.

I like Jewish cooking, Jewish music, Jewish jokes—but I'm not *serious* about it. I also like other kinds of cooking, music, and jokes (in fact, we were eating at a Chinese restaurant). I don't even mind *being* Jewish. I make no secret about being Jewish in this book, or elsewhere, and I've never tried to change my name.

I just think it's more important to be human and to have a human heritage; and I think it is wrong for anyone to feel that there is anything special about any one heritage of whatever kind. It is delightful to have the human heritage exist in a thousand varieties, for it makes for greater interest, but as soon as one variety is thought to be more important than another, the groundwork is laid for destroying them all.

This is not something I can get people in general to believe. I certainly made no impression on Sidney and Lea, so I remain a minority within a minority, and am uneasily convinced that in the land of the blind, the one-eyed man is in deep trouble.

2

The American Chemical Society was meeting in Boston in April of 1959, and I was invited to give a talk. It wasn't the usual presentation of a research paper, because I wasn't doing research. They wanted a general talk for the Division of Chemical Education (presumably because I had written a number of papers for the *Journal of Chemical Education.*

I chose to give a talk I entitled "Enzymes and Metaphor," which dealt with the manner of making the concept of catalysis clear to students by the use of colorful analogies (something I was, in any case, doing in my science writing for the public).

It was one of the few talks I've given for which I had to actually write the speech, because one of the conditions was that it be available for reprint. The written paper appeared, eventually, in the November 1959 *Journal of Chemical Education.*[1]

I gave the talk on April 7, 1959, and did well, I think. I did not actually read the speech, though it lay before me. Afterward, in the question-and-answer session, a woman rose to ask me how I would metaphorically explain a coenzyme, the portion of the enzyme that does the actual work, but does it with far greater efficiency than it possibly could if the rest of the enzyme weren't there.

It was not a planted question and it was not something I had thought of. For a few moments, I flailed about uselessly within my mind—and since my face is the mirror of my emotions, everyone in the audience must have known I was flailing.

[1] See *Is Anyone There?* (Doubleday, 1967).

Then, in sudden inspiration, I took off my identification badge, which was pinned to my lapel.

"The printing on the badge," I said, "is the coenzyme and the badge itself is the enzyme. The printing does the actual work of communicating a message, but it couldn't do that work if the rest of the badge were not there to supply the surface on which the printing appears."

I got a round of applause more, I think, for the obvious relief on my face than for anything I said. And then I recognized the questioner as Ruth Pitt, Bernie's wife.

I had not seen Bernie very often in the past year or so, but he did call me up during the worst of my troubles at the school to say there was a rumor that I was being fired, and was that so? It was a clear case of misery loving company, for his voice sounded much more animated than it usually did.

I had no objection to making him happy, so I told him the whole story, and he listened with, I think, delight. He may have been disappointed when Keefer gave in, for he would have enjoyed watching a protracted fight.

On the day of the talk, I also met Al Cooper once more, my buddy of the old days as a graduate chemistry student at Columbia. He was looking for a job again, as we had both been doing at the ACS meetings of 1947, twelve years before. I took him out to dinner that night, thankfully aware that I myself was *not* looking for a job and that, barring catastrophe, would never be looking for a job again.

3

Prior to the talks at the American Chemical Society, I had received a letter from some society official asking if I would consent to be interviewed by a reporter from the Boston *Herald-Traveler*. The implication was that it would be welcome publicity for the society.

I agreed, partly out of loyalty to my professional society and partly out of a perfect willingness to be interviewed by an important newspaper.

The reporter duly arrived, and asked a number of questions—mostly about my science-fiction writing, since that is the most colorful thing about me as far as the general public is concerned. I replied, fully and frankly, as I try always to do, and I was pleasantly surprised when, on April 6, 1959, the day before my talk, the *Herald-Traveler* ran the interview on the first page of the second section.

There was a picture of myself smiling fetchingly out of a plump

face, and an eight-column headline that referred to me as a "BU Professor." The story itself was entirely correct and did not contain a single
misquotation or error that I could find, so I was pleased enough to buy
a number of copies and spread it around a little bit.

4

On April 9 I noticed David stroking an alley cat outside our house
with every indication of love and affection, and I beamed. We were a
cat family, and I was delighted that David, without any encouragement
from us, loved cats as Gertrude and I did.

Alas, half an hour later, David walked into the house with a
stuffed-up nose and puffy eyes, and it turned out to be a lucky stroke
that I had seen him playing with the cat. Had that not been so, who
knows what exotic ailment I would have thought he had? As it was, I
recognized that although he was, voluntarily, an ailurophile, he was, involuntarily, an ailurophobe. He was allergic to cats, as Sprague was.

An antihistamine fixed him up, but we now knew, sadly, that it
would be difficult for us to own a cat—as long as David was in the
house.

5

Work continued at the usual hectic pace. I was finishing the first
draft of *The Double Planet* (a book on the Earth and the Moon) and
starting the first draft of *The Wellsprings of Life*, both for Abelard-
Schuman. I was working on the galleys of *Realm of Numbers* for
Houghton Mifflin—and I even lectured at the med school.

Even though I was no longer getting a regular salary from the med
school, I intended to do whatever was needed to justify my title. That
meant I would give an occasional lecture, if asked to do so and if the
subject were to my liking—and if I were paid.

My price was one hundred dollars per lecture. Sinex said that the
usual fee for a guest lecture was twenty-five dollars. And I said sternly
(not willing to give an inch), "Name your guest and I'll show you I'm
four times as good."

On April 13, 1959, I lectured to the class on nucleic acids, for instance, then gave a second lecture on April 16.

Not all my lectures were successes, however. On the eve of April
16, I made a trip to the Brighton branch of the Boston Public Library
to talk to a group of what they told me would be high-school students.

It wasn't; I was deceived, perhaps unwittingly. I found myself with an audience of eight-to-twelve-year-olds. I was unprepared psychologically and annoyed, so the talk was a dismal failure.

One thing I do remember was the questioning of one of those youngsters after the talk. Up went his hand and he said, "What is the second closest star, Dr. Asimov?"

I smiled inwardly. Everyone knew that the closest star was Alpha Centauri, but not many knew the name of the second closest. I did, however, and I was glad to be able to answer without hesitation.

I said, "Barnard's Star, young man, is the second closest star. It is a little over six light-years away."

The kid just looked puzzled and said, "Then what's the *closest* star, Dr. Asimov?"

"Alpha Centauri," I said, surprised that he should be surprised, "which is 4.3 light-years away."

"That's funny," said the little rat, "I thought the closest star was the sun, which is 8 light-minutes away."

The audience set up a fearful cacophony of high-pitched laughter. It was probably the pet conundrum at the junior high schools that year, and I had fallen for it.

6

Our living room was in the last stages of being decorated, rather more than three years after we had moved into the house. The wallpaper had to be put up several times because our first choice cracked every time it went up, and we had to abandon it at last for the second choice.

On April 25, 1959, the wall-to-wall carpeting was put down in the living-room, dining-room combination. Then came a large sofa and three chairs, together with drapes on the twenty-seventh. It all looked very good, and our investment in the decorating came to just about four thousand dollars.

That, however, was nothing to cry about. Even with that, and with our mortgage entirely paid off, and my school income cut off, we now had nearly fifty thousand dollars in the bank. We had more money in reserve, in fact, than we had had before we had bought the house.

7

On April 16, I had had a pleasant lunch at the Ritz with Abe Burack of *The Writer* and with Ben Benson. I was in a particularly good mood because I had been invited to attend the thirteenth annual Mystery Writers' Association's award dinner, on May 1, 1959, and Abe and Ben were going, too. I welcomed their company. I wasn't sure that, as a science-fiction writer, I would be socially acceptable to the members of the MWA, and my recent mystery *The Death Dealers* was not much of an entree for me. It seemed well, therefore, that I would be sure of at least two personal friends there.

On April 30, I went to New York and gave the completed manuscript of *The Double Planet* to Bernice Frankel, who was now my editor at Abelard-Schuman, and perhaps the nicest in the series. Her letters to me always began, "Dear Handsome Hero," and I always admire good taste in women.

I went with her to have dinner with Hal Cantor (her immediate superior) at his apartment in Stuyvesant Town—always good for a twinge of nostalgia in itself. (It had been ten years since I had moved away.) Cantor had promised me steak and potato pancakes and said his wife made the best potato pancakes in the world. He may have been right, because I didn't particularly like potato pancakes till then, and I loved them afterward.

There was only one catch to the meal, though. Just before we began, he said to me in quite a conversational tone, "Do you know Ben Benson?"

"Yes, sir," I said, "I sure do."

"Dropped dead yesterday," he said.

It took them quite a while to pacify me after that, and dinner was delayed for half an hour before I was able to eat. Ben had had a bad heart, as I knew, and he was, as I heard it, shopping in New York, and just clutched at his chest and died in the street.

8

I wasn't certain what to do. All the light had gone out of the MWA dinner for me. I even considered skipping the whole thing and going home.

On May 1, I visited Bob Mills, but found no satisfaction there. He was looking for a new job, for he felt that there was just no way of earning enough at *F & SF*, and he was as glum as I. He was supposed to go to the MWA dinner, too—and he wasn't sure if he would. We sat there, grunting at each other, until Judy Merril walked in.

She, at least, was cheerful, and jollied us along until we were both in good humor.

This was a great thing for which I will be forever grateful to her, for the Mystery Writers' Association dinner was an important one for me to attend.

Janet Jeppson was attending. She was the young psychiatrist who had stood in line to get her book signed by me at the New York convention 2½ years before and who had felt insulted by my scowling face and suggestive remark (not knowing I was in a state of kidney-stone agony).

She had heard nothing but good things about me from her brother, who had been in my class in that last teaching semester and who had heard me give my great speech on abnormal hemoglobins. Therefore, hearing from a mystery-writer friend of hers, Veronica Parker Johns, that I was to be one of the people attending the banquet, she decided to come along as a guest and meet me again—for she still admired my books.

It was a near squeak, though, for Eric Fromm was giving a lecture that night and she had to choose whether to listen to Fromm or to meet me and perhaps be insulted again. And I had to choose whether to go home in despair over Ben, or go to the dinner and be cast down over his absence.

We both decided to go to the dinner.

I realized at once that I had made the right choice. The dinner was full of people I knew. I never realized before how much the mystery world and the science-fiction world overlapped.

The Ballantines were there, for instance, all apologetic because they had been one of the firms who had rejected *The Death Dealers* and a little regretful that perhaps I no longer felt friendly with them.

I stared at Betty as though she were crazy. "What has a rejection got to do with friendship?" I asked, hugging and kissing her. She kissed me back.

Bob Mills was there, too, looking much more cheerful than he had in the office, and Hans Santesson was there, and many more. By the time the call went out that we were to sit down to dinner, I felt that I was at a science-fiction convention.

I looked at my card to see the number of the table to which I had been assigned. It was Table 3, and as I looked about, trying to locate it, Hans Santesson came over and said, "This way, Isaac. There's a young lady here waiting to meet you."

There, with the biggest possible smile on her face, was Janet Jeppson, whom I now saw (as far as my memory goes) for the first time in my life. Filled with the euphoria of having found myself, unexpectedly, at a pleasant convention of so many living friends to make up for the one who had died, I greeted her with just as big a smile and took my seat next to her. Also at the table were Bob Mills and Hans Santesson— and others whom I knew less well.

Eleanor Roosevelt was the chief speaker, and this was the only time I was ever in the same room with her. She spoke of F.D.R. and of his love for mysteries. Since I idolized both Franklin and Eleanor, it was a great occasion for me.

And meanwhile, during the dinner, Janet and I carried on an animated conversation. I thought she was charming and intelligent, and she thought I was charming and intelligent. She didn't tell me she had met me at the New York convention and how I had acted.[2]

While Eleanor Roosevelt spoke I even held Janet's hand, and she didn't stop me.

Robert Mills, on finding out that she was a science-fiction fan, asked if she read *Fantasy and Science Fiction*, and when she said she did, he asked her if she had read the just-published "Unto the Fourth Generation."

She said, "Yes."

"What did you think of it?"

I ought to have interrupted at once to say that I was the author, in order to prevent the mouse-trapping, but I must admit I wanted to hear what she would say, in case she had forgotten I had written it.

She *had* forgotten. "It had a serious flaw," she said. "The protagonist went through the experience and then, in the end, it was as though nothing had happened. He had in no way been changed by it."

And *then* Bob said I was the author, and Janet, embarrassed, tried to apologize.

"No," I said, "you're perfectly right. That *is* a flaw. I'll change it when I put it in one of my story collections." (And I did, too.)

After Eleanor Roosevelt's speech, there came the time for the awards, and when the award for the best novel of the year was awarded, I muttered (thinking of *The Death Dealers*), "I'm afraid I qualify as author of the worst novel of the year."

Apparently I said it with such sincerity that Janet's soft heart bled for me, and never after did she believe my sedulously cultivated put-on that I was a monster of vanity and arrogance.

An award for the best mystery movie of the year was handed out, too, and a Hollywood starlet arose to accept it and deliver a vacuous little speech. As one might expect of a Hollywood starlet, she was mostly breasts, and Janet (who was leastly breasts) said in a low voice, "Oh, I wish I looked like that." And my soft heart bled for her.

[2] When she did tell me, years later, I refused to believe it until she showed me the book I had signed. She also told me how amazed she was at how different I was at the banquet, and I, of course, explained about the kidney stone and about the difference the presence or absence makes.

So we were each of us impressed with the other's sincerity, in addition to all our other virtues.

When the dinner was over, I said to Janet, "There's no need to end the evening, I hope."

She said, "Wouldn't you rather stay with your friends here?"

"At the moment," I said, "you're my only friend."

She said, "I was just going home."

I hesitated. "Are you married?"

"No."

"Steady boyfriend?"

"Not right now."

"May I come along?"

It was her turn to hesitate. "Just to talk?"

"Just to talk."

So I came along and I stayed till after midnight and we just talked, and then I left and the next day I went back to Boston.

We exchanged letters afterward and corresponded on a fairly regular basis. Her letters were invariably longer and far more interesting than mine. She was, in fact, a fascinating letter-writer and always described the places she saw and the things she did, as I was incapable of doing.

She had always wanted to be a writer and she did manage to sell a short story to *Saint* under a pseudonym, and that was a great day for her. Her profession, however (she was a psychiatrist, remember), kept her busy and she didn't have the chance to just write story after story as I had done till the sheer weight of practice and persistence began to break down the walls.

In any case, when I visited New York, I would usually call to say hello and, if she weren't with a patient, we would talk a while (sometimes for quite a while).

It was a very pleasant relationship and I was always very glad I had decided to go to that Mystery Writers' Association dinner. Of course, I kept thinking that she would soon meet someone with whom she could have a more serious relationship than with me, that she would get married, and that the correspondence would then fade off—and I couldn't help but feel sorry at the thought, though I always told myself that I should be happy on her account if that happened.

On two different occasions, in fact, she told me she had met someone who seemed interesting, and on each occasion I thought surely the correspondence would fade off, and no matter how I tried to be happy for her, I was more conscious of being selfishly sorry. On each occasion, though, the thing blew over.

9

On May 3, 1959, I attended Ben Benson's funeral and drove down to Sharon to be at the actual interment. It was the first funeral I had ever attended.

10

During the month of May, I received copies of *The Clock We Live On* and *Words of Science*.

Words of Science was the first of my Houghton Mifflin books. It was a very well-made outsize book—6¾ inches by 10¼ inches—and a single copy cost $5.00 as opposed to $3.00 for *The Clock We Live On* and $3.50 for *Nine Tomorrows*. I was very pleased with Houghton Mifflin and I have never had grounds to complain about the appearance of their books. They do a good job.

By now, too, my essay series in *F & SF* was a settled thing. The eighth one appeared in the June 1959 issue, and since the magazine was soon to celebrate its tenth anniversary, it seemed a permanent institution and I had the comfortable feeling that not one month would pass without something of mine appearing in a science-fiction magazine. If nothing else there would be my monthly essay in *F & SF*.

This was important to me. I knew that I was writing very little science fiction now, but I didn't want to give up the science-fiction world. Thanks to my *F & SF* essay, I never did.

11

On May 5, 1959, the whole issue of my standing in the school—which I thought was settled—broke out again.

Sinex called me into his office and told me that Keefer felt I was using my title as a way of garnering personal publicity and that, therefore, I could not have the title. I was to be demoted to lecturer.

"What personal publicity?" I asked, utterly confused.

It was the April 6 article in the *Herald-Traveler*, which had pleased me so much at the time, and especially the headline identifying me as a "BU Professor."

I left, walked down to Soutter's office to tell him that the battle was joined again, made some phone calls, thought it over that night, walked into Sinex's office the next day, and here, in essence, is what I said. (Once again I made no notes and didn't include anything in my diary except for the phrase "long conference," but I remember it very well.)

"Dr. Sinex" (I said), "the article in question was the result of an interview by a reporter; an interview that I was requested to make by the president of the American Chemical Society, which is my professional society. I have the letter he sent me in which he said that such an interview would be welcome publicity for the society, and my answer in which I said I would be glad to oblige the society. I called him yesterday and he is willing to bear witness for me in this and to hold me entirely guiltless of seeking the interview on my own behalf.

"Second, you can read the article from beginning to end and tell me if you find a single sentence, a single word, that redounds to the dishonor of the university or that represents self-seeking publicity. As to the headline—I have no control over a headline writer. I decline responsibility for that.

"Third, if I *did* want personal publicity at the expense of my Boston University affiliation, I have an easy way of gaining it. My brother is an editor of a large newspaper in the New York metropolitan area called the Long Island *Newsday*. You are welcome to look through its files to see whether I have ever once used it for personal publicity of any kind, with or without Boston University."

Sinex, having listened to me speaking at far greater length than I have here outlined, and with much greater passion than the mere words can display, said that there would be a vote at the nominating committee the next Monday—the eleventh.

"Very well, then," I said, "you tell Keefer that what I said before still stands. I will fight this in every possible way, through the civil courts if I have to, and I will never give up."

I was about to leave when I thought of something else. "One more thing, Dr. Sinex. If this blows over, and if it seems to Keefer that if he harasses me every few months I will resign, assure him that I won't. Assure him also that he may think he will be remembered by posterity for some accomplishment or other in his medical career, but he won't. He will be remembered for no more, and no less, than what I choose to say about him in my autobiography. And that goes for you, too, Dr. Sinex." And *then* I left.

There was now nothing to do but wait for the session on the following Monday. I was certain I would be demoted to lecturer, since I suspected the nominating committee was a kind of Supreme Soviet, called into session only to confirm the voice of the Leader. That meant I would have to find a lawyer and begin taking steps, perhaps against his advice. There is no way in which I can properly describe the feeling of being, at one and the same time, enormously determined and enormously reluctant.

It wasn't necessary. On the evening of May 11, 1959, I received a phone call from Professor Hegnauer of the Physiology Department. The nominating committee *had voted Keefer down,* and I was to remain an associate professor after all. In fact, the vote was unanimous, I was told. Keefer himself, to save face, had to abstain.

And on the evening of the fifteenth, Dr. Soutter called to assure me that he was taking steps to make certain that Keefer did not continue the fight over me by taking the matter to Case.

I had won the fourth round and that really ended it, after nearly two years of intermittent fighting.

So let me keep my promise and say what I think of these gentlemen in my autobiography. I hold no malice or bitterness over the matter. I enjoyed the fight and I won it, and by relieving me of my school duties they did me a favor. Where, then, should the malice or bitterness come in?

I feel, looking back on it, that Henry Lemon misjudged the effect of my profession on the school and sincerely and honestly felt it would be for the good of the school to get rid of me. I feel that working with what seemed to him to be worthy motives he influenced Chester Keefer into thinking it was important to get rid of me. I feel that F. Marrott Sinex, new at the job, had no choice but to go along with Keefer.

Except for those three and for that short period of time, *no one* at Boston University *at any time* has treated me with anything but the greatest respect and friendship. And even Sinex, in the years since that fight, during which he remained the head of the department and my titular boss, never treated me with anything but the greatest respect and friendship.

I have, therefore, no fault to find with anyone or anything.

PART
II

The Book Race

11

Peace

1

For the first time in a long while, peace descended—no job worries, no housing worries, no pregnancies. It is nice to have such interludes now and then.

We got David his first bicycle on May 7, 1959, at which time he was still some months short of his eighth birthday. It was somewhat less than regulation size so that his feet could reach the pedals.

Like Stanley before him, he had no trouble. I anticipated training wheels, or having to walk or run beside him, but no such thing. He got on it and off he went.

It made me think that if it were that easy, I *had* to be able to master the device, so I got on briefly—but only briefly.

That night, however, I felt as though I had gotten onto another kind of bicycle, but one that I couldn't easily get off. It involved Norbert Wiener.

At some dinner party (the details are not, alas, in my diary) Norbert told me he had read *The Death Dealers* and had liked it. My heart warmed to anyone who would give me a kind word for the book, and Norbert's praise was so extravagant that I would have popped my vest buttons if I had worn a vest.

But then it turned out that Norbert wanted to write a mystery of his own and had a collaboration in his mind, so I couldn't tell how much of his praise was sincere and how much was policy. I took to avoiding him after that because, to be truthful, I didn't in the least want to collaborate on a mystery with him.

On the evening of May 7, though, I saw him perforce. It was at an initiation dinner of Sigma Xi, over which Bill Boyd was presiding. He wanted me there, so I came and sat in the front row near him to hear the speech that followed.

It was Norbert who was speaking, and his topic was the relationship between quantum theory and gravitation. I can't say if anyone in the audience understood him. Certainly, I did not—not a word.

Speakers frequently choose one person in the audience to speak to,[1] and Norbert chose me. Fixing his bulbous eyes on me with a constant and unblinking intensity, he talked. Without ever breaking eye contact, he talked. Everyone else in the audience could let his mind wander, could yawn, could nod, could whisper—but I had to look bright, wide-eyed, and interested throughout, even though I did not understand a word.

I was as limp as a new sock by talk's end and got out as fast as I could lest he waylay me.

2

I received a letter from Leon Svirsky of Basic Books, suggesting I do a book on an overview of science, and on May 13, 1959, he visited me in West Newton and spent three hours with me. He was a short fellow, with a hooked nose and a deeply tanned complexion. He buttered me up endlessly and assured me I was the only person who could handle a complete overview.

My books on various branches of science were obviously beginning to pay off, and my status as a "generalist" had come to be recognized. I was a bit frightened of the task all the same, for I was not at all sure I could handle all the sciences. Nevertheless, I am easily swayed by flattery, and I rather gave him the impression that I would agree to do it.

I must have, for I received a contract on the nineteenth and it included a fifteen-hundred-dollar advance, the largest ever offered me up to that point. By that time, though, I had cooled off, and my fright at the prospect had increased. I put the contract aside and said, in my diary, "I don't think I'll sign it for a while."

3

On May 18, I received a rather unusual item in the mail. It was a book in Russian, authored by myself—a translation of The World of Carbon.

It was sent me by an employee of the American Embassy in Moscow who happened to be "an Asimov fan" (his words) and who had come across it. He warned me that there was nothing the United States Government could do to help me collect royalties on it and, of course, I knew that.

Since then, I have had a fair number of books in Russian and in

[1] I don't. I feel the rest of the audience senses it is left out and reacts adversely. I always focus on no one but look over the heads of the audience and vary the direction in which I look.

other languages of the Soviet Union, forwarded to me in one way or another. I can't honestly say I worry much about payment in those cases. I am always somehow rather pleased to be demonstrating my success "in the hometown."

4

On June 18, 1959, David finished first grade with éclat and was promoted to the second. From then on, he progressed normally through the succession of grades.

And on the same day, I finished *The Wellsprings of Life*.

5

Just as Atlantic City is the obvious beach area to a Philadelphian, so Cape Cod is to a Bostonian. I had never made it to Atlantic City when I lived in Philadelphia, but then I had only been there three years.

Now, after ten years in the Boston area, I finally made it to Cape Cod. (Even our summer stay at Marshfield in 1958 had taken us only partway to Cape Cod.)

On June 23, 1959, we drove the full, curling length of Cape Cod and, after three hours, reached Provincetown at the tip. The next day I walked with both kids up to the top of the Provincetown monument, which was the equivalent of a climb of twenty to twenty-five stories. They showed no signs of strain at bounding upward, but I felt quite middle-aged about it. Once at the top, moreover, I had a distinct disinclination to look over the edge of the railing, but neither kid showed any signs of acrophobia, so rather than put it into their heads, I looked over the railing with them.

We were home on the twenty-fifth, and the little two-day vacation was very successful. I have always held that short vacations indulged in on impulse are generally more successful than long ones prepared for lengthily. That, however, may just be a matter of my hating to be away from my typewriter for very long at a time.

6

On June 29, I spent a couple of hours with a group of people at Allied Research in Boston, and the idea was to set up a "brain busting" session, where intelligent, creative, and slightly off-center people could consider problems and come up with solutions—for pay, of course.

I was attracted to the idea, as I invariably am to anything I have never tried, but then it turned out that I would have to apply for security clearance, and I did some thinking. As soon as I had that I would be subjected to bureaucratic regulation of all kinds; I would have to be careful what I wrote lest I give away something I shouldn't.

I therefore turned down the job, and from that day to this have never done anything that would have required security clearance.

7

I was beginning a third book for Houghton Mifflin, *Realm of Measure* dealing chiefly with the metric system.

Hal Cantor of Abelard-Schuman had come across one of my published Houghton Mifflin books and on June 30 called me to complain about it rather petulantly. I had been too cowardly to tell Abelard-Schuman myself that I was doing books for another publisher, but I had thought about the matter long enough to have my argument ready.

I told him that if I could not properly work for any publisher but the one I had first—then the one I had first was Doubleday, and I could do nothing for Abelard-Schuman. Doubleday, I said, had never complained. There are some points that are unanswerable, and that was one of them.

8

I managed to perform a more than usual feat of idiocy on July 4, so I must include it.[2] I was to go to Jerome Himelhoch's house, and that meant driving along the circumferential Highway 128 to Route 2 and then following Route 2 some distance westward.

Both 128 and 2 are major highways, and to miss one while going along the other is a feat of no mean unintelligence. I managed it.

Somehow I went right past the Route 2 turnoff without seeing it. Not content with that little bit of triumphant folly, I then refused to conceive it possible that I had missed it and drove halfway to Gloucester before I gave in to Gertrude's repeated suggestions that somehow I had left Route 2 behind.

We got to Jerry's house over an hour late and I searched desper-

[2] I had reached about this point in my first draft of the autobiography when I told my good friend Ben Bova that I was trying to include every one of my extraordinary acts of stupidity, and he nodded wisely and said, *"That's* why the autobiography is so long." It is good to have a friend. One can never rely on enemies for these home truths.

ately for a way to blame it on circumstance, fate, and the gods, but all I kept getting from everybody was, "How can you miss the Route 2 turnoff?"

9

One of the few depressing lunches I have had with Austin Olney came on July 7, 1959. I incautiously told him of the various books I had in progress, and he advised me strongly not to write so busily. He said my books would compete with each other, interfere with each other's sales, and do less well per book if there were many.

The one thing I had learned in my ill-fated class in economics in high school was "the law of diminishing returns," whereby working ten times as hard or investing ten times as much or producing ten times the quantity does *not* yield ten times the return.

I was rather glum that meal and gave the matter much thought afterward.

What I decided was that I wasn't writing ten times as many books in order to get ten times the monetary returns, but in order to have ten times the pleasure. As far as pleasure was concerned, I had not yet reached the stage of diminishing returns—so I continued to write as quickly and as copiously as ever.[3]

10

On July 15, 1959, I took the train to New York in order to deliver the manuscript of *The Wellsprings of Life* to Abelard-Schuman.

I was still undecided on the science-overview book that Basic Books wanted, and so I called up Janet Jeppson and asked for her advice. After all, I felt that a psychiatrist ought to be able to sort out my fears. I don't think that was the way she attacked the problem. She just felt it was a worthy book to do and, with blind faith, felt I could do it and told me so.

Heartened, I went to Basic Books and signed the contract.

The next day I visited Doubleday, feeling terribly guilty because I had nothing in the works for them. I saw Brad for the first time in months.

I also met a young man named Tim Seldes, who was now working

---

[3] Years later, when Austin was urging me to write some book or other, I reminded him of the time he had told me to write less, and he said, "Well, I was wrong. For some reason, your books support each other, and the more you write, the more they sell. But it's still good advice for most people."

on the science-fiction books under Brad. He was tall, thin, with angular features and a keen sense of humor. I think it was as difficult to catch him in a serious moment as it was me, and the results were sometimes uproarious—often in terms of humor, always in terms of decibels.

11

Both children attended a day camp during the summer, and on July 23 I had the pleasure of seeing David perform in a play that dealt with the siege of the Alamo. He had one line that went, "Sir, Captain Bowie has arrived with word from General Houston." He then did me proud by dying in a most spectacular fashion when the Alamo was stormed.

In their last days at camp, both kids had vague fevers and rashes that we suspected were German measles, but we were never sure.

12

Although my sessions at Allied Research came to nothing thanks to my decision not to go for security clearance, I did get to meet Arthur Obermayer, who was tall, ingratiating, and handsome. He was a bachelor and in later days I would say to him, enviously, "I guess you just sit quietly in your chair and the women fall at your feet."

"No," he said, sitting quietly in his chair, "I notice they're always surrounding you."

"Do you know how much charm and eloquence I have to exert to achieve that effect?" I said, indignantly.

"No," he said, "I wish you'd teach me."

Arthur was deeply involved in the doings of the American Chemical Society. On July 24, he suggested I host a series of weekly TV shows in which I would interview various chemists and discuss chemical subjects with them. It would be on the educational channel, WGBH, and the American Chemical Society would be the sponsor.

I more or less agreed, as I more or less agree to anything that is new, especially if the action is postponed for a few months so that I needn't think about it very soon.

13

July 26, 1959, was our seventeenth wedding anniversary, and an oddly fitting event that day was the visit of the sister of Lee Gould (through whom that first blind date with Gertrude had been arranged) and her husband, Bernard Fonoroff.

I met them for the first time on that day. Both were attractive, both were warmhearted. Bernie's predominating characteristic, however, was a kind of settled melancholy.

As for Essie, she was one of the many people I have met (usually, but not invariably, women) who are nonstop talkers.

I liked her anyway, but I must admit that nonstop talking is harder on me than on most because I happen to be a fairly nonstop talker myself, and the trouble with nonstop talkers is that they are poor listeners. I'm not *really* interested in listening to someone else for a very long time—a trait of my own which I can understand and endure—but when it's the other person who is clearly not really interested in listening to *me*, I find I can neither understand nor endure it.

14

Houghton Mifflin, on the strength of my *Words of Science*, got me a guest shot on "The Last Word," a panel show moderated by Bergen Evans, the well-known lexicographer. It was an educational show in which the panels discussed words, meanings, and usages in (it was hoped) a witty and urbane manner, which meant it had low ratings —but still it was a nationally syndicated show and that meant it would be the first time I would be seen "coast to coast."

I raced to New York for the purpose on July 30 and stayed at the Hotel Westbury, which I found to be very convenient.

I taped the show the next day, and also did a few radio interviews, being squired from place to place by a young lady from Houghton Mifflin's public-relations group who happened to be beautiful enough to look like a movie star.

I played up to the situation in my best style. When the taxis would come to a halt at our destination, Barbara Krohn (the beautiful young woman) would pay the fare, while I lolled back lazily in the seat and tried to look like a kept man who was *worth* it.

15

On August 4, I drove the family to the summer resort at which my parents were staying. They were delighted to see us, and my father put me through a very trying time as he introduced me to all his old buddies as his famous writer-son.

I learned a few things about my father on that occasion. I learned he could row a boat, for instance, and that he could *swim*. It never occurred to me at any time that my father would know how to swim. It was only with a wrench that I could make myself understand that he had not been a candy-store keeper all his life; that he had had a youth in Russia in which he had undoubtedly learned to swim in lakes and rivers. I was the one who couldn't swim. I had spent my youth in the candy store.[4]

My father could whittle, too. There was no end to his talents.

16

On August 10, 1959, I found a letter waiting for me at school that asked me to come to Cornell University on November 10 to give a talk. That, in itself, was not entirely surprising. What *was* unusual was that they offered me five hundred dollars to do so.

I had never heard or conceived of anyone being paid that much to talk, and I was convinced it was a misprint for fifty dollars. I did not want to go all the way to Ithaca, New York, for fifty dollars, though I would gladly do it for five hundred dollars. It was important, then, to find out which it was.

To write and say, "Surely you meant fifty dollars" was somehow unthinkable. It would expose my low opinion of myself, and if by some chance they were actually crazy enough to want to give me five hundred dollars, my question would tempt them to say, "Oh yes, we did mean fifty dollars."

After considerable hesitation, however, I thought of the solution. I wrote an answer that said, very formally, "In return for your offered fee of Five Hundred Dollars ($500.00), I will gladly agree to [etc., etc.]."

If they answered me with happy outcries, I was all set. If they came back with pained explanations, it was all off.

They answered me with happy outcries.

17

The next day I learned that *Satellite* had ceased publication with its eighteenth issue after 2½ years of existence. I have never learned to endure the death of any science-fiction magazine, however minor, without a pang, and *Satellite* had published three short pieces of mine.

But let's be practical. I had just sold a nonfiction article called

[4] Yes, I know. I could have learned anyway, but I never wanted to.

"The Hungry People" (on appetite, obesity, and dieting) at the rate of ten cents a word, which was better than twice what I got from science fiction, and it eventually appeared in the October 1960 *Mademoiselle.*[5]

While I didn't intend to let the rate differential prevent me from writing science fiction, neither could I help realizing that my feelings on learning of the death of *Satellite* were a matter of sentiment and not of financial fear.

18

A new streetcar line had opened that connected West Newton with the center of Boston, and I took advantage of it to take David into town and to a children's movie to celebrate his eighth birthday on August 20, 1959.

A much more anxious time came two days later when at 3 P.M. Robbie disappeared again, as she had done nearly two years before. We ran about the neighborhood distraught, calling for her, and then despairingly decided to call the police. We were certain we couldn't be lucky twice and that this time she had had an accident, been kidnaped, been . . . The mind dared not venture further.

We went back into the house to make the call and it occurred to me to look into her room—and, by heaven, she was in her bed, sleeping. Apparently she had felt like taking a nap and didn't bother telling us about it.

We had to celebrate, and the next day we took advantage of a pleasant Sunday to drive to Sturbridge, Massachusetts, some forty-five miles away, and spend five hours amid a reconstruction of colonial buildings. It was our first time there and we enjoyed it.

19

Poul Anderson and his wife, Karen, visited us on August 28. Poul is a rather tall, lean individual, with a shock of curly hair and a baby face. He is slow of speech and has a slight stammer, but those are as nothing compared to his singing voice—or, rather, the total absence thereof. Poul is very fond of singing folk songs, and the sound of his doing so will wrench the heart of any music lover—indeed, the heart of anyone with ears, and will almost instill hatred of the otherwise thoroughly lovable Poul.

Karen appeared to be the dominant one of the pair; as intelligent

[5] See *Is Anyone There?*

as he, with readier speech, a more aggressive spirit, and a tendency to *embonpoint.*

We took them out for a Chinese dinner and came back for hours of conversation. I remember two things best.

First, Poul tried to get me to pronounce his first name in Danish fashion (it was the Danish version of Paul). Despite endless repetitions I never got the vowel sound quite right.

Second was my comment that I tried to keep my library small; that an out-of-date book, or one I never used, simply consumed space I needed for other things; that there were times when an empty space was the most valuable item on the bookshelves.

Poul turned to Karen and said, "Listen to this man. He speaks pearls."

I wish it were easy to stick to this view, however. No matter how I try, books keep adding themselves to my library—and throwing away a book, or just giving it away, is so hard. After all, when I think of the long years in which I never so much as had a book . . .

Of course, you mustn't think that these books that I might keep or might throw away were great and beloved works of literature. My library was a working library, and consisted entirely of reference books. A surprising number of them consisted of books I received in the mail from fans, or from friends, or from publishers seeking quotes.

Not all these were worth keeping from a strictly utilitarian standpoint, but when a book—any book—comes inscribed to me personally, discarding it is an extremely difficult thing to do.

Some books that I bought, I periodically replaced with later editions—Webster's Biographical Dictionary, Webster's Geographical Dictionary, foreign-language dictionaries, World Almanacs and others of its kind, Bartlett's Quotations, even entire encyclopedias.

And some books were particular favorites of mine and used constantly. There was Langer's Encyclopedia of World History, for instance, and Glasstone's Sourcebook on Atomic Energy.

20

On August 31, Janet Jeppson visited the med school to see her brother who was married and whose wife, Maureen, had just had a daughter named Patti. Janet had written she was coming, so I dropped in at a laboratory in which her brother, John, was working in order to say hello. It was the first time I consciously met her brother who, except for his lighter coloring, was remarkably like my brother-in-law,

John. This other John was also good-looking, quiet-spoken, and rather introverted.

21

I had not attended a World Science Fiction convention since the fourteenth in New York three years earlier. The fifteenth had been in London and the sixteenth in Los Angeles, and both had been out of the question.

The seventeenth World Science Fiction convention, in 1959, was, however, slated for Detroit, and I was tempted. I had made it to Cleveland four years before, so why not Detroit? I wouldn't drive it, of course; I would take the train. So there I was in a roomette on Friday, September 4, 1959, on a 2 P.M. train that would have me in Detroit the next morning.

I suppose it's impossible not to have a little fantasy about finding a pretty girl in the roomette across the way and having a very pleasant conversation with who knows what added features (anything is possible in fantasies).

And that's what happened. When I settled down in my roomette who should be in the roomette across the way but a pretty girl. She smiled at me and I smiled back and we had a very pleasant conversation much of the way to Detroit. There were, however, *no* added features, because she was a nun. So much for fantasies.

As though to make up for it, almost the first thing I encountered at the convention was a fan I had never met before, a woman named Djinn Faine. She was 21 years old, 5 feet, 10 inches tall, 157 pounds in weight, and I believe her measurements were 40-25-40.

Someone (it may have been Bob Bloch,[6] but I honestly don't remember) warned me as soon as I showed up that there was a plan to bring me face to face with a spectacular woman in order to watch me faint dead away. (There was a rumor that had arisen, somehow, that I was extraordinarily susceptible to feminine beauty.)

I arranged to be introduced to her privately and asked permission to carry out a plan of my own. She was amused and agreed. Later on, when the wiseguys deliberately brought me face to face with her, I walked up coolly, put my right arm about her waist, my left behind her

6 Bob is a tall, lean fellow, who is quiet, soft-spoken, and looks rather like an absent-minded accountant, but he is very possibly the funniest man in science fiction. He's not particularly ready with a quick upward jab of the verbal knife, as Harlan Ellison is at all times, or as I am if caught offguard, but give him time and he can build up enough in the way of dry comedy to inundate anyone.

shoulder blades, bent her back, and kissed her soundly. I then walked off, dusting my hands and stifling a yawn. That is a bright moment in my memory.

I did hang around her, however, whenever I could, though a fat lot of good that did me. The line was incredibly long and, as nearly as I could tell, Djinn was equally pleasant and equally unattainable to all.

Harlan Ellison, who was still quite thin, and shorter than he seems to be now (no elevator shoes, perhaps), came up to her to ask for a dance and said, with a humility I have never heard from him, either before or since, "I suppose you wouldn't be interested in dancing with a little *vonts* like me."[7]

"I would be glad to dance with you," said Djinn, with perfect courtesy, and off they went, dancing delightfully.

For all I know this was the occasion that inspired the undoubtedly apocryphal story that Harlan once went up to a gorgeously stacked woman and said, in his customary direct manner, "What would you say to a little f——?"

And the woman looked down at him and said, "I would say, 'Hello, little f——.'"

Also dancing court on Djinn was Gordon Dickson. Gordie is a large fellow who, in person, seems rather bumbling, as though he were forever trying to gather his wits together and was in a constant state of mild befuddlement over their refusal to stay together once gathered. This, of course, is pure illusion, for if you listen quietly you find he is making perfect sense, and his writing, at least, is sharply incisive.

Gordie is still another one of those singers with whom science fiction is cursed. Like Sprague de Camp and Poul Anderson, Gordie Dickson has a singing voice of which any walrus would be proud.

On this occasion, though, Gordie wasn't relying on his singing voice but, I presume, on his masculine charm. (I suppose he has it; I'm no judge of such things.) He was clearly making every effort to ensnare the young woman. He was, in fact, *so* assiduous and *so* friendly that I assumed he was not only a long-time friend but that he was also on intimate terms with her. Naturally, I backed off. I love Gordie like a brother and he's also bigger than I am.

I thought I had guessed right when, not long after the convention, he married Djinn. But then I learned that their first meeting had been at the convention and that he had known her no longer than I had. Oh well, he was a bachelor and I was a married man.

One of the devices used to raise money at the convention was to raffle off an hour of time with a celebrity-writer, and I agreed to let my-

[7] *Vonts* is Yiddish for "bedbug." *He* said it, not I.

self be put up for auction. I was won by a young woman for seventeen dollars, which was very flattering. Her name was Mary Martin (no, not *the* Mary Martin), a dainty Dresden china figurine of a woman, a divorcee and a physician.

I led her up to my room with everyone shouting after me that I was compelled by the terms of the auction to do whatever she demanded that wasn't unprofessional or disgraceful. (No one added "illicit.")

What she demanded, however, was an hour of conversation, and that is exactly what she got, with herself in one chair and myself in another at a respectful distance. I had a lot of innocent conversation at that convention.

What with one thing and another I was up all Saturday night at that convention, and since I'm an early-morning person, I saw no point in going to bed when I finally got to my room. I just showered and went to breakfast.

Breakfast is always a deserted meal at science-fiction conventions as far as the writers are concerned—or most of them, anyway—since they're all sunk in swinish slumber after a night of drunken debauchery. Well, I had debauched with the best of them, as far as laughing and singing and joking were concerned, but I hadn't done any drinking, so I was clear-eyed and happy as I advanced toward my eventual toast and eggs and bacon.

And who should I see as I entered the coffee room but John and Peg Campbell. We gave each other the big hello and I joined them.

"I am glad to see," said Peg, austerely, "that at least one other person keeps sensible hours."

"I always do, Peg," I said.

I toastmastered the banquet on Sunday, September 6, and, as I recall, I spent part of the time making Willy Ley jokes.

Willy Ley, at the time, and for years afterward, wrote a monthly science column for *Galaxy*, as I did for *F & SF*.[8]

I said, for instance, "I happened to refer yesterday to Willy as the second-best science writer in science fiction, and I was told that that was a terribly rude comment to make under the circumstances and that I ought to apologize. Well, Willy, I don't understand what the circumstances are that made it rude, but I'll be glad to apologize right now and in public. Willy, I'm *sorry* you're the second-best science writer in science fiction."

[8] There were even periods when we sent each other postcards telling each other our plans for future columns so we would not overlap. It wouldn't have mattered if we had, though, since our styles were so different.

I also told a couple of stories that I borrowed from Randall Garrett and that may quite possibly have been true.

In one, Randall said, "Tell me, Willy, do you prefer to be called Willy or Veelee?"

And Willy, in his thick Teutonic accent (which some people said he practiced before the mirror so that he would never lose it), answered, "Veelee oder Veelee, id mages no divverenz."

In the other, Randall came up to Willy, who was sitting relaxed, with a cigar in his mouth. Randall looked sadly at Willy's majestic corporation (for he was no longer the slim youth he had been when I had met him—and neither was I), tapped it lightly, and said, "Willy, Willy, you ought to diet."

And Willy looked down upon his abdomen indulgently and said, "All righd. Vot color?"

Finally I made up a story. The night before, I said, Willy had spent hour upon hour sweet-talking the girls. (That part was true. He spoke to them most earnestly indeed, and since I had better things to do than watch him all night, heaven only knows where it all ended— though somebody told me afterward he guessed the answer to the question "Willy Ley?" was in the affirmative.)

In any case, I said he spent hour after hour and that I came up to him at last (this part is the lie) and said to him, "Willy, Willy, you'll pay for this in the morning."

And Willy looked surprised and said, "Vy? Nobody is charging."

Each time I told a Willy Ley story, I looked down the head table toward where Willy was sitting to make sure that he wasn't showing signs of anger. Since the line of notables were shaking in uniform laughter, I kept going. It was only after it was all over that I found out I had been looking down the line in the wrong direction. Oh well, Willy was a teddy bear who never grew angry at anything or anyone.

I met Avram Davidson for the first time toward the end of the convention. He had a full beard, a keen intelligence, and was a practicing Orthodox Jew. I didn't meet many.

"Next year in Pittsburgh," I said to him, raising an imaginary glass of wine, for that was where the convention was scheduled to be held.

"Next year in Pittsburgh," he echoed, automatically, and looked chagrined at once at having been lured into a semimockery of the sacred "Next year in Jerusalem," which is part of the Passover Seder tradition.

Earlier, during a discussion in which he had stressed his orthodoxy just a little too hard for my comfort, I said, when asked my stand on the matter, "I'm an atheist."

"Yes," said Avram, without batting an eye, "but what kind of atheist? A Baptist atheist, a Hindu atheist? A Seventh-day Adventist atheist?"

I got the idea. "A Jewish atheist," I said, "which means I have to fight the irrational elements in Judaism particularly."

It may seem to you, by the way, when you read my descriptions of my stays at conventions that they consist entirely of idle chatter. That is not so, of course; they are considerably more than infantile fun and games.

Science-fiction conventions have a serious purpose, one that is primarily aimed at the science-fiction reader who is given his chance to participate in a subculture that is important to him. That is why the conventions shift their site from year to year. This gives the average fan of a particular region, one who has perhaps little in the way of pocket money, a chance to attend, now and then, without having to travel far.

Most of the fans attending are young people, many of them in their teens. It is a great opportunity for them to meet those writers who are, in their eyes, legendary heroes.

There are celebrity introductions for the readers, and autographing sessions. There are fans who cart in a pile of books taller than themselves in order to get each one signed. If, for some reason, there are fans without books to sign, there is invariably the huckster room, where books and magazines (both new and secondhand) are sold in incredible profusion.

In one way, autographing became an increasing problem for me, since it supplied me with more and more work; partly because the number of my books was increasing steadily, and partly because those books were individually popular. In another sense they were not a problem, because I loved autographing. Some writers cut down on their labors by refusing to sign anything but hard-cover books, but I have never refused anything and will sign torn scraps of paper, too, if that is asked of me.[9]

When I am feeling particularly suave during the autographing sessions, which is almost all the time, I kiss each young woman who wants an autograph and have found, to my delight, that they tend to cooperate enthusiastically in that particular activity.

The conventions include talks and panel discussions on every aspect of the writer's/artist's/editor's/agent's life; on the problems of writing and of publishing; and on all the fringe areas, too, from Holly-

[9] There is the occasional joker who hands me a blank check. I just sign it along with everything else, but when the joker gets it back he finds I have signed it "Harlan Ellison."

wood to comic books. Readers are fascinated by this, since so many of them are aspiring writers.

Every talk, every discussion is thrown open to questions from the floor, which would continue (sometimes with articulate hostility) to the end of time if the question period were not arbitrarily cut off.

Yes, indeed, there are serious aspects of conventions, but the serious parts and the laughter, too, inevitably come to an end eventually.

I finally caught the 7:30 P.M. train Monday evening. I had no nun to talk to on the way back but I did have George Scithers, an active science-fiction fan, who was also returning from the convention by train. (He got off at Worcester, Massachusetts.)

It was my first extended time with him. He was an electrical engineer, an Army officer, and a good and patient listener (something I always find soothing).

I was back in Newton the next day and found Gertrude and the kids waiting for me at the station.

22

An advance copy of *Realm of Numbers* reached me on September 16. What I remember best about the book, though, is that shortly before it appeared, Houghton Mifflin had sent me a proof of the cover.

It was the first time any publisher had ever shown me a cover before actual publication. I thought it was a waste of time for I have no artistic taste, and if they expect a reasoned opinion on a book jacket, they are bound to be disappointed.

This time, though, I called Austin.

"Austin," I said, "I have the cover to *Realm of Numbers.*"

"And do you like it?" asked Austin eagerly.

"Yes, I do, Austin—except for one thing."

"Oh?" said Austin, and the temperature of the conversation suddenly dropped to subzero levels, "and what is that?"

I knew what was going through his mind. I was going to be a difficult author, with ideas of my own as to color and balance and all that sort of stuff, and he was going to have to have a fight with and displease either me or his art director or both.

"Well," I said, "you've misspelled my name."

And again the atmosphere of the conversation took a right-about turn.

"Oh my God," said Austin, for my first name was spelled Issac on the cover. Houghton Mifflin had to run a little black band over my name and then print it again, spelled correctly, on the band.

The other thing I remember about that book was that my father read it (he read a number of my books). When he was partway through, he said to me, during one of our phone conversations, that he was enjoying the suspense.

"Suspense?" I said, astonished. "What suspense?"

He said, "Well, I'm just beginning about the square root of two. Tell me, *do* they ever find an exact solution for it?"

23

On September 17, George O. Smith called unexpectedly, and then dropped in during the evening in the usual thy-house-is-my-house camaraderie of the science-fiction brotherhood. I was glad to see him, because the year before he had had a rather bad heart attack and it was good to see him up and about.

I knew that George liked to bend an elbow, so it was my plan to take him to a bar where he could have a beer or two (or whatever he wanted) and we could talk.

Since I have never voluntarily walked into a bar except when someone led the way, I didn't know exactly where in my neighborhood there were bars, but I somehow felt confident there would be one every ten yards. (All us nondrinkers are sure the world is a den of iniquity designed for drunkards.)

No such thing! I had a devil of a time finding a bar, and when I did, it seemed like such a raffish and low dive that I sat there with the greatest of unease and discomfort. George felt quite at home, however, and did not seem to think the surroundings were in any way unusual.

24

I went to New York by train on September 26, for the purpose of eventually being driven up to Scarsdale by Hal Cantor to the palatial home of Lew Schwartz, the publisher of Abelard-Schuman. Lew was quite fat, somehow the epitome of the comfortably successful Jewish businessman, but surprisingly erudite. He had the brain of an intellectual in the body of a corporation executive. I met his charming wife, Frances, for the first time on this occasion.

We were edging toward the period when sex could be spoken of with more and more abandon, and someone asked the company generally if they knew what troilism was.

I said, "Sure—sex with three people participating."

The questioner looked disappointed and said, "Ah, but do you know the derivation of the word?"

I thought I might as well be polite and let him have a turn, so I said, "What?"

"Well," he said, "in Troilus and Cressida, Troilus watched Cressida making out with Diomed."

"In the first place," I said, "he didn't watch with any pleasure; he was brokenhearted, and he certainly didn't participate. In the second place, Ulysses was also there watching, which would make it a foursome. And in the third place, it is much simpler to suppose that 'troilism' is derived from the French word *trois*, meaning 'three.'"

This was an example of reversion to type. When I was young, I used to show off in that snotty fashion all the time. Since the war I had stopped doing it, which I think was the chief reason I changed from a disliked youngster to a well-regarded fellow of mature years. But even now, sometimes—I forget.

12

Guide to Science

1

The time had come when I had to tape the first of the shows I was to do for WGBH under ACS sponsorship. Except that it cemented my friendship with Arthur Obermayer, it was nearly a total loss. I found I didn't like TV work, and I have never changed my mind since.

I went to WGBH on September 30, 1959, for the first time and spent six hours doing the first show. Since the show was only half an hour long, that was my introduction to the fact that the length of a performance and the length of the work were two entirely different things. Part of the extra time arose from the fact that the show had to be rehearsed first and then done in earnest, and that was the most bothersome thing of all. A rehearsal makes the real thing seem repetitious and dull.

2

By October 2, I could no longer postpone work on the science-overview book I had promised Leon Svirsky of Basic Books. I had signed the contract 2½ months before; I had received and banked the fifteen-hundred-dollar advance; I was even beginning to feel guilty enough over the matter to lose sleep.

That day, therefore, I began the book. I kept referring to it in my diary as *Guide to Science*, but in the contract it was called *The Intelligent Man's Guide to Science*. Leon Svirsky admitted that in naming it he had in mind George Bernard Shaw's book *The Intelligent Woman's Guide to Socialism*.

I objected to the name. I said that it would smack of elitism and condescension and would uselessly curtail the readership. Why not call it *Everyone's Guide to Science*?

On the contrary, said Svirsky, every man considers himself intelligent, whether he is or not, and the title, appealing to snobbism, would help the sales.

What I did not foresee was that in years to come I would be asked, with emotions grading from mild amusement to intense hostility, by increasingly self-aware feminists, why the book was restricted to males. Why not *The Intelligent Person's Guide to Science?*

The truth is that in 1959 neither Svirsky nor I thought of this simple piece of justice. The title was simply part of the taken-for-granted male chauvinism of the English language. I had to get out of it in later years by smiling as ingratiatingly as I could and saying that the "intelligent man" of the title referred to the writer and not to the reader.

By the time I had begun *The Intelligent Man's Guide to Science,* I had written a nonfiction book on astronomy, one on mathematics, and one on the derivation of scientific terms, so I was branching out vigorously. In the *Guide,* however, I was being asked to take almost all of science as my field of review.

It was not something to be done lightly, and I didn't take it lightly. I worked hard to make the progression a sensible one. I began with the universe as a whole and worked inward in narrowing circles till I was inside the brain at the end.

The plan for the *Guide* made it natural to present the subject in historical perspective, and I found I liked doing so.

First, it gave me a chance to present a logical unfolding of a field of knowledge, to make an exciting story out of it, with the scientist as hero and with ignorance as the villain.

Second, it made it easier for me. There is no subject so difficult and arcane that it isn't comparatively simple in its beginnings, when scientists were largely ignorant of it. I could always follow the subject up to the point where my own understanding failed—and get at least something out of it both for my readers and myself.

It was my chosen method of attack thereafter. In dealing with any difficult subject, I always began at the beginning and didn't care how long it took me to get to the subject in its present complexity.

3

On October 10, I drove the family to New York, and we used the new Connecticut Turnpike for the first time.

At his invitation, I visited Mac Talley at his Park Avenue apartment that afternoon and was impressed by its splendor.

It turned out he had an excellent idea—he wanted me to write two books, one on the human body and the other on the human brain, and he suggested we call them exactly that: *The Human Body* and *The Human Brain.* I agreed readily.

Family about 1963, I think. From left, me, Robyn, Gertrude, David.

Robyn as a pre-teener.

My Greenough Street office.

I'm holding David, who is about thirteen years old here (1964). The other two boys are fans.

Harlan Ellison and I in Cleveland in 1966. Photo by Jay K. Klein

Cleveland in 1966. I'm between Gertrude and Sprague de Camp. Photo by Jay K. Klein

Cover of the special Isaac Asimov issue of The Magazine of Fantasy & Science Fiction, *October 1966.*

Arthur C. Clarke, Barbara Silverberg, and I sometime in the 1960s.
Photo by Jay K. Klein

In 1969, picking up my mail in the Newtonville post office (posed for a newspaper story). My sideburns are just beginning to lengthen. Photo by Gilbert E. Friedberg

At my parents' golden wedding anniversary celebration in 1968. I'm standing between Stanley and his son Danny; sitting, from left, are Marcia, Mamma, Pappa, and Gertrude. The ones I don't know are Stanley's relatives by marriage.

My mother and father. I believe this was taken at their golden wedding anniversary celebration in 1968 when my mother was seventy-two, my father seventy-one.

At the golden wedding anniversary celebration, Mamma and Pappa with the six grandchildren: on top, Robyn, Larry (Marcia's), and David; on bottom, Nanette and Eric (Stanley's), and Richard (Marcia's).

The next day, Gertrude and I visited Bob and Barbara Silverberg in their apartment on West End Avenue. I was impressed by its splendor, also.

Bob was fifteen years younger than I was, and he had only been publishing science fiction for five years or so, but he was extraordinarily prolific and successful. He was far more prolific than I was, and my status at the end of my first five years of writing was as nothing compared to his.

He seemed to have worked out a perfect life for himself. He planned to have no children, and Barbara, an engineer and a devoted wife, had a job that kept her out of the apartment much of the time. The large apartment was therefore almost entirely his, and he had it filled with books and with magazines and, in short, it was thoroughly organized to revolve about his profession. And Barbara, in her spare time, acted as his secretary, proofreader, and so on.

I could not stop myself from feeling envy—at least for a while. And then I reflected that since Bob always seemed to be more or less unhappy, I had better not waste my time wishing I were in his place.

We went on to spend the evening with Stanley and Ruth in Greenwich Village. Stanley, by now past his thirtieth birthday, was also, by now, distinctly balding. I pointed out the approaching desertification of his scalp in kindly fashion, just in case he hadn't noticed, and also managed to mention the odd fact that against all precedent among the Asimov males I was keeping my hair, all of it. He, in just as kindly a fashion, mused on the fact that I would soon turn forty—something that was indeed looming most unpleasantly on the horizon.[1]

It was on that occasion, by the way, that Stan said to me, after a period of general conversation, "I notice, Isaac, that when the conversation does not concern you directly, your eyes glaze over, but that you snap to attention the moment your name is mentioned."

On another and later occasion, Stan said to me, "Isaac, you're honest, reliable, industrious, capable, intelligent, and ambitious. You have all the unlovable virtues."

The truth is, of course, that Stan is exactly the same way, but there's no denying he has always been more lovable than I have been.

4

When I received the Russian edition of *The World of Carbon* some months before, I had written to the Soviet firm that had pub-

[1] Stan and I are on terms of the utmost affection, but there *is* a kind of genial give-and-take between us.

lished it. The gist of the letter was that I knew that there was no international agreement requiring that they pay me for publishing the book or any book of mine, but that on the basis of simple justice between honest men, ought I not be paid? Surely honesty is not something that must wait for regulation by law.

I did not expect an answer, but I got one. My thesis was accepted wholeheartedly. Records were kept with meticulous honesty, the Russian publisher told me, and any time I was in the U.S.S.R., they would be delighted to see me, at which time all accumulated royalties would be paid me.

Fair enough, but I did not travel, and I doubted that I would ever again be in the Soviet Union.

However, Bill Boyd had been invited by the Soviets themselves to come to the U.S.S.R. to lecture on blood groups. He was going, and he intended to visit that very publishing house and collect *his* royalties. I promptly wrote a home-made power of attorney, giving him the right to collect my royalties as well.

I didn't think they would honor it, but they did. After some hesitation, they handed him the equivalent, in rubles, of three hundred dollars. Boyd could not, of course, take the cash out of the country, so he bought various things with the money: a billfold, opera glasses, a Spanish pin, three vodka glasses, a set of twelve rather beautiful gold-plated spoons, and so on, all of which he delivered to us on October 27, 1959.

What pleased me most was that he brought me a Soviet watch. It had clear numerals, a sweep red-tipped second hand, a loud tick (when a Soviet individual wears a watch, he wants people to know it, I presume), and it kept accurate time. Everyone warned me that a Soviet watch would break down quickly, but in all the years since it has required nothing more than periodic cleaning.

In later years, when more of my books appeared in the Soviet Union and when it didn't seem likely I was going to have a convenient intermediary going there, I wrote to the publishing firm again. I explained that I was not a traveler and that I was not likely to be picking up my royalties. I asked if they could suggest some useful way of spending the money within the Soviet Union that would serve the cause of world peace and brotherhood. They wrote back that I might consider reinvesting the money in the publishing house itself, since its chief function was to publish books on science for the general public.

I could find no quarrel with this, and I granted them permission to use my money in this fashion. I assume they are doing so to this day.

5

On November 6, 1959, we obtained a new bed for David, and Robyn inherited his old one. We gave away her crib, and it meant that for the first time in over eight years there was no crib in our place.

We were fresh out of babies, which somehow seemed to imply creeping old age. Everything, if looked at improperly, can be interpreted as a sign of aging.

6

On November 10, I drove four hundred miles to Ithaca, New York, taking nearly eight hours to make the trip, and that night I gave my five-hundred-dollar talk. It was the largest fee, by far, that I had ever received up to that point, but I didn't actually receive it. They told me they would mail it to me (and so they did, of course).

I suppose there is sense to that. A school like Cornell has to make sure a speaker arrives and gives the talk before they dare set the ponderous machinery into action that serves to eviscerate a check from the bowels of a bureaucracy. Just the same, when I got better known, and could make my own rules, I insisted on checks being ready for immediate delivery after the speech.

On the eleventh I drove to New York and took in the first few sample chapters of *The Intelligent Man's Guide to Science*. I knew that I wasn't following Svirsky's directions. He had wanted an overview of twentieth-century science, starting sharply with 1901.

Twentieth-century science rests, however, on a foundation of nineteenth-century science, which rests on a foundation of eighteenth-century science, and so on. While early science can be gone through fairly quickly, I nevertheless divided the book into large areas of knowledge and tended to start each chapter with the Greeks or, at the very least, with Galileo.

I wasn't worried about that. I had reached the pitch of self-assurance where I told myself that Svirsky could like it or lump it.

7

Once I got home, I took a break and did a third in the thiotimoline series, which I had started eleven years before. This was "Thiotimoline and the Space Age." I wrote it on November 14 and sent it off to Campbell at once.

After that, I returned to *The Intelligent Man's Guide to Science* and raced ahead, full speed. I had no trouble with the book at all. I would frequently have days in which I would write six thousand to ten thousand words without any sense of strain. I couldn't have done this without an electric typewriter, of course.

8

On December 10, we invested in an item of interior decoration on our own. We bought a piano for eight hundred dollars, and two days later it was delivered and set up for use. For the first time in my life, I had a musical instrument of my own at hand.

I couldn't play a piano, of course. I quickly taught myself to read music, based on what I remembered of "music appreciation" in the fourth grade, and learned how to tap out any tune in any key with one finger, if I had the music before me. I could never go past the one-finger stage, however. I was no Leonard Meisel, the piano-playing friend of my youth.

Gertrude had had piano lessons when she was young and had learned how to play even though she claimed she had no natural ear for music. On occasion she did play and I would listen with ravished enjoyment, but I always had to do so secretly. As soon as Gertrude caught me listening, she would become self-conscious and would have to stop.

The chief reason for buying the piano, however, was with the hope that David, or Robyn, or conceivably both, would turn out to have musical talent, or at least musical interest. After all, one needn't have to play well to find piano-playing relaxing.

Unfortunately, it turned out that neither child could manage the piano. We tried them on other instruments, too. We tried David on the trombone and Robyn on the flute and we persevered through the horrid noises that resulted with remarkable tolerance, but nothing struck a spark. Since I was certainly unmusical and since Gertrude claimed that she was unmusical, too, we could scarcely blame the kids.

9

On December 14, I did the third of the ACS television talks on WGBH, and that was the only one I enjoyed. In the first place, I had no guest, which meant that for that one time I was responsible for myself only. In the second place, through some incredibly lucky mixup, the studio in which I was supposed to rehearse was taken up by some glee club that refused to vacate until they got all their notes properly sour.

When the time came to go on, therefore, I had to go on without rehearsal, and the point was that the program was *live*. I felt triumphant. The camera started rolling and I began:

"Ladies and gentlemen, tonight, through some incredibly lucky mixup, the studio in which I was supposed to rehearse was taken up by some glee club that refused to vacate until they got all their notes properly sour. When the time came to go on, therefore, I had to go on without rehearsal. . . ." I went on to talk cheerfully on weight and mass for half an hour.

I was told later that when I delivered my first two sentences the director in the control booth turned a pale pastel green and was restrained by force from lunging into the studio to extirpate me from the face of the earth.

Just the same, the program went well, and I thought surely they would thereafter let me go on without rehearsal. But no, it was back to rehearsals and discomfort.

10

The year 1959, my first full year as a full-time writer, saw my situation not very much changed from that of the year before. Again, I published four books in the course of the year:

29. *Nine Tomorrows* (Doubleday)
30. *The Clock We Live On* (Abelard-Schuman)
31. *Words of Science* (Houghton Mifflin)
32. *Realm of Numbers* (Houghton Mifflin)

Among them were my first books with Houghton Mifflin.

As for my writing earnings for 1959, those came to $29,100. This came to some $5,000 short of the year before, but the difference was almost entirely the result of the lack of a school salary and a grant allotment. I didn't let that bother me. I was supporting myself and the family quite handsomely by pre-1958 standards, and I was content to earn $30,000 a year, give or take a couple of thousand dollars, for the rest of my life.

11

But the evil day came. On January 2, 1960, I was forty years old, and middle-aged. There is no possibility of pretending to youth at forty. To be sure, there's nothing wrong with middle age, but it comes hard to a person who is a child prodigy by profession.

Of course, I have never permitted myself to *act* old, or to admit to being old, or even middle-aged, in public. I maintain always that I am "a little over thirty" and that I am "in my late youth." I shall do that however long I live, and for however long my audience laughs indulgently at my pleasant presumption.

Once, having said I was "in my late youth" and gotten my indulgent laugh, I couldn't resist playing for a larger one by pausing and saying in a confidential manner, "I call it my 'late youth' because it's dead." I did get my larger laugh, but I'd rather not use the line.

There were four separate celebrations involving cake that day. At noon, I got cake and ice cream for the whole family, and then, in the afternoon, a friend of mine, George Christie, and his wife, Doreen, appeared with a cake of their own. George is a psychiatrist and I remember him best for his comment when someone recited a few of my eccentricities. George thought about it and then said, "Well, Isaac, being a genius, doesn't fall under the rules."

I thought it was a very sensible analysis of the situation, and wondered if there were any way I could persuade the whole world to believe this.

At a meeting, that evening, of the Interplanetary Exploration Society (which still existed in Boston, thanks to Alma Hill), cake and ice cream were served in my honor. Later, we celebrated with Blanca Batteau, a beautiful girl of Basque origin. (Her husband, Wayne, was a special favorite of John Campbell's.) Blanca was also born on January 2, but had only turned thirty-five and looked considerably younger despite the fact that she had borne six children.

My birthday gift to myself was the just-about-completion of the first draft of *The Intelligent Man's Guide to Science*. I had done something like four hundred thousand words in three months. In fact, I had already begun final copy, though there still remained a bit of first draft to do, and that final copy was moving as quickly as the first draft had.

By January 27, I was able to bring half the manuscript in completed form with me to New York for delivery to Basic Books. Svirsky read enough of it to be able to tell me the next day that he approved. He sounded, in fact, very enthusiastic.

12

The Wellsprings of Life, which I had completed the previous June and which I had confidently expected to be published in the spring of 1960, was delayed. Abelard-Schuman printed their books in Great Britain in order to save money, and a printing strike there delayed matters. I had urged Hal Cantor to have the book printed in the United States, but the need to keep costs down was paramount, and Abelard-Schuman gambled on a short strike and lost. My other books in press with them were also delayed.

I could understand the publisher's need to save money, but on the other hand, any delay in publishing a science book increased the chance of obsolescence by publication date and I was very annoyed. Again, publication delays mean a postponement of the date on which a book starts to earn its keep, and that was no great cause for joy either.

I wouldn't have minded so much if it weren't that Doubleday and Houghton Mifflin had never delayed a book on me.

13

Scholastic Magazines had purchased *Science World* from Street & Smith. I had written for the magazine both before and after the sale, and in that way met Eric Berger, a gray-haired, rock-jawed gentleman with a limp and a gravelly voice. He was warm, friendly, and a great kidder, who was not always easy to work with since he insisted on having ideas of his own that did not always mesh with mine.

He talked me into doing a series of short biographies of thirty scientists from Archimedes to Robert Goddard. I had done them and they had been published, one by one, week by week, through late 1958 and early 1959 in *Senior Scholastic*.

The obvious thing to do with them afterward was to put them together into a book. What I wanted to do was to have Houghton Mifflin do it in hard-cover as a book entitled *Breakthroughs in Science*, and then have them take care of arranging the Scholastic soft-cover version.

Scholastic, however, insisted on remaining in control. They would put out the soft-cover, negotiate the hard-cover with Houghton Mifflin, and take care of all royalty payments themselves.

Except that there would be no royalty payments. Scholastic wanted to pay me a flat sum for the hard-cover and they wanted to split that flat sum 30 per cent to Eric and 70 per cent to myself.

I had never split payment with an editor before, but the whole conception of the series had been Eric's, and I felt that was worth something, so I agreed to the 30-70 split. I drew the line at the flat sum, however. I wanted royalties.

Scholastic, with Eric as its spokesman, pointed out that the soft-cover edition would be simultaneous with the hard-cover and that that would severely limit sales of the latter. Therefore the flat payment was a "good deal" in that it would certainly amount to more than the royalties would. In other words, Scholastic would collect less in royalties from Houghton Mifflin than they would pay out to me in a flat sum, so that Scholastic was being generous.

Frankly, I couldn't believe that Scholastic was so stubbornly insistent on being generous. I told them that my hard-covers sold regardless of a soft-cover edition and I would be willing to take my chances on a royalty arrangement.

On February 9, 1960 (Robyn's fifth birthday), Eric called angrily and said that I might be willing to take my chances on a royalty arrangement, but he wasn't, and I had no right to insist on a risk he would have to share.

I considered that a low blow but I gave in. However, I arranged to have Houghton Mifflin send me sales figures on the hard-cover edition each time they sent royalties to Scholastic.

I then grimly began to calculate my royalties from statement to statement and, precisely as I had told them, the soft-cover edition did *not* affect the hard-cover sales and, after a couple of years, the royalties overtook that flat sum they paid me.

I then wrote a letter to Scholastic and informed them of this fact and reminded them that I had predicted it. I also told Eric the same thing and reminded him that his hardheaded business brain had led him into a loss that would grow endlessly from year to year, and was Scholastic still in the mood to be generous?

Each statement time, I sent a more strongly worded letter to Scholastic and to Eric, each time giving the total that I considered I had unfairly lost, and eventually Scholastic gave in. A new contract was prepared on a royalty basis, and back royalties were paid. Royalties on the book have been coming in to this day.

14

I went to New York on February 25, 1960, and visited Basic Books where Svirsky, to my utter horror, began to talk about cutting *The Intelligent Man's Guide to Science* in half to make it fit into one volume. I argued against that vehemently, and when he seemed unmoved, I left with the grim determination that this would not happen.

The next day I attended a meeting of the Trap Door Spiders as a guest of Sprague de Camp. The club, which had been the brainchild of Fletcher Pratt, survived his death. This was the first time I had attended.

Present were not only Sprague, John Clark, and Willy Ley, but also Basil Davenport, whom I now met for the first time. He was a terribly erudite gentleman who could recite any number of dirty limericks so rapidly that it was almost impossible to follow him. He seemed to be a heavy drinker, and since I never met him but on convivial occasions, I'm not sure I ever saw him completely sober. He was a very pleasant and warm person, however, and I took a great liking to him.

Because the Trap Door Spiders is a stag organization of sharply limited membership, I have occasionally noted a readiness on the part of outsiders to believe it to be the type of meeting in which naked women arise out of cakes.

Not so; it is almost unbearably respectable, and its members tend to be middle-aged, personally conservative (though sometimes politically liberal), and highly intelligent. The whole purpose of the club is to engage in conversation (that almost lost art) over food and drink.

It is customary after a TDS dinner for the guests to be grilled, but that is not as terrible as it sounds. It only means that he is to be drawn out concerning the nature of his profession and encouraged to discuss those facets of his specialized interests that might titillate the curiosity of the members present. The traditional first question is "Mr. So-and-so, how do you justify your existence?"

The club meets at 6:30 P.M., and after an hour of drinks and *hors d'oeuvres*, dinner starts at 7:30 P.M. The grilling starts at about 9:00 P.M., and by 11:00 P.M. all are on their way home. One can scarcely ask for an evening that does less harm and gives greater pleasure. On this occasion, I certainly enjoyed myself exceedingly.

Sprague invited me to join the club after the dinner was over, and I was strongly tempted to do so. It would have meant regular visits to New York, however, and although I was visiting New York on a more or less monthly basis, I wanted to remain flexible and to go when I had a manuscript to deliver or some important business to discuss—and not when an irrelevant banquet, however enjoyable, was in the offing.

15

When I got back to Boston, I found copies of *The Living River* waiting for me. It was the book I had agreed to write for Yeager three years before, and it was that agreement that had occasioned my confrontations with Keefer. Now here was the book, my first *adult* science book for the general public.

It was conceived, of course, as the first book of a pair, but under the circumstances, I postponed the second—about cardiovascular research—indefinitely.

16

There were still two chapters of *The Intelligent Man's Guide to Science* remaining to be written, but if Svirsky were planning to eviscerate the book, I had no intention of writing them. Nor, of course, would I return the advance. Nor would I discuss the matter with him and subject myself to the temptation of compromise.

On March 1, I simply started another book altogether, *Words from the Myths*. It was my intention to retell the Greek myths and point out that many English words were obtained from or were reminiscent of one or another aspect of those myths.[2]

The writing of *Words from the Myths* was perfect balm for my wounded spirit. It was forty thousand words long and took just twelve days to do.

It was the first book I wrote without any preliminary discussion with any editor. I was getting confident enough of my ability to assume that some publisher or other was bound to want any book I cared to write.

On March 14, 1960, I took it in to Austin Olney, since it was he who had done *Words in Science*, and this new book could be viewed as a companion piece. There was no trouble at all. He liked it, asked for a few very minor changes, and then I got my contract.

17

On March 11, just as I was completing *Words from the Myths*, I received a call from Svirsky. I had had not a word to say to him since our meeting in New York fifteen days before. Apparently he had come to a decision on his own. He told me he had decided not to cut the book but to publish it in two volumes.

"Fine," I said, coldly. "In that case, I will finish the book."

There was a distinct gasp from his end of the line. "What do you mean?"

"I mean," I said, "that if you had persisted in your intention to cut the book, you would never have gotten a completed manuscript."

---

2 My favorite example is this: The Greeks viewed the universe as having been created out of chaos. Chaos was not nothingness but consisted of all the matter of the universe mixed together in random fashion. Chaos was disorder. The creation of the universe was then not the creation of matter, but the imposing of order upon disorder. The ordered universe is "cosmos." Therefore anything that imposed order upon disorder is "cosmetics," and from this we get a notion of what it is that women do when they use makeup.

Once I finished *Words from the Myths* I therefore got back to *The Intelligent Man's Guide to Science*.

18

I took the children to a local TV children's show on March 21. I thought it might be an unusual experience for them and that they would like it. It was the "Bozo" show, the chief character of which was Bozo the Clown, who affected not only the usual painted face, but also a huge, bright orange fright wig.

The children saw the program on television regularly and loved it, but the television set was black-and-white. When Bozo came waltzing in, Robyn, who was sitting among the group of children with whom he intended to interact, took one horrified look at the orange wig and broke and ran to me in absolute terror.

In later years, Robyn remembered the incident well but could not bear to be kidded about it. She invariably grew defensive and tried to explain her reactions to that monstrous head of hair.

19

I was finally finishing up the definition cards for Stedman's Medical Dictionary, on which I had been working, on and off, for two years. It was just one of a number of little miscellaneous jobs that constantly plagued me. I would write entries for various encyclopedias, for instance. I did a whole series on the various elements for Grolier's Encyclopedia, a number of miscellaneous articles for Encyclopedia Americana, and so on. There was also the ongoing bimonthly column of reviews for *Hornbook*.

These little jobs were never as pleasurable as books or stories, since they were so restrictive. They were invariably closely bounded as to subject matter and length and, for that matter, deadline.

I might have routinely refused all such tasks, but they had their usefulness, too. They managed to force me into what might otherwise have been neglected byways of knowledge, which I could then incorporate into my various books.

Nothing goes really to waste, if you're determined to learn.

I had already learned, for instance, that although I was one of the most overeducated people I knew, I couldn't possibly write the variety of books I manage to do out of the knowledge I had gained in school alone. I had to keep a program of self-education in process.

In my *F & SF* articles, for instance, I went to great pains to deal with a variety of subjects, and I had to read up on them first. In the case of books such as *The Living River* or *The Wellsprings of Life* I had to do a great deal of reading. Some of the chapters of *The Intelligent Man's Guide to Science* forced me to deal with subject matters concerning which I knew remarkably little. My library of reference books grew and I found I had to sweat over them in my constant fear that I might misunderstand a point that to someone knowledgeable in the subject would be a ludicrously simple one.

Sometimes I really do make an egregious error, and I can always count on letters from my readers to correct me.

20

By now my writing had become so visibly prolific and various that I had to field endless questions from curious onlookers who began to view me as some kind of incredible phenomenon who must do it all by means of mirrors or prestidigitation.

They would ask me, for instance, whether I did not have to work on more than one project at a time in order to get all my writing done.

I always say, "Yes, I do, but only one thing at any one time." In other words, I'm not typing one book with one hand and another book with another and dictating a third all at the same time, as some of the curious seem to think I do.

Then they ask, "Do you switch from one to another?"

"At will," I say.

"What if you get a writer's block?" (That's a favorite question.)

I say, "I don't ever get one precisely because I switch from one task to another at will. If I'm tired of one project, I just switch to something else which, at that moment, interests me more."

(Of course, there are times when a deadline interferes and forces me to work on some particular item even when I'd rather not. In that case, I bring myself to do it by promising myself to work on something particularly juicy as soon as I finish.)

Another question I'm frequently asked is, "How do you keep your different projects straight?"

I can't answer that one. All I know is that what I do is the equivalent of taking one record off in my mind and putting another record on; or perhaps of lifting the needle out of one groove and putting it in another. Those, however, are just metaphors. What I *really* do, I haven't any idea.

And that brings up the question: "When you turn to a project you may not have been working on for a considerable time, do you forget what you've written or what you intend to say?"

Well, I'm not actually a superman, so I must admit that if I return to something after weeks or months have passed, I am forced to glance over what I've already written. In fact, I've learned to make simple outlines in telegraphic language of what I have done in particularly complicated books, if I have reason to think I may be leaving it for an extended period. Then, when I return, I look over the outline and start right in.

As for what I intend to do later on, that offers no problem, since I always make that up as I go along.

This absence-and-return works only for nonfiction, by the way. There are tighter constraints on fiction. If I stay away from a piece of fiction too long, and allow too many of the strands in it to become hazy in my mind, it would be better to start all over. For that reason, I generally work on fiction in a pretty steady fashion, trying not to allow too much in the way of gaps.

21

On April 18, 1960, I made the rounds of certain households to collect money or pledges for the Combined Jewish Appeal. This was at the request of a neighbor who sometimes drove me to the train station when I went to New York, so I hated to refuse.

I found it utterly humiliating. No matter how I told myself that it was not for myself I was asking money, but for a charity, I felt as though I were a beggar. Then, too, since I was not active in the Jewish social life of the neighborhood and was never seen in any temple, I was a stranger to those I called on and I sensed a certain suspicion, on their part, of my *bona fides*, and that was embarrassing, too.

I had to work several evenings before the job was completed, and then I told my neighbor I wouldn't do it again. And I never have, not only for the Combined Jewish Appeal but also for any charity. I realize that someone has to, and that it is a noble deed, but I'll have to seek nobility in other directions.

22

I drove the family to New York on April 20, and the next morning I took the final chapters of *The Intelligent Man's Guide to Science* to Svirsky. There remained only a couple of appendices to be done. Harry

Stubbs, incidentally, went over the chapters of the book to backstop me, and I couldn't possibly think of a better person for the job. No one else I know has his wide-ranging knowledge combined with his willingness to put himself out for a friend.

We got back to Newton on the twenty-fourth and found a letter waiting for me that brought me news of the Picks. It had been at the Picks' that I had been eating dinner four years earlier when I first got the news that Gertrude had found the West Newton house. Gerard and Helena had moved to Los Angeles a couple of years before, and now I found that Helena had been killed in Los Angeles in an automobile accident on February 14, and Gerard Pick had been hospitalized for two months thereafter. It was the first friend I had lost in an automobile accident; not the last.

23

I had to visit Harry Stubbs periodically to deliver chapters for his consideration and to pick up those he had gone over and annotated. On May 2, 1960, when I visited him, it somehow came up in the conversation that I had never looked through a telescope.

"Doesn't that bother you?" he asked, astonished.

"No," I said, philosophically, "what's the difference? I've seen photographs of the various astronomical objects, and I have it all in my mind's eye."

But Harry wouldn't have it so. He taught general science at Milton Academy and he had a small observatory there with a couple of telescopes in it. It was a clear evening and he got me into his automobile and drove me to the observatory. He was insistent on having the author of "Nightfall" look through a telescope at least once in his life.

He focused on a comet, which looked like a dim, tiny patch of fuzz, utterly unspectacular, and on a star cluster, which looked like a collection of glitter.

Then he focused on the Moon, and it was then I made what I consider one of my all-time silly remarks. I looked into the eyepiece, looked at Harry in amazement, and said, "My goodness, it *does* have craters."

On May 4, the last bit of *The Intelligent Man's Guide to Science* was done, just about one year after Svirsky had suggested the task and just seven months and two days after I had begun. Considering the length and the complexity of the subject material, I couldn't help but think I had done a remarkable job.

13

Back with Doubleday

1

I was at Basic Books on May 18, 1960, discussing the matter of illustrations for *The Intelligent Man's Guide to Science* and not doing a very good job of it. While I was there, a letter came in from George W. Beadle, the great geneticist, expressing strong approval of the book. That was very flattering indeed.

That did not mollify me entirely, for Svirsky had already suggested that someone like Beadle write an Introduction for the book. I did not want it. I may have written Introductions to scores of other people's books, but I have my own peculiar pride. I don't want other people writing Introductions for me.

Svirsky, however, of all the editors I have ever had, was least concerned with my feelings for the books I have written, and in the end he had his way. Of all my books, *The Intelligent Man's Guide to Science* is the only one with an Introduction by someone else, and that someone else was Beadle.

It was a very elegant and kind Introduction, indeed, and I am grateful to Beadle for that—but that doesn't matter. I didn't want an Introduction, and I wince every time I see it.

While at Basic Books, I picked up the first batch of galleys of the book, by the way, and from then on more galleys came in periodically.

I got to work on the galleys as soon as I got home and before long found, to my horror and disgust, that when Svirsky said he had decided not to cut the book, he meant that he would not cut it 50 per cent to a one-volume work. What he did do, on the other hand, was to cut it 30 per cent.

Nor was it cleverly done. To me, it seemed a hack job.

Apparently, Svirsky had for many years been an editor at *Scientific American*, and he had gotten into the habit of cutting away the fat from the writings of scientists who knew their subjects but who were relatively innocent of writing ability. That might be an appropriate thing to do, but when he tried to do the same thing on my own close-knit writing, he produced galleys that bled at a hundred joints.

I did what I could, reinserting information whose omission made passages senseless or, even worse, flatly wrong, and I tried to strike out all the infelicities he inserted and put back all the felicities he deleted. I also called him on the phone periodically and told him what I thought of his editing. I must emphasize that at no time did he ever consult me before using his blue pencil.

No matter how hard I worked, I never managed to put enough of my material back in or take enough of his material back out, and I could see, despairingly, that after all my hard work, I was going to end with a two-volume boxed book of 280,000 words that was going to make an elegant appearance, but of which I would be ashamed.

I knew that even if the book were to prove to be a success, that wouldn't help. I would still be ashamed of it.[1]

2

I spent June 10, 1960, with John Campbell and Peg. It was not as it had been a dozen years ago. I now saw him rarely, and I wrote for him rarely.

My monthly articles for *F & SF* by no means tied me down to that magazine exclusively, not even as far as articles were concerned, so I did turn out an occasional article for Campbell, more to have something in *Astounding* for old times' sake than for any other reason.

Thus the May 1960 *Astounding* had a biological article by me, "March of the Phyla," and another, a sequel, "Beyond the Phyla," in the just-out, July 1960 issue. Both dealt with evolution. He had just bought "The Matter of Space" from me, an astronomical article, which was to appear in the September 1960 issue, and as for "Thiotimoline and the Space Age,"[2] which he had bought some time before, that would appear in the October 1960 issue.

These were exceptions, however. The fact is, I rarely had Campbell in mind anymore. I had changed. He had changed. Even *Astounding* had changed, or at least its name had.

Campbell had always felt that the use of *Astounding* as the name for the magazine was undignified, and had originated merely in imitation of *Amazing*, the first magazine in the field. When he had first become editor twenty-two years before, it had been his intention to change the name to the respectable and well-defined *Science Fiction*.

[1] True is true, though. I can't say that Svirsky's changes were all bad. He introduced some modifications in my discussion of the tetrahedral carbon atom that actually represented an improvement on what I had done. That, of course, I kept in. I don't quarrel with good stuff just because it isn't mine.
[2] See *Opus* 100 (Houghton Mifflin, 1960).

Columbia Publications had beaten him to the punch with that title, however, and he could do no more than change the earlier name of *Astounding Stories* to *Astounding Science Fiction*.

Now he was making the change to *Analog Science Fact-Science Fiction*, but was doing so gradually. All through 1960, *Astounding* was fading on the cover and *Analog* kept coming forward, until finally the magazine was known as *Analog*, and is so known to this day.

Many fans objected, I among them. In fact, I have never quite managed to forgive Campbell for the change. He had complicated reasons for choosing *Analog* as the name, none of which was convincing to me, except for the trivial one that it would keep unchanged the common abbreviation of *ASF* for the magazine. And he gave up a name of memories and tradition.

Then, too, he continued to have his odd enthusiasms. Succeeding to the Hieronymus machine, which I had encountered in his basement three years earlier, was the Dean drive. This was a mechanical device whereby rotary motion could (supposedly) be converted into one-way-directional motion.

If this worked, then, instead of the expensive and wasteful rocket exhaust driving a spaceship in accordance with Newton's third law of motion, a turning wheel on board the ship, turned by any convenient form of energy, could push the ship upward against gravity and through space.

Delightful—except that the Dean drive violated the law of conservation of momentum and the law of conservation of angular momentum, and if it worked I didn't think that physicists would be able to put the broken pieces of the universe back together again.

I met Mr. Dean, the inventor, on that day, June 10, and he seemed like a very pleasant fellow—but pleasant is not enough. I have never heard, in all the time since, of anyone making the Dean drive work, or of anyone believing it would work whose expertise in such matters I would trust.

3

Walter Bradbury had left Doubleday and had moved on to the firm of Henry Holt.

That hit me very hard, and his departure accentuated the guilt I was feeling at having abandoned Doubleday myself. It had been over two years since I had taken in my last book for Doubleday, *Nine Tomorrows*. Nothing since then; not a word.

Brad had not been interested in my nonfiction, but Brad was gone. Tim Seldes, relatively unsophisticated, might be imposed on.

"Suppose, Tim," I said, eagerly, "I write a nonfiction book for you. You see, I don't write much fiction these days, but I can easily write nonfiction."

Tim said, "It's possible. I'll tell you what. Richard Winslow is our science-book editor, so after we've both had our vacations, let's all three of us get together and discuss this."

I agreed and hoped for the best.

Meanwhile, at home, I continued to work rapidly on the galleys of *The Intelligent Man's Guide to Science*, setting up index cards as I went.

4

On July 1, 1960, I received a statement from the nearly forgotten Marty Greenberg. No check; just a statement.

As was usual in these cases, I couldn't believe he had sold so few books and that he owed me so little money—but I just filed it. I had given up on the four Gnome Press books.

5

I was at this time engaged in the revision of one of my popular science books. It was the first time any of them had needed revision. Several new elements had been prepared in the laboratory, and it seemed a good occasion to update *Building Blocks of the Universe*, which had been published three years earlier.

It wasn't hard to do, since my practice in those days was to keep up a running updating of my books by marginal notations. I had developed that habit in the days of the biochemistry textbook. When the request for a revision came, on July 2, it was only a matter of a few days to send off a letter detailing all the changes that had to be made. My editors were always gratifyingly astonished at my speed, but it was actually very easy to do.

As the number of my books increased, however, it became more and more difficult to keep each one up to date. I became more and more likely to prefer to write a new book on another aspect of the subject, which could then be made to incorporate the latest findings I knew about.

6

The year 1960 was, of course, a presidential election year, and John F. Kennedy had been running hard for the Democratic nomination, with Hubert Humphrey as his chief opponent. I was in a quandary. I liked Humphrey and I thought he would make a good President. However, I also liked Kennedy, and I thought it was important that the United States get over its foolish reluctance to have a Catholic in the White House. (Also, I remembered my 1952 prediction that Kennedy would be the next President after Eisenhower "if only he weren't a Catholic.")

On the night of July 13–14, Kennedy was nominated, and eventually it turned out that the Republicans nominated Nixon. That made the choice an easy one for me. I would, in any case, have supported any reasonable Democrat against any reasonable Republican, but if Nixon were the Republican, then I would have voted for Satan if he were willing to call himself a Democrat.

In fact, I spent three agonized months fearing that Kennedy's Catholicism and Eisenhower's influence[3] would put Nixon in the White House.

7

July 26, 1960, was our eighteenth anniversary, and we prepared to celebrate the occasion by visiting Gertrude's parents in the Catskills. They were in a cabin in Livingston Manor, and we were going to join them the next day, in some neighboring cabin.

On the twenty-seventh, we drove there, and the omens were good. Instead of leaving in the sunshine and arriving in the rain, as it seemed to us we always did, we left in rain and arrived as it began to clear. Mary and Henry were waiting for us and we all dined on lobster tails.

The cabins were not far from the resort where my own parents were staying, and on the twenty-eighth and twenty-ninth we paid them brief visits. John Blugerman arrived on Sunday, the thirty-first, to complete the Blugerman reunion.

The vacation seemed to me to be rather dull since we were not at

[3] Eisenhower was retiring from his second term with undiminished popularity, and he could have had a third nomination and election for the asking had not the Republicans of the Eightieth Congress, in a fit of retroactive fury against F.D.R., initiated the Twenty-second Amendment, limiting Presidents to two terms—a biter-bit piece of business that did not fail to move me to sardonic amusement.

an actual resort where there were other people and the usual activities. The one advantage was that I didn't have to stay there continually. Since Gertrude was, essentially, with her family, I would not be leaving her deserted and alone if I took off for New York, and I was anxious to see Tim Seldes and follow up on our conversation concerning a possible nonfiction book.

My opportunity came on Sunday, August 7, when John Bluger-man, who had been joined by his girlfriend, drove back to New York with her. They took me along as passenger and I registered at the Westbury.

I spent most of the next day at Basic Books, going over the galleys that had accumulated in my absence and collecting page proofs, which I would have to take back to Newton so that I might complete the index.

8

On August 9, 1960, I finally had my luncheon with Tim Seldes and Dick Winslow. (I met Dick for the first time now, tall, slow-spoken, usually smiling.)

I wanted that nonfiction assignment and I was anxious to please. Therefore, when Tim and Dick took me to a French restaurant and began by ordering a drink for themselves I was determined, this time, not to cast a pall on the proceedings by announcing that I did not drink. Boldly, I ordered a vodka sour.

Then when, in due course, they ordered a second drink, I, even more boldly, ordered another vodka sour. By the time I finished the second vodka sour, I was, of course, drunk—or at least sufficiently sozzled for Tim to notice.

So when Dick innocently said to Tim, "Shall we have another drink?" and I said at once (determined to drink them under the table, if I had to) "Sure thing," and then cried out, "Waiter! Waiter!" Tim spoke hurriedly in French to the waiter when he arrived.

The waiter leaned over me solicitously and said, "Would ze zhentleman like some bread and buttair?"

I repelled the offer with scorn and tried to demand my third drink, but the waiter turned deaf and handed out the menus, on which I focused my eyes with badly hidden difficulty, and we all ordered. (At subsequent lunches with me, Tim never drank for fear of setting me a bad example.)

However, it all worked out well. Richard Winslow was delighted (or said he was) at the chance of editing a nonfiction book of mine, and we agreed it would be a biochemistry book for adults. Thus began my second career with Doubleday—one that involved adult nonfiction.

I came out of the lunch in high spirits and, still not entirely recovered from my drinking bout, threw myself into a taxi, directed him to my next destination and said, with great satisfaction, "Just had a swell lunch with two editors."

The cab driver (very experienced at detecting drunks, I suppose) stopped the cab, turned to me, and said, "Did they buy you drinks?"

"Yes, indeed," I said.

"You didn't sign anything, did you?"

I reassured him, but was very touched at his concern for me and astonished at his insight into the nefarious habits of editors, so I doubled the tip I would ordinarily have given him when I stepped out.

That evening I caught a bus back to Livingston Manor, and the next day, August 10, we all drove back to West Newton.

9

The Interplanetary Exploration Society (Boston branch) was still alive, as Alma Hill continued to be resolute in her refusal to allow it to die.

On August 13, Hans Santesson was scheduled to speak to us, and I attended out of a feeling of loyalty. After all, he had introduced me to Janet Jeppson a year and a quarter ago, and that was a pleasant memory.

It was fortunate that I did, for even counting myself the total audience was five, and Hans looked put out at this. He recovered, however, and treated us to a two-hour talk, which seemed excessive under the circumstances.

10

On the fifteenth, I had lunch with Austin (as usual, at Locke-Ober's), and I explained that I would be doing adult nonfiction for Doubleday, and he had no objection at all. He may even have been relieved, since he felt I was perfectly capable of bringing in two books a month and was willing to have other houses share the load.

And on August 18, I completed the index of *The Intelligent Man's Guide to Science* so that it was all done, complete, from the first word of the first draft to the last word of the index in 10½ months.

11

August 20 was David's ninth birthday, and I bought him a wrist-watch (not a very expensive one, to be sure) as a present. The next day I drove Gertrude to Birchtoft, where we had stayed for two weeks in 1949.

The idea was that she would have a three-day vacation by herself while I stayed home with the children. It was only fair. I had on several occasions gone to science-fiction conventions by myself (and was planning to do it again in a few weeks), and those were vacations for me. Why shouldn't she have one?

On Monday, the twenty-second, I took the children and two neighbor children to a place called "Pleasure Island," a large child-centered amusement park in a distant suburb, and spent five hours there. The children loved it, and a sense of fatherly duty kept me alive—barely.

The next day, the twenty-third, I took both children to see a movie called *Thirteen Ghosts* with three-dimensional effects. It was a terrible movie that packed almost as much survival difficulty into two hours as "Pleasure Island" had into five, but I managed to make it.

I took them home and was outside in the driveway with them when the telephone rang inside the house. All this time, for a period of something like fifty-five hours, whenever the children were not actually sleeping or eating, I had been holding their hands, determined to allow nothing to happen to them while I was in charge.

With the telephone ringing, however, I did not wish to run into the house dragging them behind me. Fixing them with a stern eye, I ordered them not to move a muscle for five minutes, and dashed to the phone.

It was only a neighbor calling to ask how I was making out and did I need help—food, water, shelter, anything? I was just saying triumphantly that all was going without a hitch, when Robyn came in crying with her face bloody.

In the few minutes that I had let go of her hand she had managed to trip and fall on her face in the driveway, knocking out the left front upper incisor, which she now held in her hand. I rushed her to the nearest dentist, who X-rayed her mouth and assured me that no damage was done. It was a baby tooth, of course, the root was more than half eroded away, and it would have fallen out soon anyway.[4]

Despite the reassurance, I remained in a wild state, reproaching myself over and over for having let go of her hand. The neighbors

[4] He was right. Eventually, the permanent incisor showed up and all was well.

across the street rallied round, helped me wash the kids and put them to bed, and labored to console the still-frightened five-year-old Robyn (she wasn't as frightened as I had been, the rotten little kid).

Then, over my feeble protests, they forced cake down my throat, and when that usually wide-spectrum specific didn't cure me, they insisted I swallow a jigger of whiskey neat. That did, indeed, seem to lift some of the woes of the world from my shoulders and gave me an insight into why people drink. By the time Gertrude made her usual call to see if all was well, I could say, convincingly, that all was well.

The next day, of course, the cat would be out of the bag, for I was driving up to bring her home again. I couldn't very well leave Robyn behind, and I dismissed as impractical my ordering her not to smile or open her mouth.

Fortunately, Gertrude had had a very good time and she took the tale of the misadventure (during which I stressed the dentist's certainty that all was well) with concern, but without needlessly scolding me.

12

I was planning to go to the eighteenth World Science Fiction convention, which was to be held at Pittsburgh, and I intended to go by train. There was a train strike, however, and I drove instead.

I set out on Thursday, September 1, got to Reading, Pennsylvania, where I put up at a motel and then the next day got to Pittsburgh.

Almost the first thing that happened when I got there was that I found that Janet Jeppson was attending, too. I was delighted to see her, except that when I did see her she was with Theodore Cogswell. Ted is an English teacher as well as a science-fiction writer; has deep-set eyes, a slow way of talking, a fey sense of humor, and always appears to be intensely attractive to women.

I decided I didn't approve of Janet's being with Ted; I felt she wasn't safe. When I finally pried her loose, I managed to hang about her fairly constantly and saw to it that she was secure from all the predators. I don't honestly know that she wanted to be secure from predation, but it didn't occur to me to ask her, and she was too polite to send me away.

Early on, too, I met Gordie Dickson, whom I greeted with loud outcries of joy.

"Gordie," I said, "where's Djinn?" Naturally, I wanted to see that spectacular creature again even if she and Gordie were married.

But Gordie said, morosely, "How the hell should I know?"

It turned out that they had remained married only two months and were long divorced. Djinn was not at that convention, and I have never seen her again.

Judy Merril was there—radiant—with a new flame named Dan Sugrue, an oddly morose young man (whom Judy later married and divorced).

I remember one late-night session at the convention, when someone brought his sixteen-year-old daughter and left her there in our midst, apparently unaware that he was abandoning her to the mercies of some of the raunchiest characters in the world.

She was a sweet-faced girl, more beautiful than any sixteen-year-old girl I had ever seen, and who seemed much older than her age (though that might only have been my wishful thinking). She was a considerable damper on the conversation, though, except for Dan Sugrue's attempt to tell a joke fit for her virginal ears, which, however, quickly turned out to be something capable of embarrassing even Randall Garrett and myself—which Dan nevertheless was unable to turn off.

Judy Merril looked at the sixteen-year-old girl and said, sentimentally, "Four years ago, my daughter was sixteen years old."

"Really?" I said. "No one looking at you would guess you were young enough for that."

So she hit me, but not really hard. I managed to get to my feet again with hardly any assistance.

On Saturday, September 3, I helped auction off some authors and I was bought myself (for an hour) by three kids and an older person who was acting as their sitter.

I was toastmaster at the Sunday awards-giving banquet and that meant I handed out the Hugos. Generally, I did so without excessive enthusiasm, because I was only too aware that the coming of the Hugos and the ending of my science-fiction phase had very nearly coincided so that I had never had the chance of having my most famous stories compete for the award.

The Hugo-winning novelette this time, however, was *Flowers for Algernon* by Daniel Keyes, and about this one I could not help but be enthusiastic. It was, in actual fact, a wonderful story.[5] I enlarged on its merits as I called out its name as prize-winner and waited for Keyes to show up.

"How did he do it?" I demanded of the Muses. "How did he do it?"

I then looked up at a level about nine or ten feet from the floor in

[5] It was later expanded into a novel that I didn't like as well, and made into a movie called *Charly*.

order to encounter the face of the giant whom I had never, until that moment, met.

A hand plucked at my elbow and I brought my eyes down to ordinary man-height. And from the round and gentle face of Daniel Keyes, as he reached for his Hugo, emerged the immortal words: "Listen, when you find out how I did it, let me know, will you? I want to do it again."

I took off early on the morning of Monday, September 5 (my mother's sixty-fifth birthday), and managed to miss the turnoff to the Pennsylvania Turnpike. That was even worse than missing the Route 2 turnoff on Route 128. I had to find my way back to the turnpike by alternate roads, but I eventually did.

13

I had started the book I was to do for Doubleday shortly before I had left for the convention, and I continued it after I came back. Eventually I named it *Life and Energy*, and when it came time to dedicate it, I named "Richard K. Winslow and Tim Seldes, gentlemen, scholars, and *bon vivants*." The *bon vivants* bit was, of course, in memory of the excellent lunch, complete with drinks, at which I gained the chance to do the book.

I was beginning to have trouble with dedications.

The first few were simple. *Pebble in the Sky* was to my father, who, after all, had allowed me to read my first science-fiction magazine and who had bought me my first typewriter. The second book, *I, Robot*, was dedicated to John Campbell, who had discussed each of the robot stories with me and who had helped me put the Three Laws of Robotics into words. The third book was dedicated to Gertrude, the fourth to my mother. There were other family members and then friends—Brad, Fred Pohl, Sprague de Camp, Horace Gold, Charles Dawson, who had befriended and helped me. The time even came when I could, alas, memorialize dead friends. *Lucky Starr and the Rings of Saturn* was dedicated to the memory of Henry Kuttner and Cyril Kornbluth.

Still, as the number of books increased, I had to make a numbered list of dedications, which I had to study more and more closely to see if some deserving person had been omitted, or whether enough time had elapsed for a repeat.

It is questionable, of course, as to whether a dedication is necessarily to be considered an honor. Consider the case of nineteenth-century English wit Douglas W. Jerrold. He was told that a friend of his, a prolific but third-rate writer, was dedicating the next of his numerous books to him. Jerrold sighed, shook his head, and said, "Ah, that's a fearful weapon that man has."

14

I attended another meeting of the Interplanetary Exploration Society on September 10, and drove Alma Hill there at her request. I chafed a bit about it because the meeting was in the Hotel Touraine, which was in downtown Boston. There were never parking places there and I was going to have to drop off Alma at the hotel and then either park two miles away or make use of some overcrowded parking lot. In either case, it was going to be a tedious and sweaty chore.

Alma, with that obliviousness to difficulties of which she was particularly capable, said to my mutterings, "Oh, there'll be a parking place right there."

And there was! When I drove up to the hotel, an empty place existed right in front of the main entrance. I was speechless, but Alma walked calmly into the hotel as though nothing had happened. Never again has anything like this taken place, but, of course, I've never again had Alma with me, and that may account for it.

Part of the entertainment on this occasion was my reading of "Thiotimoline and the Space Age," which had just appeared in *Astounding/Analog.* I was luckier than Santesson had been. I had an enormous crowd of twelve people hanging on my words, which were well received.

15

Later that week, Robyn entered kindergarten, and there I was—an aging prodigy, too old to have preschool children.

16

On September 18, 1960, Gertrude and I traveled to Arlington, a northern suburb, and visited Ben Bova and his wife, Rosa. Ben was an ex-newspaperman who had taken a job at Avco Research and who was writing very good science books, some of which I had read in connection with my *Hornbook* column, and had enjoyed.

Ben, whom I now met for the first time, was twenty-seven years old, about my height, had very close-cropped hair, and was enormously intelligent and witty. I took an instant liking to him, a liking that has never faltered and has only intensified.

I can even pin down the exact moment when I "fell in like" with him. I had all my life heard people describe promising children as "a regular Einstein" until the phrase, from overuse, grated unbearably on me. Bova (of South Italian extraction, although he has blue eyes), in speaking of a promising lad, used the phrase "a regular Galileo" and instantly won his way into my heart.

Rosa, also of Italian extraction,[6] was a plump girl, good-natured and much given to laughing and to talking rapidly in a rather shrill voice. We had a very good time and readily added them to our roster of friends.

17

Svirsky was after me to do a book on Mendeléev and his discovery of the periodic table of the elements. It was Mendeléev's ability to point out gaps in the table and to predict the existence of undiscovered elements, together with their exact properties, that ensured general acceptance of the table. Svirsky wanted me to call it *The Case of the Missing Elements* in order to make it fit into a series of detective-story-like science juveniles that Basic Books was doing.

I had no desire to work for Svirsky after his hacking of *The Intelligent Man's Guide to Science*. I did, however, want to do a book on the discovery of the elements. My feeling was that I would simply do it my way regardless of Svirsky's instructions and then if he didn't want it, someone else would.

I drove in to New York on September 22, therefore, to sign the contract at Basic Books. My own name for the book was *The Search for the Elements*.

On the same trip I signed a contract with Mac Talley for *The Human Body* and *The Human Brain* and finally signed the Doubleday contract for *Life and Energy*.

18

I was, of course, among the millions who listened to the Kennedy-Nixon debates. I was as tense as a freshly wound mainspring, fearful that Kennedy would make some mistake or that Nixon would not.

To be sure, Nixon, in an unfortunate attempt at makeup, had

[6] Ben insists that she is of Sicilian extraction, though I have difficulty in making out the distinction.

made himself look impossibly ugly—which is supposed by many to have decided the election then and there—but I didn't notice that. He always looked impossibly ugly in my eyes.

I could not see that either had the advantage. My comment in my diary on the morning of September 27, with the first debate having taken place the night before, was, "I thought Kennedy did the better of the two, but then I am prejudiced."

19

The Search for the Elements was not a hard job. I was thoroughly at home with the subject, and it raced along. It was another one of those books that took me two weeks to do, and on October 14 I mailed it to Svirsky.

Svirsky decided quickly that it wouldn't fit the series he had in mind. I hadn't concentrated on the mystery aspect of it, nor had I lingered over the periodic table sufficiently. What's more, it was too long and too complex.

None of this bothered me; I had foreseen it. I waited for him to give it back to me so that I could pass it on to Houghton Mifflin (for whom I was writing another in my "realm" series on mathematics; this one *Realm of Algebra*).

Svirsky fooled me, however. He said he wanted to hold on to the manuscript and consider it as an item for a somewhat older age level. Well, I had signed a contract and accepted an advance. I couldn't prevent him from doing that—but I was chagrined.

20

I did my best to introduce the children to those accomplishments I had missed. I tried to get them to learn how to swim at the YMCA, for instance. Neither proved instantly enthusiastic about it, but in the end both learned how to swim.

And on October 14, I enrolled David in a bowling tournament at the YMCA; duckpins rather than full-scale tenpins. It was a father-and-son affair and I joined him in rolling the bowling ball. He showed no real aptitude for it (and neither did I), but we continued to bowl periodically for some years and even managed to extract pleasure from it. The very occasional strike on either side was always ecstasy for both.

21

On October 21, 1960, I went to MIT to hear a lecture by Hugo Gernsback, the grandfather of magazine science fiction. It had been 34½ years before that he had put out the first issue of *Amazing* and had made my career possible. I had never met him before, and I felt it rather an honor to be slated to introduce him now.

He handed out sheets of paper to the audience before he started to speak and, knowing Gernsback's penchant for self-publicizing,[7] I assumed it was a long vita.

It wasn't. It was an essay he had written. I had a chance to read mine all the way through as I sat there on the platform while waiting for the papers to be distributed. Finally, when he began to talk, darned if that essay didn't turn out to be his *speech*. He repeated what I had just read, word for word, and pinned as I was on the platform I had to seem to be listening with devouring absorption.

Fortunately, the talk only lasted half an hour, and the hour-long question-and-answer period that followed was more interesting.

22

I drove the family to New York on October 27, and the next morning I was at Basic Books, for it was publication time for *The Intelligent Man's Guide to Science*. I finally got my hands on a finished copy, complete as a two-volume boxed set (very impressive, I must say) less than thirteen months after I had put down the first word.

To celebrate, Svirsky had me interviewed by *Newsweek* reporters, complete with a picture-taking session at the *Newsweek* building, then drove me up to his home in Ossining in Westchester County.

I had dinner with him and with his wife and then we drove down to Manhattan again, for he had tickets to the musical *Fiorello*. Gertrude met us at the theater and we enjoyed the play. After that, we went to a nightclub, and then went back to his place.

We stayed overnight with him and most of the next day. In the evening, he took us to the Yonkers races. It was the first and only time I've been at a racetrack and watched the horses run. It was pleasant as a spectacle, but I refused to bet, which I think rather spoiled Svirsky's fun. (He bet, and lost.)

There is no question but that he treated us well, and even royally.

[7] I don't resent it. I have the same penchant.

As a person, he was kind and delightful. In fact, when *The Search for the Elements* was finally published, I dedicated it to "Ruth and Leon Svirsky and October in Westchester."

As an editor, however, he was a complete failure—at least as far as I was concerned. I could not work with him on books, and no amount of personal kindness could alter that fact, though it did raise the level of my guilt feelings.

23

I drove from New York to West Newton on October 30, and in the course of that trip I had (for the first time in ten years and some seventy thousand miles of driving) the dubious pleasure of having a flat tire on the highway. The trouble was that while I knew in theory what to do to change a tire, I had no practical experience whatever and, what with my general ineptness, I dared not try.

I was on the Belt Parkway on the northeastern border of Queens and I had to make my way over desolate fields to find a telephone on which I could call the AAA. Having done so, I found I had no way of describing the location of my car. I did my best and eventually a repair truck found me after a delay caused by the necessity of having to scour a five-mile stretch of the highway in search of me. It all cost me three hours in time spent in fretting and humiliation.

Have I learned my lesson? No! To this day, I can't change a tire.

24

The next day, matters reversed themselves.

The Living River, which had been the occasion of bringing to a head the issue of the "disgrace" that my science writing was bringing on the school, proved to be not a disgrace at all.

It won the Blakeslee Award given out by the American Heart Association, having been judged the best book in that subject area in the year of its publication. On October 31, 1960, I received a plaque to that effect and a check for five hundred dollars.

I managed to let various people at the med school know of this and was quite certain it would get to the ears of Keefer and Lemon.

Despite this vindication, I did not in the least desire to go on to what I had originally planned to be the second book on the subject, the one on cardiovascular research that the Heart Institute people had originally had in mind. To have done so would have meant applying for another grant, or for the renewal and extension of the first, and I wasn't going to. I had definitely decided never to accept grant money again. Nor did I ever again hear from the Heart Institute people about it—so that was that.

25

On November 1, 1960, I received my fourteen-volume set of the McGraw-Hill Encyclopedia of Science and Technology, which I had ordered on approval. I had the option of sending it back if I didn't like it, but a quick glance told me it would be invaluable in my work, so I kept it.

I also had the option of paying for it in innumerable monthly payments, but I had no intention of giving myself the task of making out a check every month.

So I simply looked at the total, made out the check, and sent it off.

It wasn't till some days later that I realized I had performed one of my special miracles of nonintelligence. The total payment I had paid included all the carrying charges that would have been added if I had paid in monthly installments. The total for payment all at once, recorded elsewhere in the pamphlet, was something like fifteen dollars less.

Well, why should McGraw-Hill have my fifteen dollars? I sent a letter of explanation and after a long delay I got back a letter that seemed to leave the matter in the air. I sighed and decided to take up the matter personally the next time I was in New York. I made a note of the name attached to the letter. I don't remember what it was, but it was long and humorous. Let's call it, "Mitschermatscherlinklich."

And, indeed, my next time in New York, I called McGraw-Hill, asked for Mitschermatscherlinklich, and was rewarded with a burst of laughter from the person at the phone. I was eventually shifted to some particular department, asked again, and got another burst of laughter. He passed me to someone else, who also guffawed.

I got the idea I was being made fun of, which is something I rarely appreciate. When I got my fourth person, I said, speaking very slowly and distinctly, "Now, I don't want you to laugh. I am trying to reach someone to discuss an overpayment. The person I must reach has a silly name but I didn't invent it. It is right here on the letter and I shall come over in person and raise hell if you laugh at it because I'm in no laughing mood."

The person on the phone, a woman, said gravely, "What is the name, sir?"

"Just don't laugh! It is Mitschermatscherlinklich."

There was no laugh. No laugh at all. The woman said, "I am the person you want to speak to. What is your complaint?"

"*You* are Mitschermatscherlinklich?"

"Yes, I am. What is your complaint?"

I couldn't let it go at that. I had to make some sort of lighthearted sally in order to keep it from ending on this grim note. I said, "Well, a charming young woman like yourself won't remain single for long, and when you are married, you will have a beautiful name."

And she said, in rather awful tones, "I am *Mrs.* Mitschermatscherlinklich. Now can we please get on with it?"

So we did and I eventually got my fifteen dollars back, but all the fun of it was gone.

14

A Book for Each Year

1

It was time to buy a new car. My experience with the second Plymouth, with its Hy-Drive, which had required careful and stubborn babying to keep it in action, had, at least temporarily, cured me of Plymouths. This time it was going to be a Ford.

On November 5, 1960, I placed my order for a Ford Galaxie, and on November 23, I got it. I did not trade in the Plymouth, however. It was in satisfactory working shape, and Gertrude might as well have a car of her own. We became a two-car family for the first time and had a chance, at least, to use both halves of our two-car garage.

There were lots of advantages. It meant that when one of us was using the car, the other wasn't immobilized. And when one car was out of order, we weren't altogether immobilized.

It had its disadvantages, too. It meant that during a snowstorm I could no longer make do with shoveling out only one half the driveway —the *whole* thing would have to be cleared.

2

For the first time in two years, I received a science-fiction challenge I couldn't resist. It came about thusly:

The magazine *Playboy* in a recent issue had decided to have a little fun with science fiction. They published an article entitled "Girls for the Slime God" in which they pretended, good-naturedly, that all science fiction was sex and sadism.

To maintain this fiction, *Playboy* illustrated the article with fictitious funny-sexy covers of fictitious magazines. They also used quotations that they drew from a single source, a magazine called *Marvel*, which published nine issues between 1938 and 1941. It had tried (and failed) in those nine issues to make a go by introducing the sex motif. The stories dealt very heavily with the hot passion of alien monsters for Earthwomen. Clothes were always getting ripped off and breasts were described in a variety of elliptical phrases—and these were the events and phrases quoted in the *Playboy* article.

Cele Goldsmith, then editor of *Amazing*, read the article and called me at once. She suggested I write a story entitled "Playboy and the Slime God" satirizing the satire. I was strongly tempted to do so for several reasons:

1. Cele was a beautiful woman and I happen to be aesthetically affected by beautiful women.
2. I take science fiction seriously, and I was annoyed at the satire.
3. I just happened to think up a plot.

So I wrote "Playboy and the Slime God," using some of the same quotes that *Playboy* had used and trying to show what an encounter between sex-interested aliens and an Earthwoman might *really* be like.

I was a bit afraid that, not having written science fiction for two years, not since "Rain, Rain, Go Away," I might have forgotten how— but one doesn't forget. I began the story on November 4, and by the ninth it had been submitted and accepted.[1]

At almost the same time, incidentally, I updated my book *Inside the Atom* so that a revised edition might appear in 1961.

3

November 8, 1960, was Election Day. I voted in the morning, for Kennedy, of course, and that night I stayed up very late. By 10:35 P.M. I was satisfied that Kennedy was elected, but the popular margin was thin and kept getting thinner. It wasn't till well into the next morning that Nixon conceded.

It was a great relief to me. He had been Vice President for eight years and senator before that and representative before that and what I most wanted out of politics now was not to have to look at his face or hear his voice ever again. To use a phrase invented two years later by Nixon himself in a typically mawkish whine of self-pity, I longed not to have Nixon to kick around anymore.

4

On November 10, I went to MIT to listen to a talk by Louis P. Hammett. I wasn't the least interested in the subject of the talk, but he had been my professor in graduate physical chemistry, the course that I

[1] Cele rewrote the final three paragraphs of the story, and did a much better job than I had, so I let hers stand.

had to pass with a B in order to become a full-fledged graduate student back in 1939, and he had given me an A. Naturally, I remembered him with warmth.

At the end of the lecture, I felt warm enough to go up and introduce myself. I had been a teacher myself long enough to know that students who come up and say "I was in your class of so-and-so" can very rarely expect to be remembered—but I had to.

I said, "It's a pleasure to see you again, Dr. Hammett. You taught me physical chemistry twenty-one years ago. My name is Isaac Asimov."

He looked uncomfortable until I pronounced my name and then he was suddenly galvanized into interest. "Delighted to see you, Asimov. How can I get a copy of *The Death Dealers?*"

"I can send you one," I said, astonished, "but I'm surprised you've heard of it."

"It's a best seller at Columbia," he said.

And a great light dawned. When I wrote the book, I was very anxious not to have anyone think I was satirizing the medical school, so I kept my mind firmly fixed on Columbia University, its physical plant, its faculty, even some of the graduate students I had known. It never occurred to me that anyone at Columbia would recognize the descriptions, but of course they did. It became a game there, trying to guess who the various characters were, and everyone wanted a copy.

I sent one to Hammett, as promised, and eventually he sent me a note to say he had enjoyed it. I was a little uneasy, though; I didn't want some of the characters recognized.

5

On November 17, I attended a meeting of the Boston Authors' Club for the first time, as guest of one of its members, Marjorie Carleton, and was inside Boston's famed Parker House for the first time in my life.

The Boston Authors' Club (like the Brooklyn Authors' Club of nineteen years before), consisted of elderly people of minor importance in the world of literature. They were lovable people, though, and I was always delighted to be with them. I joined the club and attended a number of meetings over the next few years, always with pleasure.

6

The December 5, 1960, issue of *Newsweek* reached the stands on November 30, with a laudatory half column on me and *The Intelligent*

Man's Guide to Science. It had a picture of me that looked rather thoughtful and spiritual, if you can imagine such a thing. (I find it rather difficult to do so myself.) It was the first time there had been an item on me in a national magazine.

The Intelligent Man's Guide to Science was getting rave reviews almost everywhere. It got a very good one in the December 16, 1960, issue of *Science,* for instance, from Derek J. De Solla Price. Although it may be a case of the old lady showing her medals, I cannot resist quoting the beginning:

"Here, at last, is something new in popular science writing. For once an author has taken the whole of modern science as his oyster, and he has shown himself equal to the task without patronizing the reader, taking him for a babe-in-arms, or doing devilish damage to the contents by culling his material from thirdhand sources. For at least one reviewer who started with a considerable allergy toward all popularized science, the world will never again be quite the same."

How I loved such critical approval, and yet that did not reconcile me to Svirsky's heavy-handed editing. Nothing any critic would say could convince me that the book was not better as I had written it.

7

We got the first heavy snow of the season on December 12, and, in fact, the worst December blizzard in the history of the Boston Weather Bureau—and I got my first practice at shoveling out both halves of the driveway. I was beginning to remember that you're not supposed to shovel snow if you're over forty, and I remembered only too well what had happened to Cyril Kornbluth a dozen years before, but it wasn't always possible to hire young men to do the job on the spot, and I was rarely patient enough to wait.

Despite the blizzard, I went in to New York by bus, which I had just discovered as an alternative to train travel. At that time, the Trailways bus between Boston and New York was a rather pleasant transportation device. If you bought a ticket for one of the "deluxe" runs, you got a pretty stewardess, sandwiches, and coffee.

I spent most of my time in New York with Doubleday and with Basic Books. Svirsky was now tempting me to do a one-man multivolume encyclopedia of science for youngsters. Despite my reluctance to work with Svirsky, I remembered the pleasant time he had showed us in October and the good reviews I was now getting, and grudgingly agreed to write a sample.

8

When we visited Bernie and Essie Fonoroff on December 18, 1960, one of the guests was Marvin Minsky, who worked on robots and artificial intelligence at MIT and who had read my science fiction with enthusiasm. He was a tall man, with a bald, domed head, a delicate way of talking, and an enormously quick comprehension. In later years, I used to say that I had met only two men I was willing to concede were more intelligent than I was. One of them was Marvin.

I did not find myself drawn to Marvin's robots, by the way. It was not that there was anything wrong with either Marvin or his robots; quite the contrary. It was that I seemed to withdraw from direct contact with "science-fictional" subjects of any kind. I never had the urge to see nuclear power stations either, for instance, or rocket-launching sites.

I'm not sure why that is. Perhaps I dislike the invasion of real life into my science fiction. My robots belong to *me*, and I don't want outsiders horning in—even if the outsiders are busy inventing real robots.

Then, too, there may be a certain fear of knowing too much; a fear that that might hamper the unfettered play of my imagination and inhibit the story-making facility within me.

Third, I am not a visual person. I have spent so many bounded years in my childhood that I have grown used to having books as my window on reality. I will *read* about Marvin's robots avidly, but will be reluctant to look at one in action.

9

For the first time in seven years, we didn't have a Christmas tree at Christmas. The children had outgrown it and I celebrated the day by writing "Heaven on Earth," an article intended for my *F & SF* series. It eventually appeared in the May 1961 *F & SF*[2] as my thirty-first essay in the series.

Of all thirty-one, I thought it by far the most ingenious. In it I described a method for mapping the heavens on the Earth (in imagination) and thus illuminating a number of celestial phenomena and facts.

Writing that particular essay helped activate a feeling I had had for quite some time—which was that my *F & SF* essays, or some of them at least, ought to appear in book form. I had already written

[2] See *Fact and Fancy* (Doubleday, 1962).

thirty-one, and seventeen would be enough to make up a book of ordinary length.

I made a collection of seventeen of what I thought were my more interesting essays, including "Heaven on Earth," you can well imagine, and, on December 27, 1960, I took the collection (which I called *Fact and Fancy*) to Austin Olney. He seemed interested and I was pleased.

10

The next day I put Gertrude on a bus for a two-day visit to New York with her family, and the day after that, John McCarthy of MIT dropped around to talk about a TV panel show in which the two of us were soon going to participate.

McCarthy worked along with Marvin Minsky on computers and artificial intelligence, and McCarthy, too, was a fearsomely intelligent person. Where Marvin was bald, however, McCarthy was very thickly bearded, and beards on young men were still rare in those days.

John McCarthy was what some people might call absent-minded, but that wouldn't be accurate. He just didn't care about what went on outside the inside of his head.

In this case, for instance, he visited me on a day of light snow, and he walked in without rubbers and without bothering to wipe his shoes on the mat. He just dragged in the snow to melt into dirty water on our nice new golden carpet. I was horrified, but could think of nothing to say. (After he left I did my best to clean it up.)

While we were talking, Mary Blugerman called. Gertrude was out somewhere and Mary wanted to see if the children were well. Yes, they were, said I—when McCarthy, characteristically unconcerned with the fact that I was on the telephone, suddenly decided to continue the conversation from the living room.

"Is someone there with you?" said Mary, in what I took to be a suspicious manner.

"Yes," I said, "but it's a man with a beard. We'll be on television together next week."

"Yes?" said Mary, the suspicion more clearly marked. "You're sure it's not a girl?"

"For goodness' sake, Mary, if it were a girl do you think she would be talking while I was on the phone with my mother-in-law? Hey, John, come here and say hello."

Dutifully, John came over and said, "Hello," and I suddenly realized that he had (so help me) a soprano voice. No wonder Mary thought there was a girl in the house with me.

I snatched the phone away. "It's a man," I said, by now in a near frenzy, "but he has a high voice. His name is John McCarthy and I'll introduce him to Gertrude when she comes home."

I wasn't desperate enough to keep John overnight and make him wait for Gertrude, but she did get to meet him eventually and to note the timbre of his voice.

11

The year 1960 ended with my earnings within twenty-five dollars of the thirty-two-thousand-dollar mark, my third consecutive year in the thirty-thousand-dollar area. If I were to regard my writing alone, I had every reason to be happy, for I had topped 1958 and 1959 by a narrow margin and had set a record.

Nevertheless, 1960 fell below my *total* 1958 income (counting the last bit of my school earnings) by over two thousand dollars. If I could best that mark, I felt that I would be entirely satisfied.

There was hope that I might do exactly that in the next year, for in 1960 I had published no less than eight books, well beyond the previous record of five in 1957, and surely each should contribute to my earnings the next year. They were:

33. *The Living River* (Abelard-Schuman)
34. *The Kingdom of the Sun* (Abelard-Schuman)
35. *Realm of Measure* (Houghton Mifflin)
36. *Breakthroughs in Outer Space* (Houghton Mifflin)
37. *Satellites in Outer Space* (Random House)
38. *The Wellsprings of Life* (Abelard-Schuman)
39. *The Intelligent Man's Guide to Science* (Basic Books)
40. *The Double Planet* (Abelard-Schuman)

Four of the eight books were published by Abelard-Schuman, but I had no further books in press with them. The delays in publishing and the unsettling turnover in editors had driven me away.

It was, in a way, a shame. Hal Cantor had, by now, also left, and Frances Schwartz, Lew's wife, was in charge of the Juvenile Department. She was a pleasant, no-nonsense woman, whom I liked a lot. It was clear she was there to stay, but I now had commitments elsewhere, and the Abelard-Schuman phase of my career was over after having lasted eight years. (And I had *two* new publishers as replacements among the 1960 books—Random House and Basic Books.)

It was also true that 1960 was the first year, in the eleven in which I had so far been publishing books, in which I didn't have a single

Doubleday book published. That was a bad feeling, but I had *Life and Energy* in the works for them, and it was well along.

12

I turned forty-one on January 2, 1961, but there was no hassle about it. As I said in my diary that evening, "Forty-one isn't as old as forty." No age really is. After a while, each year is a victory, and you begin to be first relieved, then victorious, and finally (I imagine) triumphant.

13

On January 6, 1961, while on a visit to New York, I had, for old times' sake, dropped in at Henry Holt's to see Walter Bradbury. It was just a social visit. I had not come to propose a book; neither did he suggest one. I thought he looked drawn and tired.

I wasn't wrong, for on the thirteenth, I received a letter from him to the effect that immediately after I had visited him, he had resigned his position. Not *because* I had visited, you understand; that was just a coincidence. Despite the fact that Henry Holt had made him an offer he "couldn't refuse," he had not been happy there. He went on to take a job at Harper's.

14

On January 16, 1961, I received a copy of *Words from the Myths*, which I had written during the weeks of my despair over *The Intelligent Man's Guide to Science*. It was my fifth Houghton Mifflin book, and was designed after the fashion of *Words of Science*, but was in ordinary-size format.

It's a small thing, even a petty one, but I am enamored of numbers, and the book had a special significance to me. It was my forty-first book, and I received my advance copy in the month of my forty-first birthday. I had published one book for each year of my life.

It may have been about that time that I began to wonder if time and circumstance would allow me to publish as many as a hundred books altogether. It began to sound like a possible ambition. I had published forty-one books in eleven years. At that rate, it would take only sixteen years more to make up the remainder of the hundred, and with luck, I could live that long.

I mentioned this to Gertrude, who shook her head, "Maybe you can reach your goal, Isaac," she said, "but what good will it be if you then regret having spent your time writing books while all the essence of life passes you by?"

I said, "But for me, the essence of life *is* writing. In fact, if I do manage to publish a hundred books, and if I then die, my last words are likely to be, 'Only a hundred!'"

Still, I dare say that any monomania wearies people who don't share it, and even the kids had no trouble sensing my insanity in this respect.

Robyn, when she grew a little older, once snuggled into my lap and said, "Daddy, do you love me?"

Looking down into her sweet little face, I said, "Oh boy, do I love you!"

And she said (for what little girl isn't quite willing to test her father's love if she knows that she has his heart in her hand), "Suppose someone said you had to choose either me or—"

I was ready for her. I was certain she was going to say, "—either me or a million dollars, which would it be?" and I was all prepared to say, "I would rather have you, Robbie, dear, than a million zillion dollars."

But that's not what the little devil said. She knew where the weakness lay. What she said was, "Suppose someone said you had to choose either me or writing, which would it be?"

And I said, hollowly, "Why, I would choose you, dear."

But I hesitated—and she noticed that, too.

As to David, he never played games like that. He had a much more practical mind. It had been somewhere before the previous Christmas, when he was 9½, that he had begun to grow doubtful about Santa Claus. I had never tried to disillusion him in the matter because I hesitated to spoil his fun, but I was relieved when I found him becoming independently uncertain.

Finally, he said to me, "Santa Claus *can't* exist. How can anyone deliver presents to all the houses in the world in one night?"

I wondered if I ought to explain about an army of elves helping him, but decided not to compound the felony. Instead I said, "In that case, where do the presents come from?"

"There's only one way," said David. "Fathers and mothers have to do it, each father and mother for their own children. Then it can all be done in one night." He pondered a bit. "That must be why kids have to go to sleep early on Christmas Eve; so they don't catch their fathers and mothers at it."

I told him he was right, and praised him for his keen analysis, but he looked as though his fun had been spoiled just the same.

15

Kennedy was inaugurated on January 20, 1961. The weather wasn't very good in Washington, but it was worse in Boston. I had two feet of snow in the driveway.

Despite the weather, however, my heart warmed because my office in the attic was gaining new objects. We not only got in additional bookcases, matching the old, but I had brought home a second large filing cabinet. This one had originally been at the med school, but I had bought it with money on the National Heart Institute grant so that it was mine and not the school's. At least that was my contention, and the school did not seem anxious to argue the point.

16

I had a rather rude shock on February 1, 1961. Houghton Mifflin rejected a book of mine. My essay collection *Fact and Fancy* was clearly an adult book since I never made concessions in my *F & SF* essays, assuming always that my science-fiction audience, whatever the age of the individuals, was of adult intelligence. Since Austin was juvenile editor, he passed it on to the Adult Division, and they rejected it.

Austin, rather embarrassed, said *he* would be willing to do the book, but of course the essays would have to be modified to meet the needs of a juvenile audience.

I couldn't do that under any circumstances, so on February 3, I lunched with him, assured him there were no hard feelings, and took back the manuscript.

In later years, I would sometimes tease Austin about Houghton Mifflin having rejected *Fact and Fancy*, and he would always look distressed. Therefore, because I have a profound affection for him, I try not to tease him oftener than once a year.

17

The March 1961 *Amazing* came out with "Playboy and the Slime God," and this was my first appearance in any magazine with a piece of fiction in a year and a half.[3]

---

[3] Actually, I had a *fraction* of a story published in the interval. Cele had the idea of doing a round-robin story. Poul Anderson was to write the first part, ending it in a

The title, of course, was terrible, but it had been forced on me by the material I was satirizing. When Groff Conklin was considering the story for one of his collections, he asked, rather piteously, if I could come up with an alternate title.

"You bet," I said, "how about, 'What Is This Thing Called Love?'"

He was delighted and so was I, because it fit the story perfectly. I kept the new title when I put the story into one of my own collections.[4]

18

My relations with Harry Walker, the lecture agent, which had ended in 1958 after the disastrous North Leominster talk, had not ended forever, apparently. On February 6, 1961, I received a call from his office asking me to pinch-hit for a friend of mine, Gerald Hawkins, (a young astronomer I had met at the Whipples') in a speech to a Framingham women's club. I said I would, more for Gerald than for Harry.

I did, too, and it was a useful deed for me. Harry told me afterward that while the talk had been well received, some in the audience had been distracted by my habit of walking up and down the stage as I talked.

I had developed that habit in lecturing to the biochemistry class, when it had been necessary to walk back and forth to write formulas or to indicate, or modify, formulas already written. I got into the habit of walking back and forth as I talked even when no formulas were on the board.

In fact, some people in the class had complained that the swiveling of heads induced nausea. Assuming that to be a comic complaint, not seriously advanced, I said, indifferently, that they needn't watch me. They could look down at their notes and just listen.

And one wiseguy said, "Even just listening induces nausea."

I guess he said it without being able to stop himself (something that had happened to me so often), and he must have been greatly relieved when I burst into laughter.

At any rate, I recognized that what I could force on my classes I could not force upon general audiences (or should not), and since that

---

real mess; I was to take up the task and do the second part, ending it in a real mess; then Bob Sheckley, Murray Leinster, and Bob Bloch would carry on. The whole story was called "The Covenant," and it appeared in the July 1960 *Fantastic*. I think any one of the five authors could have written a better story if he had done it all himself.

[4] See *Nightfall and Other Stories*.

time I have been careful to stand in one place. Whatever parts of my body move as I make my emphatic or emotional points, my feet remain firmly planted.

19

On February 8, I got the news from Abe Burack that the National Book Council had included *The Intelligent Man's Guide to Science* as one of the nominees for the National Book Awards in the nonfiction category.

It didn't seem possible to me that I would win, however, and I was right. That year it went to William L. Shirer (on March 14) for *The Rise and Fall of the Third Reich*. It was a well-deserved win and in my diary I said, "No disgrace to lose to him."

The mere fact of nomination was praise enough for me, and it's the only nomination for National Book Awards I've ever had.

20

I took the train to New York on the thirteenth, stayed at the Westbury, and on the next day submitted my collection of essays, *Fact and Fancy*, to Tim Seldes.

I was increasingly making the discovery that "unto everyone that hath shall be given."

The more books and articles I published, the more requests I received from publishers and editors for specific additional books and articles.

There was a feeling of power there for me, but it was a power I dreaded and hated using. I remembered the feeling of rejection too vividly to want to inflict rejection. The result was that I didn't reject often enough and I regularly did somewhat more work than I could comfortably find the time to do and, rather depressingly often, did work I didn't really want to do. And when I *had* to reject out of sheer lack of time or knowledge or interest, the rejection weighed upon me and depressed me.

21

Some students from MIT had called and asked if I would give a lecture there. I agreed, and they asked my fee.

The time was not long past when I had spoken to science-fiction fans, college students, librarians, and other worthy people for nothing, and I still didn't like to charge them. However, I had learned that I was worth anything up to $500, so I thought—well, let's try.

I rather quaveringly asked for $100, and they accepted that so readily I was sorry I hadn't asked for $150.

I gave a late-afternoon lecture at Kresge Auditorium on February 22, 1961, then, basing it on my *F & SF* essay "My Built-in Doubter,"[5] which had not yet been published but was about to appear in the May 1961 *F & SF*. It was the first of a number of articles I have written in which I have denounced various pseudoscientific beliefs that have attracted the attention of the gullible and the quasi-intelligent.

It went over well and, after the talk, the young sponsors suggested dinner. I said, "Fine. There's a Howard Johnson's right on Memorial Drive, and if you'll get into my car—"

They said, "You don't understand, Dr. Asimov, we've already made reservations at Joseph's."

Joseph's was one of Boston's posh eating places, and that rather took my breath away, for it was very expensive and I had never eaten there. Did the kids know what they were doing? I said, uncertainly, "Well, if you'll get into my car—"

But they were already hailing two taxis and eventually there were six or seven of us seated around a big table at Joseph's. My conscience smote me. They were being *so* nice to me after I had soaked them a hundred dollars.

I said, deeply troubled, "Where the heck do you kids get the money to pay speakers?" for I had gathered my talk was one of a series of four for the year.

I expected them to say they gave up lunches or sold pencils on the corner, and I was quite prepared to force the hundred dollars back on them.

But one of them said, cheerfully, "We show first-run movies and collect lots of proceeds."

"*Lots* of proceeds?"

"Sure. Up to five or six thousand dollars for the year."

I mentally divided that by four and said, "That must mean you pay some of the speakers more than a hundred dollars."

"Of course," said the spokesman, apparently unaware of the enormity of what he was saying. "Wernher von Braun, who spoke before you, got fourteen hundred dollars."

I stared at him for quite a while, then I said, "Was he fourteen times as good as I was?"

"Oh *no*. You were much better."

[5] See *Fact and Fancy.*

There was nothing I could do but order roast duck (very good) and in other ways treat myself to an excellent dinner, but it all taught me a valuable lesson well worth the money I had lost. I had learned to pitch my asking price high, and my fees went up after that.

22

As February 1961 turned into March, I received three royalty statements from each of three publishers. They were from Doubleday, Abelard-Schuman, and Basic Books, and they were large enough to bring my total earnings for the first nine weeks of 1961 to over fourteen thousand dollars. When I stopped to recall that that was very nearly my total annual writing income as recently as 1957, I found it rather unbelievable.

23

On March 13, 1961, I got a call from Stanley to the effect that my father, now sixty-four years old, was in the hospital waiting for a prostatectomy. It was a rude shock, but after all, not something entirely unexpected. Trouble with the prostate is all too frequent once one passes the half-century mark, and the operation is not a too-difficult one.

Still, my father had been suffering from angina for nearly a quarter of a century now, and we were nervous.

Fortunately, the operation, which was carried through on March 20, was successful, and he came through in fine shape.

24

Doubleday accepted *Fact and Fancy*, thank goodness, and I received the contract on March 22. This meant that at least some of my *F & SF* essays would appear in collected form. What I didn't tell Tim Seldes, of course, was that, assuming *Fact and Fancy* did reasonably well, I would instantly try to foist off a second collection on him.

As though Austin sensed that Doubleday had come through where Houghton Mifflin had not, I got a contract from the latter for *Words from Genesis*. The success of *Words of Science* and *Words from the Myths* and the pleasure I had had in doing both had led me on, irresistibly, to search for other word sources I could write about.

The Bible seemed the obvious place to look, so I went through the Book of Genesis, quoting occasional verses and pointing out the English words one obtained from those passages. Again, what I didn't tell

Austin was that if *Words from Genesis* did reasonably well, I'd go on to succeeding books of the Bible.

25

On March 23, I visited MIT to participate in a panel for some reason or other that I've forgotten. It was at that time I met Cleveland Amory, who had made a name for himself with his books on New England's high society. He was tall, handsome, curly-haired, and the clear lion of the occasion.

We were to speak for twenty minutes apiece, and I came second and spoke my twenty minutes. (Years of lecturing to classes and timing myself to finish as the bell rang had made me vain of my ability to meet the time demanded of me.)

Amory came third and spoke for forty-five minutes, very wittily, and I loved every minute of it. Mrs. Amory sat between myself and him, however, and I couldn't help but notice that periodically, and with gradually increasing force, she kept surreptitiously tugging at his trousers below tabletop level. This, I supposed, was a signal that he was talking too long. He ignored it.

26

I frequently make small errors in my books (not so frequently I make not-so-small errors), and I had a rather embarrassing one in *The Intelligent Man's Guide to Science*.

In it, I had occasion to mention, briefly, the research of W. B. Castle in the matter of the absorption of Vitamin B_{12}, since it is the failure of that mechanism that brings on "pernicious anemia."

His papers on the subject (at least those I was aware of) appeared in the prestigious British periodical *Biochemical Journal*, and I assumed, therefore, that he was a British biochemist and identified him so in my book.

Someone at school told me that Castle was not a British biochemist at all, but an American physician, born in Cambridge, Massachusetts. Indeed, he worked at Boston City Hospital right across the street from the med school, and from the window of what had been my laboratory, I could see the window of his.

On March 23, I marched myself over to Boston City Hospital, found my way to his office (having called in advance and made an appointment). I explained the error and apologized and he took it in very good humor.

Fortunately I had the chance to make the correction quickly. I received a letter from Svirsky on March 29 to the effect that a third printing of *The Intelligent Man's Guide to Science* was in the works and I could make minor corrections if I wished.

Meanwhile, on March 24, I finally completed *Life and Energy*, the book I had persuaded Tim Seldes and Dick Winslow to let me do. It was a good book, the kind of biochemistry book I had been hankering to do ever since the textbook days of ten years before, and it was 120,000 words long.

27

I drove to New York on April 3, 1961. That was the day my father was scheduled to be home from the hospital, so I drove straight to Windsor Place. My father looked wan and worn but he was otherwise all right.

I then went to Doubleday to deliver *Life and Energy* and chased back at once. I planned to stay overnight at my parents' so as to be with my father as long as possible since, rather emotionally, he decided he had been near death. In fact, he asked me to give a friend a copy of *The Intelligent Man's Guide to Science* and dictated the inscription I was to place in the book. It was florid and lengthy, and it embarrassed me greatly—but in this case my father's wishes were paramount.

It was very pleasant to talk to my father, and I was delighted to see him as lively and as quick intellectually as he had ever been, but staying overnight was a bad notion just the same, for I got no sleep. My father spent the whole night trudging back and forth between bed and bathroom, as I suppose was, under the circumstances, inevitable.

28

Norbert Wiener was still after me to collaborate with him on a murder mystery. Fortunately, Jason Epstein, Norbert's editor at Random House (and another one of the fearfully intelligent people with whom my life has been filled), quite clearly didn't want this. I had a long dinner with him and Norbert on April 4, while I was still in New York, and Jason's idea was that there be a book called *Conversations with Norbert Wiener*, with Norbert at one end of a tape recorder and me at the other.

It sounded easy except that I was not at all certain that I could ask the right questions, and I had a sinking sensation as to whose job it would be to edit thousands of pages of transcript. The only thing I could do was to say "Yes" and then never push it.

It is my experience that almost nobody is a pusher. If there is a project I want done, of course, I push everybody and eventually it gets done. If there is a project I don't want done, I simply don't push and then (almost always) nobody else pushes, either, and it doesn't get done.

I didn't push this time and nothing ever happened.

29

On April 11, I made one of my rare forays into civic affairs.

The city of Newton was facing a referendum on fluoridation of the water supply and I was in favor of fluoridation, as was, of course, the dental profession. I was asked to give a talk to a local PTA in support of the law, and I agreed; I felt it my duty.

Some time afterward, one of the people in the forefront of the profluoridation movement called me to suggest I write an article for a newspaper in favor of fluoridation. I was well aware that I was not entirely an expert on the subject, and I envisioned myself as either having to do considerable research or as being converted into mincemeat by the antifluoridation fanatics.

I said to her, "Why not have so-and-so do it?," referring to a leading dentist who had been one of the group who had pressured me into giving the talk.

"Oh," she said, rather surprised at the suggestion, "surely you understand that so-and-so is a busy man!"

So I refused point-blank to do the article.

Could she have known how offensive her remark had been? The implication was, of course, that either I wasn't a busy man myself, or else that writing was so easy a job that I could toss off an article between yawns.

Both assumptions are irritating in the extreme. Writing is hard work. The fact that I love doing it doesn't make it less hard work. People who love tennis will sweat themselves to exhaustion playing it, and the love of the game doesn't stop the sweating.

The casual assumption that writers are unemployed bums because they don't go to the office and don't have a boss is something every writer has to live with. I have never known a writer who hasn't suffered as a result of this, hasn't resented it, and hasn't dreamed of murdering the next person who says, "Boy, you've sure got it made. You just sit there and toss off a story or something whenever you feel like it."

30

On April 12, 1961 (the sixteenth anniversary of F.D.R.'s death), I was absolutely stunned and delighted by the news that the Soviets had orbited a man, had sent him once around the world, and had brought him back safely.

Yuri Gagarin was the first astronaut (or "cosmonaut," to use the Soviet term) to enter space, and he was a countryman of mine. Like me, he was born in the Smolensk district of Russia.

31

The next day came the news from Elizabeth Moyers that Dean Soutter was resigning. Actually, said Elizabeth (who was an expert on office politics and who imagined it existing everywhere), he was being forced out by the Keefer group.

My conscience twanged miserably, for I knew that Soutter had fought valiantly on my behalf, and it might well be that it was that fight that had marked him down for the slaughter. On April 14, after I had given the second of my two lectures for that teaching semester, I rushed down to see Soutter and he told me essentially the same story that Elizabeth had.

Thereupon I felt it incumbent upon me to do for him what he had done for me. I called President Case and made an appointment to see him on the seventeenth. On that day I went over to the main campus and spent half an hour telling Case of the manifold virtues of Soutter and of the importance of keeping him at the school. According to my diary, Case "seemed impressed."[6]

Then on May 5, Soutter had an interview with Case, something that I had arranged, and in my diary I say that Soutter "apparently won a partial victory."

I suspect that if Soutter had been as fiendishly determined to keep his title as I had been, he would have managed. Soutter, however, had other things to do. There was a new medical school that the University of Massachusetts was thinking of starting, and Soutter was in line to be its head.

[6] On that same day, anti-Castro Cubans, encouraged by the United States, invaded the Bay of Pigs in Cuba, and the fiasco that resulted held the United States up to ridicule before the world.

So he resigned on May 16 and left, I suppose, without much in the way of regret. I had the comfort, though, of knowing I did not let it happen without striking a blow on his behalf. I do not forget favors done me.

Once he was gone, I got wearily set for a new onslaught upon myself. I even had the fugitive thought that Keefer had gotten rid of him precisely in order to take me on in a fifth round—but it never happened. I was left to myself.

15

Over the Top

1

The Wellsprings of Life was receiving reviews that were every bit as good as those for *The Intelligent Man's Guide to Science*. That gave me particular satisfaction, for *The Wellsprings of Life* was *mine*, and had not been tampered with in any way by editorial oppression.

In the April 23, 1961, *Science*, George Gaylord Simpson, the renowned vertebrate paleontologist of Harvard University, reviewed *The Wellsprings of Life* and referred to me as "a national wonder and a natural resource."

That is, by all odds, my favorite quote about myself. Years later, Lester del Rey gave me a set of calling cards for my birthday, each reading "Isaac Asimov—Natural Resource," and I said, "Why did you leave out the 'national wonder' part, Lester?"

He said, "I thought that much would embarrass anyone—even you."

It is the only time I ever knew Lester to underestimate the extent of my cheerful self-appreciation.

2

On April 15, 1961, I had received a long letter from Doubleday pointing out possible errors, omissions, and other insufficiencies in *Life and Energy*. It was not from Dick Winslow, but from his new assistant, Lawrence P. Ashmead, a young geologist from Yale, whose first task it was to handle this book.

When Ashmead showed Dick a draft of the letter (according to the story told me by Ashmead in later years), Dick stirred uneasily and said, "You can't do that. Asimov is a scientist and he'll be very annoyed at being picked on like that."

Ashmead insisted, however, and off went the letter.

Well, I did quiver a bit when I got it, but almost all the points were valid ones, and I worked away to make the necessary changes. On May 2, I drove in to New York and went to Doubleday with my corrections. I found that Dick Winslow was in the hospital with pneumonia, so I talked to Ashmead.

"Those were very good points you made," I said. "Thank you very much. Here are my suggested corrections and let me know if anything more needs to be done."

Larry Ashmead—and from then on he was only Larry to me—was greatly relieved that, despite Dick's prediction, I had not stormed in furiously, and from then on I was on his gold-star list, and we have been close friends ever since.

This turned out to be a very convenient thing for me in my future career, but I didn't foresee that at the time.

3

The next day I had lunch with Hugo Gernsback at his suggestion. He was now seventy-six years old and it was the first and only time I was ever alone with him.

I had rather looked forward to this, for I had been told he was a gourmet and knew places in New York, secret places, where one could feast like an emperor. That sparked my gluttony, and when he took me out of his office and proceeded to walk me for something like three fourths of a mile, I thought happily that he was taking me to some hidden rendezvous that he would not give away to any cabbie.

When we entered a Longchamps restaurant, I thought happily that there was a gourmet Elysium hidden in the back or in the cellar that used Longchamps as a front.

When we sat right down in Longchamps, I thought happily that this was a secret gourmet Longchamps that nobody knew anything about.

When he ordered a ham sandwich, I thought happily that this was a code for something so incredibly *cordon bleu* that no one but a few happy mortals had ever tasted it, and I ordered a ham sandwich, too.

I got a simple ham sandwich. In fact, it was rotten.

What Gernsback wanted to see me about was a new science-fiction magazine he was planning to start and that he hoped I would edit. That was something I couldn't and wouldn't do, even if he *had* treated me to a gourmet meal.

4

On May 13, 1961, the Interplanetary Exploration Society, which had died stillborn with Campbell's speech at the Museum of Natural

History 2½ years before, suffered the death of its Bostonian incarnation at last.

Alma Hill had arranged a picnic at the Arboretum and, with her usual calm assumption of cosmic subservience to herself, refused to set a definite place of meeting. "We'll meet each other," she said firmly, with the same self-assurance with which she had told me there would be a parking place outside the Hotel Touraine.

Remembering that the parking place had really been there, I took Gertrude down to the Arboretum with a certain amount of confidence. We met no one.

Others later told me they were there, too, and met no one. I don't know how many of us wandered singly and in pairs without ever crossing each other's path.

That was it. If there was ever another meeting of the society, I was not informed.

We had better luck the next day, though.

The MIT science-fiction society usually had a picnic at the Blue Hills Observatory on the first or second Sunday in May, and on the fourteenth, all four of us went there and had a wonderful time. There was lots to eat—cold cuts, cake, watermelon, soft drinks, beer, and an incredible number of other comestibles guaranteed to destroy any stomach more sensitive than mine or a college student's. There was also a traditional walk up to the top of the hill on which the observatory was situated. This I would gladly have ignored because my joy in moving upward under my own power has always been restrained. David, however, wanted to make the climb and I didn't want him to do it on his own.

After this occasion, I was always invited to the annual picnic, as was Harry Stubbs, and I went on every occasion that I could. Somehow, the custom arose of asking me to pick the actual Sunday out of the two possible and I always have, even when it was known in advance I could not attend. The superstition is that the Sunday I choose is always bright, sunny, and desirable. I can only recall one time when that superstition refused to work.

5

On May 22, I met George Gaylord Simpson, who had called me a "national wonder and natural resource." It turned out, over lunch, that he was a science-fiction fan and read my *F & SF* articles, which made his opinion of me a little less surprising.

He was particularly interested in John Campbell, whom he had never met, but of whom he seemed to be in considerable awe. I went through some of my stories about Campbell—our meeting, his penchant for outrageous opinions, his incredible agility in argument, his tendency of late toward mysticism. Then I hesitated because I didn't want to malign Campbell and yet I was overcome with a desire to epitomize him perfectly. Finally, the desire to epitomize won out and I said,

"I'll tell you something, George, that I think will describe Campbell perfectly. Suppose you meet a man who asks you what your field of endeavor is and you tell him that you are the world's greatest living vertebrate paleontologist, which is, of course, what you are. And suppose that, on hearing this, the man you meet fixes you with a glittering eye and proceeds to lecture you for five hours on vertebrate paleontology, getting all his facts wrong, yet somehow leaving you unable to argue them—you will then have met Campbell."

6

That same day, I had dinner with John R. Pierce of Bell Telephone Laboratories. He had invented the word "transistor," was working on communications satellites, and was a well-known science-fiction personality, having written for *Astounding* under the name of J. J. Coupling. He was in town to give a talk at MIT, a talk I attended.

Also at the dinner was Vannevar Bush, one of the pioneers of electronic computers, and he also read my *F & SF* articles.[1]

7

While talking to Simpson, Pierce, and Bush, all in the course of a single day, I found my desire to write science fiction suddenly activated. The next day, therefore, I sat down to write a short story. It wasn't much of one, only two thousand words long, and, considering my talk with Bush, it's not surprising it was about computers.

I called it "The Machine That Won the War," wrote it in a single session, and sent it out to Bob Mills before the day was over. Mills took it at once and it eventually appeared in the October 1961 *F & SF*.[2]

[1] Every time I met an important scientist who was a reader of mine, I was inordinately delighted. I suppose that no matter how brave a face I put upon it, there was always a little bit of shame within me that I had abandoned science for writing, and I needed the assurance, endlessly repeated, that my fellow scientists accepted my writing.
[2] See *Nightfall and Other Stories*.

8

I was making nonfiction progress as well. I had finally returned to *The Search for the Elements,* which Svirsky had said was unsuitable for his juvenile line, and had rewritten it with an eye toward adults. Naturally, that meant it grew longer and was now well over sixty thousand words long.

Having finished that chore, I finally began *The Human Body* on May 23, which I was now aiming for hard-covers with Houghton Mifflin, and then soft-covers with NAL.

I could tell from the first page that the book was going to be pleasurable for me. I experimented with a new device, which was to give the pronunciation and derivation of every anatomical and physiological term, placing these in parentheses immediately after the first use of the term and including an initial "G" or "L" to indicate whether the derivation was from Greek or Latin.

I was afraid that this might seem didactic to some and condescending to others—but I was wrong. Judging by the letters I eventually received, knowing the pronunciation removed some 80 per cent of the terrors of a word, and knowing the derivation removed the other 20 per cent.

It meant I could use the full vocabulary of the subject without ruining the readers' enjoyment, when not using it would have ruined my own. I have followed this same practice, or modifications thereof, in other books and have never been sorry.

9

On May 30, 1961, we visited the house of Rollo and Mary Silver in Brookline. Rollo was another one of the computer group at MIT, of medium height and with crisply curly hair that was receding at the temples. Mary was tall, with long hair and angular facial features, and had what I would later have thought of as a hippie approach to life. Other computer people were there—John McCarthy, Marvin Minsky and his wife, Gloria (a rather obese physician with a very attractive personality), and so on.

What really attracted my attention was the house, though, which I was to visit many times in the future. It was an old mansion that seemed full of incredible quantities and varieties of whatnots, of strange books, odd devices, and queer things I couldn't identify.

The most exciting fact was that Rollo Silver had a copy of *The*

Historian's History of the World. I had read most of it during the Navy Yard days and I remembered that reading with pleasure and longing.

I looked at Rollo's set (not entirely complete, for one volume was missing) and realized that I was not as honest a man as I had always thought I was. If there had been ten thousand dollars in small unmarked bills on that shelf and if I knew I could get away with it without ever being detected, I would nevertheless have left it there without as much as a quiver of temptation—in accordance with my father's teachings.

But my father had only mentioned money. If I had thought I could steal that set of books without ever being detected, well, who knows . . .

I did eventually (and rather falteringly) ask Rollo if he would sell it, and rather hinted that money was almost no object, but he was quite firm in his refusal.

I then tried to get it elsewhere. I saw some volumes in a department store, for instance, being used for nothing more than as objects in bookcases to help pretty display rooms. I asked if they had a complete set, and the floorwalker didn't know. I said that I would be glad to buy any volumes they had at any reasonable price and he said he would look into it for me, but despite several calls, I could never get them to fix a price.

I called secondhand stores but none of them had it, and few of them had heard of it. I left orders all over the city, but no set ever turned up. It was all very disappointing, and every time I visited the Silvers I would wander over to that set and finger it.

10

June 3, 1961, was graduation day for the med school class of '61, the last class I had taught as a fully salaried member of the faculty. There was a trace of sentiment in my wanting to attend that ceremony.

It was not sentiment alone. John Jeppson was graduating, and I knew that his sister, Janet, would be attending. She had written to tell me so, and it seemed like an excellent opportunity to see her again.

I went, and Janet was indeed there, together with her widowed mother, Rae K. Jeppson.[3] John was there, of course, and his wife, Maureen, and her mother. I was delighted to meet them all and hopped around with even more than my accustomed ebullience. Janet

[3] Janet's father, John Rufus Jeppson, had died on November 2, 1958, at the age of sixty-two—just half a year before I had met Janet at the MWA dinner.

said Maureen's mother described me as an "overgrown puppy dog," meaning it pleasantly, I think.

I sat in the very last row with the Jeppson family, and afterward we all went to a restaurant for a celebration luncheon.

11

In the evening of that day I went to Cambridge to hear Linus Pauling speak. I managed to corner him at the reception and found that he had indeed recommended me to Svirsky as the man to write *The Intelligent Man's Guide to Science*.[4] (Svirsky had told me this was so, but I thought he might merely be trying to flatter me.) Pauling said he had a copy and his wife was reading it with pleasure.

Since Linus Pauling was in the forefront of the movement for nuclear disarmament and peace, he was anathema to those who looked forward either grimly or joyously, to a nuclear war with the Soviet Union, and the speech was picketed by members of the John Birch Society.

That was my only contact, however indirect, with that lunatic-fringe group of the far right.

12

On June 6, 1961, I drove to New York to deliver the revised manuscript of *The Search for the Elements* to Svirsky.

At that period I was writing articles for the Encyclopedia Americana. One of the results of that was that I received a complimentary copy of the 1961 edition of the Americana to add to my 1942 Britannica. This meant I could turn to the Americana for postwar developments, and that was welcome indeed.

13

On June 21, I began what I planned to be the fourth *Realm* book in math for Houghton Mifflin. Having done *Numbers*, *Measure*, and *Algebra*, it seemed logical to do *Realm of Geometry*. Logical or not, I quickly realized I didn't want to. It would mean too much work with diagrams. I therefore dropped it at once, even though Houghton Mifflin had handed me a contract for it.

To mask the disappointment, I began a *Words* book instead. This

[4] That must have been immediately after he wrote me the letter about my carbon-14 article in the JCE.

time I planned *Words on the Map*—designed to trace the origin of various geographical names.

Instead of using a continuous account, as in *Words of the Myths* and *Words in Genesis*, I returned to the format of *Words of Science* and wrote *Words on the Map* as a collection of 250 one-page essays.

I had a particularly unusual opportunity to work on it intensively, as Gertrude and both children took the bus to New York on Friday, June 23, and left me at home alone for the entire weekend. I spent just about the whole of Saturday and Sunday at the typewriter, doing seventy-two of the essays.

14

On the evening of Friday the twenty-third, I attended the leave-taking party for Dean Soutter.

Keefer was there and he went out of his way to greet me, crossing the room with a wide grin and congratulating me on the reception of *The Intelligent Man's Guide to Science*. I could detect no sarcasm in his words and there was nothing to do but to shake hands with him, smile, and acknowledge his words courteously.

In a way, of course, it was a treaty of peace. Keefer could scarcely make it plainer that he considered himself to have been wrong in his attitude. My science writing did *not* disgrace the school, and my insistence on writing rather than research was for the *good* of the school. After that, though we never became friends, we were certainly no longer enemies.

Henry Lemon, who was also there, and who may have taken his cue from Keefer, also congratulated me. That was a confession of error, too, in my eyes. In his case, though, it was the last time I spoke to him or even saw him, after twelve years of first uneasy and then hostile association. Later that year he left and took a post with the University of Nebraska School of Medicine.

15

It seemed to me that the reaction of Keefer and Lemon to *The Intelligent Man's Guide to Science* was the last bit of evidence I needed to show me that that book was my nonfictional equivalent of "Nightfall."

Just as "Nightfall" had led to my recognition as a major figure in the world of science fiction, so *The Intelligent Man's Guide to Science* led to my recognition as a major figure in the field of science writing. Professionally, I had finally gone over the top.[5]

Acclaim for *The Intelligent Man's Guide to Science* was not universal, however. There had been an only lukewarm review in the New York *Times*, from a competing science writer who, I gathered, felt he could have done it better.

There was also a savage article in the June 2, 1961, *Science* entitled "In Defense of Biology" by Barry Commoner, a plant physiologist who has since become very well known for his habit of blaming the ills of the world on everything but overpopulation.

He was the retiring vice president of the American Association for the Advancement of Science, and the article was a reprint of his farewell address. I glanced at the first few paragraphs and was wondering whether I ought to read it thoroughly, when I caught my own name in print.

Naturally, I went back to the beginning and read the article with keen intensity. It turned out that Professor Commoner was tipping his lance in defense of biology against *me* and *The Intelligent Man's Guide to Science*.

What he specifically objected to was a sentence that started Chapter 10. That sentence was: "Modern science has all but wiped out the borderline between life and nonlife."

To this, Professor Commoner took violent exception. He went on, immediately after quoting the sentence, to say:

"Since biology is the science of life, any successful obliteration of the distinction between living things and other forms of matter ends forever the usefulness of biology as a separate science. If the foregoing sentence is even remotely correct, biology is not only under attack; it has been annihilated."

As it happened, the sentence to which Commoner objected was not mine. It had been inserted by Svirsky—but never mind. I had let it remain and it appeared over my name, so I was prepared to defend it.

And why not? I had never in my life either before or since heard a more stupid argument advanced by anyone supposed to be a scientist.

Imagine Copernicus to have advanced his theory that the planets, including Earth, all revolved about the Sun, so that Earth was as much a planet as Venus and Mars was. Suppose Copernicus had therefore said: "Modern science has all but wiped out the borderline between Earth and the other planets."

And suppose some geologist, instead of arguing the merits of the

[5] I still didn't like the book.

case, had chosen to attack Copernicus for threatening the existence of geology as a separate science, as though the advance of science must be stopped if it threatens to demolish the status of some scientist's specialized preserve.

Besides, it does not demolish the status of that preserve and does not affect what that scientist must view as his legal property rights. Even if Earth is but one more planet, geology remains a living science as the study of the particular planet, Earth. And even if life is but a specialized form of physics and chemistry, then biology remains a living science as the study of that particular form.

To worry about names and divisions, when knowledge itself is universal, argues a parochial mind that is incapable of seeing past the end of the nose (or perhaps not quite to the end, if the nose is a majestic one).

I defended my point of view in a brief, albeit caustic, letter, which *Science* was good enough to print. I did the same in far greater detail in an *F & SF* article named "Dethronement," which I wrote on June 29, 1961, and which eventually appeared in the December 1961 *F & SF*.

Getting my answers into print satisfied me, and I hold no further animus against Commoner, but I'm afraid I can never look upon him as a person of great intelligence.

Since "Dethronement" was in the nature of a specific attack on a specific man I was not interested in having it appear beyond the occasion for it. It is, therefore, one of exactly seven of my *F & SF* essays that I have never allowed in any of my collections.

16

David went off to camp on July 2, an eight-week camp, and not simply a day camp. He was not quite ten and it was our first real separation. It was not to a completely strange place we took him, however, but to Camp Annisquam, where we had spent vacations of our own. It had been converted under the same ownership, to a boys' camp, and we felt we could trust them to take care of David.

We received a postcard from him on July 5, and that, I think, was the first piece of mail he had ever had occasion to author. According to my diary, it "sounded fine and natural."

17

On July 6, 1961, I went to New York and stayed at the Stanhope Hotel, just across the street from the Metropolitan Museum of Art. It was the first time I had stayed there, and I rather liked it because it gave me a chance to visit the museum. I stayed at the Stanhope frequently thereafter.

I had lunch the next day with T. O'Conor Sloane III, a Doubleday editor whom I had not met before but whose name was not unfamiliar to me. He was the grandson and namesake of the man who had been editor of *Amazing* from 1929 to 1938.

Tom Sloane was interested in adding to a series of books of short biographies he was doing. Specifically, he wanted me to do a book of short biographies of 250 important scientists. It was something along the line of the series I had done for Eric Berger three years before but was to be much more extensive and was to be for adults.

The notion fascinated me and I agreed to do it.

18

On July 20, 1961, I obtained, for the first time, stationery that had my name and address imprinted on it. I've never been without such stationery since.

There was some uncertainty over the exact form of the letterhead. Should there be a Ph.D. after the name? Should there be raised lettering?

I held out for the plainest block printing available and with my name in lonely grandeur, making use of no title whatever. My point of view was that this was reverse pride. My name needed no adornment; it was enough in itself. I have held to that view ever since.

19

We took advantage of David's absence at camp to take a week off ourselves. We went to Birchtoft in New Hampshire on Sunday, July 23; we had been there a couple of times. This time we took Robyn with us.

Robyn, now six years old, was on her best behavior. She was unbelievably cute, with her blond hair in two pigtails, and was self-consciously adorable. She was the hit of the camp.[6]

It wasn't a bad time for us, either. One high point was a hayride on the evening of the twenty-fourth, during which I overcame, with difficulty, my fear that the horses might run away with us. (They were two old nags who had long ago lost any capacity—let alone will—to

---

[6] Robyn warns me that I am making myself sound like a silly, doting father, but my defense is that I *am* a silly, doting father.

gallop.) We engaged in community singing and I sang "If I Love You" with great éclat. I was in good baritone voice that evening and made the best of it. (I prefer my tenor voice myself, but my baritone is more impressive.)

We met a couple named Lucille and Matey Conrad, who were extremely compatible. Since they were at our table, we had an uproariously noisy time. In fact, when we went to see Shaw's *The Devil's Disciple* at a neighboring playhouse, the real high point was the drive there and back. I was at the wheel, but the hilarity in the car, particularly coming back, was so great that I was physically helpless half the time, and how I maneuvered the car over the country roads without killing everyone I can't imagine.

The twenty-sixth was, of course, our nineteenth wedding anniversary, and everyone made a fuss over it.

On Saturday night, there was a dance, with Robyn joining in and dancing very solemnly with a number of grown-ups, and the next day we left regretfully. It was the best vacation we had had since Chester's Zunbarg thirteen years before.

On the way home, we stopped off at Camp Annisquam and saw David for the first time in four weeks. He was delighted to see us and, of course, wanted to come home with us (par for the course in such cases), but we had to do the hardhearted thing and leave him there for four more weeks.

20

Still another new project turned up on August 8, 1961, when Roy Fisher of the World Book Encyclopedia visited me. The World Book people were going to start a yearbook and they wanted to have a staff of experts, each of whom was to review the year in their field. I, of course, was to review the year in science.

Each annual article was to be two thousand words long (or a little over that), and the pay was to be two thousand dollars. Payment of nearly a dollar a word was so stupendous a notion that I could think of no way of refusing.

I did, however, enter a firm caveat. I explained that I did not fly and that I did not like to travel; for instance, I wouldn't go to Chicago, where the World Book home office was located. What's more, I wouldn't do reportorial writing; I wouldn't interview; I wouldn't quote. All I did was to interpret results and explain concepts.

Fisher said he understood and that was all acceptable, so I was satisfied.

21

The next day, August 9, I took in *Words on the Map* to Houghton Mifflin, and, encouraged by Robyn's behavior at Birchtoft, I took her with me. We all ate at Marliave's, an Italian restaurant, and Robyn did not disappoint me. She was quite the little lady.

Soon afterward, there was another family meal. Stan and Ruth arrived with their children on August 15, and we all ate at Novak's, a central-European restaurant in Brookline that was one of our favorites. If the Olympian gods could have tasted their sauerbraten, they would have given up their ambrosia.

I remember once taking a guest to Novak's and then insisting that I do the ordering. A beautiful plate of sauerbraten and potato pancakes (with red cabbage on the side) was eventually placed before each of us.

I expected one taste and a cry of sudden ecstasy but, no, all I received was animated talk while first one mouthful and then another slid down the gullet. I was dreadfully disappointed for a few minutes, but then the guest skidded to a dead halt, stared at the plate and cried out, "What am I eating?" And from then on, there was delight.

Stan and Ruth liked it, too.

22

On one of my earlier visits to New York, Tim Seldes had told me that Doubleday had gotten a request for the Portuguese rights to the Foundation books. It wasn't surprising. By now, it was the general impression that Doubleday did all my science fiction. Gnome Press was so moribund, by this time, that no one thought of it in connection with anything.

Tim asked me whether he was to send the request to Gnome Press or give it to me.

I sighed and said, "I'll take it, but I'll just turn it down."

"Turn it down? Why?"

"Because I don't get money for my Gnome Press books. I haven't for years."

Tim looked surprised. "Does Gnome Press send you statements?"

"Erratically. Every couple of years I get one that I don't trust."

"In that case, Isaac, they've broken their contract. Get the books back from them."

"I can't do that, Tim. I'd have to sue and I can't sue Marty."

"You don't have to sue. If you'll agree to let Doubleday publish the books, we'll have our lawyers lean on Gnome Press."

"In that case," I said, "lean away."

And lean they did.

On August 18, 1961, I had lunch with Tim Seldes and Marty Greenberg. Marty was willing to give up the books in return for various minor financial items.

Tim Seldes wanted to make no concessions since Marty didn't really have any further rights to the books if we were willing to press our charge of contract violations. But that would take time and it seemed to me that the books were the thing. I wanted nothing held up for a couple of thousand dollars even if I had to pay them out of my own pocket.

So I said to Tim, in a private conversation afterward, "Take the books and run, Tim."

He did, and he wouldn't hear of my paying anything. From that time on, *Foundation, Foundation and Empire, Second Foundation,* and *I, Robot* were Doubleday volumes.

I was dreadfully grateful to Tim and also dreadfully nervous.

I said, "The cream has been taken off the book sales, Tim. You won't sell many now and I'm afraid Doubleday won't get back its investment. *Please* let me pay."

"Stop worrying, Isaac," said Tim. "We're going to make a lot of money out of these books."

How he could tell, I don't know, but they proved the best money-makers of any of my books.

Sometimes I stop to think of the money Marty could have made if he had made a real attempt to sell them, and had given me regular statements and paid me on time, so that I would write still more books for him. Other authors got their books away from him eventually, and almost each one of those books were classics in the field. Marty had been sitting on a gold mine and had not been aware of it. He went for the short-term pin money.

23

David's tenth birthday, on August 20, 1961, took place while he was still in camp. We called to make sure that they would observe it and have a birthday celebration for him. On August 27, his stint at the camp was over and we brought him home. He seemed in perfect health and spirits.

24

Not so Robyn a few days later, on September 1. Neighbors were enclosing a veranda and where eventually a thick, nonshattering pane of glass was to go, a thin and murderous pane of glass had been inserted. Robyn, of course, promptly decided to put her arm through it. We managed to get her to Newton-Wellesley Hospital, and eight stitches were required.

To this day it is difficult for me to think of it without writhing in sympathy pains. I am subject to them and when Robyn later discovered this, she thought it very peculiar and would show me off to her friends. She would wait till she decided I was unsuspecting and then she would come up with some miserable little friend of hers and suddenly produce the arm where the thin white scars and the needle marks are, to this day, faintly visible, and say, "Daddy, do you remember the time . . ."

And as soon as my face twists in agony and I begin to gasp, she turns to her friend and says, "See!"

Robyn knows the entire list of my eccentricities.

25

Oh well, down one day and up the next. The day after the stitches, the Abelard-Schuman statement arrived and, along with it, a check for fifty-six hundred dollars. That was the largest single check I ever received, larger even than any of my Doubleday statements. It was rather stupefying.

It brought my 1961 earnings to the neighborhood of the thirty-four thousand dollars I had set myself as a goal, since that had been my total earnings, writing and teaching, in the record year of 1958. Since there were still four months left to the year, I was bound to surpass the record by several thousand, so I knew I was going over the top, financially as well as professionally, in 1961.

It was about time. An overnight success I certainly was not. I had labored at my writing for twenty-three years and it was only now that I could think of myself as having made it, as being well-to-do.

Let me tell you I was delighted, and I worked happily on *The Human Body* over the Labor Day weekend.

26

The Human Body dealt with anatomy and physiology, subjects I had never taken in school. That raises a question I am often asked: "How can you write on subjects concerning which you are ignorant?"

I manage. There are encyclopedias, dictionaries, almanacs, textbooks, learned magazines, all sorts of reference materials—and I consult them.

Yet if I get my material out of other books—what do *I* contribute?

I remember once, when I was doing *Words of Science*, I was typing at school with Webster's Unabridged Dictionary before me. Matthew Derow, of the Department of Microbiology, came up behind me, watched as I leafed through the Unabridged, and finally said, "You're just copying the stuff out of the dictionary."

I said, "You're right. If you like, I'll give you the dictionary and you write the book. It's just copying, and then you can get the royalties."

He didn't take me up on it.

What I contribute to my books are (1) ease and clarity of style, (2) sensible and logical order of presentation, and (3) apt and original metaphors, analogies, and conclusions.

You don't copy any of that out of books, however many references are open before you as you type.

I am sometimes also asked, in connection with my books, whether I interview experts or solicit expert readings of my manuscripts.

The first of the two I never do. I consider it time-wasteful. Experts tend to maunder, hedge, and evade points. Besides which, there is invariably social interaction, which is totally wasteful as far as writing a book is concerned. I prefer to read in a few hours a book that an expert spent a few years writing (and would take a few years to explain, if I spoke to him).

Sometimes I do get expert readings, if I have a friend I can trust on the subject. Thus I had Harry Stubbs read *The Intelligent Man's Guide to Science* for me, and I asked Elizabeth Moyer to go over *The Human Body*.

In *The Human Body*, for instance, I had carelessly placed the spleen on the wrong side, and Elizabeth corrected that, of course, with great glee (along with a few other lesser points). She never let me forget it, either. Whenever she was feeling in exceptional spirits she would ask me to locate the spleen for her, and then tell anyone who was around that I had located it on the wrong side of the body in my book on anatomy.

I remember going to the Anatomy Department to pick up the manuscript after she was through with it, and another member of the department, John Ifft, asked me curiously if I were writing a book on anatomy. "Yes," I said, and he made no answer.

When I was leaving, however, I heard him say in a low voice that was undoubtedly not meant for my ears, "I'd bet he'd resent it if I wrote a book on biochemistry."

Svirsky, with his usual ability to disregard my feelings, sent each chapter of *The Intelligent Man's Guide to Science* to a different expert, without consulting me. I got some help in this way, but also a certain amount of annoyance.

In one chapter I discussed the matter of overpopulation and hoisted my usual warning signals of alarm. The "expert" who read that particular chapter actually had the incredible audacity-*cum*-ignorance to write in the margin, "I'd say this was God's problem, wouldn't you?"

It was the work of a moment to write underneath, "God helps those who help themselves" and to place an enormous STET over the entire passage. I was particularly watchful, come galleys time, to make sure the passage remained, too.

27

On September 7, 1961, in New York, Gertrude and I met with the Conrads (of our recent Birchtoft trip) and ate smorgasbord at the Stockholm Restaurant.

It is never wise for me to dine buffet style, for I invariably overeat. Never, though, did I overeat so badly as on that evening.

By the time I had had my helpings, and seconds, and thirds, and fourths, and had tried enough of each item to have stuffed an anaconda, I finally got down to an excellent chocolate layer cake and found, halfway through, that I could eat no more.

I stared numbly at the half I could not eat (never before or since have I been unable to eat cake) and my distress became so apparent that we all had to pay up and leave and then had to walk up and down the street until it seemed safe to do anything else.

If I have to pick one meal when I was at my most gluttonous, that was it. I don't enter this as an item of pride. I was, and still am, bitterly ashamed of that incident. Nevertheless, although I'm as careful as I can be in this autobiography to spare the feelings of others, I'm not here to spare my own.

And in any case, I learned a lesson. My weight at this time was 210 pounds. It was my peak. I didn't lose for quite a while, but I gained no more.

The next day I had a relatively abstemious lunch with Mac Talley, who had obtained tickets to *Camelot* for that night for Gertrude and myself.

28

I was in New York again on September 20, and again I had lunch with Mac Talley.

He now had the idea that I write an entire *Asimov Science Shelf*, introducing each of the various sciences in detail. He kept telling me that I was now in my forties and that was probably my peak productive decade and I should engage in a large project.

That made a rather depressing bit of sense to me. There was no way of seeing life as a whole without understanding that somewhere there was going to be a peak followed by a decline. And for the peak to come in the forties seemed reasonable.

I agreed to tackle the job and tried to reconcile myself to the downward slide that would soon be coming. It would be another and less happy version of the "over the top" I was experiencing in 1961.

16

Far over the Top

1

Tim Seldes had by now come to take the place, to some extent, that Brad had earlier had, and that, still earlier, Campbell had had. I suppose it must have been Campbell's imprinting in the first place, but I have the tendency to look upon editors as security figures and of having one editor as security-figure-in-chief.

Age had nothing to do with it. As I recall, Tim had, at one time, held a door open for me to pass through, and I shrank back. It seemed an inversion of values. The man of lesser importance held the door for the man of greater importance, and no one could possibly have been raised (professionally) by Campbell without having it firmly fixed in his head that the editor was more important than the writer.

So I said, "Don't hold the door for me, Tim. I'm not that important."

And he said, "Don't give yourself airs of humility, Asimov. My mother always taught me to hold the door open for older men."

I walked on through, but that was a horrible moment. *I was older than my editor.*

What further depths of degradation loomed ahead of the infant prodigy I once was. If I lived long enough I would become older than the President of the United States someday; older than the Pope; older than *anyone.*

Of course, I was only old in years, and I have never allowed myself to lose the innocent depravity of childhood.

Timothy was on the phone once when his secretary was out. When his other phone rang, Tim paused long enough to put his hand over the mouthpiece of the one he was talking into and said, "Make yourself useful, Asimov. Pick up that phone and keep it occupied till I can get to it."

So I picked up the phone and engaged in a very pleasant conversation with the person at the other end. It gradually grew more and more personal with regard to Tim himself. I was enjoying myself telling funny stories about Tim, who naturally grew more and more restless.

Finally, putting his hand over the mouthpiece again, he said, "Who the hell are you talking to, Asimov?"

I said, "Your sister, Marion. She says you were that way when you were little, too."

"Oh God," said Tim, tragically. He shouted into his phone, "I'll call you back in a few minutes." Then he wrested my phone from me and said, "Can't I trust you at all?"

His sister is, of course, an accomplished actress, and I said to Tim once, "Say, Tim, isn't your father Gilbert Seldes, the writer?"

"Yes," said Tim.

"And isn't your uncle George Seldes, the writer?"

"Yes," said Tim, growing a little suspicious.

"And isn't your sister Marion Seldes, the actress?"

"Yes," said Tim, now quite uneasy.

"Well, tell me, Tim," I said, innocently, "how does it feel to be the only member in the family not to have talent?"

Then I quickly put his secretary between us, as I knew he wouldn't hit her.

His secretary was Wendy Weil, and in a long series of editors' secretaries, she stands out in my mind. She was (and is, of course) six feet tall, very intelligent, and very sweet. Her figure is not a lush one, but if it were she would have been unsafe to allow in public. Men would have had to wear dark glasses to look at her.

She had a tendency toward a permanent slight stoop, partly because she had so often to talk to other women, all of whom were considerably shorter than she.

I noticed her once talking to another young woman who was a full twelve inches shorter than herself, and both were wearing rather similar costumes.

I came up and said, cheerfully, "Girls, you look like two separate species—you know, the Greater Rose-breasted Nuthatch and the Lesser Rose-breasted Nuthatch."

The short girl laughed, but Wendy only sighed. I suspect being the Greater Rose-breasted Nuthatch had its problems and that part of her tendency to stoop was to give the impression she was only five feet, eleven inches tall in order not to frighten away too many men.

She didn't frighten me, of course, which must have puzzled her, for she topped me by a good three inches. We were walking along the corridor at Doubleday, with myself being terribly gallant, when she said, "Doesn't it bother you that I'm taller than you, Isaac?"

I shrugged. "Only standing up," I said. "If we lie flat on our backs, I'm taller." Since I said that in my ordinary speaking voice, it was overheard, and the remark was repeated from end to end of Doubleday, and outside it as well, for all I know.

Wendy, of course, blushed. She was only twenty-one in 1961, and she turned a pretty pink at slight provocation, a sight that Tim was cruel enough to enjoy. At least, he never stepped in to protect her from my innocently depraved remarks.

"There is something," I once said to Tim, "so enticing and exotic about a Gentile girl."

"Like whom?" said Tim, setting up a land mine of his own.

"Like Wendy," I said, waving my arm at her with a grand gesture.

"Who," said Tim, with every evidence of satisfaction, "is Jewish."

"Jewish?" I said, stupefied.

"As the day is long."

"You mean my unattainable ideal is Jewish?" and I stared at Wendy open-mouthed.

I think Wendy dined out on that story for years, and she would remind me of it periodically. It seemed to make up for a lot.

Wendy did teach me an important lesson, though.

I always call my New York editors collect; or I did, in those days. I suppose everyone has some sort of chintzy little habit, and that was mine. I could never bring myself to make a long-distance call at my own expense.

I once called Tim because I happened to know it was his birthday, and I wanted to wish him a happy birthday.

Wendy answered, accepted the call on Tim's behalf, and said he'd be with me in a second.

"It's not important, Wendy," I said, cheerfully. "Don't bother him. I just wanted to wish him a happy birthday."

"You called him *collect*," said Wendy, scandalized, "to wish him a happy birthday?"

I could hear Tim in the background saying, "Who is it?" and Wendy said, "Isaac is calling you *collect* to wish you a happy birthday."

I heard him say, in the distance, "For God's sake, don't embarrass him." Then he got on the phone and talked pleasantly and amicably to me.

Of course I wasn't calling *Tim* collect. I was calling *Doubleday* collect. Even so, I had been brought face to face with my own cheapness and I was embarrassed, so the next time I saw Tim in New York, I apologized.

And he said, "Listen, Asimov" (he always called me by my last name in a sort of mock-hectoring manner), "we have authors who cou in drunk and have to be dried out. We have authors who come in crying because they have writers' block and we have to soothe them. We have authors who are out of plots and we have to supply one. We have authors who have agents who drive us up the wall. We have authors who can't write very well so that we have to spend weeks editing their books into something readable. You don't give us *any* of those troubles. All you want to do is kiss the girls and make collect calls. You're welcome to that, Asimov."

Just the same, from that moment on, I began to wean myself away from collect calls and, eventually, I never called a friend or an editor[1] collect again.

2

I had a tendency to turn to my editors for advice outside the field of writing, too.

For instance, I never knew what to do with money except to put it in the bank. Neither my parents nor anyone I knew in my younger years had so much money as to make a bank account an embarrassment. By now, however, I had some seventy thousand dollars in the bank, and all it was doing was making me a few thousand dollars in interest per year, most of which was taxed away by the government.

My accountant said I should invest it, and I knew that, but how?

I was told to get a broker, and I knew that, too, but who?

I asked various people if they could recommend a broker, and among others I asked Tim. He recommended two young men he was using as brokers who had made him considerable money. I took his advice (I had to take someone's advice, and he was my security-figure-in-chief), and on September 22, 1961, I went down to Wall Street and actually interviewed these brokers.

Eventually, I gave them ten thousand dollars to invest for me, and it took them only a few years to change that into about sixty-five hundred dollars.

3

Meanwhile, I was writing an experimental science biography for Tom Sloane. I chose as my subject (almost at random) U. J. J. Leverier, the nineteenth-century French astronomer. Tom approved and the book was under way.

[1] Actually, my editors are my friends.

4

On September 30, we bought a new TV set, one equipped with remote controls. It was a much better set than the old one, which had broken down frequently.

Nevertheless, the old one still worked. We put it down in the basement primarily for the use of the children, and we were now a two-TV family as well as a two-automobile family. We were taking on all the appurtenances of suburban living.

5

The New York *Times Sunday Magazine* asked me to do an article on science-fiction conventions, and I did one and mailed it to them on October 2—and they rejected it.

That was my first attempt for them, and I managed to get something out of it by writing a second and more serious article on science fiction, which they took and published in their November 19, 1961, issue under the very irritating title of "Fact Catches Up with Fiction."

Nevertheless, that didn't make things easier for me with the *Sunday Magazine* thereafter. They request an article now and then, but they reject at least as many as they accept, so that my batting average is under .500.

I wish I could say that this was the worst score I've ever made. It isn't. *Cosmopolitan* has asked me twice for an article; twice I've obliged; twice I've been rejected. Batting average, .000.

The loss is not total. I can generally sell a rejection elsewhere or cannibalize it into another article. In fact, I even welcome an occasional rejection (a *very* occasional rejection) because it makes the game more interesting.

6

My biography—a very small one—came to be written for the first time.

Sam Moskowitz was writing a series of articles for *Amazing* that consisted of biographies of various science-fiction writers of the past and present and, eventually, running out of everyone else, he came to me.

On October 17, Chris Moskowitz came to interview me on husband Sam's behalf, and I did my best to give her all the statistical material she needed. Sam himself interviewed my brother, Stanley, and I don't know who else.

The biography, about the length of a short story, eventually appeared in the April 1962 *Amazing* under the title (*his*, for heaven's sake, not mine) "Isaac Asimov: Genius in the Candy Store."

It had some mistakes, the worst of which was making Campbell rather than Tremaine express the opinion that people who sold stories free to Wollheim ought to be blacklisted. This was corrected when the article appeared in a collection of Sam's biographies, published under the title "Seekers of Tomorrow."

I think that was the first time I was called a "genius" in print, but not the last time.

Even before Sam used the term, however, I'd grown tired of it. I'd already been asked, often enough, "How does it feel to be a genius?" or, more bluntly, "Are you a genius?," or, more hostilely, "What makes you think you're a genius?"

The fact is that I've never called myself a genius, and I think the term has been cheapened by overuse into meaninglessness. If other people want to call me that, that's their problem. I myself shoot for other more meaningful and more significant goals: like being the best science-fiction writer/science writer/public speaker in the world. That is good enough for me.

7

On October 20, 1961, I met Cliff Simak, face to face, for the first time. I had been corresponding with him, on and off, for twenty-three years, but our paths had never before actually crossed.

I was no longer an eighteen-year-old would-be writer, and he was no longer a father figure of nearly twice my age. The alchemy of time had converted me into a forty-one-year-old member of an aging establishment and very nearly Cliff's contemporary. It was a delightful lunch; we kept pausing to stare at each other as though we had never been truly certain that the other existed.

8

Something new was brewing. According to Bob Mills, it started with Avram Davidson. Avram, not averse to earning some badly needed cash, bent his mind to thoughts of some anthology that would, of necessity, include a story of his. It occurred to him, therefore, that what was needed was an anthology of those short pieces that had won Hugos.[2] One of the stories that would then be included would be "Or All the Seas with Oysters" from the May 1958 *Galaxy*. It had won the Hugo for best short story at the sixteenth World Science Fiction convention, held in Los Angeles in 1958.

Bob Mills thought it was a good idea and discussed it with Tim Seldes, who was willing to accept and publish such an anthology. The question arose as to who should be editor. It occurred to one of them that it had better be a name that was as well known as possible, but also one who had never himself won a Hugo so that the book would not seem self-serving. I seemed a natural possibility, and on October 31, 1961, I got a letter from Bob suggesting the notion.

That struck me as a good idea, because I had never done an anthology and I thought it would be fun to try. What had always held me back from offering to do one was my reluctance to choose the stories myself. I wasn't certain of the value of my judgment. Here, however, was my chance to do an anthology in which I did not have to choose the stories. The stories were already chosen. All I would have to do would be to take care of some mechanical problems, such as obtaining tear sheets and permissions, and to write an Introduction.

But then another problem arose. The number of my books had now become an issue with me, and I wanted to be able to list the anthology as part of the corpus of my works. Could I do that if the book consisted simply of nine stories written by other people? If I myself had chosen the stories, I could do it; the fact that the stories were my choice would place a personal impress on the book that would justify my calling it mine.

But the stories were already chosen, and if I had neither written nor chosen the stories, how could I have the face to call the book mine?

It occurred to me, therefore, to make the Introductions both to each individual story and to the collection as a whole, very highly individual. It would then be an anthology that no one else but myself could have put together in just that way, and it would be my book.

I made up my mind that in each Introduction I was not to deal with the story at all. After all, why describe the story when it was there to be read, and why praise it when the Hugo award was automatic praise? Instead, I would deal with the author, and I would make it funny. And I would make the over-all Introduction funny, too; if I could, of course.

---

[2] Beginning with the thirteenth convention at Cleveland in 1955—the one at which I had been guest of honor—the Hugo awards had become the feature and high point of every convention.

And since the reason I was chosen was because I had never won a Hugo, I decided to make that the point of the humor. I would complain bitterly throughout the book about never having won a Hugo.

And, after all, if I complained loud enough and long enough, someone was bound to give me a Hugo for *something,* if only to shut me up.

Naturally, I said nothing of this to Tim Seldes or Bob Mills in advance.

9

Still another new project came up on November 4. I received a letter from a firm based in Los Angeles asking me to write a short science-fiction piece that would run as part of an advertisement.

They stressed that the advertisement would appear only in outlets of high prestige such as *Scientific American* and *Fortune.* They also assured me that although they wanted the piece to deal with communications, since the advertisers specialized in communications devices, the story would not be expected to tie in to the advertisement in any way.

Finally, they were offering $250 for a story that would be 1,200 words long. That meant $.20 a word, which was five times the rate a science-fiction magazine could pay me.

I was tempted and agreed to do it. The firm ran a series of six advertisements, and two of them included a story of mine. The first, which appeared in the February 1962 *Scientific American,* was in the second advertisement of the series and was called "My Son, the Physicist."[3] The second story, which appeared in the sixth advertisement of the series in the October 1962 *Scientific American,* was "Starlight."[4]

10

On November 7, 1961, I received my royalty check from Basic Books. In the previous statement, half a year before, my $1,500 advance had been paid off and there had been a little money left over. But now the bulk of the sales had been made, including lump sums from several small book clubs, and I found myself staring at a check for $27,600.

It was five times larger than any check I had ever before held. It was in itself very nearly as large as all I had made in the previous year.

[3] See *Nightfall and Other Stories.*
[4] See *Asimov's Mysteries.*

It was four times as large, all by itself, as the annual salary that Keefer felt the med school could not afford to pay a science writer.

I was glad my parents were alive to see the day, for it was a world away from that first check I had received twenty-three years ago, the one that was for $64 and had seemed so large.

Yet it had its sad side.

It was a unique check that could not possibly be repeated, it seemed to me, unless I happened to write another book like *The Intelligent Man's Guide to Science*; one that was at once as highly priced and as highly regarded, and that didn't seem very likely to me. What's more, it came at the end of a year that, even before the check arrived, was already setting a record for me.

This meant I was going to end the year with an impossibly high sum of money and that there would be no way of duplicating it ever again. The year 1961 would *have* to be my top money-making year and I was only forty-one and I wasn't ready to have my top year yet. I didn't want to spend thirty years or so (assuming I lived out a normal life-span) looking back on that one miracle year.

So I was sorry. I never wanted sudden fame, sudden wealth, sudden windfalls. What I had always wanted, and what I had so far always gotten, was a gradual increase, a little more each year, so that I would never have to feel that I was living in the anticlimax period of my life.

But there it was, so I eventually put it in the bank. And even that check didn't make me like *The Intelligent Man's Guide to Science* any better.

11

I had lunch with Bob Mills in New York on November 13. He was planning to leave *F & SF* and open a literary agency. I was sorry. I had done about forty *F & SF* essays by then and the exchanges between "the Kindly Editor" and "the Good Doctor" had become a pleasant fixture. No matter who replaced him I didn't feel that I could do "the Kindly Editor" bit ever again.

I then delivered a talk at the New York Public Library. It had been arranged through Houghton Mifflin and Mary K. Harmon was in New York for the occasion.

Mary K. (as she was always called) was a new member of the juvenile department and I was going to work more and more with her as Austin moved up to positions of higher responsibility. Mary K. was one of the most pleasant and cheerful women I have ever met. Never, in years and years of association, was there a cross word between us, or even a neutral word. All the words were cheerful, pleasant, and happy, whether in her office, or having any of innumerable lunches at Locke-Ober's.

Locke-Ober's had a room downstairs in which only men were allowed. (I don't know if that's still true in these days of women's liberation, but it was true then.) I sometimes ate downstairs when my lunches were with Austin, but I much preferred it upstairs with Mary K. or with Austin or with both.

12

Two days after I got back from New York on that occasion, I was feeling incredibly lousy, rotten enough to be unable to hide it. Gertrude wanted to take my temperature, but I fended her off until I had finished an article and driven to the post office to mail it. I promised that as soon as I got back I would let her take my temperature.

The article was "Blood Will Tell" and it was meant for the IBM house magazine *Think*, which was offering me five hundred dollars for twenty-five hundred words. I was already routinely requesting a ten-cent-a-word minimum for any article I did outside the science-fiction magazines, and often got more than that—twenty cents in this case.

Gertrude did take my temperature when I returned and it proved to be 101° and I was kicked right into bed.[5]

The next morning my temperature was normal and, bounding out of bed, I somehow managed to wrench my back, found myself (for the first time in my life) hobbling about with a bent sacroiliac, and got right back into bed.

Fortunately my back improved greatly by the next day, but from that time on, I have taken to pampering it. I began to favor harder and harder mattresses.

I remember once when Robert Silverberg wanted to make a telephone call in my place and I directed him to the phone in the bedroom. He dropped down on the bed, looked pained, and said, "Who has the bad back?"

I said, "No one, precisely because that's what we sleep on."

So my sacroiliac is fine and never gives me any particular trouble.

[5] I would have been very pleased if *Think* had taken the piece and if I could have told myself that even a fever did not affect my writing skill. Unfortunately, they sent it back for revision. After revision, however, they took it, and it eventually appeared in the April 1962 *Think*. See *Is Anyone There?*

13

One of my early *F & SF* essays, which appeared in the October 1959 issue, was "The Height of Up."[6] In it, I attempted to discuss what the maximum possible temperature might be. I don't consider it one of my better essays.

Nevertheless, a young graduate physicist at Princeton, Hong Yee-chiu, sent me a letter, which I received on November 22, 1961, telling me that reading that essay had changed the direction of his research. He began to consider what the maximum temperature might be in the world of actual phenomena—at the center of exploding supernovae, for instance—and in the process worked out a theory of neutrino formation at very high temperatures that could be a legitimate explanation for the mechanics of stellar collapse.[7]

It is difficult to describe how pleased I was at this. I suppose that anyone going into the sciences dreams of making a major discovery or of evolving a major theory someday, but that can only happen to a very few and there comes a time in almost every scientist's life when he is forced, more or less reluctantly, to let go of that dream.

I had had to let go quite early in the game. My ineptitude in the laboratory meant I was not likely to make major experimental discoveries, and I lacked the patience to see some theory safely through all its difficulties. Fortunately, by the time I let go I was succeeding in my writing career, so that the trauma was minimal.

Nevertheless, there remained the secondary dream of the teacher: If I could not accomplish great deeds in science, I might yet inspire them. Hong Yee-chiu was an example and I was so grateful that he had taken the trouble to write and tell me of what he had done.

14

It was about now, by the way, that Avram Davidson replaced Bob Mills as editor of *F & SF*. Avram was a perfectly good editor, but he and I were never as close as Bob and I had been.

I asked Avram if he wanted the essays to continue, and was quite ready to appeal over his head to Joe Ferman if Avram said "No," but he said "Yes." He also indicated that he would not welcome any continuation of the "Kindly Editor" bit, which suited me, since I had already intended to drop it.

[6] See *View from a Height* (Doubleday, 1963).
[7] Hong Yee-chiu, in after years, was the first person to make use of the term "quasar" as a shortened version of "quasistellar source."

It did seem to me that Avram's blurbs for my articles were too esoteric and, on occasion, too barbed for my tastes, and eventually I managed to persuade the magazine that my essays had become too well known a series to require individual blurbs and, rather to my relief, they were dropped permanently.

15

At the beginning of December I finally got around to writing my science review of the year for the World Book Year Book. That wasn't dilatoriness on my part. I deliberately waited in case there were any last-minute developments. I mailed it to Chicago on December 4, and eventually received word that it was satisfactory.

That same day, however, there was something that was less satisfactory. I received a letter from Roy Fisher suggesting that the editorial board get together at some mountain resort in West Virginia, on May 1 and 2 next, all expenses paid, two hundred dollars per diem, wives invited.

I was outraged. I had *explained* I didn't travel, but Gertrude was quite excited about it and wanted to go, so I rather grumblingly agreed to do it.

I consoled myself by working madly on my science biographies. I already had a notion that it was going to end up by being more than the 250 biographies that Tom Sloane had asked for, since I was writing up everyone I could think of, and each scientist suggested several others to my fevered mind. As is usual in such cases, however, I let the book find its own length (as I am doing with this book, for instance) and meant to worry about unpleasantness with editors later.

16

On December 6, I took the bus to New York and handed in the manuscript of *The Human Body* to Mac Talley. On that same day, I took the train to Baltimore, for I was slated to give a talk at Johns Hopkins on the morning of the eighth, one which, according to my diary, "brought down the house."

I had lunch that day at the Faculty Club with William McElroy and Al Nason. McElroy had been the biochemist who, back in 1948, had hired Nason and had turned me down. McElroy had never heard of me then, but the thirteen-year interval had educated him with respect to me, I was glad to see.

I am not immune to small-mindedness, so I'm afraid I felt an inner triumph that there was no way in which McElroy could hire me for *anything*, for he could not pay me enough. In fact, for this year anyway (the unique year of 1961), I was quite certain I was making more than he was—and Johns Hopkins paid me two hundred dollars for the talk, too.

17

It was now that I first heard of "Mensa." This was an organization that began in England and was supposed to include the top 2 per cent of the world's intellectuals (or that fraction of them who applied for entrance), as judged by their passing an IQ test with a sufficiently high figure.

I was invited to attend a meeting of Mensans by a woman named Gloria Saltzberg, in Waltham, who was hosting it. On December 15, I drove to her house and found, a little to my shock, that she was confined to a wheelchair.

She had been a victim of the 1955 polio epidemic, six years before, the one that had come just before the Salk vaccine was put on the market and, therefore, the one that might well be considered the last one. Yet despite this horrible misadventure, which might well have left her with an everlasting grudge against the universe, Gloria was cheerful and sweet.

We have been good friends ever since, and I never heard her repine against her fate even once. She busied herself about the house, with her handsome husband, Bill, and with three attractive daughters, and managed a full social life as well. I was mightily impressed by her. She spoke with a Boston accent as thick as my Brooklyn one, so that a Midwesterner would probably have found the sounds of our conversation amusing indeed.

To my surprise, Dr. Lewis, our children's pediatrician, walked in. (He was a good pediatrician, always quiet and calm, which, more than any medicine, is an appropriate antidote for panicky parents.)

"It's my pediatrician," I said, in blank surprise.

"Really?" said Gloria.

"Of course," I said, "I'll prove it. Dr. Lewis, say, 'There's a virus going around' for these nice people."

Dr. Lewis smiled patiently. He was used to my eccentric teasing and knew that, except when the children were at their worst and I was at my most anxious, I could always be counted on to make virus jokes.

18

On December 18, 1961, according to the New York *Times* obituary column, Professor John Lyon, of my undergraduate and graduate classes in literature, died at the age of eighty-three. I remembered his kindness to me and was sorry that in the quarter century that had passed I had never thought to write and tell him so.

It didn't help. I continue to allow people to die without my having told them what their lives have meant to mine.

19

On December 22, 1961, I sent $501 to Marty Greenberg as a final payment in settlement of our agreement, and I was through with him, literarily, forever. I saw him once or twice after that, more or less unexpectedly and by accident, and was always friendly, but our twelve-year relationship was over.

20

On December 29, we visited the Elliot Strausses (he had been a boon companion of John Blugerman in his bachelor days), and I remember one incident very clearly. I was in one room, doing something or other, and Gertrude was in the other room where, as I learned afterward, she had taken an extreme dislike to a foolish, nasal woman who had put on a world-weary pose and apparently got away with it.

Eventually I wandered into Gertrude's room and, feeling bored and irritable, I sat down in the chair next to the foolish girl, a chair that was empty precisely because no one would sit there.

Whereupon she promptly turned to me and said, "Well, here's a new one. Suppose you justify your existence to me."

And because she had caught me out of sorts, I turned upon her and said, "As the more intelligent of the two of us, I prefer to have you justify yours to me, if you can do so without boring me too badly."

Everyone laughed and she tried, rather gamely, to recover, but I was annoyed and wouldn't let her, forcing her to appeal to her husband, who smiled and said (perhaps in secret delight), "You're out of your league, honey."

What made it memorable, then, was that Gertrude approached me and hissed fiercely in my ear, "I love you." Gertrude was not a demon-

strative woman and she didn't often tell me such things of her own vo-
lition.

21

I celebrated the end of the year by taking David and Robyn to
some local ice-skating rink.

When young I had learned to roller-skate (with some difficulty)
but had never had the occasion to ice-skate. Nor had I longed for the
experience either, and as I grew older, my lust for new athletic experiences, never very great, had diminished to a clear zero.

I was always willing to have the children try it, however, and
David was eager.

I therefore rented ice skates for both of them and helped put them
on (or, more accurately, helped get someone to help put them on, for I
hadn't the faintest idea myself of how to go about it).

I then helped David out onto the ice while I remained off the rink
myself. He shuffled along, holding onto the railing, and I told him to
keep it up and he would get the idea and hoped earnestly that some
stranger would volunteer some elementary instruction.

I then turned to find Robyn and see if I could get her to take a
few tentative slides. For a moment I couldn't find her and became
panicky, and then I spied her out in the middle of the rink, skating.
She was doing it very amateurishly, of course, but she was on her feet
and quite obviously enjoying herself.

Eventually, we saw to it that Robyn had skating lessons, and she
loved them.

22

And so 1961 came to an end and I found it had been a disappointing literary year in one respect. I had published only two books:

41. *Words from the Myths* (Houghton Mifflin)
42. *Realm of Algebra* (Houghton Mifflin)

Not since 1953 had I published so few books in one year. It was
the first year in eight that I had no books with Abelard-Schuman, but
that didn't bother me. I did not particularly expect more books with
that publisher.

It was also the second year in a row in which I had no Doubleday
books, and that, too, didn't bother me, for *Life and Energy* was due for

publication in a matter of weeks and I had two other books in press with them.

Besides, the question of how many books were published was completely buried under the amazing record of my 1961 income.

For 1961, I had achieved the completely unbelievable total writing income of just over sixty-nine thousand dollars. I had known ever since midyear that 1961 was my year for going over the top, but not till the Basic Books royalty check had come in did I realize how *far* over the top I would go.

My income was twice what I had made in my previous record year of 1958 and was well over ten times my top salary at the med school. I enjoyed it even though I was certain I would never approach this figure again.

17

A Multiplicity of Books

1

I turned 42 on January 2, 1962, and scarcely even noticed the fact as I continued to work on my science biographies and as, each week, it seemed to me that I was going to exceed my allotted number of 250 biographies and my allotted wordage of 150,000 by a greater and greater amount.

I had a bad cold at this time, the worst in at least ten years, and it made me irritable.

Bob Mills had sent me a letter suggesting terms for the anthology of Hugo winners (which I intended to call *The Hugo Winners*) in his new capacity as literary agent, and I thought they were outrageous.

I visited him in his office on January 5, snuffling with my cold and too miserable to pay any attention to the fact that he had someone (whom I didn't know) in the office with him.

I said, "Bob, I'm not well, and I'm in no condition to argue. So let's put it this way." And I held up his letter, tore it into four parts, threw it in the waste basket, and got up to leave.

He stopped me and asked what I wanted. I said, balefully, "The standard Doubleday contract. I get half, the authors get half, prorated for each according to length of story, and you get 10 per cent agent's fee of my half."

That's the way it was, too.

The final terms, however, were not so favorable after all. *The Hugo Winners* turned out to be a perennial seller. Twice a year I've got to isolate its earnings from my Doubleday statement, do the necessary prorating, and send checks to authors and agents.

That is the usual task of the anthologist and I shouldn't complain, but I'm not primarily an anthologist and I have better ways of spending my time. Fortunately, Doubleday agrees with me in this and in all future anthologies I have edited, I always made sure that only my own share of the money comes directly to me and that someone else does the necessary calculations and mailings for the other people concerned.

2

With the contract for *The Hugo Winners* settled, I began, on January 11, to write the Introduction. For that, I cannibalized the article that had been rejected by the New York *Times Sunday Magazine*, making it funnier and more personal.

What I wrote, in fact, represented a complete break with any of the Introductions I had seen in any previous science-fiction anthology. Previous Introductions had been scholarly and dignified, as though the anthologists were nervously trying to justify the existence of science fiction. Mine read more as though I were clowning about at a science-fiction convention.

I had started doing this sort of thing with the humorous autobiographical Introductions to my *F & SF* essays, but this carried matters a step farther. I was not certain I could get it past Tim Seldes, but I intended to try.

3

I was slated to speak at Philadelphia on January 25 to a branch of the American Chemical Society, and it was to be formal. I was going to need a tuxedo.

I have never been known as a natty dresser and I knew nothing about tuxedos. Such was my ignorance, in fact, that once when I was invited to speak at some function and the invitation had said "black tie" I had innocently put on a black bow tie and let it go at that.

After the talk was over, Gertrude, who had been with me, asked me, curiously, "Did you notice that you were the only person at the head table who wasn't in a tuxedo?"

"No," I said, blankly. "Were they wearing tuxedos?"

"I thought so," said Gertrude.

Talking at Philadelphia, however, was like showing off before the hometown boys. I had never forgotten my essential failure at the Navy Yard, and J. Hartley Bowen, my old grandboss, was going to be there. I gathered that by now he was very proud of having been my old grandboss, and I wanted to give him further reasons for pride—so I arranged, on January 11, to rent a tuxedo.

4

My copies of *Life and Energy* finally arrived on January 15, 1962, and I greeted them with great jubilation. It was just three years and five days since my last Doubleday book, *Nine Tomorrows,* and in the interval I had published thirteen non-Doubleday books.

What a relief it was! Doubleday had been the first to publish one of my books and, with all possible respect to my other publishers (particularly Houghton Mifflin), I always thought of Doubleday as my prime publisher, and I was glad to be back with them.[1]

5

I took the complete manuscript of *The Hugo Winners*—the tear sheets of all nine stories and all the Introductions—to Doubleday on January 24.

"Glad to see you've got the stuff, Asimov," said Tim, mock-gruffly, and held out his hand for the material.

"Wait a while, Tim. I want to explain about the Introduction."

"What's to explain?"

"It's sort of personal."

"How do you mean personal?"

I evaded the clutching fingers of both Tim and Wendy and said, "Let me read it to you," and began:

"Let me introduce this book my own way, please; by which I mean I will begin by introducing myself.

"I am Isaac Asimov and I am an old-timer.

"Not you understand that I am (ha, ha) really old. Quite the contrary. I am rather young, actually, being only mumblety-mumble years old, and looking even younger."

By this time, Wendy had caught her breath and said, "You're making it up. You didn't write that."

I lifted my eyebrows. "Of course I wrote that. What's wrong with it?"

She looked over my shoulder and said, "He *did* write it, Tim."

Tim held out a magisterial hand and said, "Let me see that junk, Asimov."

I handed it over. He read the Introduction where, near the end, a passage went as follows:

"The person qualifying as editor for such an anthology would naturally have to be someone who had not himself received a Hugo, so that he could approach the job with the proper detachment. At the

---

[1] Of course, in the interim, they had obtained the four Gnome Press books, which meant that Doubleday had published twenty of my books out of a total of, up to that point, forty-three.

same time, he would have to be a person of note, sane and rational, fearless and intrepid, witty and forceful, and, above all, devilishly handsome.

"All this was pointed out to Mr. Timothy Seldes at Doubleday & Company, and that fine gentleman agreed in every particular. Once again, the stringent requirements for the post seemed to cut down the possibilities to a single individual and I accepted with that lovable modesty that suits me so well.

"And so here I have my revenge. If those wiseguys, herein included among the authors, had not been so eager to grab at the Hugos, but had modestly held back the way I did, *they* might have edited this anthology.

"I hope they have learned their lesson."

Tim read through the entire Introduction and said, "Asimov, this is all very well at a science-fiction convention, but what about the people in Dubuque?"

"The people in Dubuque," I said, assuming a confidence I was very far from feeling, "will love it. They will feel themselves inside the world of science fiction."

"I'll think about it," said Tim.

He did and, fortunately, ended on my side. The book was eventually published *exactly* as I had prepared it, and the gamble paid off.

I have lost count of the number of people who have written to tell me they enjoyed the Introductions as much as they did the stories (some said they enjoyed them more). Youngsters who were unborn when I wrote that Introduction will write letters to me that begin:

"Since you are well known to be a person of note, sane and rational, fearless and intrepid, witty and forceful, and, above all, devilishly handsome, I wonder if you . . ."

The Hugo Winners began my custom of intricate Introductions for all my story collections whether they were anthologizations of stories of others, or collections of stories of my own. *Nine Tomorrows* was the last collection I ever presented bare.

It also made it possible for other authors to produce anthologies or collections with elaborate and/or autobiographical introductions. Often this habit is traced back to Harlan Ellison's *Dangerous Visions*, and on at least one occasion some illiterate reviewer even spoke of me as following Harlan's example.

The fact is, however, that *The Hugo Winners* antedated *Dangerous Visions* by five years, and I refuse to give up my prior claim, not even to Harlan, whom I love dearly.

6

The next day, January 25, I went down to Philadelphia and gave my talk in my rented tuxedo, the first time I had ever worn one.

In the course of the talk, I told the story of my preparation of the specification on seam-sealing compounds eighteen years before and of my deliberate attempt to make it impossibly complicated. Hartley Bowen was in the audience and he loved the story. Thereafter, whenever I gave a talk in the Philadelphia area and he knew he was going to attend, he would urge me to tell the story.

Sprague and Catherine de Camp showed up for the talk and I spent some delightful hours with them afterward. Catherine seemed scarcely to have aged.

7

Mac Talley hired Anthony Ravielli to do the illustrations for *The Human Body*. I saw samples of his work and was delighted. He was expensive, to be sure, and part of the expense was to come out of my royalties, but he was clearly worth it. Ravielli's excellent drawings, which were both anatomically correct and artistically attractive, set off the book admirably.

In fact, I was so pleased at the news that, having received it on January 29, I got to work on *The Human Brain* on February 5.

If I expected this book to be a repeat of the earlier one, as far as enjoyment was concerned, I was wrong. I began with the hormones, which I could manage well enough, but once into the nervous system itself, I found myself working very near my capacity to understand. *The Human Brain* proved to be one of the hardest books I've ever had to write.

8

Before starting *The Human Brain*, however, I did something else. For Collier Books, I wrote a small science-fiction story intended for the 6-to-7-year-old.

For a brief period of time in the early 1960s, Collier Books was putting out large numbers of paperback editions, including some of my Abelard-Schuman books. I met Richard Cecil, who was in charge, and he was a tall, enthusiastic fellow who was convinced that a great deal could be done if a firm really put out paperbacks in quantity.

One of his plans was to put out a series of little books of about two thousand to three thousand words in length for the beginning reader. It was to have a limited vocabulary and I was to do the science-fiction story as part of the series. I wrote it on February 1, 1962, and called it *The Best New Thing.* (I tested it by having Robyn, who was going to be seven that month, read it, and she seemed fascinated.)

There was a pattern that I was following more and more, by the way. I had no concern about finishing one book before beginning another.

Although I had barely started *The Human Brain,* for instance, I was pushed off in another direction once my copies of *Words in Genesis* appeared on February 8. I at once began *Words from the Exodus,* in which I took the second, third, fourth, and fifth books of the Bible as my source material. And all the time I continued writing biographies for Tom Sloane.

The multiplicity of tasks didn't confuse me. I switched from book to book freely and never allowed myself to get tired of any one of them. It became not unusual for me to have as many as five or six books going in one stage or another, while writing shorter pieces in between.

It was the juggler's rhythm and I loved it.

9

We had a party for Robyn's seventh birthday on February 19, and I celebrated, if that's the word I want, by driving my car to school through a snowstorm (I was giving a small class on library use at the med school) and managed to scratch and dent my car slightly trying to park in an icy parking lot.[2] Robyn had her party, however.

10

Ever since I had visited Gloria Saltzberg two months before, she had been urging me to join Mensa. I didn't object to that. I liked Gloria and I liked the members I had met. I did object to the IQ tests, however.

In the first place, I don't really believe in IQ tests; I don't think they prove very much. Second, I felt that considering my accomplishments, my intelligence might well be taken for granted and that an IQ test was superfluous.

Gloria, on the other hand, said that passing the test was a neces-

[2] The next day, John H. Glenn orbited the Earth three times as the first American astronaut in orbit, and he didn't dent *his* vehicle.

sary formality, and why should I hang back? Surely, if *she* had passed it, I could do it standing on my head.

On thinking it over, I decided that my real hangup was the possibility of failure. I was afraid of the humiliation of turning out to be not bright enough for Mensa. Since it was also humiliating to be hanging back out of fear of failure, I applied for entrance to Mensa.

I received my copy of the test soon enough and, on the evening of February 27, 1962, went to Gloria's, opened it there, and, under her supervision, took the test.

It was *not* an easy test, and certainly no pushover. I did make it, though. The score, which I received on March 10, gave me an indicated IQ of 161, whatever that means, and thereafter I was a member of Mensa.

11

Gertrude went to New York on her own on March 13, leaving me behind with the children, and this time I was determined to have no teeth knocked out. I never let the children out of my sight.

When Gertrude got back on March 16, she was in a state of delight. She had had perfect weather. She had had a good time. And she had made a daring purchase of nothing less than a mink stole, which had set us back six hundred dollars.

It didn't bother me, since we had the money. I was delighted, in fact, that Gertrude reached that state of trust in my earning power to buy the stole even without consulting me. Between that stole and my own renting of a tuxedo, we were edging up into the middle-middle class.

12

My advance copy of *Fact and Fancy* had come through on March 9. It was my second collection of science essays (*Only a Trillion* had been the first), but the first collection of my continuing series of *F & SF* essays.

Naturally, I promptly put together a second collection of seventeen *F & SF* essays, which I entitled *View from a Height*.

On March 30, I visited Walter Bradbury at Harper's. He looked in much better shape than he had when I had last seen him at Holt, and he suggested a book on the genetic code. This was much in the news now. Ever since Watson and Crick had worked out the double-helix structure of the nucleic-acid molecule, geneticists had been successfully working out the detailed chemistry of the mechanism of inheritance.

Mac Talley had already suggested a book on the subject, and I had turned down the suggestion on the ground that news was breaking so quickly in that subject that I would be out of date before I was finished. A second, independent suggestion, however, set me to thinking.

One of the virtues of *The Wellsprings of Life*, after all, had been that I was able to bring *The Chemicals of Life* (in which I hadn't even mentioned nucleic acids) up to date.

Now if I did a book on the genetic code, I could bring *The Wellsprings of Life* up to date, for its last chapter, on nucleic acids, was now woefully inadequate.

So I told Brad I would do it, but I also told him that Mac had suggested it first and that he would have to have the paperback refusal. Brad agreed to that. Eventually I called Mac and said I would do the book on the genetic code, and I was all set.

13

Another task that was in the works involved Cliff Simak. He had been put in charge of a science page at his newspaper, and it was his intention to get series of four to six articles on particular subjects written by those of his science-fiction colleagues who had scientific credentials —myself, Willy Ley, Robert Silverberg, and so on. As long as Simak was running the page, I wrote article series whenever he asked me to (they amounted to seven altogether, one a year between 1962 and 1968). When Simak retired, so did I—from that task.

14

I had an unusual experience on April 7, 1962. The University of Omaha had asked me to lecture for them, and before I had a chance to refuse out of hand, they explained they meant a lecture by phone.

The phone company would set up a loudspeaker arrangement; I was to keep my phone open at a particular time; I was to be there waiting; they would call; I would give my lecture, be able to hear audience response, be able to answer questions, and so on.

It was an intriguing notion and it occurred to me that I might make my influence felt anywhere in the nation without having to travel a step or, for that matter, without having to do more than sit in my easy chair in my underwear.

On April 7, therefore, I did it—and found I hated it. There was simply no use doing a lecture that wasn't live. I had to see the audience, sense it surrounding me, get the response in full. Talking a lecture into a phone, I decided, was like typing while wearing boxing gloves, or making love while wearing a tuxedo.

I rejected all further such invitations whenever I possibly could.

Then on April 13, it came time to give a lecture to the biochemistry class. I was now giving one lecture a year ("It proves I'm still there," I would say). Of course, I was now a stranger to the class and they to me, and under those circumstances I knew I had a cold audience.

While that might not matter to the academic lecturer in general, it mattered to *me*. If I didn't warm them up somehow, I wouldn't get the kind of response that would make it possible for me to enjoy a lecture.

Generally, since my lectures are off the cuff, I don't remember the particular strategies I use to warm up an audience, but I happen to have a record of my opening paragraph on this occasion:

I began: "Once a year the department carefully selects a strategic moment when it is considered safe to entrust me with a lecture. Yesterday you had a biochemistry examination, and this afternoon you will have a physiology examination. Outside it is a dull, gray, miserably rainy day, and to top it off it is Friday the thirteenth—so here I am."

There was a roar of laughter and no trouble thereafter. The lecture was on trace components of the diet, not something that was apt to stir the blood unduly, but a warm audience will laugh at any of my little jokes, and when I ended, I received the applause I always consider to be my just due.

15

Mac Talley admitted that *The Genetic Code* ought to take precedence over *The Human Brain* because of the timely nature of the former.

Too timely. Neither in college, nor in graduate school, nor even in the days of the med school had I learned about the genetic code, for the very good reason that it didn't exist in those days. In our wretched biochemistry text, we didn't as much as have "genetic code" in the index, not even in the 1957 edition.

It meant I had to educate myself before I could educate the readers, but it's all right. I enjoy the process.

My method of self-education was, of course, entirely through the printed word. I did not seek to interview leaders in the field of genetic research, not even those who were well within my reach. Nor did I seek to attend lectures on the subject.

What I did do was to get recent texts on the subject, read journals, newspapers, and magazines dealing with the matter—and, in particular, pore over *Scientific American*. It meant gathering a great deal, placing it all in decent order, wringing out the fat, smoothing out the lean, and putting it all into clear and simple words.

I *think* that is what I do. Actually, I don't watch myself do it.

And whatever it is I do, I never wait until it is done before I start writing. I start at once and do my research as I write. I could never have the patience to delay the writing end of it, since it is the writing I live for. Nothing else.

16

I was having eye trouble. Nothing serious; I was just getting old. The lens of my eye was having trouble thickening itself for close vision, and in a normal eye that meant I would have become farsighted and would need special reading glasses.

I was nearsighted to begin with, so my "presbyopia" (as it is called from the Greek for "old eyes") merely produced normal vision for me at close distances, but made me farsighted if I persisted in wearing my glasses.

I had to remove my glasses to type, then when I ate, finally at all times that I was indoors, except when I was watching television. And I only needed my glasses outdoors when I was driving—or when I wanted to make sure I could recognize people at a distance.

The usual solution to such problems is to wear bifocals, but I held off stubbornly. The bottom half of the bifocals would have to be plate glass, and I decided it was easier to remove my glasses when I had to.

I am often accused of resisting bifocals because that would represent an unseemly admission of age. Well, who am I to argue? Maybe that's right.

17

On April 27, I rented a tuxedo again in preparation for our automobile trip to West Virginia for the meeting of the World Book Year Book board.

The only other members of the board foolish enough to show up were Red Smith, who handled sports, and Lawrence Cremin, who handled education. What's more, since the editor-in-chief of World Book had died on Saturday, even as we were leaving home, the session was aborted and the World Book officials were leaving at noon the next day. It was a complete fiasco.

There was one unnecessary business session the next morning, and we left as early as we could on May 2.

I was never again able to take the World Book job seriously. It seemed to me to be too apt to degenerate into corporate folly. Were it not that I couldn't quite bring myself to leave a dollar-a-word task, I would have quit by letter the instant I had gotten home.

18

Eight years before, I had suggested an anthology of science fiction short-shorts to Groff Conklin. Groff had agreed enthusiastically, and together we selected fifty of them. We had agreed that I would write the Introduction and he would do the paperwork. What we hadn't worked out was who was to do the publishing and, as a matter of fact, we could find no one who wanted to undertake the task.

The book was retired until Collier Books began buying everything in sight. I quickly suggested to Groff that he try them, and it worked. On May 5, 1962, the contract came through from Collier Books. *Fifty Short Science-fiction Tales* would be my second anthology and my fourth collaboration (after the two texts and *Races and People*).

19

On May 8, I ordered new glasses with a slightly weaker prescription that was going to ease my presbyopia a little. For the first time I chose thick black frames, and when I put them on I found something I knew at once I would never abandon.

From that day onward, every set of glasses I have had has had thick black frames, and they have become a trademark as my face became better known. If I ever changed the frames, or had a picture taken without glasses, I would be unrecognizable.

20

The galleys for *The Search for the Elements* arrived, and on May 11, 1962, I began to go through them. I found myself simply unable to believe my eyes.

I thought I could understand Svirsky's actions in the case of *The Intelligent Man's Guide to Science*, however much I might angrily disagree with them. That book had been twice as long as he had asked, and he might have felt justified in editing it heavily.

That reason did not exist in the case of *The Search for the Elements*, and he edited it just as heavily. In some places, he simply rewrote.

I went through the book, trying to undo the damage, and it was eventually published, but it was quite clear to me that I would never, *never* do business with Svirsky again, not if he could guarantee making me a millionaire. I formally abandoned the notion of the science encyclopedia for young people that had till then labored along with a desultory kind of life, and from then on when he suggested I do some book or other, the answer was a flat "No." On one occasion, he lost his temper and scolded me over the phone, but I stuck firmly to that "No."

I learned my lesson. I have made it clear to editors ever since that I was amenable to the cutting, changing, adding, and patching of books —but that I, and no one else, would do that cutting, changing, adding, and patching, assuming I agreed with the reasons advanced for it.

I may say that I have had no trouble since. My manuscripts are freely and thoroughly copy edited, but I get to look at the copy-edited manuscript and it is my privilege to change anything back if I want to, right or wrong.

Furthermore, editors may indicate in margins what they think ought to be cut or made clear, but then I decide whether or how to do it. My favorite memory is one of Larry Ashmead writing in the margin of one of my manuscripts: "I don't understand this paragraph." I wrote under it, "I do." That ended the discussion.[3]

Any editor will tell you that I am co-operative and easy to work with, but no editor will ever pull a Svirsky on me again. I'd sooner quit writing.

21

I finished *The Genetic Code* on May 14, 1962.

In it, I had developed what I considered an original system for indicating the structure of organic compounds, using zigzag lines and polygons. It was the simplest possible system for organic molecular structure. It was dramatic and easy to understand for nonchemists, and at

---

[3] An editor is, of course, privileged to *reject* a book of mine. I don't mind that at all.

the same time gave the full and accurate details of the structure (at least where considerations of resonance and electron orbitals are not involved, and they are involved only in advanced organic chemistry).

Some years later, a paper that appeared in one of the learned journals advanced this same notation. I wrote a polite letter to the author (who lived in the Boston area) pointing out the existence of the use of the notation in *The Genetic Code* and disclaiming any desire to quarrel over priority. He replied very politely, acknowledging my priority just the same.

One disappointment in connection with the book, however, was that I couldn't do it for Brad after all. Harper was unwilling to make the necessary deal with New American Library, and I couldn't help but feel that since Mac has asked me to do the book before Brad had, I had to go along with Mac. Brad understood.

Then came another disappointment when Mac had trouble finding a hard-cover publisher for the book. W. W. Norton, whom Talley tried first, rejected it on the ground that it was "written down"—which wounded me, for I do *not* write down.

22

In the spring of 1962, I won the Publication Merit Award, which was handed out by Boston University at fixed intervals. I had never heard of it until I was told on May 10, 1962, that I had won it, and that it carried with it a prize of five hundred dollars.

On May 23, I showed up at President Case's office to receive the award.

I valued it as one more vindication of my stand against Keefer.

Another kind of vindication came on June 3.

Columbia's miscellaneous groupings had long since been gathered together under the umbrella of the School of General Studies, and I, as an old university undergraduate, was now a titular alumnus of General Studies. As such, I was selected as alumnus of the year for 1962.

I had to grin. Columbia's undergraduate second-class citizen was an alumnus of the year.

Of course, I didn't consider myself an alumnus of General Studies. I considered myself an alumnus of Columbia College, whether I was recognized as such or not. Still, I went to the dinner to hear myself praised and to accept a Steuben owl as my award.

23

Gertrude and I attended a cookout on June 10, 1962. It was intended for various Newton mothers who had served with the Cub Scout organization. Gertrude had been a den mother and had served conscientiously, and I went along as prince consort.

The people involved were members of Newton's more comfortably placed society and I didn't feel at home with them. The main activities seemed to be smoking and drinking, and since we didn't drink (and I didn't even smoke), we felt out of place.

One woman, who looked more than somewhat sozzled and who had a drink in one hand and a cigarette in the other, looked at my empty hands with hostility and said, "What's the matter with *you?* Don't you drink?"

"I'm afraid not, ma'am," I said with smiling friendliness.

"And I suppose you don't smoke, either?"

"I'm afraid not, ma'am," I said exactly as before.

She frowned and said, "Well, what the hell *do* you do?"

And I said, without lowering my voice, "I f——— an awful lot, ma'am."

Whereupon she burst into shrieks of laughter, repeated the remark to everyone, and I was the hit of the evening.

24

A new project arose during lunch with Austin on June 27.

Sterling North (whom I knew only as a book reviewer for the New York *Post*) edited a series of juvenile books for Houghton Mifflin that were very successful. They dealt with American history in one way or another, and Austin wondered if I could do one of that series.

I thought for a while and then suggested that I do a book on Benjamin Franklin, with emphasis on his scientific discoveries. Austin agreed enthusiastically and eventually I named the book I was planning *The Kite That Won the Revolution.*

25

As July began we all seemed to go our separate ways. On July 1, we delivered David to Camp Annisquam and on July 3, I put Gertrude and Robyn on the bus to New York. Then, on July 5, I myself drove to

New Hampton, New Hampshire, to attend a session of the Gordon Research Conferences for the second time. This time it was I, not Lemon, who was to give a talk.

That week of the conferences was devoted to communications, so I gave what I call my "Mendel talk," which dealt with a failure in communications. I discussed the discovery of the basic laws of genetics in the 1860s, and the failure of scientists to recognize that discovery till 1900.

Except for that break I kept working busily on my biographies, and on the evening of July 8, Gertrude and Robyn were back.

26

Mac Talley's assistant that year was a young man named Ed Burlingame. He was young and eager and I liked him. He was working on *The Genetic Code* and was trying to find a hard-cover publisher. On July 12, he reported that Clarkson N. Potter would do it.

That offset the disappointment of receiving my Doubleday statement and finding it to be $1,900, the lowest in 5½ years. (That was not surprising, really, in view of the 3-year hiatus in new books for Doubleday.)

And then the Potter deal fell through, too.

I was not overwhelmed by the tragedy of it all, however. Though at no time during 1962 was I to get a monster check such as I had received the previous November, I did have forty-five books on my backlist, all of them, except the two textbooks, in print and earning money. What's more, soft-cover sales and foreign sales kept picking up, and the number of small and medium-sized checks that arrived more than made up for the lack of the monster.

Month by month, 1962 was outpacing 1961 by a good deal, and even if, in the end, it fell short because of a lack in November, there still seemed a good chance that if 1961 was to be my great year, it wouldn't be my great year by as much as I had suspected.

27

Books sometimes get shunted aside as one gains an ascendant interest over another. I had been going great guns on the science biographies, and I already had over two hundred thousand words in final copy, with plenty more to go—when I wore out and went back to *The Human Brain*, which itself had been hanging fire for three months.

I had stopped *The Human Brain* after I had finished the relatively easy part and approached the brain itself, which I simply didn't understand.

In the three-month interval, however, I had had time to cool off, to stop concentrating on the how-am-I-going-to-do-it? terror. I also collected some reading matter on the subject and educated myself a little. I had enough now to start writing about the brain, and the actual act of writing about it calmed me and made it easier to go on.

I joke sometimes to the effect that when I approach a part of a book where I must explain something I don't understand, I just type faster and faster and faster. Then, when I get to the part I don't understand, sheer inertia pushes me through.

That's not literally true, of course, but there's something to it psychologically.

28

With David at camp as he had been the previous summer, we prepared, once again, to take advantage of our temporary one-child status to go to Birchtoft. For the first time, though, I had so huge a pile of unfinished manuscripts that I began to worry about the unimaginable horror of a fire.

The house and the furniture could be replaced, but the *manuscripts*. I had seven boxes of science biographies and a box of *The Human Brain*. The imagination boggled at the prospect of having to reconstruct that.

On July 28, therefore, I took everything over to the Saltzbergs' (with whom we had come to be particularly good friends) and urged Gloria to put them in the safest place in the house, where her children wouldn't get at them.

"And in case of fire," I said, "save the manuscripts and, if there is any time left, see what you can do about your kids."

She promised faithfully and when *The Human Brain* was finally published, the dedication was "To Gloria and William Saltzberg, who guarded the manuscript."

The next day we left for Birchtoft, detouring to Camp Annisquam to see David.

Once at Birchtoft, Gertrude found, to her horror, that she had forgotten to pack certain of Robbie's dresses and her own bathing suit. I suggested that we just go into town and buy whatever we needed, but the sight of growing panic on Gertrude's face made me realize that quick shopping decisions were impossible. I therefore suggested another solution.

"Tell me exactly what you forgot and where the items are in the house," I said.

She told me, and I got into the car and raced off. It took me four hours to drive home, pick up everything, and come back, and I was the hero of the place. The various wives present obviously thought that here was a properly trained Jewish husband.

I cheated, though. Part of my willingness to do the job depended on the fact that I could pick up the day's mail while I was there. Driving 150 miles to pick up clothes we could as easily buy two miles away might be a distressing chore, but driving that same distance to pick up the day's mail was a mere bagatelle.

We had good weather that week and most of the time was spent at the lake. Even I got into a bathing suit and spent some time paddling about.

29

When we got home on Sunday, August 5, I found in the mail a letter from the World Book people strongly urging me to come to Chicago on September 11. Again, I was furious. First West Virginia and now this.

I spent several days trying to keep my anger sufficiently ablaze to write them a letter telling them I would not come. But again, they paid me a great deal of money for very little work and they were lavish with travel expenses and per diems and again I decided to do as requested.

30

Shorter trips on my own were much better. In New York on August 19, I had the big adventure of taking the Staten Island ferry. In all my years in New York I had never done that.

On Tuesday, I had lunch at the Friars Club with some people from television and I saw Groucho Marx there. I rubber-necked at him in true hick fashion, but at least I restrained myself from rushing up for an autograph. I felt that in the Friars Club show-business personalities ought to be spared that.

31

When I got home on August 21, I was shocked and puzzled to find an angry postcard from August Derleth, claiming that he had the rights to Robert Bloch's story "The Hell-bound Train," which had been included in *The Hugo Winners,* and demanding an accounting of its earnings.

I was indignant. August didn't have a leg to stand on. I had negotiated in good faith with Bob's agent, Harry Altshuler. If there was any dispute over rights, the quarrel was between August and Harry, with myself an innocent (and uninterested) bystander. I sent August a postcard telling him so.

Though August bombarded me with additional cards and even threatened legal action, I held my position and said, come what might, I would not give him any information and that he must talk to Harry Altshuler. By the end of the month, August quieted down, admitting I was right, and it all blew over. What resolution was reached between Harry and August, I don't know. I never bothered to ask.

32

On August 26, we picked up David, and the family was together again.

Two days later, we received a brand-new kitchen set, a table and four chairs, replacing at last the chipped table and three chairs that Gertrude had bought twenty years before when we were still living on Walnut Street—and which had given excellent service.

The new kitchen set was paid for out of bonus money paid me by World Book. I resented that somehow, for I felt that by spewing money over me in this fashion, World Book was corrupting me and making it difficult to hold to my principles. It forced me to come trotting to West Virginia and Chicago, for instance, and I felt ashamed.

33

We all know, intellectually, that in the midst of life we are in death. We know that at any time an unlooked-for accident, a slip, a bit of forgetfulness, a mechanical failure, something over which we have no control, no knowledge, perhaps even no direct connection with, can snuff us out.

It is something, however, we don't usually think of, for life would be insupportable if we did. Yet once in a while, it is borne in upon us despite ourselves.

On September 4, 1962, I was standing in line at the post office waiting to pick up my morning mail. There was a sudden terrific crash followed by the loud racing of an automobile engine.

It was an automobile, hard up against a telephone pole just outside the post office, with the driver slumped over the wheel. There was no mystery about what had happened. The driver had had a heart attack while driving, and was dead. Had he been pointed in a slightly different direction at the moment of attack he would have gone through the glass front of the post office and all of us in line might have been killed or, at the very least, badly damaged by flying glass.

It was nothing that could have been foreseen or guarded against while conducting life under anything like normal circumstances, and I drove home shortly afterward a shaken man.

It reminds me of a story my brother once told me. As a young reporter on *Newsday* (whose staff he had joined in May 1952), he had been told to interview a state official. Stan called him and the official told him he was about to fly to Albany and would have to be interviewed there. Stan, with a fine show of ingenuousness, asked how he might best get to Albany, hoping the official would invite him along on the private plane he was taking. The official obtusely told him the names of the airlines that plied their way between New York and Albany.

Stanley took a commercial airline and was waiting in the official's office when the news arrived that the private plane had crashed, killing the pilot and badly injuring the three passengers. It was months before the official was well enough to be interviewed—in Brooklyn.

With the interview concluded, Stanley couldn't resist saying, "You know, sir, when I asked you how I could best get to Albany, I was hoping you'd invite me to get on your plane."

The state official said, "If I had thought that was what you were after, I would have invited you, and that would have been a real stroke of misfortune. After the crash, we were told that the weight of one more passenger would have certainly resulted in all of us being killed."

I was horrified when Stanley told me this story, and I sought for ways to express that horror. Stanley made it difficult by refusing to take it seriously.

Finally I said, "But Stan, don't you realize how your death would have affected Mamma and Pappa?"

Stanley shrugged that off, too. "They would have felt lousy, but they would have survived."

"You don't understand," I said. "For the rest of their lives, they would have changed their minds and decided you had been their favorite son, after all."

That sounds like a cruel and heartless joke, because Stanley and I both knew that I was the favorite son, even though Stanley was far better to the old folks than I ever was. Stanley was the kind of fellow who never resented the fact, either.

However, it *wasn't* cruel and heartless. Stanley wouldn't let me express my suffering at the thought of having lost him, so I had to make a joke to neutralize the retrospective pain. That, in fact, is the purpose of so-called gallows humor (jokes the man, about to be hanged, makes at the foot of the scaffold), which, for well-known historical reasons, is a Jewish specialty.

18

World Book Year Book

1

On September 9, 1962, I took the train to Chicago, which I had not visited in ten years.

I was met at the station by an official of World Book and was treated as a celebrity. In fact, throughout my stay every effort was made to make me happy and comfortable. Nevertheless, I was in a rebellious state of mind and I found it all unnecessary and useless frippery.

For instance, the purpose of the meeting was to introduce the board members to the salespeople under circumstances calculated to fill them with awe and reverence. Therefore, each of the seven board members was introduced as he or she moved down a kind of runway to the stage, with the orchestra playing some selection that acted as an appropriate leitmotiv.

It reminded me, uncomfortably, of a Miss America pageant, and for a while I thought I was hallucinating when the orchestra struck up "Here She Comes, Miss America." But that was the leitmotiv for Sylvia Porter, who handled the "Economy of the Year" section. At that, it wasn't too bad, since Sylvia Porter was a comely female and, compared with the popular stereotype of the economist, was a miracle of loveliness.[1]

I made the ritual bearable for myself by speculating on what they were going to play for me. I decided it would have to be "Fly Me to the Moon"—first because it was one of my favorite songs of the period, and second because I didn't see how anyone could fail to connect that with my science-fictional character.

That wasn't the one.

The orchestra played "How Deep Is the Ocean?" thus indicating my role as science writer.

I was chagrined. No matter how various the subject matter I write

[1] I remember her best on a later occasion after I had discussed lasers in one of my reviews of the year. She told me that she had never heard of lasers till she read about them in my article, and within months everyone was talking about them. She wondered how I could be clever enough to see their importance so early. I said I wondered how she knew what to do with a dollar once she had earned it.

on, I was a science-fiction writer first and it is as a science-fiction writer that I want to be identified.

There were delicious *hors d'oeuvres* at the reception that night, and then a Lucullan banquet (I must admit I can reconcile myself better to caloric pomp than to any other variety).

I sat next to Red Smith, who did the "Sports of the Year" section. He was a very pleasant fellow. He said to me, "You could understand my review section, couldn't you?"

I said, "Yes, of course. You have a delightfully clear writing style, Red."

"Yes, but you understood the subject matter. Now, you write clearly, but I couldn't understand your article."

"Your field touches a more general human response, Red," I said, but I don't think he was soothed by that thought.

Since liquid refreshments flowed steadily and since almost everybody who drinks is willing to drink one more if the drink is free, there was considerable high-flying hilarity. Fortunately, there was considerable tolerance, also, and no one minded that I didn't drink.

The moment came, though, when it was time to return to our rooms, and it turned out, to everyone's consternation, that Red Smith, having taken just one small drink too many, was having trouble navigating.

Whereupon someone said, "Isaac, you and Red are in the same hotel. Just help him back, won't you?"

Well, I had been helped back in my time (I remembered being supported on both sides after my Ph.D. celebration fourteen years before), so I had no intention of standing on my teetotaling self-righteousness and refusing the task. On the other hand, never having done this before, I had no idea of the mechanics of controlling a slightly tottery gentleman who was roughly as heavy as myself.

As I worked him up the main steps of the hotel to the lobby, I was assailed by a new worry. I had met Mrs. Smith, who was a delightful, charming, and amiable woman and who was now, presumably, waiting peacefully in her hotel room for her husband to return. But would she remain amiable? I had seen innumerable movie comedies in which some innocent fellow, bringing a too-happy friend home, is attacked by the wife as the cause of the corruption.

By the time I had weaved Red into the elevator, I had my tactics ready. When I knocked at the door and Mrs. Smith opened it, I worked rapidly. Moving Red quickly into a chair, I said, "Gee, thanks, Red, I could never have made it back to the hotel without you."

Then I left with the speed of the wind.

Mrs. Smith, who caught the significance of my statement at once and was apparently highly amused over my miserable attempt at tact, told the story far and wide the next day, and I was the laugh of the place.

Another clear memory of the Chicago visit was the announcement to us that the unexpected success of the first issue of the Year Book meant that the World Book could raise their payment to the board members by 50 per cent. From now on, we would get three thousand dollars per article, rather than two thousand dollars.

There was no question that the Year Book was a successful operation; that all the hoopla I found so distasteful was in its way merely the hoopla of American success, and was no worse than the hoopla of a World Science Fiction convention. There was no question, too, that the Year Book people were being generous and that I owed them gratitude.

Yet what I felt was uneasiness.

When the increase was announced, the other six board members[2] maintained an admirable and professional aplomb. Poker-faced, they accepted the raise. Only my voice sounded out (for I was still the kid in the candy store whose dream of affluence was forty dollars each and every week).

"That's too much," I said.

The silence that greeted that remark was deafening.

"But I'll take it," I said, trying to recover.

And, when the time came, I did take it.

On September 12, I took the train to Boston and was home the next day, with Gertrude and the kids waiting for me at the station even though the train was an hour and ten minutes late.

2

A middle-aged woman named Helen Phillips was my copy editor on *The Human Body* and, on several occasions, I dropped in at Houghton Mifflin to work with her on the book. She was tall, thin, angular, single, and almost a stereotype of the prissy New Englander, but she had a sense of humor under her starch and she was a crackerjack copy editor—never letting me get away with anything.

On September 18, for instance, we went over the index together. It was the first time anyone had ever paid any attention to my indexes but myself.

[2] They included James "Scotty" Reston and Alistaire Cooke, by the way, whom I met for the first time in the course of this junket.

My clearest memory of her, however, is our session over the illustrations—where to place them, what captions to use, and so on. Some of the illustrations were complex enough to require having various parts labeled—and among them were the illustrations for the male genitalia and the female genitalia.

This represented a problem because Ravielli's illustrations, though superb, were done in a style that made it difficult to draw lines from object to label without getting them lost in the general array of delicate lines that made up the drawing.

We were working in a room that was not truly closed off but had walls that did not reach to the ceiling and that had a gap where the door should be. That meant that the full office noise of the rest of the floor reached us, but it didn't bother me. I'm a strainer; I strain out what I don't want to pay attention to. Apparently Helen could, too, so we worked on, oblivious to the noise.

Finally, when we hit the cross section of the male genitalia, I thought about it and said, "I tell you what, Helen, let's tackle this little by little starting with the easy parts. For instance, let's place the penis right here." (I was referring to the label.)

I spoke, as I always do, in my ordinary speaking voice, which *does* tend to rattle distant windows, and I had no sooner delivered that line when every bit of noise on the floor stopped. It was as though it were all some giant television set that had been turned off with a snap. In that sudden enormous silence, I sat, puzzled and waiting.

Finally, very slowly, as though dreading what there might be to see, a head began to appear at one side of the door, more and more and more, until an eye could be seen—and it was Austin.

"Wouldn't you know? It's Isaac," he shouted, and everyone rushed in.

"It was business," I yelled. "It was strictly business. We were labeling diagrams. I tell you it was perfectly innocent."

But everyone pretended that they had interrupted an act of fornication and I grew scarlet with frustration. Helen, I noticed, wasn't in the least put out. She smiled demurely and was completely in control.

3

On September 22, 1962, the World Book Year Book raised its head again. Once again, they were encouraging their salespeople, but this time on a local basis, and I was invited to attend the festivities at a Boston hotel. I attended and was (my diary says) "for four hours immersed in a world of babbitry and boosterism."

The end was painful. Someone from the organization arose to give a talk. He had had at least one drink too many and was, I think, unable to exercise judgment. His talk slid into the telling of jokes.

He was not a particularly good jokester in the first place, but he knew a great many, and he told them *all* at as rapid a rate as he could. What's more, they were dialect jokes, a very difficult art to master, and he was not master of it. What was still more, a number of his jokes were told in Jewish dialect, and he was not Jewish, and much of the audience was.

Now, there is nothing a Jewish audience likes better than Jewish jokes told in an authentic Jewish dialect by someone who is Jewish. There is nothing that same Jewish audience dislikes worse than those same Jewish jokes told in a phony Jewish dialect by a Gentile.

The polite laughter that greeted his first efforts choked off and froze and for something like twenty minutes (or possibly twenty hours) he told joke after joke in an atmosphere of mounting embarrassment and hostility, without even one giggle from anyone at any time, and *would not stop*. I think he could not stop.

How much damage he did the World Book cause I do not know. I would have fled the scene at the first opportunity but I was at the head table about three removed from the man and could do nothing. I couldn't even tug at his trousers, as I had once seen Mrs. Amory do to her husband.

4

Then, on September 27, the Year Book let me know that they wanted a color photograph of me. For the 1962 Year Book they had used a rather impressionistic drawing, but that wasn't good enough for them. I was perfectly willing to oblige, but they insisted on a laboratory setting, since I was doing the "Science Review of the Year."

I said that I did not work in a laboratory and had not done so in over four years and that such a photograph would be phony—but that word has no terrors for publicity people. I could do nothing but go into the med school lab, set up a fake experiment with what glassware and tubing happened to be at hand, and let myself be photographed.

It appeared in the 1963 Year Book in glory, but I never valued that photograph. Aside from the fakery of the background, which bothered me even if it bothered no one else, it caught me very nearly at the peak of my weight, and I did not admire my fat face.

5

Donald Menzel of Harvard was a deadly foe of the flying-saucer idiocy. Lyle Boyd was working with him on a book concerning the various more notorious flying-saucer hoaxes, frauds, and mistakes, but they were having trouble placing it with a publisher.

I suggested Doubleday as a possible publisher on the ground that not only were they my publishers and very decent and honest but also that they were extremely hospitable to intelligent books.

To be sure, Doubleday did take the book, and Lyle called with the news on October 2, and I was delighted. The book was eventually published and did modestly well.

What I remember best about the book, however, is that I happened, inadvertently, to see a green sheet on which editorial sales, printings, and so on were estimated. At the bottom there was a line headed something like "How brought to Doubleday?" Scrawled in was "Recommended by Asimov. No finder's fee necessary."

I pointed that out with great glee and the editor concerned said, defensively, "Oh, come, Isaac, you're one of the family."

And so I am, and I would rather have that than a dozen finder's fees.

6

I drove in to New York on October 3, 1962, and decided to take the West Side Highway for the first time and register at a motel on Ninth Avenue so that I could park my own car and have it always available. It was one of those trips, however, in which I was plagued by minor mishaps.

I hit the Bronx just as an explosion killed a number of people and I found myself suddenly, and frighteningly, surrounded by taxis and ambulances.

Then, too, I had asked a toll collector directions for reaching the West Side Highway and he had said, "Just follow the arrows to the George Washington Bridge."

I did, but followed one arrow too many and found myself *on* the George Washington Bridge. I had to penetrate New Jersey and then return.

Eventually, I went out to New Jersey on purpose to give a talk at Hoffman-LaRoche, and managed to lock my trunk key in the trunk.

The next day, it turned cool, and I had brought my topcoat with me—except that it was in the trunk, which I couldn't open.

On October 4, I met Edward L. Ferman for the first time. He was the son of Joe Ferman, publisher of *F & SF*. Ed was a shy youth and vitally interested in the magazine. The meeting was about the only bright point of that trip's business rounds.

7

On October 20, I drove to Albany to give a talk at a medical school there, and then I drove down to New York. The trip from Albany to New York was made memorable for me by the fact that some gentleman of medium importance in the audience asked to hitch a ride to New York and I agreed—and then he smoked a cigar en route.

At that time, I had still not reached the point where I sternly forbade all smoking in my home, office, or car (as I now do), and the only thing I could do was to shorten the ordeal by racing down the Thruway at eighty miles an hour.

I compensated myself the next day, which was a Sunday, by taking a cruise around Manhattan. It was the first time I had ever done that, and I would have thought, on an *a priori* basis, that there could be nothing interesting in staring at Manhattan for a round trip of forty miles. I was quite wrong. Manhattan has an entirely different aspect from the sea, and the three-hour sea journey, which carried me down as far as the Statue of Liberty (closer than at any time since my visit there thirty-three years earlier), was an extraordinary thrill.

For the first time I truly grasped, viscerally, that Manhattan was an island.

The next day I was on my rounds, but the day was dominated by the fact that President Kennedy had announced a blockade of Cuba and laid down his ultimatum demanding that the Soviet Union dismantle the missile bases they had built there. That initiated a period of a couple of days during which the world held its breath waiting to see if the long-expected nuclear war would break out.

The night of October 22, 1962, I slept, but fitfully, at the Skyline Motor Inn. I woke at hourly intervals and listened for the normal sound of normal traffic. It then occurred to me that if there *were* a nuclear war and if Manhattan *were* target zero for a nuclear bomb, I simply would not wake up—so I slept soundly for the second half of the night, and the next day drove back to Boston listening to news bulletins all the way.

By the twenty-fifth, the Soviet Union backed down and Kennedy, and the United States, won the greatest victory of the Cold War.

8

The Cuban missile crisis, however, did very little to affect the congressional elections that took place on November 6. The situation in Congress remained largely unchanged.

By far the best news of the day for me was that Richard Nixon had been roundly trounced in his bid for the governorship of California. That was widely regarded as removing him once and for all from politics. I so regarded it, certainly, and so did Nixon himself, for in a fit of cry-baby petulance unparalleled in American political history, he called a news conference and told the reporters "you won't have Nixon to kick around anymore."

That should have killed him politically if the defeat had not, and it is to the everlasting shame and distress of the republic that it did not.

9

On November 7, 1962, Eleanor Roosevelt died, and I thought sadly of the only time I had ever been in the same room with her, 3½ years before.

10

I went back to school, after a fashion, on November 19. Driven by our possession of a piano, I finally decided to take an adult-education course in the reading of music. It was a rather pleasant change in routine, but actually I learned much the same thing I had learned in fourth-grade music appreciation and had not yet forgotten.

The thing I remember best about the course, however, was the teacher, a tall, good-looking young man with a shy and engaging smile, who said to me once that he had written a concerto.

"Was it successful?" I asked.

"No," he said, "I've never even heard it."

You can write a concerto, but in order to hear it you have to persuade musicians to learn it and practice it and then play it, and that costs money. I suppose you can play a version of it on the piano and hear the "tune," but that's not the same thing.

It made me glad I was a writer. Even if I wrote something I could not publish, I could read the manuscript and there would be (questions of money and fame excluded) no difference to me.

11

I had agreed to tape a television show with Dave Garroway in New York on November 28. I had no real desire to do it, for my enjoyment in doing structured material on TV is nil, but along with me on the show was to be Nobel Laureate Edward Mills Purcell, and I did want to meet him. He was one of the men to be included in my science biographies, and I felt a proprietary interest in him, therefore.

The show fulfilled all my worst apprehensions. I was at the studio by 10:30 A.M. and the delays started. We did not get finished till 5:00 P.M. and then they wanted it done over.

I refused with unwontedly forceful language and stalked out. Purcell, I remember, was perfectly at ease. When we waited hours past the scheduled time, he stretched out on a couch and went to sleep. I think he would have been ready to repeat the show.

There was good news from Doubleday, however.

I had taken in my second collection of essays, *View from a Height*, seven months before, but Tim Seldes would not commit himself to it. He wanted to see how *Fact and Fancy*, the first book in the series, would do—and for months it moved very slowly.

On the other hand, sales did not cease, either, and by the end of November they had crept up to the point where it was quite apparent that Doubleday would not lose money on the book. Tim said, on November 30, that he would do *View from a Height*.

That was great, because it meant I could instantly put together a third collection of essays.

12

On December 3, 1962, I received the three-thousand-dollar payment for my article for the 1963 Year Book.

When the check arrived, I realized, with some confusion, that even without any check nearly like that of the Basic Books monster of the year before, I was now within less than two thousand dollars of the total income of 1961, and that it was very unlikely that I would make less than that in the twenty-eight days remaining in the year.

It was not an unpleasing thought, but it was a confusing one.

Where did the money come from? And it was a guilty one. Was I properly earning the money?[3]

13

The Human Brain was almost done, thank goodness, and I had the dim feeling that I dared not let it end without having another project under way. On December 6, therefore, I began *The Kite That Won the Revolution*, and before the day was out had put an estimated one fifth of it into first draft.

That was more or less my system. There must be no endings. Several balls must always be in the air.

14

Finally, finally, finally, *The Genetic Code* found a hard-cover home. I was told on December 8 that a firm called Orion Press would do it.

I had never heard of Orion Press before and I have never heard of it in any other connection since. Still, they put out a handsome hard-cover edition eventually, and for a number of years paid out faithful royalties until the hard-cover edition went out of print.

I am grateful to them.

15

Fred Pohl was in town on December 14, and I had dinner with him at the Statler Hilton.

For some years, Fred had been very close to Horace Gold, helping him run *Galaxy*. When Horace left both the job and the East Coast, and went to California, Fred took over as the editor.

We reminisced during that meal about the days when we had first met, nearly a quarter of a century before, and Fred said at one point, "You know, Eye, I never really planned to be forty."

"I know," I said, sadly, "but Cyril's method of avoidance is really the only possible way."

[3] It may be that this is another reason I spend nearly all day every day at the typewriter. Only by keeping a workweek something like that of my father in the candy store can I make myself feel I am earning my income and am justified in accepting it.

16

On December 15, 1962, I finally finished *The Human Brain*. It had taken me 10½ months, as compared with 6 months for *The Human Body*. I took it in to Austin Olney on the eighteenth, and three days later (my father's sixty-sixth birthday) I took him *The Kite That Won the Revolution*.

17

That year the annual meeting of the AAAS was being held in Philadelphia over the Christmas-New Year week, and I decided to attend.

While there, I listened to excellent talks on psychology, saw diverting science films, heard Loren Eiseley give one of the featured evening talks in an orotund manner, and met Bentley Glass, an important biochemist who turned out to be a fan of mine.

I also managed to get in a side visit to the Philadelphia aquarium, where I saw dolphins for the first time in my life.

December 30 was the last day of the meetings, and it was cold. The temperature stood at 2° F, and I remember walking from one hotel to another, just a few blocks, with my ears slowly freezing. Fortunately, a fellow conventioneer, with woolly gloves and pity for my ears, walked behind me and kept the gloves over them.

18

The year 1962 came to an end with six books published in its course, second only to the eight-book mark of 1960. They were:

43. *Life and Energy* (Doubleday)
44. *Words in Genesis* (Houghton Mifflin)
45. *Fact and Fancy* (Doubleday)
46. *Words on the Map* (Houghton Mifflin)
47. *The Hugo Winners* (Doubleday)
48. *The Search for the Elements* (Basic Books)

As for my annual income, that came out to a little over seventy-two thousand dollars, nearly three thousand dollars higher than what I had so confidently expected to be my Mount Everest peak of 1961.

In a way this marks an important watershed in my life. Up to the end of 1962, the money I earned was of vital concern to me and dictated the direction of my life. Even my high earnings of 1961 seemed like a one-shot, and I had no certainty that the figure would not recede and would not, perhaps, recede badly.

By the end of 1962, however, it was finally clear to me that, barring extraordinary events, I need be concerned about financial security no longer. I had started from scratch at the age of eighteen and, as my forty-third birthday neared, I had reached the level of a good living and should, it seemed to me, continue so.

It was no overnight success, heaven knows, but it was solid enough to show no signs of prospective failure provided I kept on plugging.

From this point on, therefore, I will no longer specify my income from year to year (except where some particular payment has an effect on my life), since it is no longer anything but incidental.

I will, however, continue to list my books from year to year.

19

Biographical Encyclopedia

1

My forty-third birthday on January 2, 1963, was another that passed almost unnoticed.

Though both *The Human Brain* and *The Kite That Won the Revolution* were out of the way, I was, fortunately, not without tasks to do. There were the science biographies, and these continued on and on. Every estimate I made as to how many biographies I would end with had proved too low, and now I was actually getting over the nine-hundred mark.

2

The Kite That Won the Revolution ran into trouble. Sterling North, who edited the series for which the book was intended, went over it and gave it the Svirsky treatment. I received the hacked-up manuscript on January 15.

I was horrified and wondered what I should do. On the one hand, I was dealing with Austin Olney and did not wish to anger or offend him. On the other hand, I could not and would not ever again sit still for the Svirsky treatment.

Finally, the latter won out. I visited Austin and told him I would have to have the manuscript back. North's series was a success and North was a good writer and North had improved my book—but it was no longer my book, and rather than have it published in North's version, I would dump the manuscript. It didn't matter, I said, I had other books. Naturally, I would return the advance.

Austin wouldn't hear of it. He said that Houghton Mifflin would publish the book independently and not as part of the series, and that I need not make any changes that I didn't want to make.

In the end it *was* published my way and not as part of the series (even though Sterling North called me and screamed at me in a high-pitched voice—his voice was even higher than John McCarthy's).

The Kite That Won the Revolution did only moderately well, unfortunately, and I'm quite convinced that it would have done better with North's changes and as part of North's series, but that doesn't matter. There's no law that says my books have to do well, but I have a private law that says they have to be mine. And I was proud of *The Kite That Won the Revolution*, which made little money, just as I was ashamed of *The Intelligent Man's Guide to Science*, which made a lot of money.

3

Don Bensen, a writer, anthologist, and editor, whom I had met now and then, had put together a collection of five stories from the old *Unknown* and had written to me asking for an Introduction. I had agreed readily, of course, and in a fit of delicious nostalgia for the magazine that had died twenty years before, I mentioned my story "Author! Author!," with which I had finally made *Unknown* only to have it die before the story could be published.

On January 18 I received an excited letter from Bensen. The Introduction was fine, but could I dig up the manuscript of "Author! Author!"? I promptly found it. I had started the story just twenty years and five days earlier, but the days when I allowed old manuscripts to be lost had long since departed.

I read it over and found that despite its then-topical references to wartime conditions (rationing, the OPA, and so on) it was still moderately humorous. I warned Don of its being out of date, but he said he didn't care. I therefore had Gertrude retype it for me and sent it off to him with a warning that the magazine people actually owned it.

Campbell very kindly arranged to release the story to Don. Don then paid me $200 for it, which was $50 more than I received the first time around (nor did Campbell suggest that I return the original $150).

Eventually, a new anthology, *The Unknown Five*, appeared, also edited by Don Bensen, and the lead story was "Author! Author!"[1] By the time it appeared, twenty-two years had elapsed since it was written. This was the longest interval between writing and first publication that anything of mine had ever endured.

4

On January 23, my advance copy of *The Human Body* came along, and I admired it greatly. It was easily the most beautiful book (from the design and illustration standpoint) that I had yet published.

[1] See *The Early Asimov*.

On that same day I put a new electric typewriter into use. It was an IBM Selectric, with a little "walnut" that carried the type and that moved from one side of the page to the other. No longer did the whole carriage move, and I considered that that was an enormous improvement. I don't know that the Selectric was any quieter than the old machine, but it *seemed* quieter because there was less massive motion.

Yet I felt guilty. Whatever a cowboy is supposed to feel for his horse, I feel for my typewriters. In my diary I say, "I feel like a traitor to my good old machine that gave me six years of sterling service and on which I wrote *The Wellsprings of Life, Life and Energy, The Intelligent Man's Guide to Science, The Human Body,* and many others."

And it had indeed been an excellent machine. In six years of constant use, it required nothing but an occasional cleaning, plus the replacement of one minor part.

I didn't trade it, but set it up in my second room as a spare in case anything went wrong with the new typewriter.[2] As it turned out, however, the old typewriter with its moving carriage, was not an adequate backup. Once I got used to the Selectric, the moving carriage was a psychological hazard I couldn't endure.

5

On January 23, 1963, the freshman class at the med school gathered for its first biochemistry lecture, and I gave it. For the next few years, in fact, the first lecture was assigned to me. I always spread myself and the poor freshmen invariably reacted with great excitement, thinking that was the way it would be from then on.

It never was, of course, and it made the ensuing lectures by others seem all the worse. Sometimes I felt guilty over doing that, but then I remembered that I had not voluntarily removed myself from the course, that I had *told* Keefer I was the best teacher in the school. The fault was not mine! (I had to repeat that to myself over and over.)

Sinex generally let me pick my own subject for the first lecture. On this occasion I spoke on stereoisomerism, because it lent itself to some dramatic science history, something I was quite up on because of my science biographies.

[2] That was a besetting fear of mine—that something might go wrong with a typewriter and that days and weeks and months might pass before I got it fixed. In actual fact, hardly anything ever went wrong with it, and almost always, when something did, IBM rushed repairmen to the house within hours in response to the absolute panic in my voice.

6

I had my first personal experience with plagiarism on January 29. An English professor from the University of Rhode Island sent me a story submitted to her by one of her freshman students and purporting to be an original. Fortunately, she knew enough about my work to have heard of the Three Laws of Robotics, so she sent it to me for an opinion.

It didn't require long for me to reach an opinion. It was a word-for-word copy of my story "Galley Slave."

I was cynical enough not to be appalled by the plagiarism in itself. I suspected that many youngsters faced with the necessity of producing a story and feeling the task to be impossible get the bright idea of copying someone else's story.

What did appall me was that the foolish freshman was so naïve as to think he could pass off as his own an extraordinarily complex story, intricately plotted, written by someone who, at the time, had labored for twenty hard years improving his craft. Even if the teacher had not recognized the source of the story, she would surely have spotted the impossibility of the student's having written it.

I sent back the story, explaining that it was mine, word for word, and said that undoubtedly she would feel the student must be disciplined for attempting plagiarism, but if so, I would prefer that she not inform me of what was done. She didn't. To this day I don't know what happened to the student (perhaps nothing at all).

7

Except for work on the indexes (a name index and a subject index, keyed to the number of the biography rather than the page) the science biographies were coming to an end. The book was between three and four times as long as Tom Sloane had suggested it be.

I had spent a year and a half on it—but of course it wasn't a solid year and a half. I had written four other books in that interval, including the difficult *The Human Brain*.

I worried about what Tom Sloane was going to say when he saw what I had done; I hadn't warned him en route, of course, for fear he would stop me. I wasn't afraid of being Svirskied because I wouldn't allow it. I *was* afraid, however, of being politely handed back the manuscript. I still wouldn't have been sorry I had written it because I had enjoyed it, but I would be sorry not to have it published as written, for I thought it was a great book.

By February 14, I had separated all the pages into three copies; an original and two carbons. One carbon was for myself, of course. The original filled six boxes of the kind that ordinarily held a ream of typing paper, and each carbon filled four more boxes. It meant that eventually I would have to manhandle ten boxes to Doubleday.

As usual I had to start something else before being quite finished. There was Mac Talley's *Asimov's Science Shelf*. He had wanted me to start with chemistry, but I had had enough chemistry in the textbooks and I wanted to do physics because I didn't know the subject well enough and I welcomed a chance to get to know it better.

I therefore began what I was eventually to call *Understanding Physics* on February 17, 1963.

8

Robyn was eight years old on February 19, 1963. I was aware all through her seventh year that she was at the age of Alice in "Wonderland" and in "Through the Looking Glass," and that she looked exactly like the Alice in the Tenniel illustrations. That wasn't just a father's fond pride, either. Others remarked on it too, quite independently. I hated to see the year pass.

On that birthday day, I met astronomer Carl Sagan, then of Harvard, and had lunch with him. We had already corresponded and I had received some of his papers. He was an ardent science-fiction reader.

I visualized him as an elderly person (the stereotype of the astronomer at his telescope), but what I found him to be was a twenty-seven-year-old, handsome young man; tall, dark, articulate, and absolutely incredibly intelligent.

I had to add him to Marvin Minsky and thereafter I would say that there were *two* people whom I would readily admit were more intelligent than I was.[3] We have been very good friends ever since.

9

Our house had developed a new embarrassment.

The driveway was slightly bowl-shaped and, at the bottom of the

---

[3] Once, during a conversation, Carl jokingly reminded me that I had already admitted he was more intelligent than I was. "Yes," I said, "more intelligent—but I never said you were more talented." I may have to revise that. He has written few books compared to me, but two of them, *The Cosmic Connection* and *The Dragons of Eden*, have been best sellers and, unlike most best sellers, worthily so.

bowl, was a drain. The drain was connected by a horizontal pipe to the sewer across the street. It was not a well-designed drain, for the builder (who had built the house six years before we moved in and who had been its first occupant) had undoubtedly jerry-rigged it.

That pipe would naturally get leaves in it in the fall, plus assorted debris. That wouldn't do real damage ordinarily, because the rains would wash it all through, more or less, into the sewer. In a really cold winter, however, the water in the drain would freeze, trap the debris, narrow the passageway, freeze further until the pipe was solid, and nothing would go through.

The winter of 1962–63 supplied us with the necessary freezing rain interspersed with intense cold, and by mid-January we had no drain. Further cold rain meant the accumulation of water in the bowl of the driveway. Since the wisdom of the builder had seen to it that the house end of the driveway was lower than the curb end, the water backed into the garage and, if there was enough of it, into the basement. That meant endless mopping and endless attempts to devise methods to drain the driveway into the roadway.

Naturally, under the circumstances, the heavens opened and we had nothing but cold rain through February and March. We had a purgatorial winter and it was not till the end of March that we finally managed to free the drain and flush it out with hot water.

10

I went to Newark, New Jersey, to attend a meeting of Sam Moskowitz's Eastern Science Fiction Association on March 3, 1963. John Campbell was guest of honor, so I couldn't miss that one.

Randall Garrett was there and finally I was able to clear up the misunderstanding between us and we were friends again, thank goodness.

He had a very pretty, rather plump girl with him. I remarked on her prettiness and Randall said, "I knew she was my kind of girl when I said to her, 'How do you come to have such beautiful brown eyes, dear?' and she held her hand up to the level of her forehead and said, 'Because I'm full of shit up to here.'"

Everyone took his turn in making a short speech praising Campbell, and I had my turn. I went over some of the familiar stories of our early relationship and at one point I said, "John Campbell was the first to recognize my ability." I then paused, thought a moment, and said, "No, *I* was the first, but Campbell was the second."

That got the laugh I wanted, but I wasn't telling the truth, of course. Campbell was the first.

I told of Campbell's inspiring "Nightfall" and of his building up the Foundation stories from my initial idea for a short story, and I particularly emphasized his role in working out the Three Laws of Robotics and of his refusal to take credit for them, saying that they were implicit in my stories.

Randall, in his speech, came up with what I have always considered the perfect conclusion. "Isaac says John made them up and John says Isaac did, and I say they're both right. The laws were invented in symbiotic co-operation."

I think that's it. Campbell and I, in those first three years of my writing career—the crucial and formative ones—were a symbiotic organism.

There was a slide show of old *Astounding* covers (even the name of the magazine was gone now) that had me nearly weeping with nostalgia. Then Campbell talked for half an hour and it was over.

11

On March 5, I received bound galleys of L. Sprague de Camp's new book *The Ancient Engineers* from the New York *Times*, which wanted me to review it.

I'm a sucker for Sprague's nonfiction, and if I were completely ethical I would have refused the job, for I am not impartial about Sprague and can't be. I didn't refuse it, however, and I just loved the book. I thought, and still think, it is the best book that Sprague ever wrote.

I eventually composed my review, praising it to the skies, and the *Times* told me they planned to give it front-page exposure in their Sunday Book Review section. This pleased me enormously, for it was bound to help sales of the book—perhaps, I thought excitedly, even put it on the best-seller list. Then, too, from the more selfish point of view, I had no objection to seeing my deathless prose so prominently displayed, even if that prose were devoted to praising another's book.

The only trouble was that a newspaper strike closed down the New York morning papers just about the time the review was to appear. By the time it was settled, many weeks later, there was an enormous backlog of reviews to be taken care of and my review was printed well toward the back. If it did Sprague any good, it could only have been to a minimal extent.

12

I lunched with Austin Olney, and with an editor of adult books, David Harris, at Locke-Ober's on March 7, to celebrate the official publication date of *The Human Body*. Some three thousand copies were already sold, and the advance had been paid off.

I always plump for small advances, by the way. A large advance is good because it guarantees the possession of a large amount of money. If the book does not sell well enough to pay off the advance, the author is, in theory, supposed to return the balance, but no publisher ever asks for it. The author therefore makes more money than he would otherwise make—and gains publisher ill will which, in my opinion, is a bad tradeoff. (Of course, you may be in debt and need the money of a large advance at once, and you may decide to tackle the publisher's ill will when you get to it.)

I, however, was not in debt, and never was, and much preferred an advance so chosen that it was paid off out of advance sales by publication date. My later royalties were then that much the greater and I gained the publisher's good will as well.

13

Finally, on March 28, 1963, I took in the 10 boxes of science biographies. I had done something like 970 biographies.

I made my arrangements in Tim Seldes' office and he, not being directly involved, was very amused. Having set up the six boxes of the original in plain view, I went to get Tom Sloane.

"Tom," I said, "I've got the science biographies in Tim's office. I would have brought it directly to you, Tom, but I wanted to break the news to you first that it got away from me and it's a little longer than you wanted it to be. I've got the original and the carbon, Tom, and it's in several boxes and—"

By that time we were in Tim's office and Tom saw the six boxes. His mouth fell open and he said, "A *little* longer?"

"Well, yes, Tom," I said. "It's got to be that way because I didn't arrange it alphabetically the way you wanted me to. In science, it makes more sense to arrange the biographies chronologically, and in order to make it a clear and good story, I had to include a lot of scientists."

"Okay," said Tom, being philosophical, "so we'll work with the longer version. Which of these boxes are the original and which the carbon?"

Having pushed him along that far, I broke the rest of the news.

"They're all original, Tom," I said. Lifting the four other boxes from behind a desk, I said, "These are the carbons."

The book was four hundred thousand words long, considerably longer than the Svirskyized version of *The Intelligent Man's Guide to Science* and the longest book I had yet written.

Tom rose to the occasion, though. In fact, he suggested that since I had gotten so near a thousand biographies, I ought to add enough more to make it 1,001. He said that would look good in the advertising. It meant several months' more work, off and on.

My own title was *The Biographical History of Science and Technology*. Tom Sloane vetoed that, though. He said the word "history" was poison at the box office and that "encyclopedia" was a better selling point. Furthermore, the salespeople had by now recognized that my name carried weight and they urged that it be included in the title.

The book therefore became *Asimov's Biographical Encyclopedia of Science and Technology*.

It was the first one of my books to have my name in the title (but not the last). In view of my persona as a person of cheerful self-appreciation, I always insist that I don't mind having my name in the title, but I think I do mind a little bit. At least, I always refer to the book, when I must, as the Biographical Encyclopedia.

14

One of Carl Sagan's devouring interests is the question of extra-terrestrial life, and some of the papers he had written took up that question in fascinating ways. I had seen those papers and it seemed to me I ought to write an *F & SF* essay on the subject, translating his ideas into my style and for my audience. I did that on April 7, 1963, and called the essay, "Who's Out There?"

Eventually I took it in to show to Carl himself, since I had taken his name in vain at the start of the article where I described our meeting, stressing his youth and presentability. He passed the article without trouble but, rather embarrassed, asked that I take out the personal description of himself.

I did, of course, but I was sorry. I don't know whether he felt that the accent on his youth would harm his credibility or that the accent on his good looks would harm his modesty, but he has become very well known to the public since, and his youth (modified by time, of course) and presentability are now public property, so why would it have hurt?

In any case, the article appeared eventually in the September 1963 *F & SF*, as my fifty-ninth essay in the series. "Who's Out There?" was the last of the seven *F & SF* essays never to be included in one collection or another. Partly this was because by the time it appeared I was engaged in doing a whole book on the subject treating the matter from a slightly different standpoint, but partly it was because I was a little sad over having had to change the beginning.

15

Ever since Gertrude had visited Canada in 1943, I had been promising to take her to Toronto someday so that she could visit her old childhood friends as a wife and mother, with husband and children in tow. Twenty years' waiting was long enough, and on April 13, 1963, off we went.

We spent the first night at a motel in Rochester, and on April 14 we reached Buffalo, and I crossed over into foreign soil for the first time since my arrival in the United States forty years before (and the first time ever for the children).

It was a case of nostalgia at secondhand. I drove around sections of Toronto in which Gertrude had lived as a child before her arrival in the United States at the age of nineteen. Those sections were still recognizable to her, though Toronto itself had expanded and grown both outward and upward out of all recognition since World War II. We also visited some of Gertrude's girlhood friends, as well as her cousin, Albert.

On April 15, we drove north of Toronto to the resort town of Belle Ewart, where she had spent summers as a teen-ager. It had changed and, try as she might, she could not identify the particular house in which she and her family had lived.

On April 16, we visited Niagara Falls on the way home. I'm not sure if Gertrude had ever seen them before, but the rest of us certainly hadn't. I kept being afraid that I would somehow fail to find them, knowing my own capacity to get lost under even the most favorable conditions, but once in the town, I turned a street corner and there they were, immediately in front of me.

I rather lost my breath, for the Horseshoe Falls are extraordinarily beautiful. We had come to the end of a long, cold winter and even though it was mid-April, there were still chunks of ice going over the lip. It was the last of the ice, though, for the next day there was none to be seen.

We went through the entire tourist routine. We went up in a tower to see the falls by artificial light at night. We visited the museums, read all the memorabilia, went under the falls in rubber clothing. Gertrude and the children even went over the rapids in an aerocar and went up in a helicopter. It was the children's first airborne experience and may have been Gertrude's as well.

Finally, on April 18, we crossed the bridge and were back on American soil after a hundred-hour absence. The next day we were back home, and I celebrated by putting on a final burst of speed and finishing A Short History of Biology, which I was doing for Doubleday and its soft-cover division, the Natural History Press. (It was an easy book to do since I used the Biographical Encyclopedia as my major source.)

16

Almost immediately after, I took another trip, this time without the family, and made my way into Pennsylvania Dutch country for the first time in my life.

I left on April 23, dropped off A Short History of Biology at Doubleday, then went on down to Pennsylvania. I was at Lancaster the next day, and there I was going to talk at Millersville State College, at the urging of one Professor Lingenfelter, whom I had met at my stay at Breadloaf thirteen years before. He had changed considerably in that time.

I drove back on April 25 through the Amish country, and that was worthwhile. I had never seen the Amish before and it was pleasant to be in a cultural enclave. And, of course, I yield to no one in my enthusiasm for Pennsylvania Dutch cooking. I was home again on the twenty-seventh.

17

On April 30, I turned down an offer of a full-time job as science writer at eighteen thousand dollars a year. Each time something like that happened I ached with renewed pain at all the years I had spent scrounging unsuccessfully for jobs paying far less than that. And always Keefer's remark that the school couldn't afford to pay sixty-five hundred dollars a year for a science writer would echo in my ears. Of all the events in our long fight, it was that remark, and that remark alone that I found I could neither forgive nor forget.

18

During May, my main writing project was the book on physics I was doing for Mac Talley. I could see already that it was going to be another example of my being unable to stop.

What Mac had in mind, I'm sure, was a ninety-thousand-word-book entitled *Understanding Physics*, another book of the same length entitled *Understanding Chemistry*, then *Understanding Paleontology*, and so on, until either the list of sciences or I wore out—whichever came first.

I could see, however, that by the time the ninety thousand words were up I was going to be only about one third through with *Understanding Physics*, and this time I had no intention of bringing in a swollen manuscript. I would simply do three books: *Understanding Physics* Volumes 1, 2, and 3, each with some appropriate subtitle. I would have to get Mac to go along with that, but I would present him with a *fait accompli* and hope for the best.

Meanwhile, on May 23, I received a letter from Jason Epstein of Random House. A book called *Habitable Planets for Man* had been written by Stephen H. Dole of RAND Corporation, and Jason wanted to put out a popularized version of the book, one that was cut and simplified. He wanted me to do the job.

It was something that, on the face of it, I did not want to do. I wasn't going to vet someone else's book. The subject matter, however, as described by Jason, was interesting, just interesting enough for me to ask to see the book.

It was a mistake, for when the book came I found it fascinating and I was hooked. As I read I decided that I didn't want anyone else doing the popularization. I agreed to do it, therefore, on condition that I share author's billing and get 50 per cent of the royalties. This was readily agreed to by Dr. Dole, and between June 20 and July 6, I did the revision.

I didn't want to keep the same title for the simplified book, but I didn't want to depart too widely either, for Dole's title was exactly descriptive. I suggested *Planets for Man* and that was accepted, too.

19

On May 26, 1963, after the family had spent some time in New York, I was preparing to leave for West Newton. We had a problem parking at the Blugermans'. It had never been easy, but it had grown severely worse of late. High-rise apartments had been built in the area, increasing the automobile density to the point where parking spaces simply could not be had, so that we had parked (as we always had to, now) several blocks away.

It meant getting the kids and the baggage and dragging everything the several blocks to the car, or else leaving everything and everyone on the sidewalk, and then my getting the car and driving it to where everyone and everything was waiting, and double-parking temporarily.

On this occasion, though, it was raining, and we didn't want to walk blocks in the rain with baggage, nor wait in the rain till I got the car.

The alternative was to drive into the parking lot to a point just outside the back door of the Blugermans' apartment house. The trouble with that was that the parking lot was now fenced in, with an attendant standing guard over it, and it was for the use of tenants only.

Gertrude said, "Let's see if they'll let you into the parking lot temporarily."

I explained to the attendant that my mother-in-law lived in one of the buildings and that I just wanted to park in the lot long enough to load the car and then I would leave. Being a human being, he said, "Sure."

I got the car, brought it into the parking lot, right to the door, and in fifteen minutes we were loaded up and took off—driving slowly through the parking lot to the other end, where the exit was located.

As we did so, a car, parked diagonally, pulled out in reverse. The idiot at the wheel was waving to someone on the sidewalk and did not bother to look and see whether anyone was behind him.

He hit our rear door, caving it in somewhat but not damaging it enough to prevent it opening and closing. It was a purely cosmetic dent. Naturally, I stopped and he stopped, and I frothed at the mouth a bit and expressed a clear interest in whether it was his usual custom to look north when driving south. He responded quietly and told me to send him the bill and his insurance company would pay. He didn't have his insurance company card on him, but his name and address were so-and-so.

I gave him my own name and address, though it was clear his car had suffered no damage at all, and off we all went.

The next day, at home, I drove my car into my garage and asked for a written estimate as to what it would cost to beat out the damage, describing what happened. I said, "Don't inflate it for the insurance company. Give me the honest figure."

The garage did. It came to roughly $135. I reported the entire incident to my insurance company, and then sent a Xerox copy of the estimate by registered mail to the idiot who hit me, and asked him politely to have his insurance company send me a check.

On May 29, I received a letter from the idiot's lawyer, accusing *me* of negligence, and threatening a lawsuit. My own registered letter was returned. The idiot had refused to accept it.

Well!!!

I might have remained cool since it seemed to me that the idiot, fearing that I would try to make a big fuss and sue him for his total estate plus his left arm, put the whole thing in the hands of his lawyer, who reacted in the normal legal fashion of instant attack.

But I didn't. The trouble was that Gertrude recalled that once when she was a high-school student, she had asked her father to drive her to school and he had gotten into a slight collision at a time when his insurance policy had lapsed. Even though it was all the other guy's fault (Gertrude said) it had come to a court case and her father had lost and had had to pay out money he could ill afford and it had been Gertrude's fault because he had been driving her to school. And now it was her fault again because she had asked me to drive into the parking lot.

That was it! I wasn't going to allow anyone to send Gertrude into a tailspin if I could help it.

I told her first that whereas her father had let his insurance lapse, I had not. I was fully insured.

Second, even if I were not fully insured, her father had been hard up at the time, but I was not and could well afford to pay any losses.

Third (and by now I was breathing flame), *I was not her father*, and we'd see who would pay.

I instantly saw my own insurance people, who urged me to calm down and put the whole thing in their hands. I refused. I told them I would handle it and that their only task was on no account to suggest compromise or offer to do anything but accept payment in full on my behalf.

I then wrote a letter to the lawyer telling him, after a detailed description of the incident, to go to hell and do his worst. I told him I wanted no further communication from him unless he were ready to start a lawsuit, in which case I would countersue for damages plus costs. I never heard from that lawyer again.

I next wrote to the Motor Vehicle Bureau in Albany to find out the idiot's insurance company. When the Bureau wrote in order to demand fifty cents, in advance, for the information, I sent them a check for fifty cents. By July 16, I had the name of the insurance company. (By then, Gertrude had given up. In fact, on June 21, she said she wanted a divorce, as she sometimes did in times of depression.)

I wrote to the insurance company, again detailing the entire incident in as furiously eloquent a manner as I could manage, and denounced the idiot for daring to accuse me of negligent driving. I said that undoubtedly, knowing himself to be at fault and unable to risk the results of a very likely bad record, he had probably not informed his insurance company of the event.

The insurance company wrote back and said that the accident had indeed been reported (something I did not believe, but that was not the point at issue) and further said that I was in a private parking lot reserved for tenants only and that I was not a tenant. For that reason I had no case. Nevertheless, out of the kindness of their benevolent hearts they would offer me half the money I asked for and if I did not accept that offer within a certain number of days, they would withdraw the offer.

Whereupon I wrote *instantly*, and quite a long letter. I told them not to bother waiting the certain number of days, because they could wait forever and I would not accept half the money or *any* reduction in the payment by as little as one rotten penny.

I asked them if they doubted my story or thought that I would in any way deviate from the truth for the sake of half of $135. I told them who I was, urged them to look me up in Who's Who, and to judge for themselves whether my word would not bulk larger before any judge and/or jury than that of the knave and rascal whom they represented.

I asked them if they by any chance realized that my wife's mother did indeed live in one of the apartment houses and that we had the permission of the parking attendant to enter the lot, and stay only long enough to load up and get out.

And I asked, finally, if it was their intention to face a judge and/or jury and make the claim that, since I was in the parking lot illegally, their client had the legal right to ram me. I had two children in the back seat of the car, I said, and if I received any more in the way of idiot letters, I would investigate the psychological damage done them in the collision and add that to my claim.

Therefore, I concluded, either pay me every cent or be prepared to go to court, and all the way up to the U. S. Supreme Court, for that matter, for I was well heeled and would spend any amount of money on a matter of principle.

The next thing I got from them was my money. Every cent!

Financially, it was not worth it. The time I spent in writing letters, the hours of sleep I lost in brooding over injustice were worth far more than the piddling little $135 that was at stake. It wasn't even as though the bump were a serious one. I never even bothered fixing it.

But I had to show Gertrude that whatever else I might be, I was not a fellow to be pushed around—and the suggestion concerning divorce was dropped.

There was an odd postscript. After it was all over, I got a breathless letter from the secretary of the fellow at the insurance office with whom I had been arguing.

"Dear Dr. Asimov," it said, "it was such a thrill receiving your letters. I am one of your greatest fans and I told my boss who you were and that a person like you certainly wouldn't lie . . ."

I wrote to the young woman (at her home address, of course) and assured her earnestly that every word I had said in every letter I had written had been the truth.

20

On June 12, 1963, I took the bus to New York to attend a three-day session on creativity at New York University.

Bad luck dogged me a second trip in a row. I managed to lose a two-hundred-dollar wad of cash I had carried as an emergency store. This was the largest sum of money I have ever literally lost—I just dropped it somewhere.

It took me a little time to recover.

Or maybe it took me more than a little time, for I remember very little about the conference. Just two items, in fact:

1. There was some discussion about how to detect creativity in youngsters. I said at once, "Keep an eye peeled for science-fiction readers," but no one took that very seriously.

However, two days after I got home, *The Bulletin of the Atomic Scientists* asked me to do an article on science fiction for them. I chose for my theme the use of science fiction in selecting out the creative youngster. I called it "The Sword of Achilles" and it appeared in the November 1963 *Bulletin of the Atomic Scientists*.[4]

2. Someone read a paper which listed the criteria of creativity in scientists. Criterion after criterion began "The scientist expects his wife to be . . ." or "The scientist chooses a wife who . . ."

Finally I could stand it no more and broke in and said, "The scientist might choose a husband, you know."

[4] See *Is Anyone There?*

There was a sharp intake of breath all around the table, and as I stared in surprise from one to another, I realized that they thought I was implying homosexuality.

Well, even if I were, so what! But I wasn't! I said, irritably, "For God's sake, the scientist could be a woman, couldn't she?"

And everyone exhaled in relief. What amused and irritated me was that two of the scientists sitting around the table were women, and they had been just as shocked at the thought of scientists choosing a husband as the men were.

It was 1963, and I was still alone in my feminism. Women's Liberation had not yet arisen to join me.

21

We didn't send David back to Camp Annisquam in 1963. The two summers, we decided, were enough. Though he didn't complain, our own investigation was enough to show us that he had not really partici-pated in the activities. He was a loner and that was all there was to it.

We decided therefore to send both David and Robyn to a day camp. It wasn't quite as easy on us, but it was easier on David to be with us evenings and nights, and to have Robyn along with him at the camp. That was the summer, in fact, that they both learned to swim.

20

Hugo and History

1

In mid-1963, Keefer was no longer active director of the medical center. So tenuous had my connection with the med school become that I was unaware of the exact day when his term of office had come to an end.

On June 27, I had lunch with Lewis Rohrbaugh, who was his successor and a perfect sweetheart. Had *he* succeeded Faulkner, my life would have taken a different turn, though perhaps not a better one.

Lew and his wife were both Quakers. This was referred to in a newspaper article one day, and the more formal term, without capitalization, was used. The newspaper statement was that "Dr. and Mrs. Rohrbaugh are friends." I encircled the passage and mailed it to Lew with the written comment, "A good beginning. Keep plugging."

Only once did the slightest wrinkle ever interrupt the smooth and friendly tenor of our relationship. I received a routine request to contribute money to the school. It touched the one point that never stopped being sore. I replied stiffly, in writing, that in 1957 Keefer had said that "the school could not afford to pay a science writer" and that now it was my turn to say that "the science writer could not afford to pay the school."

Dr. Rohrbaugh called me in and asked me not to hold a grudge against the school for the actions of a single individual. I said I did not in any other way. Indeed, since 1958, I had co-operated with the school in every possible way and had made every effort to let what favorable publicity I received overflow onto the school.

That one statement, however, I could not make myself forget, and while I would contribute time and effort, I would not contribute money.

Rohrbaugh accepted the inevitable. Indeed, he finally formally admitted my claim to tenure. I have in my possession now a blue card that says, "This will identify Isaac Asimov as a member of the Boston University Medical Center." It is signed by Lewis H. Rohrbaugh. There is a little line under it that says, "Expiration Date," and above that line is the typed word "Indefinite."

2

On July 15, 1963, I brought my third collection of *F & SF* essays to Tim Seldes. I called this one *Adding a Dimension*, and this time Tim had no objections and introduced no delays.

With this collection, I had brought my essays up to date. Of the sixty essays I had thus far written, virtually all that I wanted to collect had been collected. From this point on I simply waited till I had done seventeen more after the previous collection, and then handed them in with an Introduction and with any corrections or updatings that were necessary, and Doubleday would then publish a new collection. Publication became automatic; and I never again omitted an article.

I had also begun a new series of articles for Eric Berger; eight essays on different worlds in the solar system that might offer, in one way or another, environments in which human beings might survive. The first essay dealt with the Moon, and the whole was eventually called *Environments Out There*.

3

Occasionally, I took the children to a Saturday morning matinee and then sat with them. I didn't mind watching bad pictures once in a while. It brought back nostalgic memories of my childhood.

On July 20, I saw *Flipper*, which at least had a dolphin in it. There was an added feature called *The Slave*, though, set in the time of Julius Caesar, which contained some feckless sex-and-sadism, more silly than offensive.

It offended Robyn, though. She might be only 8½ but she had a strong moral sense. She turned to me and said, "Daddy, this is *not* a picture children should see."

"You're right, Robyn," I said, a little ashamed, and rose to go—but David would have none of that. He wanted to see the rest of the picture, so Robyn and I stayed and spent the time whispering to each other about how bad the picture was.

4

I spent much of the summer of 1963 looking forward to the Labor Day weekend, when I would be attending another World Science Fiction convention.

The nineteenth convention, in 1961, had been held in Seattle,

Washington, and the twentieth, in 1962, had been in Chicago. Neither had been in the realm of possibility for me. The twenty-first convention, however, was to be held in Washington, D.C., and that city I could reach. It would be my first World convention in three years.

And it was not just a matter of attending it. I had a notion about the Washington convention which I was keeping strictly to myself. There might be a Hugo involved.

After all, everyone knew I didn't fly, so that everyone also knew that the twenty-first convention in Washington would be the first one I would attend after the publication of *The Hugo Winners*, in which I had made it amply plain that I had never received a Hugo.

Surely, then, the fans running the Washington convention would see to it that I got one for *something*. George Scithers, who was in charge of the convention (he had been on the train with me coming back from Detroit four years before), had called me long before to make sure that I would be willing to sign up for a panel discussion.

I agreed at once and then said, casually, "Do you want me as master of ceremonies?"

"No," said George, just as casually. "Ted Sturgeon is going to be master of ceremonies."

That was a dead giveaway. The master of ceremonies handed out the Hugo awards at the banquet, and when I was at a convention, I was almost always master of ceremonies. The only reason I could possibly be at a convention without being master of ceremonies (it seemed to me) was if I were going to get a Hugo. I couldn't very well give one to myself, so naturally they would need someone else—and George had gone to considerable lengths to make sure that I would be at the convention, using the panel as a pretext.

I was in high good humor over this. The business about never having gotten a Hugo had started off as a joke, of course, but in the process of joking, it had ceased to be one. I really *wanted* a Hugo.

But then, just a few days before the convention, George called again. "Isaac," he said, "Ted can't make it after all because of family complications. I know this is short notice, but can you be master of ceremonies after all?"

I agreed, of course, but my heart sank. No Hugo after all!

I went to the convention at the end of August in a rather depressed state. In that state, I was suddenly aware of the passage of time and the on-creeping of age. My friends, whom I saw at conventions at intervals of some years, were getting visibly old.

One of the first people I saw in Washington, for instance, was Ruth Kyle, the girl who, as Ruth Landis, had been the very image of

Grace Kelly and who had so enlivened the 1955 convention for a number of us. Eight years had passed and she was now a plump matron.

I escaped from these evidences of mortality and from my own Hugoless state by getting away to do some sight-seeing—the Smithsonian Institution, the Washington Monument. I even took a tour through the White House.

But then on September 1, 1963, came the award luncheon and it was up to me to hand out the Hugos. I did what I could to trade on my own annoyance and I handed out each Hugo with a carefully graded increase in my level of hostility.

When Fred Pohl, that friend of my childhood, approached to pick up a Hugo on behalf of a winner, I cried out as he came bounding up, "Break a leg, friend of my childhood!"—but he didn't.

Finally, there was only one Hugo left to be awarded, and it was labeled "Dramatic Award." I didn't think anyone would be interested in that since it would go to some movie or TV show with no one involved who was personally known to anybody, so I let the audience wait while I launched into a short speech of not-so-mock annoyance.

"You know why I've never had a Hugo?" I finally said in peroration, waving my fist in the air. "It's because I'm Jewish, that's why. It's because of anti-Semitic prejudice in high places. It's because you're all a bunch of Nazis." Naturally, this got a big laugh, and I opened the envelope and found that the "Dramatic Award" typed on it had just been put there as a blind.

The final Hugo was, of course, for *me*. I started reading, "For putting the science in science fiction, Is——" and stopped cold.

I was getting a special Hugo for my *F & SF* essays.

There wasn't any question that I was surprised. The day never existed when I could fake that look of stunned astonishment on my face. The audience roared; it roared for ten minutes. When everyone died down and I caught my breath, George handed me the Hugo and I said, "You've ruined my *shtick*, damn it." (I tried to feign indignation, but I was smiling all over. I was delighted.)

Apparently, Ted Sturgeon *had* been chosen master of ceremonies because they were planning to give me a Hugo, and apparently he *had* been kept away by family difficulties.

I said, "Then why did you ask me to be master of ceremonies, George? There were plenty of other choices."

"Oh well," said George, "we thought it would be funnier that way, but I have to admit no one ever dreamed you would lead up to it so beautifully."

I said, "Didn't you think it would look peculiar to have me give a Hugo to myself?"

"Sure," said George, "but the committee decided you were the only writer in science fiction who could give himself a Hugo without being embarrassed."

"Wiseguy," I said—but he was probably right.

5

On September 5, 1963, my mother's sixty-eighth birthday, I finished the first volume of *Understanding Physics*, and within a few days I got to work on a new juvenile math book for Houghton Mifflin. This one was *Quick and Easy Math*.

The idea came to me when I tried to read a book that purported to outline methods for arithmetical calculations without pen and paper. It was quite obvious that the methods that were offered required so much memorization of partial results that no one in his right mind was going to get the answer without first being driven into his wrong mind.

What were really needed were methods for performing very simple computations in the head. I had watched people laboring over the addition of 19 and 27, over the subtraction of 19 from 51, over the multiplication of 18 and 8, and so on. Explain that $19+27=20+26=46$; that $51-19=52-20=32$; that $18\times8=36\times4=72\times2=144$, and other such calculations, and you'll have explained 90 per cent of all the calculations that the ordinary person has to do.

So I sat down to write the book, and had nothing but fun with it.

6

On September 13, I received a valuable insight into female psychology.

Robyn complained that she was tired of my scolding her. I said, "If you have kids someday—are you going to scold them?"

And she reversed direction at once without any noticeable difficulty and said, "Of course. I wouldn't want them to be spoiled."

7

It was clear that the children were old enough to accompany us on trips without being too troublesome, so on September 19 we took off on a two-day jaunt to the White Mountains in New Hampshire, a region we had never before visited.

The trip was delightful and by the next day we were at Mount Washington, the highest mountain in New England. We went up a cog railroad to the top, and then down again. The round trip took three hours and I must admit that I was not pleased with the angle of either ascent or descent, but I concentrated hard on the scenery.

When we came down it was nearly dark and it was quite obvious that it was time to find a motel and settle down for the night.

Gertrude said, "We passed some motels some miles back."

Unfortunately, it was time for one of my abysmal stupidities.

I said, "We don't want to go back."

Why should we not want to go back? It was simply my notion that one went forward, just as though there were no such thing as a strategic retreat.

I didn't bother arguing the point. I just piled everyone into the car, got behind the wheel, and drove south through gathering darkness and then through deep night. The trouble was that (although I didn't known it then) I was heading into a state forest where for twenty miles there was no habitation and certainly no motel—just wilderness, and twenty miles of the most beautiful scenery in the world, which we never saw.

Gertrude was distressed over the scenery we were missing, and the children were afraid we would never find a motel. Only I knew the *real* danger, and I dared not say a word lest I frighten everyone.

Suppose we had a flat, or some other kind of breakdown, alone in that wilderness at night?

We didn't, but I drove twenty miles with that apprehension gnawing at me and yet stubbornly unwilling to turn around and head north again.

We finally found a motel—one of the crummiest I have ever inhabited—but by then we were beggars all, and in no mood to be choosers.

Once daylight came, however, I made up for my mistake. I carefully chose scenic highways, and drove slowly through an unbelievably riotous forest. The leaves had turned three weeks early that year and we had managed to catch the turning at its peak.

We got home at 5 P.M. on the twenty-first, quite satisfied with ourselves. Even the night ride, in retrospect (*only* in retrospect), seemed like an adventure.

8

In New York, on September 27, I visited Mac Talley at New American Library and received the excellent news that he approved of my book on physics and urged me to proceed with the second part with all deliberate speed. I was only too glad to oblige.

The first part was *Understanding Physics: Motion, Sound, and Heat,* and the second part I at once decided would be *Understanding Physics: Light, Magnetism, and Electricity.* The third part, when I got to it, would be on subatomic physics.

I celebrated by taking a tour through the United Nations the next day.

9

I took in the completed *Quick and Easy Math* on October 11, and was so pleased with it that I had the impulse to do a mathematical essay for my *F & SF* series. I was further egged on to do it by an old, old text in arithmetic that I had obtained from Sinex.

It dated back to 1790 and it included instruction on "compound addition"—that is, on the addition of numbers to bases other than 10. Examples would be the addition of yards, feet, and inches, or of pounds, shillings, and pence. There were also "compound subtraction," "compound multiplication," and "compound division."

There were, in addition, tables of enormously strange units for dry measure, wet measure, cloth measure, and an indefinite number of other measures; and other tables for the conversion of one kind of state money to another kind, and all to the new federal money of dollars and cents that had just been established (to say nothing of British, French, and Spanish money).

It seemed to me that most of that nonsense we had gotten rid of with no damage to anyone but, instead, to our great benefit. It further seemed to me that it would do us further good if we could get rid of much remaining nonsense of the same sort.

The essay I wrote, "Forget It!," was the sixty-fifth in the series, and eventually appeared in the March 1964 *F & SF*.[1]

I was so pleased with this essay that on October 11, when with the Fonoroffs and the Saltzbergs, I read the manuscript aloud. The reaction seemed even more favorable than I had expected, whereupon I made another decision:

The previous spring, you see, I had been asked by the New York branch of Mensa to attend one of their meetings and give a talk. They offered to let me pick any date I chose, *any* date, and they would have their meeting then.

Between my own membership in Mensa and their eager desire to

[1] See *Of Time and Space and Other Things* (Doubleday, 1965).

adjust themselves to my needs, I could not refuse, so I bent over the 1963 calendar and chose a date in the autumn.

I had not chosen a topic, however, feeling that that could easily be left for much later, even for the last minutes. On October 11, however, I decided that "Forget It!" would be perfect as a talk to self-conscious intellectuals, and as it would not yet have been published at the time I had chosen to give the talk, it would be new to all of them.

I began looking forward to the talk with eagerness. It was coming up the next month, for when I had studied the calendar, the date I chose out of the whole year as ideal for the talk was the evening of November 22, 1963. It was only a little over six weeks in the future.

10

The happiness of doing *Quick and Easy Math* made me want to do another book for Houghton Mifflin. *Quick and Easy Math* was, in essence, one of the Realm books (I might have called it *Realm of Shortcuts*, but that had seemed too flip.) It seemed natural to me, then, that I next do one of my *Words* books.

It would have been logical to continue culling words from the Bible and, in fact, some time back, I had started the first draft of *Words from Canaan*, which was to deal with the books of Joshua and Judges. Unfortunately, *Words in Genesis* had done poorly and *Words from the Exodus* was doing even worse. Even I could recognize a lost cause, so I abandoned *Words from Canaan* and cast about for something else.

If I couldn't use biblical history, how about secular history? In particular, how about Greek history? That should be a juicy source, considering the dependence of the more learned portions of the English vocabulary on Greek.

I began to buy history books with the thought that if Greek history proved suitable for my purposes, I could then move on to Roman history, medieval history, and so on.

Once again, I checked with secondhand book stores on the possibility of getting a set of *The Historians' History of the World*, and once again I failed. That, however, was not a fatal omission, and I started work on *Words from Greek History* on October 16. (I had also begun Volume 2 of *Understanding Physics* on October 14.)

11

It was time for the annual World Book Year Book meeting, and this time, *at last*, it was in New York.

We all had our session together on October 24 and 25, and discussed possible leads for our respective stories—something that could easily have been done individually by telephone or by mail.

It involved two fancy banquets, and at one of them, on the twenty-fifth, we had grouse at "Twenty-one." I didn't enjoy it particularly, for it was so gamy that it tasted decayed.

New York was an ideal meeting place for me but not for anyone else and there was considerable dissatisfaction with having to junket in such an unjunketable area. Toward the end of the session, therefore, it was announced that in 1964 everyone would meet in Bermuda.

"Everyone but me," I said, emphatically, but no one paid any attention. The consensus seemed to be that, of course, I would go. Lots of money, lots of fun, nothing to do—how could I refuse?

12

I went to New York on November 20, since I had to serve on a panel on the future of space exploration and because afterward I had to give my talk to Mensa on the twenty-second.

The panel was, in one respect, a harrowing experience. I had found out after I had accepted that another panelist would be Wernher von Braun, and I was not an admirer of Wernher von Braun. He had worked under Hitler and would have won the war for the Nazis if he could.

I know, of course, that it might be said that he was just being patriotic or that he would have been thrown into a concentration camp if he had refused or that he had to work on rockets whatever the purpose —and for those reasons I was prepared to remain neutral where he was concerned. I did not have to be friendly.

When we all got onto the platform, therefore, I studiously remained at the end opposite from that occupied by von Braun and did my best to be unaware of his existence.

It didn't help. The moderator, anxious to introduce everyone to everyone, brought von Braun to me and began performing the introduction. There were eight hundred people in the audience watching and I had two seconds to decide what to do. I couldn't make a scene; he was holding out his hand.

I had to take it and hold it as weakly and as briefly as possible— but I did shake hands. Ever since then, I have had the queasy feeling that I have shaken a hand that shook the hand of Adolf Hitler.

The panel itself went by without incident. I spoke last and perforce went beyond the speculations of the others by speaking of the possibilities of interstellar travel.

Afterward several people, including some panelists, met with the press. I was among them. In the fifteen minutes that followed, however, no reporter bothered to address a single question to me, since I was only a science-fiction writer.

Then they took our names to make sure they were all spelled right. Finally, one reporter, addressing us en masse, asked, "Should any of you be referred to as 'Doctor'?"

I waited for someone else to speak, and when no one did, I said, dryly, "I have a Ph.D., so you can call me 'Doctor.' I'm the science-fiction writer."

13

My rounds the next day and Friday morning passed without incident, and at noon on November 22, 1963, I was at the Metropolitan Museum of Art. I remember I was standing at a small replica of the Parthenon, studying it and wondering if there were anything I could say about it in *Words from Greek History* that I had not said, when I heard someone behind me saying something about the President being shot.

I turned and, ignoring the dictates of courtesy, I said quite rudely, "Hey, what the hell are you talking about?"

He told me—and that's how I found out that President Kennedy had been shot in Dallas.

I left the museum at once and went back to my hotel room to do some thinking. Then I called up the person in charge of the Mensa meeting that night and said, "Have you heard what has happened in Dallas?"

"Yes, I have. So shocking."

"I presume, then, that the meeting tonight has been called off."

"I'm afraid not. The invitations went out long ago and there's no way we can call everyone and tell them not to come."

"But no one will come."

"Maybe not. But I hope *you* will—just in case."

"I can't give a talk tonight."

"Then just sit with us. We'll understand."

At 6 P.M., I met the Mensa people in charge at Luchow's on Fourteenth Street (in the old Stuyvesant Town neighborhood of fifteen years before) and we had a rather somber meal. After that we went to the meeting hall and, to my vast astonishment, I found it choked to the rafters with an overflow crowd.

It dawned on me suddenly that the tragic event of the day had given people eight hours of shock and horror so that escape was necessary. It's very likely that if Kennedy had not been assassinated that day, the audience would have been only half its size.

I couldn't very well refuse to speak.

After I was introduced, I said, "Ladies and gentlemen, it had been my intention to give a lighthearted talk today, but under the circumstances, I think it will be impossible for me to be lighthearted. Please forgive me, then, if I am not at my best."

There was a clearly sympathetic murmur, so I took heart and launched into my "Forget It!" talk.

My warning proved unnecessary. I had no sooner warmed up and heard my own voice in my ears (there are few sounds sweeter to almost anyone, I suppose) when the outside world drifted away and vanished. Indeed, it did so even more effectively than it would have done on an ordinary day, for the act of speaking served as a kind of opiate to deaden pain and distress. As I felt my misery leave, I grew actively happy.

And so did the audience—for the same reason, I'm sure. After the first five minutes, I was animated and funny, and the audience responded eagerly, laughing up an enthusiastic storm.

The talk was a huge success and left me with a bad case of aching conscience. Yet what could I have done?

14

I completed *Words from Greek History* on December 6, and handed the manuscript to Austin on December 10. It was longer than any of my other *Words* books, so I tried to steel myself against a request for cutting—and at home I charged ahead with Volume 2 of *Understanding Physics*.

15

My father was suffering from intestinal bleeding and was in a hospital for examination. I went to New York to see him, therefore, and visited him in the hospital on December 16. He seemed in fine shape, bright and active, though his hair (what there was of it) was now completely white. I amused him, and the other patients in the room, for several hours with funny stories from Greek history.

Fortunately, the condition proved to be not serious. He was discharged and all was well when he celebrated his sixty-seventh birthday on the twenty-first.

16

As 1963 came to an end, I found I had once again, for the second year in a row, published six books:

49. *Words from the Exodus* (Houghton Mifflin)
50. *The Genetic Code* (Orion)
51. *The Human Body* (Houghton Mifflin)
52. *Fifty Short Science-fiction Tales* (Collier)
53. *View from a Height* (Doubleday)
54. *The Kite That Won the Revolution* (Houghton Mifflin)

17

On January 1, 1964, Bernie Pitt died of a heart attack at the age of forty-five. I did not know this at the time. I did not find out until three months later, when I came across a one-sentence obituary in *Chemical & Engineering News*. I called Ruth Pitt at once and, as in the case of Cyril Kornbluth six years before, I was distressed that I had not kept in closer touch.

18

I turned forty-four on January 2, 1964, but my birthday present came, unexpectedly, the day after. One of the bookstores I had been in touch with about finding *The Historians' History of the World* actually sounded hopeful, so I called the Silvers to tell them that. After all, they, above all, knew how badly I wanted a set, and they would be glad.

But Mary Silvers, who answered the phone, said, "Don't get a set, Isaac! Rollo has been trying to get you one for a whole year and he's succeeded. It's on its way."

I couldn't believe it and she had to work hard to convince me she was serious. But it was true; Rollo called me on the thirteenth to say he had the set for me. I drove down helter-skelter, and there it was, in perfect condition; and, in fact, the same edition I remembered reading in Philadelphia twenty years before.

I hesitated. It was a complete set, and Rollo's own edition had a volume missing. For a moment I felt that I ought to offer him the missing volume, but his edition was different in appearance and the added volume wouldn't look good on the shelf—and all he wanted was the looks of the set, whereas I needed them for active reference.

Yet that was just rationalization. The truth of the matter was that I was selfish beyond belief. Here was a man who had labored to give me something I very much wanted and who had ended by giving me something that was better than he himself had, yet I knew I didn't want to let go of that volume. I didn't even make the offer *pro forma*, and if he had asked for it, I would have tried to refuse.

My conscience twinged sufficiently at this, however, to cause me to offer him untold sums for the set, but he would only accept (after considerable argument) exactly what he had himself paid—forty dollars. He wouldn't take one cent more. And even with that additional evidence of good will and kindness, I still couldn't force myself to offer him the volume.

19

The Historians' History of the World came at just the right time, for *Words from Greek History* took an odd turn.

On January 2, I had had a birthday lunch with Austin and he had asked me to take back the manuscript and cut it a bit. It was too long, he said. He also said, with some embarrassment, that he had made some suggestions—only suggestions, which I need not follow—as to which areas to cut.

I took it back resignedly, for I had expected something like that. When I went over it at home and studied the passages that Austin was suggesting I cut, I seemed to see a pattern, however. I phoned him.

"Austin," I said, "you seem to be cutting out my sections on words."

"I guess so," said Austin.

"But you're leaving the Greek history."

Austin said, "I thought the Greek history was more interesting than the words."

"That makes it sound, Austin, as though you want me to write a history of Greece; a straight history."

"Well—" said Austin.

I wouldn't let him finish. "I'll be glad to do it," and I hung up, quickly.

It was exactly what I wanted to do, and I didn't mind canceling *Words from Greek History* and starting over. In fact, it wouldn't even be a matter of canceling, for I could cannibalize a great deal of the earlier book. And now *The Historians' History of the World* would be a great reference.

The only thing was I couldn't start it right away. The second volume of *Understanding Physics* was consuming a great deal of my time, and I had also started *A Short History of Chemistry*. This latter book was modeled on the earlier *A Short History of Biology*, and, like the former book, could be gotten out of the Biographical Encyclopedia without much trouble.

20

On January 15, 1964, I traveled to Northampton, Massachusetts, to give three talks over a two-day period at Smith College. Smith was, of course, a famous girls' school, and when invited I said, jokingly, "You'll put me up in the girls' dormitory, of course."

"Of course," they said.

"I was only joking," I said.

"Well, we're not. You'll be in the girls' dormitory."

I thought about that quite a bit. I knew that sexual standards were relaxing in the colleges, but somehow I didn't think they had relaxed quite as much as all that. I girded myself for anything that might happen.

I was given a two-room suite in the girls' dormitory, but it was off in a corner, with a private entrance to the street, and no other entrance at all. So much for my fantasies.

Another thing I remember about the trip was talking to some of the girls. One of them said she was married.

"A little early, wasn't it?" I said, for she was only nineteen.

"I had to get out of the girls' dormitory somehow," she said.

"If only I could get in," I said, thinking of that private entrance.

"You wouldn't like it," she said, positively. "You may think you would, but after a while, sitting in the cafeteria and hearing nothing but high, shrill voices, like a bunch of twittering canaries, you'd begin to feel as though you'd go out of your mind if you didn't hear a baritone once in a while."

And I suddenly became aware of the canary sound of all the girls around us and got the horrid feeling that she might be right.

I think I could have endured it for a while, though—long enough, you understand.

21

When I got home on the seventeenth, I found the page proofs of *A Short History of Biology* waiting for me. Along with it was an index!

That came as a shock to me. I always did my own indexes, but it had not occurred to me to make that plain to Natural History Press.

Of course, it meant a saving of time, so I looked over the index, which had, presumably, been professionally prepared, to see if I could learn lessons in technique. I quickly found that the only lesson I could learn would be on the method of preparing a thoroughly inadequate index. Half the names in the book were not included. A number of subjects were not mentioned.

It was insupportable.

I prepared my own index as quickly as I could, but when I took it in I was told it was too late to make the substitution. I discoursed lengthily and feelingly on the general subject of stupidity and they apologized, but the book was published with the useless index, and once again I had a book I didn't enjoy.

It added just one more time-wasting task to the list. I had to see to it that no publisher, either through ignorance or through forgetfulness, ever allowed a "professional" to prepare my indexes.

22

Playboy wanted me to do a science-fiction story. Where payment was concerned, *Playboy* was *The Saturday Evening Post* of the 1960s. For a 1,000-word short-short, they would pay $750.

Their proposition was that I write the story about an illustration they were sending me. The illustration consisted of a dim photograph of a clay head, without ears, and with the other features labeled in block letters. That was all. What's more, two other authors (I think one was Fred Pohl) were asked to write stories based on the same photo.

On January 20, I wrote the story, which was eventually called "Eyes Do More Than See," and sent it off. It came back on January 28, to my discomfiture. A. J. Budrys was at that time fiction-editor for *Playboy*, and he wanted a little more emotion in the story. I made the necessary changes and sent it off on February 3, and it was rejected a second time, and this time for good!

What made it particularly harrowing was that the other two stories were accepted by *Playboy* and, when they roped in a hurry-up substitute for me, his story was accepted also. In other words, out of four stories written around the photograph, three were accepted and only mine was rejected—and twice, at that.

I had not experienced such a humiliation in my science-fiction writing since I had stalked out of Sam Merwin's office with "Grow Old With Me" sixteen years before.

A little bruised, I sent "Eyes Do More Than See" to *F & SF*, which accepted it promptly. To be sure, the payment was now only $25, but I honestly didn't mind that. I had enough money; what I wanted was an acceptance. "Eyes Do More Than See" appeared finally in the April 1965 *F & SF*.[2]

23

If the "Eyes Do More Than See" affair was a humiliation, I had the chance to gain a little exaltation elsewhere. The book editor of the New York *Herald Tribune* wanted me to review the new third edition of the Columbia Encyclopedia. He said he could think of no one else with a knowledge broad enough to make a fair assessment. Well, that alone would have been enough to put a shy grin on my face, and it drove me to make a special effort.   ·

I decided I would turn the pages and read a few paragraphs on every page. I don't know if I would really have lasted the distance, but on page 118, I came across the entry, "Asimov, Isaac." It was totally unexpected, and the effect was a lot like tripping on a step you didn't know was there.

My first thought was that I was there only because I was a Columbia graduate. I looked up other Columbia graduates who, I thought, might well be in the encyclopedia, and they weren't, so it was legitimate. For the first time, I was embedded in encyclopedish amber.

Naturally, I gave the volume a good review. Fortunately, it was worth it. If it had been a rotten job, I would have been in a real quandary.

24

Hofstra College, out on Long Island, asked me for permission to reprint something and it suddenly occurred to me that Hofstra had been the college that Irene (of graduate-school days) had attended. I told them that if they obtained Irene's present address for me they could reprint without charge; if they did not, they could not reprint at all.

They got busily to work and on February 15, 1964, I got the address. I sent off a polite letter at once, recalling myself to her memory,

2 See *Nightfall and Other Stories*.

reminding her that she had planned to have five children, and asking how life had treated her.

She answered by return mail. Of course, she remembered me, she said. When mention of me appeared in the papers, she would tell people (including her children) that she knew me in school. She actually *did* have five children, four girls and a boy, and she, her husband, and her children were all doing well.

It had been twenty-two years since I had heard from her, and I was gratified. I replied in order to bring her up to date on my personal life, and after one or two more exchanges of letters, there was nothing more to say, and we stopped.

25

Robyn was nine years old on February 19, 1964, but it was somehow I who got the birthday present. The World Book Year Book had insisted on handing out another bonus, and I was ordered to buy something up to a hundred dollars and bill them. At first, I thought there was absolutely nothing I wanted badly enough to be willing to bill them for, but then I thought of a globe—an elaborate globe.

I got one that was sixteen inches in diameter and lit up inside. It was a beauty and I was very pleased.

I was able to express my pleasure directly to Roy Fisher when he arrived in Boston soon after. I had lunch with him on February 26, and he discussed a new year book being planned, one to be devoted to scientific advances and to be called *Science Year*. I thought it was a good idea, of course, and said so. Neither of us mentioned the forthcoming Bermuda junket. I suppose he took it for granted I would come. I certainly took it for granted I would not.

Fisher wanted to eat at the Harvard Faculty Club, where horse steak was a traditional item on the menu. Fisher wanted to try it, so I ordered it also. I couldn't tell it from a poor cut of beefsteak and finished it with no more trouble than a lot of chewing. Fisher, however, could only down about a third of it. He was clearly unable to continue eating horse.

26

On February 29, 1964, I finally finished the second volume of *Understanding Physics*, and that night I celebrated by attending a Mensa meeting.

Tom Lehrer, the song satirist, attended too, and the host of the meeting turned to me for help. Lehrer had come with the express warning that he must not be asked to perform, and the host was afraid that some of the Mensa people would be unable to resist badgering the man unless there were some definite item of entertainment scheduled—so would I give a speech?

I wasn't in the least enthusiastic about putting myself up as a substitute for Lehrer, but needs must. Since it was Leap Day, I improvised a talk on the development of the calendar, dealing with the lunar year versus the solar year and the Julian year versus the Gregorian year. It went over quite well, and Lehrer was left to himself.

Nor was it a loss. Ten days later I turned my talk into an *F & SF* essay, which I entitled "The Days of Our Years,"[3] my seventieth essay in the series. It appeared in the August 1964 *F & SF*.

27

Meanwhile, I was planning to put together another collection. *I, Robot* had contained nine of my positronic robot stories, but there were two I had omitted: "Robot AL-76 Goes Astray" and "Victory Unintentional." Furthermore, in the thirteen years since *I, Robot* had been published, I had done six more robot short stories.

Together, my unincluded robot short stories came to some sixty thousand words, a little skimpy, but it was my idea that my two robot novels be also included. With *The Caves of Steel* and *The Naked Sun*, I would have a large, two-hundred-thousand-word book containing all the robot material that was not in *I, Robot*. In fact, I planned to call it *The Rest of the Robots*.

For the first time, I was collecting stories not because they were, in themselves, worth collecting, but simply because they were there. I felt that I had reached the point where my stories, *all* of them, were of interest to readers as possessing historical interest if no other kind. This was rather a matter of vanity in me, I suppose, but Tim Seldes agreed.

I therefore had Gertrude type up the early stories for which I did not have satisfactory manuscripts available, and on March 5, I took in the collection to Doubleday. I also took in the second volume of *Understanding Physics* to Mac Talley.

(While in New York, I attended, on the evening of March 6, a meeting of the Trap Door Spiders for a second time. I enjoyed myself as much as I had five years before, and again Sprague urged me to join, and again I felt it was not a good idea.)

[3] See *Of Time and Space and Other Things.*

28

Meanwhile, the news arrived that Stanley was in the hospital. He had a slipped disc and was in traction. The problem was tennis. Stanley and Ruth were both confirmed tennis maniacs, and Stanley, at least, had a variety of physical problems as a result but counted it all a reasonable price to pay for the pleasure of hitting a ball with a racket.

He was eventually operated on and put into good shape—at least sufficiently good shape to continue playing tennis and continue collecting tennis elbow and other things.

Years later, when I berated him (as I periodically did) for this aberration of his, he told me of a friend of his who died on the tennis court and was buried in his tennis costume.

I said, "You sound envious."

"It was a good way to go," said Stanley.

How idiotic!

A good way to go is to go at the typewriter and collapse with your nose in the keys. *That's* a good way to go.

Tennis, forsooth!

29

On March 18, I heard that Norbert Wiener had died in Stockholm, Sweden, at the age of sixty-nine. I was distressed, of course. He was, for all his oddness, a great man. Yet I felt a touch of relief (of which I was ashamed) that there would now be no occasion for me ever to have to fend off arranging a series of conversations with him for publication.

30

The evidence of human mortality was piling up, and I was doing some heavy thinking on the subject. A number of things contributed to it:

1. There was my father's hospitalization and his pronounced aging.

2. There was my brother's hospitalization. Even my kid brother, whom I remembered as a baby, was showing signs of falling apart.

3. I was now forty-four, two years older than my father had been when he discovered he was suffering from angina—and I was almost as

fat as he was at the time. I was now 210 pounds in weight; I had never weighed as much in my life.

4. Bernie Pitt, who was less than a year older than myself, had died of a heart attack, and British actor Peter Sellers, who was five years younger than I was, had survived a rather serious one.

I was not proof against all these considerations.

I decided on April 10, 1964, to lose a considerable amount of weight, and I quietly proceeded to cut down on my food intake.

In two months, I lost 30 pounds and brought my weight down to 180, and kept it there. I never regained the lost weight, and I think it was a good thing to do. Had I not done it the chances are I would not be sitting here now writing my autobiography.

I did not say anything to Gertrude about this, but after I had been at it for a couple of weeks, she studied me for a moment and said, "Say, are you losing weight, Isaac?"

I couldn't deny it.

31

On April 13, 1964, Gertrude and I went to the local movie house to see *Seven Days in May*. I found it difficult to react properly because I watched with a great deal of tension. That was the day when, for the first time, we left the children at home without a baby-sitter. David was 12½ and Robyn was 9.

We had in the past left them with a baby-sitter who was no more than 12 herself, but thinking of that didn't help. I was never so glad to see a movie end as I was that evening. We drove home quickly—and found the children peacefully asleep in bed.

PART III

Endlessly Broadening

21

Changes of Editors

1

On April 21, 1964, I took the family for a second trip into Canada. We were only gone two days but the sensation of being in a foreign country was much stronger this time, for we visited Quebec. Francophone Canada was another thing altogether.

David was particularly excited at the thought of hearing a foreign language spoken, but all the glamor vanished when he found that television made no sense to him in French.

My clearest memory of the trip is that of my having carefully worked out in my mind the French for "Where is the ferry?" so that I could ask the question with casual sophistication and make my way across the St. Lawrence with presence and aplomb.

I saw a likely young man, clearly intelligent, with a frank, open face, and said in my best French accent, "*Pardonnez-moi, monsieur, mais ou est la traverse, s'il vous plaît?*"

But I found I was questioning a German tourist, who couldn't understand a word I said (in either French or English) and who didn't know where the ferry was in any case. I could speak German better than I could speak French, as it happens, but this rather broke my spirit and I found the *traverse* by myself.

2

New York City was having a World's Fair again, as it had had in 1939, a quarter century before. I visited it on May 8, interrupting furious work on *The Greeks*, which I had finally begun on May 1. It was not entirely my own idea. I was doing it at the request of the New York *Times*, which wanted me to write an article on it.

I stayed for eight hours and was most impressed by what was called "the Underground Home." Since I have always liked enclosed spaces and envy small animals their snug underground dens and have celebrated enclosed societies in the Foundation series and in *The Caves of Steel*, I considered it a step in the right direction.

That evening I attended a meeting of the Hydra Club for the first time in quite a while. Among those present was Cornell Woolrich, whose use of William Irish as a pseudonym had led to my own choice of Paul French. He was sixty-one years old at the time and looked older. It was the first time I had ever met him and I tried to tell him how much I enjoyed his books, but he shrugged it off.

Before I left New York that visit, I arranged to have one more book done by Abelard-Schuman. They said they would be willing to publish my Scholastic series, *Environments Out There*. I was glad to be able to give them something, for I hadn't done a new book for them since I finished *The Double Planet* six years before.

3

I was becoming internationally known. Foreign reporters occasionally interviewed me, and foreign editors visiting the country wanted to see me.

On May 27, for instance, a Japanese reporter interviewed me by way of an interpreter who spoke English with charming hesitation. I did my best, using simple words and speaking slowly.

They then offered to take me to dinner but said they wanted to go to a good restaurant that featured typically American food. I had a momentary impulse to take them to a cafeteria, but decided that the honor of the United States required more than that. I took them to Smith House in Cambridge, where the cuisine was good New England.

The Japanese woman spoke to the interpreter, who then asked me to order the meal and to choose typically American dishes. I ordered New England clam chowder and a plate of scrod with french-fried potatoes and peas. I ordered it for myself, too, since I did not want them to think that I was trying any tricks on them.

They ate it with every sign of pleasure and occasionally spoke quickly to each other, and it struck me that to them the food was exotic and thrilling.

For dessert, I was going to order apple pie *à la mode*, but the English-speaking woman asked me if the Indian pudding on the menu was a traditional Indian dish.

"Yes," I said, "American Indian."

"Please let us have it."

"Certainly," I said, groaning inwardly. Indian pudding is cornmeal mush and I had tried a mouthful of it once and decided that it was the Red Man's Revenge.

I ordered Indian pudding all around, showed them how to add the milk and then watched them eat *that* with little quiverings of delight. I ate mine like a good boy—but haven't tasted it since.

4

On June 4, 1964, in New York, I finally picked up about three fifths of the galleys of *Asimov's Biographical Encyclopedia of Science and Technology*. It was over 2½ years since I had started the book, and now I finally saw portions of it in print for the first time.

The remainder of the galleys arrived on June 9, and on the twelfth I had completed the job of proofing. Fortunately, there was no need to prepare an index at this stage. My notion of keying the index items to the number of the biography rather than the page meant the job could be done in manuscript, and I had done it. Reading the galleys was therefore the end of my job. (I added 6 biographies in galleys, so that I ended with 1,007 biographies altogether.)

I sent it all off by registered mail to Doubleday on June 13 and made a note in my diary that the postage came to $8.10, and that it was the most expensive single item I had ever mailed.

Two days later, I was completely finished with *The Greeks*, and I took it in to Austin on the sixteenth.

5

The American Chemical Society hands out, at its annual meetings, a number of awards, medals, plaques, and other memorabilia for notable work in this or that branch of the field. Among the lesser items is the James T. Grady medal for science writing in the field of chemistry. It carried with it, at that time, a one-thousand-dollar award (tax-free), a gold medal, a bronze replica of the medal (for display while the real thing rested in the bank vault), and three hundred dollars travel expenses, since the lucky winner had to show up at the meeting to collect all this in person.

Year after year I had been nominated (along with every other chemical-science writer in America, I think), and year after year I did not get the award. Sooner or later, though, if one is patient, the society is bound to run out of one's competitors.

At any rate, on June 15, 1964, I received a letter (stamped "Confidential") telling me that the award was mine if I would come and get it. The ACS was meeting in Detroit the following April and I would have to be there.

Since I'd been in Detroit five years before for the science-fiction convention, I knew I could make it. The award seemed to me to be worth the trouble of the trip, so I accepted the honor.

6

I couldn't allow *The Greeks* to be over and done with without having started another project, and there was one immediately at hand. The third volume of *Understanding Physics* had to be done, and I began it on May 27.

It was to deal with the world within the atom, and its subtitle was *The Electron, Proton, and Neutron.* I expected it to be the easiest and the most amusing of the three volumes, and so it was. In a sense, it was a rewrite of *Inside the Atom* on a deeper level and with a more detailed and extensive treatment.

That, of course, is another factor that makes the writing of nonfiction so rewarding. You can take up the same subject at a variety of levels, from a variety of standpoints, and for a variety of audiences, getting a different pleasure out of it each time. I imagine the pleasure is similar to that which a musician gets from composing, or playing, something called "Variations on a Theme from So-and-so."

I also started a third series of articles for Scholastic. This one was rather like *Breakthroughs in Science* but was to feature the development of ideas rather than biographies. The title of the series was, in fact, to be *The Great Ideas of Science.*

I also began *A Short History of Astronomy* on June 28. It was intended to be the third in my series of *Short History* books, following biology and chemistry.

7

It was a presidential election year again, and on July 13, the Republican nominating convention opened. Barry Goldwater was the sure nominee. It was quite certain that Lyndon Johnson (who, as Vice President, had automatically succeeded on Kennedy's assassination) would be the Democratic nominee.

I was quite certain whom I would vote for. I would favor almost any Democrat over almost any Republican, but in this case the gap was unusually wide.

On the one hand, Johnson had handled Congress well (Kennedy had not) and was putting through a good deal of civil-rights legislation —of which I approved. Goldwater, on the other hand, was a hard-line conservative and, specifically, wanted to see us get deeper into the Vietnam fracas.

I was furiously against Goldwater on this point. Vietnam seemed like a mousetrap to me and I wanted to see American soldiers out of there so that the United States would be free to fight more important battles (not necessarily military ones) in more important places.

For that reason I said, concerning Goldwater, in my diary notation for July 13, "It is very important that he be *smashed*, not merely defeated, in November."

The most important personal effect of the 1964 presidential campaign was that it rather disenchanted me with Mensa.

I already had some trouble with it, since though I met a great many fascinating and interesting people at the Mensa meetings, I also met a great many irritating ones as well.

In a way, I was a marked man at the meetings. A certain percentage of the members, especially the younger and newer ones, seemed to feel that the way to establish their credentials was to take me on in a battle of wits and shoot me down.

I didn't feel the same endless necessity to take on new competitors, and I was in no mood to be an old gun-fighter forever compelled to shoot it out with any challenger who could say, "All right, Ringo. Reach!"

I began to be rather sullen and withdrawn at meetings and then discovered the last straw when it seemed to me that the percentage of Mensa people who were pro-Goldwater was just as high as the percentage of non-Mensa people who were pro-Goldwater.

It struck me that I did not particularly want to associate with people on the sole ground that they were like me in whatever quality it is that makes one do well on an intelligence test. I wanted people who more or less shared my common assumptions and universe outlook so that there could be a reasonable dialog.

So though I stuck it out at Mensa for a year and more, my attendance at the meetings became sporadic and eventually I didn't pay my dues and I let my membership lapse.

8

In New York on July 16, I brought with me my fourth batch of *F & SF* essays for Doubleday publication. I called it *Of Time and Space and Other Things*.

That evening I attended a showing of *Othello* in Central Park.

This had become a steady thing with me. There is a great deal of excitement to going to the theater in the open—to sitting down in the dying sunshine and watching it grow dark as the play progresses—to being able to see the Moon and stars change position as the play progresses—to note the scurrying of the clouds and hear the rustling of the trees and estimate the chances of rain—even having the planes drown out the dialog at times adds piquancy.

And, of course, I rarely miss the chance to see Shakespeare.

9

Each month brought me closer to the time when the World Book Year Book people would hold their meeting in Bermuda. I had to practice refusing.

Roy Fisher asked me to come to Chicago again, for some trivial reason, and this time I was not going to allow any consideration of money to deflect me. I sent off an air-mail, special-delivery letter on July 25, refusing flatly, and leaving no room for any hope that I would change my mind. They let the matter drop, and that was a good sign.

10

On August 2, 1964, I finished A *Short History of Astronomy* and the next day I took it in to the Boston office of Educational Services, a Doubleday division. It had taken me only five weeks to write it and I didn't give the matter of editorial decision any thought. I took it for granted it would be published.

I was wrong. There was a serious problem. I had begun, traditionally, with the Greeks, but not long before, my astronomical friend Gerald Hawkins (now with Boston University) had published a book *Stonehenge Decoded*, in which he depicted Stonehenge as a prehistoric (1500 B.C.) astronomical observatory of considerable sophistication. It seemed therefore that I ought to have had at least a chapter on pre-Greek astronomy.

Since I had started on the wrong foot, I did not please the editor in the rest of the book either, and by September 12 it was back on my hands with a flat rejection!

It was by no means an unprecedented situation. There had been the case of *The Death Dealers* in 1958, of course. In addition, I had, in 1959, written a book called *Only a Light-Year*, a series of miscellaneous essays on astronomy written for Abelard-Schuman as an effort to follow *Only a Trillion*.

Only a Trillion, however, had not done well enough to make Abelard-Schuman eager to publish a second in the series, and some of my offhand speculations on astronomical subjects were felt to be shaky, so I got *Only a Light-Year* back with a request for revision. I put it aside because I was busily working on *The Wellsprings of Life* and I never got back to it. The book remained unpublished.

That did not mean that *Only a Light-Year* was of no use to me. Even unpublished, it had value, for I knew I would be able to cannibalize material from it for other books. Little by little, much of the material in *Only a Light-Year* appeared in my various *F & SF* essays.

In the same way, I put *A Short History of Astronomy* away and waited, in a philosophic mood, for a chance to cannibalize it.

Meanwhile, I had plenty of other things to do. The third volume of *Understanding Physics* was proceeding at a rapid pace, for instance.

Then, too, Austin Olney had accepted *The Greeks* (with just a little cutting because it, too, was overlong), and that meant I had a whole series of history books in the works. This was so different from anything else I had done that it raised me to a high pitch of excitement.

To be sure, Austin had by now come to know me so well that when he told me he was going to do *The Greeks,* he said to me, cautiously, "But Isaac, please do me a favor and don't bring in a book on the Romans till we see how this one does. All right?"

"I promise," I said.

I try always to keep my promises, so I was determined not to bring in a book on the Romans till Austin gave me the go-ahead signal. I had not, however, promised not to *write* a book on the Romans. On August 5, therefore, I began to write such a book. I didn't work very hard or steadily on it since I had to wait for *The Greeks* to be published and to be in the bookstores long enough to show results, and that meant I would not be able to take it to Austin for over a year—but I started.

11

And again, Basic Books asked me to do a complete revision and updating of *The Intelligent Man's Guide to Science.*

For this I had to take certain precautions. I asked at Basic Books who my editor would be on this one and I was told it would be Richard DeHaan, who was newly with the firm.

"Not Leon Svirsky?" I said, in surprise.

"Leon has retired," I was told.

"Good. And is it understood that there will be no changes in what

I write without my seeing those changes *before* the book is put into galleys?"

"Absolutely."

"In that case," I said, "I will do the book."

Basic Books sent me two copies of the first edition, and I gradually took it apart, removing one page at a time, pasting each on a sheet of typing paper, and making corrections and additions in the margin, exactly as I had done on two different occasions with *Biochemistry and Human Metabolism.*

Since I had carefully kept my library copy of the first edition up to date with references in its margin (something I had also done with *Biochemistry and Human Metabolism*), the revision, which I began on August 18, went quickly.

12

On August 20, 1964 (David's thirteenth birthday), I got a call from Merrill Panitt of *TV Guide.* Apparently, the television season that was to start the next month would have a new program called "My Living Doll" in which Julie Newmar was to play a perfectly stunning robot who looked exactly like the superwomanish Julie Newmar.

Merrill wanted me to watch a couple of programs and then write a humorous commentary on it.

I watched the program (slavering over Julie Newmar and wishing I had a robot like that), wrote the article on October 13, and sold it to *TV Guide.* It eventually appeared in the January 16, 1965, issue.

My title was "How Not to Build a Robot,"[1] but I discovered that *TV Guide* almost never used my titles. In fact, for some strange reason, *TV Guide* almost always used two titles, one on the contents page and one in the body of the piece, neither one of them being mine. On the contents page of the January 16, 1965, issue, the article was called "On Robots and 'My Living Doll.'" In the body of the magazine the title was "Why I Wouldn't Have Done It This Way."

"How Not to Build a Robot" was my first attempt at humor for the general public (as opposed to my in-jokes in the Introductions to *The Hugo Winners* and to my *F & SF* essays). It succeeded; I had finally learned to be a humorist.

Certainly, the editors of *TV Guide* thought I had, and in years to come they periodically asked me for more humor pieces and, eventually, for serious pieces as well.

Then, too, I tapped a really mass market for the first time and

[1] See *Is Anyone There?*

reached millions of people who had never heard of me before and who were not really my readers. *TV Guide* forwarded at least some of the mail they received from their readers concerning my article, and I had to harden myself to a completely new level of commentary.

The humor of the article consisted in my pretense of being appalled, as a "robotics expert," at anyone having designed a robot in the inefficient shape of Julie Newmar. Some readers actually wrote to express their contempt for my inability to see the point of the program, while others seemed really upset that I should prefer a cylindrical metal body to that of Julie Newmar (as though I would yield to *anyone* in my scholarly admiration for the various good points and surface attractions of that fine woman).

13

We were off to Birchtoft again on August 23, but things were changing. The resorts of the Northeast were having a devil of a time as increasing affluence and the coming of jet travel made it easier and easier to visit the Caribbean or the Mediterranean. Fewer and fewer people were satisfied with the traditional "mountains," and resorts had to find new ways of attracting people. Annisquam had become a boys' camp, and Birchtoft was becoming a camping station. When we arrived, we found that we were nearly the only ones who attended in the traditional fashion.

Both children were with us this time, and it wasn't too bad. We had the beach, and the newly installed swimming pool, largely to ourselves.

14

Avram Davidson's stint as editor of *F & SF* was coming to an end. I was not entirely displeased, since he and I did not get along quite as well as Bob Mills and I had.

For several months, Joe Ferman had been searching for a new editor and he asked me for my recommendation. He said he wanted someone who would live in New York and be on the spot.

I said, rather desperately (for I feared he might be angling for me), "What about your son? He strikes me as an intelligent young man. He's been interested in the magazine quite a while and working on it, so he won't be an amateur."

I think I was the first to raise Ed Ferman's name in connection with the editorship. Joe looked thoughtful and said, "Well, I'll think about it."

The thinking was fruitful, for Ed Ferman became editor of the magazine with the December 1964 issue. My essay in that issue (my seventy-fourth in the series) was "A Galaxy at a Time."[2]

It quickly developed that Ed and I got along like a house afire and I have always thought it very intelligent of me to put that particular bee into Joe Ferman's bonnet. He might have selected Ed for the editorship without my suggestion—but who knows?

15

On September 14, 1964, David entered junior high school (which was located just a block and a half from our house). Once again, I passed a milestone that reminded me of the remorseless accumulation of age. I had a child in junior high school!

Actually, the situation was worse than it seemed. Our children had come relatively late in life, and when we attended PTA meetings, we found that the other parents were all younger than we were. It made us feel superannuated and we did not willingly attend such meetings.

16

Also on the fourteenth, I received a letter from Linus Pauling with reference to my article "First and Rearmost"[3] in the October 1964 F & SF. He himself, said Pauling, had frequently been caught in one mistake or another, but never in his entire career had he made a mistake of twenty-three orders of magnitude, as I had in this article. That's all he said; he didn't say where the mistake was.

I started rereading the article in a fever of panic. If I couldn't find the error, not only would I be humiliated, but also I would not be able to reprint the article in the collection *Of Time and Space and Other Things*.

I found it. I had made use of Avogadro's constant (the number of protons making up a gram—6.02×10^{23}) and had multiplied by it once instead of twice (or possibly twice instead of once—I forget). I corrected the error for the collection, and didn't know whether to be proud of Pauling's confidence that I could find the error without help, or annoyed with him for not having helped anyway.

[2] See *Of Time and Space and Other Things*.
[3] See *Of Time and Space and Other Things*.

17

The next day, September 15, I traveled down to Philadelphia to give a talk to the executives of Smith, Kline & French, a pharmaceutical firm. I was a little more nervous than I usually was. When they had asked me to come speak, they had offered five hundred dollars. In a fit of insanity, I asked for twice that and they *agreed!* Now I had to come through and make it worth the money for them, and I wasn't at all sure I could.

I had decided to speak on the topic "Four Steps to Salvation," which had appeared in the June 1961 *F & SF* as my thirty-second essay and which was one of the seven essays I had never reprinted. Fortunately, the talk went very well. I was received with enormous applause, and the fellow in charge turned over the thousand-dollar check with a broad smile on his face. (Just the same, it was a long time before I dared ask so large a speaking fee again.)

The talk had been given to a small group, and it was recorded on videotape so that it could be replayed for others in the organization who had not attended the talk. The young man in charge of the TV cameras told me he would signal me when the time came to bring the talk to a halt because the film was running out. There would be signal cards telling me how much time remained, he told me.

When I was done, he told me ebulliently, "I don't know how you did it, Dr. Asimov. You never seemed the least bit concerned as the signal cards went up. You didn't hurry, you weren't rattled, and you finished in the most natural way with just twenty-two seconds to spare."

Once again, as on so many previous occasions in my life, I missed my chance to be suavely sophisticated. I should merely have smiled and murmured, "We old-timers have no trouble in this sort of thing."

Instead, I goggled at the young man and said, "What signal cards?"

"Didn't you see them?" he said, disbelievingly.

I shook my head, "I forgot all about them."

He staggered away. People never realize how nonvisual I am.

18

I returned to New York and made my usual rounds. I had lunch with Dick DeHaan and his assistant, Patricia van Doren, from Basic

Books, on September 17, and reported on the progress I was making with the revision of *The Intelligent Man's Guide to Science*.

Pat van Doren was a large, warmhearted woman, with a boisterous sense of humor, and I particularly enjoyed her company.

I remember once, when I was walking into a restaurant with her, we met Robert Banker of Doubleday, who was walking out. I gave him a pleased greeting and introduced him and Pat to each other.

Bob said, "Now, take good care of Isaac, Mrs. van Doren. He's Doubleday's favorite writer."

"Of course I will," said Pat, warmly, "he happens to be Basic Books' favorite writer, too."

Only once was I embarrassed in her presence. Dick DeHaan, commenting on my broad expertise, wondered why I had never been on any of the quiz shows. I promptly told him of my one invitation and of my turning it down.

"Of course," I said, "I'm not really afraid that I would have been lured into anything phony. I just can't imagine myself being so foolish as to be trapped into the kind of mistake poor Charles v——"

I was about to refer to Charles van Doren, who had been persuaded to go along with the fakery of those shows and who had had trouble as a result—and remembered, too late, that he was Pat van Doren's brother-in-law.

I broke down in the middle of his name and trailed off into a hot and embarrassed silence. Pat said, "Finish what you were about to say. You're perfectly right." And not more than two minutes later, her hearty friendliness had me out of the dumps.

On the occasion of this September 17 luncheon, however, Dick and Pat gave me the publishing gossip of the day. New American Library was undergoing a great reorganization, and Mac Talley had been fired.

My heart sank. This seemed to be my year for changes in editors. Leon Svirsky, Avram Davidson, and now Mac Talley. The loss of the first two had not concerned me unduly, but the loss of Mac was a bad blow. I had been working with him now for a dozen years. He had been the first to put out paperback versions of my science-fiction novels, and it was because of him that some of my books like *The Wellsprings of Life*, *The Human Body*, and *The Genetic Code* had been written.

And there was the selfish concern that I was half done with the third volume of *Understanding Physics*, another Mac Talley project. What would happen to it now that he was leaving NAL?

I visited Mac the next day. He assured me that *Understanding Physics* would not be affected by his departure from NAL and that Ed

Burlingame would take care of me. He also assured me that he was in no trouble financially and that I need not be concerned about him.

19

The time was rapidly approaching when the World Book Year Book people would be gathering at Bermuda. I received my routine invitation and returned a quiet refusal.

On September 30, 1964, I received a very angry air-mail special-delivery letter from Roy Fisher which, it seemed to me, threatened me with being fired if I did not accept the invitation.

By air-mail, special-delivery letter, I returned an intransigent refusal.

On October 2, Fisher called me and said, "Well, Asimov, just how much money do you *want* to go to Bermuda?"

As far as I can recall, that was the only time anyone had ever supposed that I was playing games in order to gouge more money for myself. I paused for a few seconds to cool down and then said, quite calmly, I think, that no amount of money would get me to Bermuda and that if I were fired, that was it.

He backed down a little, for by that late date they had no one to do the science article of the year—so I did it, without having any trouble over my not having attended the gathering. It was, however, the last article I did for the World Book Year Book. The association had lasted five years and I was out. The next year, they had Harrison Brown as my replacement, and I think the next annual junket was in Hawaii.

I can honestly say I didn't regret the end of the association at all. On several occasions I had been lured into doing things that went against my personal grain, and the lure had consisted of money. I didn't admire myself for it and I was delighted to have temptation removed from my path.

20

I drove to Albany on October 8 in order to deliver a talk at the medical center there. I was asked to give a luncheon talk on nucleic acids, and I agreed. I knew how such luncheon talks went.

After a morning of dull, learned talks, everyone brought their spouses to lunch. They then wanted an informal, good-natured talk that would give them a few laughs and that would not be over the heads of the spouses. I'd done it on a number of occasions and was not troubled at the thought of doing it again.

I arrived early and was ushered into the room where the lectures were being given. They were deadly dull and formal, of course, and were delivered in rankly amateurish fashion, but I sat there as the rest did and avoided actually snoring. Occasionally, I looked surreptitiously at my watch to see how much more time it would be before I could eat, give my informal talk, pocket my fee, and leave.

At noon, the talks were over (so I thought), and when the chairman arose, I thought it was to announce lunch. He announced me as the next speaker.

I was confused. I got up and said in a low voice, "Aren't we going to lunch?"

"Yes," he said, "as soon as you're finished."

"But you asked me to give a luncheon talk."

"Yes, and your talk *will* be followed by a luncheon."

So there I was, unprepared, with an audience expecting a formal talk. I did my best to pump formality into my talk, but I was the only one on the program that morning to have no slides, no experimental results, nothing academic. (Years later, someone recalled that talk and said that I was the only person he had ever encountered who had tried to indicate the structure of the double helix by gestures.)

It was not one of my happier speaking occasions.

21

From Albany I went to New York, where I brought in a large batch of my *The Intelligent Man's Guide to Science* revisions. They were greeted enthusiastically because the marginal notations were typewritten.

Basic Books flattered me sufficiently on that point to get me to agree to do a book on the noble gases. These had just come into considerable prominence because Neil Bartlett of Canada had succeeded in forcing the heaviest of the stable noble gases, xenon, into molecular combination with fluorine—a feat most chemists assumed was impossible.

On that same day, November 9, I had lunch with Walter Bradbury, and once again, as in the case of *The Genetic Code*, we discussed a possible book. In this case, he suggested I do a book on the neutrino, the no-mass, no-charge particle that after a quarter century of existence as a ghost particle required for theoretical reasons only had finally been detected in 1957.

And so I added Harper's to my list of prospective publishers.

22

On the way home to New York on the eleventh, I missed my turnoff in the Bronx, for the first time in all the years I had been driving between New York and Newton. My mind, I suppose, had been wandering, but I knew I had missed my turnoff when I found myself on the to-me-unknown streets of the Bronx.

And on what day was it? The day of the fourth game of the World Series.

And where did I find myself as I wandered the streets trying to get back to the highway? —Right outside Yankee Stadium.

And when was this? Just as the game was getting ready to start and people by the thousands were converging on the gates.

Talk about traffic jams!

If I had to make an unprecedented driving blunder, why exactly there and exactly then? Obviously there is some guiding principle to the universe.

23

On October 23, 1964, I finally got my advance copy of *Asimov's Biographical Encyclopedia of Science and Technology.* I had begun writing it three years before.

24

I voted for Johnson on November 3, 1964, and settled down to listen to the results on television. From the earliest reports, it was clear that Goldwater didn't have a chance, and by 8:30 P.M. I stopped pretending that there was any doubt in the matter, recorded "Johnson landslide," in my diary and stopped making notes.

I was terribly gratified and terribly relieved. Now, I felt, we could wind down our Vietnam involvement.

What I didn't know was that Johnson had already adopted an attitude very much like the Goldwater position he decried during the campaign. The difference was that Goldwater was honest enough to state what he believed even though it would lose him the election, while Johnson faked his own views in order to win the election. In later years, I said bitterly, "Given my choice, I voted for Johnson over Goldwater, and what I got was both."

I never forgave Johnson.

25

The reorganization at New American Library was continuing. On November 19, 1964, I received a call from Tim Seldes. He was leaving Doubleday to take over as a vice president at NAL.

I was appalled. Now I would be losing Tim, too, for he was much closer to me at Doubleday than he could possibly be at NAL.

Besides, Doubleday had always struck me as a gentle, soft-sell sort of place, and having heard Mac Talley talk about what had gone on at NAL, I wasn't sure that Tim would like the change. I couldn't very well tell him not to take the job because he had already committed himself and because I didn't know any facts, only guarded comments from Mac, which I might have misinterpreted.

Nevertheless, I couldn't conceal my worry, and I asked Tim several times if he were *sure* he knew what he was doing. I asked him please to keep his eyes open and stay on guard.

He just laughed and told me to stop being a mother hen.

But at least it made me feel still more secure about *Understanding Physics*, the last word of which was written on November 22, the first anniversary of Kennedy's assassination.

26

Of course, new jobs were under way. I had started *The Neutrino* on November 26.

I had also talked Austin Olney into letting me do a book on the slide rule. This was a throwback to my decades-long irritation at my old college professor, Gregory Razran for not having told me how the slide rule worked when I had asked him, and over the fact that at no time in my education had I ever been taught to use it.

I made up my mind that others would not suffer so. I would teach them.

27

On November 24, I had agreed to talk at Columbia University the next March. Since I had left Columbia fifteen years before, I had returned only once or twice and it had become foreign territory to me. I was not foreign to the Columbia students, apparently.

I was to talk to the chemistry students in particular, and the young man who invited me told me with great glee that various faculty members would come and, in particular, that John M. "Pop" Nelson would be there. Pop Nelson had taught me undergraduate organic chemistry a quarter century before, and it was his appearance that I had taken in vain in my picture of the murderer in *The Death Dealers*.

What's more, the student referred to Pop Nelson as "Cap Anson," the name I had used in the book, and said that Nelson had read the book. I was horrified, and wrote to ask for assurance that Nelson had not been angered before I would agree to come.

28

Danny Asimov, my eldest nephew (by adoption), was going to MIT and, in fact, had had dinner with the family that autumn. He was a tall, gangly youth, quite good-looking, very bright, and highly talented in mathematics. He was grave and serious, however, and not much given to small talk.

On November 25, I received a letter from Martin Gardner, telling me that a Daniel Asimov had written him to correct an error in Gardner's long-running and popular column "Mathematical Games" in *Scientific American*. Gardner inquired if he were my son.

I explained the relationship. This was my first direct contact with Gardner, whose books I admire inordinately. He is one of the small group of human beings (Sprague de Camp and Willy Ley are two others) who are utterly rational and who, surrounded by the wonders of science, have always been able to distinguish those wonders from the malodorous glitter of mysticism.

29

At about this time, Boston University expressed a wish to collect my papers. Dr. Howard Gotlieb, the head of special collections, wrote to ask me for them and I thought he was joking.

To be sure, I had been giving copies of my foreign editions and some of my old manuscripts to the Newton Public Library as a way of getting them out of the house, but that was on my own initiative, and the library was humoring me. I couldn't quite believe that someone would *ask* for them.

Gotlieb assured me solemnly that he was serious, and so I dragged out what manuscripts and papers I had, together with some spare copies of various books in various editions, and took them down to the library. I explained that there would be more, but when I took down additional installments there still seemed to be a very small supply of material for someone who had been writing for a quarter of a century.

"Is this all?" asked Gotlieb.

"I'm afraid so."

"But what have you done with all the rest?"

"Lately, I've been giving some of the stuff to the Newton Public Library, but mostly I've been burning them."

Gotlieb turned a pretty shade of mauve. "*Burning* them?"

"You know, when they crowd up my filing cabinets, and I don't need them anymore, I get rid of them. They're just junk."

I then received an emotional lecture on the value of a writer's papers to the cause of future research. I found I couldn't believe it (I still don't), but Gotlieb was such a decent and gentle guy (plump, round-faced, always smiling) that I didn't have the heart to argue. I faithfully promised to bring in all material and not burn anything.

It took a while, though, to educate me. At one time when I took in some manuscripts, Gotlieb looked over them and (I can swear) licked his lips. "Holographic corrections!" he said. "How valuable that makes this!"

"What are holographic corrections?" I asked.

"I mean you've made corrections in writing."

I laughed. "That's nothing. I make many more corrections in first draft."

"Where's the first draft?"

"Oh, I tear up each page as I finish with it."

Gotlieb frowned fearfully. "Didn't you promise to bring in everything?"

"First drafts, too?" I said, thunderstruck.

Then, on a still later visit, it turned out he wanted the fan mail also. He wanted *everything*.

"You won't have room," I protested.

"We'll *make* room," he answered firmly.

So in all the years since then, I have been periodically flooding the Special Collections Division of Boston University Library with the most appalling collection of manuscripts in first and second draft, with galleys, page proofs, and a copy of every book in every edition; also with a copy of every magazine that contains an article of mine, with correspondence of all kinds, including fan mail, and, in fact, with anything that mentions my name.

All of it has their storage vault under severe internal pressure, and the explosion, when it comes someday, will probably wreck a half-mile stretch of Commonwealth Avenue, but my conscience is clear. I've warned them.

For the first few years, everything I handed in was submitted to an official appraiser who, at the end of the year, would send me a detailed and itemized list of everything and included the estimated value of that year's submissions so I could take an income-tax deduction. The value came to roughly three thousand dollars, which appalled me because I didn't think any of the items were worth anything at all—but I took the deduction.

When laws were passed forbidding such deductions (thanks to the abuse of those laws by politicians) and I could no longer make them, I was relieved.

30

I took in the very last of *Understanding Physics* to NAL on December 3, 1964. It had taken me 1¾ years to write the three volumes.

Then, on December 17, I completed the revision of *The Intelligent Man's Guide to Science*. It had taken me only four months of actual work, thanks to my years of careful marginal annotation of the first edition.

Also on December 17, I received a letter from Brad telling me that he was leaving Harper's and returning to Doubleday—once again shortly after I had agreed to do a book for him.

I wondered what would now happen to *The Neutrino*, but my uncertainty was quickly settled. Harper gave Brad permission to take *The Neutrino* with him, and I was delighted. It would mean one more book for Doubleday.

Although Brad continued to interest himself in *The Neutrino*, he would not be dealing with me directly. Replacing Tim Seldes as my editor was Larry Ashmead, whose acquaintance I had first made 3½ years before.

Then Larry had sent me a letter suggesting corrections in *Life and Energy*, and I had thanked him. Now he was my editor and quite convinced that I could do no wrong. My relationship with him soon grew so warm that I felt even more relaxed and comfortable with him than I ever had with Brad and Tim.

22

Fantastic Voyage I

1

I had seven books published in 1964, a more copious list than in any year since the record-breaking eight of 1960. They were:

55. *The Human Brain* (Houghton Mifflin)
56. *A Short History of Biology* (Doubleday)
57. *Quick and Easy Math* (Houghton Mifflin)
58. *Adding a Dimension* (Doubleday)
59. *Planets for Man* (Random House)
60. *The Rest of the Robots* (Doubleday)
61. *Asimov's Biographical Encyclopedia of Science and Technology* (Doubleday)

The Rest of the Robots was my first book of fiction since *Nine Tomorrows* five years before. To be sure, it was not new material but was a reprint of two earlier novels, plus eight stories that had not appeared in any of my previous books.

I hesitated over whether the eight stories, making up only one quarter of the book, were enough to warrant my counting *The Rest of the Robots* as a new book and giving it a number. I ended by giving myself the benefit of the doubt.

Just the same, I do not *always* give myself the benefit of every doubt in what must seem like my mad determination to add to the numbers of my books. In 1961, Doubleday had put out *Pebble in the Sky, The Stars, Like Dust*, and *The Currents of Space* in a single omnibus volume entitled *Triangle*. Here, though, I did not contribute a single new word and I did *not* list it as a book of mine nor give it a number.

2

On January 2, 1965, I was forty-five years old and I celebrated the day most inappropriately with a bout of intestinal flu.

3

I was in New York on January 11 and had lunch with Tim Seldes and Wendy Weil, and about midway through the meal Tim said to me, "Well, Asimov, what are you doing these days at Doubleday, now that I'm not there to keep you out of mischief?"

I told him enthusiastically about doing *The Neutrino* for Brad, and having it end at Doubleday.

"What is a neutrino, anyway?" said Tim.

So I told him. It took quite a while and, at the end of the meal, Wendy said, "You know, Isaac, during the first half of the meal you did nothing but flirt with me, and then Tim asked you about the neutrino and after that you never even glanced in my direction. It was as though I didn't exist."

I said, "But Wendy, first things first."

I said it as though I were joking, but I was quite serious. I may be the epitome of dirty-old-manhood, but get me started *explaining* something and women vanish from my ken.

The next day I had a far less satisfactory luncheon. Leo Rosten (the author of the Hyman Kaplan stories which, in my youth, I had much admired) had written to suggest a lunch, since he wanted to discuss something with me. I had eagerly accepted.

The lunch took place on January 12, 1965, and I had the rather dubious pleasure of listening to Rosten ramble on in a disconnected fashion for some two hours. He never got to any point that I thought might be worth a discussion with me, and after a while I came to the conclusion that there was no point. What he had in his mind when he asked for the luncheon I have no idea. He never got in touch with me again, and I certainly didn't get in touch with him.

4

On January 18, I received a panic call from a member of the Tufts Medical School faculty. They had begun a lecture series, and the first lecture of the series was to be held the next night. The speaker was a physician from Labrador and they had just received the news that, as a result of some serious and unexpected problem, he couldn't make it. Could I fill in? They knew it was terribly short notice, but please . . .

How could I refuse? The next day I showed up at the designated place in downtown Boston and was ushered into a large auditorium which, I estimated, could hold something like five hundred people.

When the faculty member rose to introduce me, however, what it did hold was nineteen. That was the exact count, and it included myself and the introducer. There had been no time to make the announcement of the change in speaker so that the audience I got was the one that the Labrador physician would have gotten had he been there.

What's more, when the announcement was made that I would speak, three people who had come to hear the physician and would accept no substitute rose and walked out.

I gave my talk, as best I could, to the emptiest hall I had ever addressed, and to silence, discomfort, and embarrassment all around. The organizers of the lecture series paid me my fee on the spot and took me out to a good dinner afterward, but it didn't help much.

5

Winston Churchill died on January 24, 1965, at the age of ninety. My comment in my diary was that he was "probably the last romantic hero of a major war in history. From now on there will be only two kinds of wars: (1) petty, inglorious ones and (2) quick, mutual suicide, also inglorious."

Despite the fact that Goldwater had been defeated, the Vietnam War was steadily heating up and showed every sign of continuing to do so, so that my disillusionment with Johnson was already beginning. The Vietnam War was exactly what I meant by a "petty, inglorious" war, and I kept repeating to people Joseph Fouché's famous epigram on the assassination of the Duc d'Enghien: "It is worse than a crime; it is a blunder."

6

I had a small bump on my left forearm, just about halfway between elbow and wrist. It didn't hurt or bother me in any way, but one day I showed it to my physician. He studied it for a moment and said, "Probably a lipoma—just a little growth of fatty tissue and completely harmless—but check it with a dermatologist."

I showed it to a dermatologist on February 2, who studied it and said, "Probably a lipoma—completely harmless—but check it with a surgeon."

So I went to a surgeon that same day, and he studied it and said, "Probably a lipoma—completely harmless—when do you want to have it taken out?"

"If it's completely harmless," I said, reasonably, "why do I have to have it taken out?"

"Oh well," said the surgeon, smiling cozily, "we can never tell, can we?"

And, rather to my indignation, he made an appointment for the operation on February 11.

There followed a rather uneasy period in which I made a trip to New York and worked hard on my various projects yet remained always aware that I was about to be operated on. On the evening of the tenth, in fact, I watched television with a painful intensity, until I grew aware that I somehow had the feeling that I was watching each program for the last time—that I was saying farewell to life . . .

The next morning I left at 8:30 A.M. and drove to the hospital. The operation, which I can really scarcely dignify by the name, took place between 10:40 and 10:55 A.M. under a local anesthetic. The only pain or discomfort was the prick of the needle that gave me the anesthetic. Afterward, eight stitches were taken to close the incision.

I said to the surgeon when it was over, "Well, what is it?"

And he said, "Just a lipoma—completely harmless—as I told you. But we'll have the laboratory check it, just in case."

They wanted me to stay overnight, but by 2:00 P.M. I was overcome with boredom, got dressed, walked out, and went home.

On February 19 (Robyn's tenth birthday) I returned to the surgeon to have the stitches removed. By that time the lab report was in and I asked what had been reported.

"Just a lipoma," said the surgeon. "Completely harmless."

"Let me see the actual report," I said.

There it was: "Lipoma."

I watched television that night like a man reborn.

7

On February 18, I finished the book on the slide rule and took it in to Austin on the twenty-third. My title for it was *Realm of the Slide Rule* but Austin changed it to *An Easy Introduction to the Slide Rule.* On March 8, Austin agreed to do my Scholastic series *Great Ideas of Science,* which by now was completed, as a book.

8

On February 27, I passed two milestones. Gertrude and I went with David to the Boston Museum of Science and left Robyn at home entirely on her own. She remained alone for five hours in what was apparently complete comfort.

On that same day, I bought a tuxedo all my own for those inevitable occasions, once a year or so, when I would have to wear one. It was, specifically, for the upcoming ACS convention and my Grady Medal award, but I did take it, rather sadly, as a sign that I was growing old and stuffy.

9

Roy Fisher was in Boston on March 3, and asked to have dinner with me. I assumed it was in order to tell me, formally, that I was not part of the group at the Year Book any longer. Well, that was so, but it was not what he had come to tell me. He was after my agreement to do an article on the genetic code for the new year book, *Science Year*. The payment would be at the usual World Book level, but I disregarded that. I asked if any trips were involved, and when he assured me that none were, I agreed to do it.

10

On March 10, I was in New York and gave my talk to the Chemistry Department at Columbia University. I saw Dawson for the first time in years and asked him if he had read *The Death Dealers*. He said he had but when I asked him if he liked it, he said (honest as always) that he did not. I was a little abashed and decided not to tell him that I had modeled the hero on him.

Pop Nelson was there, too. I had been so certain, seven years before when I had written the book, that he was dead that I had not hesitated to model the murderer on him. He had already seemed to be an old man in 1939 when I was in his class, but I suppose he must only have been sixtyish then.

He was well in his eighties now and he seemed quite pleased to see me though I couldn't be certain that he knew who I was or that he was quite clear as to his role in the book. I told him how much I had valued my class with him and I think he got that. I certainly hope so, for he was dead before another year had passed.

The talk went very well (Stanley was in the audience and it was the first time he had ever heard me speak, I think) but I refused all payment, even for my travel expenses. Somehow I felt I owed them that much for having used the department in my book without permission.

11

It was still possible to get me to write a science-fiction story.

The fifteenth anniversary of *Galaxy* was coming up and Fred Pohl wanted a story out of me for it, and the cover story at that. In March he sent me a proof of the cover he planned to use and suggested that with the cover as inspiration, it would be easy to write the story.

It wasn't. I looked at the cover, which featured a large, sad, space-helmeted face, with several crude crosses in the background and with a space helmet balanced on each cross. I could make nothing of it at first, and I had to rattle the contents of my skull for hours before I could come up with something satisfactory.

On March 15 and 16, I wrote the story, the first fiction I had written in over a year, and decided it wasn't bad. I called it "The Last Tool," sent it in, and Fred took it at once.

When it appeared in the October 1965 *Galaxy*, however, Fred, as was always his wont, had changed the title to "Founding Father."[1] For once, though, the change was for the better. It harked back to the book by the same name about Joseph Kennedy, the head of the Kennedy clan, and it fit the story perfectly, and with even sadder irony than "The Last Tool."

12

I finished *The Neutrino* on March 24, and promptly started *The Noble Gases* for Basic Books.

Then, on April 2, the entire family took off for Detroit. We planned to drive by way of Niagara Falls, our second visit there, and our third April in a row that would see us in Canada. At 2 P.M. on the fourth, we had completed our trip across the Canadian shore north of Lake Erie and were in Detroit. There we visited Gertrude's Aunt Sophie, Henry's younger sister. It was the first time I had ever met her, and the family resemblance was strong.

April 5 was the big day. I gave a luncheon talk, the first I ever gave with the children in the audience. David, in particular, enjoyed himself, and after that he pushed hard to attend any talk I gave. I never knew how much he understood of my more esoteric talks, but he always laughed heartily in the right places.

This was a puzzle to me, for though he had grown interested in sci-

[1] See *Buy Jupiter and Other Stories.*

ence fiction, he would never read any of my books. He would shrug with embarrassment when I questioned him about this and would say, "I don't know. They just sound too much like you." Yet when I pointed out that he liked my talks when I *certainly* sounded like me, that didn't help.

What I remember best about that luncheon was the fact that I suddenly became aware that Robyn had a nearly full glass of chocolate milk right at her elbow and very nearly at the end of the table. I was in agony, expecting each moment to have the glass crash with a spray of chocolate milk over everyone around. Yet I couldn't stand up and shout to her lest she startle and knock over the glass. Nor could I bring myself to get up, walk over, and humiliate her by moving the glass.

I stared in her direction, therefore, till she looked my way. Catching her eye, I then lifted my own glass ostentatiously and placed it in a different spot and Robyn, instantly taking my meaning, moved her glass to the middle of the table.

Robyn *did* read my books on occasion. I remember the first time she did so, when she was not very much older. She came to me, one time, with the sad announcement that she had nothing to read.

"Read one of my stories," I said.

"Your stories aren't for kids," she said.

"I have a story about a little boy," I said. "How about that?"

"Where?"

I got a copy of *Nine Tomorrows* for her, opened it to the story "The Ugly Little Boy," and said, "Here, Robyn, read this."

Off she went to her room, from which she emerged on several occasions to tell me that she was on page so-and-so and it was great. Then there was quite a long lapse, and when she finally emerged, her face was red and swollen and tear-streaked, and she fixed me with a woeful look and said, "You didn't tell me the ending was sa-a-a-ad!"

As a father, I hugged her and consoled her, but as a writer I was delighted.

Anyway, that night in Detroit, I donned my tuxedo, left the kids with Aunt Sophie, and took Gertrude to the formal dinner at which I received my gold medal.

The next day, we left Detroit and stopped off in the Rochester area so I could give another talk. Then, on the eighth, I managed to get a ticket for speeding on the New York Thruway.

13

An Easy Introduction to the Slide Rule was different from most of the other books I had written in that it had to have illustrations. To be sure, my textbooks, as well as *The World of Carbon*, *The World of Nitrogen*, and *The Genetic Code* all had to contain chemical formulas, but these could be set up in type, or they could be drawn by any amateur with a drafting set.

For the slide-rule book there had to be a number of illustrations of the slide rule, one or more to every page almost, and it had to involve photography.

I had made rough sketches of what the illustrations would have to look like, and I bought a slide rule that was particularly clear and would lend itself to photography. Then, on April 20, 1965, along with Walter Lorraine, the art director at Houghton Mifflin, I went to a place where photographs of the slide rule could be taken, with only those portions showing that were absolutely necessary.

I adjusted the slide rule to the positions desired and, for three hours, photo after photo was taken. It was interesting at first, but the interest quickly wore away.

14

A science-fiction movie was in the process of being made, one called *Fantastic Voyage*. It dealt with a device that shrank normal objects to microscopic size. A submarine and five crew members are then placed in the bloodstream of a human being (an important scientist) so that an operation can be carried through from within, saving his life.

Bantam Books had obtained the rights to a paperback novelization of the movie and they got in touch with me to do the job. They would supply me with the screenplay and I could use that as the basis for the novelization. They would pay me a flat sum of five thousand dollars for the job. No royalties.

I turned down the proposal out of hand. Hackwork, I said. Beneath my dignity.

They kept after me and, on April 21, I had lunch with Marc Jaffe and Marcia Nassiter of Bantam Books. When enough flattery had been expended on me, I agreed at least to read the screenplay. That was fatal, for I liked it and felt the urge to write the novel. To be specific, I didn't want anyone else to write the novel because there was going to be a chance to make use of a lot of anatomy and physiology and I was afraid that anyone else Bantam might get would ruin the job.

One thing bothered me. The ending, as it was to appear in the movie, was fatally flawed. The crew had to get out of the body within an hour because the miniaturization would only last that long. Expansion to normal size would kill the patient, of course. The crew did manage to get out at the very last second, but the submarine was left inside.

At a subsequent meeting, I told Jaffe I would have to change the ending.

"Why?"

"It leaves the submarine inside," I said. "The sub will expand and kill the patient."

"But the submarine is eaten by a white cell."

"So it expands inside the white cell."

"But the submarine is digested."

"A white cell can't digest metal, and if it could, that would only re-arrange the atoms and— Marc, trust me, that submarine has to get out."

Marc said, unhappily, "All right."

I said, "And there has to be an understanding that the Hollywood people won't change the ending back, or interfere with any other changes I make."

Marc said he would see to it, and on that basis I agreed to do the novelization.

It was a lucky thing I made that stipulation, for there were numer-ous inadmissible points in the movie as it was made. There was no consideration of surface tension or even of the fact that air was made up of atoms and molecules and wasn't a continuous fluid.

I did my best to correct the worst of the flaws, but there were some that were intrinsic in the whole notion of miniaturization, which is, of course, basically impossible even in theory, in my opinion.

Before I began the book, I had to have Doubleday's permission, since I had never done a science-fiction book for anyone but them. On April 29, when I took the completed manuscript of *The Neutrino* to Brad, I broached the subject of *Fantastic Voyage* and found there was no trouble at all. In fact, it was Doubleday that had suggested my name as a possible author to Bantam.

And on May 5, I finished *The Noble Gases*. It had been an easy book to do.

15

I met an enthusiastic young man, Richard Hoagland, at about this time. Our first contact was by phone. He was anxious to see me and had all sorts of plans and projects in mind. He had an eager spirit that was very contagious.

When we finally made personal contact, I was taken aback to find him a thin, narrow-chinned youngster of nineteen; extraordinarily bright, though, and filled with enthusiasm for space.

Somehow he persuaded me to do a television show in Springfield, and I drove out there on May 6, taking David with me. Hoagland, who ran the planetarium at Springfield, showed it to us in detail (to David's great delight). Hoagland also talked a good deal about Mariner 4, which was on its way to Mars to take photographs as it flashed by.

I avoided becoming overcommitted at that time, for I sensed even then that Hoagland, like many utterly enthusiastic people, might have a reach that slightly exceeded his grasp.

16

In New York, on May 13, I was visiting Bob Mills, out of friendship rather than business, and listened to him talk to one of his clients who apparently needed money badly.

When Bob got off the phone I said, smugly, "Aren't you glad, Bob, that I'm just here as a friend and cause you no trouble?"

"You cause me plenty of trouble," said Bob.

"What trouble?" I demanded.

"Listen, Ted Sturgeon has been trying to have the job of novelizing *Fantastic Voyage* for months, and only last week I found out you had the job."

I said, "But Bob, how did I know that Ted was after it? I wouldn't have dreamed of taking the job if I knew Ted wanted it. Call him up, Bob, call him up."

Bob called him and I got on the phone. "Ted," I said, "I didn't know you were after *Fantastic Voyage*. As far as I'm concerned, you can have it. I'll call Bantam Books right away and tell them you'll do it and that's okay with me."

I then called up Bantam Books right there in Bob's office, so he could hear exactly what I said. I got Marc Jaffe.

"Marc," I said, "I don't think I ought to do *Fantastic Voyage*."

"Why not?"

"I wasn't aware that Theodore Sturgeon wanted to do the novelization."

"Who says he does?"

"He does. I've just spoken to him on the phone and I would like you to let him have the job. I'll be glad to sign over the contract."

Marc paused. Then, suspiciously, "Why are you offering to do this?"

I said, "Because Ted Sturgeon is an old friend."

In my innocence I thought this was an unanswerable argument, but Marc said, "You're a peculiar writer. You come right over here."

So I did, and there were quite a few people waiting for me. I felt surrounded.

Marc said, "Why are you trying to get out of the contract, Isaac?"

"I'm not trying to get out of the contract, Marc. It's just that Ted would like to do it and he'll do a marvelous job."

Marc said, "We need a scientist for this. You were the only person ever considered for the job. You didn't beat out anyone because if you didn't do it we were going to drop the project."

It was the argument on their side that was unanswerable. I said, chastened, "I'll do the book."

Then I had to call up Bob Mills to tell him what Marc had said and to ask him to call Ted and explain to him, as diplomatically as he could, that Asimov might promise but he couldn't deliver.

On May 26, Bantam concluded the final details with Twentieth Century, which was doing the motion picture, and on May 31, I began work on the novelization.

One problem that arose in connection with *Fantastic Voyage* involved a hard-cover edition. Bantam Books owned the rights to a paperback edition only, and novelizations of movie scripts invariably came out in paperback only as throwaway publicity devices for the movie.

This, however, was precisely what I didn't want. It would be humiliating to have one of *my* books so subservient to a movie. I had therefore told Bantam Books that there would have to be a hard-cover edition. Bantam warned me that a hard-cover edition would have to be negotiated with the Hollywood owners of the screenplay and that there was nothing in the contract compelling them to give me any part of the royalties.

At that moment, I didn't care. I said, even if the hard-cover earned me not a penny, there had to be a hard-cover edition. So Bantam Books said they were sure Grosset & Dunlap would do such a hard-cover edition and I said that would be fine.

Then, on June 2, Marcia Nassiter called me and said that Grosset & Dunlap would *not* do a hard-cover edition.

By that time, though, I was making extremely good progress on *Fantastic Voyage*, and it was clear to me that with the movie script to guide me, completing the novelization would be a snap. I didn't want to drop the project, therefore. Instead, we would simply have to find some other hard-cover publisher.

17

Meanwhile, I was also working on another revision of *Inside the Atom* for Abelard-Schuman. This time I made the revision a thorough-going one and was primed for the task by my work on the third volume of *Understanding Physics* and on *The Neutrino*. I finished that job on June 3.

Having done that, I returned to my book on the Romans, which I had allowed to hang fire while engaged in other jobs.

18

Other projects were arising. The Atomic Energy Commission put out small pamphlets on various aspects of nuclear energy for distribution to the public, without charge. It was an educational service on the part of the government.

I was asked to do one such pamphlet on the genetic effects of radiation. I knew something about the subject but was afraid that I didn't know enough to put something out under the official aegis of the AEC. I explained this but the AEC at once told me that the eminent geneticist, Theodosius Dobzhansky, was going to be part of the project and that he would backstop me. They went on to say that Dobzhansky had suggested my name because he thought I was the best science writer in the world, bar none.

I wasn't proof against *that* kind of flattery, and with Dobzhansky helping out, I couldn't go wrong. Besides, it was only to be ten thousand words long or so, and it would be a public service.

I had lunch with Dobzhansky at Rockefeller University on May 14, and it scarcely needed any urging from him to get me to agree. I said I would start as soon as I had a chance.

In another direction, the magazine *Science Digest* had a column called "Please Explain," in which some question in science was answered in five hundred words. Apparently they farmed the job out, and in May they asked me to do one.

Apparently I gave satisfaction, for they asked me to do another and then another and then still another. Finally, without my ever having agreed to it, I found that I was running the column. Eventually, the title of the column was changed to "Isaac Asimov Explains."

19

The hard-cover edition for *Fantastic Voyage* continued to elude me.

I was somehow confident that Doubleday would do it if I asked them to, but Larry Ashmead regretfully told me it was impossible. The paperback rights were gone, which meant an important source of revenue was eliminated. Second, Doubleday would have to deal with the Hollywood people rather than with me, and they didn't want to do that.

Marcia Nassiter told me that W. W. Norton might be willing to do the hard-cover edition, but that fell through, too. I began to feel as I had in the days, three years before, when I was trying, and failing, to get a hard-cover edition for *The Genetic Code*.

About the only way I could cheer myself up was to work hard on my book on the Romans whenever my discontent with the *Fantastic Voyage* situation prevented me from actually working on that book.

I was being cautious with Roman history, by the way. I hadn't gotten far along before I saw there was no way to hold that history down to some length Austin would be willing to accept, and I didn't want to end up doing any cutting, as I had in the case of *The Greeks*. (I *hate* having to cut books; I don't mind making them longer.)

For that reason I decided to write only half of Roman history and call the book *The Roman Republic*. Then, at some future time, I would write the other half and call it *The Roman Empire*. Each book, I figured, would be seventy thousand words long or so, and that would be fine. In this way, I would slip a two-volume history right past Austin.

(Of course, he still didn't know I was writing even the first of those volumes, for I had promised not to present him with any more histories till we saw how *The Greeks* fared.)

20

In New York, I had lunch with Dick DeHaan, Pat van Doren, and Arthur Rosenthal of Basic Books on July 16, 1965. Arthur Rosenthal, the publisher, was a tall man with a large and majestic nose. I took a liking to him at once.

Dick DeHaan had spent considerable time urging me *not* to do the index to the revised edition of *The Intelligent Man's Guide to Science*.

"Why should you do it?" he said. "Your time is valuable and should be spent in writing, not in nitpicking index cards. Besides, we'll have a specialist do it who can do a much better job than you can."

I tried to explain that I *liked* indexing, but he kept saying that no writer could approach his own book with sufficient detachment to do a good index. In the end, much against my will, and despite my experience with A *Short History of Biology*, I reluctantly let myself be argued into having someone else do the index.

Later in the meal, Martin Gardner joined us. He had just done *The Ambidextrous Universe* for Basic Books, a book that worked its way up to the overthrow of the law of conservation of parity in a steady and systematic way. I had read the book, and loved it, and had, indeed, modeled the development of my own book *The Neutrino* as closely after Gardner as I could.

This was the first time I had met him in person. He was a white-haired, pink-skinned, soft-voiced fellow of medium height and as delightful to talk to as he was to read—not so much for any sparkling wit as for the cool rationality of his point of view and for his utter intellectual integrity.

I tried to explain to him what his books meant to me, and how closely I tried to model my own style on his.

"That's strange," he said, gravely, "I try to model my style on yours."

Later in the luncheon, Martin said to me, "Isaac, if you want real fun, pick some book you really like and know, and annotate it."

He himself had put out annotations of *Alice in Wonderland*, of *The Ancient Mariner*, and so on. I had all these annotations and had enjoyed them enormously.

What chiefly pleased me about the remark, however, was that I had anticipated him. Only that morning I had had a longish session with Tom Sloane.

Asimov's Biographical Encyclopedia of Science and Technology was doing far better than he (or I) had anticipated, and he was urging me to do another "big book."

I had thought rapidly, for I wanted to nail Tom down while he was in the mood. I thought of my aborted biblical series for Houghton Mifflin; of *Words in Genesis*, *Words from the Exodus*, and the never-completed *Words from Canaan*.

Why not start all over, on the adult level, and do a guide to the Bible as I had done a guide to science, touching only on the nontheological aspects? I suggested that to Tom in general terms.

"Why not a book on the Bible, Tom?" I said.

"What kind of book?" Tom had asked, cautiously.

"I'm not sure. Let me think about it." I was unwilling to specify before giving Tom a chance to get used to the general idea.

But Martin's suggestion rang a responsive answering chord within me. I hadn't thought of it that way, but what I was planning was a sort of annotation of the Bible. If I could make that work, I would annotate other books.

21

I finished *Fantastic Voyage* on July 23, 1965. The job had taken not quite two months. I finished *The Roman Republic* on July 28.

I still had no hard-cover publisher for the former, but Marc Jaffe told me, when I called him on the twenty-seventh, that he had happened to have lunch with Austin Olney, who had sounded interested in the book. This rather astonished me, since Houghton Mifflin had never published a single book of science fiction, so that I had not even considered them as a possibility. If Austin were interested, however . . .

I at once took in a carbon for him to read.[2]

On August 2, I went to see Austin. The ostensible reason for the visit was to look at the final illustrations to the slide-rule book, but I disposed of that quickly and then said, "How is *The Greeks* doing?" (It had been at the bookstores for about two months.)

"Pretty well," said Austin. "The reviews seem satisfactory and the sales are fine."

"Remember that you said I shouldn't submit a history of the Romans until we found out how *The Greeks* was doing? Does this mean that I can start work on the Romans now if I want to?"

"Yes," said Austin, heartily, "you can begin any time."

"And bring it in whenever I'm finished."

"Whenever you're finished."

"Good," I said, and got my briefcase, which I had surreptitiously placed just outside the door when I entered lest its bulk raise suspicions. "I've just finished it. Here it is!" and I handed him the manuscript of *The Roman Republic*.

---

[2] At about this time, I conducted a very successful experiment, by the way. I took the entire family to Merriewoode—the resort on the island at which Gertrude, Henry, and I had stayed some years before—and left them there from July 24 to August 7. This gave me two weeks of bachelor existence in which I could work steadily and undisturbed on my various projects. That was more of a vacation for me, by far, than if I had gone to Merriewoode with the family.

He stared at it with astonishment and I said, defensively, "You said not to *submit* a book on the Romans till we saw how *The Greeks* did. You didn't say I couldn't *write* it."

He burst out laughing and I was home safe. In fact, I took advantage of his good humor to ask how he liked *Fantastic Voyage*.

He admitted he liked it very much but he wasn't sure whether Houghton Mifflin could promote it effectively since they had never done any science fiction.

I took a chance. I *had* to have a hard-cover edition and so I had to try the hard sell. I said, "Nothing to it, Austin. Just make sure that my name is printed clearly on the cover and that's all the promotion you'll need."

"It's not that easy, Isaac. We can't count on a paperback sale because Bantam has it already and as soon as the paperback comes out there'll be no hard-cover sales at all."

"Not so, Austin," I said. "That may be the common wisdom of the literary marketplace, but it doesn't work with my books. My hard-covers sell at an unbroken rate, whether soft-cover editions are available or not."

"Are you serious?"

"Absolutely. I had a book called *I, Robot* published fifteen years ago. It has appeared in several paperback editions over the past ten years. To this day, *I, Robot* is selling briskly in hard-cover edition."[3]

"Really?"

"A minimum of two thousand copies a year. How many copies would you want to sell of *Fantastic Voyage* in hard-cover?"

"At least five thousand," said Austin.

"I promise you it will sell at least eight thousand."

Austin was clearly impressed, and by August 9 he had agreed, probably with some qualms, to do the book.

And at home I began work on the Bible book. My working title was *It's Mentioned in the Bible*, and I stopped at virtually every proper name to talk about its significance. I remember having a wonderful time speculating on the location of the Garden of Eden and on the significance of its four rivers.

22

As long as I didn't have a hard-cover haven for *Fantastic Voyage*, the fact that I would get no money for it didn't matter. Once the

[3] And it still is, to *this* day.

haven was found, however, I found myself resenting the fact that the Hollywood people owned the book *in toto* and were entitled to all royalties on the hard-cover. The Science Fiction Book Club (a Doubleday division that did not confine itself to Doubleday books) wanted to use the book, and all its royalties in that edition would go to the Hollywood people, too.

I decided this shouldn't be. *Fantastic Voyage* would be the first novelization of a movie in history (as far as I knew) that would appear in hard-cover, and that was entirely due to me. Houghton Mifflin wouldn't have taken the chance on anyone else. Why should I not get something? I therefore asked Austin to put some pressure on the Hollywood people to reserve some fraction of the royalties for me.

23

There was another American Chemical Society meeting coming up in September. This time it would be in Atlantic City—a place much easier to reach than Detroit had been. I was asked to give a talk that would be part of a symposium on "Atmospheres in Space Cabins and Enclosed Environments."

It was the work of a moment for me to reply that I knew nothing about the subject, and the work of another moment for them to reply and assure me that they understood this but that they wanted me to give the last talk of the session, a speculative and entertaining one on future developments in the field.

Somehow it is always taken for granted that however little I may know about a given field, I can always speculate learnedly and fruitfully on future developments in that field.

Since I hate to disillusion people too much on the subject of my universal knowledge, I usually allow myself to be flattered into something on the second push, and I did in this case.

Again, as on the occasion of my talk on "Enzymes and Metaphor," six years before, I would have to write my speech, for it would be slated for eventual publication. On August 17, 1965, I wrote what I called "There's No Place Like Spome."

Spome was my abbreviated form of "space home," and I spoke, of course, of large, artificial starships that were self-contained worlds—an anticipation, in a fumbling sort of way, of Gerard O'Neill's concept of space settlements some nine years later.

24

Even while I was writing the speech, Wendy Weil called in some agitation. "Do you remember warning Tim Seldes against joining New American Library, Isaac?"

"I warned him to exercise caution," I said.

"Did you know anything you didn't tell him?"

"I knew that Mac Talley had been fired, but Tim knew that, too. I was afraid that they were the kind of firm that might do it again, that's all."

"Well, they did. They've just fired Tim."

Tim Seldes had been on the job for only nine months.

25

Ed Burlingame was no longer with New American Library. He had taken a job as editor-in-chief of a small publishing firm called Walker & Company. It was a family-run concern under Samuel and Beth Walker.

I visited the place for the first time on August 26, 1965, in order to see Ed, and he and I went out to lunch. Sam Walker joined us—tall, dark, good-looking, and genial. (I didn't get to meet his wife, Beth, until some later occasion. She was a tall, blond beauty, very outgoing and bouncy and with a most infectious laugh.)

Gertrude, who was with me in New York this time and was out shopping, had called me just before lunch, and I urged her to join us. She did, and this was one of the few occasions when I took her on my rounds with me. She visited Doubleday and Bantam after lunch.

Naturally, the lunch with Burlingame and Walker was not entirely for the purpose of stuffing calories into me. They wanted a book. Burlingame suggested a book on quasars, the mysterious, far-distant, starlike objects that were very compact, a light-year or less in diameter, yet that shone with a hundred times the brilliance of a galaxy.

Burlingame spoke of a "little book" on the subject. I explained, however, that in order to do a sensible book on quasars—or at least in order for *me* to do a sensible book on quasars—I would have to explain a number of things first, and it would end up as a big book.

I did this in order to avoid committing myself to doing any book at all, but Ed blocked me off neatly. "Do it your way, Isaac," he said, "and let the book find its natural length."

I said I'd think about it, but I knew they were going to land me. (I think I'm the most easily landed writer in the world. I spent too many years trying to storm the gates of the literary fortress to be able to resist entering when the portcullis is down and I am being waved inside to the blare of trumpets.)

Indeed, even as I hung back coyly, it occurred to me that I had all the material in my ill-fated *A Short History of Astronomy* at my disposal. That book had been gathering dust for a year, and it was time to cannibalize it.

My willingness to do the book was further increased when Ed, who had nursed along my *Understanding Physics* volumes at NAL, told me that Walker & Company would do the hard-cover.

The exhilaration produced by this piece of news induced me, finally, to begin *The Genetic Effects of Radiation* for the AEC. It had been nearly four months since my lunch with Dobzhansky, and I couldn't delay it much longer.

26

At noon on September 5, 1965, my father called from New York.

"Hello, Pappa," I said. "Why are you call—*oh* boy!"

I felt a little sick. I had meant to call, but I had gotten tangled with my typewriter, and once I'm typing, time has no meaning. It just slips away.

My father said, "How is it you didn't call Mamma today?"

It was my mother's seventieth birthday.

"Pappa, I was busy typing. I meant to call, but I had to finish something . . ."

It didn't help. First he discussed the matter for a long time, and then my mother got on the phone (clearly, she had been crying) and she discussed the matter for an even longer time. I was thoroughly informed on the subject by the time they were through.

Later that day I called David and Robyn to me and told them that in later life I didn't want them ever to feel they had to call me on my birthday, or on any other special day. They could call me just when they needed money or something; I felt that would induce a sufficient number of calls.

27

At lunch with Austin on September 7, I discovered that *F & SF* had agreed to run a cut version of *Fantastic Voyage* as a serial. I was delighted. It would mean my longest fictional appearance in a science-fiction magazine since *The Naked Sun*, nine years before.

My pleasure was short-lived. It was not I who had the power to give approval to the sale, and not Houghton Mifflin either. It was the Hollywood people. Actually, it was a gentleman named Otto Klement, but he was only a name to me. I never met him.

Apparently, Klement (along with Jerome Bixby, who had once been editor of *Planet*) had written the treatment that became the screenplay. Who else was involved I don't know, but it was Klement who apparently controlled the rights, and it was Klement who vetoed the *F & SF* sale. There wasn't enough money in it.

I was furious. *F & SF* had offered the kind of money one expected of a science-fiction magazine and couldn't pay anything more. But who else did Klement think would buy the story for serialization?

My hands, however, were tied, and I just had to resign myself to no first serialization at all. But then, it wasn't fatal; it wasn't even unprecedented. There had been no first serialization for *Pebble in the Sky* or for *The End of Eternity*, after all.

23
Fantastic Voyage II

1

Boston was an active center for science-fiction fans. In addition to the MIT science-fiction group with whom I shared an annual picnic on the first or second Sunday of each May, there was the New England Science Fiction Association (NESFA), which had its monthly meetings. I attended these whenever I could, and Harry Stubbs, Ben Bova, and I were the professional "stars" of the organization.

In September 1965, NESFA decided to host a regional convention, which it called Boskone (and which was to become an annual and, at times semi-annual affair). Boskone was a word familiar to those who had read E. E. Smith's classic *Galactic Patrol* and one that was close to the more usual Boscon, for Boston convention.

I was chagrined because the Boskone overlapped the Atlantic City convention of the ACS, where I had to give my talk on spomes, but I managed a little of Boskone, anyway. On September 11, I took the whole family to the convention. We lunched with Ben Bova, Harry Stubbs, and Forry Ackerman, and then we dined with Fred Pohl and Lester del Rey.

And the next day I had to leave for Atlantic City and was distressed about it. I hated to abandon the warm womb of science fiction for the cold impersonality of a convention of meaningless, faceless individuals.

I was wrong!

During my stay at Atlantic City, I found that my nameplate made me as readily recognizable on the boardwalk as in the halls of a science-fiction convention. It was rather a revelation to me; I was as well known outside science fiction as within it. It was the last time I ever feared going unrecognized at any large gathering of people with any pretensions to intellect or professionalism.

2

On Monday, September 13, I attended the symposium "Atmospheres in Space Cabins and Enclosed Environments." At least I was there for the half that was given after lunch.

The auditorium seated about three hundred, but only some sixty people were present and there was a constant movement of individuals going out as they lost interest and other individuals coming in on the forlorn chance of finding interest. (This is a common situation in all scientific conferences I have ever attended and, as nearly as I can tell, speakers are used to it, take it for granted, and, being nonprofessional, are too uncomfortable to begin with to be any the worse for the constant shuffling of feet.)

I, however, watched with painful interest, for I was the last speaker on the schedule and it seemed to me that there were more drifting out than in and that the audience was slowly and inexorably growing smaller. I kept extrapolating, and decided that by the time I rose to speak it would be to face an empty hall, and was that what I had left Boskone and come to Atlantic City for?

But then, in the course of the talk of the speaker who preceded me, the trend reversed itself. More people drifted in than drifted out, and this tendency became more pronounced. Soon no one at all was leaving, and the incoming people formed a thick and steady stream. By the time the speaker sat down and my name was announced, the room was full.

That made up to me my embarrassing experience at Tufts Medical School eight months before. There I had someone else's audience; here I clearly had my own, an audience that differentiated between me and the other speakers at the symposium.

I was completely satisfied and gave an energetic and enthusiastic talk[1] without ever referring to the manuscript that lay before me. When it was over (there were no speakers following, which was a wise bit of organization) members of the audience crowded around me for my autograph, precisely as though I had never left Boskone.

While I was talking and signing I became aware of a woman waiting patiently on the outskirts. I assumed she, too, was waiting for an autograph and, unwilling to make her wait forever, I beckoned to her to come closer.

She did and said, "Do you remember me, Isaac?"

[1] I called it my "spome talk" and gave it on numerous occasions afterward.

I stared at her for a moment. There was nothing about her that stirred the vaguest flicker of memory, not her face, not her voice, nothing—but it occurred to me that only one person would *expect* me to remember her. It was my puppy-love date of college days.

I said, "Good heavens! Irene!"

It *was!* There she was, a forty-seven-year-old grandmother with nothing at all left of the girl I had last seen twenty-three years before— but I was delighted to see her just the same for the sake of the memory.

I met her husband, who was tall and who had middle-aged attractively, and could see at once that she had done far better for herself than she could have with me.

I insisted on having them join me for dinner, and we had lobster at a fancy restaurant with myself joyfully picking up the check. (I had come a long way from the time, over a quarter century before, when Irene had introduced me to my first restaurant and I had reluctantly spent eighty cents.)

We walked back along the boardwalk, and the tail end of a hurricane converted itself from a light drizzle into a steady rain. We were all soaked, and when I got back to the hotel I found Harry Schwartz, my old Boys High fellow student (and now a well-known writer for the New York *Times*), waiting for me.

I took him up to my room, where I stripped to my shorts and distributed the remainder of my clothes in order to let them dry. Then I sat on the bed, while Harry sat in the one chair and we talked. The only trouble was that I couldn't light the floor lamp. I fiddled with it and tapped it and tried to switch bulbs with a bathroom fixture, but nothing helped—so I called maintenance.

In the middle of our talk, a maintenance man arrived, looked at the lamp, picked up the loose cord, and plugged it into a socket. The light went on at once.

Harry collapsed in hilarity. "The great interpreter of science, Isaac Asimov," he kept gasping, "has been stumped by an electrical appliance that wasn't plugged in."

I pointed out, rather pettishly, that it had been well within *his* competency to solve that problem too, and he hadn't, but he ignored that elementary fact. I gathered he intended to spread the news the next day, and he probably did.

I said, as I looked ruefully at the state of my dishabille, "Anyway, it's lucky that the maintenance man came in and found *you* here instead of a woman, or what would he have thought?"

Harry said, imperturbably, "I think the situation makes a worse appearance this way."

But this was before Gay Liberation and I didn't understand the statement until some time later, when extensive puzzling over his remark finally elicited the explanation.

The next day I stumbled on Charles Dawson, my Ph.D. professor, in the early morning, and had breakfast with him. In the evening, I attended a banquet at which I gave a short after-dinner talk, spent some more time with Irene and her husband again afterward, and it was all over. On the fifteenth, I left.

I was rather satisfied. For a quarter of a century I had been nursing a wistful dream, and now it had come to a quiet end. There is no cure for a golden girl of the past that is better than being brought face to face with the alchemy of the decades. And yet age doesn't alter everything. Irene was as sweet, gentle, and charming as ever.

3

On September 18 I finished *The Genetic Effects of Radiation* and sent it off to Dobzhansky, who approved it without trouble, and on the twenty-second, I received an advance copy of the revision of *The Intelligent Man's Guide to Science*. The title of the latter was changed, rather inevitably, to *The New Intelligent Man's Guide to Science*. The new title and the extensive nature of the work done on the revision kept my conscience quite tranquil when I added it to my list as a new book.

The revision was about 20 per cent longer than the first edition (for I had restored much of what Svirsky had hacked out) and it was in a single volume, and a very good-looking one at that. I exulted over the fact that the Svirsky disgrace had finally been eliminated, but not everything was satisfactory.

I studied the index that DeHaan had not let me do, but had given to an "expert."

It was dreadful; simply dreadful. It left out a great variety of things that should have been put in. It was the slapdash job of someone working for money instead of for his own book, and never again was I fooled by any talk of expertise in indexing.

When I later discovered that I had been charged five hundred dollars against royalties for the privilege of having that rotten index made, I was ready to choke DeHaan. I felt as though a small part of the Svirsky mantle had fallen upon him.

4

I was making excellent progress on *It's Mentioned in the Bible*, and the completion of *The Genetic Effects of Radiation* touched off the need to start another book. There was the book on quasars I had promised Ed Burlingame. In order to explain quasars, I felt I had to explain the red shift. In order to explain that, I had to explain spectroscopy, and thus, going back and back, I found myself beginning with the Assyrian Empire.

In fact, I had to explain so much that there was no way in which I could call the book *Quasars*. Instead, I called it *The Universe* when I began it on September 27. Into it went large cannibalized portions of my rejected earlier book *A Short History of Astronomy*. (Nothing is wasted.)

5

Two days later, on the 29th, I had lunch, for the first time, with people from still another new publisher—Ginn & Company, a large, Boston-based textbook firm.

It was their plan to do a series of science texts for children at the grade-school level, a separate text for each grade from the first to the eighth. They wanted me to work on the five books representing the fourth through the eighth grades, as part of a large team.

I shuddered at the thought. The two textbooks I had done at the med school had put me off such things forever; nor was I anxious to work with a team, either. I took refuge behind the cowardly evasion of "Well, let me think about it."

It wouldn't be so bad if the evasion worked, but it so rarely did. Usually it just meant that whoever was after me, stayed after me. Certainly the Ginn & Company people did.

6

On October 7, 1965, I had lunch with Tom Sloane and Larry Ashmead in New York, and was able to show samples of the Bible book. I was taken aback by Tom's unenthusiastic reception of the book, and I guess the sudden fall in my spirits was quite noticeable.

After lunch, Larry told me, when we were by ourselves, that if Tom did not want to do the Bible book, Anchor Books (a Doubleday division) might be willing to do it and that he would speak on its behalf. I brightened up at once.

The next day I went to Newark to tape a talk show with David Susskind. It was my first nationally televised talk show since "The Last Word" with Bergen Evans six years before.

This one was devoted to science fiction, and along with me were Lester del Rey and Ray Bradbury. It was the first time I had ever met Ray Bradbury, though of course we knew each other well enough from our writings to be on a first-name basis at once. Neither he nor I would fly in airplanes, so since I lived in Newton and he in Los Angeles it was clear we couldn't meet often.

The session was not successful. Lester was in one of his talkative moods and gave neither Ray nor myself much chance to do anything but stare at the ceiling, and Susskind had a list of questions, silly in themselves, from which he lacked the wit to depart. It meant that all the interesting starts that any of us made were muffled and killed when he asked the next silly question.

7

For a while I had still another column going; this one with *Cavalier*. *Cavalier* had a section in which different people spent a few hundred words expressing some abrasive opinion of theirs, and I had a lot of abrasive opinions. They wanted me, therefore, to air one of them every once in a while.

My first article for them was written on October 11, 1965, and dealt with long hair, something that was already becoming the mark of rebellious youth. I pointed out that the conservatives objected to long hair on a young man because, among other things, it made him look like a young woman. Nevertheless, one clear distinction between the faces of the sexes was the beard, which the male could grow and the female could not. Yet the conservatives objected to beards, too.

What it amounted to was that conservatives wanted the male to shave his face so that he would remove the natural distinction between himself and the female, and then to cut the hair on his head to set up a nonnatural distinction.

My second article supported the anti-Vietnam War stand with sardonic sarcasm against the double-talk of the prowar multitude.

I looked forward to many months of making fun of knee-jerk conservative attitudes, but, alas, *Cavalier* changed owners and policies, and I only managed to get four or five articles into it before they went off somewhere else.

8

November 5, 1965, was the publication date of *The New Intelligent Man's Guide to Science*, and Arthur Rosenthal of Basic Books hosted a cocktail party for me in honor of the occasion. In the movies, writers always have cocktail parties on publication day, but that did not happen to me until my sixty-fifth book.

This is not a complaint. I don't like cocktail parties, even when they're in my honor; *especially* when they're in my honor. I don't drink, and when I am being honored I have to spend all my time being gracious and smiling and can't get off in a corner and eat *hors d'oeuvres*.

Nevertheless, the party was a success. The entire family was there on both sides, except for Mary Blugerman. My friends in publishing and writing were all there, and even some friends from the past, such as Sidney Cohen.

The Rosenthals and we had a quiet Japanese dinner afterward, and I had *sushimi* (raw fish) for the first time.

Earlier that day I had presented Tom Sloane with my final version of the first chapter of *It's Mentioned in the Bible*, a longish chapter dealing with Genesis. It was my intention to get him to commit himself to a contract, or to reject it outright so that I could seek another home for it.

9

We were home late on the night of November 7, and at 5:21 P.M. on the evening of November 9 the electricity blanked out in our house. Gertrude had just finished cooking dinner (I've always had dinner early, a holdover from the Navy Yard days when work was finished at 4:30 P.M.), and she was in fact going to the table with plates of food when it happened.

We had candles in the house, thank goodness, thanks to the big hurricanes of a decade before, and we ate by candlelight in the gathering dusk as I waited for the lights to go on.

I quickly grew annoyed. There was no storm; it was a beautiful night with a full Moon rising; yet night fell completely and the lights did not turn on. It was clearly not our house alone, for the street lights were not on and the other houses in the neighborhood were dark as well.

I called the electric company, with no luck. The line was busy, and it stayed busy.

I thought a sizable section of the city might be out and I was certain that if I could only listen to the radio I'd find out what was happening, but the radios we had all ran on house current, which was out, and we had no battery radios.

Gertrude and the children didn't mind. They had lit a number of candles and were playing cards, and the fact that they didn't mind simply increased my own irritation.

Then I had a brilliant idea. I went down to the garage, started the car, and turned on the radio.

For some reason I had trouble finding a station. There was nothing but feeble static. I searched the bands in growing mystification and finally got a very weak voice that spoke of the electricity being off in all New England and New York.

I was horrified, and could imagine only one cause. I turned off the radio and the car engine, walked upstairs, and calmly blew out every candle but one.

I then called Gertrude to one side and said in a low voice, "The electricity is out all over New England and New York and I don't know where else. This may be a nuclear attack. There's nothing to do but wait for instructions."

So we waited all through the first part of the night of the Great Blackout of 1965, fearing that at any moment soldiers might come through ordering us to evacuate or that the glow of a mushroom cloud might appear on the horizon.

But, of course, it was just a failure of the power grid, and at 12:45 A.M. the power returned, having been off for 7½ hours. In New York City, the power did not return till dawn (though the Blugermans had no loss of power at all in their section of the city).

The next day, when everyone swapped stories, Gertrude and the children were furious with me. It seemed that everyone else had had a wonderful and exciting time, having fun in the darkened city—and only we had cowered under the threat of nuclear devastation.

"Who told you to be a science-fiction writer?" demanded David.

10

On November 15, Gertrude called me from the high school where she was taking a class. In leaving the parking lot, she had gotten tangled with a cigarette she had dropped, and before she had caught the wheel, she had made mild contact with a parked car, enough to dent it. It was a brand-new car, too.

I drove out quickly in my car and told Gertrude to get into my car and drive home in it, while I stayed behind and took the blame. Gertrude wouldn't; the fault was hers and she wasn't going to shirk it.

We waited nearly an hour on a cold night before the woman showed up who owned the car. We told her what had happened, and Gertrude was so visibly upset that the woman actually spent time consoling her. We, of course, said we would pay all repair bills and, in the end, when the bill arrived, we had our insurance company pay every cent at once.

I mention the incident only because I have earlier told in detail the story of my ferocious fight against someone who had hit us in a parking lot, and I wouldn't want anyone to think that we ourselves were never to blame for accidents. However, when it was our fault, we admitted it and took our lumps, financial and otherwise.

11

I was in New York on November 23 and had lunch with Tom Sloane, who was still indecisive over *It's Mentioned in the Bible*. I was exasperated.

I was also exasperated over the situation with *Fantastic Voyage*. Otto Klement was being difficult over the matter of fixing some definite share in the hard-cover royalties for me. I had no hold over him and I felt like a fool for ever having agreed to a novelization.

At least there was a new project. Judy Dikty, an editor at Follett Publishing Company, a Chicago-based firm, wrote a letter in which she asked for a book on the basis of personal friendship. She was the wife of Ted Dikty, a well-known science-fiction fan who had been co-editor of *The Best Science Fiction Stories: 1949*. This had anthologized my story "No Connection." It was only the third time I had had a story anthologized, and I remembered it well.

I complied. You can't let a pal down, even if it's only the wife of a rather tangential pal. Besides, the request was not a difficult one.

Judy wanted me to write a book on the Moon, one that was aimed at the eight-year-old level, and she said thirteen hundred words would be enough. It was just a few words on each page, along with a sketch that they would take care of. She sent me an outline of the topics to be covered.

It only took me part of two days to do the book, even though it ended being twenty-five hundred words long. In that time I was able to prepare and include rough figures indicating what I thought the sketches ought to be like and to divide the writing into appropriate sections. I was done on December 12 and mailed it off the next day.

12

I had still another session with Tom Sloane on December 16, and it was even more unsatisfactory than the one before. *Still* he had come to no decision on *It's Mentioned in the Bible*. Instead he began, very enthusiastically, to try to talk me into doing a book on modern engineering triumphs, such as the large and graceful arch that had recently been built in St. Louis.

To me the suggestion was absolutely untenable on two grounds. First, it would require travel. I could scarcely write about the St. Louis arch without going to St. Louis to look at it and inquire about it—and I simply wouldn't do that.

Second, and even worse, it was perfectly clear to me that Tom wanted me on another project so I would abandon the Bible book, and I wasn't going to do that, either. I said "No" quite firmly, and that was it. I went off quite depressed.

The next day, though, I visited Bantam Books, and Marcia Nassiter came up with news that absolutely flabbergasted me. Otto Klement had indeed managed to find a first serialization for *Fantastic Voyage*. *The Saturday Evening Post*, no less, was going to run it as a two-part serial.

I was abashed. To be sure, *The Saturday Evening Post* wasn't the giant it had been in the 1930s, but it still paid far better rates than *F & SF* would, and I had been captious indeed about turning down the latter. It made me feel that the Hollywood people had a great deal more practical sense than I had, and I didn't particularly enjoy that feeling.

13

Every once in a while, *F & SF* ran a special issue devoted to one particular writer. The September 1962 issue was for Theodore Sturgeon, and May 1963 had been for Ray Bradbury.

Ed Ferman had been after me for quite a while to collaborate in a special Isaac Asimov issue, and he wanted it for the October 1966 issue, which would be the seventeenth anniversary issue of the magazine. The difficulty was that the author being honored would have to write an original story for the issue.

I finally agreed and on December 19 began to write "The Key." It was a Wendell Urth story, my first in ten years and my fourth altogether. I completed it on Christmas Eve.

Meanwhile, I was also putting together a new anthology for Doubleday. The Juvenile Division wanted an anthology of science-fiction stories involving children, and they agreed to do all the scutwork of obtaining permissions and making payments, while I wrote all the Introductions and included my own "The Ugly Little Boy." It was not a difficult job, and my part was done on December 22. We decided to call the book *Tomorrow's Children*.

Then, too, I put together seventeen more *F & SF* essays for my fifth collection—*From Earth to Heaven*.

14

December 31, 1965, marked another milestone-of-aging for me.

According to the copyright laws, the copyright held good for twenty-eight years. At any time in the last year, the copyright could be renewed for another twenty-eight years by filling out an appropriate application and sending off a small check.

My first published story, "Marooned off Vesta," had been copyrighted on December 31, 1938, and December 31, 1965, was the twenty-seventh anniversary of that date. Between December 31, 1965, and December 31, 1966, that copyright could be renewed. If I failed to renew it by the latter date, the story went into public domain and anyone could thereafter publish it without payment to me.

I didn't wait, of course. I filed my copyright application on December 31, 1965. Then, using the proper reference books at the Boston Public Library, I looked up the registration dates of the next two stories, "The Weapon Too Dreadful to Use" and "Trends." I knew, with a sigh of resignation, that for the rest of my life and with steadily increasing frequency, I would be applying for copyright renewals.

15

I published only five books in 1965:

62. *A Short History of Chemistry* (Doubleday)
63. *The Greeks* (Houghton Mifflin)
64. *Of Time and Space and Other Things* (Doubleday)
65. *The New Intelligent Man's Guide to Science* (Basic Books)
66. *An Easy Introduction to the Slide Rule* (Houghton Mifflin)

I was not particularly downcast by the small number of published books in 1965. I had many books in press and was quite certain that I would do considerably better in 1966. Besides, though my income had remained at a fairly stationary level over the preceding four years (a satisfactorily high one, of course), it made another one of its surprising jumps in 1965. That year was the first in which my earnings surpassed the hundred-thousand mark—something I had difficulty believing even with the figures staring me in the face.

16

We spent New Year's Eve in Worcester at the house of people Gertrude had met at Merriewoode, and we left the children at home alone. It was the first time we had ever done so on New Year's Eve, knowing we'd be out most of the night, but we had grown quite confident. After all, David was fourteen and Robyn was nearly eleven.

The New Year's Eve party degenerated (or rose) into a marathon joke-telling session in which I starred, first because I had a copious supply and could tell them well, and second because I was the only sober person in the bunch. In fact, I remember that night chiefly because it was the time that I told the most spectacularly successful joke of my career. It was my short caveman joke, which goes as follows:

***

A cavewoman came running to her husband in the greatest possible agitation.

"Wog," she called out, "something terrible has just happened. A saber-toothed tiger has gone into my mother's cave and she's in there. Do something! Do something!"

Wog looked up from the mastodon drumstick at which he was gnawing and said, "Why should I do something? What the devil do I care what happens to a saber-toothed tiger?"

***

Combine the fact that most husbands have less than kindly feelings toward their mothers-in-law with the fact that those particular husbands at the party were sloshed, and you can expect a big laugh—but I didn't expect one *that* big. It went on and on, feeding on itself, and the joke session came to an end. No one could even start a joke without the laughter beginning again.

17

On January 2, 1966, I was forty-six years old, and I celebrated by preparing an elaborate bibliography of my published work for the special Isaac Asimov issue of *F & SF*. In addition, inspired by the somber thoughts with which my birthday, and the copyright renewal, had imbued me, I wrote a poem (well, a bit of comic doggerel) for the issue as well.

After all, I was forty-six and I had been a published writer for twenty-seven years. If a person had started reading science fiction at the age of nine, as I had, he might be thirty-six years old and yet have been reading my stories for all his literate life. A person like that would have to feel I was a very aged man, and so I wrote the poem about someone who met me and expressed that belief. I called it "I'm Still in the Prime of Life, You Rotten Kid." (When it appeared, Ed fitted it into the table of contents of the magazine by calling it merely "The Prime of Life"—something I always thought was a mistake.)

18

There are also advantages to aging. On January 8, 1966, I persuaded David to shovel the driveway after a snowfall of moderate depth, while I took the ease to which old age entitled me.

19

I gave up trying to get Tom Sloane to give me a contract on *It's Mentioned in the Bible*, and on January 17 I followed Larry's suggestion and consulted Gene Eoyang, an editor at Anchor Books.

Unfortunately, Eoyang turned out to be one of those fellows who talks volubly but not with the completest coherence. It was not with entire certainty that I gathered he would put through a contract on the Bible book.

At least *The New Intelligent Man's Guide to Science* was doing as well as its predecessor. It was already going into its third printing.

20

Otto Klement had, of his own accord, been willing to grant me half the payment from *The Saturday Evening Post* for their version of *Fantastic Voyage*. The contract did not require him to pay me a cent.

That further cooled my suspicions of him, especially since I had to admit he had earned his half by refusing to sell it to *F & SF* and selling it for nearly six times as much to *The Saturday Evening Post.*

The Saturday Evening Post warned me that it would cut the novel to half its length, so I did not dare read it when it appeared, nor have I ever dared read the first serial version at any time since.

The first installment appeared in the February 26, 1966, issue of *The Saturday Evening Post.* It came out every other week now, not every week as in its golden days; and it cost twenty-five cents an issue, not five cents.

The title of the story was on the cover: "New science-fiction serial, FANTASTIC VOYAGE, Inside the human brain"—but my name wasn't. In the magazine were eight nonfiction pieces and two (only two) fiction pieces—a good indication of what was happening to fiction generally. The other fiction piece, "The Prodigal Fool," was by Isaac Bashevis Singer. It was a special Isaac issue, apparently.[2]

The second and final installment was in the March 12, 1966, issue. Again the story's name was on the cover, but not mine. The price went up to thirty-five cents with that issue. I am quite certain that *Fantastic Voyage* had nothing to do with *that.*

21

My royalties from Doubleday were steadily increasing as the number of my books on their backlist increased. The royalty statement I got on January 28, 1966, included a check for nearly eleven thousand dollars, which was the largest check I had ever received, except, of course, for that monster Basic Books item in November 1961.

22

On February 3, 1966, the Soviets made the first soft landing on the Moon and obtained photographs of its surface *from* its surface. These were the first surface photographs of any world other than the Earth.

I felt exhilarated enough to tackle the last bit of *The Universe* in a fury of work and finished it on the fifth. It was one hundred thousand words long and had taken a little over four months to do. I was very

---

[2] Oddly enough, I was rather annoyed. Isaac is not a common name, and in the science-fiction world any reference to "Isaac" is a reference to me. I had gone to a lot of trouble to hang onto the name, and I hated having another Isaac who was a writer, and I particularly hated having him share the issue with me.

pleased with it, but although it had begun as a book on quasars, I didn't get to quasars till the final section of the last chapter.[3]

Walker & Company agreed with my optimistic estimate of *The Universe*. After they had a chance to read it, they voluntarily added a thousand dollars to my advance.

As soon as I saw *The Universe* about done, I started *The Roman Empire*, of course.

23

On March 1, 1966, I received an advance copy of the hard-cover edition of *Fantastic Voyage*. I had done the writing so rapidly and the movie was worked on so slowly that even though the script was done and the movie was in progress when I first started the job, the book came out half a year before the movie was slated for release.

This gave rise to the totally unjustified notion that the book came first and that the movie was made from it. I have corrected this as often as the mistake surfaces, but I can never seem to wipe out the notion altogether.

Meanwhile Austin had succeeded in persuading Klement to let me have 25 per cent of the hard-cover royalties, which was fair enough, considering that the book was not really an original production but was modeled closely on someone else's script. However, Klement had wanted to arrange to have the full royalty paid to him and that it would be left to *him* to pay me my 25 per cent.

I didn't want that. I did not want an unnecessary stop added to the payment route if I could avoid it. I wanted the 25 per cent direct from Houghton Mifflin and asked Austin to insist on that firmly, and Klement gave in. That was the last point of dispute over the book with Hollywood.

On March 1, also, I finally got the contract for *It's Mentioned in the Bible* from Eoyang. I had been grimly working on it for about seven months and was one third finished. It was a considerable investment of time and effort to make without a contract, but I didn't mind taking the risk. I was enjoying the book too much to quit—still, I must admit that with the contract finally signed, I felt much better.

---

[3] This is not unusual for me. In *The Neutrino*, I laid the foundations so carefully that it was not till exactly half the book was done that I could begin a chapter entitled "Enter the Neutrino." When Brad went over the manuscript he wrote in the margin at this point, "At last!"

24

I had lunch with Austin on March 7 and he told me that *Fantastic Voyage* had already sold six thousand copies even though the official publication date was still two weeks in the future. I was all grins and relief.

"Do you have any doubt that we'll make the eight thousand I promised?" I asked.

"None at all. In fact, I am quite certain we will sell far more than eight thousand."[4]

Austin seemed quite calm about it, since he apparently felt that if I said that that was the way it would be, that was the way it would be. I, on the other hand, less stanchly certain of my own wisdom, was nearly hysterical with relief.

25

I had dinner with Carl Sagan on March 19. With him was his fiancée, Linda Salzman, an extraordinarily attractive young artist, rather shy and soft-spoken, and quite obviously deeply in love with Carl. I took to her at once.

Earlier I had left a carbon of *The Universe* with Carl for his expert reading. I felt he might pick up some errors that I could well do without. After dinner, we spent time at our house and I plucked up the courage to ask him about it.

"I haven't had time to look over it yet, Isaac," he said. "I've been awfully busy."

I said, with a strained smile, "Of what importance is your work, Carl, compared to my manuscript?"

Carl looked at me thoughtfully and said, "You're joking, Isaac—except that you're not *really* joking, are you?"

There was no point in trying to fool Carl, so I wiped the smile off my face and said, "No, Carl, I guess I'm not joking."

Within ten days he had the manuscript back in my hands with some very useful pinpointings of error; none, thank goodness, major. He was also quite lavish with his praise of the book, which I dedicated to him and to Fred Whipple.

---

[4] And so we did. It has sold steadily in hard-cover ever since, and the coming of a soft-cover edition, as I predicted, made no difference whatever in sales.

26

March 21, 1965, was the official publication date of *Fantastic Voyage*, and the entire first printing of seventy-five hundred copies was gone. I had to wait for a second printing before I could get my author's copies over and above the one advance copy I received.

27

The Ginn & Company people were continuing to lay siege to me with reference to the science series for grade schools. They explained it all very carefully to me over dinner on March 30. A successful school text, they said, was equivalent to an annuity; it could make a great deal of money over the indefinite future with periodic revisions.

In fact, figures in the millions of dollars were freely discussed, and it was pointed out that I could leave a continuing estate that would take care of my children after I had moved on to the big typewriter in the sky. Though I didn't want to do the series—in fact, I desperately didn't want to do it—I found it a lot harder to resist the prospect of becoming a millionaire than I would have thought.

For myself, even millions lacked attraction at the price of working on such a project. After all, what would I do with a million dollars? I already had a couple of typewriters and all the typewriter paper I needed, together with pens, reference books, and so on. I must admit, though, that the thought of leaving my family well taken care of was an appealing thought.

And while thinking, I did a second book in the Follett series of astronomy books for eight-year-olds. This one was *Mars*.

28

On April 4, I attended a seder at the house of Essie and Bernie Fonoroff. It wasn't a very profound seder from the religious standpoint but it was the first that David and Robyn ever attended. David read the traditional "four questions" as the oldest boy there, but he read them in English, of course. And the food was good, as it always is at a seder.

I couldn't help but think it was the first seder I had attended since the one in Hawaii, and that one was twenty years before!

Where the devil did the time go?

29

I was giving numerous small talks at this time, usually involving not much travel, generally taking me no farther afield than Connecticut or New Hampshire. On April 23, 1966, I talked at the University of New Hampshire, and it turned out to be the first warm day of the season.

The dean took us on a tour of the campus, and the young coeds greeted the warm Sun (after a New Hampshire winter) in an explosion of bikinis. Since it was Saturday and a largely classless day, the bikinis were spread out on the lawn with insignificant fractions of the young women's bodies inside them.

The dean took no notice of it. In fact, no one seemed to, except, of course, me. I surveyed the scene with the greatest satisfaction and paid little attention to what the dean was saying. No one seemed to notice my behavior either, except Robyn, who indignantly reached up to put her hand over my eyes.

At another talk, in Westminster, Massachusetts, on the twenty-fifth, I met Burnham Walker for the first time in eight years. He was sixty-five now, white-haired and wrinkled, but as sharp and as dryly humorous as ever.

And on April 30, I was part of a panel at Boston College. We were ushered about by a young, good-natured priest, who at one point herded us all into an elevator. I was last and hung back, motioning him to enter the elevator ahead of me. For a while, we did the Alphonse-and-Gaston routine, but the young priest was responsible for getting us everywhere on time and dared not delay, so he finally got on the elevator first, saying to me, "All right, you win the struggle for humility this time."

He then said, "There's an old joke about the priest who said, 'I'm the most humble person in this room and I'm proud of it.'"

30

On May 2, 1966, one of Ginn & Company's executives invited Gertrude and me to their Beacon Street home, and then to a marvelous French meal at a nearby restaurant.

It was the first time we had ever been in one of the old aristocratic homes of Boston and, according to my diary, "it was fascinating in a horrifying sort of way."

I was not proof against this sort of treatment. These upper-class attentions had their effect on my candy-store soul, and by the time the evening was over I knew I was going to be involved in the project.

All I could do was to hope there really were millions of dollars in it. Anything less would not pay me back for the trouble I was getting into. I knew that much even as I said, resignedly, "All right. I'll do it."

31

May 8 was the day of the annual MIT science-fiction society picnic. As always, I picked the day, and for the first time my choice lacked magic. It rained.

The picnic was held indoors at MIT with impossible mountains of food, which I dutifully tried to make inroads upon, but without the true fervor of the ancient days, since I was determined never to let my weight get more than a couple of pounds over the 180 mark.

It had one interesting side effect, however. I was able to examine the society's science-fiction library, which had a complete collection of the various magazines. I found the August 1929 issue of *Amazing*, which, I remember, had been the first science-fiction magazine I had ever read (thirty-seven years before) and which had inspired me to use the fortunate word "science" in *Science Wonder* to win my father's approval. I even cast my eye over the first few paragraphs of Harl Vincent's "Barton's Island," the first science-fiction story I ever remember reading—but that magic was gone too.

32

Arthur Clarke was working with Stanley Kubrick to put out a motion picture called *2001: A Space Odyssey*, and Kubrick, who was investing millions in what must have seemed a very dubious venture (for *good* science fiction might well be poison at the box office), was searching for ways to promote it properly.

One way was to get a group of high-prestige individuals to make the movie respectable by having them submit to movie-camera interviews in which they would speak on such subjects as the possibility of extraterrestrial life.

I was one of those approached, and I spent hours on May 18, 1966, doing the interview in one of the rooms in the Anatomy Department. Elizabeth Moyer watched sardonically, but I think she was impressed with my seriousness and aplomb. She had never seen me under any conditions when I wasn't being more or less effervescent—even in the dark days of my fight with Keefer eight years before.

Afterward, I heard that Carl Sagan had been approached and had refused to co-operate since no money was involved. It made me uneasily aware that I had given myself away for nothing and had exposed myself as valueless by the only measure Hollywood valued—money. But it was for Arthur Clarke, I told myself, and you can't let a pal down.

33

In New York, on May 20, I had lunch with Janet Finney of Random House, for whom I had written *Satellites in Outer Space* seven years before.

I came early (I always do) and waited calmly at the table till Miss Finney arrived, merely seven minutes late, which was really nothing. I was accustomed to much worse than that.

She hastened to the table and called out to me as she came, "I'm sorry I kept you waiting, Isaac."

I called out in reply, "That's all right, Janet. I kept myself from growing impatient by thinking of your lovely face and basking in the anticipated warmth of your arrival." You know, just the thing any writer would say to his editor.

And a waiter, who had been passing by, stopped as though he were poleaxed, looked at my cheerful, blue-eyed, Slavic countenance in puzzlement, and said to me, "Pardon me, are you Italian?"

"Only with women," I said.

Janet Finney had a new suggestion for me—a book to be entitled *Twentieth Century Discovery*, which was to deal with scientific advances since 1900. It was rather like Svirsky's original suggestion to me except that this new book was to be for teen-agers, was to be only fifty thousand words long, and was to deal with only five or six specific topics.

I agreed readily.

34

My sense of having a teen-age son was growing stronger. We sent David on a visit to the Blugermans in New York, and he made the trip there and back by bus—alone.

Then, on June 3, he and I went to a baseball game at Fenway Park. It wasn't David's first game at all (he had even gone to games entirely alone, rather than with other boys), but it was the first we had attended together. And it was my first since those days thirty years before when I lived and died according to whether the Giants were victorious or defeated.

The game was between the Boston Red Sox and the New York Yankees and I rooted for the Yankees, since anything else would have been treasonable. David, on the other hand, rooted for the Red Sox. I had to force myself to remember that Boston was David's hometown. It seemed unnatural somehow.

35

Not all my books were successful, of course, but that spring, I hit a new low.

For some months I had been working on a book called *Background to Modern Biology* for the Educational Division of Houghton Mifflin. Those were the days when an attempt was being made to revolutionize the teaching of biology and to put it on a firmer biochemical and biophysical basis for the high-school level.

The trouble was that the high-school biology teachers were having trouble teaching the new biology since they didn't understand it themselves, and what I was supposed to do was to write a book that would teach the teachers. I readily agreed to it and in the process of working on it I had several lunches with Haven Spencer, who would be editing the book, and who was, in his own way, as delightful as Austin himself.

But the book took on a life of its own, as my books always seem to, and when I showed Haven samples of first draft it was clear that wherever it was going, it wasn't aimed at any destination that would serve to "teach the teachers." By June 27, it was clear that there was no chance of saving it, and the project came to an end by mutual consent.

All my more disastrous rejections, such as those for "Grow Old With Me," *The Death Dealers*, and *A Short History of Astronomy* had come at least after the book was finished. In the case of *Background to Modern Biology*, I was rejected partway through first draft.

It was embarrassing, but it was not the end of the world. I consoled myself by continuing busily and happily on my book on the Bible.

24

Second Hugo and Special Issue

1

We spent the first two weeks of July 1966 on a lake in Concord, Massachusetts, having agreed to rent the summer house of a casual friend for that period of time.

It was a rather disastrous experiment. The house was not comfortable and the surroundings were not pleasant.

In fact, I have blanked out most of that episode and remember only one incident out of those two weeks. One evening (I didn't even record which one in my diary), Robyn came running to the house shouting, "Daddy, Daddy, a flying saucer! Come look!"

I rushed out of the house to see. I was, and am, a firm disbeliever in flying saucers as extraterrestrial spaceships. I'm perfectly willing to believe in unexplained atmospheric phenomena, though, and I was curious to see what my eleven-year-old Robyn would consider to be a flying saucer.

It was a cloudless twilight. The Sun had set and the sky was a uniform slate gray, still too light for any stars to be visible; and there, hanging in the sky, like an oversize Moon, was a perfect featureless metallic circle of something like aluminum.

I was thunderstruck, and dashed back into the house for my glasses, moaning, "Oh no, this can't happen to me. This can't happen to me." I couldn't bear the thought that I would have to report something that really looked as though it might conceivably be an extraterrestrial spaceship.

I came out with my glasses and it was still there; it was *not* the figment of the overheated imagination of an eleven-year-old girl and the myopic suggestibility of a doting middle-aged father. But now the shape was beginning to distort slightly.

It was becoming slightly elliptical, then more so, then rather lopsidedly so, then black markings began to appear—it was turning broadside and it was a Goodyear blimp!

I was incredibly relieved!

2

July 26, 1966, was our twenty-fourth wedding anniversary, and we celebrated it in rather a different fashion. A convention of some type of engineers was meeting at MIT and were to be shown a preview of the movie *Fantastic Voyage*. My family and I were invited.

It wasn't entirely appropriate since I had nothing whatever to do with the movie, but I was curious to see it and so, needless to say, were the children.

It was a good picture. I was a little embarrassed when some of the engineers in the audience snickered at a few of the science-fiction touches, but then as the picture continued, they were caught up in it and the snickers stopped.

As for myself, I got my first look at Raquel Welch. She was the heroine, and it was her first starring role. One of the inducements that had been used in trying to persuade me to do the novelization was an offer to fly me to Hollywood and introduce me to Miss Welch.

I had never heard of her and all I knew was that I was not going to get into any airplane.

"If you want me to do the novelization," I had said, "then promise *not* to fly me to Hollywood."

Now, as I watched the motion picture, I wondered if I had been entirely wise. There are worse things than being in an airplane, I thought, and not meeting Raquel Welch was surely one of them.

I was particularly impressed by the scene in which Raquel was attacked by antibodies. Those antibodies had to be stripped from her body before they killed her, and four pairs of male hands moved instantly to her breasts to begin the stripping—and there was room there (it appeared to my fevered vision) for all eight hands.

When the movie ended, the spaceship had been left behind, inside the white cell, and Robyn turned to me and said at once, "Won't the ship expand now and kill the man, Daddy?"

"Yes, Robyn," I explained, "but *you* see that because you're smarter than the average Hollywood producer. After all, you're eleven."

David, who never read my books ordinarily, insisted on a copy of the book version of *Fantastic Voyage* as soon as we got home. He read it, I think, without stopping to breathe and when he was through, I said, "How did you like it, David?"

He said, indifferently, "It was just like the movie, but more stretched out."

My son, the critic!

3

That summer it was Robyn's turn. It was she who was going to spend eight weeks at a camp, as David had done for two years running some six years before. Robyn was older now than David had been when he had had his experience—but Robyn was a girl and seemed more fragile. I *hated* the notion.

We took her down to the camp, somewhere in Cape Cod, and left her there the very day after we saw *Fantastic Voyage*. Before the day was over I had written her a letter.

The next day we called her and received the news that she didn't like the food. We took that bit of news with equanimity, since what youngster ever likes the food at camp? We also got the news that she had already gone horseback-riding and that she loved it and that they had received instruction in how to jump clear in case the horse decided to lie down and roll over on them.

I instantly gave her instructions to stay away from all horses, but she insisted that she loved them and she would jump clear.

I was not consoled.

The particular camp had been chosen for Robyn because of the glowing recommendation of some slight acquaintance whose own daughter, a friend of Robyn's, was going. That daughter promptly got homesick and the slight acquaintance quickly brought home her precious darling at once, leaving Robyn behind with her morale shattered.

Robyn called us and begged to be taken home also, but we were hardhearted and would not give in. "Make new friends, Robyn," I said, firmly.

We never spoke to that slight acquaintance again.

4

Brandeis University had been fairly close to our apartment in Waltham and it was not very far away from our house in West Newton. We had been using it more and more as a cultural center, regularly going to see plays being staged there, for instance. Gertrude took summer courses at Brandeis.

On August 1, 1966, Gertrude and I, together with some of our friends, all visited Brandeis to hear a talk by Stanley Kauffman, the drama critic of the New York *Times*. It was a very good and enlightening talk and the women in our group were enthralled and clearly delighted with the speaker.

Something in my memory stirred. It seemed to me Kauffman used to work for Ballantine Books once and I had met him. Incautiously, I said so, and all the women, including Gertrude, whispered excitedly that they wanted an introduction after the talk.

"I'm not sure he's the one. I'm not *sure*."

"Well," said someone in the group, "what's the difference? He'll know *you*, anyway."

No, he wouldn't. Why should he? But they wouldn't listen.

After the talk, I was more or less forced to bend my reluctant steps toward the stage with half a dozen excited people following me, and with a very clear picture in my mind of a notable who didn't know me and who would favor me with a haughty stare, and with the total humiliation that would follow.

There was someone talking volubly to Kauffman as I approached, and I was in no hurry to interrupt. For my part, the conversation could be continued indefinitely till the people waiting behind me grew weary and demanded to be taken home.

Then Kauffman, lifting his eyes, waved a hand, and said in a quite matter-of-fact fashion, "Hi, Isaac," and went on talking.

I cheered up tremendously and pushed forward in a bustling way, cut out the fellow trying to talk to Kauffman, and introduced all my friends.

I was very disappointed and rather outraged when Kauffman left his job with the *Times* not long afterward. I kept telling myself there was no connection.

5

We visited Robyn at her camp at the midterm break on Sunday, August 7, and it was a virtual repeat of the time we had visited David under similar circumstances. Robyn asked piteously to be allowed to come home, and we refused stonily. I had the urge to tell her that the refusal hurt me far more than it hurt her, but she wouldn't have believed me.

When we left, it did occur to me that if something happened to her during those last four weeks, and if I had to spend the rest of my life thinking that *if* I had taken her home . . .

But then if I took her home and something happened to her there, I would have had to spend the rest of my life thinking that *if* I had left her at camp . . .

You can't win.

6

On August 10, I was in New York and took the complete manuscript of the Old Testament portion of *It's Mentioned in the Bible* to Doubleday.

I also dropped in at *F & SF* to get the original of the cover of the October issue of *F & SF*, which was to feature me. The illustrator, Ed Emshwiller, had drawn me from a photograph, and I was quite accurately pictured.

My image, like a bust, was shown on a pedestal that enclosed a large metal coil representing science, and a typewriter representing literature. In the background was a giant representation of a cell, which I supposed represented the med school.

Staring at the typewriter was a Sherlock Holmes figure who represented my science-fiction mysteries; a saluting robot, who represented my robot stories; and a beautiful, unclothed, red-headed girl, who must have represented some other aspect of my life, but I don't know exactly what.

About the only thing I could find fault with was the fact that Ed, unable to tell the color of my eyes from a black-and-white photo and unable to remember that color from those times he had met me (at the convention in Detroit in 1959, for instance) made them brown whereas, in actual fact, they are as blue as the western skies.

I obtained the original that day, and it is still on the wall of my office.

7

I obtained a copy of the 1966 issue of the Encyclopaedia Britannica on August 16, and finally I could replace the old 1942 edition that my father had bought shortly before I had left for Philadelphia twenty-four years before.[1]

8

We celebrated David's fifteenth birthday, on August 20, by putting him on the bus for a second solo trip to the Blugermans' in New York, and for a few days both children were away from home.

[1] I got the 1966 issue when I was forty-six. By an odd coincidence, my father had obtained the 1942 issue when *he* was forty-six.

We attempted to take advantage of the situation by having a little holiday of our own on our way to Robyn's camp to bring her home. On the recommendation of the Fonoroffs, we drove to Falmouth and then drove our car onto the ferry that would take us to Martha's Vineyard.

We had never visited it before and were delighted with it. There was only one trouble. It had never occurred to us that we ought to call ahead and make reservations in advance. It was deep in the summer season, and when we called the hotels, quite ready to pay any price, for money was no object, we found that money was also of no value when all rooms were filled.

We spent hours in a vain hunt and then, come midafternoon, had to make our chastened way back to the ferry slip and get a ferry back to the mainland. For a while, in fact, it seemed that we might not be able to find room on a ferry that day and we would have to spend the night sleeping in the car, but it didn't come to that.

It ended well enough, though. We put up in a hotel in Falmouth, and it had a heated swimming pool, which Gertrude used with considerable enjoyment.

And the next day was my real holiday, for we went to Robyn's camp and finally picked her up to take her home.

It was a joyous ride home, for she sang all the songs she had learned at camp and told us endless stories about girls we didn't know and what she had done and said and what they had done and said. I could have listened for days on end.

About the only drawback was that Robyn had been responsible for her own bathing for eight weeks, and her own clothes-washing, and the hot-water situation had been so erratic that she must have skipped both whenever she could. The atmosphere in the car was therefore quite close and I speculated on the desirability of burning all her clothes when we got back and of having Gertrude scrub down Robyn's little hide with a wire brush.

Actually, a lot of soap and steaming water seemed to do the trick as far as Robyn was concerned, and the clothes washer handled her clothes without actually breaking down under the strain.

The next day, David came home and the family was together again.

9

Understanding Physics arrived in its Walker & Company hardcover edition on August 26, 1966. It was in three separate volumes and looked very good indeed. They appeared no less than 3½ years after I had begun writing the first volume.

I had to consider whether to number the books in my list as a single book or as three. After all, when *The Intelligent Man's Guide to Science* first appeared in 1960, it was in two volumes, yet I considered it only a single book. However, I had written the latter as a single book and had written the former as three books—and each of the three volumes of *Understanding Physics* was longer than my average novel or my average history; so I counted it as three books.

I had a new thing going, too. So far I had published six books of science essays from the science-fiction magazines. The first one, *Only a Trillion*, had been from *Astounding*; the next five were from *F & SF*. Of late, however, I had been writing science articles for a wide variety of non-science-fiction magazines, for the New York *Times Magazine*, *Mademoiselle*, *Think*, *True*, *Petroleum Today*, and so on and so on.

Why not a collection of this miscellany? Why not get them together between two covers for those who liked almost anything I wrote? I had suggested this to Larry Ashmead and he had agreed in his everamiable way, so on August 27 I began putting the articles together. The title of the new collection was *Is Anyone There?* It was taken from the title of one of the articles included at Larry's suggestion.

10

The twenty-second World Science Fiction convention in 1964 had been in Oakland, California, and the twenty-third, in 1965, had been in London. I was unable to attend either, of course.

In 1966, however, the twenty-fourth World Science Fiction convention was to be held in Cleveland, as it had been in 1955 when I had been guest of honor. Then I had gone alone; this time I took the family.

We left on Thursday, September 1, stayed in Syracuse overnight, and were in Cleveland on Friday afternoon. We stayed at an old hotel and were put up in an old and terribly depressing room, with closets that were (I do not exaggerate) six inches deep.

Gertrude was furious, and it was almost like our first trip to Hilltop Lodge, twenty-three years before, when it had seemed there would be no way out but to go home.

The same lucky thing happened as at Hilltop Lodge. Then it had been Lester Weill; now, as we went down to the lobby to demand a better room or, if one did not exist, to go home, we met Harlan Ellison, bubbling over with enthusiasm and charisma.

To me he was just a little, sharp-featured guy, highly intelligent and as lively as quicksilver; but to women, somehow, he was a lot more than that. God knows what they see, but they see it. In five minutes flat, Gertrude was filled with delight and I could see that even Robyn was sparkling.

We had dinner with Harlan, and he kept us all thoroughly amused. We then attended parties till 5 A.M. and all was well. Even our closets seemed bearable.

At one of the parties, Evelyn del Rey was sitting on a windowsill and greeted me with some sardonic statement. She and I were always fencing when we met, and she was quick-witted enough to force me to extend myself.

This time I didn't feel like being extended. She had been Evelyn Harrison before she had been Evelyn del Rey, and she had been at the New Year's Eve party a dozen years before. I had kissed her then, and I had never forgotten that. I thought of it now, and since we were alone in the corner—or at least since everyone was talking to someone else—I said to her on impulse,

"You know, each time I see you I remember the time at Roz Wylie's New Year's Eve party when I kissed you. It was the first time any girl kissed me quite like that, and it meant a lot to me. I didn't think any girl ever would, so I'd rather not cross swords, Evelyn."

She looked at me with her defenses all down and said, "You remember that?"

I said, "Of course."

She said, "I didn't think you did."

From then on, for the rest of her life, she never fenced with me again. We were, whenever we saw each other, always warm friends.

There was no mystery to it. She had remembered and she had thought the episode had been of so little importance to me that I did not remember it, and she resented that. I have always been sorry, and annoyed at my own stupidity, that I had not made it perfectly clear long before. I could then have avoided mangling her self-esteem.

11

I met Gene Roddenberry at the convention, and we were all shown a preview of the new TV show "Star Trek." I must say that I watched it without any notion of how important it would become to science-fiction fandom. No breath of prescience stirred within me.

12

At 1 P.M. on Sunday, September 4, someone decided that Harlan and I ought to share the stage and engage in an impromptu battle of wits. Harlan was quite eager to do so, being quite confident that he could demolish anyone, and I was quite reluctant to do so because I was quite confident of the same thing. However, I couldn't very well back away, partly because I didn't want to seem to be a coward and partly because everyone kept telling me that I was the only person at the convention who could keep up with Harlan-in-full-cry, and I turn soft as a grape under flattery.

Harlan is a lot more voluble than I, but a lot less flexible. He is prone to use vulgar language and cannot prevent himself from doing so. My own strategy, then, was to deliberately lead the chain of insults as close as I could to obscene implications without using a single improper word, quite sure that Harlan, in his eagerness to go me one better, would find himself stuttering over obscenities.

In the end, though, Harlan began to tell the story of an encounter between himself and Frank Sinatra, in which Harlan had stood up to that show-business despot and had come off the winner. I willingly suspended the dialog to listen, and in the end we all cheered him as the worthy representative of the science-fiction fraternity; I, loudest of all.

That was the first of a series of encounters between us at conventions. It was all in good fun and was intended as in-humor for in-people, but some of the more unsophisticated fans inevitably assumed the battle to be a serious one and Harlan and me to be the deadliest of enemies. As it happens, of course, we are buddies, and though we live three thousand miles apart, one of us frequently calls the other for advice or help, and we never fail each other. Yet I must forever assure people we are friends, and I'm sure that so must he.

13

That same evening was the award banquet and Sprague de Camp, who was guest of honor, delivered a sober and interesting speech. I myself, as usual, was on the dais, for I was to hand out the Hugos—but this was a matter of only academic interest to me for once, since I had already gained a Hugo three years before in Washington, and one was enough to establish the principle.

Yet one thing of mine was nominated. The organizers of the convention had the intention of awarding J. R. R. Tolkien a Hugo (at least I think they had the intention). Tolkien's Lord of the Rings trilogy was out now and it had taken fandom by storm.[2]

The convention organizers, therefore, proposed a Hugo nomination in a new category, the "Best All-time Novel Series." They defined a "novel series" as consisting of at least three interconnected novels, and advanced Lord of the Rings as an example of what they meant, which, to me, was a clear hint as to how they wanted the voting to go.

However, to make it look unforced, other series were nominated. These included Heinlein's Future History series; E. E. Smith's Lensman series; Burroughs' Mars series; and my own Foundation series.

I felt that Tolkien was certain to win, and fairly so, and that Heinlein, Smith, and Burroughs all had enough devotees among the young fans attending the convention (and who did the voting) to give each a good shot at second place. Foundation, I honestly felt, would finish in last place, and I grieved at being the sacrificial lamb. I was reconciled to losing, but I hoped against hope that Burroughs or Smith would manage to place fifth. I would be delighted to make fourth.

When it came time to hand out that award, however, the organizer of the convention hastily whispered to me that Harlan wanted to handle the novel series item and said, in a shamefaced manner, "We had better let him. You know Harlan."

I certainly knew that Harlan was capable of creating a giant-size fuss if he didn't have his way, and I didn't want him spoiling the banquet, so with what grace I could muster I gave way.

Harlan came dancing up, made a few rapid remarks that had everyone laughing, and then announced the nominees and *omitted* the Foundation series.

I called out from my seat, in real outrage, "Hey, Harlan, at least *mention* the Foundation series."

Harlan didn't even hear me, or at least he made no sign that he had. He reached for the envelope, tore it open, waited the inevitable heartbeat for the sake of suspense, and said, "And the winner: Isaac Asimov for the Foundation series."

I thought it was Harlan's idea of a joke and sat there without moving and looking rather annoyed until everyone started laughing, and I gathered I had really won. And there were Gertrude and the children beaming, and everyone still laughing and applauding, and I got up to accept my Hugo, thoroughly and utterly speechless.

I don't think the organizers of the convention had thought anyone

[2] It had taken me by storm, too. Since it came out I have read it, and *The Hobbit*, four times and have liked the books better each time.

would take the award away from Tolkien, and it was the first indication
I had had, the first really *convincing* indication, since the first of the
Foundation series had appeared twenty-four years before, that the series
was so popular. In fact, I suddenly realized that just as "Nightfall" was
the most highly regarded science-fiction piece among the shorter
lengths, *The Foundation Trilogy* was the most highly-regarded science-
fiction item among the longer lengths.

That I could bear off the prize, so to speak, both long and short,
seemed utterly improbable to me, yet I had done it, and I remember
feeling utterly delighted that John Campbell was alive to see it. It
seemed to justify the faith he had had in me when I was eighteen and
when no one but Campbell himself could have seen anything at all in
"Cosmic Corkscrew."

According to my diary, "The evening was one great, gorgeous triumph! I spent hours laughing, hugging, and singing, and didn't go to
bed till 4 A.M."

And the next day we left for home.

14

I was typing up all the articles for *Is Anyone There?* rather than
using tearsheets, and I wasn't finished till September 14. The book
ended being 105,000 words long, half again as long as my usual essay
collection.

What seemed even more important to me was that on September
15 I began my *hundredth F & SF* article. I had continued the series,
without missing an issue, for over eight years. The hundredth essay,
"Impossible, That's All," dealing with the speed-of-light limit to veloc-
ity, was to appear in the February 1967 *F & SF*.[3]

15

The paperback version of *Fantastic Voyage* came out in September
and I received copies on the seventeenth. The motion picture was
released at the same time, of course, and my connection with it was
mistakenly assumed. Some fans wrote excitedly that my name had been
left out of the list of credits, and I had to write soothing letters to them
assuring them I had not been cheated.

One of the Boston movie houses encouraged misapprehension by
sporting a big sign that read, "See Boston University's own Isaac
Asimov's movie *Fantastic Voyage*."

[3] See *Science, Numbers, and I* (Doubleday, 1968).

I called up the Boston offices of the movie producers rather anxiously in order to disown this and to ask them to ask the movie house to take down the sign. The producers just laughed and said that if it helped bring in customers, it was perfectly all right.

16

More important to me than the movie that month was the special Isaac Asimov issue of *F & SF*, the October 1966 issue.

It contained my story "The Key"[4] and my poem "The Prime of Life,"[5] along with the bibliography I had prepared which, though it covered ten magazine pages, was only a partial one, even for those days.

In addition it contained my 96th *F & SF* essay, "Portrait of the Writer as a Boy,"[6] in which I described the beginning of my writing career in 1938.

This was my first piece of straight autobiographical writing of any length, but I did not consult my diary. I had the incidents clear in my memory, I thought, and, being proud of my memory, it did not occur to me to go any farther. In later years, when I did consult my diary while writing something more elaborate than an *F & SF* article, I was rather astonished and embarrassed to discover that my memory had played me false in several minor respects.

Finally, the special issue on me contained an Asimov-related cartoon by Gahan Wilson, and a biographical sketch of myself and of my character by Sprague de Camp, who praised me far more highly than I deserved.

17

At the 1966 World Science Fiction convention, *If* had won a Hugo as best magazine. It was a sister magazine of *Galaxy* now, and Fred Pohl edited both. Fred had the notion of putting out a special "Hugo Winners issue," one to which as many of the winners would contribute as possible.

He laid siege to me for a short story, and I agreed. (In my state of euphoria over the Hugo, how could I refuse?) I began a story I called "Billiard Ball" on September 21. It was a seven-thousand-word murder mystery that made use of general relativity. I liked it—and so did Fred,

---

[4] See *Asimov's Mysteries*.
[5] See *The Bicentennial Man and Other Stories* (Doubleday, 1976).
[6] See *Science, Numbers, and I*.

who didn't even change the title. It appeared in the March 1967 *If,*[7] which bore "Special Hugo Winners Issue" on the cover.

18

It seemed almost superfluous to attend the Boskone one month after that triumphant Cleveland convention, but I did, of course. My brother and his family happened to be in Boston at the time, and on October 1, all of us—four adults and five children—had dinner. It was a remarkable gathering of the clan.

While the Boskone was in progress I also wrote *Stars,* the third little book on astronomy in the Follett series.

I was working on a new history, too. I had done Greece in one volume and Rome in two, and I had no intention of letting Houghton Mifflin off the hook. The natural subject for the next book was Egypt, and so I was writing *The Egyptians* with feverish speed.

19

Lloyd Roth (of Columbia University days) was in town on October 11, and Gertrude and I took him to dinner. It was then that he told me of our first meeting, when I was trying (and, for a while, failing) to get into graduate school.

He remembered his end of it far better than I did, and I assume he remembered it correctly. At any rate, I did not have that portion of the tale in the diary, and what I told about that meeting in *In Memory Yet Green* is based on what he told me that day.

20

My mother had passed her seventy-first birthday on September 5, and was operated on for cataracts on October 26. It was a successful operation and, with glasses, she continued to see perfectly well.

On the day of the operation, Ginn & Company, having assembled its "team" for the grade-school science texts, gathered them together for the initial conference. There was an initial dinner on the twenty-sixth followed by two days of conferences.

There were three groups of people involved. First the authors. There were myself and Roy Gallant, who were to do the texts from four to eight, inclusive. Roy was an excellent science writer, whose

[7] See *Asimov's Mysteries.*

books I had read and enjoyed. He was neatly dressed, of moderate height, and reminded me, irresistibly, of Clifton Webb.

Then, too, there was Jean Bendick, who was to do the texts from one to three, inclusive. She was short, round-faced, vivacious, and gave an impression of almost girlish good humor.

There was a group of editors and advisers from the academic community, of whom J. Myron Atkin of the University of Illinois was head. He was bearded and very quick. Three others, whom I recall particularly, were Ed Kormondy, Irvin Ramsey, and Jean York.

Finally, there were people from the Ginn & Company staff. There was Ben de Luca, rather short and good-natured, and capable of a quick recovery. I remember once, when we asked for the suggested contract to include provision for an advance, he smiled and said something about that not being company policy.

Thereupon I opened my mouth to say that in that case it was not my policy to do any work for them, but he anticipated my statement and said so smoothly that it almost seemed part of the same sentence, "but, of course, we'll do it anyway."

I admired his aplomb.

There was Jack Chase; large, stout, and very serious; and there was James Ashley, who was newly hired just to take over the project. He was a tall, thin, young man, very gentle and unsure of himself just at first, but quickly learning to take charge.

I was amazed how quickly the group learned that it was impossible for me to be serious and how, inevitably, almost anything would serve to remind me of a joke. In fact, Jim Ashley got to the point of starting each session (and we had a number of them in the years to come) with "What's today's joke, Isaac?" Then he would invariably collapse when I told one.

It was all dreadfully dull work, generally, and I could only support it by infusing it with just a tiny bit of convention hilarity. I suspect that most of the others welcomed it, though a few would occasionally look uneasy.

21

When "The Key" appeared in the special Isaac Asimov issue of *F & SF*, I was well aware that it was the fourth of my Wendell Urth stories. Ten years earlier, when I had written three in rapid succession, I had decided that when I had enough I would put out a hard-cover collection of them—but then years had passed in which I wrote little science fiction and I knew that I was never likely to accumulate the ten stories or so I would need for a book.

The thought occurred to me, though, that the Wendell Urth stories were not the only ones that could be considered mysteries, if the term were defined fairly broadly. I suggested to Larry Ashmead the possibility of putting together a collection of these science-fiction mysteries, and he agreed at once.

I even suggested using the title *Asimov's Mysteries*, and Larry accepted that, too. I felt that the *Mysteries* part of the title would attract mystery readers who were not interested in science fiction particularly and that my name would be sufficient to drag in the science-fiction fans. On October 29, I began putting the stories together.

At the same time I was deep in the New Testament portion of the Bible book.

22

I had been an associate professor of biochemistry for eleven years now, and every once in a while it did cross my mind vaguely that it would be nice to be a full professor.

It could be done. There was no one at the university now who saw me as anything but an asset to the school, and there was no feeling against the promotion—provided I did some work and gave some classes.

I myself was willing to accept almost any professorial title—"Professor of Science Communications," for instance—and expected no pay. However, I would not take any classes. I simply lacked the time or the desire.

On November 4, 1966, I had lunch with Dean Gus Wiebe of the School of Communications and discussed the matter, but, as always before and since, we came to this irresolvable difficulty. They had to have some time in exchange, and I simply had none to give.

As a result I continued to be nothing more than an associate professor of biochemistry, and I resigned myself to that status as permanent.

23

I had become a member of the American Academy of Arts and Sciences, which met monthly at an old mansion on the border of Brookline. The mansion was an extraordinary piece of evidence of a sumptuous way of life in a day when the rich paid no income tax and the poor had to barter their labor for bare subsistence—a day I hope will never return, no matter how well off I become. I was particularly fascinated by the library, which was huge and, by and large, unreadable.

The procedure was always the same. There was a period of drinks, *hors d'oeuvres*, and talk. This was followed by a very good dinner, and then by a serious talk on some heavily intellectual subject by someone who was, usually, not an accomplished speaker.

I usually enjoyed it despite the stiffness of the assemblage, but of all the sessions I attended over a period of some five years, I remember the one on November 9, 1966, with the most satisfaction. That was the day Gertrude and I sat down at an empty table. Some of the young women who actually ran the day-to-day workings of the organization came in with, apparently, permission to join the dinner festivities. There seemed room only at my table so, hesitantly, they asked if they might join us.

I welcomed them joyfully, and the table was jumping all through the meal. After that, I invariably made some effort to find some way to join the staff rather than my fellow academicians at some table, but it never happened again.

I suspect I am not really an academician at heart.

24

On November 19, 1966, I was at a party concerning which I remember nothing except that I was introduced to someone as follows: "Isaac Asimov—John Updike."

Now, I know perfectly well that one John Updike is a luminary of American letters, a writer far beyond my own poor ability to emulate—but John Updike is not a unique name, and I hesitated. What if I expressed delight and reverence and it turned out to be John Updike the local veterinarian.

Updike, however, had no such problem. Since he had heard of Isaac Asimov, he knew that this must be *the* Isaac Asimov. To have two people with a name like that passed the bounds of credibility.

He therefore said at once, "Say, Asimov, how do you manage to write all those books?"

At once I was certain he was Updike the writer and I was ashamed to have let him make the advance. I felt myself to be professionally subordinate and I ought to have beat him to the punch and expressed the proper respect. It was too late, now. I passed off his question jokingly and we exchanged some mild conversation, but I remained upset.

I determined, therefore, not to let pass the next opportunity of being properly humble toward my betters. As it happened, the chance came the next night.

Boston University was dedicating a new library, the Mugar Memorial Library (named for a large contributor), and I was involved, since Howard Gotlieb (my curator, who lovingly collected all my papers) was a moving spirit behind it.

I showed up and wreaked my usual havoc among the *hors d'oeuvres* until I spotted Max Shulman across the room. He had written some best-selling humor books (*The Feather Merchants, Barefoot Boy with Cheek*), which I had enjoyed, and was the originator of at least one TV situation comedy, "Dobie Gillis," which I was fond of.

Fortunately, I knew what he looked like and there was no question that he was *the* Max Shulman.

I therefore walked up to him and said very diffidently, "Mr. Shulman, my name is Isaac Asimov and I want to tell you how much I enjoy your books."

No chance! I got as far as "My name is Isaac Asimov—" when he broke in and said, "Say, Asimov, how do you manage to write all those books?"

I gave up.

25

My father turned seventy on December 21, 1966, and there I was approaching the end of my section on the gospels in my Bible book. When I had told him I was working on a book on the Bible, he had been dubious, and I had shied off from explaining that that would mean the New Testament as well. Eventually, of course, he would have to know.

I carefully sent him (and also the Blugermans) a copy of every book I published and I could scarcely refrain from sending him a copy of my book on the Bible.

26

I spent the last week of the year in Washington, attending the AAAS conventions. I was slated to give a talk on the twenty-ninth, but it was a minor one.

I heard an excellent talk by Lynn White on the history of technology on the twenty-sixth and an even better one by George Wald on the chemistry of vision on the twenty-eighth. The talk by Wald, I felt, was the best I had ever heard up to that time. Wald spoke without notes and is the only speaker I have ever heard who, I was willing to admit, was better than I was.

27

The year 1966 ended with a publication list of twelve books, more than I had ever had before in a single year, far surpassing the previous record of eight books in 1960. It was a rather queer feeling that I had managed to average a book a month. There had been jokes prior to this about the "Asimov book of the month," but 1966 was the first year in which I managed to make the joke come literally true. The list follows:

67. *Fantastic Voyage* (Houghton Mifflin)
68. *The Noble Gases* (Basic Books)
69. *Inside the Atom, Revised Edition* (Abelard-Schuman)
70. *The Neutrino* (Doubleday)
71. *The Roman Republic* (Houghton Mifflin)
72. *Understanding Physics I: Motion, Sound, and Heat* (Walker)
73. *Understanding Physics II: Light, Magnetism, and Electricity* (Walker)
74. *Understanding Physics III: The Electron, Proton, and Neutron* (Walker)
75. *The Genetic Effects of Radiation* (Atomic Energy Commission)
76. *Tomorrow's Children* (Doubleday)
77. *The Universe* (Walker)
78. *From Earth to Heaven* (Doubleday)

I suppose, looking at the list coldly, that I was helped along to my record output by an increasingly liberal attitude concerning what constituted a "book." Thus, *Inside the Atom* was still basically what it had been when I had listed it as Book No. 19, ten years before, but I decided that the rewriting had been extensive enough to make it sufficiently new to be listed.

Then, too, I might have considered *Understanding Physics* to be one book instead of three, and *The Genetic Effects of Radiation* was a relatively short pamphlet.

In each case, however, I decided in my own favor because the number of books had become important to me. A strict interpretation might have given me as little as eight books for the year, and the fact is I wanted my twelve.

28

I celebrated my forty-seventh birthday on January 2, 1967, and Robyn helped me celebrate by taking me to the local Brigham's and treating me to hamburgers and ice cream at her expense. She had been saving up her allowance for the purpose. She was very excited and was the complete hostess.

25
"You Are *the Field*"

1

Occasionally it has occurred to some publishing house or other to have me do a younger version of some adult book I had earlier done. Occasionally I even promised to do so—and then backed out. There were always new projects occupying my time, and an adaptation never seemed interesting enough to compete with them.

Walker & Company, however, suggested a juvenile version of *The Universe*, and somehow I found that project interesting. On January 19, 1967, I began the process of cutting *The Universe* to a third of its length without leaving out anything essential. I called the new version *To the Ends of the Universe*.

2

You can't write as many items as I do without having some of them turn up in strange places or under strange conditions, and every once in a while something unprecedented would happen. I received an announcement from a Unitarian church in Bedford that my story "The Last Question" would be part of the services on Sunday, January 22.

That was more than I could resist, and since the weather that Sunday was not threatening, I drove my car to the northern suburb (where, a dozen years before, I had considered the possibility of a job), quietly entered the church, and took a seat in the rearmost row.

The minister read the story with considerable verve, and when he came to the end with the Computer-as-God saying, "Let there be light!" the organ let go with a crash and the effect was tremendous.

The minister had recognized me when I entered, so my attempt at anonymity failed. He wouldn't let me get away without having me join the coffee-and-cookie session afterward. I wasn't exactly loath to stay, however, for I never mind being made much of.

3

I had lunch in New York on January 27, with my brother and two other people from *Newsday*. We talked about the possibility of my writing articles for syndication by them, and afterward I had forty-five minutes alone with Stan. It was the first time we had ever been so long a time together, the two of us alone, since he had become adult.

Stanley was thirty-seven years old now. He had risen to the post of assistant managing editor at *Newsday*, and was soon to join the faculty of the Columbia School of Journalism on a part-time basis. We found ourselves to be completely compatible, each understanding the other's sense of humor, and each at complete ease with the other.

4

Harlan Ellison was editing a giant anthology of original science fiction for Doubleday, one he was calling *Dangerous Visions*. In it he was deliberately seeking ground-breaking material, consciously trying to shatter the mold set by John Campbell and his school (including myself) almost thirty years before.

Over and over he asked me to contribute something to the volume and each time I refused. My excuse was that I lacked the time, and that was true enough. My *real* reason, however, was that I couldn't face trying to write a story that would pass muster in the 1960s, when such talent as I had suited only the 1950s.

I felt that I didn't measure up any longer and I didn't want to prove it.

I offered, instead, to write an Introduction, and Harlan, rather than not have my name in the volume at all, agreed. I wrote the Introduction on February 4, 1967. In fact, I wrote two. The first dealt with my notion of how science fiction had changed in the 1960s. The second, entitled "Harlan and I," recounted the first meeting between us, fifteen years before. (Harlan later added a footnote insisting I was exaggerating, but I was not. My description of the meeting is completely accurate.)

Writing the Introductions did not really soothe me. In every other respect I had bounded forward in the 1960s. I had moved ahead in quantity, quality, and variety. In science fiction, however, I was convinced I was a has-been.

I had witnessed the phenomenon before. There had been great and prestigious science-fiction writers in the 1930s, writers I had revered and loved. When the 1940s (and Campbell) came, however, the writers of the 1930s moved out and a new group (including myself) moved in. I recall wasting precious little sympathy on them. They were the dinosaurs and we were the mammals and that was it.

Now it was I who was one of the dinosaurs, and there was a New Wave of mammals, whom I scarcely knew and who wrote in ways I could scarcely understand.

The more I thought of it, the less I dared to compete, and I might well have retired from the field permanently and might never have written one word of science fiction after "Billiard Ball" but for one remark.

I was attending a small science-fiction event in Newark on March 5, and was sitting in a bar with the del Reys, the Pohls, and the Silverbergs.

Evelyn del Rey said to me, "Why don't you write science fiction these days, Isaac?"

I squirmed a bit and said, sadly, "Evelyn, you know as well as I do that the field has moved beyond me."

And she said, "Isaac, you're crazy. When you write, you *are* the field."

I could make no coherent answer. Never, since my early days with John Campbell, had I received such encouragement when it was so badly needed.

To be sure, I didn't go on to turn out a massive output of science fiction—but never again thereafter was I *afraid* to write science fiction. If I had to, or if I felt like it, I wrote it, and if there were even the slightest danger of my feeling self-doubtful, I would mutter to myself, "Isaac, when you write, you *are* the field."

5

The previous fall, *TV Guide* had asked me to do an article reviewing the new science-fiction programs that had sprouted on television. I produced a humorous article entitled "What Are a Few Galaxies Among Friends?," and it had appeared in the November 26, 1966, issue of the magazine.

I made fun of the scientific illiteracy in silly programs such as "Lost in Space," "It's About Time," and "The Time Tunnel." I made some mention of "Star Trek," too. I said of it that it "seems to have the best technical assistance of the current crop," but I did wax a little jovial over one particular blooper.

That was when I ran into the "Star Trek" phenomenon. The viewers of the other shows didn't mind my comments (it may be they didn't know how to read), but the "Trekkies" were heard from at once. Even Janet Jeppson wrote me an angry letter.

Surprised, I watched the program and could see that it had its points. It was certainly the most intelligent science fiction I had seen yet on any of the visual media.

I began to feel that I had worked to harm something I should have labored to save, and for the first time I approached *TV Guide* and asked to do an article. They agreed, and on February 15 I turned out "Mr. Spock Is Dreamy," in which I was funny, but in which I managed to say a lot of nice things about "Star Trek."

It was published in the April 29, 1967, *TV Guide*, and Janet sent me a mollified letter. It also established my friendship with Gene Roddenberry, the producer of the show, and I felt enormously better.

It was in that article, incidentally, that I first referred to Robyn as "my beautiful, blue-eyed, blond-haired daughter." I have been doing that periodically ever since.

6

Occasionally someone wanted to work for me as a graduate student, but, of course, I was doing no research and took no graduate students. It was more difficult to explain why I would not serve as an adviser on some project or other, but usually I managed.

But then two young women from Radcliffe called me and said they wanted to do a term paper on science fiction and their professor had agreed provided they got an adequate adviser. They had suggested me, they said, and their professor had said that would be fine. I promptly said that it might be fine for them and their professor, but it wouldn't be fine for me because I wouldn't do it.

They asked to come see me and I said, "Very well, you can come see me, but I won't serve as adviser."

On February 16, they came to see me, and it was clear they knew my weakness. Each was a beautiful girl. I don't mean attractive; I mean beautiful. They simpered and dimpled at me and somehow I agreed to be their adviser. For the remainder of the semester, they would come over occasionally to ask questions and show me what they were writing. I looked forward to it.

7

On February 18 I visited the home of people I didn't know simply because they had a Soviet guest who wanted to meet me. I went with some misgivings, but the guest could speak English quite well enough to butter me up. He told me that in a recent poll in the Soviet Union, I had placed third in popularity as a science-fiction writer. A Soviet writer had finished in first place, and Ray Bradbury in second.

I loved to hear it, for it's nice to make good in the hometown. I have heard similar tales ever since. Eventually, a friend of mine, just returning from a visit to the Soviet Union, told me that he was told, quite seriously, that of all American writers, science-fiction or not, I was in second place only to Mark Twain. (If there's any American writer I don't mind being in second place to it's Mark Twain.)

8

The next day was Robyn's twelfth birthday and I returned her birthday present to me by taking her to a Chinese restaurant. It was just she and I. No one else was welcome.

9

On March 15, 1967, I finally finished the book on the Bible. I had been working on it for over a year and a half.

I was sorry I was done, actually. It had been a great deal of fun from the first verse of Genesis to the last verse of Revelation, and my feeling was that now that I had done the work, I could do a *really* good job if, with the overall knowledge I had gained, I were to start over. I think that was the first time I ever felt the urge of revision that keeps so many authors working through so many drafts.

I resisted the urge, however. I had too many other things to do.

10

The history books had become virtually an obsession with me. Having finished *The Egyptians*, I began, on March 22, another, on the other region of ancient civilization, the Tigris-Euphrates. This book I eventually called *The Near East*.

The history books were chancy in a way. I was accepted as a science-fiction writer and no one could doubt my credentials as a scientist, but what made me a historian? I expected the reviews would reflect this.

I had schooled myself to withstand bad reviews, after the time of Henry Bott. Eventually I even learned to dump bad ones directly into

Stanley and I at the book-and-author luncheon on Long Island where I made my "Stanley who?" speech.

Ben Bova.
Photo by Jay K. Klein

Robert Silverberg.
Photo by Jay K. Klein

Fred and Carol Pohl.
Photo by Jay K. Klein

At Boskone, 1969.
Harry Stubbs (Hal Clement) and I.
Photo by Jay K. Klein

I am between Anne McCaffrey and
Damon Knight (Kate Wilhelm is peeking out
under Damon's beard), in Toronto
in 1970, I believe.
Photo by Jay K. Klein

Sitting next to me are Judy-Lynn and
Lester del Rey—Infinity Con, 1972.
Photo by Jay K. Klein

John Campbell in the last year of his life. Photo by Jay K. Klein

Boston convention, 1971. I'm handing Ed Ferman a Hugo. Photo by Jay K. Klein

Boston convention, 1971. Cliff Simak is on the right. Robyn (age sixteen) is next to me. Photo by Jay K. Klein

Toronto, 1973. I have just won the Hugo for The Gods Themselves. *Lester del Rey, toastmaster.* Photo by Jay K. Klein

A typical lecture shot. This one is at a science-fiction convention. I don't remember which; it could be Toronto in 1973. Photo by Jay K. Klein

Me in foreign parts! June 1973, disembarking in Canary Islands and looking nervous.

Janet and I in Toronto in 1973. Photo by Harvey L. Bilker

the wastebasket and to keep only the good reviews. (Since I never showed my reviews to anybody after my first try in 1950, is there any reason I have to keep them even-handed?)

One review of *The Roman Republic* and *The Roman Empire* in the New York *Times* of May 7, 1967, did try my temper, though. The reviewer seemed surprised that I dealt so largely with war and politics instead of with economics and sociology. Apparently he objected to my writing an interesting book when I might so easily have written dull ones such as, presumably, he did.

For days I tottered on the brink of writing him on the matter, and then decided it was useless to say anything. I should, instead, *do* something; and what I should do was exactly as I pleased regardless of reviews. What successful writer, after all, has not, on occasion, received bad reviews—and who remembers the names of the reviewers?

(The same day I began *The Near East,* I also began another small book in the Follett series. This one was on light and I called it *Light.*)

11

The Boskone was held twice a year, and on April 1 I attended the vernal portion of the festivities. The next day I received the E. E. Smith Memorial Award (Doc Smith had died on August 31, 1965, at the age of seventy-five) or, as it was more popularly called, the "Skylark."

Awards in science fiction were beginning to proliferate. One could not write as much as I did, and attend as many conventions, without accumulating plaques, statuettes, and assorted testimonials. Some I put on walls, some were placed on shelves or in bookcases. As objects, they are troublesome and get in the way. As evidence, constantly before my eyes, of the affection and appreciation of my readers, they are priceless.

12

My first chance to put Evelyn del Rey's dictum into action came now. A periodical called *Abbottempo,* put out by Abbot Laboratories, a respected pharmaceutical firm, for European distribution, asked me for a two-thousand-word science-fiction story. It was to be on a subject of medical interest and something that physicians would find at once interesting, amusing, and thought-provoking. I had almost replied with an automatic refusal when Evelyn's remark occurred to me and, as it happened, I thought of a plot that would fit the prescription perfectly.

On April 10, 1967, I wrote "Segregationist"[1] at a sitting, and the editor took it without any trouble. The story dealt with heart transplants, and at the time it was written it was entirely science-fictional. Once again, however, as in the case of "Everest," fourteen years before, science caught up with me. By the time the story appeared, in December 1967, heart-transplantation was an accomplished fact.

Whereas "Everest," however, meant nothing if the failure to climb the mountain were subtracted, "Segregationist" still had meaning even if the heart transplant were not taken into account.

Once the story appeared, by the way, *Abbottempo* sent me a boxed collection of the magazine, with one copy in each of the eight languages in which it was published: English, French, Spanish, German, Italian, Japanese, Greek, and Turkish. It was the first time anything of mine had appeared (to my knowledge) in either Greek or Turkish.

It was my first intention to keep that set intact as a valuable bit of Asimoviana, but I broke down. There was an article on some horrible disease in that issue, with some impossibly emetic photographs to go with it, and they were present in every language. I could not stand the photographs and, eventually, took out my story and destroyed the rest of the magazines very thankfully.

I had had a similar problem some months before in doing an article on the juvenile hormone in insects, and the use it might have as a specific insecticide without harmful side effects on other forms of life.

Writing it was simple, except that the articles I had to read to bone up on the subject were filled with stomach-turning insect photographs. I moaned to Gertrude that I might have to refuse to do the article and that I would lose an easy fifty cents a word.

Gertrude said, matter-of-factly, "Don't look at the pictures."

Now, why didn't I think of that?

I began the article without further trouble of any kind on January 31, 1967, and it appeared in the May–June 1967 issue of *Think*, the in-house magazine of International Business Machines Corporation. They ran it under the title "The Insecticide That Turns a Bug Against Itself." I never included it in any of my collections but I cannibalized it eventually to form the first section of the book *Twentieth Century Discovery* that I was planning to write for Random House.

13

Gertrude was still driving the old pink-and-white Plymouth Hy-Drive I had bought in 1954. It had traveled seventy-six thousand miles

[1] See *Nightfall and Other Stories*.

and was a dreadful thirteen-year-old deathtrap that was well overdue for replacement. We bought a new Plymouth Barracuda in its place and it was delivered on April 11, 1967. For the first time in her life, Gertrude had a brand-new car all her own.

My own Ford was not as old as the Hy-Drive, but it had seen its best days.

On April 16, I took it (with the family inside) to Fairfield, Connecticut, to give a talk at Fairfield College, and then we headed south. Two days later I was traveling along the Skyline Drive, surrounded by the gorgeous scenery of the Shenandoah Valley in Virginia.

On the morning of Wednesday, April 19th, I discovered I could not start the car. I called in reinforcements in the form of employees of the motel I was staying at, and after half an hour and united efforts, we got it started. I blamed the trouble on the thin air of the mountain heights and was not unduly disturbed.

We went to the Luray caverns, which we enjoyed enormously (it was the first time any of us had been in a limestone cave), and then we went northward through Washington, where we spent a couple of days sight-seeing. By Friday we were out on Long Island, visiting Stanley and Ruth.

Saturday morning, the twenty-second, I was all set to go home, and again I couldn't start the car. It surely wasn't the mountain heights this time, for there are no mountains on Long Island.

In a complete dither, I did the only thing I could think of: I called Stanley. I had every faith in him. I was merely brilliant; he was level-headed, and that, in an emergency, is worth a great deal more.

He came down in his car, without complaint, and asked me if I had gas. Of course I had gas, I assured him. I've never in my life not had gas, I added. Then he tried to start the car and failed.

"What do we do?" I asked forlornly.

"We call a gas station," he said.

"On a weekend?"

"We try," he said, firmly.

We went to a phone booth and I fed him dimes and we got nowhere. Some stations were closed, others were not equipped with mechanics, others had mechanics who would not come to my car but demanded I bring it to them.

Finally, Stanley leaned back in exasperation and said, "How is it, Isaac, that someone who is the genius you claim to be, isn't bright enough to join the AAA?"

At that, I said indignantly, "What do you mean, not bright enough. I'm a member of the AAA. Here's my card."

He gave me a very strange look and didn't even bother to ask me why I hadn't told him that to begin with. He called the AAA and they had a tow truck out to my car in almost no time.

For the first time in my seventeen years as an automobile driver, my car was towed away. Apparently my spark plugs were utterly used up. I had neglected to replace them at the last ten-thousand-mile checkup because I hadn't had the checkup. The auto mechanic said he couldn't understand how it had managed to start every time but two over the preceding six months.

After that we headed for home, and on the Connecticut Turnpike the power steering conked out and I had to be towed *again*. No tow at all in seventeen years, and then two in one day for unconnected reasons.

Once I finally got back to Boston, I took my car to my own repairman at the first opportunity and inveighed bitterly against the Fates. I was very eloquent indeed, but my repairman, a man with no poetry in his bosom, said, "Doc, you gotta understand this car is wore out. Don't yell at it. It done its best."

I recognized the justice of the remark, and though I told him to overhaul the car and put it into tip-top condition, I began to look for another one.

14

While the car was being repaired, I went to school in a taxi. After all, I had promised my two beautiful Radcliffe students that I would be there on April 25 to look over their dissertations, and a promise is a promise.

After I had gone over their papers, it occurred to me that I might as well make use of them for transportation. After all, I had been of considerable service to them, and they might as well make part of it up to me. So I asked them to drive me back to Newton.

"We'd love to," they said, "but our car only seats two."

I was surprised. "Don't try to get out of it," I said. "No car only seats two."

"Come look at it," they said.

Down I went with them and they were right! They had a tiny MG that was about the size of a baby buggy and there was no way of squeezing more than two people into its single tiny seat.

While I stared in dismay, one of them said, "Of course, if you're willing, I'll drive, and Toni can sit on your lap."

"All right," I said, cheering up at once. Crowding into that front seat with my two beauties struck me as an elegant way to travel.

No sooner said than done, and off we went. Toni, who sat on my lap, was the taller and larger of the two, and I should judge she weighed a buxom 140 pounds. If a 140-pound sack of wheat had been draped over my knees, I'm sure my legs would have gone to sleep in ten seconds. As it was, my circulation continued unimpeded and I never felt the weight at all. It's a curious physiological phenomenon I can't explain.

We must have made a curious sight as we barreled down the Massachusetts Turnpike—a tiny car with two beautiful young women filling it completely and the head of a middle-aged man poking out from between them.

As we approached the first toll booth, I called out, "Pay the money, girls, and I will pay you back when we get to my house."

"We don't have any money," they said.

"No money?" I said, stupefied. "How can you get by without money?"

"Oh, someone always helps out," said the driver, cheerfully.

That remark offered me an insight into the strange world in which beautiful young women live. I struggled to get out the necessary coins. It was very difficult, weighed down as I was by 140 pounds of female flesh and blood, but it had its compensations.

When we were finally home, I invited the young women into the house for Cokes and called out to Gertrude to say hello.

She wasn't there; she had gone out shopping. I hadn't expected that. I turned uneasily to the young women and said, "My wife's out shopping. I'm sorry, but I honestly didn't know that the house would be empty. We'll leave."

"That's all right," they said, coolly, "we'll have our Cokes."

I wasn't sure that it was flattering to have them so completely certain that I was entirely harmless, but I served them their drinks.

15

Howard Gotlieb, my curator at Mugar Memorial Library, had decided to put up a display of Asimov books, presenting a copy of every single one, some in different editions, all suitably inscribed, and in chronological order from 1 to 80.

The only book he didn't have and couldn't get was *The Death Dealers.* Howard appealed to me, and I was helpless. I had no spare copies at all, only my own library copy, which I had had bound in hard-cover.

Howard pleaded for it and, very reluctantly, I let him have it, asking him over and over again to guard it with his life. He promised, and put it prominently in one of the cases, along with a card describing it as a very rare copy, personally bound by the author, but as otherwise existing in paperback form that was out of print and could not be obtained.

On April 27, 1967, there was a formal opening of the display—eighty books in seventeen years, an average of five a year. Many people from Houghton Mifflin showed up, including, of course, Austin, Mary K., and Walter Lorraine. To my surprise, Sam Walker of Walker & Company arrived. He was in Boston on some errand or other and took the trouble to drop in; I was pleased and touched.

16

Robyn was growing up. We had frequently taken walks together, going hand in hand here and there in the neighborhood, talking and skipping and joking and singing.

Now things were slacking off. She began to disapprove of my more elaborate effervescences and finally demurred at taking walks with me altogether.

"Why not, Robyn?"

"You're my father, Daddy."

"Of course I'm your father. That's why we should take walks."

"No. The girls might see me."

"So what?"

"You're not supposed to walk with your father."

"Why not?"

"Because the girls don't do it."

"Who cares? We do."

"Well, we shouldn't."

And we didn't. She had grown too old for it. The trouble was, I hadn't.

17

And then things grew worse. On May 1, Robyn broad-jumped at gym in school, breaking the school record, but landing so hard that she apparently sprained her right ankle and couldn't stand on it. As they carried her off, she called out, "Did I break the record?"

That, I suppose, was the true mark of the achiever, but she should have asked, "Did I break my leg?" because she had.

We took her to the Newton-Wellesley hospital, where they X-rayed her ankle and found she had sustained a hairline fracture of the tibia just above the ankle. It was a tiny, unnoticeable break, but on went the cast just the same and it would stay on, said the doctor, for six weeks.

I was in despair. It was the first broken bone to anyone in my immediate family in my whole life, and I tried to drown my unhappiness in work. There was a little astronomy book for Follett, *Galaxies*, and I put together some stories of mine for New English Library, a British firm. The collection was called *Through a Glass, Clearly*, and it was for distribution in Great Britain only.

18

By May 3, Robyn seemed quite herself, except for the broken leg, of course. In fact, she seemed pleased at the romantic position of being in a cast and getting some time off from school, so I took a chance and made the trip to New York that I had been planning for the fourth.

I had a long lunch with Larry on that day and he wondered if I'd ever considered doing an autobiography. I admitted I had been thinking of doing one for years but always came up against the difficulty that my life had not been an exotic and unusual one. "But someday I will," I promised.[2]

At Walker & Company, Sam Walker, having gone over the exhibit of my books at Mugar Memorial Library the week before, inquired of me concerning *The Death Dealers*. He had noticed that it had appeared only in paperback and that it was now out of print.

Might it not be possible to do a hardback copy of it, he wondered? I was delighted at the thought. My failure with *The Death Dealers* was somehow the literary equivalent of my failure to get into medical school, and I wanted another chance.

Of course, I would have to seek a reversion of rights from Avon, but I didn't think that would present any difficulties—and it didn't.

19

When I returned to West Newton, I found Robyn, to my relief, still in high spirits. In fact, on May 8 she returned to school by taxi (one would be provided every day in consequence of her having suffered the injury in the course of a school activity—I had paid insur-

---

[2] Actually, Austin Olney had asked me even earlier if I had ever thought of doing one, but I don't remember the occasion and apparently did not make mention of it in my diary. Then, too, later on, Paul Nadan of Crown Publishers actually offered me a contract to do so, even though I had never written anything for Crown.

ance for that privilege), and that added mightily to her sense of importance.

On that same day, I gave a talk for a group organized by my friend Arthur Obermayer. He knew me well enough to have it at Boston's Playboy Club, and that marked the first time I had ever been inside the halls of such an institution.

I found the bunnies very delightful indeed, but apparently Arthur knew me well enough to have arranged for all the bunnies to vanish after dinner, when I was to give my talk.

20

On May 24, I began a new book for Basic Books, where I was now working directly with Arthur Rosenthal, the publisher. I suggested doing a book on photosynthesis—which would give me a chance to do biochemistry. He was willing and I used *Photosynthesis* as my working title.

Somehow I took it for granted that by the time the book rolled off the presses, it would be called *The Green Miracle* or *The Food Factory* or something like that. It wasn't. It came out as *Photosynthesis*. In fact not only was the word on the cover, but it was also repeated four times, one under the other, as though printing a Greek-derived five-syllable word four times made it any easier to pronounce or understand than if it had been printed only once.

"Arthur," I said uneasily, "how can the book sell well with that ridiculous title?"

Arthur said, "It's got a good book jacket."

It did. Under the quadruple title was a photograph of the Sun, peering through a tree in full leaf. "That is a good photograph," I said.

"I'm not talking about the photograph," said Arthur. "If you'll look under the photograph, you'll see your name printed very clearly—and spelled correctly."

It was nice to have a publisher's confidence, and, indeed, the book did moderately well.

21

The month of May was ending in absolute chaos. Robyn was still in her cast, of course, and Gertrude, who had been suffering chronically from arthritis, suddenly began a siege in which it was acute. She could scarcely move. On top of that, John Blugerman called from New York to tell us that Henry Blugerman had lung cancer and would have to be operated on.

Naturally, that would be the month in which my speaking schedule was particularly heavy. Seven talks had been scheduled, and the final one was on May 31. It was to the American Heart Association in downtown Boston.

That morning a friend called, and when he remarked on the sadness in my voice, I seized the chance of listing my woes. I ended by saying, "The only one around here beside myself who isn't in a bad way is David. Thank goodness, he's in good health."

I then hung up and I hadn't as much as removed my hand from the phone when it rang. I answered and (you're ahead of me, I know) it was from the school to tell me that David was running a slight temperature and was being sent home.

I would have liked to cancel the talk that night, but you can't do something like that. Talks were show business to me, and the show must go on. Nevertheless, I was too upset to feel I could be trusted at the wheel of my car. I called a taxi and had it take me downtown.

There was a cocktail party first and, for the first time in my life, I deliberately had three drinks in an effort to get high before giving my talk. I felt I would not be able to give it cold sober. Perhaps because I had the need to get drunk (or thought I did) the drinks did not affect me at all as nearly as I could tell.

I got up to give the talk, sober—and found I did not need the drinks after all. The act of speaking elated me. In fact, I found so much relief in speaking, and felt so removed from all the disasters of the month, that I did not want to stop. I knew that when I stopped all would come back to me.

I continued fifteen minutes longer than I ought to have, and if I thought I could have persuaded them to listen, I would have spoken all night. As it was, it was one of the best talks I had ever given.

Then, of course, things improved. By the next day, David's fever was gone, Gertrude's arthritis cooled down to the point where she could leave the house—and on June 2, Robyn's cast was removed.[3]

---

[3] Adding to the gloom of May was the gathering crisis in the Middle East. The Arab states were assuming a threatening posture, and Israel seemed to be without a friend in the world except for the United States. Although I was not, and am not, a Zionist, I wasn't quite ready to see Israel destroyed, and I worried about that. Then in the first week of June, Israel launched a pre-emptive offensive and smashed Egypt, Syria, and Jordan in what came to be called the "Six-day War." The world situation thus improved as my personal affairs did.

22

I was waiting for my new car, and rather than use the old one, I drove to New York on June 8 in Gertrude's Barracuda, which handled like a dream. When I arrived in New York, I called home and found that the new Ford was waiting at the dealer's.

It was just as well. Had the new car come a day sooner, I would have been tempted to drive it to New York, and it made more sense to drive it about locally and work out the bugs before risking it on a long trip.

All was going smoothly with respect to *The Death Dealers*. Avon allowed the rights to revert to me, and Walker & Company gave me a contract.

On June 9, I visited Henry Blugerman in the hospital. He seemed in good spirits as he waited for the operation, and I was glad of that, for he was a gentle, kindly soul beloved by all.

23

On June 13, I finally picked up my new Ford. It was the fifth automobile I had bought and I felt rather inordinately wealthy with *two* 1967 cars in my garage.

More important was the fact that on June 15, Henry survived what seemed a successful operation. One lobe of his left lung was removed and the doctors expressed the hope that there might be a complete recovery. Henry was seventy-one years old at the time and it seemed reasonable to hope for another decade of life.

And meanwhile I had written my 109th *F & SF* essay, which eventually appeared in the November 1967 issue of the magazine. It was the 17th essay of a new series and I promptly began putting together a sixth collection, to be called *Science, Numbers, and I*.

24

There was a change of editors at *Hornbook*. This seemed a chance at last to end a duty I was finding increasingly onerous. I had not wanted to abandon the previous editor, Ruth Hill Viguers, who had brought me in as reviewer, but with her gone, there was no reason I needed to continue. I had been working on the column for nine years now, and enough was enough.

Nor did my conscience hurt me. I suggested Harry Stubbs as a successor, and he agreed to serve. Harry was much better at it than I was. He read the books more carefully and thoughtfully than I did, and anyone who read his columns could see that he enjoyed preparing them more than I did.

25

The appearance of *Fantastic Voyage* in *The Saturday Evening Post* had belatedly filled me with the ambition to get something of mine into the dying shadow of that magazine before it was too late. I wrote a fifteen-hundred-word short-short for that purpose, one I called "Exile to Hell,"[4] and I sent it in on June 21, 1967.

I was rejected, however, just as I would have been by the *Post* in the 1930s and 1940s. Only then did I begin to remember my neglect of Campbell. In the ten years that had elapsed since he had published "Profession" in the July 1957 *Astounding,* I had sent him only one piece of fiction, and that was "Thiotimoline and the Space Age," and that was only semifictional at best.

Feeling like an ungrateful hound, I sent in "Exile to Hell" to Campbell and he took it. For old times' sake, I was delighted. It eventually appeared in the May 1968 *Analog* (the first bit of fiction of mine to appear in the magazine under that name) with a typical Campbellesque blurb that gave away the point of the story.

26

Time magazine was noticing me. A reporter came to interview me on June 26, and two days later a photographer came to take pictures for the magazine.

The July 3, 1967, issue then carried the story—two columns, along with a good-looking and dignified photograph of myself. *Time* treated me with considerable praise, including some quotations from myself in which I treated me with considerable praise as well.

According to Larry Ashmead, one of the Doubleday editors rushed into his office and said to him jubilantly, "Have you seen the story on Asimov in *Time*? It's filled with charming Asimovian immodesties."

For years thereafter, I used the phrase "charming immodesties" to refer to my own estimates of myself, until I found the phrase "cheerful self-appreciation," which suited me still better.

Another spinoff rested on the fact that Boston University had just

4 See *Buy Jupiter and Other Stories.*

gained a new president, Armand Christ-Janer.[5] He had just taken office on July 1, and in his first week, while leafing through *Time*, he found one of his faculty featured there.

He sent me an excited hand-written note, which I received on July 9, and on July 20, at his invitation, I went to the main campus to see him. We spent twenty minutes together and he told me (according to my diary) "how grateful BU is to be associated with me."

I thanked him and smiled to myself at the thought of how the situation had changed in the ten years since my struggle with Keefer.

[5] He was younger than I was by a number of years and it took me aback to find I had reached the time in life when I was older than my college president.

26

Asimovian Immodesties

1

I had lunch with Tim Seldes and Wendy Weil in New York on July 7, 1967, and that was one of the occasions on which an event took place that fueled the rumor that I have a photographic memory. (I don't. It's just a pretty good memory.)

It seems that I had once read in *The Historians' History of the World* that Abd er-Rahman III, the greatest King of Muslim Spain, who had reigned fifty years with great success and prosperity, had confessed that in all that time, he had had only fourteen happy days. It seemed a remarkable commentary on the human condition, and I remembered it—especially since I myself had had far more than fourteen happy days.

A couple of weeks before my lunch with Tim and Wendy, I had bought a paperback book of quotations edited by George Seldes, Tim's uncle. I like books of quotations and tend to buy them when I see them. This one, however, was filled with quotations that were expressed in such turgid and unmemorable prose that (even though I agreed with virtually all the liberal sentiments) I threw the book away.

It did, however, have the Abd er-Rahman III quotation under "Happiness." It went something like this: "I have reigned fifty years at the height of prosperity and power, loved by my friends, respected by my subjects, and feared by my enemies, yet in all that time I have known but fourteen completely happy days." I noticed that quote because until that time I had thought I was the only person in the world who knew it.

At the lunch I said to Tim, "I just bought your uncle's book of quotations."

"Really," said Tim, "and did you notice the mistake in the very first item?"

Well, I hadn't. I knew that Tim asked me that only to puncture the rumor that I had a photographic memory, and the fact was that I hadn't the faintest idea what the first item in the book was. Thinking rapidly, however, I recalled that in the Introduction to the book (I read

Introductions) it stated that the paperback (which I had bought)
differed from the hard-cover edition in listing quotes alphabetically by
subject rather than by author. If in the hard-cover the listing were alphabetically by author, then the Abd er-Rahman III quote was probably first.

Thinking that through took only a few seconds, so when I said,
calmly, "Yes, I did," it sounded as though there had been no pause at
all.

Tim said, disdainfully, "You're bluffing. You don't even know
what the first quotation was."

"Yes, I do," I said. "It was Abd er-Rahman III's statement: "I
have reigned fifty years . . ." and I completed it with reasonable accu-
racy.

Both Tim and Wendy were now staring at me, and Tim said,
"And what was the error?"

"Although Abd er-Rahman III is quoted as saying he reigned fifty
years, they give his dates of his reign, and he died after reigning only 49
years," I said (having happened to notice everything about that fascinating quotation). "That's not really a mistake, however. He was
counting the years by the Mohammedan lunar calendar, in which there
are only 354 days to the year."

I then went on (remembering another item I had noticed), "The
quotation is only first in the hard-cover, of course. In the soft-cover it is
on page 441 and under . . ."

Tim could stand no more. He leaned across the table, seized my
lapel, bunched it, drew me toward him, and said loudly, "Asimov, to
choose a phrase at random—you're a *prick*."

I couldn't have done it for any other quotation in the book, and it
was sheerest luck that Tim had picked on it.

2

After dinner on July 11, Robyn, whose cast had been removed
nearly six weeks before and who had since then been running and
jumping in an ecstasy of freedom, tripped on our lawn and sprained the
same ankle.

Ordinarily, we'd have thought nothing of it, but I dared not take a
chance under the circumstances, and insisted on putting her in the car
and taking her to the hospital.

She wept bitterly and said she didn't want a cast again.

I reassured her. "It's nothing, Robyn," I said. "We're just going to
make sure and then he'll bandage it and you'll just limp for a day or
two and you'll be as good as new."

I remained as cheerful as I could manage while the X rays were taken, and then I joined the doctor who was studying the results.

"Well?" I said, anxiously.

The doctor said, "I can't be certain. I can't tell whether the mark is just what was left by the old fracture or whether she has opened it again."

"What do we do then?"

"In a case like this, the only thing we can do is play it safe. The cast goes back on."

I said, "I can't tell her that."

"You'll have to," said the doctor, quite coldly. "Do it now and I'll get the materials ready."

I walked into the room where Robyn was waiting with tear-streaked cheeks. I was under the impression I appeared cheerful, but Robyn took one look at my face and broke into a loud wail. I could take no more. I ran to her and put my arms around her and when the doctor came in, we were both clinging to each other and both crying.

The doctor said, impatiently, "Come on, now," and on went the cast. He said, "We'll only keep it on a couple of weeks, and then we'll take another look."

I took Robyn home in such a mingled state of shock and despair that I could only sit down at the typewriter and, one after the other, turn out three *F & SF* essays on the metals. They were "The First Metal," "The Seventh Metal," and "The Predicted Metal," my 110th to 112th essays in the series. They appeared in the January, February, and March 1968 *F & SF*.[1]

I also began a new history book on July 22. Having done five books on ancient history now, I felt the need to move into medieval times, and started one on the aftermath of the fall of the western provinces of the Roman Empire. I eventually called it *The Dark Ages*.

Robyn's cast was still on when, on July 26, Gertrude and I celebrated our silver wedding anniversary. Then, on the twenty-eighth, we visited the hospital again. The cast was removed, the X rays were taken again, and the cast was *not* replaced. That was the day of the real celebration.

3

It was a little annoying to have so many people thinking that *Fantastic Voyage* was made from my novel, when, in actual fact, the electronic media seemed utterly uninterested in anything I had written.

[1] See *The Solar System and Back* (Doubleday, 1970).

There had been the abortive sale of "Evidence" to Orson Welles twenty years before, but that had been less than nothing.

On August 11, 1967, came a more substantial nibble. I received a letter from John Mantley, the producer of the long-running and very successful television show "Gunsmoke." He was interested in my robot stories.

I no longer had to worry about such things personally. Doubleday controlled the subsidiary rights to all my robot stories, thanks to *I, Robot* and *The Rest of the Robots*, and I merely referred Mantley to them.

There followed a liberal education in the glacial speed with which Hollywood moved. It took a couple of years before a contract could be worked out and option money could be paid.

4

On August 14, I drove the family to Craigville Inn on Cape Cod. A writers' conference was being held there and I had been invited to give some talks and to enjoy a week on the Cape with my family. We accepted gladly.

To my surprise, I met Jack Rubinson there. It was he who had introduced me to the Futurians twenty-nine years before. He was Jack Robins now and had changed so little that I had no trouble recognizing him. With him was his wife, a talkative woman whom I had never met before and who wrote humorous confession stories. I don't think much of the genre and, from my conversation with Mrs. Robins, I couldn't believe she would turn out anything worthwhile.

I was wrong. She read one or two of her stories at the conference and they were really funny. I enjoyed them.

David celebrated his sixteenth birthday on August 20 at the inn, and the next day we went home.

5

The twenty-fifth World Science Fiction convention was being held in New York in 1967. It was the first time the convention had been held in that city since 1956 (the convention at which I had met Janet Jeppson for the first time and during which I had been tortured by a kidney stone).

Now, in 1967, it had been five years since I had had a troublesome kidney stone, and I was the proud owner of two Hugos and was virtually an elder statesman in the field.

On September 1 I took the family to New York, and that evening we had dinner with Gene Roddenberry and his wife. Since the children watched "Star Trek" with fascination (and so did I), they were fearfully impressed at my easy cameraderie with Gene.

Not everything about the convention was friendly, however. Harlan Ellison had written a "Man From U.N.C.L.E." segment in which a character was alleged by Judy Merril to be modeled on herself in a defamatory way. During the convention, Judy had Harlan served with a summons in preparation to suing him, and I spent some time going from one to the other, trying to get Harlan to apologize or Judy to reconsider.

It was a case of shuttle diplomacy years before Henry Kissinger made it famous. The only trouble was that my effort did not succeed. Neither would bend.

On the night of September 3, we and Henry Blugerman, too,[2] had dinner with the de Camps. It was quite a sedate affair, and as we left, I saw a bunch of my convention buddies (including Lester del Rey, Fred Pohl, and so on) seated at a long table and just getting ready to begin theirs.

For a moment I was inclined to regret my own family involvement and to wish I were with the group. It turned out just as well. Although our dinner had passed without incident, the group could not get service, and when the salads came, after long delay, they were the wrong ones. Lester del Rey, unable to get his salad changed, lost his temper and scaled it across the restaurant as though it were a Frisbee, and then all left.

The next night, the Hugo awards banquet was even more of a shambles in some ways. Harlan Ellison was master of ceremonies (rather to my chagrin, for I felt that I had a stranglehold on that post any time I was there), and he did not conduct it properly. He was very witty and funny, but he kept the stage interminably and made it a Harlan evening, which was not what it was supposed to be.

Taking their cue from him, those whom he finally allowed to speak, also went on forever. Sam Moskowitz got up and stolidly insisted on a ten-minute eulogization of an award-winning fan, ignoring the restlessness of the audience. Finally, when Lester del Rey arose to make his guest of honor speech, there was no time left and he could only say a few words.

---

2 Things had not worked well with Henry after all. The initial euphoria after his operation gave way to gloom when it turned out that the cancer had metastasized and was inoperable. He was undergoing X-ray treatment, but things looked dark.

The next day we went home, stopping at Windsor Place first to greet my mother on her seventy-second birthday.

6

On September 11, 1967, David entered high school and Robyn entered junior high.

The new freshman class started at the med school that day as well, under a new system whereby they didn't take separate subjects so much as a generalized hash. That meant that I didn't give my "traditional" first lecture of the biochemistry course at the beginning of the spring semester. I gave it at the very beginning of the year. It went over with great success.

That afternoon, the med school was giving a reception in honor of the new president, Christ-Janer. Ordinarily, I would not have attended, but I happened to be at the school, thanks to my morning lecture, and I had met Christ-Janer about six weeks before and had liked him. So why not?

All the students had been invited but, by and large, it was the eager and unsophisticated freshmen who attended. Since I was the only faculty member they had yet met, a number of them clustered about me and told me what a good lecture it was.

"Yes," I said, expansively (and let myself be overwhelmed with the desire to commit a "charming Asimovian immodesty"), "and you fellows think all the lectures will be that good. Well, it will take you about six weeks to wake up to the fact that mine will be the *only* good lecture you'll get, and by that time it will be too late for you to get your money back."

There was dutiful laughter at that and some more praise for my lecture.

Just then the dean passed and I called him over, nudged the young man who had been most lavish in his praises, and said, "Tell the dean what my lecture was like this morning."

The young man said, "It was great, Dean. Terrific!"

"And Dr. Asimov says," came the clear voice of a young woman from the rear, "that it's the only good lecture we'll get and that by the time we find that out it will be too late to get our money back."

There was a rather awed silence and I felt myself turning a distinct brick-red. I said, in a rather choked voice, "You shouldn't have said that, young woman."

"I didn't," she said artlessly. "You did."

The dean took me off the hook by saying, matter-of-factly, "I think Dr. Asimov is right," and passed on.

But then it was too late for the administration to do anything to me anyway, short of my committing some heinous crime.[3]

7

The very next day, my Asimovian immodesties hit me over the head again. Boston TV station WHDH sent a crew over to photograph me in my office for a sort of "the writing machine at work" program.

As it happened, on the door of my office I had a collection of funny cards I had picked up here and there, cards that read "Genius at work," or "Just treat me as you would any other genius," or "It's hard to be humble when you're as great as I am," and so on.

Since no one but the closest personal friends ever visited me in my attic, it was obvious that it was just a private joke. It wasn't till the interview was over that I realized the cameras were focusing on the cards one by one.

"Hey," I said, "don't photograph those."

"Just for laughs among ourselves," said the head interviewer, soothingly.

But when the program was shown some days later, those cards flashed on the screen one after the other throughout the introductory remarks.

8

On September 14, 1967, I actually began to put typewriter to paper on the first section of what I was scheduled to do for the Ginn science series—a year and a half after I had formally agreed to work on the project.

I began with a heavy heart. The Ginn & Company people continued to talk in terms of millions of dollars, but I grew to believe that less and less.

[3] A British professor once told me that anyone with tenure at a British university could be fired summarily for one of only two reasons. "These are," he said, "first, gross immorality on the office furniture—I think it's all right on the floor—and second, and worse" (here he paused impressively), "pinching the tea-things."

9

I met David Gerrold for the first time on September 17. He was only twenty-three years old, tall, skinny, boyish, beaky-nosed. He was entering science fiction by way of "Star Trek" and had done *The Trouble with Tribbles*, probably the most popular single show in the series. He was one of the new generation of TV-SF writers who knew not the magazines.

10

On October 17, I took in the completed manuscript of *The Dark Ages* to Houghton Mifflin, and two days later I drove to New York and took *Twentieth Century Discovery* to Janet Finney at Random House.

11

I continued to review books occasionally, a job I always detested but sometimes found it difficult to refuse—especially if it were the New York *Times* that asked me to do the reviewing.

On October 24, I reviewed a book called *The Way Things Work* for them. It was the translation of a German book and I was impressed by it.

As usual when I was given enough space to spread myself, I tried to make the review a more or less independent essay that might be interesting in itself as well as informative about the book. I think, on the whole, that this was the best review I ever turned out. It appeared on page 3 of the Sunday Book Review Section of the November 19, 1967, *Times*.

As it happened, the book did surprisingly well; better, in fact, than the publishers had expected. I found this out when, in an interview with a New York *Post* book columnist, the editor of the book said something to the effect that "after Asimov's review of the book in the *Times*, sales took off."

I'm always glad to help a deserving book, but I was just human enough to wish that a book reviewer as effective as myself could be found to write about *my* books. (Actually, when I first started my stint with *Hornbook*, I was handed a Paul French book to review. I hesitated for a moment—just a moment—and then disqualified myself.)

After that, I grew more reluctant than ever to review books. I did not want that particular position of power—or to find out that I really didn't have it, either.

But thereafter I began to receive sets of galleys, more and more frequently, with an editorial request for some comment that might be used in publicity. I refused these (or ignored them) as often as I could, but sometimes either the author or the editor was someone I could not refuse. Then, too, the book itself sometimes managed to get me spontaneously enthusiastic. It happens then that I may, eventually, break the record for the number of different books that carry approving statements by a particular author.

I cannot honestly say that my approval helps the books, but apparently the editors think so, because requests still come in every week.

It's a matter of perverse Asimovian immodesty on my part that my own books rarely have approving comments on them from other people. I won't have it, you see, though sometimes editors, less proud than I am, slip them in without consulting me.

12

John and Peg Campbell were in Cambridge, and I visited them on October 26. Peg's daughter, Jane, was also present, along with her husband and son.

John might be a grandfather now, but he never changed. I never saw him without finding the years drop away. I was a teen-ager again, listening to him lecture once more. With the years, I grew a little more amused, a little less awed, but only a little.

Among other subjects that day, we talked about Wayne Batteau and his research on the physiology of hearing. (It was Wayne's wife, Blanca, who shared birthdays with me, and both of them helped me celebrate my fortieth, seven years before.) The next day I discovered that even as we had been talking, Wayne had died of a heart attack in Hawaii. He was fifty-one years old.

I attended a memorial service for him on October 30, the first since that for Ben Benson, eight years before, and thought, rather woefully, that, provided I continued to survive, these occasions would become more and more common, until they would grow to dominate my life.

13

I usually enjoyed myself at meetings of the Boston Authors' Club, but November 10 was one occasion when I did not. I had gone with

Gertrude and some guests because it was the annual banquet and the club put its most elegant foot forward that day.

At the last minute I was asked to sit at the head table, and I deserted Gertrude and my guests to do so. That was bad. I don't generally succumb to self-importance in that particular way, but I do fall short of perfection now and then, and on this occasion I could not resist—or, at any rate, I did not.

Retribution struck at once, for it was an Asimovian immodesty that was in no way "charming." I was placed at the end of the head table where there wasn't really room for me, and the woman already at the end resented the crowding. At least she looked at me with disfavor and, for the most part thereafter, ignored me. She clearly didn't know who I was and as clearly didn't care.

I sat there, therefore, essentially alone, twiddling my fork, watching Gertrude and my guests enjoying themselves at their table, and feeling like an incredible ass. It was only my sense of justice (which kept telling me that I was getting exactly what I deserved) that kept me from feeling even worse.

Eventually, the woman at my left, feeling perhaps that she couldn't ignore me completely, turned to me and said, with very much the air of one throwing a bone to a dog, "And what do you do?"

"Write," I said, briefly.

She looked at me with disdain and said, "Since you're a member of the club I can guess that much. *What* do you write?"

I stubbornly refused to unbend. "Anything," I said. "You name it. I write it."

She wasn't going to play guessing games. She sniffed audibly and turned to her neighbor on the other side. After a few moments, I heard her say she was thinking of giving up smoking. She said, "You remember those boulders of cigarette smoke lying around the lung vacuoles in the movie *Fantastic Voyage*—"

I said quickly, "You named it. I wrote it."

She turned. "What?"

"You mentioned *Fantastic Voyage*. I wrote the book," I said, haughtily. (It was the only time I ever implied that the movie had been made from my book.)

"*You* wrote *Fantastic Voyage?*"

"That's right. I'm Isaac Asimov."

It stirred her up a bit, and that made two bits of childishness on my part in one evening.

14

On November 14, 1967, I was in Philadelphia, where I gave a talk to a branch of B'nai Brith. At 8:00 A.M. on the fifteenth, I was on the road, and by 1:30 P.M., I was back in Newton. It took me 5½ hours to negotiate that 300-mile trip.

David had to go to the eye doctor for a routine examination. The eye doctor was in Brookline, the adjacent town. We left at 3:30 P.M., and just as I pulled away from the garage, flakes of snow began to fall. It turned into freezing rain, and the pace of traffic slowed, while its density increased. I was within half a mile of the eye doctor when I decided there was no way in which I could make it, and I maneuvered the car into a homeward path.

I was too late!

The homeward rush hour was beginning, and no one was prepared for so early a sleetfall. Minor accidents spread like the bubonic plague; cars stalled; long lines of traffic stalled.

I did as everyone else was doing, which was to turn out into any street that seemed open—*any* street—hoping that some way might be found that would take me home.

I found myself in areas that were completely unfamiliar. I was inching down streets that might have been in Fargo, North Dakota, for any recognizable landmark I could see. At one time I slid helplessly down an incline while the car at the bottom tried frantically to get out of the way—and then I had to try frantically myself as the car behind me came slipping and sliding down upon me.

I managed. At no time did I make contact with any other car.

At no time, however, was it possible for me to stop anywhere and find a telephone on which to call home and announce we were alive. And the ice was becoming covered by wet snow, which made the going still harder.

Eventually I drove the car into a deserted filling station to get off the road, stepped out, had David do the same, locked the car, and began trying the houses in search of a private phone. It took several attempts to find someone who would answer a doorbell and allow strangers to come in. Finally, we found the apartment of a Mr. and Mrs. Francis Nolan.

They allowed us in, had us take off our wet shoes, and supplied us with slippers. I used their phone to call Gertrude and assure her we were well (she had already been calling the police and the hospitals). The Nolans then fed us soup, gave us the best seats in the living room, and insisted we relax and watch television.

When the traffic finally died down, their oldest son went out with us and, together with some friends who were at the Good Samaritan work of directing and helping cars, they pushed me out of the filling station, onto the road, and pointed me toward Washington Street.

It still wasn't easy driving, but the lines of cars were gone and I was home, quite exhausted, at 9:30 P.M. It might have taken me 5½ hours to do 300 miles earlier in the day, but in the evening it had taken me 6 hours to cover 21 miles.

Six days later I returned to the Nolans, and with me were some signed books and a quart bottle of the most expensive whiskey I could find (I have no way of judging whiskey but by the price) as a thank offering.

15

A year and a half earlier, Marion K. Sanders of *Harper's* had asked for an article on the origin of the universe. It appeared in the March 1967 *Harper's* as "Over the Edge of the Universe," and eventually I put it into one of my own collections under the title "The Birth and Death of the Universe."[4]

I had liked the article when I wrote it, and it was pleasant to have it in as prestigious a magazine as *Harper's*, but the most delightful spinoff came on November 21, 1967. On that day I learned that it had won for me the Westinghouse-AAAS prize for science writing, a prize that was to be delivered a month later at the annual meeting of the AAAS.

And meanwhile, having completed *The Dark Ages*, which dealt primarily with what would later become France, Germany, and Italy, I took up the history of Britain in the same period and called it *The Shaping of England*.

16

My Bible book was in press now and it was clear that my working title *It's Mentioned in the Bible* would not do.

On December 4, Larry phoned to ask if I would mind if it were called *An Intelligent Man's Guide to the Bible*. I reacted enthusiastically. I thought it was an excellent idea since I felt that it would

4 See *Is Anyone There?*

in that way borrow luster from *An Intelligent Man's Guide to Science* and, if the Bible book did well, to lend luster as well.

"However, Larry," I said, "I think we had better check with Basic Books and make sure they don't mind."

It turned out to be a good thing we did. I was sure Arthur Rosenthal wouldn't mind, but he did. In fact, he reacted with quite uncharacteristic anger and even threatened a lawsuit.

I was chagrined and said, "Never mind, Larry. I have a better title. Presumably, science is accessible only to the intelligent man, but the Bible is, or should be, accessible to everyone. Let's call it *Everyman's Guide to the Bible.*"

Larry agreed but then, some time later, he got back to me with the news that the sales staff had argued that Random House had a line of Everyman books and that Doubleday didn't want to give the impression that the book was published by Random House.

He said, "The salesmen want to have it *Asimov's Guide to the Bible.* They say *Asimov's Biographical Encyclopedia of Science and Technology* is doing very well, so we ought to keep that formula."

I said, weakly, "But I'm a scientist and therefore have a right to put my name on a collection of science biographies. Wouldn't it be presumptuous of me to put my name on a book about the Bible?"

But Larry said, "If you're presumptuous enough to write a book on the Bible, be presumptuous enough to put your name on it."

That was it. The book would be *Asimov's Guide to the Bible.* It was to be the third book to have my name in the title, and this one embarrassed me. If it had not been for Arthur Rosenthal's surprising intransigence, it wouldn't have happened. There are limits to my "charming Asimovian immodesties."

I eventually asked Arthur what his objection had been, since both books were, after all, by me. Arthur said it would have given rise to confusion as to publishers so that orders, being sent to the wrong publisher, would be lost. And since Doubleday was the larger publisher and the more closely associated with me, Basic Books would have been hurt the more badly.

17

I could not forget my dead book *Words from Greek History.* To be sure, I had converted it into *The Greeks,* but in the process I had lost my treatment of the words.

It occurred to me that I could try again and do one-page essays this time, as I had done in the cases of *Words in Science* and *Words on the Map*. Nor need I confine the words to those involving Greek history. I could use words that referred to any age and any area. I could then call it simply *Words from History*.

I began that book on December 17.

18

The AAAS meetings for 1967 were being held in New York, which was fortunate because I was required to show up in person for the Westinghouse Prize.

I got that prize on December 27, complete with a reception and a banquet that all the prize winners attended. On accepting the prize I said, dryly, that it was customary for all winners to suffer unaccustomed attacks of modesty and to ascribe the victory to chance acquaintances and various strangers. I hoped, therefore, that the audience wouldn't mind too much if I shyly admitted that I had worked hard for the prize and deserved much of the credit myself.

I didn't get much in the way of laughter. I think the audience was too puzzled by my outlandish attitude to laugh.

Henry Blugerman was the only family member to be present, and I was intensely pleased to have him there. I didn't know how many more times I would see him.

Janet Jeppson was at the convention, too, and I persuaded her to join myself, Carl Sagan, and Linda for dinner on December 30. It worked out very well and was the pleasantest part of the convention. The next morning I took the train for home.

19

The year 1967 saw eight books published:

79. *The Moon* (Follett)
80. *Environments Out There* (Abelard-Schuman)
81. *The Roman Empire* (Houghton Mifflin)
82. *Through a Glass, Clearly* (New English Library)
83. *Is Anyone There?* (Doubleday)
84. *To the Ends of the Universe* (Walker)
85. *Mars* (Follett)
86. *The Egyptians* (Houghton Mifflin)

20

I turned forty-eight on January 2, 1968. I was so old by now that I scarcely noted the change in age from one year to the next.

It was a bad winter in other ways. The sleetstorm on November 15 had been the harbinger for considerable nasty snow, and a wet snow-storm that had struck Boston while I had been in New York at the AAAS meeting caused the roof to ice up under the shingles. Water began to leak into the house.

Beginning with January 10, we had to keep every pot and pan in the house on various timbers in the eaves in order to catch the drops and keep them from getting into the house proper. To get into the eaves we had to enter from my rooms in the attic and progress care-fully, in stoop-shouldered fashion, to place the containers, then, when they were sufficiently full, to retrieve them (without spilling them), empty them, and replace them.

Robyn was a godsend at this time. Since she was the smallest in the family and the most agile, she could maneuver in the cramped space much more easily than could anyone else. Sure-footedly she kept up a running fight against the melting ice, and was cheerful enough about it to keep up everyone's spirits.[5]

It was Gertrude who made the key suggestion—which was to turn off the heat upstairs. Of course! I didn't mind low temperatures and I could always work in a sweater. Off went the heat, and the leaking slowed down to a trickle within a matter of an hour. Come spring we reshingled the roof.

All this inevitably slowed me down, but I did manage to finish *Photosynthesis* on January 13. I had worked on it, on and off, for eight months, and it had not been an easy book to write, but to this day I think it the best possible book on the subject that could have been written for popular consumption.

21

On January 18, 1968, I received my author's copies of the Walker & Company edition of *The Death Dealers*. Finally, after ten years, my ill-fated book had found a hard-cover home. I didn't count it as a new book, of course, even though I had persuaded Walker to give it *my* title

---

[5] Robyn was old enough now to earn money as a baby-sitter for other, younger children.

and call it A *Whiff of Death* in its new life. After all, except for the title and for a very few minor changes to keep the book from smelling too strongly of the 1950s, it was exactly what it had been.

This time it was no failure. Walker & Company eventually sold out at least two printings, arranged for a new paperback, and managed a number of foreign editions.

22

My book *Twentieth Century Discovery* met with a sudden reverse, on the other hand.

Janet Finney of Random House sent it back on February 5 with a request for changes, saying that she had marked the places she thought might be cut. Since the book was not unduly long, I wondered what places she could be referring to. I found out soon enough.

In every chapter, she had indicated the deletion of any paragraph that referred to work done before 1900.

This was impossible. She could only have made the request because she knew nothing about science. One cannot deal with any aspect of science by starting cold at some arbitrary date. There has to be some indication of the state of the art at the time, and this must involve some brief reference to events that came before.

I might have argued about this, but I didn't. My experience with Svirsky had forever sensitized me to any heavy-handed or unreasonable demands for cutting. I phoned Janet Finney and explained that the changes requested were so extensive that it was clear that the book was not publishable. I was therefore withdrawing it from consideration.

Miss Finney accepted that with clear relief—as though I had done the unexpected, but gentlemanly, thing.

23

On February 5, the same day on which the bad news from Random House had arrived, Gertrude and I went to see the stage show *Plaza Suite* with George C. Scott and Maureen Stapleton. We loved it and Gertrude wanted very much to meet Mr. Scott. In the intermission she suggested that I make my way back to the dressing room and ask to see him, using my name as a passport.

I refused with horror. "What good will my name do?"

"Maybe he's a science-fiction fan," said Gertrude.

But I shook my head. I refused to try to ride my name into the man's dressing room, and Gertrude was disappointed.

After the play we went into a restaurant just a few yards from the theater for a late-night snack, and as we were finishing the waitress said to us in tones of great excitement, "George C. Scott and Maureen Stapleton from the play next door are eating here."

I gave up. I know when the Fates are conspiring against me. I said to Gertrude, "Okay, let's go back there. I'll ask for an autograph, and if he knows me, I'll introduce you."

We walked to the rear of the restaurant where not only Scott and Stapleton were sitting, but about a dozen other people as well, all of them, presumably, involved with the play. As we approached, they looked at us rather stonily; they were clearly not overwhelmed with delight at having their privacy invaded.

I held out my *Playbill* uneasily and said, "Mr. Scott, I wonder if you and Miss Stapleton would care to let me have your autographs. My name is I-saac A-si-mov."

I pronounced my name with exaggerated care so that they would have no chance of hiding behind a misunderstanding. Scott and Stapleton, however, remained utterly unmoved and signed the *Playbill* in bored resignation. I knew that to introduce Gertrude would have all the effect of sound in a vacuum.

And then one of the young men arose from his seat at the table and cried out, "Gertie!"

Gertrude stared for a moment and cried out in her turn, "Natie!"

It was her Cousin Nathan, whom I had never met. They hugged each other, talked rapidly, asked after each other's immediate family. Nathan introduced her all around and Scott and Stapleton shook hands with her and smiled graciously, while I stood in the background shifting from foot to foot.

It didn't last long, but the chance of being husband to a celebrity gave me a useful lesson in humility.

24

On February 15 I went to New York and dropped in on Mac Talley who had, by now, established a new firm, Weybright and Talley, with his father-in-law. Naturally, he wanted a book from me and was full of ideas, but I already had a book for him. I asked him to look over *Twentieth Century Discovery*.

I then went on to Doubleday, where Larry Ashmead astonished me.

He told me that they were experimenting with different designs for the book jacket of *Asimov's Guide to the Bible,* and in one case they used a selection from the book in an oval on the back.

With clear embarrassment, Larry said, "The only thing, Isaac, is that I don't like the quotation. I think it is poorly written."

I was as embarrassed as he. Larry had *never* disliked anything I had written. He had *always* praised everything I had done, even when I myself was uncertain as to its merits. For something of mine to be so bad as to force an unkind word out of him must mean that it was bad beyond belief.

"May I see it, Larry?" I said.

He took me to the Art Department and showed me the cover. I read through the passage and said, with infinite relief, "This isn't me, Larry."

"It's not from the book?" said Larry, stunned.

"No, this must be some material that was just lying around, and they included it just to get a general idea of how the cover would look."

We asked, and that was indeed what had happened.

Larry flushed and tried to apologize for having thought me capable of such bad writing.

But I was triumphant and said so. "Listen, Larry," I said, "I didn't trust your opinion of me. I thought that even if I wrote something bad you would say it was good. But now you found something bad you thought was mine and you told me so. From now on if you say something of mine is good, I will believe you."

25

Henry was in the hospital again. I visited him on Friday, February 16. His memory seemed to be fuzzy, but except for that he seemed fairly well. I told him I'd be going home on Sunday and that Gertrude would be in on Monday to see him.

I did go home on Sunday, but, alas, there was no Monday for Henry. Even as Gertrude was packing for the trip, Henry died of a stroke at 8:45 P.M. on February 18, 1968, about a month before his seventy-third birthday.

It was Gertrude who answered the phone call from John, and I knew from her gasp what had happened. Afterward she sat with her head against the wall, crying softly, and I held her hand and wondered, in vain, how I could possibly console her.

What bothered me most was that it was I, not she, who had seen Henry shortly before he died.

It was the first death in our immediate families.

Gertrude had, of course, planned to go by bus, but that would no longer do. In the morning, I drove her to the airport and she and David took the shuttle plane to New York (the first plane trip for either, though they, and Robyn too, had taken a little ride in a helicopter once).

I did not let Robyn go. It was her thirteenth birthday and I wanted her to celebrate it outside the shadow of death.

I took her out for a fancy dinner and did my best to make the evening pleasant for her. The next day, the twentieth, I drove her to New York and we attended the funeral on the twenty-first.

A number of the Blugerman family had gathered. Gertrude's Aunt Sophie (Henry's sister) came in from Detroit, and her Cousin Albert from Toronto. My mother and father also arrived, along with Stanley and Ruth.

That afternoon, I drove back to Newton with both children, leaving Gertrude behind with her mother.

26

In January, I had received a request for a science-fiction story from *Boys' Life*. They sent me the proof of an illustration and asked me to write the story around that. Poul Anderson was being asked to do a story from the same illustration.

The job wasn't easy since the illustration was not very representational. It showed a head and, above it, circles containing designs of one kind or another—very little more than doodles. I remembered my embarrassing failure at that sort of thing four years before in connection with "Eyes Do More Than See," but took the chance, anyway.

I wrote a two-thousand-word story that I called "The Proper Study,"[6] and on February 23, 1968, I received word of acceptance. Poul's story was also accepted, and both appeared in the September 1968 *Boys' Life*.

On Sunday, February 25, I finished *Words from History* and, on the same day, Gertrude returned from New York by air. She was bearing up well and so, apparently, was Mary.

27

I tried not to commit myself to speaking engagements in the winter months, unless they were so close to home that the weather made little difference or it were understood that in case of snow I could not

[6] See *Buy Jupiter and Other Stories*.

come. What was dreadful in that case was when it threatened snow, but did not actually do so.

That was the case on February 29, 1968, when I was scheduled to give a talk to Girl Scout leaders in a moderately distant suburb. Snow was predicted and the clouds were lowering, but by 4:20 P.M., at which time I could no longer delay my departure, it had not actually begun. I had no choice but to drive in.

I wasn't really sorry, for it was a pleasant occasion and the Girl Scout leaders proved a very indulgent audience even when, out of puckishness, I predicted the increasing necessity of sex education and the coming time when Boy Scouts and Girl Scouts would form a single organization, with one of the jobs of the leaders being that of regulating and channeling sexual experimentation. (Perhaps they didn't take me seriously.)

From the podium, I commanded a view of the windows and, about halfway through the talk, I could clearly see the snowflakes beginning to drift down, and memories of November 15 smote me sickeningly in the pit of my stomach.

My impulse was to wind things up quickly and run for my car to make it home before it got too bad.

Professionalism, however, reigned supreme, and my strong urge toward a premature ending kept me going longer than normal as a way of refusing to give in. I spoke for an hour and twenty minutes—then had dinner with the group.

Virtue triumphed! Though I had to drive through the dark and the snow, I got home safely.

27

Guide to Shakespeare

1

With *Words in History* done, I needed another project, and one was ready to hand. It was impossible for me to do a guide to the Bible without thinking of what to do next in the same line. Well, what is the only literary production in the English language that can compare with the Bible? Correct!

For several months I had been playing with the thought of doing a guide to Shakespeare along the lines of my guide to the Bible. I would devote a chapter to each play, telling the plot and quoting those passages that I wished to annotate.

The trouble was that I didn't quite have the nerve to suggest it to Larry. The Bible book had not, after all, been his idea, but had been something I had tried, unsuccessfully, to foist on Tom Sloane. Larry had taken it over because of his prejudice in my favor. That didn't mean he would want to do another book of the same kind, and I hesitated to spoil our perfect relationship by putting him under the necessity of refusing an idea of mine.

Yet it boiled up within me and, on March 1, 1968, I decided on a compromise. I would do one of the plays and bring it in as a sample. Larry could then have a better idea of what I intended than from my verbal description alone.

I chose Richard II to begin with and began by quoting the opening line, "Old John of Gaunt, time-honored Duke of Lancaster." Why "Gaunt"? For that matter, why "old"? The extreme age of John of Gaunt is stressed in the play, and the character playing him is always made up to look 110 and totters around in what seems the last stages of physical decay—but the real John of Gaunt died at the age of 59.

It didn't take me long to find out that Shakespeare was going to be even more fun than the Bible.

2

Robyn came to me on March 6 with a little fantasy she had written. I read it with amazement. It was very good considering that she was only thirteen. I typed it up for her, without making any changes except to straighten out the spelling, punctuation, and grammar, and it read even better.

Even allowing for the prejudice of a doting father, I was convinced that I could not have done as well at thirteen. I sent it in to Ed Ferman, not thinking of it as a possible sale but only hoping that Robyn would be excited at getting a letter from an editor (and, of course, I asked him to write directly to her).

Ed sent it back to Robyn in the course of time with a kind and encouraging letter, and he also wrote to me to say that if it had been available for the special Isaac Asimov issue he would indeed have run it as an added Asimovian item.

After that I was in a quandary. I wanted very badly to encourage Robyn, because I honestly thought she had the potential of being a good writer. Yet how was I to encourage her without being counterproductive?

I had some sober talks with her about the rewards and difficulties of a writer's life. I discussed the special case of someone who was the child of a successful writer. On the one hand, doors would open that otherwise would not. On the other hand, there would be something to live up to that would represent a distorting pressure.

Robyn, however, made it quite plain that her opinion of the writer's life was based on mine, and that she thought it was a disease that, once it took hold, would drive everything else out.

I assured her earnestly that not all writers were like me; that it was possible to write and to live also. I said I wouldn't press her or hound her, but if she should feel the urge to write, to do so, and I would help her all I could.

She promised, but I can only suppose she never felt the urge. At least, she never came to me with another story. I have never ceased to regret this, and to wonder how I might have arranged things better.

3

The year 1968 was a presidential election year and I was heart and soul with Eugene McCarthy in his effort to replace President Johnson as Democratic candidate for that year. It didn't seem possible to replace a sitting President, but I felt it was important to make a noise, if only to force Johnson, should he run and be re-elected, to bring the Vietnam War to an end. To that end, I contributed money to the McCarthy campaign and joined rallies on his behalf.

In February, the North Vietnamese and Viet Cong launched the so-called Tet Offensive. Though it was beaten off, it startled and disheartened all Americans with its show of enemy vigor. It was clear that we had been lied to by the Administration and that, short of a nuclear bombardment, we would not win the war.

On March 11, McCarthy won a surprisingly large percentage of the vote in the New Hampshire primary. I was delighted—and astonished. It hadn't seemed to me possible that he would do so well.

4

On March 14, I had lunch with Larry in New York and gave him the manuscript of *Twentieth Century Discovery*, which Mac Talley had bounced earlier in the month.

Naturally, I told Larry that Random House first, and then Weybright and Talley, had rejected it, and that this might be because of its intrinsic deficiencies. Larry simply smiled and said he would read it and judge for himself. Of course, he took it.[1]

That same evening I taped a segment on "The Johnny Carson Show" in New York. I was on with Gore Vidal, who fascinated me. He seemed totally composed and self-assured, and spoke with the consummate ease of an actor.

Johnny Carson, himself, however, I thought less of. He ignored me completely when he arrived before the show. Then, on greeting me on the air, he pronounced my first name "I-ZAK," with equal emphasis on both syllables, instead of "I-zik," with the first syllable accented. A minor sin, surely, but I was on network television and I think the least a host can do for his guest is to ascertain the correct pronunciation of his name.

My impulse on being addressed, "How are you, I-ZAK?," was to answer, "Fine, and how are you, JOE-NEE?" I lacked the nerve, however, and have regretted that ever since.

5

Some years earlier, Damon Knight had begun an organization termed the Science Fiction Writers of America, and usually abbreviated as SFWA. I joined as a matter of course.

In 1965, SFWA began the custom of an annual award for stories in four classifications: novel, novella, novelette, and short story. The award was a transparent plastic parallelopiped with, inside, a rock and a

---

[1] It did quite well, though, both in trade sales and subsidiary sales, and Doubleday made a nice profit on it, so that Larry's judgment was justified.

swirl of grains designed to look like a spiral galaxy (or, in more old-fashioned nomenclature, a spiral nebula). The award was called the Nebula.

On the evening of Saturday, March 16, 1968, I attended the Nebula awards banquet in New York and enjoyed it very much. It didn't matter that I had nothing in nomination. As an elder statesman, I was treated with reverence even by my fellow writers (there were no fans at the SFWA functions). I didn't at all mind being treated with reverence, and my only regret was that I had to leave by midnight, since I was planning to drive back to Newton the next day.

6

On March 21, 1968, I lectured in Kresge Hall at MIT under the same sponsorship for whom, over a decade in the past, I had talked for one hundred dollars. This time I charged them six hundred dollars. It was still less than half the fourteen hundred dollars that Wernher von Braun had charged on the previous occasion, but I was making progress.

Nor did I allow my conscience to hurt me over the fact that the sponsors dined me well. Not only did I go to Locke-Ober's cheerfully with them, but also I brought David and Robyn with me. I knew they were still getting a bargain.

7

On March 23, I completed my sample treatment of *Richard II* and mailed it in to Doubleday. I was crowding Larry a bit, considering how recently I had put *Twentieth Century Discovery* in his hands.

It was clear I was suffering over Larry's penchant for accepting everything of mine he could find and fearing he would get in trouble over it. Larry therefore assured me he could not actually accept anything. Everything went before an editorial board, so that responsibility was spread broadly.

It made me feel much better.

8

We attended the showing of an old Clifford Odets play at Brandeis on March 31. It was set in Depression times and dealt with true love shattered by joblessness. Afterward, we were settling down for a discussion when someone rushed in with the news that in a television address, President Johnson had announced he would de-escalate the war and that he would not run for re-election.

The Tet offensive and the Eugene McCarthy campaign had done their work.

There was a loud roar of triumph from the audience (which was very largely of the liberal persuasion), and not the least of the shouters was I. I felt Johnson had brought his own political destruction on his own head by his dishonest handling of the Vietnam crisis. That we were about to change King Log for King Stork, I wasn't smart enough to foresee.

9

On April 6, 1968, Carl Sagan and Linda were married, and Gertrude and I attended the wedding. I was a little more involved than I had expected to be. Carl and Linda were married by a rabbi (a little, I think, to Carl's irritation, as it had been to mine under similar circumstances twenty-five years before), and the rabbi needed a formal witnessing of the marriage certificate. What's more, he needed someone who knew his father's Hebrew name, and not some Americanized version thereof.

It turned out that I knew my father's Hebrew name, so there I was witnessing the document as Isaac ben Judah, son of Judah ben Aaron.

In his little sermon, the rabbi spoke of the beginning of the universe, but put a religious cast upon it. Carl told me afterward that he had been hoping to get some mention of the big bang, and was disappointed that he had not.

At the reception afterward, I was happy indeed, for the *hors d'oeuvres* and cake were excellent. What I remember best, however, did not make me happy. I met Carl's parents, and his mother said to me, calmly, "And how are your grandchildren, Dr. Asimov?"

What did she *mean*, my grandchildren? I knew perfectly well that I was old enough to have grandchildren. At forty-eight, I could easily have had a twenty-five-year-old daughter who might just as easily have had a five-year-old child. Just the same, I *didn't* have any grandchildren, and she might just as easily have sneaked up on it by first asking if I had children, then how old they were, and *then*, if it seemed likely, whether I had grandchildren.

I said, freezingly, "I am *not* a grandfather."

Mrs. Sagan said, "There's nothing wrong with being a grandfather."

"Undoubtedly. I just happen not to be one."

"Mr. Sagan and I have never been so happy as since we've had grandchildren."

"Look, be delirious with happiness for all I care, but I am not a grandfather."

Despairing of the effects of pure logic, I was looking about for something hard and heavy to reinforce the point I was making, but Gertrude pulled me away.

10

Esquire asked me for a science-fiction story (I was quite accustomed, by now, to getting requests from miscellaneous places), and on April 16 I wrote a four-thousand-word story called "The Holmes-Ginsbook Device."[2]

I wrote it as a satire on *The Double Helix*, which James Watson had published not long before, and which, despite its difficult scientific subject (the working out of the structure of DNA), turned out to be a best seller. The reviews, which stressed and greatly exaggerated the notion that it spoke of scientific connivery and sexual adventure, undoubtedly contributed. If so, the readers must have been heavily disappointed.

In any case, in "The Holmes-Ginsbook Device" I stressed the connivery and sex in an indirect fashion and thought I had achieved something screamingly funny. I was dreadfully disappointed, therefore, when *Esquire* rejected it.

There was no use sending it to *Analog*, for I couldn't believe for a moment that Campbell would consider using anything that treated sex as lightheartedly as "The Holmes-Ginsbook Device" did. (It was the first ribald story I had written since "I'm in Marsport Without Hilda," eleven years before.)

I sent it therefore to *Galaxy*, where Fred Pohl finally wrote to tell me that I had overdone the humor and suggested I cut it in half. He said he hoped I wouldn't take the Harlan Ellison attitude that no word of my precious prose must be touched.

I replied that I wasn't in the least like Harlan in this respect. But since the story was intended to be a satire of a specific book, I did not want the point eviscerated by cutting. However, I said, I recognized the value of Fred's comments and agreed that the story, as it stood, was not publishable in *Galaxy*, so why didn't he send it back, with no hard feelings on either side.

I thought no one could possibly be more agreeable and sweet than

[2] See *Opus 100* (Houghton Mifflin, 1969).

I was, but Fred Pohl wrote that I *did* sound like Harlan and that he would take the story as it was.

It finally appeared in the December 1968 *If*, and was another of the stories in which the public did not agree with my own jubilant estimate. As in the case of "Strikebreaker" I had thought it would be hailed with enthusiasm. It wasn't. It went unmentioned and unnoticed.

11

On April 18, I was staying at Howard Johnson's at Eighth Avenue and Forty-eighth Street, on the occasion of one of my New York visits. I was walking briskly toward the hotel when I was attracted by the movie stills in front of a pornographic movie house. Hard-core pornography was flaunting itself openly (a far cry from the days, thirty years before, when LaGuardia had closed down the comparatively innocent burlesque houses), but I was not used to it. In fact, they embarrassed me.

On this occasion, it suddenly occurred to me that I was alone, that I was adult, that it was legal to show these films and see them, and that there could be no reasonable objection to my looking at the stills. So I did, and very carefully, too, but I must admit I got very little out of them.[3]

My long study of the stills must have given someone wrong ideas as to my intentions and needs, however, for as I turned away a young girl of, I should judge, no more than nineteen, and quite pretty, rushed toward me, saying, "Hello-o-o-o. How are you?"

My first thought was that it was someone I had met at one of the numerous conventions I attend. The pattern is plain and I had been subjected to it before. I meet a young girl, whom I hug and kiss and make eyes at, and she naturally expects me to remember her forever (even though, from my own point of view, it is merely suave behavior in public). Naturally, I would wound such a young woman's feelings deeply if I admitted I didn't know her from Jezebel, and I didn't want to do that.

So I grinned and said, "I'm fine. Well, well, what are you doing here?" I felt that as the conversation progressed, I would figure out where I had met her and get a dim idea as to who she was.

She seized my hand and said, "Come, I will show you a nice thing," and tugged at me.

---

[3] I did not go in to see the film, of course, and had no desire to. To this day I have not seen a pornographic film. I prefer my pornography in three dimensions and with myself and a woman as the only actors and spectators. That's just a personal predilection, of course. Others can do as they please.

I followed in confusion and it was not until she led me into a hall-way and placed my hand on her abdomen that I realized that, at the age of forty-eight, I was being accosted by a prostitute for the first time in my life. (I'm only brilliant; I never said I had good sense.)

Looking back on it, I realize I might have said haughtily, "Unhand me, woman, I do not wish paid caresses."

Or I might have said, "My dear young woman, let us not stay here in this filthy doorway where, at any moment, I will be mugged. I have an expensive room not half a block away with two clean double beds in it. There I will scrub you down with plenty of soap and warm water and then we shall see what is best to do."

In actual fact, I did neither. Sudden illumination broke in on me and I gibbered. Literally! I just went "Buh-buh-buh-buh-buh" and started trying to pull away.

I must have looked so terrified that the girl's gentle heart smote her and she didn't even try to collect anything for the feel of her abdo-men, but let me go. I dashed out, made it to Howard Johnson's at a dead run, and threw myself on one of the beds, panting.

It had been a very frightening experience.

Why was I frightened? How should I know? I'm only reporting the facts.

12

Over the weekend, the New York regional convention, the Luna-con, was being held, and I seized the opportunity to attend.

It was on this occasion that I met Judy-Lynn Benjamin, who worked for *Galaxy* and *If* under Fred Pohl. She's a very short girl and a little heavy, and has the most enormous brain of any woman I've known. Quick, articulate, quite merciless in her opinions, she soon gave me the irresistible impression that she was the real heart and muscle of *Galaxy*.

At least, on a later occasion, I said just that jokingly from the plat-form when Fred Pohl was in the audience, and he threw something at me. He didn't look as though *he* were joking, from which I deduced that my attempt at fun had struck a nerve.

13

Tony Boucher died on April 29, 1968, of cancer. He was fifty-seven years old. He died in California, so there was no question of my attend-ing the memorial service or the funeral.

I was distressed, for on those occasions when we had met, notably at the Cleveland convention, thirteen years before, which he had toastmastered, we had gotten along like bosom buddies, and because, thanks to our wide separation and my own dislike for travel, I had only met him three or four times altogether.

I had, as always, my own method for insulating myself against the miseries of life. I worked along, more or less madly, on various sections for the Ginn science series, and when I felt my spirit fraying over that particular unloved task, I would move on to various sections of the Shakespeare book and take a soothing vacation.

14

On May 4, Gertrude and I, along with another couple, went to Brandeis to see a magnificent collection of old Bibles. Having spent so much time on *Asimov's Guide to the Bible,* I felt I had to see it.

At one point we were looking at a Jewish Bible published in Spain before the expulsion of the Jews. It was open to the seventh chapter of Isaiah, and was in Spanish, except for one word that was in Hebrew and stood out like a sore thumb amid the rest.

My friend said to me, "Why do they have one word in Hebrew?"

Having spent some time on that very point in my Bible book, I said, "That's the verse that, in the King James, goes, 'Behold a virgin shall conceive, and bear a son.' The only trouble is that the Hebrew word is *almah,* which does not mean 'virgin' but 'young woman.' If the Jewish publishers were to translate the word correctly they would seem to be denying the divinity of Jesus and they would be in serious trouble with the Inquisition. Rather than do that, or translate it incorrectly, they leave that word in Hebrew."

I said all this in my usual speaking voice and in very much the manner in which I would have delivered a lecture at school. While I was talking (at somewhat greater length than I report it here), the nearest security guard approached and listened curiously.

I didn't notice that, but my friend did, and (like most of my friends) he overestimated the importance of my name. He therefore said to the guard with reference to me as I passed on to the next exhibit, "Do you know who he is?"

And the guard said, "God?"

My friend needn't have laughed *that* hard.

15

My father had truly retired some years before and had spent his time rather dully at home. Without work to do, without close friends or ties to the community, he returned to religion; not out of conviction, but because it was something he knew, something to do, some way of meeting other people with whom he had something in common.

He found an Orthodox synagogue that he could reach (he knew nothing about any other variety of Judaism and would have scorned them anyway, if he did) and spent much of his time there. He couldn't help but turn back to the dietary laws and to various other tedious points of ritual, which made life hard for my mother.

On those rare occasions when I saw him in these last few years, I found it difficult to keep from berating him for this. It had been his free-thinking that had made it possible for me to live without a religious prison, and I hated to see him move back into the cage again. But I knew his motivation, and even the synagogue was better than an utterly empty life.

It was getting more difficult for my parents, though, to endure the New York winters and the problems of running the apartment house. For a number of years before Henry's death, he and Mary had spent each winter in Florida, and that seemed attractive to my parents—but why just the winter? Why not sell all the apartment houses and take what money they realized and spend it on retirement in Florida? Surely their money would last the few remaining years of their lives.[4]

In 1968, with the time approaching when they would be leaving for Florida, my parents wanted one last gathering. They didn't know the exact date of their marriage any more than they knew the exact date of my birth, but 1968 was the Golden Wedding year, so they just picked a convenient day.

We celebrated it at Stanley's house on Long Island on May 19, 1968. We were all there, the entire family: Stanley and Ruth, Marcia and Nick, Gertrude and I, and all seven grandchildren, with my mother and my father presiding in full parental glory.

And glory it was. They had come to the United States, some forty-five years before, without money or education, and had managed by

---

[4] When they explained this to me, I pointed out that they needn't worry about their money lasting. If it did not, I would take over their expenses myself. And, of course, my father instantly stiffened and said, as I had heard him say countless times when I was an adolescent, "God forbid I should ever have to come to my children for money." And he never had to.

nothing more than hard work and dogged determination to raise three children, see all three married and with children in their turn, see their two sons completely educated and each in a position full of honor and prestige.

We sat around the table at a midday meal, and Stanley and I took turns in telling funny reminiscent stories about our parents. I remember I read selections from my *F & SF* essays that happened to mention my father, notably the one that was the prelude to my ninety-third *F & SF* essay, "Balancing the Books,"[5] which had appeared in the July 1966 issue of the magazine.

No shadow of unhappiness fell on that day, and when we pulled away to drive home to Newton, I waved joyfully at the two old folks and tried not to wonder if I would ever see them again.

16

On May 31, 1968, Gertrude and I drove down to Martha's Vineyard. Things were completely different from the way they had been on our first disastrous try, three years before. In this case, we had new friends, Bert and Jean Rudnick, who had a summer house on the island and who had arranged to have us rent a cottage for the weekend. They came with us, moreover, and were ready to drive us around and take care of us.

The cottage was comfortable, even luxurious, and under the Rudnicks' guidance, everything went well. We even discovered that Harry Schwartz (whom I had last seen in Atlantic City three years before) was on the island, so we had another friend.

We were home on June 2, with the memory of the early fiasco wiped out.[6]

17

In the larger world outside, disaster struck on June 5, when Robert Kennedy was assassinated by a Palestinian named Sirhan Sirhan. Suddenly, events about-faced.

Although I liked Eugene McCarthy and had voted for him in the

---

[5] See *Science, Numbers, and I*.
[6] While we were waiting to go on the ferry for the return ride, Harry Schwartz and I whiled away the time talking. We had nearly made it onto a ferry when the guards signaled it was full and we would have to wait for the next one. Then the word went out that there was room for one more car, but only a compact, and a Volkswagen pulled out from behind us and got on. Harry said, "Don't worry. God will get him for that."

New York Democratic primary on April 30, 1968, I had no illusions that he could be nominated. I did think, however, that Bob Kennedy was sure of the nomination and of the subsequent victory, and that suited me.

Once he was gone, I could see no one on the horizon who could make a successful run. That meant we had to face the possibility of a Republican President, and from nowhere had come that dreadful man whose political death and burial seemed to have taken place six years before. It seemed that Nixon would be the Republican nominee again, and with Robert Kennedy gone, he might be elected.

But life must continue. My nephew Danny was graduated from MIT on June 6, and I finished *The Shaping of England* on the eighth. And David was taking driving lessons.

18

Another network talk show turned up on June 14. On that day I taped a show with Dick Cavett. Debbie Reynolds sat next to me, and we even danced a bit after the taping—the only time I've ever had a Hollywood star in my arms.

The show itself was not aired till some weeks later, and at that time there was a special interruption because President Johnson was signing some bill with tedious formality. It wiped out half my stint and all of Debbie Reynolds'.

19

On June 28 we took Robyn to Cape Cod for another eight-week stay at a summer camp, not the same one as the year before. It was much easier for me this time, and Robyn, with the experience of the previous year behind her, was excited and pleased to be going.

As for David, he was doing a short stint at Houghton Mifflin as a mail-delivery boy. It wasn't much of a job, but it gave him his first practice in earning wages—at just the age at which I had had my own first practice in this direction at the Columbia Combining Corporation.

What made Robyn's leaving a little more bearable was that Larry Ashmead called that day to say that Doubleday had finally decided to issue a contract for what was to be called *Asimov's Guide to Shakespeare*. It's just as well they did, for I had been working hard on it ever since I had handed in my *Richard II* sample—not because I was so certain that Doubleday would agree to it, as that I simply couldn't help it.

Of all the books I have ever worked on, I think *Asimov's Guide to Shakespeare* gave me the most pleasure, day in, day out. For months and months I lived and thought Shakespeare, and I don't see how there can be any greater pleasure in the world—any pleasure, that is, that one can indulge in for as much as ten hours without pause, day after day indefinitely.

It had occurred to me two months earlier that although I had no fewer than nine books on my list that contained collections of stories that had appeared originally in the magazines, from *I, Robot* to *Asimov's Mysteries*, my most famous short story, "Nightfall," now twenty-seven years old, did not appear in any one of them. It had appeared in eight anthologies that I was aware of, and had been translated into German and Italian, but I had never made use of it myself.

I had therefore suggested to Larry that I put together a collection of stories that I had not previously collected and call it *Nightfall and Other Stories*. On the same day that Larry told me of the contract for *Asimov's Guide to Shakespeare*, he told me that one for *Nightfall and Other Stories* would also be put through.

It did not take me long to put the new collection into shape, and on July 10 I took it to Doubleday.

20

On July 19, 1968, Groff Conklin died at the age of sixty-four. It was he who had been the first to anthologize a story of mine in *The Best of Science Fiction*, twenty-three years before. I had collaborated with him on the anthology *Fifty Short Science-fiction Tales*, which had been published five years before. On the all-too-few occasions on which we had met, we had found ourselves compatible in all areas from science fiction to politics—with the one exception that he was a chain smoker.

21

Each year, my connection with the Brandeis summer program was growing stronger. From an interested spectator, I came to give lectures of my own. In the summer of 1968, I agreed to give a "course," five lectures on five successive mornings, beginning with July 29.

I enjoyed it. I liked the temporary sensation of being faculty; I liked the elaborate cocktail parties (with *hors d'oeuvres*) and dinners. I even liked the lectures, in which I simply gave the five sections of my book *Twentieth Century Discovery*.

During the second week of the summer program I gave one more lecture, in the evening, on August 4. On that evening Roy Machlowitz of Navy Yard days dropped around. I hadn't seen him for some twenty years.

Even while the summer program was on, I began a new book. I had carried the history of Rome past the barbarian occupation of the western provinces in *The Dark Ages* and *The Shaping of England*. Now I wanted to carry on through that same period in the eastern provinces in which the imperial tradition continued unbroken.

In other words, I planned to write a history of the Byzantine Empire, and, on August 3, I started a book I called *Constantinople*.

22

On August 9, I received a royalty check from Doubleday that was nearly twenty thousand dollars. My Doubleday royalties were going up steadily, and although my 1961 check from Basic Books remained the record, I began to suspect for the first time that it would not stay a record indefinitely.

23

On August 16, I taped a show with Walter Cronkite, who was narrating a program on the future, one called "The Twenty-first Century." I was rather excited about this, for I admired Cronkite extravagantly.

I sat down in a chair across a low, round table from him, and while the technicians fiddled with the light, I wondered whether I could say, "My father will be very thrilled, Mr. Cronkite, when he finds out you've interviewed me."

It seemed so childish a remark that I didn't dare make it. I was afraid Cronkite would call off the whole thing in disgust.

My hesitation gave him the chance to speak first. He said, "Well, Dr. Asimov, my father will be very thrilled when he finds out I've interviewed you."

24

I brought Robyn home from camp on August 19, and how delighted I was, though her separation from me was not as traumatic the second time.[7]

---

[7] In fact, looking back on it now, I don't remember the second summer in camp at all. Were it not for my diary record, I would have been willing to swear under oath that she had only been at summer camp once. It shows the importance of a diary to keep your life from slipping away into the mists of forgetfulness.

The next day was David's seventeenth birthday, and on it he took his driver's test and passed. His driver's license was surely a sufficient birthday present for him, but we celebrated in addition with a big dinner at a Chinese restaurant.

David was having trouble at the high school, incidentally, and it was clear to us that he would need smaller classes and more individual attention. It meant private school, and we began investigating some. Finding one that was suitable did not promise to be either quick or easy.

25

On August 28, I drove the family to the airport. Gertrude and both children took the shuttle to New York, it being Robyn's first flight. I stayed at home and worked on the last few plays for the first draft of *Asimov's Guide to Shakespeare*, and on the interminable sections I had to do for the Ginn science series.

Meanwhile, the Democrats held a nominating convention in Chicago, one that was marked by rioting and by police violence. They nominated Vice President Humphrey to run for President and Senator Muskie for Vice President against the Republican nominees, Richard Nixon and Spiro Agnew.

I had long admired Humphrey as an outspoken liberal, but as Vice President he had loyally supported Johnson in every stage of his utterly wrongheaded approach to the Vietnam War. Humphrey had, moreover, failed to denounce the police actions on the streets of Chicago. With reference to the competing candidates I therefore said, gloomily, in my diary for August 29, "A plague on both their houses."

I couldn't keep that up, though. There was no way I could ever bring myself to vote for the unspeakable Nixon, or even to abstain and cost him an opposition vote. I knew that I would have to vote for Humphrey.

26

My parents were now down in Florida. It had been their intention to go by train because, as my mother told me on the telephone, "Pappa says you don't go on planes."

I spoke to my father rather firmly and told him that my neuroses were not something to be imitated. They went by plane, therefore, making their first trip of this sort.

On September 5, 1968, my mother turned seventy-three, and I

called them in Miami Beach, where they were now living, presumably permanently. We exchanged letters now and then, and I made it a practice to call them once a week.

Stanley and Ruth went to visit them in Florida about this time, but I knew that I would never go, and that unless they came back to the New York area, at least on a visit, I would not be seeing them anymore. It was a queer feeling.

27

The med school was engaged in a huge building program that had begun while I was still an active member of the faculty. Now, nine years after I had ceased being active, Building A, which had housed the Biochemistry Department for decades, was losing its function. It had been twenty years earlier that I had first walked into the building and met Burnham Walker, and now the department was shifting to one of the new buildings.

On September 9, I gave my usual first lecture of the year and did so in one of the new buildings for the first time.

28

Al Capp suddenly re-entered my life very briefly. Over the years we had seen each other only very occasionally. In 1964, I had seen him once or twice during the Johnson-Goldwater campaign when he, like I, had been ardently anti-Goldwater.

A change had come over him, though. I don't know what it was or how it happened. I met him at the Whipples' a couple of years after the Goldwater campaign and it was as though someone new were inhabiting the body.

It was not just that he had become disillusioned in his liberalism; he had joined the enemy camp with enthusiasm. In fact, we all spent the whole evening that time at the Whipples' arguing the matter of civil rights for blacks, and Al took up what seemed to me to be a distressingly anti-black stand. I argued with him vehemently on that occasion.

I became very sensitive thereafter to his strip "Li'l Abner," which, it seemed to me, now had sequence after sequence that made fun of student viewpoints, of antiwar sentiment, and of the campaign for civil rights. None of this is against the law, of course, or even necessarily immoral, but Al Capp's humor seemed to me to be rather vicious, and I writhed.

Finally, when it seemed to me that his current sequence was making unfair fun of a fictional minority group that could only be equated with the blacks, I dashed off a one-sentence letter to the Boston *Globe*, in which the strip appeared. It went, "Am I the only one who's grown tired of Al Capp's anti-black propaganda in his comic strip, 'Li'l Abner'?"

On September 9, 1968, the *Globe* ran the letter. I was pleased, but didn't give the matter much thought.

On September 10, at 3:00 P.M., the phone rang and Al Capp was on the line.

"Hello, Isaac, I saw your letter in the *Globe*. What makes you think I'm anti-black?"

"Hello, Al. What do you mean, what makes me think you're anti-black? We argued all evening on the subject at the Whipples'."

"Can you prove I'm anti-black in a court of law?"

"Perhaps not, but I wouldn't try to."

"You're going to have to."

I sobered up at once. Till then, I thought we had been bantering each other. I said, "Al, are you saying you're going to sue me?"

"Of course I am. I can't allow you to libel me in this manner."

I said, "Well, wait. Are you going to suggest an alternative to a lawsuit?"

Al said, "Yes, you'll have to call off the Black Panthers."

"Come on, Al, I'm not the head of the Black Panther movement."

"Well, you'll have to write a letter of apology to the Boston *Globe*, saying that I'm not anti-black, that you regret having wrongfully accused me, and you'll have to make sure that the *Globe* prints it."

"All right, Al," I said, thoroughly chastened and very scared. I had never been sued, and the mere thought of being involved in this kind of legal fracas turned my blood to cherry juice and my spine to jelly.

I went up to my office, put the paper in the typewriter, and began to write an obsequious letter of apology.

It wouldn't come. The words simply wouldn't type out. I *wanted* to apologize and get off the hook, but my typewriter would not co-operate. After a while, I realized that what it amounted to was that I would rather be sued and go through hell than apologize. I felt that I was in the right, and I was not going to back down.

So I called a lawyer friend.

He laughed. "Capp can't sue you," he said, "unless he sues the Boston *Globe*, too. They printed the letter."

I said, "But I sent it to the letter column intending it to be printed."

"That makes no difference. You didn't force them to print it. They printed it of their own choice. If they choose to print a libelous letter, they are as guilty as the letter writer, so you just call the *Globe*, tell them Capp is threatening a suit, and let them worry about it.

"Besides, Isaac, you can say anything you want to about a public figure, unless it is something you know is untrue and you say it maliciously in order to do him harm—and that's very difficult to prove. Al Capp is a public figure, and so are you, by the way, so both of you are fair game."

I felt a little better, and called the *Globe*. I spoke to the editor of the letter column and *he* laughed and told me not to worry, repeating almost exactly what my lawyer friend had said. He said the paper's lawyers would take care of it.

They did. At 3:00 P.M. on September 11, just twenty-four hours after Capp's call, the letter-column editor called to tell me that Capp had cooled down. It had been pointed out to him that a sentence in the letter column was easily forgotten, but that if he chose to make a lawsuit out of it, it might become a *cause célèbre* and he would be made to seem, rightly or wrongly, the spearhead of anti-black sentiment in the United States. He saw the justice of that and dropped the whole thing.

It was over, but for twenty-four hours I had been a very frightened person. Taking a strong stand and refusing to back down may seem very fearless, but behind it there was sheer terror.

29

The Al Capp affair had an unexpected side effect. For twelve years Gertrude and I had had a running fight with the junior-high students who used our street to walk to and from school. We attempted to keep them from noisily congregating on the sidewalk outside our house.

It had been an endless and a losing fight. The attempt to drive them away insured their making a point of trying to hang about our place. Though we could go out and make them move on, it meant being at our windows twice a day, and churning up our adrenalin, and going out and arguing. For them it was merely a bit of excitement.

We could never work out what to do, and then on September 11, the *Globe*'s letter-column editor called just as the youngsters were going home from school and Gertrude was out there arguing with some of them. I came out of the house in the very best of spirits over my rescue from a deadly and expensive lawsuit, and called out to Gertrude, "Everything's all right. Go inside and I'll take care of this."

And I did! Bursting with good humor and ebullience, I talked to the kids for the first time with affection. I joked with them, kidded around, sparred a little with one of them, put my arm around the shoulders of another, told them (in answer to a question) how many books I had published and why that meant I was eccentric and had to have quiet. In no time at all they were eating out of my hand.

I don't know why, in twelve years, I had never tried it before. It wasn't as though I hadn't had hints . . .

For instance, once, when I went to mail letters at the mailbox, which happened to be right at the corner of the school, a group of youngsters were about the mailbox.

They looked threatening to me, distinctly gangsterish. As I approached, trying to seem calm, I was certain one would pull a switchblade on me, or that they would refuse to let me near the mailbox, or that they would destroy the mailbox after I had deposited my letters.

As I approached, wary and tense, one of them said, "Hello, Dr. Asimov. We're reading *I, Robot* in class, and we like it a lot."

At once I could see they were a group of little boys, soft-faced and gentle, intelligent and eager.

"That's good, fellas," I said. "Keep plugging and get good marks." They opened the mailslot for me in very Boy Scoutish fashion and all was well.

There were other examples of this, too—so why did I insist on setting up a war between myself and them?

That was the good aspect of the Capp affair. Finally, I learned. We never had trouble with the youngsters again. They virtually tiptoed past the house, and I made it a practice to be outside once in a while, to wave to them and kid around a bit.

30

It was about this time, too, that I began once more to experiment with facial hair. Increasingly conscious that more and more men were altering their hair styles and that only quite old men were retaining the older look, I began to shave my cheeks lower down.

Little by little I extended my sideburns, and by the time of the Al Capp incident they were halfway down my cheeks.

They continued to extend and to grow bushier and, eventually, they reached the angle of my jaw, while the individual hairs grew to be two inches long or more. They became a permanent feature of my face, and it is now difficult to believe early photographs that show me without sideburns.

31

By September 25, 1968, I had completed the first draft of my annotations of all but five of Shakespeare's plays, and I had about half a million words done. I had been working on it, on and off, for half a year, and I could resist no longer. I wrote an Introduction and began final copy of those plays I had done.

28

Approaching the Hundredth

1

On September 26, 1968, I had lunch with Austin, Mary K., and Walter at Locke-Ober's. Austin said, "You must be approaching your hundredth book, Isaac."

I said, with satisfaction, "Yes, indeed, the advance copy of *The Dark Ages*, which I received last week, is the ninety-second."

"And how many are in press?"

"Seven," I said.

"That brings it to ninety-nine," said Austin. "What are you planning for your hundredth book?"

"Nothing special," I said. "It hadn't occurred to me that there should be anything special."

"There's got to be," said Mary K., "and since we're suggesting it, we've got to have it."

I promised to think about it and even joked that it should be called *Opus 100*, but they took the joke seriously, and that became the name.

I decided quickly that the only appropriate format for the hundredth book would be to include passages from as many as possible of my first ninety-nine books, stressing the variety of subjects I had covered, and to include autobiographical comments.

Austin agreed heartily.

2

Rusty de Camp, Sprague's son, with whom, twenty-three years before, we had had a harrowing baby-sitting experience, was now a staid engineer, as severely straight as Sprague himself, and very like Sprague in appearance, except for his reddish hair.

Rusty was living in a Boston suburb now, and since Sprague and Catherine were visiting him, I joined them on September 28. Rusty had married a divorcée with several young children, so that Sprague and

Catherine (now sixty, but both as good-looking and ageless as ever) were instant grandparents.

3

Asimov's Guide to the Bible was four hundred thousand words long, and I was quite aware that Doubleday planned to publish it in two volumes. The natural way of dividing it was to put the Old Testament in one volume and the Apocrypha plus the New Testament in another.[1]

For some reason, Doubleday decided not to publish both books at the same time, but to do so in successive falls—perhaps to take advantage of two different Christmas seasons. On October 5, I finally got the first volume, *Asimov's Guide to the Bible: The Old Testament*, more than three years after I had started writing it.

Naturally, I sent a copy to my father in Miami Beach, quite relieved that the book did not include the New Testament. That didn't help much, though. My father phoned me to tell me that he had gotten to page 7 and then had closed the book and would read no more. Although he didn't go so far as to actually excommunicate me, I decided right then that when the second volume arrived I would not send it to him.

4

There was no difficulty in doing *Opus 100*. The autobiographical portions were sheer pleasure, and by October 17 I had a sizable sample to present to Houghton Mifflin for their consideration.

I knew there would be the mechanical difficulty of obtaining the books from which excerpts were to be included (or typing them up, if necessary) and of getting all the permissions, but that would be just a matter of time and tedium, and Houghton Mifflin promised to do the necessary scutwork.

5

I had become sufficiently conscious of the longevity of my career to make a note in my diary on October 21, 1968: "This is the thirtieth anniversary of my first professional sale—'Marooned off Vesta.'"

The next day I set off on a drive by myself to Columbus, Ohio,

---

[1] I included the Apocrypha so that I could deal with I and II Maccabees, which are valuable historical documents well worth annotating.

where I was slated to give a talk and receive a plaque. The payment for the talk, a mere $250, was by no means sufficient to justify so long a drive, but I wanted the plaque. It was from the American Society for Information Science.

I was in Columbus by noon of the twenty-third, and found that the society had arranged for me to have a penthouse suite at a fancy motel. It was a much more elaborate one than I required, but it was a welcome sign of their eagerness to treat me well.

When it was finally dinnertime I found myself at a gathering of just about a thousand people, who filled a huge dining room from end to end. It was rather daunting. I had never had so large an audience sitting at tables; they make a far more impressive crowd than the same number sitting tightly packed in an auditorium.

What's more, the master of ceremonies, a large, fat man, had a number of items of business to dispose of and, quite unexpectedly, proved to be a very good and entertaining speaker.

I was cast down at once, for a good preliminary speaker wears down the audience and uses up its laugh potential. I had been planning to give my Mendel speech, which was made to order for information people, and now I went over it in my mind to see how it could be spiced up and more effectively belted out.

The gentleman on my right, noticing perhaps that I was looking glum and abstracted, said, "We're looking forward to hearing you, Dr. Asimov."

I said, my glumness not assuaged, "I may not be any good."

"I know you will be, since I've heard you before and you were terrific."

"Oh? Where did you hear me?"

"At the Gordon Research Conferences a couple of years ago, where you addressed the Information Division. That's what gave us the idea of inviting you now. You gave a speech about Mendel at the time."

I stared at him with horror. "Are there many people here now who heard me then?"

"At least half, I should say."

I had just ten minutes to prepare another speech in my head. That wasn't what bothered me; ten minutes was ample time.

But think! If the gentleman on my right had not made his spontaneous comment, I would not have known this important fact of audience overlap. I would have gotten up, given the same speech that a large number of them had heard, and it would have been a complete and embarrassing frost.

Instead, when it was time for me to talk, I told them exactly what had happened in such a way as to get them laughing, and then gave a completely different talk on the future of communications, which was a huge success.

Since then I have been very conscious of this danger of duplication and have not relied on finding out by accident. I have, whenever possible, asked the people in charge about the likelihood of audience duplication.

6

November 5, 1968, was election day, and I voted unhappily for Humphrey. I was afraid that Nixon would win, and he did—by a more narrow margin than I had expected. What's more, Congress remained Democratic.

I was dreadfully depressed, convinced that a Nixon presidency could only mean misery for the United States, and glad that I was slated to give a talk to a group of librarians in Foxboro, Massachusetts, on November 6. It would help take my mind off Nixon.

To librarians, I invariably give personal talks—about me and my books—and they just as invariably love it. In the question-and-answer period that followed, one librarian rose to make a statement that I have never forgotten:

"Dr. Asimov," she said, "I just want you to know that in our branch, your books are the most frequently stolen."

There was widespread laughter and I said that this seemed to indicate that either my readers were particularly dishonest, which I doubted, or that once having one of my books in their possession they couldn't bear to give it up on any account—something for which I couldn't blame them.

7

On November 9, I finished *Opus 100*, and on November 10, I put together my seventh *F & SF* essay collection, *The Solar System and Back*.

On November 21, the day I took *The Solar System and Back* to Doubleday, the secretaries presented me with a sweatshirt on which lettering had been placed that read "Isaac Asimov Is a Genius." The intent was to embarrass me, of course, and they succeeded. I was never able to wear that sweatshirt, although the time was to come when Robyn would wear it with complete lack of concern.

8

At a meeting of the American Academy of Science on November 13, I was part of a conversational group that was joined by Nobel Laureate I. I. Rabi, whom I had never met before. He at once began talking, and I listened with becoming reverence.

When Rabi was done speaking, I began to say something, and Rabi, wanting belatedly to add a remark to his own comments, began to talk again, ignoring me. I fell silent, out of respect. When he was through, I began again, and darned if he didn't interrupt me a second time. I fell silent again, but now I was seething. He had consumed my store of respect.

When he was through, I made a third attempt at saying something, and when, for a third time, he interrupted me, I simply raised my voice and ran over him. Rabi stared at me as though he now saw me for the first time, raised his arm, and *struck* me.

I staggered a bit and finished my comments. I was terribly tempted to hit him back, but he was older than I was and smaller, so I couldn't.

9

Life was becoming a mosaic of old and new friends. On November 22, I had lunch with Walter Sullivan, the science writer for the New York *Times*, and met him for the first time. He was tall, slim, with a reddish complexion, a shock of white hair, and an air of complete gentlemanliness. He proved a perfectly marvelous person.

In the evening, I talked at the Hunter College Playhouse as a favor to my old friend and mentor, Dr. Dawson, and had dinner with him beforehand. At the playhouse, I met Morris Joselow, who, twenty years before, had helped me back to the lab after I had celebrated my Ph.D. by getting drunk.

10

The growing up of the children was introducing concerns. David drove Gertrude's car solo on November 29, and I could see that he would be wanting to do so with increasing frequency—and that in a few years, Robyn would be making her demands.

As it was, Robyn was having occasion to use the phone more and more, and between her and Gertrude, it was becoming difficult for me to receive my business calls. It seemed logical to arrange for two phones in the house, and on December 9 it was carried through. We became a two-phone family as well as a two-car one, and I had one phone all to myself.

11

On December 12, I was slated to give a talk at the Masonic Temple in downtown Boston. I had never been inside and I was amazed at its rococo interior. I decided it would be pleasant to speak in what seemed to be a Hollywood notion of Cleopatra's palace, but I was taken down into the basement, where everyone sat on planks thrown over wooden trestles before long wooden tables in a room with white-washed walls and hissing radiators.

I sat there uncomfortably for an interminable period, and the organizer of the occasion said to me after a while, "Dinner is delayed."

"Why?" I said.

"We're having a Chinese meal being delivered from Woburn, and I suppose it is being delayed in traffic."

That struck me as astonishing. We were at the very edge of Boston's Chinatown, one of the best in the country. Why send out to Woburn?

He went on to say, "Will you speak now, please?"

"*Before* the meal?"

"Yes."

"But I'll have a hungry audience and the meal will arrive in the middle of the talk and it will be impossible."

"Can't help it," he said, got up, and introduced me.

It was exactly as I said. I had a hungry, unresponsive audience, and halfway through, the dinner arrived and the clanking of cutlery distracted everyone. I had to bring my talk to a halt as soon as possible.

And what of the Chinese meal that had been sent for from Woburn and that had been the cause of the delay? It was about the worst I had ever eaten. One of the dishes had been heated in distinctly rancid fat, and the remainder, if not actually rancid, was completely undistinguished.

12

Tom Sloane wanted an updating of *Asimov's Biographical Encyclopedia of Science and Technology*. I did not. I wanted a complete overhaul. Now that it had done so much better than expected, I wanted to improve it in several ways that would require a complete re-setting, and I held out for it.

Tom gave in, and on December 13 I received two copies of the book, which I then proceeded to cannibalize. I added material to almost every biography, added two hundred additional biographies, and, in particular, made the whole thing chronological without exception. (In the first edition, I had listed some biographies as footnotes to other biographies, something I later decided was a thoroughly bad idea.)

13

We finally found a private school for David, on the Connecticut shore some twenty miles east of New Haven. We visited it on December 18, and decided it would be perfect. There was an enormous tuition, of course, but we expected that.

14

I spent the last week of the year in New York attending a meeting of the Modern Languages Association. That would not have been the sort of thing I would do ordinarily, but science fiction was being taken up by academe, and there was a panel of science-fiction writers scheduled, one that included myself and Fred Pohl, plus some others.

The Silverbergs and del Reys were present, as were Judy-Lynn Benjamin and Phil Klass (the latter writing excellent science-fiction humor and satire under the pseudonym of William Tenn).

I made the comment in the course of the session that I didn't think I had ever made any successful prediction in my science-fiction stories. From the floor, Phil said that, on the contrary, in my story "Trends," I had, in 1939, predicted popular opposition to space exploration, an opposition that no one else had foreseen and that had actually developed.

After that, I frequently gave that as an example of one of my successful predictions and, in fact, have a talk I entitle "The Science-fiction Writer as Prophet," which virtually always gets a standing ovation from college-student audiences.

15

I had eight books published in 1968:

87. *Asimov's Mysteries* (Doubleday)
88. *Science, Numbers, and I* (Doubleday)

16

On January 2, 1969, I turned forty-nine years old, and for the second time, I was caught unawares by a surprise party. (The first time had been on my 35th, fourteen years before.)

This time it was at the home of a friend, and it was Gertrude who stalled me by pretending to have a bad backache. Then, just as I thought we couldn't go at all, it cleared up in time for us to be the last ones there. When I walked in, simply expecting some dinner and conversation, everyone yelled "Surprise!" and a birthday cake appeared out of nowhere.

17

In the course of the Modern Languages meeting in December, Judy-Lynn and I had spent a couple of hours at some bar and she had introduced me to a drink called the "grasshopper." It was green, pepperminty, very delicious, and just as effective in getting me high as was any other form of drink—more effective, since I liked it so much I was always tempted to dare Fate by ordering another.

On that occasion she had suggested I write a robot story about a female robot. I said that my robots had no sex.

She said, "You can write around that, Asimov." (She had a mock-gruff way of speaking that reminded me very much of Tim Seldes.)

"I'll think about it," I said.

This was usually my way of getting rid of a subject, but in this case, I really did think about it, and on January 10, 1969, I started "Feminine Intuition."[2] It was a positronic robot story with Susan Calvin herself as heroine, the first story in which she appeared since I had written "Galley Slave" over eleven years before.

As it happened, Ed Ferman had asked me quite some time before to write a story for the forthcoming twentieth-anniversary issue of *F &*

[2] See *The Bicentennial Man and Other Stories.*

SF, and I had promised to do so. This seemed just the thing. I sent the story to Ed and it eventually appeared in the October 1969 *F & SF* as the lead novelette.

The trouble was that it never occurred to me that in suggesting the gimmick, Judy-Lynn had a lien on it for *Galaxy* or *If*. I never thought of her as an editor, only as a friend, and I honestly accepted her remark as a friendly suggestion and nothing more.

Consequently when, a few months later, she said, "Ever do anything with that female-robot idea, Asimov?" I was very pleased to be able to say that I had.

"Yes, indeed," I said, innocently. "I wrote a Susan Calvin story based on the idea, and Ed Ferman took it for the twentieth-anniversary issue of *F & SF*."

Judy-Lynn opened her eyes wide. She may be very short, but her temper is easily seven feet high, and she has a vocabulary to match. "You mean you gave Ed Ferman *my* idea."

"Did *you* want it, Judy-Lynn?" I said, weakly.

"Of course I wanted it, dummy. Do you think I'm going to waste good ideas on you so *other* people can get it?" At least that was the gist of her remarks, which went on and on. I just shriveled.

Don't think she ever forgot, either. She may have forgiven me because she has a soft heart and she knows I'm not very bright, but she never forgot.

From then on, she made it her business to play practical jokes on me.

She would send me fake advance copies of magazine covers of issues in which a story of mine was to appear. On those covers my name would be misspelled, and panicky calls would come from me at once.

She would send me reviews of products of my pen, which she would get Lester del Rey to write, and which she would arrange to have set up in print as though it had appeared in a newspaper. Lester would design the reviews so as to puncture every single one of my little weaknesses, and when I received them I would call up in rage to find out what paper it had appeared in and who had written it.

She would write letters under the pseudonym of Fritzi Vogelgesang and announce that Judy-Lynn had been fired and that she, Fritzi, was the replacement, so that I would send puzzled letters asking why Judy-Lynn had been fired and, of course, being very pleasant to Fritzi, who sounded like a nice girl.

To cap it all off, she arranged to have me informed, indirectly, that she and Larry Ashmead had just had a secret wedding and were off on their honeymoon. I spent the rest of the day calling up everyone who might have some chance of confirming or denying the news, but everyone was under instructions to give me ambiguous information.

On every one of these occasions people who knew what Judy-Lynn was doing would say, "Asimov will never fall for that."

Judy-Lynn would always say, "Sure he will. That dummy will fall for anything." She would then bet a dinner that I would fall for it.

I never failed her. She collected free dinners for as long as she could find a sucker to bet on my intelligence.

18

At a meeting of NESFA on January 12, 1969, all of us were greatly excited over the prospect of an actual manned landing on the Moon that year. The Apollo program had been aiming at that, and astronauts had been successfully skimming its surface and then returning.

We reminisced over the many stories that had been written about first landings on the Moon, and I said, "This is the year in which there ought to be an anthology of such stories."

There was an outcry to the effect that I ought to edit one, but I demurred and said, "No, Harry Stubbs ought to edit it, since he has never done an anthology, but I'll be glad to write an Introduction to it."

It worked out that way. I suggested the anthology to Larry Ashmead and he agreed. The anthology, *First Flights to the Moon*, edited by Hal Clement, was published in 1970. I did write the Introduction and, what's more, two of my stories, "Trends" and "Ideas Die Hard," appeared in it.

19

Early in the year, I had gotten a letter from Beth Walker, of Walker & Company, suggesting a new book. That was nothing new, but this time it was one that she swore I could write in one day so that I need not try to fend her off by pretending I was buried in work.

Her idea was that I write an ABC book; an "A is for Apple pie" book, except that every letter stand for some word that had to do with space. There would be two words for each letter, in fact, one for the capital letter, so to speak, and one for the small one. There would thus be fifty-two words, each one explained in a sentence or two for very young readers (or their parents), and Walker & Company would take care of the necessary illustrations. It was to be called *ABC's of Space* and it would be published in the year when it looked very much as though we would reach the moon.

It seemed like a novel idea, and I'm easily trapped by anything new. I agreed to do it. I did it all in one day, as Beth had said I would, on January 15.

I knew very well that there would be requests for other ABC books, following, but even in the process of doing the first I lost much of my enthusiasm. Having two words for each letter is artificial and wrong. "S" is such a common opening letter that though I chose "satellite" and "splashdown," I had to leave out "space," "Saturn," "star," and so on. On the other hand, "Y" is an almost impossible letter to find words for, and I had to use "yaw" and "year." Any system that, in a discussion of space, includes "yaw" and omits "star," has to be bad.

20

On January 20, 1969, Richard Nixon became the thirty-seventh President of the United States, and I did not watch the Inauguration on television. In fact, for years to come, I never watched television when Nixon spoke. I found I could not endure either looking at his shifty face or listening to his unctuous voice.

21

On January 31, 1969, David completed the first semester of his junior year in high school, and that was his last day in the public-school system of Newton, which he had been attending for 12½ years.

On that day, we drove him down to the private school in Connecticut and left him there. Of course, we expected to see him in the summer and during vacations but, by and large, he would be away from home the year and a half, and possibly two, that it would take him to complete high school.

Now that he had been with us for 17½ years, we found it difficult to contemplate so prolonged a separation. It wasn't, however, quite as bad as we had thought it would be. We called him regularly, and vacations came oftener than we had expected. On February 14, only two weeks after he had left, he was home for a weekend.

And on February 19, Robyn was fourteen years old.

In one respect, Robyn took over David's tasks, and that was with respect to the snow. It was a very bad winter. December had seen bad rainstorm after bad rainstorm (five inches on one flooded day), and then January had seen the snow—the worst collection of snow since the March we had moved into the house thirteen years before.

It was Robyn who bore the burden. She handled the snow shovel with skill and ordered me off the grounds officiously. "You're nearly fifty, Dad!" (Who asked her?)

It helped that she was beautiful, too.

The city would send snow plows to clear the street, and once you had cleared your own driveway, the city plows would come along and carefully push the snow from the piles existing on either side into your driveway. The edge of the driveway would then be filled with hard and heavy lumps of ice that broke backs and hearts in the removal. This routinely happened two or even three times, and you knew that the midget brains and rusted hearts of the men at the plows rejoiced.

But when Robyn had cleared off the driveway and stood there with her yellow hair framing her pink and beautiful face on which there would appear a sweet and helpless look—why, the cretins lifted their plows clear of the ground and not a piece of ice littered the driveway.

22

I drove to New York on March 13 and took in about half of the Shakespeare book in final copy; then on to Philadelphia, where I was on "The Mike Douglas Show"; then back to New York on the fifteenth, where I attended the Nebula awards dinner, with Judy-Lynn as my date.

Anne McCaffrey was in charge of the awards, and that placed her in a dilemma, for she was getting one of the Nebulas and she didn't like to award it to herself. (I couldn't understand why. I had awarded myself a Hugo in Washington six years before, and it hadn't hurt in the least. In fact, I enjoyed it.)

In any case, she asked if I could come up and award it to her, and I agreed on condition that I give a short five-minute talk.

She said, "Certainly!"

After all, she and I got along famously. Anne is a large, buxom, Junoesque woman with a beautiful shock of prematurely Irish-white hair, a flashing wit, and a spectacular soprano singing voice. It had become traditional at any convention that we attended together for us to do community singing together at a piano, ending with "When Irish Eyes are Smiling" and holding the final note.

I always lost. She could hold that note louder, and longer, and more beautifully than I—or, I should think, than anyone who wasn't a professional singer.

Anyway, here was my chance to sing alone. I said that everyone's name had a pattern of syllables and stresses that fit into some popular song, and my little Nebula talk that evening consisted of giving examples.

I fit "Isaac Asimov" and "Little Buttercup" and sang, "For I'm Isaac Asimov/Dear Isaac Asimov/Sweet Isaac Asimov, I."

Then I fit "Judy-Lynn Benjamin" and "Lullaby and Good Night" and sang, "Judy-Lynn/Benjamin/Come to bed/It's no si-in."

Then, having set up my little game, I fit "Anne McCaffrey" and "San Francisco" and belted out,

"Anne McCaffrey/Open your golden gate/I can no longer wait/ Frustratedly, dear."

Before I could quite finish she came storming up to snatch the Nebula from me, shouting, "You can't trust a tenor! You can't trust a tenor!"

I followed her back to her seat, shouting, "I'm a baritone, too."

The dignity of the occasion was effectively ruined.

23

Alexei Panshin had won the Nebula for his novel *Rite of Passage* and, as it happened, he and his fiancée needed a ride to Boston. I said I could take them but I wanted to stop off in Connecticut to visit David and they were willing to accept the delay.

I picked them up the next day and it made for a very pleasant trip. Even the stop to visit David was unexpectedly pleasant since it turned out that he had read, and liked, *Rite of Passage*. Alexei could but beam and give him two more books.

David came to West Newton for a two-week visit on March 21. He was in time for Boskone and I drove him in to several sessions of the convention. On one occasion, I let *him* drive *me* home.

24

World Publishing wanted me to do a children's science-fiction book for them, and it came to me that I had written just such a thing, seven years before. It was *The Best New Thing*, which I had written for Collier Books. They had accepted it, contracted for it, paid me an advance—and then times had gotten hard for them and they had never published it.

I wrote to them on March 17 to ask for a reversion of rights, which they granted. On April 2, in New York, I had lunch with Ann

Beneduce and Chaucy Bennetts of the Juvenile Department of World Publishing.

Chaucy had once been a copy editor for Doubleday and I had met her in that capacity. She had done a particularly good job on one of my manuscripts and I got to tell her so.

Since that occasion, I had discovered that Chaucy was a cousin of Janet Jeppson, since Janet mentioned her in her letters. Chaucy was as tall as I was and in her younger days had been remarkably beautiful.[3]

I showed them the manuscript and they suggested some minor changes. I made those changes, and by April 17 World Publishing had accepted it, so that *The Best New Thing* gained a new lease on life.

25

Things come in bunches. On April 8, I had lunch with Emilie McLeod of Atlantic Monthly Press. She was rather the opposite of Chaucy in appearance—tall, thin, and angular, but she was also lively and intelligent.

Emilie wanted nonfiction rather than fiction, but also for grade-school children. I promised a children's book on *What Makes the Sun Shine?*, which was the actual title proposed, but warned her that it might be quite a while before I would have a chance to start.

26

I was back in New York for the Lunacon. John Campbell was attending and I spent more than an hour with him and with Peg in their room, along with some others. We all talked, or rather Campbell talked and the rest of us occasionally interposed. It was quite like old times, and I could almost smell the old pulp magazines. I hadn't had such an extended time with Campbell for at least a dozen years.

Even better was spending some time the next day with Evelyn del Rey and getting to tell her how much her remark about me being *the* field had encouraged me and how much it had made it possible for me to continue writing science fiction.

She and Judy-Lynn persuaded me to have a grasshopper and then, when I showed signs of wanting a second, they encouraged me to have that. After two grasshoppers, though, the signs of drunkenness became

---

[3] I eventually saw photographs of her when she was young and in show business, and in my eyes she looked quite like Maureen O'Hara—better, if anything.

so marked that they did exactly what everyone always did under such circumstances—they banned all liquor from the table.

27

We had made friends with a Muriel and Howard Hirt, both of them teachers and both very fond of traveling. They had been to India several times, were fascinated by it, and, in fact, when we visited them, an Indian meal was invariably served.

They were planning to go to Great Britain in the coming August and they suggested that Gertrude and Robyn go with them. (It meant flying, so there was no use asking me.) It seemed like a good idea all around, especially since neither Gertrude nor Robyn had ever been to Europe. On April 18, I sent in the money for a down payment on the travel fare.

That same day, I was interviewed under what, to me, were the most flattering circumstances yet. A reporter from the New York *Times* wanted the background for a feature story on myself and my writing habits for the Book Review Section. The reporter was Lewis Nichols, an older, portly man getting on toward his retirement. He was efficient at his job; he asked intelligent questions quietly and took down the answers briskly. I enjoyed the interview, and I don't always.

28

I drove down to Philadelphia with Gertrude and Robyn on April 21, when I was slated to give a talk at the University of Pennsylvania. "The talk was a screaming, howling success," with a standing-room-only crowd, according to my diary.

What made it most interesting, though, was that for the first time in a quarter century, I met some of my Navy Yard friends. Bernie Zitin was in the audience, along with his wife and son. His son looked so like him that, for a moment, I thought it was Bernie himself, miraculously unchanged over the decades, till I noticed the real thing, with iron-gray hair, standing next to him.

Even more astonishing was Leonard Meisel, whose nose was unmistakable, but who was no longer bone-thin. Indeed, he was almost plump.

I couldn't believe it; I had always thought his excessive thinness was glandular and not subject to change. He seemed to enjoy my surprise and told me that his mother had steadily complained about his thinness until the day came when she began to complain steadily about his fatness.

"I don't recall," he said, "that there was ever a day when she caught me en route and said, 'Lennie, today your weight is just right.'"

The next day we visited *TV Guide* at Radnor, Pennsylvania, where the editors crowded around to see my beautiful, blue-eyed, blond-haired daughter and to admit my description was accurate. We had lunch with them, and then, in the evening, had dinner at the Zitins', with Meisel as another guest.

On the twenty-third, we left Philadelphia, deliberately choosing a route that would lead us past Wingate Hall, which we had left twenty-four years before. Although downtown Philadelphia was built up and aglitter with glass-and-aluminum skyscrapers, West Philadelphia had deteriorated badly. Wingate Hall was still there, however, and we located the windows of our apartment as we passed. Robyn stared curiously at this place where her parents had lived a decade before she was born.

We drove on farther to the Pennsylvania Dutch country, where we stopped at a restaurant that featured home-style meals. That is, you sat down at a meticulously clean wooden table with strangers. Introductions were made all around and then platter after platter of food was placed within reach and everyone helped himself ad lib. One of the platters was pork and sauerkraut and I nibbled at it cautiously, never having tasted sauerkraut and having avoided it deliberately because of the sound of its name. I discovered it tasted like coleslaw, only far better, and in no time I had devoured a gallon or so.

The next day we drove to Poughkeepsie to visit the Fonoroffs, where they were now located since Bernie had a job with IBM—and then home. All in all, it was one of the most successful trips we had made as a family.

29

I had been called by a faculty member of Boston University to ask if I could give an address at the forthcoming initiation of new Phi Beta Kappa members.

It touched a sore spot, which I thought I had long since conquered. Certain honors had eluded me in my school career. I had not made the Arista in high school and I had not made the Phi Beta Kappa in college.[4] I had not thought of it for years but suddenly the prospect of cheering on new Phi Bets got to me.

[4] Of course, Seth Low Junior College did not have a Phi Beta Kappa chapter and Columbia College wouldn't consider me for one since I was an outer barbarian.

I said, coldly, "I'm sorry, but that might be embarrassing since I'm not a Phi Beta Kappa myself."

"Bless you," said the faculty member, cozily. "We don't mind."

I said, still more frigidly, "You don't understand. *I'm* the one who minds."

Later that day, she called me back to tell me that at an emergency meeting of the council, I had been voted in as an honorary member. Well, that would do. It amounted to blackmail, I suppose, but I wasn't going to be choosy in my method for gaining what I believed to be a just end. I agreed to give the talk.

On May 2, 1969, I showed up on the main campus in order to be initiated. It turned out to be a little more embarrassing than I had counted on. Pecks and bushels of bright young, downy-cheeked collegiates were standing around in scarlet robes, and there was I, the only ancient, in a black robe—an old crow trapped amid a flock of tanagers.

There was some secret material delivered only to the initiates, with all parents and other visitors banned, but I have forgotten it all, including the secret handshake by which one Phi Bet was to recognize another (during periods of oppression, I suppose, when open avowal of membership might lead to a concentration camp).

Then, when the visitors returned, we went up on the stage one by one to be invested and to get our Phi Beta Kappa symbol. As I came up, grinning broadly, the woman who handed me the tieclip with symbol attached, whispered, "I'm dreadfully sorry, Dr. Asimov, but after the ceremony, please give it back and we'll get you another one with your name spelled correctly." I looked at the symbol handed me and there was my name—Isaac Isamov.

"That's all right," I said. "I'll keep it."

She found out why when I gave my talk to the new members, a talk that was full of phrases like "We Phi Bets . . ." and ". . . a Phi Bet such as myself."

In the talk, I told exactly how I had become an honorary member, with some humorous exaggeration, right down to being handed the misspelled symbol, and then gave my reasons for insisting on keeping it.

"It will come in handy," I said. "Naturally, a Phi Bet like myself is, above all, modest, and I would never think of thrusting forward my Phi Betitude in the faces of those less fortunately situated. Still, when I am wearing my tieclip, I can always point to it and say in an aggrieved tone, 'Look at how my name is spelled on this thing.' They will look and say, 'That's terrible. What is it?' And I will say, 'Oh nothing. Just an old Phi Beta Kappa symbol. Pay no attention to it.'"

There followed the best laugh of the evening, one that was well worth the misspelling.

Of course, it has turned out that I never wear the darn thing. I just wanted to be a Phi Bet for my own satisfaction. As far as others are concerned, just being Isaac Asimov (correct spelling) is enough, I guess.

30

Someone at Western Publishing had the idea of doing an anthology of science-fiction stories that could be useful in science classes. Stories would be chosen in which interesting scientific points were made (or violated). Each could be discussed by the editor, and topics for further discussion could be suggested.

It struck me as a good idea. Although I found anthologies a drag, this one seemed to be in a good cause and to offer me an interesting opportunity to talk about science. I agreed.

On May 4, when I attended the annual MIT picnic, I made an arrangement with some of them to make Xerox copies of particular stories from the magazines they had in their science-fiction library. They would send me the Xerox copies and I would do the rest. The anthology that resulted was eventually to be called *Where Do We Go From Here?*

31

On May 9 I was in New York, having lunch with Beth Walker. Apparently she was highly pleased with *ABC's of Space*, for she insisted I do an *ABC's of the Ocean* in the same format. I finally agreed, but with markedly less enthusiasm than I had in the first case.

Later that day, I went down to Brooklyn to talk at Brooklyn Polytechnic Institute. I had been driven down to Brooklyn for the occasion, but I was willing to take the subway back to Manhattan. I agreed to do that with the casual self-confidence of the person who was brought up in New York and to whom subways were a home away from home.

Alas, I had not used the subways in two decades and they had changed enormously. The lines had been shuffled around, and the maps were especially designed for incomprehensibility even when they weren't covered with graffiti. I managed to get lost, to overshoot my mark, and to have to ask my way back.

It was incredibly embarrassing and I have rarely used the subways since.

32

David arrived on a weekend's visit on May 16, and on the eighteenth, I took him to a NESFA meeting in Somerville. He had not been with us the previous month, when we had seen our old apartment in Philadelphia, so this time I drove him past our old apartment in Somerville, which I myself hadn't seen since we left it eighteen years before. It was the apartment in which David had been conceived, after all, so he stared at the building curiously as we passed.

33

On June 1, we were in Binghamton, where I gave a commencement address at Harpur College, a branch of the State University of New York. It was the first commencement address I ever gave, and as I sat on the stage in full academic regalia, and watched innumerable students advance to get their diplomas, I thought rather wistfully of my refusal to attend my own commencements, even that for the Ph.D., twenty-one years before.

Now here I was, going through the same foolishness where I was not personally involved. And it was only the first. Since then, commencement seasons have never passed without my being in academic robes on some platform or other.

29

Farewell to My Father

1

The Hirts, who were looking forward to their trip to Great Britain with the female portion of the Asimov family, had suggested another trip in combination, but on a far smaller scale, and one in which I could join them.

Their idea was that we visit the Concord Hotel in the Catskills, an old-fashioned but very elaborate Jewish resort. I did not really want to go, since I would much rather be home where I could work on the last stages of my Shakespeare book, but that seemed insufficient reason to deprive Gertrude, so I didn't argue the matter.

We left on Friday, June 6, with Howard Hirt driving and myself rather in a state of melancholia at what I was convinced would be a wasted weekend.[1] In a kind of hectic reaction to that I began to tell jokes, more because any resulting laughter might perhaps ease the compressed ball into which my stomach had tightened than for any other reason.

Muriel Hirt enjoyed herself tremendously and said, "Isaac, why don't you write an *Isaac Asimov Jokebook?*"

I laughed and said, "Who'd publish it?"

She said, "I should think anything you write would get published."

In a way, she was right. I thought about it and a marvelous idea occurred to me. I could pass the weekend writing jokes. While everyone around me was going through all the horrifying ritual of vacationing, I could be managing to work.

The Concord Hotel was as dreadful as I feared it might be. It was as gigantic and impersonal as a Manhattan apartment complex, and all its "vacation" appurtenances were crowded into uselessness. Nor were my fellow vacationers to my liking. At our table there was a couple who had read *Portnoy's Complaint* and were astonished that I had not.

"How can you not read a book," they demanded, "that is on the top of the best-seller list?"

---

[1] We left Robyn behind on her own, but we had done that on our earlier trip to Binghamton, and it was quite plain that she could manage perfectly well.

"For the same reason," I said, "that I didn't read *Mein Kampf*, even though it was on the top of Germany's best-seller list."

After that, there was no conversation at the table.

However, I borrowed a fistful of hotel stationery, and all that weekend I scribbled down jokes. Even while at the nightclub (the largest in the world, they said, and *certainly* the most brainless and noisiest) I saved my sanity by scribbling. I think some of the people near me thought I was an FBI agent taking notes, but I didn't care.

By the time I got home on Sunday evening, I had quite a sheaf of papers with handwriting all over it. The next day I typed it all up and went on to type additional material as well. It was not only jokes I was writing, but commentary as well. The commentary was not only on the jokes themselves, but also on my notions concerning the nature and function of humor, and on the techniques of telling jokes successfully.

2

On June 10 I had lunch with Bill Boyd. He had long since been divorced. He had a new companion whom he was planning to marry, and with her, he would leave Massachusetts permanently for a warmer climate.

It meant that I would, quite possibly, never see him again, and that was a matter of regret to me. It had been twenty-two years before that I had first met him face to face. It was through him that I got my post with the med school and it was with him that I had done two books and gotten my entree into the world of nonfiction books.

3

I took my collection of jokes to Austin on June 12. It was only first draft and only a small portion of what I was planning to write, but I wanted him to get some idea of what I was doing.

He looked a little uneasy when I began to tell him how I came to be writing a jokebook, but he was far too polite to say nasty things. I suspected he would, in the end, take the book—and he did. Muriel Hirt's casual remark in the car thus came to fruition and, indeed, when the book was published, I dedicated it to her.

4

Carl Sagan was a patient at Massachusetts General. It didn't seem as though he were in any particular danger at first, and when I visited him on June 18, we joked easily and made arrangements to have dinner, all four of us, when he got out.

Then complications set in and he remained in the hospital for weeks. I visited periodically and sat with a rather distraught Linda and did my best to keep her calm. He recovered completely, of course, but it did keep him from participating in the forthcoming attempt to land a man on the Moon.

Things were even more ironic in another way. On June 24, I received a call from Judy-Lynn to the effect that Willy Ley had just died at the age of sixty-two. Willy had spent almost his whole life enwrapped in rocketry. He was the world's leading writer on the subject and from his teens he had had the one overriding ambition to see human beings on the Moon—and he died six weeks before the attempt was to be made.

5

I went to a Boston studio on July 7 to participate in a panel show and found, a little to my embarrassment, that Al Capp was a fellow panelist. We talked together easily, however, and neither one of us made any reference to that one-day conflict the previous September.

6

On July 17, I did another panel show, in New York this time, with Rod Serling moderating. Rod Serling, who had entered the science-fiction scene with his popular "Twilight Zone" series on television, introduced me as the "Peck's bad boy of science fiction."

I wasn't sure what he meant by that, but I think he was influenced by my suave manner toward the young women attached to the studio. Also influenced by that may have been Fred Pohl, who was a fellow panelist, and who said (when the cameras were not on), "Isaac Asimov turned into a dirty old man at the age of fifteen."

It was an exaggeration, but I didn't object. It was the first time I had heard myself described as a "dirty old man," but I merely took it to mean that I was over forty and liked women, and that I showed that liking every chance I got. Since this is all true, I am perfectly willing to bear the title; I even use it on myself without qualms.

7

On July 20, I returned to Newton, and that evening, Neil Armstrong and Buzz Aldrin successfully walked on the Moon. I was enthralled, as was the whole world.

I couldn't help but remember that in "Trends," written three decades before, I had had the first Moon flights (without an actual landing) take place in 1973 and 1978. Reality had outstripped me by a full decade, and the real thing was far more complex and detailed than my fictional descriptions.

8

On July 25,[2] my typewriter had broken down. By now I had two Selectric typewriters, having traded in the older model with the shifting carriage as unusable once I got used to the dancing walnut.

It was a Friday, and it happened right after the close of the business day, which meant that I would have to wait till Monday morning to get IBM to send a repairman. Had it been my only typewriter I would have been very unhappy, but as it was, I merely moved the ailing typewriter into the other room, brought in the backup typewriter, and continued working. I felt a little uneasy at having only one working typewriter, but it was only for the weekend.

But on Saturday (our twenty-seventh anniversary) the *second* typewriter broke down also, and I went completely wild. To have invested over a thousand dollars in *two* typewriters and to have them *both* collapse on me simultaneously and on a *weekend*. Well, it just seemed too much.

It was with difficulty that I restored myself to near sanity and, that evening, with nothing else to do, I took the family to dinner and a movie. Coming out of the movie, we encountered Carl and Linda Sagan in the lobby. He was just out of the hospital after seven weeks, and I had to admit that there were misadventures worse than malfunctioning typewriters, and I was rather ashamed of myself.

On Monday, July 28, first thing in the morning, I finally managed to get in touch with IBM. The people there knew me and knew very well the intensity of my devotion to work and the level of my anxiety about the welfare of my typewriters. When the IBM man at the repair desk heard that *both* my typewriters were out, he at once swore that he would have someone at my place within the hour, and I thanked him brokenly.

In less than an hour, the bell sounded at the front door and I bounded down the stairs with gladness and relief.

What I had totally forgotten was that several days before I had

[2] It was Stanley's fortieth birthday, a sober thought considering that I could remember the day of his birth quite clearly.

made arrangements to have Israel Shenker, a feature writer of the New York *Times*, visit me for an interview, and when I threw the door open, there he was with his wife.

He introduced himself and I stared at him blankly for a moment, unable to absorb anything other than the fact that the IBM man wasn't there. Then I remembered and said grumpily, "Oh it's you!" which is scarcely the right way to greet an influential reporter.

I took them up to my office and for a couple of hours they interviewed me while I grew more and more restless because the repairman did not come. I had to excuse myself and try to call IBM now and then, but the line was always busy and it was all I could do not to break down right in front of Shenker. Naturally, I had to explain all my typewriter troubles to him. I could no more have refrained from doing that than I could have refrained from sneezing if my nose tickled.

By the time the Shenkers had left, the repairman had still not come and, in fact, he did not arrive till 1:00 P.M. What had happened was that he had gotten his directions mixed and had gone to a street of the same name as ours in Brookline.

Once in my office, of course, he fixed both typewriters in a very short time and all was well. I cooled down at once and even felt guilty over the bitter remarks I had made to Shenker concerning lousy service, because, actually, this was the first time that an IBM repairman had not come instantly on being summoned.

9

On July 30, I received my Doubleday statement, and the check came to nearly forty thousand dollars. At last, after eight years of steadily building royalties, Doubleday had surpassed that check from Basic Books.

I had made enormous progress in a decade. That one check was greater than my entire annual income for 1960.

10

Meanwhile, the Brandeis summer course was beginning and I was again involved, though not quite to the extent of the previous year. I was, however, due for an evening talk on August 6.

Gertrude would not be there for that talk. She would be attending the first week, but then she and Robyn would be going to Great Britain and I would be doing the second week alone. Actually, I rather looked forward to being alone in the house for three weeks, with a chance of getting enormous quantities of work done.

On Saturday, August 2, at 2:00 P.M., I drove Gertrude, Robyn, and the Hirts, with all their baggage, to the airport and left them there. At 6:45 P.M., Gertrude called from Kennedy Airport, where they were scheduled to take a plane across the Atlantic.

11

The next day, August 3, the Sunday New York *Times* ran the Lewis Nichols interview of me, the one that had been done the previous April. It took up a full page in the Book Review Section and was very good. What particularly pleased me was that toward the end he included a tribute I had paid my father for buying me a new typewriter even before I had made my first sale, as his evidence of faith in my perseverance and ability.

I promptly called my parents in Florida to ask if they had seen the *Times* yet. They hadn't, and my mother, who answered the phone, said my father wasn't feeling well. I asked to speak to him and he seemed annoyed at my mother for having overdramatized the situation.

He said, "So I have pains. I have pains all the time now; and I've had it for years. Sometimes it's a little worse, sometimes a little better, and finally I'll die. So what? When I die, I die."

"Yes, Pappa," I said, "but how do you feel *now*?"

"Not so bad. She's just making a fuss. I'll send her out for the *Times*. That will give her something to do."

Later on in the day, he called me. They had obtained the *Times*, read the article, and my father was very pleased. Of course, he did his best not to be sickening about it, since he always prided himself on his stoical approach to life,[3] but he rarely fooled me.

[3] Some years before, I heard Shelley Berman do a comic routine on "The Ed Sullivan Show." He played his own father, whose accent, intonations, idioms, personality, and retail store were exactly like my own father's. It made me feel queer, and when the routine was over I called my father long-distance.

My father answered and I said, "Hello, Pappa. It's Isaac. Did you hear Shelley Berman on the TV just now?"

"Yes," said my father, and nothing more.

Rather at a loss for words, I waited, then finally said, "I heard him, too, so—so —so I thought I'd call and ask how you are."

There was another pause, and my mother said, "He's fine."

I was astonished. "Mamma!" I said, "what are you doing on the phone? Where's Pappa?"

My mother said, "He's in the corner, crying. What did you say to him?"

So much for my father and his stoicism.

That night, I attended the opening banquet of the second week of the Brandeis summer course, and all was well and hilarious.

12

On Monday, August 4, 1969, things fell apart.

At 8:45 P.M. that evening I was on the phone and the operator broke in to tell me that someone else was trying to reach me on a life-and-death emergency. There were three things it could be: Gertrude and Robyn, David, or my mother and father.

Stupidly, turning cold all over, I said, "Life and death?"

I heard my brother's voice break in, "Tell him it's Stanley calling."

That meant my mother and father. I broke off my conversation, was connected to Stanley, and I said, "What's the matter?"

It was a useless question. I knew what had happened.

That afternoon, my father had died, a little less than a year after he had gone to Florida. That day of the golden wedding anniversary celebration was, after all, the last time I was ever to see him.

At least I had spoken to him the day before. He had indeed felt poorly then. He felt worse on the morning of the fourth, was taken to the hospital, and died there in a matter of hours.

He was seventy-two-years and seven months old at the time of death, and had survived the onset of his angina pectoris by thirty-one years. He had remained mentally alert to the very end and was never bedridden till the last day. It was a source of great solace to me that on his last full day of life I had spoken to him (and so had Stanley, in connection with the *Times* article) and that he himself had read the article and had seen that I had appreciated what he had done for me and that I had let the world know.

I was grateful then, and have always been since, to Lewis Nichols for the excellent article he wrote and to the chance that made it appear the day before my father's death, rather than the day after.

13

It did not occur to me for a moment to try to get in touch with Gertrude and Robyn in Europe and get them to come home. It would have been a silly and heartless thing to do, and I do not believe that death should interfere with life.

If, by disrupting their vacation, Gertrude and Robyn could have restored my father to life, I would have them disrupt it at once—but to disrupt it merely for useless ritual? Never! Nor did I bother David.

On August 5, I drove to New York, for Stanley had had our father's body brought to Long Island for burial on the sixth. The services were extremely simple and my brother and I, quite deliberately, eschewed all ceremony.[4] Stanley wouldn't even look at the body, maintaining that our father was alive only in our memories and in the consequences of the deeds he had done. The body that had been our father in life, he said, was nothing in death. I agreed with him intellectually—but I took a last look.

My mother was not present because she was still in Miami Beach, having been hospitalized as a result of the shock of my father's death, and Ruth was with her. Marcia and Nick were away on vacation and we didn't know where they were, so we couldn't reach them. All the children were deliberately kept away.

But then, unexpectedly, Larry Ashmead walked in. He had taken the trouble to find out where the services were, and had made the trip. The best way to describe anyone is to give an example of the kind of thing he would do, and this was characteristic of Larry.

My father's body was then taken to a cemetery lot he had long ago bought out on Long Island, and Stanley, I, and the rabbi went out, following the ambulance, to hold vigil over the interment.

It pleased me that Stanley and I carried enough weight for the death of our father to be commemorated in small obituaries in the various metropolitan area newspapers. Could my father have imagined, when he arrived in the new land, fifty-four years before, that his death would make the newspapers?

There was one unpleasant result of the obituaries. Marcia returned from her vacation the next day and, before we could reach her and break the news to her carefully, some casual acquaintance, learning of the death from the newspapers, expressed her sympathy. That was Marcia's first knowledge of the death, and it was a bad blow.

After the funeral, I raced back to Brandeis University. When Stanley had called me with the news of my father's death and the suggestion I come to New York, I had said, dazedly, "But I've a talk to deliver on the sixth."

"Break it," he said.

"I can't break a commitment," I said, still dazed. "I never have."

"You've never had a father die," said Stanley, coldly.

So I canceled. They understood. Yet even so I raced back, hoping that I might make the talk and spare myself the disgrace of a cancel-

---

[4] It was on this occasion that I finally apologized to Stanley for having thrown his rubber ball over the roof thirty-two years before, and found that he didn't remember the incident at all.

lation, however impeccable the reason. (Another thought, too: Giving the talk would enable me to include an encomium on my father, and I desperately wanted to do that.)

I *did* get back in time, but a replacement speaker had been selected, and I couldn't upset that.[5] I was in the audience when my replacement gave his talk, and ended by announcing that he would not accept the four-hundred-dollar fee the talk carried but would donate it to Brandeis to establish a Judah Asimov Scholarship Fund. Grateful (for I would not have had the brains to think of that independently), I rose to match the sum. Others contributed various sums, so that in the end nearly twelve hundred dollars was in the fund.

Ever since then, I have maintained the fund with an annual payment so that my father's name from year to year is attached to the helping of some deserving student. It pleases me that my father, who had so much difficulty seeing to the education of his children—but who managed to the full extent of his abilities—should be involved in such education for others after his death.

It would be nice for me to think he is somewhere in heaven, looking down and feeling proud and pleased, but I do not think so. I do not believe in existence after death, but I am still alive, and *I* feel proud and pleased.

14

The death of my father seemed to sensitize me to the manner in which my life seemed to be falling apart. Gertrude and I had been talking divorce, and when she left for Great Britain there seemed to be some feeling that when she came back we would take serious steps in that direction. The prospect seemed dank enough in itself, but with my father dead, it seemed more than I could live through.

During the day, I worked steadily and grimly on the Shakespeare book, and that helped anesthetize me, but the nights were dreadful.

And on the night of August 10–11, having fallen asleep at last, I woke at 2:00 A.M. with the old, familiar abdominal pain. It was the first kidney-stone attack of consequence I had had since 1962 and the *worst* since the first diagnosed attack in 1950.

I sat up in bed, rocking back and forth, then out of bed when sitting proved impossible, tottering back and forth with both hands pressing my abdomen, dizzy with pain and conscious of the fact that I was

[5] Afterward, I gave an informal talk (without fee) in the lounge for those who cared to spend additional time exercising their eardrums, and included some words on my father then.

alone in the house. There was no one to call for an ambulance, and if it got worse, I might possibly be unable to call one for myself.

I am frequently sorry for myself—who is immune to that?—but I don't think I have ever been sorrier for myself than that night; at least, at those moments when the pain didn't make even self-pity impossible.

After a couple of hours, though, the pain slowly died and I got a couple of more hours of exhausted sleep before waking and driving into town, utterly worn out, in order to have my first upper left molar fitted for a crown. It was the first time I had ever had to have a crown.

Without the kidney-stone pain in the way, I had full scope for self-pity. It was not just my father dead—my kidney stone—the dentist's chair. In the nine days since Gertrude and Robyn had left, I had heard nothing from them. Gertrude had difficulty writing letters, I knew, but Robyn had promised to write. Had something happened to them?

15

That was the low point. When I got back to the house, there was a postcard from Robyn dated the fourth, and she was all right. (The next day there arrived a letter dated the eighth, and everything was still all right.)

Then, too, on August 11, I heard from Janet Jeppson.

August was the traditional vacation month for psychiatrists, and Janet was vacationing in New England. She called me to ask after my health.

What she didn't know was that Gertrude was away, that I was alone, that my father was dead and my kidney stone alive, and that I was *desperate* for something to do to keep myself from drowning in self-pity.

I suggested lunch, and she agreed. After lunch, I suggested that we park one of our cars in my garage and do a little touring together in the other car. She agreed again and through perfect summer weather, we went up to Concord, visited historical sites and, in particular, wandered through the cemetery to look at the graves of Emerson, Thoreau, and others.

It was wonderful. The smallest things pleased Janet—the graves— the names—the flowers and bushes—the stores we passed. Everything animated her and she seemed to think that I was responsible for it all— for the weather—for the smooth working of the car.

I was so ravished at the thought that I was making someone happy that I was perfectly willing to accept all the credit. Nor did I tell her of my kidney-stone attack of the previous night, lest the apprehension that the pain return cast a damper on her happiness. Every once in a while I would remember and fear that some twinge might force me to grimace and give me away—but it didn't.

We spent all afternoon together, then had dinner. I persuaded her to stay another day, picked her up the next morning, and visited Salem and Marblehead, looking at old houses and old streets and finding quaint places in which to eat.

It was a marvelous two days; two days without a care; two days in which everything I did seemed right and in which I got instant feedback of pleasure and happiness from someone in whom I was trying to induce pleasure and happiness.

And it came when most I needed it. The pain of my father's death seemed soothed, and the expectation of the pain of my kidney stone seemed muted, and, with Robyn's letters also having arrived, the fears for disaster in Europe seemed deflated.

It put me right back on the track. When Janet went on her way on August 13, I could go down to New York, quite my old self.

16

My purpose in visiting New York was to tape a segment of a David Frost talk show. Some days earlier I had been called by one of the staff of the show who wanted to discuss possible lines of questioning. It was at a time when I was concerned with my father's death and I was not my usual tactful self.

I snapped out, "I have no time for that, sir. Just tell Mr. Frost he can ask anything he chooses. I will keep up with him, never fear."

I suppose that put Frost on his mettle. When I came out on the stage, on August 15, bowing and smiling and seating myself with an attitude of being completely at my ease, he said, with neither warning nor preamble,

"Dr. Asimov, do you believe in God?"

That rather took my breath away. It was a dreadful way of putting a person on the spot. To answer honestly, "No," with millions of people watching, could arouse a great deal of controversy I didn't feel much need of. Yet I couldn't lie, either. I played for time, in order to find a way out.

He said, "Dr. Asimov, do you believe in God?"

And I said, "Whose?"

He said, a little impatiently, "Come, come, Dr. Asimov, you know very well whose. Do you believe in the Western God, the God of the Judeo-Christian tradition?"

Still playing for time, I said, "I haven't given it much thought."[6]

Frost said, "I can't believe that, Dr. Asimov." He then nailed me to the wall by saying, "Surely a man of your diverse intellectual interests and wide-ranging curiosity must have tried to find God?"

(Eureka! I had it! The very nails had given me my opening!) I said, smiling pleasantly, "God is much more intelligent than I am—let him try to find me."

The audience laughed its head off and, to my relief, Frost changed the subject.

He essayed one more probe into mysticism by saying, "Do you consider it possible, Dr. Asimov, that there may be forces and energies in the universe we have not yet discovered?"

"If so," I answered, "we have not yet discovered them."

He also asked me whom I would like to see President of the United States after I had made my dissatisfaction with Nixon perfectly clear. I said I admired Senator McGovern—and eventually I received a thank-you note from the senator for that.

I will admit, though, that I had an attack of superstition after the taping. I had often stated that I didn't think that God, even if he existed, would be angry with an honest atheist who voted his convictions. Would he, however, tolerate a *wiseguy* atheist?

Of course, no lightning bolt had struck me on the spot when I virtually dared him to find me, but the show was only a taping. What would happen when it was actually aired on September 5? I could only wait.

17

David's eighteenth birthday came on August 20, 1969, while he was still in his Connecticut school. He came home on a visit on the twenty-second, however, and the next day, exactly on schedule, on the twenty-third, Gertrude and Robyn were back and the family was together again.

Such was everyone's relief at the reunion that any mention of divorce went by the board.

The twenty-seventh World Science Fiction convention was coming up, however, and we were split up again almost at once. Not that *I* went. It was the second in a row I could not attend. The year before the convention had been in Oakland, California, and now it was slated for St. Louis, Missouri.

[6] That wasn't really a lie. I had come to what was, for me, a satisfactory answer to the question many years before, and since then I hadn't given it much thought.

David, however, who had been attending Boskones and NESFA meetings, was anxious to go, and I felt he needed some sort of glamorous vacation to balance Robyn's having been to Europe. When Harry Stubbs said he was taking his kids and would be glad to keep an eye on David, that was it. David went off with the Stubbses to St. Louis by plane on August 28, and returned on September 2, having had a great time.

18

Even my writing was cause for depression in these unfortunate months; at least a particular piece of writing was.

A few months earlier, Theodore Macri of Doubleday had phoned to ask if I would write a science-fiction story that could serve as the basis of a movie. I didn't want to, because I don't like to get tangled up with the visual media directly, but I hate to refuse Doubleday.

The result was that I eventually had dinner, on June 25, 1969, with a representative of a particular studio, and he outlined his needs.

He wanted the story set in the deep sea, and so far I was willing. He went on, however, to discuss the characters in the story and I realized, with a sinking heart, that I could not do that story. I couldn't bring myself to say "No" outright to him, over a dinner he was paying for. All I could do was to write a story I felt like writing and to hope they would like it.

For ten weeks, on and off, I brooded over the task, particularly at night, and finally, on September 2, I tore myself away from the Shakespeare book and got to work on a story I called "Waterclap."

It went slowly and painfully and it wasn't till October 1 that I had completed the first draft. Nothing in the story was anything like what the studio representative had outlined for me, and I felt that the first draft would be sufficient for the studio to come to some decision. If, for some reason, they liked the story, I would do final copy and we'd be in business.

I took it in to Doubleday on October 9. They had already signed the contract with the studio and a good-sized advance had been paid over. Doubleday would, in its turn, pay my share to me at next royalty time.

I asked Ted Macri if Doubleday would return the advance if the story proved unacceptable.

"We don't have to," said Ted. "The advance is unconditional. If they don't like your story we still keep the advance."

I couldn't allow that. I knew very well I had not tried to write an acceptable story on the studio's terms, and to keep their money would be dishonest. I said, "Ted, I *want* the money returned if they reject the story, but you can take the Doubleday cut out of my royalties."

Well, Doubleday wasn't going to do *that*. They never humored me in that respect. Ted agreed to pay the money back, if necessary, but absolutely refused to take anything out of my royalties.

The studio *did* reject the story and Doubleday *did* send back the advance and I was overwhelmed with relief.

19

My kidney stone did not go away. The dull back-pain was always there, worse some times than others, and always with the threat of periods of no-warning acute agony hanging over me.

September 5 was the day on which "The David Frost Show" with my let-God-try-to-find-me wisecrack was to be aired, and at 5:00 A.M. on that day I woke with the familiar agony.

There followed a nine-hour period of unbearable pain, the worst and most prolonged I have ever experienced. At one point, I could only gasp, "All right, God, you found me! Now let go!"

In the early afternoon, Gertrude finally forced me into her car and drove me to the hospital. I didn't want to go because I was afraid I would miss "The David Frost Show," which I knew was by all odds the best I had ever done on a national talk show—but I was in no position to resist effectively.

I was examined and the doctor filled a hypodermic with what I knew was morphine but, as he approached, the pain ebbed away. Whatever it was the kidney stone was doing, it stopped doing it.

I said, vigorously, "No, don't. Don't use the hypodermic. The pain has stopped. It's really stopped." I must have seemed like a faker afraid of the needle, but no one with an acute kidney-stone attack can sit up in bed and smile. The pain had to have left. (Try it yourself and see.) The doctor had no choice but to let me go home, and I managed to catch "The David Frost Show."

20

There was a memorable fallout from that show.

I was with a group of people about a week later, and one of them said, "I saw you on 'The David Frost Show.'"

I assumed a modesty I did not feel, and simpered.

A young man of nineteen was part of the group and he said, with

genial insolence, "And what did you do, Dr. Asimov? Read commer-
cials?"

With a haughty determination to squelch the young cockerel at
once by a thrust too outrageous to parry, I said, "Not at all! I was demonstrating sexual techniques."

"Oh," he said, smiling sweetly, "you remembered?"

I was wiped out completely.

21

September 5 was also my mother's seventy-fourth birthday. She
was no longer in Florida. Recovering from the shock of my father's
death, she had been discharged from the hospital, and Stanley had
brought her home with him to Long Island.

He found a hotel in Long Beach that specialized in housing elderly
people, and made sure it was a respectable and decent place and that
she had a good and comfortable room, with a staff that would take care
of it and her. It was only six miles from his home and from *Newsday*
and he could be there in ten minutes in case of emergency.

On September 6, I drove the entire family to Long Island and we
visited the hotel, which we could see, with our own eyes, was a satisfactory place. My mother was there waiting for me. It was the first time
I had seen her since the golden wedding anniversary celebration a year
and a half before. She looked haggard and was, of course, in a teary,
hand-wringing mood, but we took her to a fancy restaurant and made
much of her and she cheered up marvelously.

Then we went back to the nearby motel at which we were staying
that night. I unloaded the baggage from the car, but, as was usual with
me, I spent time checking and rechecking whether the trunk door was
locked, whether the car lights were out, and so on. By the time I picked
up the baggage, the rest of the family had gone on ahead and were
through the door.

It was difficult for me to open the door, laden down as I was, so I
thought I might just as well go around it through the opening next to
it.

Except that it wasn't an opening, but a clear pane of unmarked
glass, and I went right through it.

God still had his finger on me, apparently, but not with malice.
Just as the kidney-stone attack had lifted in time for me to watch the
show, so the pieces of glass that shattered all around me, almost miraculously avoided me and left me only with some minor cuts on the back
of the left hand and on my left knee.

By that time, Gertrude had returned to see what was keeping me and, in horror, ran to the registration desk for help. A policeman was there with a police ambulance. He whisked me quickly to the ambulance, cleaned my wounds, made sure there was no glass in them, added disinfectant, and bandaged them.

I said, "It's a good thing, officer, the motel maintains an ambulance."

"It doesn't maintain an ambulance," he said, as he finished binding me. "I was here on another call, and I was just about to leave when you staggered to the desk."

How's that for luck?

I went back to the desk, in order to clear up one thing. "That was an unmarked pane of glass," I said, "but I'm not going to sue you. However, if you try to charge me for damages, I will sue you till your eyeballs bubble. Is that clear?"

There was no charge for damages.

I sent off a letter of commendation to the Nassau Police Department, praising the policeman who had treated me, and I trust that was entered on his record.

The next day we drove home, and on September 8, David went back to his school and I gave my annual "first lecture" at the medical school.

22

On September 13, I gave a talk at a book fair sponsored by the Boston *Globe*, and with my usual indifference to such matters, I didn't realize it was Rosh Hashanah. It wouldn't have mattered at all except that a couple of days later I received a phone call from a young man, who was a stranger to me but who had apparently seen a notice in the *Globe* that I had spoken at the book fair and who felt he had a right to ask me why I had spoken on Rosh Hashanah.

I explained politely that I hadn't known it was Rosh Hashanah, but that if I had, I would still have spoken, because I was a non-observing Jew. The young man, himself Jewish, flung himself into a self-righteous lecture in which he told me my duties as a Jew, observant or not, and ended by accusing me of trying to conceal my Jewishness.

I felt annoyed. I thought I had caught his name when he started the conversation, but wasn't sure. I had caught enough, however, to feel confident of my next move. I said, "You have the advantage of me, sir. You know my name. I didn't get yours. To whom am I speaking?"

He said, "My name is Jackson Davenport."[7]

"Really? Well, my name, as you know, is Isaac Asimov, and if I were really trying to conceal my Jewishness as you claim I am trying to do, my very first move would be to change my name to Jackson Davenport."

That ended the conversation with a crash.

23

There was a total eclipse of the sun coming up the next spring, and the path of totality would cross parts of the American East Coast in Maine, North Carolina, and so on.

Look magazine was planning to capitalize on this with an article on total eclipses and asked Larry Ashmead if he could recommend someone to do the article. Larry always recommends me, of course, *whatever* the subject.

On September 18, 1969, I was in New York to see several editors of *Look* on the subject. They did not know me and were uncertain as to my qualifications.

They explained that they wanted an article that would tell their readers what to expect and what to watch for during totality. I nodded my head and said, "I can do that."

One of the editors said, "You understand that we want it scientifically accurate but written so that someone's maiden aunt could understand it."

"That's my specialty," I said, calmly.

They still seemed uncertain and finally one of them said, "How about telling us what a total eclipse of the sun is like?"

I spent some fifteen minutes telling them, and did so with such effectiveness that there wasn't a dry eye in the house.

When I was through, they were thoroughly satisfied and said, "Good! Go home and write an article just like that."

I left with a great sense of relief, for I very much wanted to do the article. It would be my first article for a national picture magazine (a dying field, thanks to television), it would be a simple article to do, and they were paying seventy-five cents a word.

What I had feared was a single question: Dr. Asimov, have you ever *seen* a total eclipse of the sun?

Honesty would have compelled me to answer in the negative, and the whole thing would have been ruined. As it was I wrote the article,

---

7 I'm not using his real name, obviously, but his real name was just as Anglo-Saxon, I assure you.

which I called "The Sun Vanishes,"[8] and it was taken without question. In fact, the editor of *Look* called to thank me personally and to tell me how good the article was and how little editing it required. It appeared in the March 10, 1970, *Look*, just in time for the eclipse, which took place on March 7.

24

On Friday, September 26, Gertrude left for New York, and just as she was leaving, I felt the kidney-stone pains start again. It was the third and longest attack in this cycle, lasting twelve hours—though it was perhaps not as intense as the one on the fifth.

This time, at least, Robyn was with me, and she was entirely comforting and helpful, though she later admitted she was scared to death.[9]

Then on October 5, while I was in New York, I finally passed the kidney stone. It left me just eight weeks after the first attack, and while it was not as large as the first one had been, and while it had not lingered within me as long, it was certainly the most painful one I had ever had.

25

On October 7, 1969, I taped a "To Tell the Truth" program. I was the real Isaac Asimov, while two others joined me as fake ones. We all answered questions designed to elicit which was the real one. I had to answer truthfully (while yielding minimal information) while the fakes could lie to beat the band (while remaining plausible).

Garry Moore was master of ceremonies, while the panelists were Bill Cullen, Orson Bean, Joan Rivers, and Joan Fontaine. Joan Fontaine was the only one who guessed correctly—on the grounds that I wore glasses, and anyone writing so many books would have to wear glasses.

After the show was over, the contestants and the panelists mingled a bit and I got to kiss Joan Fontaine on the cheek.

26

When I got back home, I discovered that Western Publishing had changed their minds and did not wish to publish *Where Do We Go*

[8] See *Today and Tomorrow and—* (Doubleday, 1973).
[9] When Gertrude returned, she had Lee Gould with her, the girl who was with us on the original blind date, twenty-seven years before. Lee was now separated from Joe.

From Here?, the anthology of science-fiction stories intended for science teaching.

I was puzzled, since it had been their idea in the first place. I called them and asked what the objection was. I was told that there was some question as to how it might be promoted.

"What's the problem?" I said. "Just make sure that my name, correctly spelled, is on the book jacket in large, clear type."

They didn't feel that would be sufficient, so I said, rather impatiently, "Very well, then send me a letter in which I am given all rights to the anthology and you can forget it."

I then sat down at once and wrote a letter to Larry, described the anthology, and asked if he would be interested. Of course, he was, and another book that started somewhere else ended with Doubleday—one more book that did well with Doubleday, too.

30

Two Books for Each Year

1

In the single month of October 1969, no less than five books of mine were published. The first was *Nightfall and Other Stories*. It was my ninety-eighth book, and since I was still forty-nine years old, it meant I had now published two books for each year I had lived.

Then came *Asimov's Guide to the Bible: The New Testament*. I thought rather sadly that my fears about my father's reaction to it had been needless. He had not lived long enough to see it.

And then, on October 16, 1969,[1] my hundredth book, *Opus 100*, was published. It had taken me just thirteen years (early 1950 to early 1963) to publish my first fifty books, and not quite seven years (early 1963 to late 1969) to publish the next fifty.

My father had not quite lived to see the day; he had only lived to see me publish ninety-seven books; but my mother was still alive. I continued sending her books as they were published, for she maintained the family library. She left much of it with my brother, but she took the later ones to her hotel room in Long Beach and she insisted on receiving the new ones as they came out.

2

On the evening of October 16, Houghton Mifflin threw a cocktail party in honor of *Opus 100*, one that was even more elaborate than that which Basic Books had given for *The New Intelligent Man's Guide to Science* four years before.

It was now the turn of all our Boston friends to attend, and all did —as well as some from New York. Hilarity was unconfined, and not the least delightful aspect of the evening was that Austin was able to announce that *Opus 100* had sold four thousand copies as of publication date and had earned back its fifteen-hundred-dollar advance plus nine

---

[1] On that same day the New York Mets won the 1969 World Series. I was by no means any longer a baseball fan, but the Mets did rouse in my heart a small echo of the vast love for the Giants that had existed there three decades before, and I felt it was an appropriate concatenation of events.

hundred dollars over—which wasn't bad for a book that was not much more than snippets of this and that.

Afterward, the Houghton Mifflin contingent took Gertrude, Robyn, and me to a magnificent Locke-Ober dinner, which I had trouble eating in view of how well I had done myself on the mountains of *hors d'oeuvres* at the cocktail party.[2]

3

I finally completed the revision of *Asimov's Biographical Encyclopedia of Science and Technology* after having worked on it, on and off, for nearly a year. That was October 18.

My pleasure that day was muted, however, by the appearance of Israel Shenker's interview with me on the first page, second section, of the New York *Times*. That sounds great, but it was based on the July 28 interview when I was waiting for my typewriters to be fixed. As a result, my complaints about IBM were featured.

This disturbed me, for I had no real complaints about IBM. That July 28 had been the only time when a repairman hadn't been at work double-quick, and the reason for the delay in that case was understandable. I fired off a letter to the *Times* explaining this, but they never printed it.

The next day, however (a Sunday!), I got a very perturbed phone call from the regional director of IBM asking me what had gone wrong, and why I had been so disturbed. I explained and sent him the carbon of my letter to the *Times* and I'm sure he felt better as a result.

I had not learned at that time (nor have I learned since) to be cautious of what I say to reporters.

4

On October 23, I was on Boston's local TV outlet of the Columbia Broadcasting System to be interviewed in connection with *Opus 100*. Sam Levenson was also present and I met him for the first time.

Meeting him had significance to me. My style of speaking and my kind of humor were often compared, by those who heard me, to this or that Jewish comedian—Jackie Mason, for instance. More frequently

[2] Not long after that, Houghton Mifflin and Doubleday ran a joint advertisement in the Sunday *Times* Book Review Section pushing *Opus 100* and Doubleday's new book *The Solar System and Back*. I was told it was the first time in history that two competing publishing houses had published a joint advertisement and that it came about only because I was so personally popular with both houses.

mentioned than everyone else put together, however, was Sam Levenson. I wasn't entirely overwhelmed with the comparison, though; I like to think I'm one of a kind.

Sam Levenson seemed to be having an off day that time. At least he told a joke that got no laugh at all and he was visibly irked. Since I was writing my book on humor at the time, I was quite certain I saw where he had made the mistake, though, of course, I didn't say anything.

We were on together, and the conversation turned to the Moon landing. Levenson said to me, "You've heard of the Israeli astronauts, of course?"

That was my cue to say "No" so that Levenson could tell the joke, but still thinking of his mistake in the earlier joke and unwilling to hear him mangle another, I said, "Yes, I heard it," in a flat, declaratory way that signaled the end of that topic.

Annoyed, he said, "All right, then, *you* tell it." The ball was suddenly and unexpectedly in my court. (Served me right, of course.)

I said:

"An Israeli and an American were discussing the recent landing on the Moon by Armstrong and Aldrin. The Israeli said, 'That was all very well, but not very spectacular. We Israelis are going to launch an expedition that will place astronauts on the Sun.'

"The American said, 'Are you crazy? On the Sun? How will the astronauts withstand the light? the heat? the radiation?'

"The Israeli said, 'Don't be a fool. We'll send them at night.'"

It got a perfectly satisfactory laugh.

5

A gentleman named Jules Power was after me to do a TV special, something that so far had been completely outside my purview. He insisted, however, on showing me the films of insect (and other) microphotography which would make up the special. I thought they were very beautiful and effective and allowed myself to be persuaded. On October 24, I began the job.

It wasn't difficult from the standpoint of sheer writing, but it was humiliating. In television, the picture comes first, and the writer is its slave.

So though I did the job and the special ("The Invisible World") was eventually on television, was replayed several times, and earned me a satisfactory amount, I did not enjoy it and did not look for ways to repeat the experience.

6

Toward the end of the month of October, Robyn came back from school with a coal-black kitten, which she said she had rescued, by main force, from other kids who were "torturing it."[3]

Gertrude and I had not had a cat since Putschikl of sainted memory, twenty-one years before, and, given David's allergy to cats, it didn't seem we could ever have one. But David was away at his school and we could keep it a little while anyway, so Gertrude and I both fell all over ourselves to pat the little thing and feed it and make much of it.

The kitten was grateful and adopted us at once and we were perfectly willing to be adopted. By November 3, I took it to the vet and had him examined and given the necessary shots, so it was clear we intended to keep him.

Robyn named him "Satan," and that name he kept. I thought that a thoroughly black cat (even the vibrissae were black) would be uninteresting, but that proved not to be so. In the end, we found black to be so beautiful that we were sorry for people who owned cats whose pristine blackness was in any way interrupted.

(When David visited, we had to keep him supplied with antihistamines, and the cat had to be kept away from him and from his room as much as possible.)

7

On November 10, I finally finished *Asimov's Guide to Shakespeare*, just one and a half years after I had begun writing the first experimental section on *Richard II*. It was six hundred thousand words long and I knew it would have to be published in two volumes. I planned to have one volume treat of the plays with some connection to English history, from *King Lear* to *Henry VIII* and the other treat of all the remaining plays.

Then the next day I wrote *ABC's of the Ocean*, all of it in one day.

8

One other piece of writing obtruded itself.

I have always been a mystery fan since the days of "The Shadow"

[3] Later on, we grilled Robyn thoroughly and discovered that by "torturing it" she had meant that the kids at school were fighting each other for the privilege of playing with the kitten and were trying to snatch it from each other.

back in the 1930s, and I read *Ellery Queen's Mystery Magazine* regularly.

EQMM routinely ran stories by never-before-published writers, and I always read them with chagrin since it bothered me that they managed to make it while I never did. The few times I had submitted stories to *EQMM* (the last time was "What's in a Name?," fourteen years before) I was rejected.

When reading the new issue on November 12, 1969, I got very pettish, sat down, and dashed off a fifteen-hundred-word short story I called "As Chemist to Chemist" and had it in the mail two hours after I had begun.

It was a delightful story in my opinion, but even so I was astonished when only a week later I got my notice of acceptance. It appeared eventually in the May 1970 *EQMM* under the title of "A Problem in Numbers."

Like *The Death Dealers*, "As Chemist to Chemist" was a straight mystery in which all the characters were chemists and in which the solution hinged on chemistry. I still hadn't made the break from science fiction altogether.

9

On November 13, I went to New York to take in *Asimov's Guide to Shakespeare* and the revised Biographical Encyclopedia to Doubleday, and *ABC's of the Ocean* to Walker & Company.

I then drove on to Philadelphia the next day to attend the Philcon, the regional science-fiction convention of the Philadelphia fans, which is held every November.

On the evening of November 15, as I got out of the elevator at my floor, quite late at night, a large, plump, comfortable-looking, and attractive woman got out of the other elevator and gave me a very warm "Hello."

I was feeling happy, as I usually do at conventions, and gave her just as warm a "Hello" in return.

She said, "Would you like company?"

This time I was a sophisticated man of the world and I knew at once that I was dealing with a prostitute. I was no longer the babe-in-the-woods I was the year before.

I said, pleasantly, "I would love company, but my wife is in my room there."

She said, "Oh heck, why did you bring her?"

I said, "If I had known I was going to meet you, I wouldn't have."

She seemed pleased, and I went on to my wifeless room, perfectly content with the way I had handled it.

10

I still had "Waterclap" in first draft. The rejection by the movie studio did not bother me and it had been waiting for six weeks only because I had other things to do. On November 26, however, I finally revised it and began to put it in final form.

The next time I was in New York, on December 3, I submitted it to *Galaxy*, which now had a new editor. Fred Pohl had been replaced by Ejlar Jakobsson, though Judy-Lynn remained as managing editor.

Jakobsson read it, liked it, and accepted it at once. It eventually appeared in the May 1970 *If*.[4]

11

In a way, some acceptances are worse than rejections.

A newspaper syndicate asked me to do an article on how one goes about writing a hundred books. (A hundred books makes you much more of a curiosity than ninety-nine does.)

But how do I describe the method? I do it because I love to write and I know how to write, and how can I transfer either the love or the ability from my brain into another?

I proceeded, therefore, to write a humorous article entitled "How to Write a Hundred Books Without Really Trying." The syndicate took the article with minimal hesitation, paid me generously—and then never published it.

Having paid for it, they were within their rights not to publish, but that irritated me more than a rejection would have. With a rejection, I might have sold it elsewhere; this way it was simply buried, and unavailable for subsidiary use such as inclusion in a collection.

12

Robyn was now old enough to have a boyfriend, a shy young man of her own age who apparently was never called anything but "Junior." And she still retained the ability to volley back the conversational ball with strength to spare.

[4] See *The Bicentennial Man and Other Stories*.

One day she came back from school all excited. She jumped up and down and said, "Guess what, Dad? Guess what?"

I said, without looking up from the book I was reading, "You're pregnant."

And my fourteen-year-old daughter calmed down at once, assumed a world-weary pose, and said, "No, I'm not. Junior and I take precautions."

Once again, I was wiped out.

13

In the last week of the year, I attended the AAAS meetings, which were being held in Boston. I gave two talks, one on science fiction and one on the origin of life, both on December 27. It pleased me that both my fictional and nonfictional aspects should thus be recognized.

14

When the year 1969 ended, my publishing mark for the year was eight:

95. *Photosynthesis* (Basic Books)
96. *The Shaping of England* (Houghton Mifflin)
97. *Twentieth Century Discovery* (Doubleday)
98. *Nightfall and Other Stories* (Doubleday)
99. *Asimov's Guide to the Bible: The New Testament* (Doubleday)
100. *Opus 100* (Houghton Mifflin)
101. *ABC's of Space* (Walker)
102. *Great Ideas of Science* (Houghton Mifflin)

15

The year 1970 opened in very unpleasant fashion with the least happy New Year's Eve party I ever attended. The host was a lawyer whom I had always found rather obnoxious. On this occasion, he told a long, involved story about how he had frustrated a streetcar conductor who had tried to get him to put out his cigarette.

When he was all through, I said, "I think your behavior was disgusting. It would have been an act of common decency for a lawyer to obey the law and to put out his cigarette."

Well, that settled the direction of the conversation for the next two hours, during which I stubbornly stuck to my guns and made, I believe, a lifelong enemy. I say "I believe" because I never saw him again and therefore can't tell for sure.

16

I may have been a little on edge because I knew that on the next day, January 2, 1970, I would be fifty years old. Nevertheless, I did not take my fiftieth birthday with nearly the tragic upset with which I had greeted my fortieth, ten years before.

In fact, I was rather in a good humor that day. It was cold but sunny. Gertrude, herself in a good humor, made me an excellent breakfast and we all looked forward to a birthday dinner with the Houghton Mifflin group. This had been arranged at the cocktail party for *Opus 100* back in October, and Austin had been reminding me of it periodically ever since.

We showed up with both children (David was home on vacation) and had an excellent dinner. Just before we ordered dessert, Austin said, "Listen, let's not order dessert here. I know a great place in the neighborhood that has special desserts."

I was enjoying myself greatly and I had no desire to move, but Austin was the host and Gertrude said at once, "That's a great idea!" I couldn't oppose it, therefore.

I got up reluctantly and we all moved out into the cold. I hadn't the faintest idea where he was taking us, especially since we moved into the nearby Boston-Sheraton Hotel, which I knew well, and which had no place, to my knowledge, that featured marvelous desserts.

Austin led us beyond its street-level restaurants and up to the third floor. Could there possibly be a hidden patisserie or something on the third floor that was known only to the *cognoscenti*?

Then Austin opened a door and the first thing I saw was a hugely magnified photograph of my own smiling countenance, and just beyond it I spied Larry Ashmead—in the flesh.

I stopped dead in my tracks with my mouth open and slowly looked about. It was another surprise party, this time organized by Judy-Lynn Benjamin. She had been to the October cocktail party and had arranged it all with Austin, which was why he had been feverishly reminding me of the birthday dinner.

It was my third surprise birthday party and the third time I had been taken utterly by surprise.

The del Reys were there, as was the onetime Futurian, Dick Wilson. Carl and Linda Sagan were there, also Marvin and Gloria Minsky (so that Carl did not fail to point out that I had in the same room with me the two men I conceded were more intelligent than I was). The NESFA group was there, too.

All handed me small presents of inconsequential nature and humorous significance. This included a photograph of Raquel Welch in dishabille sent me by Harlan Ellison, with an inscription on it (purportedly by Raquel) to the effect that she was sending me the photo because she would do *anything* for Harlan.

Lester del Rey made a little speech in which he assured me that fifty was the beginning of the end and that from there on in everything was downhill (he was fifty-five).

As for Judy-Lynn, she bustled about supervising everything and was delighted in the extreme that all had gone so well. She kept saying, "Caught you by surprise, eh, Asimov?"

17

I completed *Constantinople* on January 16. It was a long time writing, much longer than usual for my histories, because so much of my time was spent on the Ginn science series sections. All through 1969, I had kept working on them, never with pleasure.

18

My new Doubleday book, *The Solar System and Back*, had been set for publication, quite deliberately, on January 19. That was the twentieth anniversary of the publication of my first book, *Pebble in the Sky*. As it happened, *The Solar System and Back* was my fortieth Doubleday book, so that the firm had been putting out an average of two books a year by me over those two decades.

Not to be outdone by Houghton Mifflin, Doubleday was going to give a cocktail party in honor of the occasion. Gertrude and I drove to New York on January 19 for the purpose, leaving Robyn home alone, as we now tended to do regularly.

It was a very successful occasion. Larry Ashmead came to our hotel room to escort us to the party. Stanley and Ruth were there, having brought my mother with them. Judy-Lynn was there, of course, and Wendy Weil, the Silverbergs, and so on. The del Reys were not there. They had left, or were about to leave, on an extended vacation down South.

The next day was not so good. After an early-morning stint on the "Today" show in connection with the new book, I hurried back to the hotel, stepped on a manhole cover that was covered by a thin, slick, and invisible layer of ice, and went flying.

I came down hard, and badly banged my left knee. For a while, as I lay there, I thought I had broken it. The only way to test the matter was to try to struggle to my feet, and I found I could manage. I limped, with great difficulty, the five blocks back to the hotel, but I knew I could not have managed that at all if there had been even a hairline fracture.

I therefore (limping steadily) went through all the functions of the day, including two newspaper interviews, a segment of "The David Frost Show," and an after-dinner speech.

On January 21, we drove home, where I began a new history. I returned to ancient times and decided to do one centered about the ancient Hebrew peoples. I called it *The Land of Canaan.*

19

Then came shocking news. On January 29, Robert Silverberg called me. The del Reys, in their travels in the South, were in a bad automobile accident in Virginia the day before. Lester had been hurt but was in good shape. Evelyn, however, had been killed!

It was a dreadful blow. Those of my friends and relatives who, in recent years, had died, had died of disease. But now a young woman (she was only forty-four) had died in a violent accident. What's more, she was a woman with whom I had grown to feel warm friendship over the past few years, whom I considered had given me inspirational help at a crucial moment, and whom I had last seen at my fiftieth-birthday party less than four weeks before and now would never see again.

I worked, anesthetically, that much harder on my books. There was not only the Ginn science series (yes, it was continuing) and *The Land of Canaan* and my jokebook, but I was also revising *The Universe* and working on the television special, "The Unseen World."

20

On February 12, I drove to New York, for I was going to do a segment on "The Dick Cavett Show" the next day.

It worked very well. Seated next to me was a truly beautiful English actress who seemed perfectly natural, and quite unaware she was gorgeous. Her presence buoyed my spirits and I was more nearly myself than I had ever been on television. This had its disadvantages, for I was sitting next to this gorgeous woman, with whom, of course, I was my usual suave self—quite forgetting that millions of people, and my own family, were watching.

At one point, Dick Cavett said, in response to something I had said, "You're quite a romantic, Isaac." He was using the word in its proper meaning, opposing it to "realistic."

I, however, took it up in the popular meaning and leaning toward my fair neighbor, said, "Yes, I am, and talking of romantic, dear, what are you doing tonight after the show?"

Dick said, "Come, come, Isaac, don't get horny on my time."

Everyone laughed.

After the show there was, of course, no romantic interlude involving myself and the actress. I did, however, try to express my appreciation of her beauty and she said, "I think you should meet my mother."

I took that to mean that I ought to tackle women my own age (and, of course, I was undoubtedly older than her mother was). She, however, seeing my face fall and the eager light die in my eyes, realized how I had interpreted her remark.

She threw her arms about me, hugged me tightly, and said, "No, no, I just meant that my mother is more beautiful than I am—even now."

It was easy to forgive her, for she was undoubtedly the *nicest* raving beauty I had ever met.

21

After the taping was over and I had cooled down a bit, it occurred to me that some of my statements on the show might easily be misinterpreted. The show had been only taped, but it would be shown a few hours later that same night. I therefore called Gertrude to try to explain, in advance, what had happened on the show and to assure her that I had just been euphoric.

It didn't help.

After 1969, which had seemed to consist, in retrospect, of one long slide toward divorce, there had been an upturn, a kind of pleasant Indian summer, a glimmering twilight that had lasted six weeks and included my fiftieth birthday.

But then, with that unfortunate Cavett show, everything went to pieces again and the downward slide was reinstated.[5]

On February 18, I had lunch with Stanley, who was in the city on

[5] Robyn was also annoyed with me. She had been watching the show at Junior's house, with his family and, she explained to me with Victorian *hauteur*, she had been extremely embarrassed by my crass behavior.

business, and I discussed my marital problems with him. He was a tower of sympathetic strength, though carefully refraining from taking sides. Since then I have frequently called him when, for one reason or another, I am down in the dumps. He never fails me. He's a good man.

22

February 19, 1970, was Robyn's fifteenth birthday. I had the feeling it might well be the last she would spend with an intact family, and in an agony of guilt I tried to make it a good one for her. I took her into town, where we ate at a fancy restaurant called "The Top of the Hub" at the top of the Prudential skyscraper. We then took in a wax museum and made a tour of various jewelry stores to try to repair an opal ring she had.

On that occasion I gave my last name to a jeweler, who spelled it A S I M O F. I said impatiently, "The last letter is a V, a V."

He changed the last letter, looked at the name, and said, "I see. You spell it the way the writer does."

23

On February 21, Gertrude decided to visit her mother, coming to that decision on rather short notice. I took her to the air terminal and she gave me the impression she might not return. During her absence I worked on my various projects and began What Makes the Sun Shine? for Atlantic Monthly Press.

On the twenty-fourth, when she hadn't returned, I assumed she must be serious and would not. I visited a lawyer and asked him to write her a letter, making the first tentative move toward a divorce. Gertrude, shocked and angered by the letter, returned on the twenty-eighth, but this time I held firm. The downhill slide intensified.

24

I had a lesson in the generation gap on March 1. I took Robyn to see the play Hair.

I hated it. It was incredibly noisy and poorly organized, and the small bit of nudity onstage was clearly intended to make up for its deficiencies.

Robyn, however, loved it, seemed not to mind the noise and, at the end of the play, moved up on the stage (along with some other members of the audience) to dance to the tune of "Let the Sunshine in."

25

On March 5, I went to Philadelphia to give a talk at Chestnut Hill College. It was not till after I got there and found myself inundated in nuns that I discovered it was a Catholic girls' school.

"Oh my goodness," I said blankly.

"What's the matter?" said an elderly nun. "Don't you like Catholic girls?"

"I *love* Catholic girls," I said, "including nuns, but I was all set to give a talk on population. What do I do now?"

"You give it," said the nun, firmly. "We can use it."

I took her at her word, and gave a rousing talk on the dangers of overpopulation and on the necessity of lowering the birth rate. It was to an overflow crowd (with some people sitting on the stage because there was no other room), and the talk was enthusiastically received.

26

I was putting in most of my work on the jokebook now, which was to be called *Isaac Asimov's Treasury of Humor*. It meant being funny and lighthearted at the typewriter while my personal life was steadily darkening, but this is not as inappropriate as it sounds. It was the escape to the typewriter that made life bearable.

On March 14, I drove to New York to attend the SFWA awards dinner, but that turned out badly, too. The dinner was terrible, and the service was worse. Carl Sagan, who was guest of honor, found that the slide projector would not work, and that made it impossible for him to give his talk effectively. Nor was my own talk particularly good.

27

I was inundated with speaking engagements that spring. On two successive days, March 17 and 18, 1970, I gave talks in the Providence/Fall River area. I took David with me each time (he was home on vacation), and he enjoyed them both.

I had worked out a variation of my talk on population and tried it out for the first time on the seventeenth, when I spoke at Brown University. It was received so well that I thought I would try it again the next night at Bristol Community College to see if I could polish it further.

During the dinner that preceded that second talk, I noticed that David was talking animatedly with the people on either side. This was gratifying, for he tended to be withdrawn, and I found it pleasant to have him participating in the social whirl. I listened to find out what it was that had fired his interest so, and discovered that he was giving everyone within earshot a play-by-play account of the talk he had heard me give the night before. Naturally, it had never occurred to me to tell him I was giving the same talk on this night as well.

28

The Boskone was held on March 28, and it was my first opportunity to see Lester del Rey since Evelyn's death. He was clearly not quite himself yet, but Judy-Lynn hovered about him to make sure things were as comfortable for him as possible.

On the twenty-ninth there was an eight-inch snowfall, which broke up the convention and scattered everyone into a panicky homeward journey. Lester and Judy-Lynn were driving to New York together and I was under considerable tension when I couldn't reach them in New York that evening. The weather, however, had forced them to stay on the road overnight and they didn't get back (quite safely, though) till the next day.

29

I drove to New York on April 8 and took the manuscript for *Where Do We Go From Here?* to Doubleday. I also brought in a new *F & SF* essay collection, the eighth, called *The Stars in Their Courses*.

I was part of a panel arranged by Diane Cleaver of Doubleday. The idea of the panel was to work out some standardized future background around which a number of writers could do stories. I didn't see how it could possibly work, but I was willing to collaborate on the chance that I was wrong.

On the morning of the ninth, when we got together to begin the day's work, it turned out that one of the panelists, at the last minute, could not come, having stayed up all night with a sick child.

Poor Diane was in tears and, racking my brain, I said, "Let me call Bob Silverberg, Diane."

I called him, explained the emergency, and he got ready at once and came down from his home in the Bronx. He was a tower of strength and the best panelist by far. The panel didn't accomplish anything but at least Diane was happy.

One of the panelists, by the way, was Kurt Vonnegut, whom I now met for the first time. Over a glass of beer that evening (I had ginger ale) he said to me, "How does it feel to know everything?"

I said, "I only know how it feels to have the reputation of knowing everything. Uneasy."

30

On April 14, I lectured at Salem State College and finally managed to get a payment larger than the check I had once received from Smith, Kline & French. My fee on this occasion was $1,275, and I had grown blasé enough to pocket it without a qualm.[6]

On April 19, I gave my population talk to World Federalists in Wilmington, Delaware. I took time out to visit some world-renowned gardens not many miles away, and even though a very light rain started falling, I enjoyed them.

Natural wonders do not usually appeal to me, but I remembered Janet Jeppson's pleasure in such things in New England the previous August, and the beauty of lawns, trees, and flowers had a soothing effect on me, at this time when life at home was so hard.

The next day, I drove to Pennsylvania State College, where I was to give a talk to help celebrate "Earth Day." Phil Klass, who was a professor at the school, introduced me. He spoke for fifteen minutes and was very funny indeed—to my alarm. How would I match him? And he was speaking for nothing, while I was charging four figures. As his talk went on, my spirits grew lower and lower.

Finally he ended with a peroration that went something like this: "But don't let me give you the idea that Isaac Asimov is a Renaissance man who has done everything. There are many things he has not done. For instance, he has never sung *Rigoletto* at the Metropolitan Opera."

I cheered up at once. I walked on to the stage to a polite patter of applause that clearly indicated me to be an anticlimax. I faced the audience and, without warning, sang "Bella Figlia del'amore . . . ," launching into the Quartette from *Rigoletto* in as dulcet a tenor as I could manage. With that I got a bigger laugh than any Phil had had—one

---

[6] Also on this day, I took poor Satan to the vet to be castrated. The difficulty was that he was beginning to spray his home territory to warn off competing cats, and the odor warned *us* off.

that he had unwittingly planted for me, of course—and I was home safe.

The next day I gave my third talk of the trip, at Drexel University in Philadelphia, and there I met, once again, Hartley Bowen of Navy Yard days, along with his grown son.

31

The IBM house magazine *Think* wanted me to write a science-fiction story for them. They even had the gimmick. They gave me a J. B. Priestley quote that went, "Between midnight and dawn, when sleep will not come and all the old wounds begin to ache, I often have a nightmare vision of a future world in which there are billions of people, all numbered and registered, with not a gleam of genius anywhere, not an original mind, a rich personality, on the whole packed globe."

Think asked me to use that quotation as the basis for a story and, on April 26, I finally got around to writing a story I called "2430 A.D."

I used that date because I had calculated that at the present rate of population growth, the world would by that year (assuming no disaster) be one globe-girdling Manhattan, stretching its skyscrapers-without-end over land and sea alike.

To my surprise, *Think* sent the story back, explaining that they had meant me to refute the quotation, not support it. They had never *said* so, however. Ordinarily, I would have written a stiff letter and told them to go to Hades, but times were too hard for me now to work up emotional intensity in new directions. I told them I would try, but I couldn't get to it right away.

32

On May 18, I gave a talk to a group of people meeting at a new posh motel that had been built only about a mile from our house. The master of ceremonies asked if he might read from our correspondence in introducing me. I shrugged and said he might. I didn't have the faintest memory of what was in the correspondence, but assumed it contained nothing disgraceful.

Well, it did, in a way. The man in charge of the lecture arrangements had written me saying that the fee I asked for was twice what they usually paid, and I had answered that I was twice as good as anyone else they could get—so they agreed to the fee.

Now I sat there, while my introducer read all this and I could watch the audience turn grim as they realized they were being soaked to pay for some joker who claimed to be twice as good as the next guy.

I had then to get up and prove my contention to what was now a hostile audience. I quickly switched to my Mendel speech, which had never failed me, and gave it as rousingly as I could. It was quite obvious by the time I was through that it had not failed me this time either, and that I had proved my point.

33

On May 31, 1970, I gave my second commencement address; this one at Bridgewater State College in Bridgewater, Massachusetts. On this occasion I received my first honorary degree, that of Doctor of Science.

PART
IV

Breakup and Rebirth

31

Back to New York

1

Divorce had come close enough to make it seem advisable to me to find an apartment for myself, one small enough for me to handle and yet large enough to hold my library.

I found such an apartment in Wellesley, in the same development in which Jim Ashley of Ginn & Company lived. Not only did the apartment seem right, but also Jim would be around to serve as a friend and companion in the hard period of adjustment—and as a guide to bachelor living. Furthermore, I would be no more than five miles from the house, so that I could see the kids and be available for emergencies.

On June 8, however, the lawyers met and it became clear that Gertrude would allow only a separation and that on hard terms. I had to change my plans about the Wellesley apartment and consider a more drastic move.

I could not get a divorce in Massachusetts against Gertrude's opposition without a messy court trial in which I alleged cruel and inhuman treatment—and I wouldn't do that.

I would have to go to another state where no-fault proceedings could be instituted and where I could set up a legitimate residency. California and New York were the only two possibilities and, of the two, I chose New York. New York would be closer to my children; it was the place I was brought up; it was where all my major publishers (except Houghton Mifflin) were based.

I began making plans for the move and called the various people I knew in New York for suggestions as to where I might live. Among them, I called Janet Jeppson. Janet, with her usual efficiency, tackled the problem promptly and sent me a list of suggestions.

On June 12, I drove to New York to look at the various possibilities, and of them, the Oliver Cromwell Hotel on West Seventy-second Street seemed best. It was rather decayed, but was still quite presentable, and it had a coffee shop where I could have light meals. They offered me two possible apartments, one on the twenty-second floor, and one on the third. The third floor seemed preferable to me, since it was the darker of the two and I like to work under artificial light.

There were two rooms so that I could keep the arrangement as in my attic, and an air conditioner could be installed in one of them. There were, in addition, a bathroom, a kitchenette, and ample closet space for a bachelor. I put down a month's deposit to begin on July 1, then drove home. On June 13, I finished *Isaac Asimov's Treasury of Humor*.

2

Things went rapidly thereafter. At 8:30 A.M. on July 3, 1970, the movers came and took out my bookcases, my books, my desk, and my filing cabinets, and by 2:00 P.M. they drove off. I put my typewriters, my manuscripts in progress, and a variety of other materials that I either would not trust to the movers or wanted available for immediate use, into my car.

Then I waited. Gertrude was off shopping and I did not want to sneak away in her absence and have her come back to an empty house. She returned and I said good-bye. I had already said good-bye to Robyn (and assured her that the separation did not include her, and that I would stay her father my whole life), and I even managed to find Satan and say good-bye to him. As for David, he had been visiting us, and I was taking him back to the school en route to New York.

And so I left, twenty-eight years and four months after I had met Gertrude and just twenty-five days short of our twenty-eighth anniversary.

I dropped David off at his school and then drove on to New York. I was going to be a New Yorker again after twenty-one years in Boston and its suburbs.

3

I pulled up at the Cromwell Hotel and found Janet waiting for me. She helped me unload and I found that she had, of her own accord, filled my kitchenette with cutlery, some pots and pans, and some staples such as coffee and canned goods.

How badly I needed that sign that someone cared!

It didn't take us long to unload, but when we came down, there was a ticket on my car for twenty-five dollars for illegal parking. I would have to do something about that, but meanwhile I put my car away in a garage and then . . .

What?

It was toward evening and my two rooms were empty except for the hotel furniture—a couch and some chairs in one room, two beds and two bureaus in the other. I had my typewriters and paper and manuscripts, but my library would not be there for a week, very likely, and I wasn't sure I could type in a strange place, laden down, as I was, with the guilt and gloom of having left my wife and children. What's more, it was the Fourth of July weekend and I couldn't look forward to visits to the familiar environs of Doubleday, Walker, Basic Books, or any of the rest.

Then Janet said, rather hesitatingly, as though afraid she might be misinterpreted, "You know, my apartment isn't far away and you're perfectly welcome to spend time there over the weekend, if it gets too lonely for you out here."

It was a good-hearted offer and I didn't even try to pretend I was worried about being a bother to her. I accepted.

The first night in the hotel was a more frightening time than any I had spent since my second night in the Army, twenty-five years before, but on the Fourth, I took Janet at her word, and visited her as early as I dared. We walked about the neighborhood, spent some time in Central Park, and talked. The next day she drove me up to Westchester, and we visited her mother's house (her mother was not there at the time) and drove about, sight-seeing. It was a device to help fill my mind with something other than fright.

By Monday, the sixth, the weekend was over and Janet had to go back to work (her office was in her apartment), but then so could I. I invited Larry Ashmead to dinner, then brought him to my new apartment. It was nothing much, but it was home.

It had its drawbacks. The beds were anything but comfortable, and the sound of imperfect air conditioners reverberated through the bordering alleys and made any chance of sleep marginal even with earplugs.

On July 8, I received my first mail at the Cromwell and I finally got back to work. It was impossible to work on my large projects without my library, but there was the matter of the science-fiction story for *Think*. Since they had rejected my story "2430 A.D.," in which I supported Priestley's quotation of the nightmare world of the future, I wrote "The Greatest Asset," which looked at the other, optimistic side of the coin. I mailed that to *Think* on the ninth.

That day, also, I visited Walker in the morning and Judy-Lynn Benjamin in the evening. Judy-Lynn, as it happened, had an apartment within walking distance of the Cromwell.

Finally, on the tenth, the movers arrived and my furniture and library were unloaded. Naturally, it was unloaded into the middle of the rooms, with the books all in cardboard cartons so that my library was there only potentially. By Sunday, July 12, however, enough of it was unpacked and in order so that I could really get to work if I wanted to.

Fortunately, I didn't have to plunge into deep water at once. I had the page proofs of *Asimov's Guide to Shakespeare*, and that meant I would have several days of work at indexing—undemanding work that I loved.

The index was completed, for Volume I at least, on July 16, so I took it in that day to Doubleday and had lunch with Larry. That afternoon, Janet drove me out to Jones Beach, where we saw a showing of *The Sound of Music* in the open. In the cast was Bruce Bennetts, the handsome young son of Chaucy, Janet's cousin.

4

On July 17, David arrived from his school to visit me, anxious, I was sure, to reassure himself that he still had a father. I showed him my Cromwell apartment, and that evening I took him with me to a meeting of the Trap Door Spiders.

It was the third meeting I had attended as guest, and this time it was Lin Carter (a prolific writer of science fiction and fantasy) who invited me. It was great and David and I both enjoyed ourselves.

Once again, I was invited to join the Trap Door Spiders and now, since I lived in New York and could easily attend meetings, there was no reason for me to refuse. I joined the club with great satisfaction.

The next day I drove David to Long Beach and we both had lunch with my mother. She was terribly glad to see me and terribly disturbed to hear the news of my separation. On the nineteenth, David returned to school.

5

By July 22, the index to the second volume of *Asimov's Guide to Shakespeare* was done, but I received some upsetting news, too. *Think* rejected "The Greatest Asset" and, what was worse, decided to take "2430 A.D."[1] after all. It was as though "The Greatest Asset" was so bad that it made "2430 A.D." look good by contrast.

What bothered me was this:

Whenever there is some radical change in my way of life, I always

1 See *Buy Jupiter and Other Stories*.

fear that it might reflect itself in my writing; that I might find myself unable to write, or, at any rate, be unable to write anything salable.

As it happened, "The Greatest Asset" was the very first piece of writing I had done in New York and it had been rejected in favor of something I had written in Newton.

I called John Campbell, therefore, and made a date with him for July 27. I saw him then and it was *still* like the old days. It was a new office, but Campbell was still Campbell, delighted as ever to see me. Working for him was Katherine Tarrant still.

I told him the full story of "The Greatest Asset" and asked him if, under the circumstances, he wanted to see it.

He said, in true Campbellesque fashion, "*Think* has its own needs and its own judgments, and I have mine. Let me see it."

He took a week or so, and then accepted "The Greatest Asset."[2] Once more, Campbell had been of important aid to me. My first piece of writing in New York had been sold and my superstitious fears were allayed.

It helped me in my work on a number of small items—an article for the *Reader's Digest Almanac*, an Introduction to a collection of old stories (nineteenth century and before) about reaching the Moon, and so on. These all sold in the end, and my regular columns for *F & SF* and *Science Digest* didn't miss a beat. There really was nothing to worry about.

6

August 4, 1970, was the first anniversary of my father's death, and the year had brought vast changes, but life went on.

Months before, I had suggested to Mary K. that I do a true sequel to *Words of Science*, one to be called *More Words of Science*, and I had actually done an experimental one-page essay for the book on the evening before I left Newton (the last bit of writing I did in the house) on the word "ablation." Now, in the Cromwell, I began work in earnest, and by August 8, when I stopped to draw breath, I had done ninety-three words, each involving a one-page essay.

7

My move to New York had thrown my lecture schedule into disarray. My lawyer, Don Laventhal, had strongly advised me to stay out of Massachusetts for fear of legal complications. This meant I had to can-

[2] See *Buy Jupiter and Other Stories.*

cel some talks I had already agreed to give (notably another session at Brandeis in July and August), but whenever possible I promised to replace the canceled talk with another at a later period, which I would give without charge.

On August 9, I was able to travel on my first lecture trip to somewhere that was not in Massachusetts. Since my own car refused to start (it needed a new starter, it turned out), Janet drove me to Hartford, and that evening she and I took a tour through Mark Twain's house in Hartford. It was like a re-creation of that happy time in New England the previous August. My heart melted with joy at the thought that I could be with Janet any time I wanted to (when she wasn't seeing patients).

The next day I talked at the University of Hartford and it went over very well.

Being with Janet so much, finding it so easy to make her happy, finding it so easy to be happy with her—all of that meant I was falling in love with her (and she with me). Little by little, as time went on, I spent more and more of my nonworking time in her apartment until finally I moved into her apartment (to all intents and purposes) and used the Cromwell only as a working office.

8

Austin sent back the manuscript of *Isaac Asimov's Treasury of Humor* on August 13. He disapproved of my arrangement, or, rather, lack of it. I had written the jokes as they occurred to me and he wanted me to divide them up into a number of categories and had even done some of the rearranging to show me what he meant.

It meant that the commentary would have to be rewritten and that would take several months, but I had to admit that the suggestion was an improvement, and I did want to put out a good book.

9

I taped a David Frost segment on August 19. It was my third with him. This time, Frost asked me at one point if I could play a musical instrument.

"No," I said, regretfully,[3] "but I've taught myself to tap out tunes on the piano with one finger."

"Would you like to be able to play a piano on television?"

[3] I often say there are two things I regret not having learned as a youngster: how to speak Russian, and how to play some musical instrument.

"Yes," I said eagerly, for I thought they would now hook up some electronic marvel whereby I would fake fiddling with the piano keys while somehow the beautiful strains of the "Moonlight Sonata" would sound out.

Not so. During the commercial, they dragged out a piano and when the cameras went on again, Frost said, "Go ahead. Tap out a tune with one finger."

Talk about stage fright! I managed to tap out "Dancing Cheek to Cheek" with trembling fingers and it was only after it was all over that I realized I might just as well have sung it, too. Then I could say that I had sung on television as well as played.

10

The twenty-eighth World Science Fiction convention, in 1970, was being held in Heidelberg—the first time ever in a non-English-speaking country. I couldn't go, of course, but a kind of stay-at-home convention was being held in Toronto, and I had agreed to serve as co-guest of honor along with Anne McCaffrey.

David, having gone to St. Louis the year before, wanted very much to go to another convention. He arrived in New York on August 20, which happened to be his nineteenth birthday. He (and also Anne McCaffrey's eighteen-year-old son) went with me to Toronto, where David had a room for himself and was on his own.

I met Judy Merril there for the first time in ten years. She had gone to Toronto some years back and meant to reside there permanently. She was a grandmother now.

It was also a pleasure to be with Anne McCaffrey and we, of course, had our usual singing contest with the usual result. I lost. We were back home on the twenty-fourth.

11

On September 4, Janet and I went to downtown New York, where, on Fourth Avenue, there were numerous secondhand bookstores. We browsed through them endlessly and I came up with a secondhand Modern Library edition of Lord Byron's *Don Juan.*

I had read the first couple of cantos in college, but I had never read the whole thing (or at least the sixteen cantos Byron had written —he never finished it). It struck me that since I could rarely sleep through the night at the Cromwell, I could use the time to read *Don Juan.* Who knows? It might put me to sleep.

I tried it that very night, and only got through the Dedication and into a few verses of the first canto before I realized that nobody could possibly get the full flavor of the poem without understanding all the allusions Byron was constantly making to current affairs, to recent history, and to classic learning.

I remembered Martin Gardner's recommendation, and fell into an absolute lust to annotate *Don Juan*.

There was no rush, of course, since I still had a great deal of work on the revision of *Isaac Asimov's Treasury of Humor* and in the doing of *More Words of Science*.

I kept it in mind, though. Never fear.

12

September 5, 1970, was my mother's seventy-fifth birthday. I drove out to Stanley's place. He had brought my mother there, and all three of us drove out into the depths of Long Island to the site of my father's grave.

Stanley had arranged for a stone to be put up there on the anniversary of the death. On one half it said "Judah Asimov, 1896–1969"; on the other side, "Anna Rachel Asimov, 1895–   ."

I thought it rather grisly to have a grave waiting and the entire inscription already made with only a ghostly hand raised on high and waiting for the final chipping. It didn't affect my mother that way, though. She simply wept and said that she was only waiting to be laid to rest at his side.

13

For the first time, on September 7, Janet and I established a social relationship, together, with someone who was primarily a friend of hers rather than of mine.

This involved Lorna Levant, the second daughter of Oscar Levant. Lorna had worked with Chaucy for a time, which was how Janet had gotten to know her. Lorna was now moving into a small apartment half a block from the Cromwell. Janet helped her move, as she had helped me two months before, and that night we took Lorna to dinner.

14

On September 10, I had lunch with Larry Ashmead and I advanced my notion of annotating *Don Juan*, explaining that it was the greatest comic epic in the English language, and perhaps in any language, and that its wealth of contemporary and classical allusion, which had made it all the funnier to an educated man of the 1820s, was lost on us a century and a half later.

Larry put it up to the editorial board and in due time I heard that they were willing to let me go ahead. In fact, I couldn't help but notice on Larry's desk a comment (handwritten) by Betty Prashker, one of the senior editors. All it said in connection with the *Don Juan* annotation was, "Oh let Isaac have his fun."

Little things like that make it clear why I have always loved Doubleday.

15

I had a haircut on September 16. In itself, that was nothing unusual. I have had hundreds of professional haircuts in my lifetime. That one, however, was my last.

My sideburns were doing fine, except that there was an annoying touch of gray at their upper boundary,[4] and now I let my hair grow, too. After this, my hair grew down thickly about to the middle of my neck, in waves. Left to myself I would have let it grow indefinitely, but Janet gets itchier as it grows longer and, eventually, she insists on cutting it—and is very good at it.

There continued to be no sign of baldness after the fashion of my father and brother, although I must admit that in front-center, my hair is not as thick as it once was.

16

On the evening of September 16, Janet and I had dinner at the Russian Tea Room with members of her family. Chaucy Bennetts was there and with her was her married daughter, Leslie. Leslie was twenty-one years old, tall, blond, beautiful, *zaftig*, and intelligent. Janet had described her to me as beautiful, and she was right. In fact, Leslie seemed to me to be a somewhat larger version of Robyn.

17

On September 18, I went down to the traffic court in the morning to discuss the matter of the twenty-five-dollar ticket I had received im-

[4] That gray did not go away, but spread until, eventually, my sideburns were nearly all white a few years later.

mediately upon my arrival in New York, eleven weeks before. I explained it had been a temporary park in an unloading zone, but that I was unloading with the permission of the hotel; that I was moving in at that very moment and couldn't take the car to the garage till it was emptied.

The person hearing my case admitted my innocence and, in honor of that innocence, reduced the fine to ten dollars—that being the going payment for the crime of being innocent. I felt it was useless to attempt more and paid the ten dollars.

18

There was another family day on September 19. Janet drove me to her mother's house in Westchester again, and this time her mother, Rae, was there. I had seen her at her son's graduation, nine years before, and she remembered the occasion perfectly.

Rae was shorter than Janet, but resembled her quite a bit in facial appearance. Rae was gentle and ladylike, and felt bound to tell me that she disapproved of divorce and was sorry for Gertrude. I told her quite honestly that I disapproved of divorce, and that I was sorry for Gertrude, too, and even more for my children.

Chaucy dropped in and with her this time was her husband, Leslie.[5] He was rather elderly and very quiet, a gentle soul with a heart of gold who reminded me, a bit, of Henry Blugerman.

That evening we were back in New York, and Stanley and Ruth visited. They met Janet for the first time and all four of us had a long conversation in my apartment after dinner. When we left to walk Stan and Ruth to where their car was parked, Stan lagged behind with me to say in a low voice, "Where did you find her? She's a pearl."

Well, I knew *that*.

19

I finally had the courage on September 21 to call West Newton and ask to speak to Robyn. I had seen David on two different occasions but had not seen Robyn since I had left West Newton. It had been two months since I had spoken to her.

She sounded well, and friendly, and I assured her that I would take

[5] The same name for father and daughter is undoubtedly a cause of great confusion. Chaucy's original name was Shirley, like her father's, and she had changed it, in part to avoid the confusion—then went on to inflict it on her daughter. I've never quite understood that.

care of her as I always had. From that time on, we remained in constant close touch.

20

Finally I received the advance copies of *Asimov's Guide to Shakespeare* in two volumes, and elaborately boxed. In view of the fact that each volume was some three hundred thousand words long, I felt justified in counting each as a separate book.

They were the first books to be published while I was in New York, though, of course, they had been written in Newton.

When the remainder of my author's copies arrived, I sent a set to Gertrude and one to Mary Blugerman. I had made a verbal agreement that separation, divorce, or whatever, I would keep sending each a copy of each of my books.

21

On September 27, Janet and I visited Judy-Lynn Benjamin. Lester del Rey was visiting, too, and it seemed to me that Judy-Lynn was as effective in consoling Lester in his travail as Janet was in consoling me in mine. From that day forward, I was more or less sure that Lester and Judy-Lynn would eventually marry.

And as though to balance that, I got the news that Ben and Rosa Bova were splitting up.

22

There was the usual amount of editorial splitting up, too. Ed Burlingame was no longer editor-in-chief at Walker, but had moved over to Lippincott. We had lunch on October 5. Ed had carried me from New American Library to Walker and seemed quite ready to carry me to Lippincott as well, but I was drowned in work and was in no position to take on another book at the moment.

After all, I was working on *The Land of Canaan* and on *More Words of Science* and on the revision of *Isaac Asimov's Treasury of Humor* and was beginning *Asimov's Annotated Don Juan*.

There was no question that the move to New York was inhibiting my writing. Quite the reverse. Writing was moving along more quickly than ever and would keep on doing so, partly because various publishers were closer to me and partly because the very atmosphere of New York was more stimulating.

23

Larry Ashmead called me on the evening of October 9. There was a hitch, he said, in the *Don Juan* book. My heart sank—I was enjoying it so much that I didn't want to be made to stop.

Apparently, the hitch was that the Doubleday editorial board had decided to make it a large, fancy, expensively illustrated and boxed book.

I was appalled. "You'll lose your shirt," I said. I had *told* them I didn't expect the book to sell, and had begged them to do it on the cheapest possible paper with the cheapest possible binding.

"Just the same, that's how they want to do it," said Larry. "The hitch is they can only give you a small advance."

I said, promptly, "I don't care if they don't give me any advance at all, as long as they let me do it."

But they did give me an advance.

24

Janet and I took the Metroliner to Washington on October 18. We bought seats in the club car and it was quite luxurious having a private swivel chair to one's self with a little table to write on. In time to come, however, we learned that ordinary coach was better. We could then sit together, rather than separately. Besides, half the club car always permitted smoking, whereas many coaches were completely non-smoking.[6]

The occasion for the trip was a speech I was to give at the twenty-fifth graduating class of Montgomery Community College. The only place large enough to hold the festivities was Washington Cathedral. The people who were in charge of us, Dr. and Mrs. Miller, with their young daughter, Lesley, showed us through the cathedral, hosted us at a very pleasant dinner, and then gave us an auto tour through Washington after dark. Janet loved it all and somehow, seeing everything through her eyes rather than my own, made it all sharper, clearer, and more beautiful to me.

The next morning, I gave my talk from the high pulpit in the ca-

[6] Janet didn't smoke and was as opposed to smoking as I was. I had had enough cigarette smoke at home for a lifetime, and once in the Cromwell I refused to allow anyone to smoke within the premises of my apartment. I persuaded Janet to forbid smoking in her office, too. Some of her patients were petulant about it, but they all gave in.

thedral and, apparently, the solemnity of the surroundings had its effect on me, for I gave a much graver speech than I usually do.

It sometimes happens that after I have given a speech that has been taped, a transcript of it is sent me for editing. I dislike that, for it is intensely embarrassing. No matter how good an extemporaneous speech may be, it becomes full of bad grammar when written down, with incomplete sentences, sudden changes, and backtrackings of subject.

Eventually, though, I received a transcript of my Washington Cathedral speech and I found I didn't have to do a thing to it. "Apparently," I said to Janet, "when I spoke from the high pulpit, God put words into my mouth, and He speaks very good English."[7]

25

There was the first hint of movie interest in *The Caves of Steel* on October 21. My own interest at that was kept under control. I knew the routine—options, and renewal, and talk, and perhaps even a screenplay, and then nothing.

26

In Gettysburg, Pennsylvania, on October 22, Janet and I seized the opportunity to visit a Doubleday printing plant at Hanover. It was fascinating to see how books were made, and how much was involved *after* I had finished the piddling little matter of completing a manuscript.

The personnel came out happily and grouped themselves around me under the impression that I was a famous author, and I loved every minute of it.

The next day I gave two talks at Gettysburg College—my Mendel speech and my population speech—and then we went home through Pennsylvania Dutch country. We stopped at York and Lancaster, visiting old colonial homes in each city, and then ate at the restaurant where, a year and a half before, I had been introduced to sauerkraut.

[7] One of the Trap Door Spiders is Roper Shamhart, an Episcopalian minister. Some years later, he was telling us about the Washington Cathedral as the Vatican of American Episcopalianism and of his visit there on one occasion.
"Did you ever preach from its high pulpit?" I asked.
"Of course not," said Roper.
"I did," I said.
I was going to let it go there, but Roper insisted rather strenuously on an explanation, and I had to give it. I feared he might brain me with his crucifix if I did not.

27

I finished the revision of *Isaac Asimov's Treasury of Humor* on November 1, a year and a half after the trip to the Concord Hotel that started it.

I found I didn't have to mail it, however. I took it down to the offices that Houghton Mifflin maintained in New York, and they had it delivered in a special mail pouch that got it out to Boston at once.

(Doubleday also offered me a pleasant convenience. I no longer had to deliver my papers to Howard Gotlieb at Boston University Library. I took them to Doubleday instead, and Doubleday packaged and mailed them for me. Of course, I missed the delightful lunches I had with Gotlieb on those occasions.)

28

November 3, 1970, was Election Day and, since I had established residence requirements, I could vote. To my intense satisfaction, Nixon was unable to swing either house of Congress into Republican control.

In New York State, however, the Republican senator and his Democratic challenger fought each other to a virtual tie, allowing a third candidate, James Buckley, a hard-line conservative supported by Nixon and Agnew, to sneak in with a plurality, to my great unhappiness.

29

The next day I gave a talk at the Universalist church that was only a short distance northward on Central Park West. Janet and I walked it—but in a driving rain. My shoes and socks were drenched and I had to stand in them for over an hour to give my talk. The result was foregone—my worst cold in nine years.

On that occasion, though, Marcia and her younger son, Richard, were at the talk and it was the occasion for Marcia to meet Janet for the first time.

30

Science fiction surrounded me in New York. I saw Bob and Barbara Silverberg for the first time since I arrived in New York on November 16, and for a while we, the Silverbergs, Judy-Lynn, and Lester made a steady sixsome. On that day, I also saw Ben Bova for the first time since I had come to New York and he confirmed the fact that he was separated and seeking a divorce.

31

On November 22, I drove to Long Beach to see my mother, and this time I took a rather trembling Janet with me. I reminded her that I had come without compunction to meet *her* mother. Janet was afraid, however, that my mother might disapprove of her not being Jewish.

"My father might have," I said, "if he were alive, but my mother won't. You'll see."

My mother didn't. She took an instant liking to Janet (everyone does), and all was well.

32

Then came Thanksgiving on November 26. It was customary for Chaucy Bennetts (an excellent cook—very much along the lines of Mary Blugerman) to give a big family feast on that day, and I was invited. Chaucy and Leslie were there, of course, and young Leslie, too, together with her brother, Bruce, whom I had seen onstage, at a distance, four months before, but whom I now met at close range for the first time.

Leslie's husband, Bill Boggs, was present also; tall, curly-haired, very good-looking, and an aspiring television personality. Add Janet, her mother, and myself, and there were eight people at the feast, all completely happy.

Certainly, I was. It was the first time, somehow, that I felt completely accepted in a family circle in a holiday atmosphere. It gave me an odd feeling of warmth I had never experienced before.

Young Leslie had a youthful Yorkshire terrier whose name was Moose and who was so small and fuzzy that I suspected there was nothing under the fur but a pair of eyes. At one point, when we were watching *Oklahoma!* on television, I threw myself on the floor next to young Leslie, to watch more comfortably. Moose (who adored her mistress, and vice versa), presumably supposing I was attacking Leslie, emitted a startled "woof."

This created a sensation, for Moose had never barked before. Thereafter, of course, having made the discovery it had vocal cords, Moose continued to yap now and then. I never liked to take credit for this.

33

I was slated to give a talk at Rhode Island College on December 2[8] and when we got to Providence at noon, there was none other than Austin Olney waiting at the desk of the Holiday Inn for us to arrive. He knew that I was avoiding Massachusetts, and supposing I wasn't likely to get any closer to Boston for a while, he came down to Providence to meet us.

It was a tremendous pleasure to see him after a five-month hiatus. We had lunch together and he met Janet—for the first time. As I said in my diary, "He was quite taken with Janet, but then, small wonder."

It turned out that Austin, too, was separating from his wife. It was as though it had only taken my own separation to shake all the marriages I knew asunder.

On the way back from Providence the next day, we stopped in Mystic, Connecticut, and looked over some of the old ships there. Janet, who always insisted she was of Viking descent (she is half Swedish, one-quarter Danish, and one-quarter English), is almost quixotically attached to ships of any kind.

34

There was unpleasantness, too. Don Laventhal and Gertrude's lawyer had come to a settlement along lines I privately thought were completely reasonable. Gertrude, however, hired a new lawyer, an aggressive one named Monroe Inker. His first move, on December 10, was to freeze my Houghton Mifflin income, less than a week before my royalty statement was due. I realized, with considerable regret, that I was in for a longer and messier involvement than I had hoped for.

35

I had now become brave enough to have Janet participate in my business functions. I had been afraid that my being seen in public with Janet might give rise to the possibility of accusations of adultery, but Janet said she was not afraid of such accusations. In fact, said Janet, after living forty-four years of as proper and circumspect a life as one could imagine, the thought of being accused of all sorts of immoral actions was rather exciting.

[8] That morning I said to Janet thoughtfully, "This is the 165th anniversary of the Battle of Austerlitz—and nobody cares." For some reason, she thought this was a very funny thing to say, and kept quoting it to everyone.

Thus, on December 14, when Larry had dinner with me again, he had it at Janet's place, and Janet prepared the dinner. It was Janet's first occasion as formal hostess on my behalf.

And the next day, I had lunch with Richard Dempewolff, editor of *Science Digest*, and Janet joined me. For the first time she was with me at a business luncheon.

36

I was working on a second anthology of Hugo-winning stories. The first anthology covered the nine winners over the seven-year period from 1955 to 1961. Since then, the tendency had been for Hugos to be awarded for more and longer stories, and in the seven-year period from 1962 to 1970, there were fifteen prize-winning stories with a total wordage just twice that of the first set.[9] Larry asked me when I was going to prepare the second volume, and I shook my head sadly.

"I've won two Hugos since the first volume, Larry," I said, "so I don't qualify as editor any longer."

"That's silly," said Larry.

"You don't understand. The first volume was in Tim Seldes' day, and I was asked to be editor only because I had never received a Hugo. How can I do a second volume when I have now had Hugos?"

"Why not?" said Larry.

"People might think it was queer."

For that he had an unanswerable argument. "Who cares?" he said.

So that was it. I took in the completed book (at least I took in my various Introductions, plus the front matter and back matter) on December 17. I left it up to Doubleday to get copies of the stories themselves.

Remembering well my experience with the first volume, I was careful to arrange to have Doubleday take care of all the bookkeeping. This was not the usual practice of publishers in connection with anthologies, but Doubleday was as anxious to keep me from wasting time on bookkeeping as I was.

37

David arrived on December 18 for his third visit. He told me he was arriving on a particular train at Grand Central, and I was there waiting for him. The train arrived, but David was not on it. Anxiously, I wondered if he might have missed the train and would come on the

---

[9] I inadvertently left out one of the 1970 winners, so that the second volume contained only fourteen stories.

next one, and only after I had waited for nearly an hour, did it suddenly dawn on me that David wasn't familiar with New York and
might have arrived at Penn Station.

Before chasing down there, I called the Cromwell to ask if by any
chance David had called trying to reach me. He hadn't. He was there
in person, sitting in the lobby and waiting for me. Arriving at Penn Station, indeed, and finding no one there waiting for him, he had made it
to the Cromwell via the subway system, which was pretty good of him
seeing that he was unfamiliar with the routes and that I myself had
lately been lost on it.

32

The Sensuous Dirty Old Man

1

I had another feast at Christmas, this time at Rae's house, with the entire family, as at Thanksgiving. I was a little on edge, though, for Robyn was coming in by bus the next day and I was fearful of missing her, of something going wrong.

Nothing did. She arrived at 3:15 P.M. on December 26, and I was there at the bus station to meet her. I had not seen her in almost half a year and she was as beautiful and as ebullient as ever.

For four days, she and I ate at good restaurants, saw movies, went window shopping (and real shopping), and wandered around the streets of New York City. On Tuesday the twenty-ninth, Larry Ashmead took us both to lunch at Sardi's, where Robyn desperately wanted to see a celebrity, but where we didn't see the ghost of one.

Finally, I put her on the 1:00 P.M. bus on December 30. She had been with me for ninety-three hours and I had loved every hour of it. My only regret was that I did not, as yet, consider it judicious for her to meet Janet.

2

Finally, the traumatic year of 1970 was over. During that year, I had published only six books, fewer than the number in any year since 1965, but the events of the year had nothing to do with that. It rather reflected the amount of time I had spent on Shakespeare and on the Ginn science series.

The six books were:

103. *The Solar System and Back* (Doubleday)
104. *Asimov's Guide to Shakespeare, Volume I* (Doubleday)
105. *Asimov's Guide to Shakespeare, Volume II* (Doubleday)
106. *Constantinople* (Houghton Mifflin)
107. *ABC's of the Ocean* (Walker)
108. *Light* (Follett)

All of them had, of course, been written in West Newton.

3

January 2, 1971, was my fifty-first birthday. We had celebrated New Year's Eve at Judy-Lynn's and we retaliated by taking her and Lester to dinner as a birthday celebration.[1]

Then, on January 4, I had a delayed birthday lunch with Chaucy Bennetts. She no longer worked for World, which was undergoing a complete reorganization, and she had to leave *The Best New Thing* behind. She was now working for Lothrop, Lee & Shepard, the Juvenile Division of William Morrow & Company. She was eager to have me do something for Lothrop, and I promised I would as soon as it became feasible. Once more an editor was carrying me from house to house like a contagious disease.

4

David Ford, an actor, lived in Janet's apartment house, exactly two floors higher than she did. He was a reader of mine, and hearing that I visited the place regularly, kept his eyes open for me. When he caught me in the lobby, he hailed me, and the upshot was that he arranged to have us see the stage play 1776 in which he was appearing.

We went on January 7 and enjoyed ourselves tremendously. (Ford played Dickinson of Pennsylvania, the villain of the piece, and did a good job. He went on to play John Hancock in the movie version.)

Afterward, we met Ford at Sardi's for a late-night snack, then visited his apartment for a while. We discovered that he had filled it with an incredible supply of minutiae—as one example, an old-fashioned penny gumball machine complete with gumballs.[2]

He told us that he had once had a repairman in his apartment and had had to leave to walk his dog. On his return, he was convinced that the repairman must have taken something in his absence, but he could not be certain, since he himself did not have a full count of all the miscellany he possessed, and he could not possibly tell if anything were missing or not.

[1] That has become a tradition. My birthday wouldn't be one without Judy-Lynn and Lester.
[2] I used it, popped the gumball into my mouth, and promptly cracked off a piece of my lower left first molar.

5

John Ciardi was in town on January 9, with his wife, Judith, and Janet and I had dinner with them. He was a large fellow now, quite stout; not at all the slim charmer of twenty-one years before. But still a charmer, with a voice as beautiful as ever, and my equal as a jokester— with the added advantage of being able to handle a variety of accents. Janet was fascinated by him.

Ciardi had made a new name for himself with his translation of Dante's *Divine Comedy*, and I told him of my own two volumes on Shakespeare, and the fact that I was getting unpleasant reviews from Shakespearian scholars (when they deigned to notice me at all), since they resented my invasion of their field. I added, gloomily, that I expected similar treatment from the Byronians when *Asimov's Annotated Don Juan* came out.

"Screw them," said Ciardi. "Pay the bastards no attention, and do as you please." Then, with a sudden note of caution, "But stay away from Dante."

I finished *Asimov's Annotated Don Juan* two days later, and took it in to Doubleday on January 12. With that out of the way, I was ready to begin another revision of my *Guide to Science*.

6

On January 15, 1971, I attended my first Trap Door Spiders meeting as a member. It was a stag organization, so I could not take Janet, but there were other kinds of meetings. . . .

There was, for instance, a local science-fiction convention in New York not long after, one that had been set up by some eager young fans, and I persuaded Janet to come to it with me.

Janet was quite nervous and camera-shy, so she had extensive practice in dodging, for there were numerous young people with cameras who seemed to find me as irresistibly photogenic as the Taj Mahal. On the other hand, it gave her a chance to socialize with a number of the science-fiction writers whom she had read but had never met.

In particular she met Harlan Ellison, for the first time, and found him as charming and as charismatic as Gertrude had found him in Cleveland four years before.

Janet and I, Judy-Lynn, Lester, the Silverbergs, Harlan, and a few others all had dinner at a Greek restaurant on the evening of January

23. Harlan sat at the head of the table, and Janet sat at his right hand. He wore a black leather jacket, which suited his little tough-guy image perfectly, but as the temperature rose, he decided to remove it. Underneath was his shirt adorned with little Mickey Mouse figures. Janet (a psychiatrist, after all) saw at once that what I said was true—that if you could survive long enough to get past Harlan's prickly porcupiny exterior, you would find that inside he was a soft-as-mush pussycat.

Earlier in the day, Lester del Rey and Bob Silverberg had carried on a dialog on the stage, discussing the ins and outs of science fiction. Bob maintained, with a certain amount of justice, that the human aspects of science fiction had to outweigh the science. At one point, he asked why anyone should be overly concerned with some trivial matter concerning—here he groped for an example and seized upon the first thing that occurred to him—concerning plutonium-186, he said.

In the audience, I laughed, for, of course, there is no such thing as plutonium-186 and there can't be.

After the dialog was over, I said to Bob, "There can't be any plutonium-186."

Bob, who knew that very well, shrugged it off as unimportant.

I said, "But just to show you what a real science-fiction writer can do, I'll write a story about plutonium-186."

"Go ahead," said Bob, coolly. "I'm putting together an anthology of original short stories, and if you write one that meets my minimum standard of literacy, I'll publish it."

And there it was. I hadn't really been serious about writing a story concerning plutonium-186, but Bob had inadvertently converted it into a dare and I was forced to give the matter thought.

Meanwhile, I had done a third book in the ABC series for Walker. This one was *ABC's of the Earth*, and I finished it on January 26.

7

David had finally completed his stay at the private school. He had been there just two years and graduated with his high-school diploma at last. It was clear, though, that no purpose would be served in trying to send him to college, and he himself had no urge to go.

I drove to his school on January 29, picked him up, and drove him back to West Newton. Well, not quite.

Mary Silver (whose husband, Rollo, had obtained *The Historians' History of the World* for me) had long since divorced him and married a thin, self-possessed, superarticulate fellow named Jack Patrick. She was now Mary Patrick and they had been close friends of mine in my last years in West Newton.

Afraid to face Gertrude, I didn't quite dare to take David home. I took him to the Patricks instead, therefore, and Jack took him home, while I scooted back to New York without stopping. It had been my first venture back into Massachusetts since I had left seven months before.

8

Once David was home, more or less permanently, there was a question as to what to do with Satan. On the one hand, it was very difficult to subject David to the permanent danger of allergic difficulties; and on the other, it seemed difficult to get rid of a cat that everyone loved.

The solution seemed to be to give him to *me*, at least temporarily. Indeed, I had planned to pick up Satan when I delivered David but I hadn't dared do that. Instead, Jack Patrick promised to deliver Satan when he next went to New York.

On February 9, Jack appeared, with Satan and with various appurtenances such as cans of cat food and a litter box. I was delighted to see Satan but he, of course, did not remember me. It had been seven months. He wandered about my Cromwell apartment for hours, vainly seeking Robyn, and once when the voice of some woman sounded in the hall, he ran to the door in wild expectation and was, of course, disappointed.

Eventually, I took him to Janet's apartment since Janet, fortunately, loved all living things. She took as good care of him as Robyn would have.

Janet had also a beloved hamster, Cheeky, with whom she played every evening in order to give it exercise. When she did that, Satan had to be securely shut away in another room, since his interest in Cheeky was purely nutritional.

On the other hand, Cheeky was the perfect cat-sitter. If we put the hamster cage on the top shelf of a closet and left the closet door open, Satan would sit below, never taking his eye from the cage, while his tail twitched in endless patience.

9

I took the train to Philadelphia on February 12 to do a local television talk show there and Janet, who did not come with me, told me to be sure to take her young cousin, Leslie, who was living in that city, out to lunch.

I didn't have to be asked twice. Taking a beautiful young woman to lunch is precisely the thing for which I had been designed by the gods. After lunch, I caught the train back.

There was one disconcerting moment, though. As I walked Leslie from her apartment to the restaurant, a young man in a passing automobile leaned out the window and shouted "Hello, Dr. Asimov." I was beginning to be recognized in the street, something that has been happening with greater frequency ever since.

I chafed a little. I said to Leslie, "This is perfectly legitimate. You're Janet's cousin and she *asked* me to take you to lunch. Suppose, though, you were some beautiful girl I was taking to some nefarious rendezvous. I don't want to be recognized on the street."

But Leslie said, "Never mind, Isaac. It will keep you virtuous."[3]

10

On February 6, I had started the science-fiction short story I was planning on plutonium-186 and that I eventually called "The Gods Themselves." That was from the Friedrich Schiller quotation: "Against stupidity, the gods themselves contend in vain," which, as it happened, was the theme of the story.

I was counting on a five-thousand-word length, but it got away from me. This was unusual since I had been writing to order for so many years now that I could count on myself automatically delivering five thousand words when five thousand words was requested. And I don't mean fifty-one hundred words, either.

By February 14, however, I had done ten thousand words and was still going. On the other hand, it was the first time since "The Ugly Little Boy," thirteen years before, that I felt the true thrill of writing science fiction. I didn't want to stop, and I decided I wasn't going to. Let it go on to its natural length.

11

I had to go to Boston for a session with Gertrude's legal representatives. It was purely routine but it was dreadfully worrying. Any brush with the law has to be.

---

[3] Sometimes, recognition can be useful. Once, in Washington, I ran for a taxi and my hand came to rest on its door handle just as the hand of a competing runner did. The young man who owned the other hand said, "Why, it's Dr. Asimov." I said, "Yes, it is, and surely you won't take the taxi away from me." His hand dropped from the door handle as though it were red-hot. It was a shame to pull rank like that, but I needed the taxi.

I went to Boston by train on February 18 and visited Houghton Mifflin for the first time in nearly eight months, to the excitement of all. I had dinner with Austin.

The next day I was interviewed by the lawyers, and survived. What bothered me, though, was that it was February 19, 1971, and, therefore, Robyn's sixteenth birthday, and I was unable to see her. I spoke to her on the phone at South Station while waiting for the train that would take me back home. It was the best I could do.

12

On February 21, Satan managed to get out the kitchen window of Janet's apartment and we found him meowing on the ledge, with a sheer drop of twenty-three stories two inches behind him. We fixed his attention on some food, while Janet reached out very carefully and, with a rattler-quick lunge, seized his collar in a death grip. We lugged him in by main force, and closed the window tightly.

Then we both collapsed. What would have happened if we had had to report to Robyn that her cat had dropped to its death, neither of us cared to visualize. It was the only occasion on which Satan was in any danger all the while he was with us.

13

Rae Jeppson came to town on February 23, and Janet and I took her to dinner. Then we took her to my apartment at the Cromwell, and showed her my books. (By now my books filled two good-sized bookcases in their various English-language hard-cover editions, and I had been forced to affix small numbered cards at the bottom of the spines of each one so that I could find any particular one that I needed, without too much trouble.)

I think Rae was very relieved to find that I did indeed have an apartment of my own.

14

On February 26, I helped host a Trap Door Spiders dinner for the first time. George Scithers was cohost. There were always two hosts, to share the increasingly horrendous cost of restaurant meals. The total restaurant bill came to $250 that day, and it kept rising steadily with time.

15

I finished "The Gods Themselves" on February 28, and found it was twenty thousand words long, just four times as long as it was supposed to be.

Since Bob Silverberg's anthology was being done by Doubleday, it occurred to me to show it to Larry Ashmead. It was not inconceivable that, if he liked the story, he might allow Bob to make the anthology fifteen thousand words longer than had been planned so that "The Gods Themselves" might be included without having to eliminate any of the other stories that would otherwise be bought.

Larry read the story at once and there was no question that he liked it. He phoned me and told me that anthologization was out. He wanted the story expanded into a novel.

I didn't want to expand it into a novel, however. "The Gods Themselves" fit the twenty thousand words perfectly and if I tried to pump it up to three or four times its length, I would ruin it by making it incredibly spongy.

I thought very rapidly and said, "Look, Larry, the story involves an energy source that depends on communication between ourselves and another universe, and it ends downbeat. What I can do is retell the story from the standpoint of the other universe and still leave it downbeat. Then I can take it up a third time in still a third setting and this time make it upbeat."

"Are you sure you can do this?" said Larry.

Well, I wasn't. I had just made that all up on the spur of the moment, but it wouldn't have done to say so.

"Absolutely positive," I said (well, if I couldn't, I wasn't Isaac Asimov), so on March 8, 1971, I dropped in at Doubleday and signed a contract to do the novel.

16

Meanwhile, a couple of weeks earlier, I had received a letter from Eleanor Sullivan, managing editor of *Ellery Queen's Mystery Magazine*, asking me if I wouldn't write another story for them.

I had written "As Chemist to Chemist" for *EQMM* a year and a half before and had never tried them again. After all, I had achieved the goal of selling to them, and I wasn't writing much fiction of any kind.

Just the same, once I was *asked* to write a story—and at a time when I was actually enjoying writing fiction—I decided to try.

I had to think up a plot, and I remembered David Ford's story, the one in which he felt he had had something stolen from him, but in the vast miscellany that was his apartment, couldn't be sure what it was, or even whether anything was. The thought of hiring a detective to find not something that was missing, but *whether* something was missing, intrigued me.

Then, too, it also occurred to me that, as an unusual background, I might use the Trap Door Spiders. I could have a similar organization, which I would call "The Black Widowers," have similar members, and a similar routine. I would have my characters modeled on Sprague de Camp, Lester del Rey,[4] and so on, and I would have a guest who would be grilled.

Where I departed from reality was to have the guest come up with a mystery, something that never happened at any Trap Door Spiders meeting. I also invented a waiter, who solved the mystery. The waiter's name was Henry and I did not consciously model him on my deceased father-in-law. Rather, he was an incarnation of Wodehouse's immortal Jeeves.

I called the story "The Chuckle," and it was unusual in that it was the first really straight mystery I had ever written. Until then, all the mysteries I had written had been true science fiction like *The Caves of Steel* or "The Singing Bell," or had at least had a strictly scientific background, like *The Death Dealers* or "As Chemist to Chemist."

"The Chuckle" was the first story I ever wrote (and published) of any length, in which the setting, the gimmick, and the resolution did not involve science in any way.

I finished it on March 6 (it was only four thousand words long) and I took it in, personally, to the offices of *EQMM*, which I now visited for the first time. I also met Eleanor Sullivan for the first time. Constance DiRienzo also worked for the magazine, and I remembered her well from the days, a dozen years before, when she worked for Bob Mills at *F & SF*.

Eleanor had blond hair and Connie dark hair, but both were coquettish and witty and I discovered quickly that, quite apart from selling stories, I would always have a good time talking to them and engaging in the delightful game of flirtatious *double-entendres*.

---

[4] Naturally, the resemblance would only be in appearance and mannerisms. I must admit that I never actually asked their permission to be taken in vain, but once it was done they raised no objections—though, as nearly as I could make out, they restrained their enthusiasm.

Eleanor read the story at once and liked it. She sent it on to Fred Dannay (Ellery Queen) who also liked it, and came back quickly with the request that I emphasize and make more important the background machinery of the Black Widowers.

I was delighted to do that, and it was then taken at once.

It appeared, eventually, in the January 1972 EQMM under the changed title of "The Acquisitive Chuckle."[5] Dannay had a habit of changing titles. In this case, I liked the change and kept it.

Dannay ran the story as the lead in the issue and his blurb began as follows: "The first of a brand-new series—about the Black Widowers and the piquant problems that challenged them monthly." Above that was a heading that said, "The first of a NEW SERIES by Isaac Asimov." (Capitalization is EQMM's.)

I had never thought of the story as the first of a series, and Dannay had never told me that he thought of it so. It simply appeared in that fashion in the magazine as a *fait accompli*. But that made it a challenge and I decided to try more of what I instantly began to think of as the "Black Widowers stories."

It wouldn't be easy. Each story would have to be told during a banquet; each would have to be analyzed in armchair fashion, with the solution (always by Henry) sufficiently forceful to be accepted at once.

I managed. In the end the Black Widowers stories grew to be more in number than those of any other series of stories I had ever written—and the most enjoyable for me.

17

I had lunch with Beth Walker on March 12, 1971. Present also was a new editor, the well-known science writer for the grade-school levels, Millicent Selsam.

Millie was five years older than I was, which was wonderful, for I was beginning to find it embarrassingly difficult to find people older than I was. (A fine thing for a child prodigy to have to encounter.) She was very prim in appearance and would always laugh at my outrageous remarks only after the ten-to-fifteen-second delay it took her to get over her surprise at them.

At this moment, though, being fresh at the job, she was being a new broom. She had gone over *ABC's of the Earth* and had thrown out about a quarter of my definitions on one ground or another, something that effectively put me into a sour humor.

The women ignored this and began to talk to each other animat-

[5] See *Tales of the Black Widowers* (Doubleday, 1974).

edly concerning the amazing success of such how-to porn books as *The Sensuous Woman* and *The Sensuous Man*. I maintained an annoyed silence, still brooding over my mangled *ABC's of the Earth*.

Finally Beth turned to me and said, "Why don't you write a dirty book, Isaac?"

I said, rather loftily, "Because I don't write trash."

Then I thought of my own particular *shtick*, which is the ardent flirtation with every woman in sight and said, "Besides, what do I know about sex? All I could write would be *The Sensuous Dirty Old Man*."

"Great!" said Beth, with enthusiasm. "Then you'll do it."

"What do you mean, do it? That was a gag."

"Sure you'll do it," she said, and began to make plans.

I ignored the whole thing because I couldn't believe anyone would be serious about such a thing. In my notation in my diary for that day, I talked only about what had happened to *ABC's of the Earth*. Not a word about *The Sensuous Dirty Old Man*.

18

At the convention back in January, one of the fans present had told me of a Gilbert and Sullivan Society that met at monthly intervals in New York. I found that attractive since I had been a G & S fan since childhood, and had seen every one of the plays except *Utopia, Limited*.

On March 15, 1971, Janet and I attended a meeting of the society, which I enjoyed greatly even though I found myself in the humiliating position of being in the midst of fifty people, each one of whom knew their G & S better than I did. I put down ten dollars for membership at once.

19

Meanwhile, I had another science-fiction task on my hands. I had promised Bob Silverberg a story for his anthology of originals, and I had failed. At least I had written "The Gods Themselves" and it was not a short story, but a novelette doomed to grow to a novel. I had to write something else for Bob.

I did. I wrote a sixty-seven-hundred-word short story entitled "Take a Match"[6] and finished it on March 21. After a slight revision, he took it. It appeared in his anthology *New Dimensions II*, published by Doubleday in 1972.

[6] See *Buy Jupiter and Other Stories*.

20

There seemed no end to the odd tasks I could be talked into. The magazine *Psychology Today* was planning to do a college textbook on psychology with that same title. On March 18, 1971, they approached me with the suggestion that I join the team and provide each of over thirty chapters with little five-hundred-word Introductions. These might be science-fictional, philosophical, or historical items, provided they related to the subject matter of the chapters.

It seemed just odd enough and crazy enough to be interesting, and I eventually agreed to tackle it.

21

I woke at 2 A.M. on March 19 with my old nemesis, a kidney stone. The pain mounted and reached agonizing proportions between 8 and 10 A.M. It then remained largely quiescent until 4 A.M. on the twenty-fourth, when I finally passed it after staying awake and drinking water all night. After my experience a year and a half before, I considered this a minor episode.

During the quiescent period, Janet and I visited my mother at Long Beach on the twenty-first, then drove to nearby Woodmere, where Judy-Lynn's family dwelt.

There Judy-Lynn and Lester del Rey were getting married in a strict Jewish ceremony with Fred Pohl (whom Janet now met for the first time) as best man.[7]

From this time on, Lester considered himself Jewish but always refused to admit he had converted. He had simply been accepted, he said, without himself having made a move.

Ever since there has been a game between us that consists of my pointing out that he can't be a Jew since he has never been circumcised and his insisting that the Bible, properly interpreted, forbids circumcision. We are not, however, allowed to play this game (and other similar ones) when Judy-Lynn and Janet are present because they claim that the endless squabbling is wearisome.

---

[7] Judy-Lynn, who knew that I was totally eager to see her marry Lester, convinced as I was it would mean happiness for both, confessed later that she was strongly tempted to pull one more let's-have-fun-with-Isaac trip by interrupting the ceremony to say it was all a gag arranged to fool me. She said that the pleasure of seeing me drop to the floor in a faint was something she could deny herself only through the certainty that her mother would drop to the floor in a companion faint.

Actually, it's not squabbling, it's just friendly banter, but it's hard to convince anyone of that.

22

I finished the second revision of my *Guide to Science* on March 23 and promptly began a history of nuclear energy for the Atomic Energy Commission. It was eventually called *Worlds Within Worlds*.

23

On March 25, Janet and I drove to Shippensburg, Pennsylvania, in the south-central part of the state. When I unpacked in the motel, I was astonished to find rubber boots in my suitcase, the kind that came halfway to the knee. I hadn't packed them.

I said, "Where did these come from, Janet?"

She said, a little embarrassed, "I packed them."

"What for?"

"In case of snow."

I stared at her. We were planning to drive to Virginia the next day, after I had given an evening and a morning talk at Shippensburg State College. We would visit Williamsburg and then backtrack to Richmond, where I would give another talk at a Town Hall meeting.

I said, "Snow? In Virginia? At the end of March?" I laughed heartily and Janet looked rather abashed.

We were on our way the next day and as we crossed the Potomac River, the first snowflakes began to fall. As we made our way to Route 95 and headed down toward Williamsburg, the snowstorm grew thicker and heavier.

I tried to joke about it for a while, but as the miles passed, my joking grew lamer and I fell silent. My silence turned into anger. Janet, watching me closely, decided it was perhaps unsafe to let me remain behind the wheel and begged me to let her drive. I did, and she drove the last hour through terrible weather.[8]

We finally ended in Williamsburg where, apparently, it was the worst spring snowfall in twenty years. There were a good eight to nine inches of very wet snow on the ground, and when I opened the car door, it shoved the top of a snowbank flat and a level surface of snow,

---

[8] In *her* diary, she went on and on about the *beauty* of the snowfall, and I guess that's the difference between us—and one reason I love her.

drenched and saturated with ice water, revealed itself. It was impossible to step into.

Janet was ready. Wordlessly, she reached behind and handed me the boots, which she had placed on the back seat, just in case. Wordlessly, but with steam emerging from each ear, I put them on.

And then Janet found she simply could not maintain the silence. She said, in a small voice, "Aren't you glad I brought them?"

That did it. I turned on her, face contorted with fury, pointed a finger at her, and said, "Darn it, if you hadn't packed them, it wouldn't have snowed."

But she only laughed. I don't think she believed in my calm and scientific appraisal as to the causes of snowstorms.

It turned out surprisingly well, however; very well, in fact. The next morning dawned bright and mild. The snow was melting rapidly and the little green leaves were showing on the branches of trees between fluffy bits of snow. The going was sloppy but, with boots on, what cared I for that? In fact, the weather had kept the number of tourists down and we saw Williamsburg under ideal noncrowded conditions.

In the afternoon, we drove to Richmond without any trouble, and I spoke to an estimated three thousand people—my largest audience by far up to that time. I began with, "I am delighted to be in Richmond, snow capital of the United States," and had them all in a good humor at once.

In the audience, and coming up to see me afterward, was George Kriegman, the psychiatrist at Camp Lee, twenty-five years before, now long in private practice. Also there was Phyllis Roberts, who had taken phase rule with me in graduate school thirty years before, and now long a divorced woman.

We got home on March 28, and found Satan in perfect shape, having been fed by a neighbor. Satan was delighted to see us, meowed at us constantly (either scolding us for leaving or telling us how glad he was to see us, we couldn't tell which), and followed us around faithfully the whole day.

24

The Nebula Award banquet on April 3 had Marvin Minsky as a guest speaker and Lester del Rey as the master of ceremonies.

I was asked, once again, to hand out awards, the Nebulas this time, and I made a giant-sized blooper. In one of the categories, top votes were for "No Award," which meant that no one got the Nebula that year in that category. For some reason I cannot understand, I ignored that and read out the name of the top author—who was only in second place, and did not qualify.

The mistake was corrected, but the author whose name I read out was devastatingly disappointed and I was just as devastatingly embarrassed. My desire to hand out awards was effectively quenched. I have been called on to do so on occasion since, but I have never again minded having someone else picked for the purpose.

25

Ralph Daigh, editor-in-chief of Fawcett Publications, called me and invited me to lunch on April 6. I agreed, of course, even though I knew he would undoubtedly ask me for a book that would be difficult or impossible to do in view of the state of my commitments.

On the fifth, however, he called to change the arrangements and asked if I would go Dutch treat with him. I was astonished but I said, "Certainly, Mr. Daigh."

On the sixth, I showed up at the Regency Hotel at the agreed-upon time and met Ralph in the lobby. He took me into a back room where there were people lined up to pay for tickets. I reached for my wallet and Ralph waved it away. "You're my guest," he said, impatiently.

Now I was doubly astonished. I said, "I thought you said we were going Dutch treat."

Ralph looked chagrined. "Have you been thinking for twenty-four hours that I'd invited you to lunch and wouldn't pay for you? You're my guest. It's the name of the organization I was mentioning; this is the Dutch Treat Club."

That was my introduction to the club that is for men in any aspect of the communications profession. It meets every Tuesday for lunch at the Regency. Each lunch features an entertainer and speaker, and although everything seems unhurried and is invariably pleasant, the sessions last only from noon to 2 P.M.

After the lunch was over, Ralph promptly nominated me for membership and I was voted in at once. It was the second stag organization of which I had become a member.

26

Lester del Rey celebrated his conversion (or acceptance) into Judaism by setting up an elaborate seder, which Janet and I attended, along with the Silverbergs and Lester's ex-mother-in-law.

It was Janet's first seder. She found the intricate ceremonial confusing, but the Passover food was, as always, absorbing—and I absorbed it thoroughly.

Lester did the cooking. He is undoubtedly the best male cook in science fiction, and I imagine he himself would insist he was the best cook without any qualification of gender required.

27

On April 12, I finished *Worlds Within Worlds*. It was another one of those books that got away from me. The AEC wanted it to be ten thousand words long, which was the appropriate size for one of their pamphlets, such as *The Genetic Effects of Radiation*.

It turned out to be thirty thousand words long, however, so I split it up into three parts, and sent each off separately. The AEC agreed to publish it as three pamphlets. No sooner was that done than John Sullivan of the AEC persuaded me to promise a half-size pamphlet of five thousand words, one that was to be called, eventually, *Electricity and Man*.

John Sullivan and I had established friendly relations and we had had lunch several times when he was in New York, or I in Washington. One of the reasons for the friendliness was that he, too, was trying to get a divorce and was running into the same problems and unhappiness that I was.

The first time I heard that, I looked curiously at him and said, "Aren't you of Irish descent?"

"Yes, of course. With a name like Sullivan, what else?"

"But are you Catholic?" (Walter Sullivan of the New York *Times* wasn't.)

"Yes, I am."

"Then how can you be getting a divorce? Isn't divorce forbidden by the Catholic Church?"

Sullivan smiled. "There's a loophole. Haven't you heard of the loophole?"

"No," I said, firmly. "I don't know of any loophole."

"I'm a *bad* Catholic," said Sullivan.

28

Janet and I attended the Lunacon, and on the evening of April 16 we spent hours in Campbell's room, along with Judy-Lynn. We spent more time with Campbell on the next day and then said good-bye cheerfully. Janet found him exasperating—but fascinating.

29

I sometimes consent to take part in a book-and-author luncheon. I generally don't enjoy them because I'm usually only one of three or more authors and invariably (it seems to me) the least well-known to the general audience.

There was one coming up on April 22, 1971, however, that I couldn't refuse because it was being sponsored by *Newsday* and because Stanley himself asked me to do it. I agreed, but I said he would have to send a limousine to Long Beach to pick up my mother for the occasion. Stanley said, "Why not? She's my mother, too."

I was there on April 22, but without Janet, who had to remain with her patients. My mother was there and sat in state at a table with Stanley, Ruth, and Larry Ashmead. Speaking ahead of me were Barbara Tuchman, who had written a series of popular histories, and Stephen Birmingham, who had written *Our Crowd*, about the rich German Jews of New York.

I was definitely low man in that combination. Birmingham, in particular, wowed the crowd, which consisted, I should say, very largely (perhaps 80 per cent) of middle-aged Jewish women. As usual, I thought glumly that I would be unable to follow the Birmingham talk with any degree of success unless I worked up a smash opening.

I rose at last (the final speaker) and said, "I don't have the advantages of Stephen Birmingham in addressing this audience, because I have never written anything that had any connection with Jewish tradition, Jewish history, or Jewish life. However, I have an advantage over Stephen that makes up for everything else. I have a Jewish mother, who is sitting in the audience now. Mamma, stand up and take a bow."

My mother promptly did this and accepted the round of applause very graciously—and I knew that I had my audience where I wanted them.

I then said, "My brother is also here, at the table with my mother. He's Stan Asimov and he's assistant publisher of *Newsday*.

"Of course, I wouldn't say that my mother plays favorites, for how can a Jewish mother play favorites?" (Knowing laughter from the audience.) "Still, I am the first-born, and you know what that means. For instance, when this shindig was being prepared, my mother said to me, 'Isaac, will it be possible for me to sit with you?'

"I said, 'No, Mamma, I'll be on the dais. You'll sit with Stanley.'

"And my mother said, 'Stanley who?'"

That, as you can imagine, got me home safe, for it got right in among the ribs of the women in the audience. It helped that my mother rose to her feet, completely outraged (need I say the story was a complete fiction?), and shook her fist at me.

Afterward, I signed a satisfactory number of books. Someone even went over to my mother and asked for her signature on the book, also, and she signed with no trace of embarrassment.

When Stanley got back to his office that afternoon, he found his name covered over with a sign reading, "Stanley who."

30

Beth Walker kept hounding me over my silly remark about *The Sensuous Dirty Old Man* and finally got it through my head that she was serious. She really wanted the book.

"It would just be a gag book," I said, weakly. "It won't really be pornographic."

"I know," she said.

"And it can't be a long book, because the gag wouldn't support a long book."

"I know," she said.

So I had to do it. I spent just one weekend on it, April 24 to 26, working in Janet's apartment and trying not to let her see what I was doing. (I was afraid she would be outraged and horrified.)

It was only sixteen thousand words long, and at that, longer than I thought it would be. When I was finished with it, it seemed so funny to me and so inoffensive (since it was just my general level of flirtatiousness put on paper) that I let Janet read it and she, too, thought it funny and inoffensive.

I took it in to Walker on April 26, and they approved it as well and rushed it through with amazing celerity. I had an advance copy of the book in my hands on June 2, just thirty-seven days after I had brought in the manuscript and only eighty-one days after I had used the phrase at the March 12 lunch.

What made the book particularly important to me was that it was the first book I had had published that was written after I had come to New York.

Having finished *The Sensuous Dirty Old Man*, I returned to *More Words of Science*, which had been lying dormant for a while.

33

The Gods Themselves

1

May 1 had come to have a particular meaning to me since it had been on May 1, 1959, that Janet and I had met at the Mystery Writers' of America award dinner and had begun to correspond.

In a way, it was our anniversary, and we celebrated by visiting the Silverbergs in their rambling mansion up in the Bronx, and having dinner there. Then, late at night, we watched Nelson Eddy and Jeanette MacDonald in *Maytime* on television. (Janet is an Eddy-MacDonald fan; I prefer Fred Astaire and Ginger Rogers.)

2

On May 2, I finally got started on the second part of *The Gods Themselves*.

Larry had shown the first part to a paperback house and they had expressed interest, but had said, "Will Asimov be putting some sex into the book?"

Larry said, firmly, "No!"

When Larry told me this I instantly felt contrary enough to want to put sex into the book. I rarely had sex in my stories and I rarely had extraterrestrial creatures in them, either, and I knew there were not lacking those who thought that I did not include them because I lacked the imagination for it.

I determined, therefore, to work up the best extraterrestrials that had ever been seen for the second part of my novel. There were not to be just human beings with antennae or pointed ears, but utterly inhuman objects in every way. And I determined to give them three sexes and to have that entire section of *The Gods Themselves* revolve about sex—*their* sex.

That is exactly what I did, and I began to feel myself moved by the story I was writing.

I would have gotten along faster, had I not also felt the urge to write a new history, my tenth. This one took up where *The Dark Ages* left off and continued the history of France through the Hundred Years' War. It was eventually called *The Shaping of France.*

3

I attended the Dutch Treat Club banquet on May 6. This was an annual affair, with tuxedos required. Anything with tuxedos turns me off, but Larry Ashmead was going and so was Ferris Mack (Tom Sloane's boss), and I felt it would be necessary to go.

Bob Hope was the chief item on the entertainment agenda, and since Ferris introduced us I had to shake hands with him—which put me in the position of shaking hands with a man who shook hands with Nixon.

Ferris is a round-faced fellow, always smiling, never serious, and extremely lovable. He passed me in the hall one time and said, "Can't stop, Isaac. I'm on my way to see a real writer."

I said, "Send Larry and let him see a real editor."

You can't fool around that way if you don't like a guy.

4

Our time with Satan was coming to an end. We had had him for fourteen happy weeks, but Robyn couldn't stand his absence any longer and we had to give him up. David, apparently, would have to endure his allergies.

On May 11, I drove to Boston with Satan. I had him in a carrying case for the first hundred miles and he wailed all the way. I finally had to stop and let him out. I knew that being in a moving car might panic him and cause him to scratch me, but I steeled myself against that possibility. After letting him out, I allowed him to inspect the car thoroughly, and then began to drive along the highway, slowly accelerating to full speed.

Satan was indeed terribly frightened. He placed himself on the top of the front seat immediately behind my head and leaned against my neck with his full weight in order to make as much contact as possible. He kept one paw on the window ledge to steady himself and kept his horrified eyes on the road. We drove that way for a hundred miles while I did my best never to change either direction or speed too rapidly.

This time I drove to the house. Gertrude was there but remained inside. Robyn came out to take Satan and drool over him while I drooled over her.

The next day I visited the med school for the first time in ten months, and before going home on May 13, I took both David and Robyn out to dinner.

5

My speaking schedule took me to Ohio toward the end of May. On the twenty-seventh, I talked at Cayahoga Community College, near Cleveland, and we were driven through the suburb of Parma where (our driver told us) all houses were built with pink flamingos on the lawn, and it took an additional payment of a hundred dollars to have the flamingo omitted.

On the twenty-eighth, we drove to Newark, Ohio. Janet had been rather glum about the Ohio trip till she read in the guide books that the state contained Indian mounds. That brightened her, for Indians were another passion of hers.

There were some particularly good mounds in Newark, and we drove around the town trying to find them. Unfortunately, the town was riddled with construction, half the streets were closed to traffic, and we only succeeded in getting lost.

We gave up eventually and went to our motel in disappointment. There, Janet opened the blinds to see what the view from our room was like and found herself staring at the Indian mounds just across the way. A golf course had been built on the site and the mounds served as hazards.

On May 29, we stopped off at the rose gardens in Hershey, Pennsylvania. It was a little too early in the season for roses, to be sure, but the whole town smelled of chocolate and for me at least that was better than roses.

The next day we were home.

6

I did a Dick Cavett segment on June 3. It was my fourth time with him. This time I was publicizing *The Sensuous Dirty Old Man*, so I came out with a bra over my eyes, since that was the way in which I was pictured on the book cover.

That bra-covered photograph was a device to hide my identity. The book came out as having been written by "Dr. A.," since *The Sen-*

suous Woman was by "J.," and *The Sensuous Man* was by "M." There was no real secret intended, though. The Walkers announced my real name even before the book was published, and on the Cavett show I took off the bra as soon as I could.

It was the silliest thing I ever did on television and I was sorry I had agreed to do it even as I stepped out onto the stage.

7

On June 10, we drove to Troy, New York, where I was slated to give a commencement address at Rensselaer Polytechnic Institute the next day. That night we had dinner with administrators and trustees, and the "Trojan ladies" (as we called them between ourselves) didn't know quite how to introduce Janet or how to describe her relationship to me.

Thereafter, I introduced her firmly as my fiancée. Nor was it a lie, since by then it was perfectly understood between us that we would marry as soon as we could.

The commencement went well, and I got a second honorary degree, again a Doctor of Science.

8

Action on the divorce was very slow and nothing could be done to speed the "law's delay." On June 17, I was in Boston again. My Massachusetts lawyer, George Michaels, and I sat with Monroe Inker and the judge who would be hearing the case, and nothing much was agreed upon except a further delay. However, Inker agreed to lift the freeze of my Houghton Mifflin income.

I had dinner with Robyn that night and the next day had lunch at Locke-Ober's with Mary K. for the first time in a year. I also visited Elizabeth Moyer at the med school.

9

My nephew, Larry Repanes (Marcia's older son, and a tall, handsome lad), graduated from high school on June 24, and I was driven out there to give a commencement address. Marcia had volunteered me.

10

On June 28, I did *Electricity and Man* for the AEC, as I had promised, and sent it off the next day.

With that done, I had lunch on June 30 with Peter Lacy of Reader's Digest Books. They were doing a large and elaborate book on the men and women of the Bible, and I agreed to write some articles for it.

11

Larry Ashmead's birthday falls on July 4, and every year he throws a huge birthday party at his summer place far out near the eastern end of Long Island. We were invited to the 1971 celebration, and on July 3 (the anniversary of my return to New York) we drove there. It was a peculiar feeling to drive for three hours and still be on Long Island.

On the way home, we stopped off at Long Beach and had lunch with my mother. She was getting along well at the hotel but was visibly more feeble than she had been when she arrived. She was a little unhappy about having to associate with old people and told me a circumstantial tale of talking to a woman who was nearly ninety years old and who, even as they were talking, collapsed and died.

My mother said, self-pityingly, "Everything happens to your mother."

I said, perhaps insufficiently sympathetic, "Come on, Mamma, something happened to the poor old lady, too."

12

By July 6, 1971, I had completed the second part of *The Gods Themselves*. It was thirty thousand words long and was the most unusual story (it was complete in itself, actually) I had ever written. Certainly Dua, the heroine, who, in physical nature, was apparently semigaseous, was the most interesting and sympathetic character (in my opinion) I had ever created.

I took it in to Larry on the eighth, took time out to do *Comets and Meteors* in the Follett astronomy series, and then got to work on the third part of *The Gods Themselves* at once.

13

On and off, people at the New York *Times* were trying to get me to do periodic articles for them on science. The rock we split on, however, was that I wanted a completely free hand, and no matter how much they promised I would have one, it was clear that what they really wanted were articles tightly tied to the news.

For instance, there was a botulism scare at the time, and so they asked me to do an article on botulism. I wrote it promptly and mailed it in on July 9, then called the editor at the *Times* in order to tell him it was in the mail and to bask in his approval at my speed.

Not at all. He said, indignantly, "What do you mean, you put it in the mail? I want it now. Bring in the carbon."

And I did, by taxi. That kind of newspaper life, however, is not for me.

14

On July 11, 1971, Janet and I drove to Philadelphia, where I was to tape a segment of "The Mike Douglas Show."

At 7:30 P.M. (as I discovered later), while we were standing under the awning of the Bellevue-Stratford Hotel, waiting for Bill Boggs (Leslie's husband) to get us and take us to a play, John Campbell died in his home.

Campbell had badly hardened arteries, not in the least helped by the fact that he had been a chain smoker all his adult life. He was watching television when his abdominal aorta gave way and he died peacefully. In fact, when Peg entered the room, she didn't know he was dead until he failed to answer her or in any way respond to her.

He was sixty-one years old and I had known him, and had been infinitely beholden to him, for thirty-three years.

When I learned about Campbell's death after I returned home on the twelfth (Judy-Lynn called me), the shock was second only to that I had experienced on learning of my father's death, two years before.

And rightly so, for Campbell had been my literary father. I can't imagine what might have become of my life without him, and though for fifteen years (ever since the dianetics business) my relations with him had been somewhat distant, I never for a moment forgot what I owed him.

As it turned out, "The Greatest Asset" was the fifty-sixth and last item I had sold him, and our session at the Lunacon three months before was the last time I had ever seen him.

I wrote an obituary for him for the fan magazine *Luna*, but Lester del Rey, who also wrote one, thought of the perfect title. It was "Farewell to the Master," which had also been the title of a great story by Harry Bates in the October 1940 *Astounding*.

On July 14, I picked up Lester and Judy-Lynn, along with Gordon Dickson and Harry Harrison, and drove them all out to Westfield, New Jersey, for the memorial service. (Campbell had been cremated the day before.)

There was no religious observance. Each of us had a role fixed for us, and mine came closest to religion when I read the Twenty-third Psalm. We then all went back to Campbell's house, where Peg insisted that there be no sorrow and no moping.

We left at 3:30 P.M. I took the del Reys home and as we went east on Seventy-second Street, Lester directed me to turn right on Broadway. That was an illegal right and I was stopped by a policeman and ticketed even before I had completed the turn. A crestfallen Lester offered to pay the fifteen dollars, but I jubilantly told him it was well-worth fifteen dollars to me to be able to tell the story far and wide of how know-it-all Lester had directed me into a traffic trap.

15

It had been a rough day, and I looked forward to going to Janet's for a steak dinner and then attending a showing of *Timon of Athens* in Central Park. Quite late in the day, however, some people from the Health Physics Association called to remind me that I was going to talk to them that night.

"Tonight?" I said, energetically. "You mean tomorrow night."

No, it was tonight. In two separate letters, the date had been set as July 15, but it was July 14, just the same. The letter writer had made a mistake.

I called Janet, who was just about to put the steak in the broiler. Back it went into the refrigerator, and a hurry-up call to the Shakespeare-in-the-Park people postponed our tickets till the next night. I washed, dressed, and hastened out to the Manhattan hotel where the talk was to be given. I had copies of the letters with me to show them what they had done, and they were properly contrite.

I managed to give a very good speech, but they surely didn't deserve it.

16

I was in Washington to give a talk on July 21 to a group of public-relations people. Formal dress was required, and since it was deep summer, I had to buy a dinner jacket and a blue dress-shirt to go with it. It looked good and Janet was in predictable ecstasies but I was distressed at the step-by-step manner in which I was retreating into fussy formality.

17

I did a talk show for the Canadian Broadcasting Corporation on July 24, and met Abbie Hoffman, a counterculture hero, on that occasion. I was not impressed.

In fact, I felt rather sorry for him and others like him. They had ridden a wave of emotion to its crest and when it broke and receded, it left them stranded in some no-man's-land of the spirit from which (I suspected) they would never find their way back.

18

I went again to Central Park on July 28 to see *Two Gentlemen of Verona* and warned Janet that it was a very poor play.

I frowned, though, when I looked at the *Playbill* and found that the cast of characters was not canonical. Then, as the play started, Thurio emerged and, in a high tenor, sang "Love in Bloom." "Can it be the trees that fill the breeze with rare and magic perfume?" he warbled.

I turned to Janet and said, censoriously, "That's not Shakespeare."

Janet said, apprehensively, "They must have made changes. Don't be angry."

I was angry, though, and it took me half an act to calm down sufficiently to realize that a bad play had been changed into a terrific rock musical; that I hadn't been appreciating what I was hearing.

I hopped to my feet and shouted, "Start over—from the beginning. . . ."

No one listened, but I loved it anyway. I never saw an audience leave a theater happier. (It had been opening night, you see; I hadn't been warned what I would hear.)

19

The next day I was interviewed (by telephone) on a Dayton, Ohio, radio station. After the interview, the station accepted questions from the audience, questions I was to answer. A woman's voice said, "Who, in your opinion, did most to improve science fiction?"

I was about to answer, "Me," and play for the laugh when, remembering what had happened the month before, I remorsefully stuck to the truth and said, "John Campbell."

"Good," said the voice, firmly. "He was my father."

20

My ninth collection of *F & SF* essays was ready for delivery to Doubleday on August 2. I called it *The Left Hand of the Electron*, from the title of one of the essays included.

And I was working madly on the third portion of *The Gods Themselves*.

21

John Ciardi had talked us into going to the Breadloaf Conference. He had been its head for many years now and I was to go with full faculty status and was to give talks on how to write nonfiction and to get paid for doing so. Naturally I had told Ciardi I didn't know how to write nonfiction, but he merely grunted at me.

I was not quite finished with the third part of *The Gods Themselves*, and Janet argued me into putting as much of it into final copy as possible and then handing that in with an outline of what remained to be written so that it could be finished for me if "anything happened."

I protested that I didn't know exactly how it was going to end, but Janet knew that I had the solution to the problem and told me to put that at least on paper. So I did—begging Larry not to read it unless he heard I were dead, and found the rumor confirmed.

On August 18, 1971, Janet and I drove to Middlebury, Vermont, twenty-one years after my only previous attendance at Breadloaf.[1] I remembered nothing of the physical plant or of the routine, but I quickly fitted myself in.

[1] David, whose birth had prevented my planned return the year after that occasion, turned twenty years old while I was at Breadloaf this time.

John Ciardi held court before and after dinner and we all gathered around him for drinking, smoking, and talking. Since I neither drank nor smoked, I had to make up for it with the third item, and night after night, it became a matter of John and I one-upping each other.

It was John who won, and at the very close, too. As I was leaving after the two-week session, I took his hand and said, "Farewell, O minor poet."

And without missing a beat, he said, "Farewell, O major pain-in-the-ass." I was wiped out again. (I have never dared keep score of the number of wipeouts I have suffered.)

We met one particularly pleasant couple there. Al Balk was the other lecturer on nonfiction. He had been with *Saturday Review* and I had sold him an article on communications in the future, "The Fourth Revolution,"[2] which had appeared in the October 24, 1970, issue of the magazine.

He was a tall, rather plump person, calm and pleasant. His wife, Phyllis, was gentle and shy, and countered my outrageous remarks with a soft, "Oh honestly." Their two pretty daughters were with them, and all four occupied a cottage rather off the beaten path.

I didn't loaf while at Breadloaf. I did an article on the biblical heroine Ruth for Reader's Digest Books, and also did an article for *The Saturday Evening Post* which, having died, had undergone a resurrection. In its new body, it was being published in Indianapolis and went in heavily for a nostalgic re-creation of the American mood before World War II.

They had asked me to do an article on the metric system, and I did one that was strongly prometric called "How Many Inches in a Mile?"[3] It eventually appeared in the Winter 1971 issue of the magazine.

At one point, I put in a collect call to *The Saturday Evening Post* to discuss some matter in connection with the article, and at my mention of my name, the operator gasped out, "Oh sir—oh sir—oh sir—"

I rather enjoyed her gasps, and she sounded young and beautiful.

Another memory is of my picking up a copy of *The Reader's Digest* someone had left behind in one of the bathrooms and leafing idly through the jokes. I suddenly found myself reading an anecdote about *my mother* taken from *Isaac Asimov's Treasury of Humor*.

It was the one about my mother's encounter with the teacher at night school, when the teacher said, "No wonder you're such a good

2 See *Today and Tomorrow and*—
3 See *Today and Tomorrow and*—

writer," and my mother had countered with, "You mean no wonder my son's such a good writer."

I called my mother at Long Beach at my first opportunity to urge her to get a copy of the magazine.

"I saw it," she said, indifferently. "Some of the women here showed it to me."

"Well, what did you think?" I asked, rather pleased that she had lived to see me confer immortality on her.

But she said, indignantly, "I'm pretty mad. They made it sound like a joke. It was a true story!"

"Of course it was, Mamma," I said. "What do stupid magazines know?"

22

My duties at Breadloaf were by no means a sinecure. Not only did I have to give talks, I also had to read material submitted to me and to discuss it intelligently and helpfully both with the students in private and with the class in public.

The weather was miserable, too. The first two days were summery, but after that there came a stretch of cold, blustery, rainy weather. On August 23, John Clark (my science-fiction buddy and fellow Trap Door Spider) arrived, for he attended Breadloaf every year. He came dressed in sport shirt and short pants, got out of his car, and turned blue. That was the last I saw of him in summer costume.

Every member of the faculty took his turn in delivering an evening speech to the entire student body. My turn came on August 28.

I had noted with some discomfort that each faculty member read from his works at some point in his speech.

I had not brought any works to read from, but I had done the article on Ruth. I therefore gave my talk on the Book of Ruth as a commentary on intolerance, went on to the parable of the Good Samaritan, and ended with my own discussion of love overcoming the barriers of difference in "The Ugly Little Boy."

Of all the talks I had ever given, that one was the best.

I do not look at an audience, as it happens, I always focus in midair; but I *listen* to them. From the rustling, the coughing, the laughing, the murmuring, I have my way of judging the effect of what I am saying, and I adjust to suit. None of it is conscious; it is an unconscious and unspoken dialog between myself and my audience and, when it is working well, it guides me and I cannot miss.

But if you were to ask what I listen for that tells me that I am exactly right, I would answer, "Silence!"

There are rare times when an audience falls entirely silent, when there is not a laugh, not a cough, not a rustle, when nothing exists but a sea of ears—and then I know I have reached speaker's heaven.

I haven't achieved this more than four or five times in all my life, but the one time I remember most clearly of all was that August 28, 1971, when I talked on the subject of intolerance at Breadloaf. And when I finished by quoting (from memory) the final climax to "The Ugly Little Boy," the silence was finally broken, for I heard sobbing.

I got the first standing ovation (I was told) that Breadloaf had ever seen.

The whole thing was summed up afterward when one of the students came to me and, with absolutely no sign of sarcasm at all, said, "Thank you for a wonderful sermon, Reverend."

I eventually wrote a version of the talk as my 161st *F & SF* essay, "Lost in Non-Translation,"[4] which appeared in the March 1972 *F & SF*.

We left for home on August 31.

23

The two weeks at Breadloaf were so successful that the twenty-ninth World Science Fiction conference that followed almost immediately in Boston was almost an anticlimax.

It was the most smoothly run convention I ever attended, thanks to the hard work of Sue and Tony Lewis, who ran it, and who were my friends from the old NESFA days.

Janet didn't come with me, reluctant to interfere with the reunion I was bound to have with my children, and the del Reys promised her they would take care of me. And so they did; they scarcely ever let me out of their sight. They even arranged to have the room next to mine, and we had breakfast together in their room every morning.

The Hugo awards banquet on September 5 (my mother's seventy-sixth birthday) was the high point of the convention. I sat at the dais, for I was going to hand out the Hugos, and Bob Silverberg was the toastmaster (and an excellent one—no one is better that he at sardonic humor).

Robyn, radiantly beautiful, was at my side, knitting calmly. Good

4 See *The Tragedy of the Moon* (Doubleday, 1973).

old Cliff Simak, now sixty-seven, was guest of honor and, in the course of his talk, he introduced his children, who were in the audience. Robyn whispered to me, "You're not going to introduce me, are you, Dad?"

I whispered back, "Not if you don't want me to, Robyn."

"I don't." She knitted a while, then said, "Of course, if you want to refer casually to your beautiful, blue-eyed, blond-haired daughter, you may do *that*." So I did.

Bob Silverberg made frequent references to the argument that had taken place in St. Louis in 1968 when Harlan Ellison had taken up a collection to pay for some damage inadvertently done to hotel property and, on collecting more than the required sum, had calmly assigned the excess to his own pet project, a science-fiction class at Clarion College.

Bob therefore made frequent mock announcements of various objects that would be "donated to Clarion" and got a laugh each time.

When it was my turn to stand up and give out the awards, I couldn't resist invading Bob's turf by singing a limerick I had hastily constructed while listening to the toastmastering. It went:

> *There was a young woman named Marion*
> *Who did bump and did grind and did carry on.*
> *The result of her joy*
> *Was a fine bastard boy*
> *Which she promptly donated to Clarion.*

The audience saw where it was going halfway through the last line and the roar of laughter drowned out the final three words.

In the course of the banquet, Lester presented a moving encomium on John Campbell. He is excellent at that sort of thing and constantly threatens to deliver one on me if it becomes necessary; and that does provide me with a marvelous incentive to outlive him if I can.

I was back home on September 7, and the next day I finally finished all of *The Gods Themselves*. It had taken me seven months, and it was ninety-three thousand words long.

24

My poor mother was going downhill. She was beginning to suffer from congestive heart failure and had to be hospitalized periodically. I visited her at the hospital on September 8, and my heart smote me at her feebleness and helplessness.

25

Of course, the completion of *The Gods Themselves* meant the beginning of other projects. There was another Follett astronomy book, *The Sun*, but that took next to no time. I needed something else.

A British publishing house had asked if I had some early stories that had never been collected, which they could reprint. I wrote a letter to them to the effect that such early stories did indeed exist but that they were not good enough to reprint.

Then I thought better of it. It seemed to me that though the stories were poor compared to the work I did later, they were not as poor as all that. Besides, they had a certain historical interest,[5] and if they were published in strict chronological order, without any revising, they should show an interesting progression of proficiency that might be of use to beginners. Finally, if I surrounded them with autobiographical detail, there could be added interest.

I consulted Larry, who agreed wholeheartedly with me and instantly arranged for a contract for what we both felt should be called *The Early Asimov*. I began it on September 10, 1971, and for the first time I turned to my early diaries to check on events.

26

Lew Schwartz of Abelard-Schuman died on September 12, 1971. He and I had not been really close, but we had never quarreled. After he had inherited my book *The Chemicals of Life* when he bought out Henry Schuman seventeen years before, he had gone on to publish thirteen more of my books, and had been the first of my nonfiction publishers.

27

A planetarium in the Midwest had conceived the notion of doing a version of my story "The Last Question." The whole thing was to be narrated, word for word, from my story, with the dialog being recited by different people. This was to be accompanied by appropriate special effects on the planetarium dome.

On September 15, I was taken to Yonkers, New York, by a repre-

[5] I have never pretended I don't understand my importance in the history of science fiction.

sentative of the planetarium, and there my reading of the story was recorded. I pointed out that my thick Brooklyn accent would not sound well in midwestern ears, but they brushed that aside as nonsense. They must have changed their minds, however, for they never used my narration, but chose a person whose pronunciation was General American.

In the end the planetarium version was shown not only at the Abrams Planetarium, which had had the original notion, but also at many other planetaria around the nation. It was, I believe, successful everywhere, and although the payments I requested from the planetaria were modest, "The Last Question" eventually earned more in its planetarium incarnation than it ever did in print.

28

Analog had remained without an editor for the ten weeks since Campbell had died. Between the backlog Campbell had built up and Katherine Tarrant's handling, it continued smoothly, but a new editor had to be found, eventually. The publishers brooded over the possibilities and consulted a variety of people.

They consulted me, for instance, and I told them I thought that of all living science-fiction personalities the one who most nearly resembled Campbell in ability and character was Lester del Rey. I think they tended to agree with me, but Lester was fifty-six years old now and they wanted a younger man.

Ben Bova, who was only thirty-eight, was my second choice, and on September 29, Ben called me to tell me he was in New York being interviewed by Condé Nast. Janet and I spent the evening with Ben and, in the end, he got the job.

That was delightful. It meant he stayed in New York at least part of the time, and there simply is no one I like more than I like Ben.

29

I finished *The Early Asimov* on October 4, 1971, only three weeks after I started. The book was two hundred thousand words long, but most of it consisted of my early stories, of course, and only the autobiographical passages, not more than 10 per cent of the length of the book, had to be written.

The book covered the eleven years prior to the publication of *Pebble in the Sky*, the eleven years during which I wrote for science-fiction magazines exclusively. Of the sixty stories I had written in that interval, twenty-two had already appeared in collections I had published earlier. Twenty-seven stories appeared in *The Early Asimov*.

That left eleven stories that I reported as lost and non-existent. Of these, one, "Big Game," was discovered by a fan, Matthew B. Tepper, among the manuscripts I had given to Boston University, and I published it later. A second, "The Weapon," had been published in *Super Science Stories* under a pseudonym and had been utterly forgotten by me until I did the research for this book and *In Memory Yet Green*. It is included there.

The remaining nine are gone irretrievably.

30

The divorce proceedings were still hanging fire. Sixteen months had passed since I had left West Newton, and there had not even been a separation hearing.

There had been six postponements of such a hearing for one reason or another, but finally one on October 13 seemed hard and fast.

I drove to Boston on the twelfth and stayed with my lawyer, George Michaels. When we went into town the next day, however, we found that Gertrude's lawyer had asked for a postponement once again. He had requested it and received it after I had started for Boston.

It meant I would have to turn around and drive home again and then return to Boston the next week on the new hearing date. This was very depressing, for I had no way of knowing whether there might not be a repetition of what had just happened then.

31

The news that Ben Bova was to be the new editor of *Analog* made me want to write a story for him.

"The Greatest Asset," which I had sold to Campbell just eleven months before his death, had still not appeared. It did appear in the January 1972 *Analog*, one of the first under Ben's editorship, but that was not the same thing.

I therefore began a science-fiction story on October 14, which I called "Mirror Image." It was a six-thousand-word mystery that involved Lije Baley and R. Daneel, my detective partners of *The Caves of Steel* and *The Naked Sun*. I took it to him over lunch on November 4 (his first official editor's lunch with a writer).

Ben bought it (my first sale to him) and it eventually appeared in the May 1972 *Analog*.[6]

A much more important potential sale was that of *The Gods Themselves*.

Unfortunately, in the crucial three months during which *Analog* was without an editor, that magazine could not buy the novel for serialization. At that time, moreover, *Galaxy* was going through a bimonthly phase and could not serialize, while *F & SF* was not large enough to publish a ninety-three-thousand-word novel without cutting it.

It looked as though *The Gods Themselves* would have to do without serialization, when Judy-Lynn had a brilliant idea. Since the novel was divided into three parts, each one of which could stand on its own as a separate story, why did it have to appear in successive issues of a single magazine?

Galaxy's sister magazine, *If*, was also bimonthly but appeared in alternate months. The first part of *The Gods Themselves* could appear in *Galaxy*, the second in *If*, the third in *Galaxy* again. I was willing and that was how it was arranged.

Before the agreement was made formal with Doubleday, however, Ben Bova took over as editor at *Analog* and was all set to make the purchase at a thousand dollars more than *Galaxy* could pay. I was chagrined for I would have enjoyed the additional money and *Analog* had the greater prestige—but I had given my word to Judy-Lynn, and having done so I was bound more tightly than by mere contract.

So *The Gods Themselves* eventually appeared in the March 1972 *Galaxy*, the April 1972 *If*, and the May 1972 *Galaxy*. The issue of *If* with the second part (with the trisexed extraterrestrials) sold out completely, I was told.

32

Harry Walker, who had once served as my lecture agent in Boston thirteen years before, had transferred his home base to New York, and had his offices in the Empire State Building. Once again, he persuaded me to accept him as my agent by showing me that he would be able to get me fifteen hundred dollars for a talk.

On October 16, for instance, I drove to Alfred, New York, to talk at Alfred University, a talk he had arranged. We drove back the next

[6] See *The Best of Isaac Asimov* (Sphere Books, 1973).

day over Route 17, through a succession of hills that were covered by the most magnificent autumn foliage I had ever seen. It was as though the entire Earth had been turned into a Persian polychrome rug designed by a mad weaver.

34

My Thyroid

1

I drove to Boston again on October 19, 1971, to face the separation hearing. I was obviously in a highly nervous state for I managed to spill my breakfast of scrambled eggs and bacon right into my lap before I had had so much as a forkful. At 2 P.M., though, I was in the court-room and ready.

I saw Gertrude for the first time since I had left home—474 days—and didn't recognize her at first. She had lost some weight and, as usual, looked very trim and attractive.

Monroe Inker put me on the stand and kept me there for two hours and then for two hours more on the morning of the twentieth.

It was a very uncomfortable experience, my first time as a witness under oath in a courtroom, and I remember very little of the details. I was asked if I ever kept a budget and I said, "No. We just spent the money for whatever we needed."

The judge intervened to say, "Whether you had the money or not?"

And I forgot he was the judge, turned to him in outrage, and said, "I am not now, nor have I ever been, in debt by as much as a cent."

At another time, I was asked who I thought owned the money I had earned during marriage. I answered, "I always considered any money either of us earned during marriage to be the result of commu-nity endeavor and to belong to each of us equally."

Afterward, George Michaels said that admission would not help my case, but I shrugged and said, "It was true, George. I could say nothing else." There was no answer to that.

The hearing lasted till the twenty-sixth, but I was allowed to go home on the twenty-second.

In the course of the hearing there were reporters from the Boston papers present. I kept wondering what the devil they could get out of the hearing. There were no allegations of immorality, cruelty, or scan-dal of any kind. The whole argument was over the size of the settle-ment.

I found out, though. When I visited Austin on the evening of the twentieth, he said, "I heard over the radio this morning that you were making $205,000 a year."

I was stupefied. He had to be telling the truth because the figure was right—at least for 1970.

What had happened was that at the trial my income-tax statements for the previous six years were placed in evidence, with no objection at all from myself or my lawyer since they were honest documents, and the news media had picked it up.

The Boston *Herald* of October 20 had an eight-column headline (on an inside page) that read, "Science-fiction Writer Bares Income of $205,000." (How incredible it seemed in cold print!)

I came back to New York, rather shattered and well aware that it would now take additional months before any actual decision could be reached.

2

It seemed rather significant to my fevered spirit that Janet's little hamster, Cheeky, died of old age on October 24. (Hamsters only live three years at most.) We buried him along the side of the Palisades Parkway on our way to Schenectady to give a talk at the Freedom Forum.

3

I was slated to give a talk at the University of Bridgeport on November 3, in a ceremony in honor of John Dalton, the English chemist who had worked out the atomic theory of matter in 1803. Also invited was a local physicist of advanced years named Dennis Gabor.

On November 2, the winner of the 1971 Nobel Prize in physics was announced and it was Gabor, for his development of holography. I called up the University of Bridgeport at once to ask if Gabor would still show up. They said, yes, he had promised to. I asked if they wouldn't rather have him make the major presentation under the circumstances, but they wanted matters to continue as had been planned.

Of course, they couldn't continue *exactly* as planned. It was to have been a quiet ceremony with no outside interest but, at a day's notice, it became a rip-roaring affair with television cameras all over the place.

I had not planned to do anything special. I was going to deliver an off-the-cuff, easygoing talk as I always did. Now, though, I found the cameras trained on me and had to try to talk as though they weren't there.

It wasn't easy, but Gabor helped a great deal by being completely pleasant and at ease. He did not seem to mind sitting back and playing second fiddle to me in the ceremonies.

4

More Words of Science had been delayed by my work on *The Gods Themselves*, but on November 10 I finished it, nearly a year and a half after I had begun it.

5

On November 15, I visited the offices of the American Schizophrenia Association (they were pushing to have me attend a convention), and in the elevator I encountered a gray-haired fellow. I looked at him curiously and gave in to the irresistible impulse I have of spotting similarities and announcing them.

I said, "Did anyone ever tell you, sir, that you resemble Norman Mailer in appearance?"

"Yes," said the stranger, calmly. "I get told that now and then."

Over lunch, I announced this curious similarity, and the ASA people promptly told me that Mailer maintained an office in the building and that I had undoubtedly met the man himself.

Well, that explained the resemblance.

6

Fred Pohl and I participated in a late-night talk show with Long John Nebel on November 12. After it was over, a phone call came through for me at the station. It was Danny Metta from the old Decatur Street days, thirty-five years before, the one who had married Mazie, who had given me my first instruction in touch typing.

They came to visit me at the Cromwell on November 17. I hadn't seen them since the days at Windsor Place before Pearl Harbor, but Danny, despite his baldness, was quite recognizable. Not so Mazie, who was plump and four times a grandmother. I dare say I did not bring back any memories to them either, with my long, graying hair and with my bushy, whitening sideburns.

7

On November 16 I received the January 1972 *EQMM* and discovered, for the first time, that Fred Dannay was announcing "The Acquisitive Chuckle" as a series.

I had to come through. I even suspended work on *The Shaping of France*, which was in the home stretch, to write "Ph as in Phoney."[1] It, too, involved the Black Widowers, and I added one additional character, based on Trap Door Spider fellow member Don Bensen, who, nine years before, had anthologized my story "Author! Author!" Again I had a mystery that only Henry, at the end, could unravel. The Black Widowers series, and the tales of their banquets, had come into being.

Fred Dannay took the story at once and it appeared in the July 1972 *EQMM*. Dannay changed the title to "The Phoney Ph.D." in order to avoid a conflict with Lawrence Treat, who wrote a series of stories with titles on the order of "X as in Xylophone," but I changed the title back when I placed the story in my collection.

8

Again, Janet and I had a magnificent Thanksgiving feast at Chaucy's on November 25. It was a repeat of that of the year before, but this time Bill Boggs was not there. He and Leslie had split up.

9

Although Janet and I were becoming closer and closer and although she was beginning to participate fully in my social life, she also had a world of her own.

As a psychiatrist (and psychoanalyst) she was an important figure at the William Alanson White Institute, and she had a social life involving the institute. On December 4, 1971, I went, as her escort, to a Chinese dinner given by one of her colleagues and, for the first time, I met her friends and associates. It was the final outside-world link between us.

10

I finished *The Shaping of France* on December 15, and went on at once to the fourth of my ABC books for Walker. This time it was

1 See *Tales of the Black Widowers*.

ABC's of Ecology. I managed that between December 17 and 19, but was determined to do no more. They were simply not pleasant to do, far too artificial in structure, and each did less well than the one before.

11

Janet, being a physician, was constantly nervous about the state of my health, and kept urging general checkups. I, having been brought up to believe that you saw a doctor only as a last resort, felt indignant at the notion of seeing one when I was demonstrably in good health.

Janet had now, however, discovered an internist named Paul Esserman, through the recommendation of one of her friends, and was completely satisfied with his thoroughness and with his diagnostic know-how. She insisted on my going to see him.

I went through some kicking and screaming, but she kept up a rather relentless pressure, and on December 16, 1971, I showed up, more or less sullenly, at Esserman's office. Janet came along to make sure I didn't cut and run.

Esserman was tall and pudgy, with a smiling, soft-featured face, and a very soft voice that would dissolve into a little laugh when he was pleased.

He went over me in great detail, while I submitted scowlingly, and he finally said, "You are in great shape, Isaac."

"I could have told you that at the start," I said.

"Except for a thyroid nodule."

"What thyroid nodule?"

"Well, bend your head back here at the mirror. You see?"

I bent my head back and there, at the right side of my neck, was a clear bulge that was not present at the left side.

"I never saw that before," I said, startled. (Nor had I ever felt it when shaving, though after that day, I felt it every time and couldn't understand how I had missed it before.)

Paul said, "It's probably been there for years, and it's probably nothing important, but it will have to be investigated. Don't worry, I'll make all the arrangements."

We left in considerable depression. I knew very well what a nodule could be and that "probably nothing important" didn't fool me a bit. It could also be cancer.

As for Janet, she was now really upset that I had not routinely had medical checkups at frequent intervals. Surely one of them would have picked up the nodule at an earlier stage.

But you can't go back in time. We just had to follow up on it now.

12

What could I do? I threw myself into my work and even managed to have the happiest Christmas of my life.

Janet and I went to Westchester for the Christmas feasts at her mother's and at Chaucy's, and I took with me the galleys for the new edition of the *Guide to Science*.[2] With me also were several thousand index cards, and for many hours I sat in the room that had once been Janet's father's study working on the indexing, marking, paginating, and alphabetizing while everyone else went around on tiptoes to make sure the great man was not disturbed at his task.

I enjoyed every minute of it because I knew it wouldn't last. Eventually, when everyone was quite used to me, there would be no hesitation whatever in interrupting me at my giant labors in order to get me to collaborate in some trivial household task.

13

I was also involving myself in still another treatment of the biblical Book of Ruth. I had written about Ruth first for the Reader's Digest Press book. I had then given my Breadloaf speech on the subject and had devoted an *F & SF* essay to it.

I now wanted to do a whole book on it for young people, one in which I quoted the book, verse by verse, and, in effect, annotated it. As far back as September, I had talked to Larry about it and he had directed me to Tom Aylesworth of Doubleday's juvenile section. Aylesworth agreed, and on December 28 I began *The Story of Ruth*.

14

We celebrated New Year's Eve at the del Reys. The Silverbergs were there, too, but they were planning to sell their rambling mansion in the Bronx and move out to California. More and more, the science-fiction world was centering in California. With so much science fiction in the movies and in television and with the magazines seeming less important every year, there was a natural drift of writers westward.

2 There was a question as to what to call the new edition. We couldn't very well call it *The New New Intelligent Man's Guide to Science*. Rosenthal, after all the fuss he had made about Doubleday using *The Intelligent Man's Guide to the Bible*, now backtracked and used the Doubleday formula. He decided to call the book *Asimov's Guide to Science*. Doubleday, fortunately, was more good-natured about it than Rosenthal had been in connection with the Bible book.

15

I had nine books published in 1971:

109. *The Stars in Their Courses* (Doubleday)
110. *Where Do We Go From Here?* (Doubleday)
111. *What Makes the Sun Shine?* (Atlantic Monthly Press)
112. *The Sensuous Dirty Old Man* (Walker)
113. *The Best New Thing* (World)
114. *Isaac Asimov's Treasury of Humor* (Houghton Mifflin)
115. *The Hugo Winners, Volume II* (Doubleday)
116. *The Land of Canaan* (Houghton Mifflin)
117. *ABC's of the Earth* (Walker)

16

I was fifty-two years old on January 2, 1972. With my thyroid nodule looming over me, I became uncomfortably aware that William Shakespeare had died on his fifty-second birthday.

However, even at the worst of my charming immodesties, I couldn't convince myself that Shakespeare represented a precedent for myself.

17

I had been attending the Dutch Treat Club luncheons more often than not ever since I had become a member, and was enjoying them tremendously. On January 4, 1972, I was even the entertainment, giving a half-hour talk that was well received. (It was a humorous talk about myself and my writing habits.)

18

Paul Esserman had made the necessary arrangements for investigating the thyroid nodule. On January 10, I went to the offices of Manfred Blum, an endocrinologist, who made quite certain that what I had was an enlarged thyroid and nothing else.

A week later I underwent the crucial test in which I drank a solution containing radioactive iodine. The iodine is taken up promptly by the thyroid and will not appear in any quantity anywhere else in the body. My neck region was then scanned for radioactivity.

If the nodule is "hot"—that is, if it takes up iodine—it would be a good sign, since active thyroid tissue might enlarge for many reasons other than cancer. If it is "cold" and does not take up iodine, it would be a bad sign, for a cancerous organ is quite likely to lose its specialized abilities.

Blum explained this to me. He said, "If it's cold, then there is a somewhat better chance that it might be—uh—that it could—"

I said, dryly, "Doc, it's permissible in this case to use the word 'cancer.'" (After all, no circumlocution was going to fool me.)

By January 24, I had the answer. The nodule was cold and Blum told me that statistically the chance of cancer was about one in twenty. It meant that I would have to be on thyroid pills the rest of my life, not so much to supply me with thyroid, but to supply sufficient outside thyroid to cause the body to suppress the gland itself. If the gland shrank on treatment, I might be able to avoid surgery.

I accepted the pills, but I did not for one moment feel that I would have a chance of avoiding surgery. With a one in twenty chance of having cancer, no surgeon would resist the fun of going in and seeing.

19

I continued methodically on my various projects, just the same. I had finished the first draft of *The Story of Ruth* on January 14, and on that same day I began a book I had promised to do for Chaucy.

The book was *Jupiter*. NASA was sending out Pioneer 10 to make a close pass at Jupiter, and it seemed to Chaucy and to me that it would be ideal to have a book on the planet published at the time of the pass.

On that same day, I was cohost at a Trap Door Spiders Meeting with Al Balk as my guest. Adding to the festivities on that day was the fact that Sprague, having survived a prostatectomy, was present and clearly in fine shape.

Then, over the next two days, I put all of *The Story of Ruth* into final copy (it was only twenty thousand words long) and brought it to Doubleday on January 17.

20

Elyse Pines, who a few years before had inveigled me into talking at Brooklyn Polytechnic, had come up with an interesting idea.

Though "Star Trek" was no longer on television as a living program, reruns could still be seen on local stations, and interest in it seemed to be growing steadily. Elyse watched the reruns faithfully, and so did many of her friends (and so did Janet)—so why not organize a "Star Trek" convention?

She and others got to work at it, and on the weekend of January 22–23, the convention was held at the Statler-Hilton. Elyse expected some four hundred to register. In actual fact, she got twenty-five hundred.

I attended and met Gene Roddenberry again after a five-year hiatus. Janet came with me and we had dinner at the Americana with him and with his new wife.

After dinner, Janet went home. She cannot endure the noise and crowding of large meetings as I can. Besides, most of my time under such conditions is spent autographing books, which I enjoy, but which is rather dull as a spectator sport.

21

Despite lectures, books, conventions, and even dinner at the house of Phil Gelber, an old Navy Yard buddy of thirty years before who now lived in Metuchen, New Jersey, the matter of my thyroid continued to haunt me.

On February 4, Paul Esserman had made an appointment on my behalf with Carl A. Smith, a surgeon.[3] Smith examined me, and came to the same conclusion that Esserman and Blum had. The nodule was probably benign, but the chance of cancer was high enough to warrant a look at it. The urgency was not high, however, the hospital beds were filled, and it might take some months before an operation could be scheduled.

I said, rather dry-mouthed, that I was in no hurry.

I might have been in no hurry, but Esserman was. He was influential and he used his influence. On Tuesday, February 8, I got the news. Shortage of beds or not, they had one for me, and I was to go into the hospital the following Saturday.

I had four days to get my spirits into shape. I had never before, in my fifty-two years of life, faced an operation under general anesthesia, and the prospect was a frightening one. Suppose I was one of those very few who were unexpectedly sensitive to the anesthetic? Suppose I went under and never came out again? Suppose, in fact, that I only had four days to live?

I called Stanley. He had undergone operations on his spine in con-

---

[3] That morning I read of the death of Chester Keefer the day before, at the age of seventy-four. My struggle with him, now fifteen years in the past, no longer stirred me, however, and I read the obituary with detachment.

nection with a slipped disc some years before, and that was a much more dangerous situation than a thyroidectomy, which was not, on the whole, a difficult operation. Had he been frightened? If so, how had he overcome it?

Stanley listened to my fears sympathetically and said, "The trouble, Isaac, is that you're feeling no symptoms. Your thyroid is giving you no pain so that there is no reason for you to *want* the operation. When I was waiting for my operation, I suffered excruciating back pains, and one of my legs was numb. I looked forward to the operation as a deliverance, but you don't have that advantage."

I had to work it out some other way. I kept myself busy. At that time I was working on *Asimov's Biographical Encyclopedia of War and Battle*, a book I had talked Larry into letting me do; a book that was to be along the lines of the earlier, *Asimov's Biographical Encyclopedia of Science and Technology*. It was, in essence, to be a military history by way of biographies of military leaders. That kept my mind engaged during the day.

The nights were more difficult, and on the night of February 11, I finally worked it out. It wasn't that I feared the process of dying—dying under anesthesia was the easiest way to go. Nor did I fear the consequences of dying. I wasn't afraid of going to hell. The imminence of death woke no sudden twinges of either religion or superstition within me.

The trouble was, it seemed to me, that I was only fifty-two and that I would be scorned as having died prematurely. I would suffer posthumous embarrassment, dying at so young an age. Everyone would say, "He didn't get to finish his life work because he was too much of a weakling to live out a normal life."

And I thought: What the heck, I'd published 117 books and had over a dozen more in press. That was more than almost anyone could do in a full lifetime of a hundred years. And I did it all from scratch, by myself, without inherited wealth or family connections. What more was I supposed to do? If I died, I died, but no one could possibly scorn me for what I had done with life.

And with that, a great calm descended on me, for I had made my peace with death (with a quiet death, not unduly prolonged or agonizing, at least) for all time. I went into the hospital on February 12, 1972, quite cheerfully.

I took a portable mechanical typewriter with me, and on February 13 and 14 I wrote my third Black Widowers story, "Truth to Tell."[4]

[4] See *Tales of the Black Widowers*.

Larry Ashmead visited me on the afternoon of February 14, and I gave him the manuscript of "Truth to Tell" and asked him to see that it got out to *EQMM*. I also asked him to explain that I was in the hospital for an operation as an explanation of why I did not take it in personally. (I didn't want Eleanor and Connie to think I would lightly miss a chance to go in and flirt with them).

"Truth to Tell" was accepted at once. In fact, a very concerned Eleanor called me while I was still in the hospital to tell me of the sale and to ask after my health. It appeared in the October 1972 *EQMM* under the title of "The Man Who Never Told a Lie," but I used my own title in the collection.

I did have the rather silly notion that perhaps the story was taken because of sympathy for poor Isaac (silly, because that's not how editors' minds work), but later on, Allen J. Hubin bought it for his collection *Best Detective Stories of the Year, 1973*, and *he* didn't know I had written it in the hospital. So I relaxed.

22

At 10:20 P.M. on the night of February 14, I was persuaded, over my objections, to take a sleeping pill, since the operation was scheduled for the following morning. I said I would sleep fine without one and that I had never taken one, but the nurse was following the rules, and down it went.

I was up at 5:00 A.M. even so. I shaved, cleaned my teeth, showered, and so on, and I remember taking a long look at my smooth and unmarked throat, knowing that I would never see it unmarked again.

At 6:00 A.M., the nurse came in to give me injections.

"What's that?" I said, suspiciously.

"Just tranquilizers," she said, "to keep you calm."

"I'm perfectly calm," I said. "Take them away."

She didn't listen, either. She jabbed me.

By 7:00 A.M. the injections had removed all my cares and woe and I was hilarious. I am *always* hilarious when I have no cares and woe.

They came to get me and insisted I be wheeled through the corridors in a cart even though I assured them I could walk perfectly well. While they wheeled me, I felt happy enough to sing Villon's rallying cry against Burgundy from *The Vagabond King* and did so in a loud and resonant baritone.

I heard one nurse say to another, "Have you ever come across *this* reaction to medication?"

In the operating room at 8:00 A.M., I watched with happy interest as they placed intravenous tubes in the veins of my left hand (something that, without tranquilizers, would have horrified me). Then in came Carl Smith, with a green smock and a green mask, and his eyes twinkling with the joy all surgeons feel at the prospect of cutting into quivering, living flesh.

"Carl," I shouted, "Come here."

Then I intoned:

> Doctor, doctor, in your green coat,
> Doctor, doctor, cut my throat.
> And when you've finished, doctor, then,
> Won't you sew it up again.

By then a desperate anesthesiologist was through and I was told to count backward from one hundred. I don't think I got past ninety-four. One of the residents told me afterward that my last words were "Doctor, help me."

Carl Smith told me afterward that it was a terrible thing for me to have recited that doggerel to him, for he stood there with his knife at my throat, trying to stop laughing, so that he could cut with a steady hand.

He said, "You were depending on my steady hand. Why did you try to make me laugh?"

Could I explain I would do anything for a laugh?

What I did not properly appreciate at the time (thank goodness) was that the recurrent laryngeal nerve might be involved; that if so, it would have to be excised and that I would be hoarse for the rest of my life, and my lecture career would be ended; that Carl was the kind of surgeon who would excise it remorselessly at the least suspicion of cancer.

The resident told me that the operation, a simple one, proceeded in an atmosphere of conversations and relaxation until Carl began to examine the recurrent laryngeal nerve millimeter by millimeter and then "you could hear a pin drop."

I was on the operating table for four hours, since the thyroid had to be checked for the nature of the growth. It *was* malignant; I had a papillary carcinoma. Out came the entire right half of my thyroid, but the recurrent laryngeal nerve was in perfect shape and stayed in.

I came to in the recovery room without any of the "Where am I?" bit. I knew exactly where I was and what had happened, and my first words were, "Are my parathyroids safe?" (These are small glands near the thyroid, which I didn't want to lose since they are more nearly vital to life than the thyroid is.)

Back in the hospital room, Janet was waiting for me in the greatest tension and ran to meet the cart that was carrying me. She had already been told that I was fine. She stayed with me for a while and I said to her, woozily, "I'm not sure I'm all right, Janet. I don't feel like doing any typing." (The next day, though, I managed.)

At 5:00 P.M. of the operation day of February 15, George Michaels, who happened to be in New York, came to visit. He had news of the separation suit. The day before (on February 14, 1972—which, by an uncomfortable coincidence, was the thirtieth anniversary of the blind date on which I had met Gertrude) the judge had handed down his decision.

And so, on February 14, 1972, nineteen months after I had left West Newton, I was legally separated. By the law of New York State, one year after that I could qualify for divorce.

23

February 19, 1972, was Robyn's seventeenth birthday, and again I was unable to see her. This time I couldn't even talk to her on the phone, for my throat hurt and I was under orders to speak as little as possible. Stanley undertook to call her on my behalf.

That same day, Carl Smith removed the fifteen stitches he had made to close the incision, and admired the scar greatly. (Surgeons always admire their own scars just as writers admire their own books.)

I left the hospital at 2:00 P.M. on the nineteenth, seven days to the hour after I had entered.

Just before leaving I sneezed and there was a period of horrible pain in my throat. With the wisdom of hindsight I later realized that the sneeze had disrupted some internal tissue and had caused my throat tissues to fill with fluid so that it swelled up as though I had a giant goiter. It was not a serious situation and slowly, over the weeks, the swelling went down. I thought at first it was a natural consequence of the operation.

On February 20, I actually went to the Cromwell over Janet's protests. I just couldn't survive without looking at my mail, and by the twenty-third, I was putting in a full day of work and completed the last of the little Introductions for the chapters in the textbook *Psychology Today*.

24

At this time I had my two Selectric typewriters both in use, one at the Cromwell and one in Janet's apartment. This meant that if either one of them broke down, I could not work unless I shifted my base of operations. I therefore ordered a third Selectric so that I could have a backup at the Cromwell, where I did about 80 per cent of my work, and it arrived soon after my operation.

Eventually, I got a fourth Selectric so that I could have a backup in Janet's apartment as well.

Janet also had an electric typewriter of her own, and we had the small hand-typewriter I used in the hospital.

This meant we owned six typewriters altogether, which makes perfect sense as I've described it, though most people seem to think it an odd situation.

25

On February 25, I visited Carl Smith's office for my first postoperation examination. He seemed staggered at the edematous swelling of my throat. "What have you done to my scar?" he demanded.

I tried to explain about the last-minute sneeze, but he wouldn't accept that. He said, "Have you been straining yourself? I told you not to strain yourself."

"I haven't been straining myself," I said, indignantly, "I've been very relaxed."

"Have you had sex?"

"Of course I've had sex."

"Aha! I told you not to strain yourself."

"Sex is no strain. For you, maybe, Carl; but not for me."

26

Millicent Selsam of Walker & Company came up with an excellent idea for a series of small books for the grade-school audience. They would be on science history and would have titles that would go *How Did We Find Out About———?*

I seized upon the idea eagerly. They would not have the artificiality of the ABC series, and science history had become a specialty of mine. Millie suggested *How Did We Find Out the Earth Is Round?* and *How Did We Find Out About Electricity?* as two possible titles for such books, and I agreed to do both.

I got to work on them soon after getting out of the hospital, and by March 6 they were both completed.

I was also working on a new history book for Houghton Mifflin. This one was my first to deal with modern history and covered the period of exploration and colonization of North America. I called it *The Shaping of North America* and it carried the history forward to 1763, when the Treaty of Paris ended the French and Indian War and left Great Britain supreme on the northern half of the continent.

27

On March 2, Robyn called and I spoke to her for the first time since my operation. She was taking a course in science fiction at her high school, and one of the books she was studying was *Foundation*.

28

I had not missed any speaking engagements as a result of my operation, except for a book-and-author luncheon that had been scheduled for the very day of the operation and that I was to have done without pay.

The first paid speech to come up was at Drew University in New Jersey, where I was supposed to talk on both March 3 and 4. Both Carl and Paul recommended that I cancel. If I overstrained my voice, they said, I might lose it altogether and not be back to normal for a year.

I stubbornly insisted on going, however. I could not bear to cancel. I promised I would whisper into the microphone.

I really meant to. I explained the situation to the audience, and I did actually begin in a whisper. On each occasion, though, I quickly forgot and, within five minutes, was talking in my ordinary energetic fashion. Fortunately, I didn't lose my voice.

The last echo of my operation came on March 9, when I completed my 166th *F & SF* essay. It dealt with the thyroid gland and I called it "Doctor, Doctor, Cut My Throat."[5] It appeared in the August 1972 *F & SF*.

[5] See *The Tragedy of the Moon.*

35

Janet's Breast

1

On March 13, 1972, I began the fourth Black Widower story, which I called "Go, Little Book,"[1] and took it in the next day to the delight of Eleanor and Connie, who made a big fuss over me. It appeared in the December 1972 *EQMM* under the title of "The Matchbook Collector."

2

Rae Jeppson visited Janet's apartment on March 18 and by a very fortunate coincidence I had only the day before received advance copies of my new *F & SF* collection, *The Left Hand of the Electron*, which I had dedicated to Rae. She was, of course, very pleased.

As for Asimov's *Guide to Science*, advance copies of which reached me on April 5, that was dedicated to Janet in large print—the first of my books to be dedicated to her. And that was appropriate, for it had been her eloquent encouragement in her letters, twelve years before, that had emboldened me to agree to do the first edition of the book.

3

Harry Harrison had undertaken to put together an anthology of original stories to be called *Astounding* and to serve as a memorial to John Campbell. The idea was that a number of authors were to write new stories of the type they had written for him.

Harry approached me on the matter, and I said I would write one more thiotimoline piece. On March 21, I did, "Thiotimoline to the Stars,"[2] and it appeared in the anthology.

[1] See *Tales of the Black Widowers*.
[2] See *Buy Jupiter and Other Stories*.

4

Gertrude wanted to discuss our financial situation with me.

I drove to Boston on April 6, and after lunch with Austin and Mary K., went to West Newton and, for the first time in twenty-one months, walked into the house I had bought sixteen years before.

I saw Robyn's room, which had been remodeled since I had left, and I was able to greet Satan who, of course, stared at me suspiciously. There was no sign of any memory at all.

I took the whole family to dinner, and that evening and the next morning Gertrude and I talked about the situation, but there was no meeting of minds.

I had promised that when I was in town, I would stop off at Newton High School and talk to Robyn's science-fiction class. I imagined I was to talk informally and at my leisure with a small class in a small classroom. When I showed up at the high school, however, I found the entire student body in the auditorium.

It was rank exploitation, and Robyn was as surprised as I was. She, too, had thought that only her class was involved. What could I do? For Robyn's sake, I went through with it, and even smiled.

5

On April 16, we drove to Rochester to see the planetarium version of "The Last Question." I was astonished at my own reaction to it. Though I knew the story (of course) and though the narration and dialog suffered by not being handled by professional actors, the effect built and pyramided.

I didn't write the story with clever attention to technique; my stories work themselves out with no conscious interference from me. Just the same, the six episodes of the story were successively briefer, more sweeping, and more chilling, just as though I had deliberately planned them that way for effect. Then the final episode slows and waits—and the planetarium dome grew dark and stayed dark for over two minutes while the last paragraphs of the story were recited in a quiet increase of tension, and the audience was absolutely silent.

Even I, who knew what was coming, waited, scarcely able to breathe, and for the others the final, sudden creation of the universe must have done everything but stop the heart.

It was a terrific show; in fact, it was that show that finally convinced me that "The Last Question" was the best story I had ever done and (my private conviction) the best science-fiction story anyone had ever done.

We then went on to Cleveland, where I talked at Case Western Reserve and where I got a standing ovation, but there was something better than that:

In the hotel restaurant, Janet said, "There's a woman there who looks just like Julie Newmar."

I refused to believe her. I had seen Julie Newmar in the musical show *Li'l Abner* where she played Stupefyin' Jones and where she stupefied *me*. I used to watch her play Catwoman on the "Batman" show, and while Batman was immune to her blandishments, I wasn't.

Then we read in the paper that Julie Newmar was in a play that was opening in Cleveland (it flopped). Janet really had seen her.

The next day, April 19, we encountered her again, and this time I took my courage in both hands and addressed her. It was easier than I could possibly have expected. She was a very nice woman, unaffected and natural. She turned out to be a science-fiction fan and seemed to be as much gratified at finding herself in my presence as I was at finding myself in hers.

On April 20, we were at Chillicothe, Ohio, to see the Great Serpent Mound, which delighted Janet, and then it was back to Columbus for a talk at Ohio State University on the twenty-first. We were invited to a student dinner where everyone sat on the floor, pulled pieces of boiled chicken out of a huge pot, and a number of people smoked marijuana.

I exclude Janet and myself. We were offered drags as the joints made the circuit but we turned them down politely. It was the first time I had ever been part of a group whom I knew to be smoking pot, and I felt uncomfortable.

6

I drove out to Long Beach on April 25, picked up my mother, and took her to the Long Beach Library.

The librarian there, finding that my mother lived in a hotel in Long Beach, was assiduous in his attentions to her and, of course, I had to talk at the library when he asked me to, if only to give my mother one more time in the limelight.

My poor mother enjoyed herself extremely and was very sad when it was time for me to leave. She was afraid each time I left that it would be the last time she would see me—and so was I, for she was clearly growing feebler. (I never told her about my operation.)

7

Then in May, it was Janet's turn. She detected a lump in her left breast, and somehow the light began to go out of life. A lump in the thyroid is one thing; the thyroid can be removed in whole or in part and, except for a thyroid pill every so often, life goes on unchanged in appearance and in fact.

A lump in the breast can be quite another thing. Even if life goes on, it can be at a terrible price.

Naturally, we tried to assume that it was only a cyst, only something benign, and we did our best to live normal lives while checking the matter out. On May 14, for instance, we drove to Westchester and took Rae to lunch in order to celebrate Mother's Day, and we gave her no cause to suppose we were uneasy.

We awaited further investigation—and decision.

8

The previous March I had written a piece on my views on feminism for *Harper's Bazaar*. It sat on the editor's desk for two months before I was finally invited to lunch to discuss revisions.

On May 15, I was at the restaurant at precisely noon, that being the time of meeting. The editor was late, of course, but I'm quite used to that, and it didn't bother me. At 12:16 P.M. she showed up and I expected the usual apology, which I was prepared to brush aside genially.

This editor was of sterner stuff. She strode in, favored me with a displeased look, and said, "Well, you're early, aren't you?"

I stiffened and decided we would have trouble coming to an agreement on the revision.

Later, she asked me why I wrote science fiction, and before I could give her any of my usual, and very cogent, reasons, she decided to answer her own questions by saying, "I suppose you write science fiction because you don't have the courage to face the real world."

I told her through teeth I labored to ungrit that I faced the real world very well indeed and wrote books in many fields other than science fiction.

"Oh," said she, "how many books have you written?"

"One hundred and twenty-two," I said, enunciating clearly.

"Well," said she, not in the least disconcerted, "you must be very hard to live with."

I left that lunch quite determined that I would not revise the article and that she could wait till hell froze over for it.

When I came back to the Cromwell, however, there was a request in the mail from the Publishers-Hall newspaper syndicate asking me to do an article for them on a subject of my own choosing, but mentioning one or two newsworthy science topics.

I fired back an answer at once, asking if I might do an article on guilt provokers, and describing the lunch I had just had.

I got a phone call the very next day from Richard Sherry of the syndicate. "If you can make the article as funny as you made the letter," he said, "let's have it."

My depression and anger lifted at once at the thought I could get it all out of my system by writing about it (ah, the advantages of being a writer).

I wrote the article, "Guilt," at a sitting on May 31. I told not only the story of the lunch, but also a few others, including that of Carl Smith's blaming me for my edematous neck. Then just to show that I sinned as well as having been sinned against, I told the story of our trip to Williamsburg when I accused Janet of bringing on the snowstorm by packing my boots. The article was accepted at once and appeared in numerous newspapers around the country in the following summer.

So mollified was I at writing the article that I was able to revise the article for *Harper's Bazaar* as requested, and it appeared in the August 1972 issue under the title of "No More Willing Baby Machines."

I am not planning to include "No More Willing Baby Machines" in any of my collections, but "Guilt" is another matter.

After the appearance of *Isaac Asimov's Treasury of Humor*, I planned a follow-up book containing additional jokes, plus a collection of my humorous articles. "Guilt" would surely be an item.

I had mentioned this at Breadloaf the previous summer, and John Ciardi had suggested the title—*Isaac Asimov Laughs Again*. I eventually got a contract for it from Austin Olney and even got to work on it. Other work got in the way, though, and the book has been hanging fire for years.

So has *Asimov's Biographical Encyclopedia of War and Battle*, which went into Coventry at about this time and never emerged. These are not phases of writer's block, in any way. What happens is that I take on too many projects for even my workaholic capacity, and some items simply go to the wall. I know they're there, though, and someday, if I live long enough . . .

As far as my nonhumorous essays are concerned, I was having no problem. I was putting together another collection of those that appeared elsewhere than in *F & SF* and called it *Today and Tomorrow and—*.

9

Richard Hoagland, the young man I had met in Boston eight years before and who was then running a planetarium in Springfield, showed up, rather unexpectedly, on May 23. He had a new project under way. This was to arrange a cruise on the *Queen Elizabeth* 2 to Florida to witness the launching of Apollo 17 in December.

Apollo 17 was to be the last manned trip to the Moon and the only night launch. I was intrigued, even though I shuddered at the thought of going as far afield as Florida. I promised to consider the possibility of going.

It was a relief to turn from that to something more mundane. I wrote a fifth Black Widowers story, "Early Sunday Morning,"[3] which eventually appeared in the March 1973 *EQMM* under the title "The Biological Clock."

On May 29, I finished *The Shaping of North America*.

10

I drove to Alfred University on June 3. This time I was to get an honorary degree. They had offered me a Doctor of Science but I pointed out that I already had two of those and asked, diffidently, if it were possible to get a Doctor of Letters instead. They agreed and I was delighted, since Litt.D. was by now far more appropriate a tribute to my life's work than a Sc.D. was.

I was not the commencement speaker, however; Rod Serling was. He was getting a degree of Doctor of Humane Letters.

11

My first five *F & SF* collections were now out of print in hardcover, though each had a living soft-cover edition. Larry phoned to tell me that some firm wanted to put out limited editions of each of them for very limited money. This would, of course, tie up the books as far as other use was concerned.

At lunch on June 6, I suggested an alternate scheme. Why not ab-

[3] See *Tales of the Black Widowers*.

stract from each of the books enough articles on a given topic to put out a new essay collection to be named *Asimov on Astronomy, Asimov on Physics,* and so on? I would supply each book with an Introduction, and index, and update each article where necessary.

"Good," said Larry, "and we can add illustrations, too, if you will write the captions."

I agreed.

12

The galleys of *Asimov's Annotated Don Juan* had arrived and been taken care of, and I expected to see the book itself before long. I strongly suspected, though (despite Doubleday's optimism), that the book would not do well and that, thereafter, I would not be able to stick them with a similar book. The thing to do was to stick them with one *now*, before the returns were in on the first.

On June 14, 1972, therefore, I began *Asimov's Annotated Paradise Lost,* and, in no time at all, I was lost in the pleasurable dissection of a great literary classic once more. And I persuaded Doubleday to go along with me on this.

13

The Gilbert and Sullivan Society for its June meeting was planning a rendition of *Trial by Jury* to be given in strictly amateur fashion by the members themselves—and guess who was going to be the Counsel for the Plaintiff?

I had accepted lightly enough because I knew the Counsel's solo, "With a Sense of Deep Emotion," and, of course, I can sing quite adequately.

When they gave me a copy of the music with my part underlined, however, I discovered to my horror that I had a number of minor things to sing that I knew nothing about, including my part in a very complicated sextette.

For a couple of months, I did my best to learn it. I visited Jocelyn Wilkes (a large soprano with a silver voice and a golden heart who could sing Katisha better than anyone in the world, I think), who tried to teach me the part, and I attended a rehearsal as well. Everyone else, however, knew every note, and when June 16, 1972, rolled around, I managed to get onto the stage in a kind of paralytic fit.

I believe I sang my way through the operetta, but I have no memory of it whatever.

It was the only time in my life I ever had stage fright.[4]

14

On June 19, I had lunch with President McGill of Columbia University at *his* request. I was delighted to agree, but I did make the condition that Professor Dawson be invited as well. He joined us and for two hours I rather gloried in the long way I had climbed since the days, thirty-five years before, when I had been a second-class student at the university.

15

For six weeks now, we had been living with the lump in Janet's left breast. Both Paul Esserman and Carl Smith were cheerfully convinced that it was benign, but there was no way out but to go in and look at it. The operation was to take place in July, and I was desperate for activities that would keep her mind off the matter.

I had, for instance, received an invitation to attend a seminar on the future of communications that was to be held at the Institute of Man and Science at Rensselaerville, New York. Ordinarily I would not have accepted, but it was a chance to get out into a rural atmosphere and divert Janet, so I agreed.

On July 3, we drove there and found it to be a wonderful place, well beyond our expectations. It was countrified and Janet lost her fears for a while as we explored rural roads and waterfalls, listened to interesting talks, and met fascinating people.

On the night of the third, a gentleman named Beardsley Graham delivered a talk on the future of television cassettes that was utterly stimulating. "In the future," he said, "the book will not be a pile of grimy manuscript pages, but a neat television cassette, and men like Isaac Asimov will be out of business."

I was sitting in the front row, and I jumped, of course. Everyone laughed.

On July 5, it turned out that the gentleman slated to give the eve-

[4] The day after this arduous task of mine, five burglars slipped into the national Democratic headquarters at the Watergate apartment complex in Washington and were caught. No quiver of premonition came to me as to the importance of this (as it seemed) utterly trivial event.

ning talk was unavoidably delayed in London, and Duncan Mac-
Donald[5] asked if I would give the talk instead.

"But I have nothing prepared," I said.

She said, "You don't have to be prepared. We know you can improvise."

I can never resist flattery. That night I picked up Graham's remark
about television cassettes putting me out of business and gave a rousing
impromptu defense of the book. It went over very well, and after we returned home, I incorporated the talk into my 171st *F & SF* essay. I
called it "The Ancient and the Ultimate,"[6] and it appeared in the January 1973 *F & SF*.

Since I had also thought to bring the hand typewriter with me to
Rensselaerville, I also improved each shining hour by writing my sixth
Black Widowers tale, "The Obvious Factor," and on returning home I
wrote a seventh, "The Pointing Finger."[7] They appeared in the May
1973 and July 1973 issues, respectively, of *EQMM*.

16

Victor Serebriakoff, the founder and High Panjandrum of Mensa,
was arriving in New York on one of his periodic visits to the United
States, and I received an invitation from Margot Seitelman, the maid-
of-all-work of the New York section, to come and meet him. For
three years now I had allowed my Mensa dues to lapse and I had assumed my association with the organization was over but, as it happened, I was curious to meet Victor.

On July 12, Janet and I attended the meeting. Victor was short,
plump, bearded, charming, and highly intelligent. He also had the ability to tell jokes in cockney, and that won him a secure niche in my
heart.

I met a number of other interesting Mensans, some of whom
remembered my talk on the day of John Kennedy's assassination nearly
nine years before. In particular, there was Marvin Grossworth, taller,
plumper, balder, and more bearded than Victor and just as intelligent
and charming.

Victor asked me why I had allowed my membership of Mensa to
lapse, and when I found myself at a loss for words, he told me that I

---

[5] Despite her name, she was a woman, and a charming one at that. She had interviewed me on the radio once in Boston, nearly twenty years before, and it was for
that reason she had thought of me in connection with the seminar and invited me.
[6] See *The Tragedy of the Moon*.
[7] See *Tales of the Black Widowers*.

was once again a member and that if I would prefer not to pay my dues, he would pay them for me.

Well, I couldn't allow that, so I promptly said I would pay my own dues—and I was once again a Mensa member.

Victor also urged me to visit Great Britain under Mensa auspices and give some talks. My aversion to travel had been growing steadily with the years and I was all set to refuse flatly and eternally, but Janet seemed to blossom at the thought of visiting Great Britain. I thought of the forthcoming hospitalization and rather gave the impression that I might go someday. This was taken by Victor to be a flat acceptance.

17

I had met Anita Summer, who was working for the Leonard Lyons column, because she was a science-fiction fan and we had both attended the same science-fiction convention. We got along well, and among the fringe benefits was an invitation she wangled for me to attend a cocktail party given in honor of the contestants in the Miss Universe competition.

On July 17, then, I found myself wandering about delightedly among a number of tall and gorgeous women and was particularly taken with Miss Wales.

Anita said to me, "Are you going to write a story about this, Isaac?"

"Of course," I said.

I wasn't serious, but as I thought about it, it seemed to me that I could. Four days later, I wrote my eighth Black Widowers story against the background of a "Miss Earth" contest, with a Miss Wales playing a key part. I called it "Miss What?,"[8] but it eventually appeared in the September 1973 *EQMM* under the title of "A Warning to Miss Earth."

18

Janet entered University Hospital (the same one in which I had had my thyroidectomy nearly half a year before) on July 23, and on July 25 underwent exploratory surgery.

We were not certain when she would go under the knife, and she promised to call me before she let them roll her away. At 3:00 P.M. she called me, and at three-twenty I was in her room with a copy of Wodehouse's *Cocktail Time* and settled down to wait.

[8] See *Tales of the Black Widowers.*

I expected her to be back at 5:00 P.M. with the good news of some-thing benign. By 5:15 P.M. I was frowning, and by 6:00 P.M. I was downright anxious. I could get no news out of anyone except that she was still in the operating room.

Anxiety grew, hope dwindled. Chaucy arrived at 7:30 P.M., and by then I had run out of hope altogether. I knew what had happened, and I finally forced a resident to tell me the truth. There was a small malig-nancy, and Carl Smith, a determined cutter, was performing a radical mastectomy of the left breast. I was shattered and depended heavily on Chaucy for support.

Doctors and nurses begged me, then ordered me, to go home, but of course I refused, even though Chaucy had to leave eventually. I would not leave without seeing Janet, I said. It was nearly 1:00 A.M. be-fore they went down to get her, and I insisted on going with them.

Janet was only woozily awake, just barely alert, but she knew what had happened. "I'm sorry," she said—apologizing to me.

After that, they virtually kicked me out bodily. I made my way home, oppressed and stunned, and well aware that with the passing of midnight it was my thirtieth wedding anniversary.

19

I spent the next thirty-six hours in heavy dependence on Chaucy, on Larry, and on the del Reys. When I arrived at the hospital on the twenty-seventh, I found Janet in tears and despair. The sedation had worn off sufficiently to let her know that she would have only one breast as long as she lived, unless she lost that one, too; that she was forty-five years old and, in her own eyes, plain; that she had no legal hold on me; and that I would now, as soon as was convenient, take my-self off and find a younger, prettier, two-breasted woman.

I tried feverishly to tell her that this wasn't so; that I was with her come what may; that she hadn't abandoned me because of my thyroid, and that I wouldn't abandon her because of her breast; that what pleased me in her was beyond the reach of the surgeon's knife. It didn't help. She was in no mood to listen to such things.

So I stood up, rather desperately, pointed my finger at her, and said, "Listen! What's all the fuss about? If you were a showgirl, I could see where taking off the left breast would be tragic. You would be all unbalanced, and you would fall over to the right side. In your case, with your tiny breasts, who cares? In a year, I'll be looking at you and squinting my eyes and saying, 'Which breast did the surgeon remove?'"

To my relief, she burst into laughter. Indeed, when Carl Smith came to examine her, she told him what I had said and he burst into laughter, too.

I can't take credit for adopting the right therapy. Gallows humor comes naturally to me (the "doctor, doctor, cut my throat" bit). As it happened, Janet's profession made that kind of cruel medical humor seem natural to her. Besides, no amount of sincere profession of love on my part would convince her; but *joking* about it did. If the missing breast meant so little to me that I could *joke* about it, then perhaps she could rely on me.

Thereafter, I kept up a determined cheerfulness each day when I visited her and never referred to the operation in anything but a joking way. In no time she was on her feet, visiting other patients in the ward to cheer them up.

Meanwhile, I called Carl one evening and received a detailed account of what Janet's chest would look like so that when I saw it I would not wince. Janet knew that I was queasy and would neither look at nor listen to anything that was medically gruesome. One wince from me, therefore, would undo everything. It was a long time before she could let me see her bare chest thereafter, but when the time came that I insisted she do so, I was old stoneface himself, perfectly calm.

20

I kept myself frenetically busy while Janet was in the hospital. I agreed to do two more of the *How Did We Find Out About———?* series for Walker, and while Janet was away I went rapidly through *How Did We Find Out About Numbers?* and took it in.

Janet was kept busy, too, by the constant stream of people who came to visit her. Even Austin Olney came in from Boston just to see her.

21

Janet's forty-sixth birthday came on August 6 and found her still in the hospital. Chaucy and Les arrived with a cake and we made as merry as we could, but merriment is naturally limited for a newly breast-less woman.

Janet was herself surprised at still being in the hospital and tackled Carl on the matter. He hesitated and finally admitted that she could go home, but that he had to protect her. "You know what Isaac is like," he said.

It turned out that he was still thinking about my edematized neck, brought on (he firmly believed) by my own animal lust. He was apparently convinced that I was some kind of sex maniac and would damage Janet.

Janet reassured him that I was a pussycat, and he reluctantly consented to let her go home. On the seventh, I spent hours getting the apartment into shape for her, changing the sheets on the beds, running clothes through the laundry in the basement, and so on. Any competent housekeeper could have translated my three hours of hard labor into thirty minutes.

On August 8, I brought Janet back home after sixteen days in the hospital.

22

The next day, Robyn (rather unexpectedly) arrived and met Janet for the first time, at last. I was a little fearful of how it would go, for Janet was terribly apprehensive of meeting with a daughter's disapproval of the woman-who-stole-her-Daddy and of the effect of that disapproval on a doting father. She was also very aware of how unattractive she must seem with her arm in a sling and herself so altogether an invalid.

Our fears were groundless. Robyn was perfectly sweet and gentle.

Janet and I had long-standing tickets for Shakespeare in the Park. It was to be *Much Ado About Nothing* this time, on August 10. Janet felt she simply couldn't go and persuaded me to take Robyn instead. I don't think Robyn had ever seen serious Shakespeare before and I was apprehensive that the language would throw her for a loss. Again, my fears were groundless. The play was magnificently done, and Robyn laughed all the way through and enjoyed herself tremendously.

I continued my policy of joking, of course. The del Reys visited on August 13, talking volubly about everything but breasts. At one point, Judy-Lynn talked of a singles bar and said to Janet, "Have you ever been at a swinging singles?"

"Been at one?" I interposed. "She *has* one."

Judy-Lynn instantly began to berate me, but Janet said, "Oh leave him alone. He's just bragging. It isn't large enough to swing."

(That night, by the way, Janet's mother, who had been visiting her home state of Utah for a month, came home and we broke the news to her of Janet's operation.)

36

Breadloaf and Statendam

1

Breadloaf was coming up again. I had done sufficiently well the previous year for John Ciardi to insist I come again in 1972 "and every year thereafter."

I had agreed, of course, but, after the mastectomy, Janet felt she simply wasn't up to it, and there was no way in which I could back out so late in the game. I had to go without her. Young Leslie was going, though, so I picked her up in Westchester and took her along.

I was in the same room as the year before and again there were the sessions with Ciardi, the lectures, the meals—everything, but without Janet. My evening talk on August 25 went well enough, but it fell far short of my talk of the previous year.

One woman, who had not been at Breadloaf the previous year, said that she had heard I had given a marvelous talk at that time, one that had reduced the audience to tears, and could I tell her about it?

I said I could scarcely deliver an hour talk for her, but I could give her a brief summary.

Moving one person is harder than to move a hundred, since the hundred interact. Nevertheless, when I came to the "The Ugly Little Boy" peroration, I pulled out the stops and gave it in full and when I was through, one fat tear welled over a lower eyelid and rolled down her cheek.

I was home on August 30, and I was so glad to see Janet, you can't imagine. On September 2, I drove her to Ciardi's place in Metuchen, New Jersey. Present were a few of the other faculty members so that Janet could have at least a small and distant taste of Breadloaf that year.

I was hoping that the year after I could make it up to her but, as it turned out, 1972 was Ciardi's last year as director of Breadloaf.

I never returned either. I rather thought they would ask me to come back and that I would refuse out of loyalty to Ciardi. However, they must have anticipated this and never gave me the chance to do so.

2

September 5 was my mother's seventy-seventh birthday. She was rather tearful about it when I called her and refused any celebration of the day. She talked only about my father, now dead three years.

3

I put together *Asimov on Astronomy*, the first of the recyclings of my *F & SF* essays, and brought it in to Doubleday on September 11.

Two days later, I had lunch with a pleasant woman who wanted to do an article praising the usefulness of direct-mail advertising (which she wouldn't let me refer to as "junk mail"). She had called Stanley first in order to find out where I could be reached and had asked him what he thought I would charge.

Stanley then called me to warn me that he had said I charged a dollar a word.

I was horrified. "Listen," I said, "I charge a quarter a word."

He said, "What you need is an intelligent business manager. She's willing to pay a dollar a word. Surely it would take that much to get you to praise junk mail."

True enough. It would take more than that.

I called the woman and told her that unless she could convince me that direct-mail advertising was useful and good, I couldn't write an article to that effect no matter how much she paid me. It was at lunch on September 13 that she educated me on the matter and I had to admit I had been too ready to accept the stereotype.

I did write the article later that month—four thousand words for four thousand dollars. It was the first time I had ever earned a dollar a word. My title was "The Individualism to Come," and it appeared in a special section of the New York *Times* on January 7, 1973.

The thrust of the article was that in the coming age of computerization, direct-mail advertising could meet the needs of individuals, rather than masses, and that computers were therefore a humanizing force and not a dehumanizing one.

A couple of months later, I incorporated this thesis into my 175th *F & SF* essay, "By the Numbers,"[1] which appeared in the May 1973 *F & SF*. It was one of my most controversial essays, and I received a number of indignant letters from readers who would not accept my view of computers as benign.

[1] See *The Tragedy of the Moon.*

4

I finally finished *Jupiter* on September 14, and instantly began on the second volume of my history of the United States. The first had been *The Shaping of North America* and the second was *The Birth of the United States*.

I began dealing with this birth in a presidential election year, and I was in deep despair over this one. Nixon and Agnew were, of course, running for re-election. The Democratic nominee was McGovern, of whom I approved, but who, I felt, couldn't win. While Janet was in the hospital, the Democratic vice-presidential nominee was forced to withdraw, and any feeble chance of defeating Nixon was gone.

I attended a McGovern rally on September 20, and contributed money, muttering gloomily to Janet as I did so, "I better give him the money now, for he will sink without a trace in November."

Then on the twenty-third, I attended a party in which it seemed to me that even people I would have expected to be liberals were turning to Nixon. It was more than I could bear.

"Nixon is a crook," I said. "A common crook. He never told the truth in his life." But no one believed me.

5

Janet was working on a science-fiction novel. It was by no means the first novel she had written. She had written two mystery novels in the years before I came to New York as well as a number of science-fiction stories but had been unable to sell them. She had, however, sold a mystery short story (under a pseudonym) to Hans Santesson, who then edited *Saint Mystery*.

Janet was rather anxious to have me help her with her novel, but I refused absolutely to have anything to do with it. In the first place, if I helped and she then sold the novel, she would never believe that she had done it by herself. She would always suppose it had been my touch that had done it, however small that touch had been.

Besides, I didn't want the risk of petty squabbling over endless literary details upsetting the warm and even tenor of our relationship. I had witnessed too many unpleasantnesses in marriages between writers.

I insisted on keeping to my own books, and on October 13, I completed *How Did We Find Out About Dinosaurs?* for Walker.

6

On October 14, I started my ninth Black Widowers story, "The Lullaby of Broadway."[2] The puzzle there involved mysterious bangings in an apartment. There I was working off my frustrations over mysterious bangings in Janet's apartment. The apartment house she lived in was fine in many ways, but it seemed to have been built of sound-conducting concrete. Any noise in one apartment resounded hollowly in all other apartments, and no one could tell where the noise came from.

I submitted it to *EQMM* on October 30 and, to my considerable astonishment, it was rejected. I had sold eight Black Widowers stories to *EQMM* over a period of a year and a half, and this was my first rejection.

Yet the rejection was only a limited catastrophe. I had every intention of having Doubleday publish a collection of Black Widowers stories once I had enough to fill a book, and it would actually be useful to have some stories included that had not seen prior publication. I therefore put aside "The Lullaby of Broadway" for that purpose.

7

Richard Hoagland's suggestion for an Apollo 17 cruise was still alive, somewhat to my surprise. The notion of having it on the *Queen Elizabeth* 2 had fallen through, but there was a chance of doing it on one of the Holland-American liners. On October 19, Richard hosted a cocktail party on the *Rotterdam* to help sell the cruise, and for the first time in my life I was on board a modern luxury liner.

I was amazed to find carpets and elevators aboard ship and, indeed, everything resembling a particularly fancy hotel. My desire to take a cruise was suddenly intensified, and from then on I was quite certain I was going. (Janet had been on liners before. In fact, she had crossed the Atlantic on the *Rotterdam* itself at one time.)

8

I drove to Camden, New Jersey, on October 21 to speak at a college there, and realized only at the last moment that I didn't have the name of the motel at which I was to be staying. Janet, who favored meticulous preparations, was surprised that I hadn't been more careful

---

[2] See *Tales of the Black Widowers.*

about this but I said it didn't matter. I knew where the college was and once we got there they would direct us to our motel.

The trouble was that it was Saturday and the school was a community college, which meant no one lived on campus and it was empty. I finally discovered a library and an inhabitant librarian and asked how I might find the gentleman who was in charge of the lecture.

He was not on the campus, of course, and a long checking of records turned up the fact that he had just moved, that he had left no forwarding address, and that he had an unlisted phone number. I realized that I had committed another Asimovian imbecility and that I had brought Janet and myself to a city under conditions where I did not know what living arrangements had been made for us, and couldn't find out. Janet did not say one recriminating word—but she didn't have to.

Desperately, I said to the librarian, "Look. Suppose you had to put up a speaker at a hotel or motel. Which would you use?"

She told me. It was seven miles back along the road I had taken to the school, seven miles of rough, small-town driving. I made it, grimly determined to stay at that motel whether it was the correct one or not, and if the school couldn't find me, the hell with them.

It was the correct hotel. My reservation was waiting for me.

About an hour later, the man in charge of lecture arrangements called, blissfully confident I would be there. I said, trying to hide my exasperation, "See here, how is it you never included the name of the motel in our correspondence?"

And the idiot responded, "But you never asked me."

9

For many months, there had been desultory discussions concerning a projected book to be called *Our World in Space*. Chiefly, it was to be a large coffee-table book filled with paintings of space exploration by a superlative artist named Robert McCall. McCall wanted written matter to be included, and he wanted me to do it.

At first McCall discussed the matter with Doubleday, but Doubleday wouldn't offer McCall the deal he wanted, so he moved on to New York Graphic. I thought that meant I was abandoned, but not so. He still wanted me. I was reluctant, but I had difficulty refusing. The book would be beautiful and the writing would be easy, since it would be on subjects I had dealt with before.

A minor irritation, however, was that the royalties were to be split

60–40 in favor of McCall and that he was to get top billing so that the book would be by McCall and Asimov.

I decided to talk it out with McCall over lunch. I would tell him that he could have one or the other. If he wanted a 60–40 split, the book would have to be by Asimov and McCall. If he wanted McCall and Asimov, the royalties would have to be split 50–50. I intended to be quite firm about it.

McCall was a tall, sandy-haired, freckle-faced fellow who was gentle and pleasant. I liked him a lot, but business was business!

So at lunch, I said, "Bob, now here's the situation. . . ."

And McCall said, "Before you say anything, Isaac, I just want you to remember that you have already published about 130 books and this book we're talking about is my—very—first—one."

I sat there speechless for a moment, and then gave in. It was McCall and Asimov and it was 60–40 his favor. I'm a lousy businessman, but that night I slept peacefully, and I wouldn't have if I had insisted on having it my way.

On October 23, I knocked off the first of the six chapters.

10

On the gray morning of October 27, Janet looked out of a north window of her apartment and said, "You ought to tell the Cromwell people to do something about their incinerator, Isaac. It's belching out black smoke."

Wordlessly, I rushed for my coat.

"What's the matter?" she asked.

"The Cromwell doesn't have an incinerator," I said, and was out the door.

It was a fire, of course, but it was brought easily under control, and my side of the building was untouched. My apartment didn't even smell of smoke, but it was a fright. I carried insurance, but there was no way that money alone could replace the complete set of my books or my manuscripts in progress—or even my library.

11

I gave up my Ford on October 29. It had been developing chronic troubles and it was silly to pay large garage bills for two cars when we needed only one. Thereafter, we made do with Janet's Plymouth, which was smaller and, in terms of mileage, newer.

It was another relic of my Boston era to vanish, and I was nostalgically sorry.

12

On November 7, I voted first thing in the morning—for McGovern, of course.

For the first time in thirty-six years, I did not listen to election returns, since I knew that Nixon would win big and thought that McGovern would carry no more than three states. I wasn't masochistic enough to want to wallow in the details.

The reality proved to be even worse than my pessimism suggested. McGovern carried only Massachusetts and the District of Columbia.

I got a very small amount of consolation out of the fact that Nixon, in his self-centered paranoia, had concentrated so entirely on a personal victory that no effort was made to insure a Republican victory one foot outside the Oval Office—so that in the face of an enormous presidential defeat, the Democrats nevertheless retained control of both houses of Congress.

I said to Janet, unhappily, "Johnson won a similar landslide in 1964 and had destroyed himself by 1968, but that was because of the Vietnam War. Now the Vietnam War is ending in an American defeat that Nixon is going to pretend is a victory, and the American people will fall for it. I don't see *anything* that can possibly give him the fate he deserves."

I didn't have the faintest suspicion that the "anything" had already taken place and that the Watergate time bomb was ticking relentlessly. By now, of course, the actual burglars were coming up for trial, but I had no reason to think that it would go any farther than their conviction.

13

I was in Rochester on November 9, with the prospect of a talk to the New York State Librarians Association the next day. I was in a two-room hotel suite with (at the moment) nothing to do. Janet had gone to sleep and I sat there with the strong urge to write a tenth Black Widowers story—and I had not brought a typewriter with me.

I was tempted to try to write the story with pen and ink, but it seemed to me that this would be far too tiring and that the mechanical detail of moving my hand to form the letters would interfere with the creative process.

I was desperate enough to try, though. I used the hotel writing paper provided guests and began to write—and continued to write—and kept on writing till the story (the first draft, at least) was finished.

I rushed into the next room and woke Janet. "Janet," I said, "you know how noisy writing is. Well, it isn't the writing that's noisy, it's the *typewriter*." When I wrote by pen and ink, I was conscious of writing in a profound and, to me, an utterly unaccustomed silence.

From that point on, I never took my typewriter with me on trips but relied on pen and ink if I wanted to write.

This particular tale deserves a better conclusion, however. I called the story "Yankee Doodle Goes to Town,"[3] and though I thought it one of the best Black Widowers I had ever written, Fred Dannay didn't think so. To my considerable surprise, it was rejected, and I put it aside as an unpublished item to be included in my eventual collection.

14

New projects kept springing up. There was now an annual volume of Nebula award story collections, which included runners-up, and was thus different in nature from the Hugo awards volumes, which came out at five- or six-year intervals and included only the winners. Furthermore, the Nebula award stories were edited by different big-name writers each year.

The eighth volume of the Nebula award collections, due out in 1973, was to be edited by myself—at least, so the Science Fiction Writers of America (which was in charge of the awards, and of the volume) wished. I pointed out that I edited the Hugo awards volumes, but they said there was no conflict of interest there.

Since the Nebula awards volumes were published by Doubleday, I agreed—and found out only later that the SFWA had recently shifted publishers and were now working with Harper & Row. I consulted Larry Ashmead and, with his customary amiability, he said it would be perfectly all right for me to do it for Harper's.

On November 13, therefore, I had lunch with Victoria Schochet of Harper's and arranged the details.

That same night, Janet and I had an elaborate dinner with Mac Talley at Trader Vic's and I found myself agreeing to do an elaborate book on the polar regions of Earth.

Then, on November 21, Austin Olney came to town and, over din-

[3] See *Tales of the Black Widowers.*

ner, suggested I do a book on the history of the telescope, and I agreed to that, too.

Before the month was over there was one more item:

Arthur Rosenthal was no longer with Basic Books, but had moved to Boston. Basic Books was now a subsidiary of Harper & Row, and in charge was Erwin Glickes. I had lunch with him on November 27 and he wanted a large book on nutrition along the lines of *Asimov's Guide to Science,* and I agreed.

When I was going to find time to bring all these agreements to fruition, I couldn't say.

15

On December 1, 1972, *Asimov's Annotated Don Juan* was published, nearly two years after I had completed it. (The delay was occasioned by the artist, of course.) It was a beautiful book, though an expensive one, and eventually won a prize for its design.

Doubleday was sufficiently pleased with it to throw a little luncheon party for Janet and me in its honor. Sam Vaughan, the president of the Publishing Division, and Walter Bradbury were there. So was Larry, of course, and, at my invitation, the del Reys.

It went very well, and the Doubleday people were pleased with the advance sale. I was not overoptimistic, however. I was glad that *Asimov's Annotated Paradise Lost* was safely done and in production. Doubleday was going to do it in the same style as *Asimov's Annotated Don Juan* but without artwork and without a box. So much the better.

16

On December 4, Richard Hoagland's cruise came to pass. Janet and I got on the *Statendam,* which was the *Rotterdam's* little sister. For the first time in my life, I got on a ship voluntarily to embark on an ocean voyage and discovered I liked it and was not afraid.

Along with us on the ship were Ted Sturgeon (with his most recent wife and son), Robert and Ginny Heinlein, Marvin Minsky, Fred and Carol Pohl, and Ben Bova.

Along with Ben was Barbara Rose, a young woman with whom he was clearly and desperately in love. In fact, some time before, he had said to me, clearly bemused, "You know, Isaac, I think I'm in love with a nice Jewish girl, of all things." I had then replied, "For goodness' sake, Ben, you're Italian; you don't have to. Quick! Run!" But he didn't.

I scarcely blamed him. Barbara was a vital brunette, with a pretty face, lovely eyes, and a stunning figure. She was outgoing and an energetic talker.

Among nonscience-fiction personalities present were Ken Franklin, an astronomer who had first detected the radio emissions of Jupiter. He was short, plump, curly-haired, and quizzical—a straight-faced jokester. There was also Hugh Downs, best known as Jack Paar's sidekick on the latter's late-night talk show.

The first evening, Janet and I went out on board to see the ship go past Manhattan, by the Statue of Liberty, and under the Verrazano-Narrows Bridge, and there we encountered Norman Mailer, still another member of the group. This time I knew who he was and introduced myself.

By the time we went to bed, I knew I was not prone to seasickness, and that we could luxuriate freely in our two-room suite. (The ship, alas, was only half full, which meant the owners were running at a loss, but those of us on board had all the more space, and excellent service.)

While I was on the *Statendam*, I wrote my 176th *F & SF* essay, "The Tragedy of the Moon,"[4] which appeared in the June 1973 issue of the magazine. I also did my eleventh Black Widowers story, "The Curious Omission."[5] Both items were done in pen and ink.

It was quite clear that the world generally was not taking the cruise seriously, perhaps because of the large leavening of science-fiction people on board. A New York *Times* reporter who seemed to be there largely because Norman Mailer was, seemed unhappy about the whole thing. Katherine Anne Porter was aboard, too, which meant that all outsiders felt it incumbent upon them to refer to the cruise as "a ship of fools."

By December 6, we reached Florida and anchored seven miles off Cape Kennedy. The giant rocket stood out against the flat Florida coast like a misplaced Washington's Monument.

The day darkened; night came; clouds banked on the eastern horizon; and there was a continuous display of faraway lightning-without-thunder ducking in and out of the distant thunderheads. Launch was scheduled for 9:53 P.M. and there had never been any hitch, any hold, any delay in an Apollo launch.

This time, however, at thirty seconds before launch there was a hold that continued—and continued—

Midnight came and went and we were into December 7, the thirty-

---

4 See *The Tragedy of the Moon* (Doubleday, 1973).
5 See *Tales of the Black Widowers*.

first anniversary of Pearl Harbor, and no one seemed to be aware of this bit of ill omen but myself. In a short time, the launch would have to be postponed to the next night, the ship would have to move away, and we would miss the sight.

At 12:20 A.M., the hold was lifted and the countdown proceeded to zero. A cloud of vapor enveloped the rocket and I held my breath for fear Pearl Harbor Day would do its work.

It didn't. The rocket slowly rose and the vast red flower at its tail bloomed. What was surely the most concentrated man-made night light on an enormous scale that the world had ever seen blazed out over the nightbound shores of Florida—and the night vanished from horizon to horizon.

We, and the ship, and all the world we could see, were suddenly under the dim copper dome of a sky from which the stars had washed out, while below us the black sea had turned an orange-gray.

In the deepest silence, the artificial sun that had so changed our immediate world rose higher and higher, and then—forty seconds after ignition—the violent shaking of the air all about the rocket engines completed its journey across the seven-mile separation and reached us. With the rocket high in the air, we were shaken with a rumbling thunder so that our private and temporary daytime was accompanied by a private and temporary earthquake.

Sound and light ebbed majestically as the rocket continued to rise until it was a ruddy blotch in the high sky. Night fell once more; the stars were coming out, and the sea darkened. In the sky there was a flash as the second stage came loose, and then the rocket was a star among stars; moving, and moving, and moving, and growing dimmer. . . .

In all this, it was useless for me to try to say anything, for there was nothing to say. The words and phrases had not been invented that would serve as an accompaniment to that magnificent leap to the Moon, and I did not try to invent any. After all, I had nothing more at my disposal than the language of Shakespeare.

Some young man behind me, however, was not hobbled by my disadvantage. He had a vocabulary that the young of our day had developed to express their own tastes and quality and he used it to the full.

"Oh *shit*," he said, as his head tilted slowly upward. And then, with his tenor voice rising over all the silent heads on board, he added eloquently, "Oh *shi-i-i-it*."

To each his own, I thought.

17

The rest of the cruise had to be anticlimactic, but on December 9, we reached St. Thomas, in the Virgin Islands, and Janet and I toured it with considerable interest. It was my first time on a distant island portion of the United States since my stay on Hawaii twenty-six years before.

Ben and Barbara left the cruise at that point to do some traveling on their own and to return to the United States by plane. Norman Mailer also left, and with him all reporter interest, such as there was.

Joining us, however, were Carl and Linda Sagan. Carl gave several magnificent talks on the new knowledge of Mars gained from the Mariner 9 probe. Since the reporters were gone, however, nothing of this appeared in the public print. Instead, Norman Mailer's earlier speech, a rather silly one suggesting ESP experiments on the Moon and offering the possibility of a spirit world surrounding Earth, received the full treatment.

We were in Puerto Rico on December 10, and again we toured the island. This time Janet and I took separate tours, she to visit a rain forest, and I to visit the great radio telescope at Arecibo.

Fred Pohl gave a marvelous talk on December 11, while Bob Heinlein's I thought rather wandering.

On December 13, we were home again. On the whole, Janet and I had had a wonderful time and I felt, with delight, that she had been compensated for having missed Breadloaf four months before.

18

My article on the cruise, which was written for the New York Times at their request, was rejected. I was not utterly surprised. My batting average with the Times was .500 at best.

Fortunately I had a solution for virtually all nonfiction rejections. Later that month, I rewrote it, at greater length, as my 177th F & SF essay, "The Cruise and I,"[6] and it appeared in the July 1973 issue of the magazine.

As for "The Curious Omission," which I had written onboard ship, Fred Dannay rejected that (my third Black Widowers rejection in a row).

[6] See The Tragedy of the Moon.

19

Someone representing Woody Allen called me and asked if I would look over a movie script Allen had written. It happened to be science fiction and Allen was uncertain whether he had handled it correctly, so they needed the word of an expert.

Ordinarily, I would have denied being an expert and ducked the responsibility, but I am a great fan of Woody Allen's and I wanted to see the script. I wasn't disappointed. Since I was able to picture Allen perfectly, sight and sound, reading the script was like seeing the movie, and I howled over it. I called the fellow who had sent me the script and tried to give him my opinion, but he suggested lunch.

I had lunch with Woody Allen and two of his friends on December 20, and when Allen asked me about the script, I told him flatly that it was terrific.

Did it need changes? he wanted to know. No, I said, it was perfect. Was I sure? Yes, of course I was sure. Allen protested that he knew nothing about science fiction. I said that if he refrained from telling people that, no one could possibly guess.

I was getting a little uneasy, though. After all, I was pushing as hard as I could to get Allen to do the picture and *he* would be putting the money into it. What if I were wrong?

Allen must have been getting uneasy, too. Did this guy, Asimov, really know what he was talking about? "How much science fiction have you written?" he asked.

Feeling a little nervous, I said, "Not much. Very little, actually. Perhaps thirty books of it altogether." Then, diffidently, I explained in a half whisper, "The other hundred books aren't science fiction."

Allen turned to his friends. "Did you hear him throw that line away? Did you hear him throw that line away?"

Apparently my skill at showmanship (was that what it was?) convinced him. He asked me to serve as technical director for the movie, which meant going to wherever it was he was shooting it. I refused and recommended Ben Bova instead (who took the job and did very well).

Finally, Woody Allen said to me, "Well, how much do I owe you?"

I said, "I enjoyed reading the script so much, Mr. Allen, that you don't owe me anything."

I rather thought that Allen would at this point force more money on me than I would have had the nerve to ask for—but I was wrong. He said "All right," and that was that. I never got a penny.

The movie, as it happened, was *Sleeper*. It came out, in accordance with my recommendation, just as Allen had written it, and I was right, thank goodness. It was the most successful picture he had made up to that point and I was sure I would get a letter of thanks, but I never did.

20

I was also involved in a project originated by Gerald Walker of the New York *Times*. He was incensed over what he considered the rotten way in which publishers promoted, publicized, and sold their books, and it occurred to him that writers, in protest, ought to walk up and down Fifth Avenue with books in a pushcart, peddling them to passersby. The trick was to show that even *this* would produce more sales than publishers could.

Gerald asked me to join in. I had no complaints against my publishers, who were making me much more money than I had ever dreamed I could earn—but I felt it important to show solidarity. Just because I was doing well didn't mean I oughtn't pitch in for those who weren't.

So I contributed books to "Operation Pushcart" and was on hand to help with the festivities. It took place on December 23, 1972, at Fifth Avenue and Sixtieth Street, and, alas, it was a fiasco.

It rained heavily and the participating authors all huddled miserably under umbrellas. Since there were no passersby, we had to buy each other's books. When we finally tried to move the pushcart down Fifth Avenue despite the rain, policemen stopped us on the grounds we didn't have peddlers' licenses. And, of course, reporters were on hand to put scoffing stories in the newspapers.

21

Christmas wasn't so good. Chaucy was preparing a feast, as usual, but she had the flu, and her son Bruce, in the early-morning hours of December 24, was rather badly hurt in an automobile accident. Under the circumstances, festivities were canceled.

22

During 1972, I had published no less than fifteen books, outdoing the previous record of twelve, in 1966. They were:

118. *Asimov's Biographical Encyclopedia of Science and Technology* (Revised Edition) (Doubleday)

119. *The Left Hand of the Electron* (Doubleday)
120. *Asimov's Guide to Science* (Basic Books)
121. *The Gods Themselves* (Doubleday)
122. *More Words of Science* (Houghton Mifflin)
123. *Electricity and Man* (Atomic Energy Commission)
124. *ABC's of Ecology* (Walker)
125. *The Early Asimov* (Doubleday)
126. *The Shaping of France* (Houghton Mifflin)
127. *The Story of Ruth* (Doubleday)
128. *Ginn Science Program—Intermediate Level A* (Ginn)
129. *Ginn Science Program—Intermediate Level C* (Ginn)
130. *Asimov's Annotated Don Juan* (Doubleday)
131. *Worlds Within Worlds* (AEC)
132. *Ginn Science Program—Intermediate Level B* (Ginn)

The three Ginn Science Program books were for the fourth, fifth, and sixth grades. (I received copies of the remaining two, for the seventh and eighth grades, shortly after the beginning of the new year, so that they were included among my 1973 books.)

The Ginn Science Program books were finally published more than five years after I had written the first word of my share—and, in my opinion, they fizzled. Considering the amount of time and work I had put into them, the money they earned was completely trivial.

23

I began the new year of 1973 by putting together my tenth collection of *F & SF* essays, *The Tragedy of the Moon*, and on January 2, 1973, I celebrated my fifty-third birthday very quietly.

24

On January 5, 1973, I attended the annual meeting of the Baker Street Irregulars, a society of Sherlock Holmes enthusiasts, whose attitude toward the "sacred writings" was a curious mixture of high dedication and low camp.

I went as the guest of Edgar Lawrence (one of the Trap Door Spiders), who was also a Baker Street Irregular. I went, to be honest, to scoff, but I remained to enjoy myself.

Once again, as in the case of the Trap Door Spiders and the Dutch Treat Club, my appearance as a guest led to a suggestion that I join as a member, and I did. It came to be my third stag organization, one of which, the Dutch Treat Club, met weekly; one, the Trap Door Spiders, monthly; and one, the Baker Street Irregulars, met annually.

At this first meeting, I encountered Robert Lowndes, who had been a Futurian with me thirty-five years before and who, as an editor, had bought a number of stories from me. He had become quite gray and quite stout—but then so had I.

I also met Banesh Hoffman, a physicist from Queens College, whose book *The Strange Story of the Quantum* I had read and had admired extravagantly.

25

I took in *The Tragedy of the Moon* and *Asimov's Annotated Paradise Lost* on January 8, and arranged matters concerning a third book.

I had by now done a hundred "Please Explain" columns for *Science Digest*, and for years it had been understood between Larry and myself that when the hundred mark was reached, Doubleday would put out the collection.

Doubleday, however, had done six books of mine in 1972 and had no less than four more books of mine in press. I was acutely conscious that since I had come to New York I had tended to overlook Houghton Mifflin. I asked Larry's permission to give "Please Explain" to Houghton Mifflin, and he agreed.

At noon that same day, I went to Brooklyn to give a talk at Public School 88. It was not the sort of thing I usually did, but this school was near Windsor Place, and the condition was that I be driven about the old neighborhood—where I had last lived twenty-five years before.

This was done, and I was rather overwhelmed to see that the old candy store, which my father had owned for sixteen years and in which I had worked for six, was desolate, abandoned, and boarded up.

Finally, in the evening, I went to a birthday party for the old vaudevillian and stand-up comedian, Joey Adams. I found myself in the same room with a number of show-business people, including Ginger Rogers, Jan Peerce, and Tiny Tim. What really rather overwhelmed me with mortification, though, was that Roy Cohn, the sidekick of Senator Joseph McCarthy and who figured prominently in the television hearings nineteen years before, walked into the room. This time I managed to avoid an introduction, and I didn't have to shake the hand that had shaken the hand of McCarthy.

26

I finished *Our World in Space* for New York Graphic on January 14 and *Please Explain* for Houghton Mifflin on January 22. I therefore instantly started on the book on polar regions for Mac Talley. The title for that was, eventually, *The Ends of the Earth*.

27

The Vietnam War came to an end on January 24, 1973, four days after Nixon's triumphant reinauguration. Nixon used the catch phrase "peace with honor" to describe it. To me it seemed that the very same peace could easily have been arranged at any time in the previous ten years, nor did I see how any phase of our part in that deplorable affair could be equated with "honor."

It bothered me enormously that so much of the country considered him a hero for ending a war that he had uselessly continued for four years. What's more, in a few weeks a number of our prisoners of war returned and were orchestrated into repeating "God bless our commander-in-chief" so that Nixon's popularity polled at an all-time high, and I felt myself to be suffocating in frustration.[7]

And still the Watergate time bomb ticked, and I remained completely unaware of its importance. The Watergate burglars had, all but one, pleaded guilty, and that seemed to end it.

28

A British publishing firm, Sphere Books, was doing a series of *The Best of—* books, featuring various science-fiction writers, and they wanted to do a collection of my stories.

I checked with Larry Ashmead to find out if Doubleday would be willing to allow this.

Larry said, "Only if Doubleday can do an American edition."

I said, "But Larry, all the stories have already appeared in one or another of my Doubleday collections."

Larry had the perfect answer for this. He said, "So what?"

I went over the list of stories Sphere Books wanted to include. I took out one or two I thought I could do without; I put in one or two

[7] On January 22, 1973, two days before the cease-fire announcement, Lyndon Johnson died, as though he could not survive the war he had so mistakenly escalated.

that were particular favorites of mine. Then I added "Mirror Image" so that I could have a very recent story included that was *not* in any of my Doubleday collections, and on January 28, I did the Introduction for the book.

29

I had lived at the Cromwell now for nearly three years and was reasonably content. It served quite well as an office and, of course, I ate and spent much of my time at Janet's place.

It meant making a five-block trip from one to the other, and then back, at least once a day, which was bothersome on occasion when the weather was bad, but was good exercise.

Shortly after I moved in, though, the Cromwell, for economic reasons of its own, began a changeover from a hotel to an apartment house. Changes took place, all of which were for the worse for me.

The coffeehouse in the lobby vanished and was replaced by a drugstore. There had been a maid who had come in daily to look at the dust and occasionally supply me with fresh towels and bedsheets. She vanished, too, and after that, though the apartment remained neat and orderly, the dust gradually accumulated.

Worst of all was the noise. The manned elevators were converted to self-service, and the kitchenettes in every unit were being rebuilt and upgraded. This meant banging, day in and day out, better or worse depending on which apartments were being worked on.[8]

On February 1, 1973, my own kitchenette was upgraded and that really drove me wild.

Family problems were also worrisome. My mother was in the hospital again—it was in-and-out with her now.

As for Robyn, she had applied to four colleges, been accepted by each one, and had decided to go to Windham College, in Vermont. I brooded at how inaccessible she would be to me, and worried about how she would survive the Vermont winters.

[8] At one point, I approached the honest workingman who was banging away just outside my apartment and said, petulantly, "How long will this take you?" He looked me up and down and said, "How long did it take Michelangelo to do the Sistine Chapel?" I burst into laughter and didn't mind his banging after that.

37

Eclipse Cruise—Alone

1

The success of the *Statendam* cruise had made ocean travel seem delightful to me. I was pleased when another opportunity arose.

A gentleman named Phil Sigler was organizing a cruise in which a ship would cross the Atlantic in the summer of 1973 and anchor off the African coast at a spot that would allow its passengers to observe a total eclipse of the Sun. He approached me and asked me to join as one of the notables. If I would agree to give four talks, then not only would I get a free passage for Janet and myself, but there would be a generous stipend as well.

I couldn't resist. I agreed to go.

Since landings were planned at the Canary Islands and at Dakar, I would need a passport. (Janet had one.) By February 8, I had my passport photos and had visited the passport office to make arrangements for one. It was the first time in my life that I ever had a passport of my own—fifty years to the month after having arrived in the United States on my father's passport.

Oddly enough, Robyn was also requiring a passport. She was going off on a skiing trip to France with a group of students. That created alarm and despondency within me, but she went and returned in perfect safety and had a good time. She celebrated her eighteenth birthday on February 19, 1973, while she was in France.

2

On February 20, I was in Larry Ashmead's office when a group of Soviet publishers entered. They were visiting Doubleday in connection with the agreements finally being set up between the Soviet Union and the United States for the regularization of the copyright situation between the two nations.

Larry courteously introduced me and there was a noticeable stir among the Soviets. They recognized the name and I was instantly invited (through the interpreter) to visit the Soviet Union someday.

It was pleasant, fifty years after I had left the Soviet Union as a young child, to be invited back as a celebrity whose writing was well known there. Nevertheless, I knew that the likelihood of my visiting the Soviet Union was very small. As long as I didn't fly, the logistical problems were all but insuperable.

That same day, the *Statendam* cruise produced another delayed effect, for I began my twelfth Black Widowers story, "Out of Sight."[1]

Its background was a cruise much like the one I had been on. It dealt with a table of six people just like the one I had actually sat at, and the key incident was the spilling, by the waiter, of a cup of hot chocolate into the lap of one of the women (something that had actually happened to Janet).

Fred Dannay accepted this one, the first of my Black Widowers to be accepted after three successive failures. It appeared in the December 1973 *EQMM* under the title of "The Six Suspects," though of course I used my own title in the collection.

Once I had finished "Out of Sight," I decided I had enough Black Widowers stories for a book. I therefore wrote an overall Introduction plus Afterwords for each story, and took *Tales of the Black Widowers* to Doubleday.

Tales of the Black Widowers was to be a Crime Club book, so that I had finally cleared the hurdle I had stumbled over so badly with *The Death Dealers* fifteen years before.

It meant that Michele Tempesta was my editor for this one. She had been working in Larry's group for some years. In fact, I had dedicated *Today and Tomorrow and—* to her, using a phrase that could be interpreted salaciously, if one wished. I got my advance copy on March 6, and when I pointed this out to her, she was chagrined— not at the salacity, but at not having seen it herself.

3

Ed Ferman, the editor of *F & SF*, joined forces with Barry Malzberg, one of the more spectacular of the new generation of science-fiction writers, to prepare a new anthology of originals. They were planning to ask certain writers to prepare stories that would carry some particular category of science fiction or other to the ultimate level. They asked me to do a robot story, and after some hesitation, I agreed.

I then had to think of a way to write what might be considered an ultimate robot story.

[1] See *Tales of the Black Widowers*.

There had always been one aspect of the robot theme I had never had the courage to tackle, although Campbell and I had sometimes discussed it. The laws of robots refer to human beings. Robots must not harm them and they must obey them, but what, in robot eyes, is a human being? Or, as the Psalmist asks of God, "What is man that thou art mindful of him?"

So on March 6, 1973, I began a robot story entitled, "That Thou Art Mindful of Him."[2] It appeared in the anthology, which was entitled *Final Stage*. It also appeared in the May 1974 *F & SF*.

4

Although *Tales of the Black Widowers* was now in press, I had no intention of putting an end to the series.

I was going by train to Wilmington on March 15 to speak at the University of Delaware, and it occurred to me that I might make the time on the train pass more quickly and pleasantly if I used it to think of a plot for the thirteenth Black Widowers story.

Unfortunately I had my plot while I was still in the station and I had to pass the trip otherwise. Once I got back, I wrote it, calling it "When No Man Pursueth."[3]

For the first time I put myself into one of the Black Widowers stories. Although it is based on the Trap Door Spiders, and although I am a member, none of the Black Widowers is modeled on me, although I mention myself (under my own name) on occasion, as a friend of Emmanuel Rubin (who is modeled on Lester del Rey).

In "When No Man Pursueth," however, the guest was one Mortimer Stellar, a prolific writer of many books in many fields. I made him arrogant, vain, nasty, petty, and completely self-centered. (When Janet read the story, she was furious with me.)

Fred Dannay took the story and it eventually appeared in the March 1974 *EQMM*.

When the preceding Black Widowers story, "Out of Sight," had appeared in the December 1973 issue, Dannay said in the blurb that it might be the last of the series. This meant that I received a number of indignant letters from readers who objected to my ending the series and I was glad to be able to tell them that another story had been written and was in press.

[2] See *The Bicentennial Man and Other Stories.*
[3] See *More Tales of the Black Widowers* (Doubleday, 1976).

5

It was necessary to send me an advance report on the Nebula award winners for 1973 so that I could prepare the award anthology I was editing for that year. Only items in the shorter categories were to be included, but the people in charge carelessly included the winner in the novel category, too.

The winner happened to be none other than I, myself, since *The Gods Themselves* won the 1973 Nebula for the best novel of the year by a heavy plurality. It would have been more exciting if I had found this out at the banquet, but it was exciting enough as it was. It was the first Nebula I had ever won.

6

On the morning of April 3, 1973, I said to Janet, "I had a peculiar dream last night."

"What was it?" said Janet, who is, of course, professionally interested in dreams.

"I dreamed," I said, "I had prepared an anthology of all those good old stories I read when I was a kid and I was getting a chance to read them again."

Janet said, "Why don't you prepare such an anthology?"

I was about to say: Who would publish it? as I had done in connection with the suggestion of a jokebook four years before.

This time I didn't. I thought: Why not?

As soon as Doubleday had opened for the day I called Larry. I pointed out that it would be a semi-autobiographical collection, like *The Early Asimov*, that it would deal with the decade of the 1930s (as *The Early Asimov* dealt with the 1940s), and that it would describe the manner in which those early stories shaped my thinking. It would be of historical interest in two ways, therefore, and would be a vital item in any science-fiction library.

Larry let himself be talked into it.

Of course, I needed the stories, but for that I had my good friend Sam Moskowitz, whose collection of science-fiction magazines was second only to that of Forrest J. Ackerman.

I called Sam and asked if by any chance he were working on an anthology of the stories of the 1930s. He said, "No. I would love to if I could find a publisher, but I can't."

I said, "I've found a publisher. Would you mind if I prepared such an anthology?"

He said, "More power to you."

"There's more," I said urgently. "Sam, could you get me copies of the magazines containing a list of stories I will give you?"

Goodhearted Sam said, "Oh sure!" and in three weeks he had them, every one, with word counts and copyright information and comments on each. In two weeks more I was able to complete my commentary on the anthology, and by May 10, 1973, the book was complete. It was an enormous book, far longer than I had told Larry it would be, because it ran away with me. It ended up nearly five hundred thousand words long.

In connection with the book, I was anxious to get hold of my high-school graduation book and a copy of the literary semi-annual containing "Little Brothers," which I had written thirty-nine years before. On April 4, therefore, I visited the Boys' High librarian, Mrs. Dorothy Kephart, and eventually she got both items for me. I talked Doubleday into using my high-school graduation picture for the book jacket of the anthology, which I eventually called *Before the Golden Age*.

And while I was working on the anthology, I completed *The Birth of the United States* and began work on both my second collection of recycled essays, *Asimov on Chemistry*, for Doubleday, and on *How Did We Find Out About Germs?* for Walker.

7

Carl and Linda Sagan had moved from Harvard to Cornell, and on April 12 I visited Cornell and met them again. The occasion was a round-table discussion I held that night with Carl, with Thomas Gold, and with Fred Hoyle. They were three astronomers of the first magnitude, and I felt enormously out of place, but nobody seemed to mind except me.

8

What the Trap Door Spiders constantly needed were new members, and I was delighted to be the occasion for one. On April 27, Lester and I cohosted a session (at Lester's house, with Lester preparing a magnificent meal) and brought in Ken Franklin as my guest. I had met him on the *Statendam* and was sure that he would be just the sort of guest we needed. He was more. The membership loved him, one and all, and he was eventually voted in enthusiastically.

9

The Nebula awards banquet was held on April 28. The suspense was spoiled for me, of course, but as editor of that year's Nebula anthology I was asked to give a talk.

Harlan Ellison was toastmaster and put on a magnificent show. He pointed out everyone in the audience and did the Don Rickles bit, insulting each one brilliantly. Naturally, each insultee could hardly wait for his turn and was terribly afraid Harlan would skip him or her or might be too gentle.

In only one place did Harlan rouse resentment. He referred to an editor of the female persuasion as an "editress." The young woman objected vehemently. Harlan might have apologized good-naturedly and proceeded, but that wouldn't be Harlan; he chose to stand his ground and fight.

Since I am a feminist, I felt Harlan was in the wrong, and when he finally introduced me, with the appropriate insults, I rose and said:

"Harlan's quarrel over the use of 'editress' reminds me that the basic word is almost always used for the male sex, and the derived word for the female, so that we have 'princess,' 'actress,' 'aviatrix,' 'mistress,' and even 'Jewess' and 'Negress.' However, there are occasionally words used for the female in its basic form and for the male in derived form. These are not well known so I will give you an example, thus: 'Harlan is a yentor.'"[4]

The place rocked, Harlan laughed harder than anyone, and my disappointment at knowing in advance I had won the Nebula was made up for.

10

Now at last the Watergate affair was coming unraveled. On March 19, 1973, one of the men involved in the burglary, James McCord, wrote to Judge Sirica of the involvement of White House people in the Watergate break-in, and the New York *Times* finally began to run Watergate material.

I read it all with amusement but couldn't believe that it would do anything but pinprick Nixon.

[4] To those of you who are innocent of New Yorkese, I must tell you that *yente* is a Yiddish word meaning a scolding, shrewish woman.

At the annual meeting of the Baker Street Irregulars, January 4, 1974. To my left is Robert Fish, to my right Banesh Hoffman. Directly above Fish is Edgar Lawrence.

Robert Stack and I on "The Mike Douglas Show," about 1973.

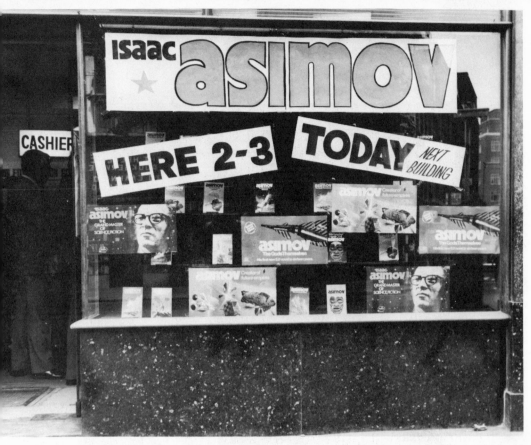

Bookstore window in London during my 1974 visit there.

The 1976 Lunacon. Typical shot of me at a science-fiction convention. That's Ted White, at that time editor of Fantastic *and* Amazing *magazines, to my left with the "guest" badge on.* Photo by Jay K. Klein

In 1976 at home, standing in front of a bookcase containing hard-cover, English-language editions of my books, in chronological order, no exact repeats. Photo by Jay K. Klein

From left, Victor Serebriakoff, me, Marvin Grosswirth: Mensa bigshots on June 22, 1976.

In 1976, in my library at home.

Commencement address, Haverford College, May 17, 1977. Next day is my coronary. Photo by
Edward J. Bonner

Receiving the Hugo for "The Bicentennial Man" in late 1977.

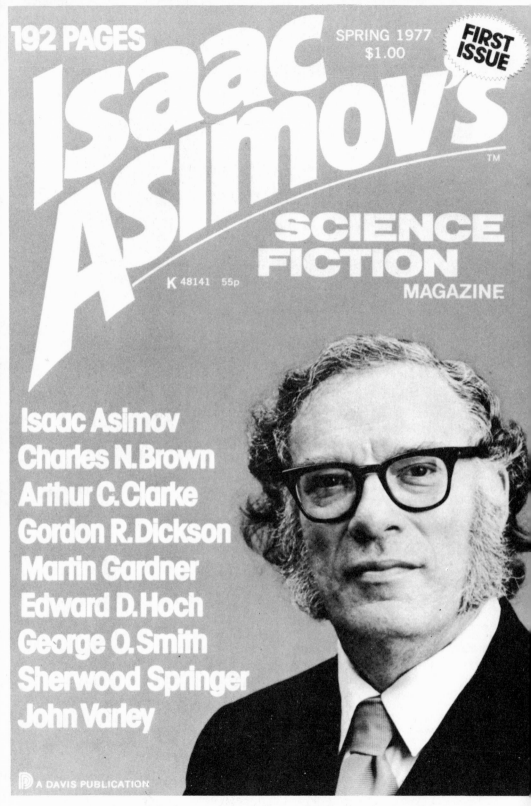

192 PAGES

SPRING 1977
$1.00

FIRST ISSUE

Isaac Asimov's

K 48141   55p

SCIENCE FICTION MAGAZINE

Isaac Asimov
Charles N. Brown
Arthur C. Clarke
Gordon R. Dickson
Martin Gardner
Edward D. Hoch
George O. Smith
Sherwood Springer
John Varley

A DAVIS PUBLICATION

Cover of the first issue of Isaac Asimov's Science Fiction Magazine.

My feelings changed on April 30, when I was so curious to hear what Nixon would say concerning Watergate that I forced myself to listen to him and to look at him on television for, I believe, the first time since his phoney "Checkers" speech twenty-one years before.

When he was through with this speech, in which he announced the resignation of his top flunkies, H. R. Haldeman and J. D. Ehrlichman, I knew we had him. It seemed to me Nixon would never have let Haldeman and Ehrlichman go except to save the one person he loved more than everything else in the world put together—himself. That meant that if the investigation continued persistently enough, it would find at the center of the web, not this underling or that, but Nixon himself.

From that point on, I took to combing the *Times* from cover to cover every morning, skipping only the column by Nixon's minion William Safire. I sometimes bought the New York *Post* so that I could read additional commentary. I listened to every news report on the radio.

I read and listened with greater attention and fascination than in even the darkest days of World War II. Thus my diary entry for May 11, 1973, says, "Up at six to finger-lick the day's news on Watergate."

I could find no one else as hooked on Watergate as I was, except for Judy-Lynn. Almost every day, she called me or I called her and we would talk about the day's developments in Watergate. We weren't very coherent and mostly we laughed hysterically.

Once, in the course of a speech to the Dutch Treat Club, I heard Gore Vidal speak of "needing my Watergate-fix" every morning, and I knew exactly what he meant.

11

At the annual Mystery Writers of America award banquet on May 4, I met Frederic Dannay for, I believe, only the second time. Although I had sold him stories, he ran the magazine from Westchester and it was Eleanor Sullivan with whom I dealt directly.

Later that evening, at the Plaza Hotel, I chanced to meet the great mime Marcel Marceau, who (it turned out) was a science-fiction fan and a reader of mine. He invited me to attend a show he was giving in New York, and I went on May 6.[5] Since Janet had a migraine, I took Judy-Lynn instead, and that may have been the first occasion on which we did what we came to call "talking Watergate."

[5] Science fiction was *such* a small and disregarded field when I began, but through the years it has gained me entry everywhere.

12

The Saturday Evening Post wanted a short story. I had already sold them a couple of stories that had appeared in some of the minor science-fiction magazines years before. What they wanted this time, however, was a new one.

Janet was suffering periodic migraine headaches at this time. She had always been subject to them occasionally, but in the spring of 1973 they had become frequent, and during one of them, she had managed to make dinner—and a particularly good one.

I wondered sadly if the migraine had been the reason, and that made me think of a robot who was out of order and who, *because* he was out of order, was a creative genius. On May 7, therefore, I dashed off a sixteen-hundred-word short-short that I called "Light Verse."[6]

I was anxious for *The Saturday Evening Post* to understand it was a new story so, in my covering letter, I stressed the fact. "This is not an old story," I wrote. "I wrote it this very day."

The editors of the *Post* took the story at once and wrote me saying they couldn't believe I had done the story in only one day.

It reminded me that I should be careful about admitting the speed with which I write. Some editors can't believe a story is good if it is written in a day; it has to be sweated over for a year and a half, perhaps. Actually, the story didn't take me a full day. It was in the letter-box two hours after I had started it.

It was published in the September–October 1973 issue of *The Saturday Evening Post*.

My fourteenth Black Widowers story, "Quicker Than the Eye,"[7] was begun on May 31, and eventually appeared in the May 1974 *EQMM*.

13

The college commencement season of 1973 carried me to Worcester, Massachusetts, where I talked at a community college, and from there I went to Boston to see the children.

Robyn had a driver's license now, and with all the self-confidence of the eighteen-year-old, insisted on chauffeuring me. There was something infinitely frightening about being driven by someone you insist on

---

[6] See *Buy Jupiter and Other Stories.*
[7] See *More Tales of the Black Widowers.*

picturing as a little girl cuddling in your arms. That was on June 3, and the next day, June 4, 1973, Robyn was graduated from high school.

14

It was four years before that Publishers-Hall syndicate had bought my article "How to Write a Hundred Books Without Really Trying" and then never published it. (It was that which had given me the notion for the Black Widowers story "When No Man Pursueth.")

A chemical-engineering magazine, *ChemTech*, had asked me for an article, for which they could not pay, and it occurred to me that I might get this old article back from Publishers-Hall. Since it had already been paid for, I wouldn't mind having it published without additional repayment.

I got the release from Publishers-Hall on June 7, and it eventually appeared in the March 1974 *ChemTech*, but by then the title had to be changed to "How to Write 148 Books Without Really Trying." Then, when I finally included it in one of my collections, the name had to be changed again, to "How to Write 160 Books Without Really Trying."[8] This illustrates one of the minor problems of being prolific.

15

On June 9, 1973, I began the book on the history of the telescope that I had promised Austin, a book that was eventually called *Eyes on the Universe*.

The idea for this had originated not with Austin, but with a corporation that was interested in helping to construct a large telescope that was to be placed in orbit about the Earth. This would, in my opinion, be an important tool for the advancement of astronomy, and I was eager to do what I could to help it along.

My big fear rested in the fact that I understood very little about the nuts and bolts of scientific instruments, so the corporation, to help me out, sent me a huge crate of literature on the subject. There's never any difficulty in self-education, if you're really interested.

16

The eclipse cruise was approaching, and embarkation was slated for June 22. It meant missing the crucial part of the Watergate hear-

[8] See *Science Past—Science Future*.

ings by the Ervin committee—the testimony of John Dean—but there was actually something that worried me more, and that was Janet's health.

Not only was there the problem of the migraines, but also she had become conscious of a "bruit," an abnormal sound in one of her neck arteries. She feared the possibility of a clot there and of a consequent stroke.

Paul Esserman had sent her to the appropriate specialist, who was talking about an angiogram. This involved the injection of a dye into an artery and the X-ray study, in detail, of the circulation through the brain. It was not a pleasant, nor an entirely safe, procedure. The doctor scouted the need for immediate testing, however, and told her it could be done after the cruise.

But we worried.

17

I drove to Boston on June 17 and talked to the American Society for Medical Technologists, and the next day drove to the suburb of Lexington to talk at Ginn & Company.

Janet stayed home, for she did not like to accompany me to Boston. She felt that if I had the chance to see my children, she would be in the way. I argued against that, but she insisted.

It was my custom, when I was out of town alone, to call back after stages that involved traveling so that she would know I was safe (she was always apprehensive about something happening to me when she was not there to protect me).

At about noon on June 18, 1973, therefore, I called her to tell her that I had negotiated the dozen miles or so from Boston to Lexington and was in one piece.

She seemed lethargic on the phone and told me she had just awakened. I knew that she had a 1 P.M. patient scheduled and I was concerned over her apparent sleepiness. Furthermore, she seemed not to understand what I was saying, or else she would forget what I had just said and ask me to say it again.

I became rather exasperated and urged her to wake up. She assured me she was well and I had to hang up at last.

I gave my talk at Ginn & Company and I was no sooner done than I got a message from Chaucy to call Paul Esserman, as Janet was ill.

Apparently something had happened that morning that had left her in a daze and a semicoma. Had I not called, she might have sunk into a coma too deep to respond to the doorbell when her patients came. I *did* call, however, and that roused her just sufficiently to answer the door. She was unable to deal with them, but one of them, noting that Janet was really ill, and knowing the name of her internist,[9] called Esserman's office.

The patient also managed to get Chaucy's name out of Janet, as a relative who could be notified. The patient called Chaucy, who was already in a state of alarm, for she had happened to have called Janet that morning and, like myself, had been perturbed over how strange Janet had sounded.

Chaucy came at once and relieved the patient, who then left. Chaucy managed to elicit from an increasingly comatose Janet that I was at Ginn, and Chaucy sent off the message to me. By then, Esserman's partner, Howard Gorfinkel, had arrived, and soon after, an ambulance came. Janet was in University Hospital only a couple of hours after I had talked to her.

Gorfinkel's first thought, judging from Janet's condition, was that she had taken pills of some sort. He tried to find out what she had taken and asked Chaucy to look about for some note. Chaucy was furiously indignant at the thought that Janet might have made a suicide attempt, stressing the fact of Janet's happiness with me, but Gorfinkel (wisely perhaps) doubted my gift for inspiring total happiness and continued the search. No note was found.

When I called Esserman in great panic, after receiving the note, Esserman asked, very gently, if perhaps Janet and I had quarreled. It was my turn to be indignant, for I saw at once what was in his mind. "We *never* quarrel," I kept shouting into the phone. "It's *impossible* for me to quarrel with Janet."

Then I got into my car, and with everyone at Ginn & Company shouting at me to take it easy—to drive carefully—to stay calm—I did no such thing. I drove to New York at a steady eighty miles an hour.

When I got to the apartment, I found blood in the bathroom, and deduced that Janet had had a stroke. I called the hospital and was told that she was in the intensive-care unit and that I could not talk to her —and I was now certain she had had a stroke. Through my head ran miserable images of paralysis and death.

I took a taxi to the hospital, found out on what floor the intensive-care unit was, and came out of the elevator like a rocket. Paul, Howard, and Chaucy were all there waiting for me, and they blocked my passage. I was not to see Janet till they had talked to me.

It turned out that a diagnosis had been made when a neurologist had taken a spinal tap and had found blood in the cerebrospinal fluid.

[9] By a fortunate chance, Janet had once recommended Esserman to her.

She had had "subarachnoid bleeding." This was bleeding into the outer membranes of the brain, rather than into the brain itself, through the rupture of a tiny artery. That accounted for all the symptoms (and probably for the blood in the bathroom), and it was *not* a stroke.

Nevertheless, it was serious enough. She would have to have an angiogram and, very likely, brain surgery. It would be a long procedure and "life threatening," and that was the whole story, and if I calmed down I could see Janet.

I saw her. She was hooked up to an intravenous food supply and to various instruments. Her eyes were open and she recognized me and said, just as she had on the occasion of the mastectomy, "I'm sorry."

I took her hand, unable to speak, and she said, "I spoiled everything."

She meant the eclipse cruise, of course, which was four days in the future, and Esserman told me that she kept saying that she would have to leave in four days and couldn't stay in the hospital.

I finally went home and stayed up all night, entirely unable to sleep. I called up Rae and told her the situation, explaining that it might be very bad—and fearful that Rae might consider it some kind of visitation on Janet for taking up with a married man.

Rae, however, was very consoling in that respect and thanked me for having made Janet happy.

I called Phil Sigler on June 19 and told him I could not go on the cruise, explaining why. He sounded despairing at the news, saying I was his star, but what could I do?

I spent most of the nineteenth at the hospital holding Janet's hand. She would drift in and out of sleep, and her memory was not working at all. She was not clear as to why she was in the hospital, and over and over again she said to me, "Do I have metastatic cancer? Am I dying?"

I would say, quietly, "No, dear. You've had subarachnoid bleeding, and you'll live."

She would close her eyes, contented, and then she would open them and ask about cancer again and I would repeat my answer. It happened over and over and I felt that if it happened often enough it might stick. I was prepared to repeat it all day.

Then, after one answer-and-response, she opened her eyes and said nothing. Anxious to continue the repetition, I prompted her by saying, "Are you afraid of something, Janet?"

And she said, in very woebegone fashion, "I'm afraid you'll leave me."

I tried to reassure her.

18

On the occasion of the mastectomy, I had expected good news and had received bad. The situation was reversed this time.

On the twentieth, Janet had her angiogram, and all (quite unexpectedly) turned out to be well. The bursting arteriole had, in bursting, apparently healed the condition (don't ask me how), and her cerebral circulation was absolutely sound. There would be no brain surgery, for there was nothing that needed to be done, and she was promptly taken out of the intensive-care unit.

On June 21, I visited her in an ordinary hospital room. She was no longer comatose (though still without much memory), and I was so relieved I could scarcely endure my happiness.

Paul Esserman said to me, "You'll be going on the cruise, then?"

"Not on your life," I said. "I'm not leaving her in the hospital."

Paul said, in his soft way, "I'm afraid you'll have to, Isaac. Doctor's orders."

"But I can't."

"It's all she talks about—how she spoiled the cruise for you and now you won't see a total eclipse. We've got to keep her calm and relaxed and we can only do that if you go on the cruise."

So I called Phil Sigler and said I would go after all, and he sounded as though I had restored him to life. I told him that the condition was that arrangements be made to have me call Janet at the hospital from the ship every day. He promised (and kept that promise).

19

On June 22, 1973, I got on the ship. Marci Sigler, Phil's vivacious and good-looking wife, came to the apartment house to make sure I was coming and personally saw me on board.

The ship was the *Canberra*, which was much larger than the *Statendam*. Among the notables on board were two of the astronauts, Neil Armstrong and Scott Carpenter. With Scott was his clever young wife, Maria. Also present were Walter Sullivan, Frank Branley of the Hayden Planetarium, and George Hamilton of the Fels Planetarium in Philadelphia.

Unlike the *Statendam* cruise, this one was filled to capacity. There were twenty-five hundred passengers aboard, all involved with the eclipse, and I think the only empty bed on the ship was one of the two in my room, the one that Janet was to have occupied.

There were seven at our table: the Carpenters, the Sullivans, the Branleys, and myself. Janet was to have made the eighth, but her chair remained empty throughout the trip.

It was a hectic table, for I had to keep my mind off Janet, and I did it by a constant running fire of conversation, jokes, and *double-entendres*. The others naturally rose to the occasion, particularly Maria Carpenter, so that the table was by far the noisiest in the place.

For that matter, I kept the whole cruise in a continual state of excitement, for I was in an overflowing state of effervescence.

I gave four talks on the history of astronomy—all of them off the cuff, but using my book *The Universe* as raw material. I gave each of them twice, since otherwise there was no possibility of reaching the entire audience.

I was also part of a seminar at one point, and during the course of it, I said, "At the table where I'm sitting—and, as luck would have it, I was placed at the noisiest table on the ship . . ."

Walter Sullivan, who was also part of the seminar, stared at me in horror as I said that, and cried out, indignantly, "But Isaac, you're the one who makes it noisy."

"Ah," I said, "that explains it. I wondered why I was always at the noisiest table wherever I go."

At another point during that seminar someone in the audience asked me if I had read an article on tachyons in *Saturday Review*, and with great satisfaction I was able to reply, "Read it, sir? I *wrote* it."

Neil Armstrong was at the next table, and he had the most charming ten-year-old son, intelligent, lively, freckle-faced. I asked Neil if he would sell me the kid. He thought about it and said, "Yes, if you'll promise to drop him overboard after you buy him."

I reported that to the kid who said, wisely, "That sounds like Dad, all right."

One time at dinner, the young Armstrong boy came over and said, "Listen! What word has the letter combination XYZXYZX?"

We had been playing word games, but this one stopped us cold. For some ten minutes, an absolute silence hung over the table as all seven of us tried to think of a seven-letter word with that pattern of letters. I thought of "Sensens," the trade name of a preparation sold to mask bad breath in my youth, rather like "Tic-Tac" today. That was a proper noun, however.

Finally, I decided to go through the alphabet and see if I could think of the word by a systematic search through my mind. I began with A and instantly the word popped into my head.

And just as instantly, I threw up my hands and shrieked, "AL-

FALFA!!!" The scream resounded through the large dining room and the whole enormous room fell silent.[10] The next morning at breakfast someone came over and said to me, "Everyone in the place knows the answer. It's 'alfalfa.' But what's the question?"

20

Naturally, I called Janet every day. It meant finding my way to the small radio room, waiting my turn, and waiting while the radioman (with a thick and beautiful Scots burr) made contact. Then, finally, I could speak to her. I calculated afterward I spent a total of twelve hours in that little room.

Janet's memory was still largely out of commission, and each day I had to explain where I was and why. She always sounded cheerful, however, and insisted she was doing well. One day I called Paul Esserman instead, just to make sure that Janet knew what she was talking about. He assured me she was all right and I asked him to explain to her that I had used up my daily call on him.

I also put my time to good use by writing a fifteenth Black Widowers story, "The Iron Gem,"[11] onboard ship. I eventually sold it to *EQMM*, and it appeared in the July 1974 issue under the title "A Chip of the Black Stone."

21

On June 28, we docked at the Canary Islands, and I got off the ship and walked around a bit. I didn't take any tours largely because I have a besetting fear of somehow not getting back to the ship on time and having it leave without me. In fact, when we stopped off Dakar on July 1, I didn't get off the ship at all. I could, however, see the coast from shipboard, and it was a strange feeling to know that I was gazing at Africa.

Janet was back in her apartment on the twenty-ninth after eleven days in the hospital, and I talked to her there. She had the services of a live-in nurse, so I felt she was secure.

22

On June 30, it was eclipse time. A sandstorm over the Sahara produced a windblown sand haze in the sky and there were clouds besides.

[10] The Armstrong youngster said he was thinking of *entente*, but I told him that was French and "alfalfa" was much better.
[11] See *More Tales of the Black Widowers*.

The *Canberra*, however, managed to find a place where there was a hole in the cloud cover, and all over the decks of the ship, tripods and telescopes and cameras had sprung up overnight like a growth of weeds. I was one of the few without equipment of any kind.

The sight of the total eclipse was wonderful. There were two things that were unexpected. The eclipsed Sun, with its corona spectacularly visible, looked smaller than I expected, and at total eclipse, it did not seem to be night but, rather, twilight.

I was excited enough to be shouting wildly at the moment of eclipse. There were people there with tape recorders, and I was allowed, afterward, to listen to the deathless prose that issued from my lips.

One exclamation was, "Yes, that's it. That's it. That's the way it's supposed to look," as though I were congratulating the cosmic director who was running the show.

The other, when the brighter stars began to be visible was, "That proves it. The stars *do* shine in the daytime."

To me, the most exciting split second was the reappearance of the Sun. For five minutes of totality we waited and then at the western edge of the Sun there was a flash of light. The "diamond ring" effect lasted for a bare moment. The blaze broadened, and in two seconds one could not look at the Sun anymore.

The whole thing was a spectacular success. Now, if anyone ever asked me to write a description of a total eclipse, as *Look* had asked me to do, four years before, I would be an experienced person in the field.

23

Yet there was something that was, for me, an even more exciting moment.

There were musicians onboard ship who were arranging an amateur musical show in honor of the Fourth, and I went up to watch rehearsals. At one point, I couldn't help but sing along in a very low voice. It wasn't low enough.

Someone came up and said in surprise, "Do you sing baritone?"

"Of course," I said. (The surprise was natural. My speaking voice tends to be tenor.)

"Sing this, then," he said, and thrust a piece of sheet music into my hands. Apparently he thought I could read music.

I put it away and said, "Tell me the words and play the music."

He played it on the piano and sang it after a fashion. Then he said, "Now you."

I sang it while he held his breath to see if I could make the high note—which I reached effortlessly—and thereafter I was part of the rehearsals—and was full of stage fright.

On July 4, we put on our show, and finally I sang "Dear one, the world is waiting for the sunrise. . . ." to thunderous applause and considerable surprise. Many people thought I was mouthing the words while it was being sung on a record player.

On July 7, there was another showing, and I not only sang "Dear one," but also "Old Man River" as an encore. Then when they wanted still more, I rebelled, and said I did not want to sing baritone anymore, but would sing tenor. I sang "Venezuela" (which I had heard in Chester's Zunbarg, twenty-five years before) at the top of my range.

That was really a triumph. I sang both baritone and tenor to the same audience on the same evening and did it well each time. It's a good thing I'm a compulsive writer. Otherwise, wild horses wouldn't have kept me out of show business.

24

We docked in New York at 9:30 A.M. on Sunday, July 8, 1973. The Siglers arranged to have customs go through my baggage onboard ship, but when I tried to get off I was stopped. No one would be allowed to disembark, I was told, till all the baggage was removed, and that would take hours. I tried to explain that I was carrying my own baggage and that it had already been checked by customs and that I had a piece of paper to prove it. No one would listen.

I waited about fifteen minutes and then, driven mad by the fact that I could *see* the apartment house, I got my baggage and marched off the ship, disregarding the official who was shouting after me, presented my paper to the customs people, and got a taxi. I was in Janet's apartment at 11:15 A.M., hours before anyone else on the ship got off.

Janet, whom I now saw for the first time in sixteen days, seemed quite herself, though weak.

25

Eventually, I went to the Cromwell and found that, in my absence, a new door had been placed on my apartment (part of the shift from hotel to apartment house) and that the new girl at the switchboard knew nothing about any key for it, or any mail that might be waiting for me. She didn't even know that I was living there.

I had to wait till the next day before things returned to normal.

On July 17, the progress of the Cromwell changeover reached the point of an imminent abandonment of the switchboard. I had a private phone installed, therefore. It saved me the trouble of having people go through the switchboard (which was sometimes troublesome to reach). On the other hand, it meant I had no one to ward off my calls when I wanted that done, and I had no one to take messages. I therefore hired an answering service, the same that Janet used.

As a result of the cruise, by the way, I wrote two *F & SF* articles, my 183rd and 184th, entitled "The Eclipse and I" and "The Dance of the Luminaries."[12]

[12] For both, see *Of Matters Great and Small* (Doubleday, 1975).

PART
V

*Ageless Love
and Aging Heart*

38

Second Marriage

1

Judy-Lynn was no longer with *Galaxy*, but had joined the staff of Ballantine Books. There, one of her duties was the editing of anthologies of original stories, and she was after me to do a story for her.

On July 22, 1973, I began "Stranger in Paradise" for her, completed it on the twenty-ninth, and handed it to her. It was a sizable effort, ten thousand words long, and she promptly rejected it!

With considerable indignation, I took it over to Ben Bova on the thirty-first, and later that day he called me and asked me if I were sitting down. Rather irascibly, I answered that I wasn't.

"Well, sit down," he said, and then he rejected it, too.

I retired the story in considerable agitation. The growing speed with which my experience and position had made it possible for me to write stories and get editorial decisions meant that in the space of merely ten days I was able to write a novelette and get two rejections— and from my closest friends, too. It was the first shorter piece of fiction that had been rejected by more than one editor in thirty-one years; the last had been "Victory Unintentional."

It might have been a more significant blow and affected me more deeply were I not so prolific. As it was, all my other projects were doing well.

2

Janet's birthday was approaching and I was anxious to make it a good one. The year before she had celebrated her birthday in the hospital and had missed Breadloaf later in the month. Then this year she had been hospitalized again and had missed the eclipse cruise. Insofar as one could make up for all that, I would try to arrange it.

The day before, Sunday, August 5, I made my weekly phone call to my mother. I had hoped she would not have noticed that the day before was the fourth anniversary of my father's death, but she had noticed it and was very sad. I did my best to console her and promised I would be visiting her very soon, but she wept at her loneliness without him.

And then came August 6, Janet's forty-seventh birthday, and at the Cromwell I did one or two things I could not neglect and then rushed to Janet's to begin the celebration.

At least I began to rush over, but even as I was leaving the door, the woman at the switchboard (which was in its last weeks of existence) called out that there was a phone call for me.

She hooked me in to the phone in the lobby and it was my sister, in tears. She had just been called by the police. My mother was dead. She had died peacefully in her sleep in the early hours of the morning, and some member of the family would have to identify her or she would be taken to the morgue. My brother couldn't be reached (it turned out that he was off playing tennis with Ruth), Nick was at work, and Marcia was too unstrung. I assured her that I would go.

I went to Janet's apartment, then, in a somber mood. "I'm sorry, Janet," I said, "but the birthday will be a lousy one again. My mother just died."

Janet brushed aside her birthday as of no consequence, commiserated with me, and together we drove out to Long Beach. I identified my mother for the police and I remained till the medical examiner arrived to certify a natural death, and the people from the funeral home arrived to remove the body.

My mother had died four years and two days after my father, and just one month short of her seventy-eighth birthday.

Her death didn't affect me as badly as my father's had. The slow deterioration of her health had made the event inevitable, her sad and lonely life without my father had made it welcome to her, and I had to recognize that prolonging its meaninglessness was not what she wanted.

Soon after my mother's body was removed, Stanley and Ruth, and then Marcia and Nick, arrived.

Stanley said he would take care of the bills and details in connection with the hotel in which my mother had been living. He was the executor of the estate and knew the terms of the will. Since we three children were the only legatees, Stanley suggested that we remove my mother's belongings from the apartment now, arrange some of the stuff for disposal to charitable agencies, and divide the rest.

I could not bear to take part in the division. I did take one ballpoint pen (I cannot resist pens), but nothing more. Stanley and Marcia divided the rest in perfect amicability.

While that was taking place, my deep depression stirred the inevitable gallows humor within me and I said, suddenly, "If Mamma had only known that all six of us were going to be here today, she would have waited." It got a rather hysterical laugh.

My mother was eventually buried in the plot just next to my father, and the headstone had an additional date carved into it.

Nor was there any trouble over her will. My mother had insisted, over my protests, on leaving everything to her three children, divided into equal thirds. I had told her that I didn't need any money and to cut it into equal halves for Stanley and Marcia, but she wouldn't even consider cutting me out of the will.

After her death, I told Stanley that I would not accept my share and that he was to arrange to have it divided into two for himself and Marcia, making whatever legal arrangements were necessary. I said I wouldn't even take my share long enough to give it to them, lest that involve tax problems.

Stanley arranged matters with his lawyer, who sent me a letter suggesting I get a lawyer of my own to protect my interests.

I replied that I needed no lawyer since I had no interests that could conflict with Stanley's.

The lawyer asked Stanley if it were possible I really meant that and Stanley assured him that he and I took the business of being brothers quite seriously.

3

I kept myself busy with work on *Eyes on the Universe*, and on August 14 I began my sixteenth Black Widowers story, "The Three Numbers,"[1] which sold instantly (despite "Stranger in Paradise" I had not lost my touch). It appeared in the September 1974 *EQMM* under the title "It's All in the Way You Read It."

Then, on August 19, Janet and I went to Rensselaerville, where we had had such a pleasant time the year before. This time I was, in a sense, fulfilling the Duncan MacDonald role and running the discussions, which were based on ethical questions arising from my science-fiction stories. The weather was perfect and it was all much more like a vacation than a seminar. For Janet, particularly, the surroundings were ideal.

While we were there, David turned twenty-two, and my present to him was the money with which to buy an automobile for himself.

[1] See *More Tales of the Black Widowers*.

4

We were home on the twenty-third and prepared for the thirty-first World Science Fiction convention, which was to be held in Toronto. That was a little far for me, but *The Gods Themselves* had been nominated for a Hugo and I wanted to be there on the chance that it might win.

En route we stopped off at Niagara Falls, where I had the odd sensation of being a seasoned traveler. Janet had never seen them, but it was my third visit there, and I squired her around. By the afternoon of August 31, we were in our hotel in Toronto.

The Hugo awards banquet was on the evening of September 2, 1973, with Bob Bloch giving the guest-of-honor speech and Lester del Rey toastmastering. The Bovas and Pohls were at our table, along with Gordon Dickson.

It was a prize-winning table, indeed. Ben won the Hugo for best editor, and Fred Pohl won in the best-short-story category for a story he completed that Cyril Kornbluth had once started. Fred therefore had two Hugos, one for himself and one for Cyril. And, of course, I won the Hugo for the best novel, thanks to *The Gods Themselves*.

Afterward, I went up to Ben Bova's suite to help celebrate. I had promised Janet, who favored early-to-bed, since we would be on the road the next day, that I would only stay for fifteen minutes. After an hour had passed, however, she called to make sure I was all right, and we begged her to join us.

In ten minutes more there was a knock at the door and I said, jubilantly, "Janet is here" and threw the door open, dashing through.

Ben opened the real door to let Janet in, while I emerged, shamefaced, from the closet. Ben at once gleefully informed the assembled multitude that "the greatest mind in science fiction" couldn't tell a closet door from a hall door.

We did leave the next day and were home by September 4.

5

On September 5, I heard from Robyn. She was at Windham College in Putney, Vermont, and was beginning her college career there. She had given away Satan before she left for college, and we would see him no more. (And on that day, my mother would have been seventy-eight had she lived.)

Meanwhile, Janet had finished her science-fiction novel, *The Sec-*

ond Experiment. That might never have happened but for her siege in the hospital with her subarachnoid hemorrhage. Filled with a sense of the briefness of life, she decided she just had to use the summer to get the novel done.

Then, too, once again Austin had come in from Boston and visited her in the hospital while I had been off on the cruise. Her memory had improved to the point where she seized the opportunity to tell him the plot of the novel. He had been interested and had urged her to finish it and let him see it.

On September 11, Janet handed a copy of the novel to Ben Bova for possible serialization. Ben rejected it, but found much good in it and suggested a rewrite. I persuaded Janet to try it on Houghton Mifflin before revising, and get a second opinion. Doubleday was the logical choice, actually, since Houghton Mifflin did no science fiction (except for *Fantastic Voyage*), but Austin had expressed interest in seeing it, and it would be only courteous to let him see it.

6

While I had been at the Toronto convention, word had come to us that Tolkien had died. I had by then read the Lord of the Rings series three times with great pleasure and had, moreover, a certain feeling of guilt at having beaten it out for a Hugo seven years before.

I decided, therefore, to write a seventeenth Black Widowers story centered about Tolkien as my way of showing homage. I called it "Nothing Like Murder"[2] and took it in to *EQMM* on September 17. Not entirely to my surprise, it was rejected. Fred Dannay quite rightly pointed out that his readership was not likely to be sufficiently acquainted with Tolkien to make the story a fair one for them.

The story did not remain retired for long, however. A month later, Ed Ferman asked if I had a story for him by any chance. I said that I had a story based on Tolkien, but it was neither fantasy nor science fiction. He asked to see it and on October 11, I mailed it to him. To my considerable surprise, he took it and it appeared in the October 1974 *F & SF*. It was the first Black Widowers story to appear anywhere but in *EQMM*.

I waited for loud complaints from the *F & SF* readership, but they did not come, and Ed eventually told me he would welcome additional Black Widowers stories now and then, if they had some sort of scientific theme.

[2] See *More Tales of the Black Widowers.*

And in the meantime I had done, *How Did We Find Out About Vitamins?*, my sixth in that series for Walker.

7

Although the success at Rensselaerville and Toronto had gone some way toward making up to Janet the loss of the eclipse cruise, more had to be done. It had been over a year since I had vaguely promised Victor Serebriakoff that I would consider a trip to Great Britain, and now I decided to go through with it. On September 18, I began to check with a travel agent on possible arrangements for a round trip to Great Britain the following June.

8

The editors of *The Saturday Evening Post* asked me to do a story about Benjamin Franklin. It was to be a fantasy, in fact, and I was to have a conversation with him in which he and I discussed the contemporary world situation.

I was taken with the notion. After all, I had written a book on Franklin (*The Kite That Won the Revolution*), and I was a great admirer of old Ben. So I agreed and wrote the story, which I called "The Dream," on September 19. I sent it off to the *Post*, which accepted it without trouble.

It pleased the people at the *Post* sufficiently to make them want to elaborate on the idea. In the first place, on September 28, a photographer was sent to the Cromwell to take photographs of me in bed, presumably carrying on my dream conversation with Ben Franklin. They ran the photographs with the story, which appeared in the January–February 1974 issue of the magazine.

Then, the approaching Bicentennial of the Declaration of Independence fired the imaginations of the *Post* editors, and I was asked to do further dreams involving Ben Franklin, further conversations in which I was to develop a kind of Franklinesque wisdom calling for peace and co-operation among peoples as a way of celebrating the Bicentennial.

I favored that, too, and wrote three more three-thousand-word dreams, which I simply called "The Second Dream," "The Third Dream," and "The Fourth Dream." They were published in the April 1974, the May 1974, and the June–July 1974 issues of the magazine, respectively. The names under which they appeared were, respectively,

"Benjamin's Dream," "Party by Satellite," and "Benjamin's Bicentennial Blast."

By that time, though, the *Post's* dreams had exceeded all bounds. They wanted me to travel around the country in order to interview people and then to work those interviews into the dreams. That I flatly refused to do, and the scheme ended with the fourth dream. One of the editors did a fifth dream, I know, but I don't know if anything happened thereafter.

Nevertheless, the first Franklin piece and the favorable reaction of the *Post* led me to begin the third volume of my history of the United States. This was to cover the Civil War and I called it *Our Federal Union*. I began work on it on September 26.

9

My year of official separation from Gertrude had come to an end a half year before, but negotiations for a divorce had been going on but slowly ever since. I was anxious to avoid another court battle, but to do that we would have to come to some agreement on financial settlement, as everyone must, sooner or later.

On October 7, George Michaels, my Boston lawyer, was in town, and he and his wife, Barbara, had lunch with Janet and me, and he brought us up to date on developments.

The occasion was overcast not only by the general unpleasantness of the topic, but also by the fact that, the day before, Egypt and Syria had taken advantage of Israel's preoccupation with Yom Kippur to deliver a surprise assault on Israel.

Life went on, however. Janet submitted her novel to Houghton Mifflin on October 8, thus keeping her promise to Austin three months before. On that same day, I got the news that *The Caves of Steel* was under a movie option. That made two active options, since *I, Robot* was still under option after four years—that option having been regularly renewed.

10

I had been in touch with Robyn at her college and found that she was depressed and homesick—about par for the freshman year. Still, I felt it necessary to see her. I was slated to give a talk in Rhode Island on Sunday, October 14, and I decided to go by way of Vermont.

I drove to Putney on the thirteenth, and if Robyn was unhappy, there seemed no sign of it. She looked radiantly beautiful to me and she had a very happy dinner with Janet and me at the motel at which we were staying.

After I drove her back to her school, though, I discovered that the faint malaise I experienced during the meal was developing rapidly into a definite case of intestinal flu. By the next morning I was clearly, and badly, ill. Janet had to drive me to Cranston, Rhode Island, for I was absolutely incapable of handling the wheel.

It was the first time in my twenty-three years as a public speaker that I ever fell ill on the way to a talk.

I managed a two-hour nap before the talk, but it didn't help much. I was forced to give the talk while running a considerable temperature. The audience seemed enthusiastic, and Janet assured me afterward that I had seemed completely normal, but I myself knew the difference between what I gave and what I could have given if I'd felt well. I had to attend a reception afterward and be as gracious as I could be without letting on that although I seemed friendly and lively as I sat there, I would fall down if I tried to stand up.

The next day we drove back to New York, with Janet doing most of the driving. At home I finally allowed her to take my temperature and I was feverish, of course, so I stayed in bed for the day. I was up and around in time to take a trip to Washington on October 17, however, and to deliver a talk there.

11

On October 20 came the Saturday-night Massacre, in which Nixon fired Archibald Cox, the special prosecutor, and the top two men of the Justice Department in a sudden couplike attempt to abort the Watergate investigation.

Since I remembered the days of Nazi Germany and since my opinion of Nixon could not be lower than it was, I was convinced that Nixon was planning an outright dictatorship and would place the nation under martial law.

I could scarcely believe it when Nixon backed off, but I could not believe that this was the result of any ethical misgivings on Nixon's part. It had to be only a lack of courage.

For a while, though, I was in despair, and it was at this time that the Ginn people decided to approach me on the matter of my treatment of evolution in the science series. They were losing out on adoptions because some school systems objected to the inclusion of evolution. Ginn wanted the word "evolution" omitted and "development" used instead.

Furious over the approach (as I thought) of dictatorship and repression, I decided that I would make no compromises with obscurantism. On October 21 and October 24, I sent off scathing letters absolutely refusing to agree to this. I said that I didn't care if I didn't make one penny out of the books, but I would not compromise my scientific integrity. If they removed "evolution" they would also have to remove my name from the books.

"Evolution" stayed. The science series continued to do poorly.

I went on to do *The Solar System*, the seventh in my series of small astronomy books for Follett.

12

November was an eventful month.

The matter of a divorce finally came to a climax. For months, it had looked increasingly as though there might be another trial. My lawyers welcomed it since they were certain the judge would not raise the alimony above what it then stood.

I didn't want that. I wanted to repeat my original considerably higher offer, and my lawyers, shaking their heads at my quixoticism, did as I asked them to. Gertrude finally accepted that, and on November 16, 1973, I was divorced. It came 21 months after my separation, nearly 3½ years after I had left Newton, and 31¼ years after my marriage. The whole process had cost me $50,000 in legal fees.

Although I had wanted the divorce, it was a traumatic procedure all the way.

What made it worse was that Robyn was ill—seriously ill. It had begun only about two weeks after I had seen her at Windham College. It appeared first as a sore throat, fever, a sense of weakness. It developed into tonsillitis, and she was put in the school infirmary.

She did not improve and then they discovered that she had a low white-cell count and could not find the cause for it. Without the white cells she was in a constant state of low-grade infection.

There was no question but that she would have to have her tonsils out, but that could not be done until she had recovered from the present infection.

I kept up a constant drumfire of phone calls to the infirmary and to her doctor and finally I asked the big question. Since white cells were involved, I said, "Can it be leukemia?"

He said, "We can't rule it out."

I said, in agony, "Don't say that."

He said, coldly, "Look, man, I've *got* to say that." He was right, of course.

Gertrude went up to Windham College, got Robyn, took her back to Boston on November 16 (the very day the divorce went into effect), and put her in Children's Hospital. I had to fight off the superstitious feeling that Robyn was being punished for my divorce.

On November 17, even while crucial tests were being conducted on Robyn's bone marrow to check out leukemia, I had to drive to Atlantic City to give a talk to the American Association of University Women. I never came closer to rebelling against my show-must-go-on compulsion.

But things turned better. By the nineteenth, the test had definitely removed leukemia from the list of possibilities, and under penicillin treatment Robyn began to improve. By November 21, she was home with Gertrude with the white-cell count rising, and I could breathe again and look forward to a more pleasant Thanksgiving than I had thought possible a few days earlier.

13

In fact, I could begin to think of marriage. Janet and I got our blood tests on November 21, and the next day we had the Thanksgiving feast at Chaucy's.

Over the Thanksgiving weekend I worked on a little book that the NESFA fans in Boston wanted to put out. The next Boskone was going to have me as guest of honor and they had started the tradition of putting out a small book of writings by the guest of honor. I suggested I put together eight stories from the 1950s that I had never collected, with appropriate commentary, under the title *Have You Seen These?* They agreed.

On the twenty-fourth, I mailed off *Have You Seen These?* That day, I also bought Janet a wedding ring.

14

Janet and I had a small problem as to just how we were going to get married. Neither one of us wanted a religious wedding of any kind, and it was our idea to get a civil wedding at the Municipal Building. All our friends advised us against this, however, on the ground that the atmosphere of such a wedding was dismal and would not make for a happy memory.

We went down to the Municipal Building on November 29 to get our wedding license and we had to agree that it was no place to get married.

Fortunately, we lived just a few blocks from the headquarters of the Ethical Culture movement, and officials of that movement are empowered to perform weddings. Janet therefore made the necessary arrangements with Edward Ericson of Ethical Culture for the purpose.

Oddly enough, although Janet and I had been closely bound and very much together for over three years, almost since my arrival in New York, the prospect of actual marriage seemed to upset her.

At least when I arrived from the Cromwell for dinner on the twenty-ninth, I found Janet weeping. In agitation, I asked what was wrong.

"I don't know," she said. "I feel as though I'll be losing my identity."

I said, urgently, "Don't look upon it as losing identity; look upon it as gaining subservience."

It worked just as well as my remark after her mastectomy had. She burst out laughing and cried no more.

We spent the next day waiting. The wedding was going to take place in Janet's apartment, in the living room, under the avocado tree that she had grown from seed. The only ones present aside from ourselves and Ericson were to be Al and Phyllis Balk, whom we had met at Breadloaf three years before and who would serve as the necessary witnesses.

At 4:00 P.M. all was ready. Janet had taken the phone off the hook so that there would be no unwelcome interruptions. The sun was sinking toward the horizon and reddish light shone through the slats of the venetian blind, making parallel streaks upon the wall we faced.

The light slowly faded as Ericson spoke briefly and finally pronounced us married at 4:30 P.M. on November 30, 1973. We all drank champagne, and Janet put the phone back on the hook. She had barely taken her hand away from it when it rang. It was Austin Olney, unaware that we had just gotten married, calling to say that Houghton Mifflin would publish Janet's novel, *The Second Experiment* (subject to some revision). It was the most auspicious possible beginning for our marriage.

All five of us then went out for a wedding dinner, and finally we came back to the apartment as man and wife, 17 years after our first brief meeting at the 1956 convention, 14½ years after our first real meeting at the Mystery Writers' of America dinner, and 3⅓ years after I had come to New York.

<h1 style="text-align:center">15</h1>

As a newly married man, once again, my first piece of writing was "The Second Dream" for *The Saturday Evening Post*, and my first social engagement was lunch with Lester and Judy-Lynn on December 2.

My first speaking engagement was on the evening of December 2, when Janet and I drove out to South Orange, New Jersey, to talk at Temple Israel.

I introduced Janet very proudly as my wife, and to Janet's mortification this meant she was promptly backed into a corner and made to listen to chatter about children and the PTA.[3]

The rabbi was delighted at hearing that we had been married on Friday at sunset. He said, "You married as the Sabbath arrived. That is a very good omen."

On December 4, I visited *Family Health* to discuss an article they wanted me to write (which I never got to, as it happened) and they brought up the matter of another article they had asked me to write over half a year before.

They had, at that time, asked me to do an article on some medical emergency bravely met and endured by myself or by some member of my family. I had said at the time that the only example I knew personally was Janet's mastectomy, but I didn't want to write about that until after we were married, since the story would not have a happy ending unless I could prove it did not prevent the marriage.

At our December 4 meeting the editor said, "Where do we stand on your fiancée's mastectomy?"

I said, "We married four days ago. I can write it now, provided she gives her permission."

Janet hesitated, quite naturally appalled at having her misfortune spread over the pages of a magazine. I made two points, however:

First, the story of the successful survival, emotional as well as physical, from such an operation might help others.

Second, to describe the survival, without once mentioning God as either cause or refuge, might be a blow for humanism.

She agreed, and even added a few paragraphs of her own, under the name "Janet Asimov."

The article, entitled "Mastectomy: A Husband's Story" appeared

---

[3] On future similar occasions I therefore tried to work into the conversation, as early as possible, the fact that she was a psychiatrist.

in the December 1974 *Family Health*, while Janet's addendum appeared as "Facing Up to It."

16

While Robyn's illness and my own divorce and remarriage filled the last months of 1973 for me, I could not help but be aware of the energy crisis. In the wake of the Yom Kippur War, the Arab bloc had imposed an embargo on oil shipments to the United States, Japan, and western Europe, and a confused American public suddenly found itself queuing up at gas pumps.

Not only did this raise questions in my mind as to how I was going to reach those places I had to reach in order to give talks, but also I was suddenly bombarded with requests to write articles on various aspects of the energy crisis.

My own favorite article of that type was the one I wrote, unrequested, for *F & SF*. It was my 188th essay, entitled "The Double-ended Candle,"[4] and was published in the June 1974 *F & SF*.

17

Comet Kohoutek was coming. Through the last months of 1973, it had been expected eagerly, for it had been sighted so far out in the solar system that it was clearly a large comet that might be making its first pass through the inner solar system.

This meant it might be a bright one, if it were of appropriate composition, icy, rather than rocky. Naturally, the dramatic assumption was that it would be icy and brilliant.

A half year before I had written an anticipatory piece called "Watch for the Christmas Comet,"[5] which had appeared in the December–January 1974 issue of *National Wildlife*. I had been cautious enough to qualify and say, "Comet Kohoutek, on its way now, may prove to be a superbright . . ." Despite the inclusion of that careful "may," I believed that it *would* be superbright.

Consequently, when it was announced that there would be a three-day "Cruise to Nowhere" on the *Queen Elizabeth* 2 to see the comet at its peak, I eagerly signed up. Again, it would make up to Janet a little for her having missed the eclipse cruise. Besides, it would serve as a honeymoon trip.

We embarked on December 9 and it was the first time on the QE2

---

[4] See *Of Matters Great and Small*.
[5] See *Science Past—Science Future* (Doubleday, 1975).

for either one of us. Janet, who loved all ships, promptly formed a lasting attachment to this one.

The weather disappointed us. It was cloudy and rainy wherever the QE2 went, and no one ever had a chance to look at the comet. This, as it turned out, was just as well, for Comet Kohoutek was a terrible disappointment. At its brightest it was barely visible to the naked eye, since it did not, after all, have the proper composition. It was too rocky to be bright.

Janet and I didn't care. We were in a state of honeymooners' bliss, walking about the ship so entwined that it's a wonder we didn't trip over each other's feet.

We attended the various lectures, and on December 10 we entered the auditorium to hear Kohoutek himself. As we sat down, Janet said, "It's so good to go on a trip just to enjoy ourselves; one where you don't have to work and give a talk."

As she said that, it was announced from the stage that, unfortunately, Kohoutek was in his cabin, immobilized by seasickness. Janet, unable to bear the disappointed hum that swept over the audience, elbowed me sharply in the ribs and said, "Get up and volunteer to give a talk."

I did, and found myself on stage in thirty seconds, forced to improvise a talk out of nothing. I said to Janet afterward, "But you had just told me how wonderful it was that I didn't have to give a talk."

"Volunteering one is different," she said.

18

Abelard-Schuman was no longer a separate entity, but had merged with larger firms. Frances Schwartz was still running it, however, and she asked me to do a book that UNICEF (the children-oriented agency sponsored by the United Nations) was interested in. She wanted a book on population for youngsters.

She said, rather plaintively, "As soon as I began working for Abelard-Schuman, you stopped writing for us."

That had been only a coincidence, of course, but it was one that smote my conscience. Besides, population was one subject that was particularly dear to my heart. I agreed, therefore, and on December 14 I began a book that was eventually entitled *Earth: Our Crowded Spaceship* and that was to appear under the imprint of John Day, now a sister firm of Abelard-Schuman.

About this time also I wrote my eighteenth Black Widowers story,

"No Smoking,"[6] which eventually appeared in the December 1974 *EQMM* under the title "Confessions of an American Cigarette Smoker."

And even though Comet Kohoutek had fizzled, it had aroused enough interest in comets generally for Walker to want *How Did We Find Out About Comets?*, which I began on December 27, and which was the seventh of that series.

In fact, the only flaw in the generally happy first month of our marriage was Robyn's continued indisposition. Although she was no longer seriously ill, she was by no means well enough to be risked in Vermont, and she was kept at home waiting for the tonsillectomy that would follow upon the doctor's go-ahead signal. Then we could hope for a permanent recovery.

Every week that passed, though, made it clearer that her freshman year at college was a washout and would have to be repeated.

19

In the year 1973, I published fifteen books again, equalling the 1972 mark. They were:

133. *How Did We Find Out the Earth Is Round?* (Walker)
134. *Comets and Meteors* (Follett)
135. *The Sun* (Follett)
136. *How Did We Find Out About Electricity?* (Walker)
137. *The Shaping of North America* (Houghton Mifflin)
138. *Today and Tomorrow and—* (Doubleday)
139. *Jupiter, the Largest Planet* (Lothrop)
140. *Ginn Science Program—Advanced Level A* (Ginn)
141. *Ginn Science Program—Advanced Level B* (Ginn)
142. *How Did We Find Out About Numbers?* (Walker)
143. *Please Explain* (Houghton Mifflin)
144. *The Tragedy of the Moon* (Doubleday)
145. *How Did We Find Out About Dinosaurs?* (Walker)
146. *The Best of Isaac Asimov* (Sphere)
147. *Nebula Award Stories Eight* (Harper)

20

I had a quiet celebration of my fifty-fourth birthday on January 2, 1974, and the next day dared the gas crisis by driving to Middletown,

[6] See *More Tales of the Black Widowers.*

New York, to give a couple of talks. For once it was not the snow I worried about but the gasoline. There was, in fact, light snow, not enough to be bothersome, and by stopping wherever we could for whatever gasoline we could get, we managed.

And on January 4, I attended my second Baker Street Irregulars dinner, this time as a full member.

21

On January 9, 1974, Robyn had her tonsillectomy. All was well at first, but then her white-cell count began to drop and once again the fever returned, so that there was a replay of the terror of November.

No, not quite. This time at least, we knew it wasn't leukemia, although no one could offer a real alternative. The best guess was that her white cells had developed a sensitivity to some chemicals (including the tetracyclines) and she had better be cautious in this respect. In any case, she was home by the sixteenth.

It was the last straw as far as her freshman year was concerned. Nor did Windham College in any way co-operate with her. Despite several requests on her part and several promises on the part of the faculty, there was no attempt to make it possible for her to work on her courses at home. It seemed clear to me that once Windham College collected tuition, they were no longer interested in the student beyond that.

It became plain to me, then, that not only would Robyn have to repeat her freshman year, but also it would have to be at some college more reasonably concerned for its students than Windham was. For my own part, I urged Robyn to attend some college closer to home so that in case of sudden health problems she not be forced to rely on callous strangers.

It was at this time I wrote an article about Robyn for *Seventeen*. The editor, Ray Robinson, told me that they had published articles about the effect of divorce on daughters, but they wanted one on the effect of divorce on fathers of daughters.

I was willing to comply, although I warned Ray I would have to get Robyn's approval of the finished product before I could submit it. I wrote "To My Daughter," therefore, on January 9, the day of her tonsillectomy, and I must admit it was a rather sentimental piece, for Robyn was always (as far as I was concerned) just about a perfect daughter.

After she had recovered from the immediate ill effects of the operation and was at home, I sent a copy to her. She called me up on the nineteenth to say that it would be all right to publish it.

Well, I thought so, and she thought so, but Ray didn't think so—

he rejected it. (Fortunately I had warned Robyn of that possibility.) Ray said he wanted one to reflect the anguish of the father a bit more, but there was nothing I could do about it. Through the separation and the divorce my relationship with Robyn remained perfectly loving, and whatever anguish there was did not involve her.

I put the article to one side and eventually seized the opportunity to publish it in one of my collections.[7]

22

Galaxy had a new editor, Jim Baen. He was a young man whom I had never, to my knowledge, met. He called me on January 23 to ask if I had any science-fiction stories I could submit to him.

"Sorry," I said, "I don't have anything." Then I remembered. "I do have something," I said (thinking of "Stranger in Paradise"), "but you wouldn't want it."

"Why won't I want it?"

"Because it's been rejected by Judy-Lynn del Rey and by Ben Bova, so I assume it is a stinker."

"May I see it and judge for myself?"

That was only fair, so I sent it to him and the next day he called and said he wanted it.

"Are you sure?" I asked, fatuously.

"Of course I'm sure," he said, and it ran in the June 1974 issue of *If*.[8]

I worried, on and off, that Jim, in his eagerness to have an Asimov story, had taken a bad one, but later in the year my old Futurian friend, Don Wollheim, chose it for his Best of the Year anthology, and I knew that Don wouldn't take a bad Asimov story for the sake of the name.

23

I felt very much a living monument when I found that Joseph Patrouch, Jr., of the University of Dayton, had written a book called *The Science Fiction of Isaac Asimov*. (He had given a three-point course at the university with that precise title, too.)

Patrouch had sent sample chapters to Larry Ashmead, who had liked them and who had asked me if I would mind if Doubleday did a book of that nature. I said that Doubleday had my full permission to go ahead and that the book did not need to be a panegyric; if there was

[7] See *Science Past—Science Future*.
[8] See *The Bicentennial Man and Other Stories*.

negative criticism, that was all right, and there was no necessity to show me the manuscript in advance.

Larry disregarded that. On January 28, he sent me the manuscript and I read it, at a sitting, in four hours, with the phone off the hook. No manuscript ever absorbed me more, not even one of my own. Patrouch was not completely favorable, but even when he turned thumbs down, he did so reasonably.

I returned the manuscript to Larry, correcting only one date as a factual error and making not one other request for modification.

24

I attended a "Star Trek" convention on the February 16–17 weekend, and something like fourteen thousand fans attended! I was incredibly lionized. It was impossible for me to move two steps in any direction without being halted for autographs.

It made me feel so all-powerful that at one point I tried to jump up onstage in one agile leap. But I was fifty-four, not twenty-four; I missed, fell down, and banged myself up a bit. I then had to limp up the stairs with difficulty. It taught me a much-needed lesson.

25

Robyn was nineteen years old on February 19, 1974, and her health was at last quite back to normal. In fact, she had gotten herself some sort of temporary job that involved considerable driving.

She always had the capacity to find temporary jobs when she was idle, and always had the willingness to work at them.

39

Great Britain

1

It was definite by now that we were going to Great Britain in June, and on February 23, we spent the evening at Marvin Grosswirth's talking to Victor Serebriakoff about it.

I firmly rejected his plan of having Mensa pay all my expenses. For one thing, I wanted to go first class, and I didn't want to be inhibited in my enjoyment thereof by worry over British Mensa's financial welfare. I was willing to have Mensa arrange an itinerary for us and supply us with a car and chauffeur, provided we paid all expenses, including that of the car and chauffeur. Victor looked puzzled, but he agreed.

2

On February 28, I went to Boston to attend Boskone as the guest of honor. For the first time, Janet accompanied me to Boston. She was my wife; why not? And so my Boston friends met Janet now.

At this time David was in the hospital briefly with some sort of viral infection, and I seized the opportunity to visit him. In the preceding two years, it seemed everyone had been taking turns at the hospital: I once, David once, Robyn twice, Janet twice.

3

On March 15, I wrote my 193rd *F & SF* essay, "Skewered!"[1] It was on a mathematical subject that always elicited considerable mail, so that I would have written more of them if I only knew more math. Since it was a seventeenth essay, it meant I could put together another collection, my eleventh, which I called *Of Matters Great and Small*.

[1] See *Of Matters Great and Small*.

4

On April 2, we left for a lecture tour westward. Our first stop was California, Pennsylvania, not far from Pittsburgh. It was a small town that had apparently been founded by a bunch of Forty-niners heading westward under the doughty banner of "California or bust." When they busted in western Pennsylvania, they founded a town named California and turned defeat into victory.

When I parked my car there and got out, a young man passing on a bicycle called out, "Hello, Dr. Asimov."

I said, "How do you know I'm Dr. Asimov?"

He said, "The newspaper said you'd be coming in today and I don't figure there would be *two* strangers in town." That was keen logic.

I gave my talk there on the evening of April 3, and that night we were kept awake by a terrific thunderstorm in which the lightning flashed continuously and the sky was a steady rumble while the rain came down as though it couldn't wait to flood us.

We were fortunate it was no worse. There were tornadoes not far to the west, and one of them destroyed Xenia, Ohio.

5

I had done several articles for *Family Weekly* and they were putting on a fancy luncheon at the Plaza for April 21, and I was invited. I felt it would be worthwhile for me to go and yet I didn't think I would enjoy being trapped with hundreds of strangers, so I asked Janet to come with me. She, ever obliging, did so.

Once there, it proved considerably more interesting than I thought, for there were well-known television personalities included in the crowd. I even met Roy Fisher of the World Book Year Book days a decade earlier. Joyce Brothers, the television psychologist, was at our table.

Once settled at the table, and finding some of our companions were congenial, I looked at the booklet before me and realized it was an awards luncheon, and that we were sitting right near one end of the head table at which, presumably, the awards winners were to be found.

I looked up curiously to see who they were and there, at our end of the table, not six feet from where we were sitting, was Alan Alda, the star of the M*A*S*H show.

As it happened, that was Janet's favorite show and she was very deeply enamored of Alan Alda. I wanted to tell her who was sitting so near her before she could find out for herself and, of course, I found I had lost my voice. I just yammered and finally managed to say, "Alda! Alda!" and pointed.

Janet looked up, puzzled, and her eyes widened. She said, excitedly, "It's Alan Alda."

"You want his autograph?"

"You'll embarrass me."

"Of course I won't." I bounced up. "Mr. Alda," I said, "I'm Isaac Asimov."

He said, "Why aren't you at home writing a book?" so I knew he knew who I was.

"It's my wife's fault," I said. "She's deeply in love with you and she's sitting right there and wants your autograph."

Janet colored a pretty beet-red, and Alan Alda said, "Poor woman," and signed.

Then Janet said I had embarrassed her. How, for goodness sake?

6

Robyn agreed with me about starting fresh in a school nearer home, and had no desire to return to Windham, which, in any case, she had disliked extremely.

The choice lay between Boston College and Boston University. I favored Boston University myself—my own school—but Robyn said that Boston College was closer to home, smaller, in better surroundings, and seemed more comfortable. —So Boston College it was.

7

There was a dinner at the Regency Hotel (where the Dutch Treat Club and the Baker Street Irregulars met) on May 2, one that was devoted to environmental causes. Barry Commoner was one of the speakers, but I remembered his article in *Science* thirteen years before, and took care not to get close enough to be introduced.

The dinner was excellent, but after it was over, two cigars and three cigarettes were lit in my vicinity and I simply got up and left. I wrote a letter afterward to the man who had invited me and explained that I thought human beings who considered themselves committed to the preservation of the environment should not pollute and, far more important, should not pollute the air of their nonsmoking neighbors with the stench of carcinogenic smoke.

I got no answer.

8

I finally finished *The Ends of the Earth* on May 7, after sixteen months of very much on-and-off work on it, and delivered it to Mac Talley.

9

Watergate kept heating up steadily, and a constant diet of it for over a year had not sated me. Nixon sank ever deeper into a quagmire of his own making, and his endless retreats struck me as somehow similar to the steady decline of Hitler in the last two years of World War II.

I was looking forward to his impeachment, conviction, and removal from office as a salutary lesson to all future Presidents to take seriously and honestly their oath to uphold the Constitution. Consequently, I could scarcely bear to miss any news broadcast.

On May 10, 1974, when I was returning from a dinner in New Jersey, I hastened, in order to get home before midnight and the last news broadcast of the day. Walking into the apartment at a quarter of midnight, I turned on the radio at once so that I would not forget.

My attention was caught at once by the statements being made by whoever it was on the program in progress. I listened for a while and called out, "Janet, there's a joker here spouting my ideas."

Janet came in, listened two seconds, and said, "It's *you*, Isaac."

And so it was. About a month earlier I had taped an interview with Casper Citron and had forgotten about it. It was running now and as usual I didn't recognize my own voice when unprepared for it.

10

I had been invited to give the commencement address at Boston University School of Medicine. There was no fee, but that didn't bother me. It was the most spectacular demonstration yet that I had been right in my quarrel with Keefer (seventeen years in the past) and that the school now recognized my value.

We drove to Boston on May 18, and had dinner with Austin Olney. David joined us and now met Janet for the first time. He was no longer living at home, but had a small room of his own in a rather run-down section and was looking about for better quarters. It seemed an appropriate step toward independence, and I approved.

The next day I gave my commencement talk. It was the first med school commencement I had attended since the one, thirteen years before, at which John Jeppson had graduated.

We drove back to New York, taking Robyn with us. Once back, I was anxious to begin making the rounds of New York with her, but on the twentieth she was tired and perhaps a little feverish and I was paralyzed with terror that she might be having a relapse.

She lay on the couch in the living room reading, and I sat at the dining-room table, unwilling to let her out of my sight—so unwilling, in fact, that I wouldn't use my typewriter but, using pen-and-ink, wrote a science-fiction story that *Boys' Life* had requested. The story was "The Heavenly Host," and it appeared in the December 1974 issue of *Boys' Life*.

She was feeling well the next morning, however, and for four days she and I went sight-seeing—Central Park, Metropolitan Museum of Art, NBC, and so on.

At NBC, I had been working on and off, for some months, with a producer, Lucy Jarvis, writing a special on the cult of youth for television. I didn't enjoy it any more than I had enjoyed doing "The Unseen World."

Naturally, when I did arrive at NBC for story conferences, I eased my unhappiness by engaging the various pretty young ladies in light-hearted banter, and my role was clearly that of the "sensuous dirty old man" concerning whom I had written.

When I took Robyn to NBC on May 22, the young women in Lucy Jarvis's office were horrified. There I was with my arm around a very young woman of spectacular appearance and with every evidence of extreme affection on my part—and the instant feeling was that I was flaunting every canon of good taste by bringing my latest starlet-conquest with me.

There was an almost palpable explosion of relief when I introduced Robyn as my daughter.

11

Robyn left on May 24, and that night Lester and I cohosted a Trap Door Spiders dinner at Lester's place. Once again I did well. My guest was Martin Gardner, and he was just as good at captivating the membership as Ken Franklin had been the year before. Martin was voted in, and I was not backward at pointing out to the general membership the high quality of my guests.

12

The trip to Europe was now almost upon us, and the thought of long travels and of three weeks away from home was unsettling—so I wrote something to keep my mind off it. Specifically, it was my nineteenth Black Widowers story—a Christmas story called "Season's Greetings."

Alas, it was rejected, and since its plot was such that there wasn't the faintest hook on which to hang an *F & SF* submission, I retired it and saved it for the next collection, in which it eventually appeared.[2]

13

On May 30, 1974, we boarded the *France*. I was at sea for the fourth time in a year and a half—four different ships of four different nationalities, since the *Statendam* was Dutch, the *Canberra* Australian, the *QE2* British, and the *France*, of course, French.

There were strong rumors that the *France* was going to be decommissioned. It was indeed going to take an extra day in making its crossing in order to save on fuel, since the price of oil had gone up steeply since the episode of the embargo. This upset our itinerary somewhat and, for a while, led us to think the trip would be washed out altogether.

And, indeed, on the last day of the crossing, the news became definite that the *France* would be decommissioned.

It was a quiet crossing, consisting almost entirely of eating, as I recall. The dining room was so arranged that the passengers made an entrance, sweeping down the stairs, dressed as though each one were starring in a Hollywood musical. Janet grew restless since we were dressed as though we were eating at a neighborhood restaurant, but I told her that on the *Canberra*, I (with no wife to ride herd on me) had dressed casually at all times, wearing sneakers even to the captain's functions.

I spent some time writing my twentieth Black Widowers story, "The One and Only East."[3] This one Fred Dannay eventually took, and it appeared in the March 1975 issue of *EQMM*.

[2] See *More Tales of the Black Widowers*.
[3] See *More Tales of the Black Widowers*.

14

On June 5, 1974, we disembarked in Southampton and I was in England for the first time, since, as a three-year-old child, I passed through it on my way to the United States, fifty-one years before.

Steve Odell of the Mensa organization was there waiting for us in a car hired for the occasion. He had worked out the itinerary of our sight-seeing tour and was to chauffeur us about (driving carefully on the left side of the road).

He drove us through the New Forest, where wild ponies had foaled, so that Janet was ravished by the sight of colts here and there. She also enjoyed the sight of the immemorial beeches. We were driven to Salisbury, where we were placed in an excellent hotel, and went to see Salisbury Cathedral.

I was instantly immersed in English history and I realized clearly that my youth, spent as it had been hip-deep in books written by English writers, had made me culturally an Englishman.

I was determined to try all the English items of diet even though it killed me (for I had heard many stories of the poor quality of the English cuisine). I began with steak-and-kidney pie at the hotel in Salisbury and loved it. There was a rich "gattoh" (accent on the first syllable) for dessert. It tasted like good cake to me and it was quite a while before I grasped that a gattoh was the naturalized version of the French *gateau*.

(On the whole, the food I ate in England was delightful from beginning to end as, of course, was the food I ate onboard ship. In the course of the trip I gained 10 pounds, my greatest departure from my stabilized weight of 180 in the 10 years since I had lost 30 pounds. Fortunately, I lost it in the month following my return and got back to 180 pounds.)

Steve, at my request, even took me to a pub in Salisbury, where I cautiously ordered a sherry. I hoped I would see a game of darts, but no one played that evening.

On the morning of June 6 (the thirtieth anniversary of D-Day), Steve drove us to Stonehenge, which was every bit as impressive as I thought it would be, especially early in the morning on a featureless plain with ourselves almost the only ones violating its ancient brooding.

We went on to Avebury and then to Bath, where we were taken through the Roman ruins. We went out to the Forest of Dean at the Welsh border, where we stayed in a hotel that Queen Elizabeth I had once visited.

It had been raining on and off all day, mild sprinkles that never lasted long and were not very annoying. Interspersed were sunshine and summer clouds. After dinner, Janet and I took a walk among the beeches of the forest and the bluebells on the ground, until another sprinkle drove us under one of the trees.

The Sun was out even while it sprinkled, and a rainbow appeared in the eastern sky. Not one rainbow either, but *two*. For the first time in my life I saw both the primary and secondary bows, separated, as they should be, by a distance of ten degrees of arc. Between them, the sky was distinctly dark, so that, in effect, we saw a broad band of darkness crossing the eastern sky in a perfect semicircle, bounded on either side by a rainbow, with the red side of each bordering the darkness and the violet side fading into the blue.

It lasted several minutes and we watched in perfect silence. I am not a visual person, but that penetrated—and deeply. Two months later, in fact, the incident inspired my 197th *F & SF* essay, "The Bridge of the Gods,"[4] which eventually appeared in the March 1975 *F & SF*.

On June 7, we drove to Gloucester, visited the cathedral there, then drove through charming little towns in the Cotswolds and admired the neat and orderly English countryside as much as we admired the polite and quiet people we met everywhere.

We finally got to Stratford-on-Avon, where I filled myself with Shakespeare, sausage rolls, pork pies, and canal locks. That evening we saw *King John* at the Stratford theater.

The next day we went down to Oxford, and that evening we saw a robin (the English robin and not our own finch) who observed us for a long time and seemed to think us a curiosity. We also heard a nightingale, which was perched on a TV antenna.

The next morning was Sunday the ninth, and we wandered about a nearly deserted Oxford on our own, peeping into the various colleges and listening to a cacophonous medley of church bells in a stubborn competition that seemed to go on forever.

At one point we tiptoed into Trinity College and listened to the services that were going on. Without warning, I became aware of a plaque on the wall honoring the memory of Samuel J. Wilberforce, the bishop who had debated evolution with Thomas Henry Huxley and, in my excitement, I shattered the silence by exclaiming to Janet, "Look, there's Soapy Sam."

Then we were taken to London, where my work would begin. We were staying at Brown's, a wonderful old-fashioned London hotel, but the room was unsatisfactory and Janet was depressed.

I urged her out into the streets of London for a pleasant walk and

[4] See *The Planet That Wasn't* (Doubleday, 1976).

a chance of finding a good English dinner somewhere. Unfortunately, it was still Sunday and London was closed down. At Piccadilly Circus, I spied an open restaurant and we made for it—and it turned out to be an American-style pancake place.

But we made a satisfactory meal of it and the next morning changed rooms.

There followed some five days of endless interviews here and there, with surpassingly pleasant interludes. We had lunch on a boat anchored in the Thames, and Panther Books made a fuss over me. They told me I was their best-selling author.

"Your best-selling science-fiction author?" I said in disbelief.

"No," they said, "our best-selling author of any kind."

On the evening of the tenth, Victor Serebriakoff was host to us at a dinner at his club. The next day I spoke at Kings College and wore my red jacket, explaining that I intended to join a fox hunt. The students let that go but were puzzled by and fascinated with my bolo tie, something I had taken to wearing when Janet explained that she found my clip-on bow ties ridiculous.

I had shepherd's pie for lunch at the college, and that afternoon there was an elaborate Doubleday reception in my honor. Present among others were science-fiction writers Jim Blish and John Brunner. We all had a fancy dinner at an Italian restaurant.

Janet went off to do some sight-seeing while I was busy with my talks and interviews, visiting the gardens at Kew, for instance.

On the morning of the twelfth, however, she and I did some sightseeing in combination, visiting the Royal Institution, which was only a block from Brown's and where I saw Faraday memorabilia. We then went to Dickens' house and even stopped off a bit at the British Museum.

In the afternoon, I signed books for ninety minutes at London's largest bookstore, with fans queuing up in good order for blocks.

That evening I attended a science-fiction fan-club meeting at a bar, one that had the air of an impromptu convention. Ruth Kyle was there. She and Dave Kyle were living in England at that time, and Dave was recovering from an appendectomy.

It made me conscious of the passage of time. Nineteen years before she had been Ruth Landis, the young girl who had helped make memorable the Cleveland convention at which I had been guest of honor. Now she was a plump matron who seemed completely out of place among the fans—while I was carrying on precisely as I had at Cleveland.

On the thirteenth, Steve took me by train to Birmingham, where I signed books for three hours at four different bookshops. We stayed at an American-style hotel. I told Steve I could tell it was American-style because it was civilized enough to have washcloths. Steve said, in his reserved English manner, that Englishmen carried their own washcloths because they could never tell where strange washcloths had been. It put a new light on the matter.

Finally, on Friday the fourteenth, I gave my talk to Mensa, the talk for which I had originally been asked to come to England. Dave Kyle was there, fresh from the hospital. So was Jay Kay Klein, who for twenty years had been attending almost every science-fiction convention of any importance with his camera, taking endless photographs. Arthur Clarke introduced me in a hilarious speech and set a level of quality I did my best to maintain. The proceedings were recorded and I believe Mensa made a respectable sum selling copies.

On that occasion it was announced that I had been appointed one of the two international vice presidents of Mensa. It was a purely honorary position, but I worried about it, since I wasn't sold on the idea of anything as artificial as IQ as a proper way of marking off a group of people who might, too easily, come to think of themselves as "superior."

As a direct result, I wrote my 195th *F & SF* essay, "Thinking About Thinking,"[5] in which I carefully expressed my disenchantment with IQ tests. It appeared in the January 1975 *F & SF*, and I rather thought that its appearance would lead to my being drummed out of Mensa, but nothing happened.

On Saturday, June 15, we were on our own, having said good-bye to Steve Odell the evening before after nine days of constant association.

We decided to visit Westminster Abbey, but between sleeping later than we had planned, and deciding to walk rather than take a taxi, we managed to get to a large boulevard along which a procession of cavalry, with the men in red uniform and plumed hats, riding gallantly on beautiful horses,[6] were passing by. It was a celebration of the Queen's birthday and suddenly there came an open carriage, and Elizabeth II, plainly visible and recognizable, came by waving to us and, presumably, to the other people watching. That was an utterly unplanned bit of sight-seeing.

We then got to Westminster Abbey and, moving about unguided, we found the graves of Newton, Rutherford, Darwin, Faraday, and

[5] See *The Planet That Wasn't*.
[6] There was an equine concomitant one rarely hears described in connection with gallant men parading on beautiful horses. The boulevard was filled with fresh horse manure.

Maxwell in a cluster. They were five of the ten scientists I had listed as the all-time greatest in my article "The Isaac Winners,"[7] which had appeared in the July 1963 *F & SF*.

That evening we had a farewell dinner at Simpson's with Victor, at which I ate a saddle of mutton and a treacle tart, and then we saw *Pygmalion* with Diana Rigg (whom I adored in the TV show "The Avengers"), and we loved it. Victor took us backstage and we got to meet Miss Rigg, who was wearing a dressing gown with, clearly, nothing underneath it.

And that was it. On the morning of Sunday, June 16, we took the train to Southampton and boarded the QE2 for the journey back to the United States.

15

We enjoyed the QE2 even more than we had the *France*. We ate at the Queen's Grill, the poshest of its restaurants, and were better fed than we ever had been in our lives. The gods on Olympus can keep their ambrosia; I will take the chocolate soufflés in the Queen's Grill.

The trip west was even quieter than the trip east had been. At one of the dinners, when the neighboring tables were all stiff and silent, and I was looking out at the ocean, I constructed a limerick and, on impulse, recited it. I said:

> *There was a young girl of Decatur*
> *Who went out to sea on a freighter.*
> *She was screwed by the Master,*
> *An utter disaster,*
> *But the crew all made up for it later.*

Everyone laughed, and the reserve broke down at once. I was delighted and wrote down the limerick. Thereafter, I began making it a practice to construct limericks whenever I was trapped in company and bored, and from then on I always wrote them down.

Finally, on Friday, June 21, we were back in New York and at our apartment, after twenty-three days' absence. The trip to Great Britain had been a smashing success in every way.

In fact, the only irritation of the trip was the absence of Watergate material. Ship's news and the English newspapers seemed to find it completely unimportant, and I had the terrible feeling that it had suddenly vanished. It was with great relief that, on my return, I discovered that Nixon's troubles had continued to mount steadily.

[7] See *Adding a Dimension*.

16

Richard Repanes, Marcia's younger son, graduated from high school on June 25. The entire family came to Manhattan afterward and we treated them to dinner.

Additional family meetings came on the twenty-eighth, when Janet and I drove out to visit Stanley and Ruth so that we could all attend a showing of "The Last Question" at the Vanderbilt Planetarium on Long Island. It was my third watching, since I had seen it first in Rochester and later on in Philadelphia.

We stayed over at Stanley's house that night. When I found I was having trouble falling asleep in a strange bed, I found *Treasure Island* in the bookcase and began to read it as a possible soporific. No chance. I stayed awake all night and finished it.

17

Ben Bova had finally achieved his divorce also and, while we were off in England, he and Barbara were married. On July 5, the four of us celebrated with a dinner at Luchow's.

18

On July 14, we went to Rensselaerville for our third year, and again it went off perfectly. On July 18, we were back in New York, and I did the last bit of *Our Federal Union,* finishing it on the twenty-first.

That meant I immediately began *How Did We Find Out About Energy?* for Walker.

19

On July 24, 1974, I was interviewed at CBS and spoke solemnly and seriously of the problems of overpopulation, energy depletion, pollution, and so on. When the interview was over, the interviewer, putting away his recording equipment, asked me why, if everything was as I said, society was doing nothing about it.

I said, "Everyone has certain short-term goals, and if these are met, each person is satisfied and refuses to worry about long-term survival. Even I myself, for instance, have my short-term goals. If some all-powerful genie were to offer to wave a wand and solve all the world's problems, but only on condition that Nixon get away with it—I would hesitate, because right now the most important thing in the world to me is the saving of the American system of government through the impeachment and conviction of the scoundrel in the White House."

At this point, a young woman entered and said, "I heard what you just said, Dr. Asimov, and I want you to know that the Supreme Court has just voted 8 to 0 against Nixon. He will have to deliver the tapes."

I was utterly jubilant, completely forgetting my predictions of universal disaster within a generation.

It seemed to me the absolute end for Nixon. The House Judiciary Committee was debating the impeachment resolution and would certainly approve it, and the House as a whole would certainly approve it, too.

Then with the tapes in the hands of the prosecution I felt no doubt at all that there would be ample evidence of Nixon's criminal behavior and that the Senate would therefore vote to convict him.

20

August 1, 1974, was "Non-Parents Day." At least Ellen Peck of the National Organization of Non-Parents ("NON") had established it so. Since she had gotten the idea from a remark I had made on a "David Frost Show" once, she hailed me as the "father of Non-Parents Day." I crowned the two non-parents of the year with laurel wreaths in Central Park.

It was a small crowd and the ceremony was utterly undistinguished, but I felt a little uneasy. The reporters were there and I wasn't sure about Robyn's reaction. I called her that evening to assure her that my advocacy of non-parentism involved no personal animosity against her. She laughed and told me not to worry—that she agreed with my views on the matter.

21

The New York *Times* was instituting a new feature in its magazine section, and I had a telephone request to contribute a short mystery story. On August 4, I wrote what I considered a delightful short-short entitled "Little Things," and sent it in.

To my astonishment, the *Times* turned it down. I sent it to

EQMM, which took it at once and published it in their May 1975 issue. It was the first time in five years that *EQMM* had published a story of mine that was not a Black Widowers story.

22

Finally, on August 6, Janet could celebrate a birthday (her forty-eighth) that was not overshadowed by hospitalization and death. We had a fancy dinner, and took in a show. The excitement was raised to higher pitch by the fact that the Nixon tapes had now made quite clear the extent of Nixon's crimes, as I was sure they would. My comment in my diary for August 5 was, "Nixon has owned up to being a crook and a liar, which is news that is something like thirty years old."

But then, on August 8, Nixon gave up the fight and resigned. Spiro Agnew had resigned ten months before as a result of proved wrongdoing that had nothing to do with Watergate. It turned out, therefore, that in 1968 and again in 1972, the United States had elected two men for the highest offices of the land who had been shown, independently, to be criminal.

I was dissatisfied. Nixon's resignation preserved his pension and numerous perquisites, and I was not impressed by the argument that it had spared the nation an ordeal. To my way of thinking, the ordeal was necessary to make certain it would never happen again. I felt that by taking the easy way out, we were storing up trouble for ourselves in the future.

23

On August 9, Stanley and I met with a Russian woman who brought news of my Uncle Boris, my father's youngest brother, who, it seemed, was still alive in Leningrad when she had left the country, but who was trying to get to Israel. Eventually, Stanley tracked him down in Israel, and there has been correspondence since. Some of the very early material in *In Memory Yet Green* was obtained from him.

24

Sprague de Camp was in the hospital and, apparently, in a bad way. On August 10, we picked up the del Reys and drove to Villanova, Pennsylvania, where we had dinner with Catherine, and visited Sprague at the hospital. He seemed thin and drawn and more than half inclined to think he was dying—but fortunately he made a good recovery.

25

I had enough miscellaneous science essays now to put together another non-*F & SF* collection, *Science Past—Science Future*, and I took it in to Doubleday on August 12. It was my fourth such book, if we count *Only a Trillion*, published seventeen years before, prior to the start of my *F & SF* essay series.

Then, on August 15, a young woman named Naomi Gordon came to see me at the Cromwell. She had an idea for an elaborate anthology that would take advantage of the gathering furor over the Bicentennial celebration that would be on us in two years. The anthology was to be called *The Bicentennial Man*, and ten famous science-fiction authors (of whom I was to be one) would contribute original stories based on that theme.

I said I might do this and asked her to get the matter more firmly established and then come back. I was certain she would not manage it and that I would not see her again.

26

A new project had arisen. American Airlines had an inflight magazine called *American Way*, for which I had written a humorous article called "Solutions!" nine months before, and which had appeared in the January 1974 issue of the magazine.

It had occurred to John Minahan, the editor of the magazine, that what was needed was a monthly column oriented to "change"—that is, to views of the possible future. It also seemed to him that I was the person to do the column.

I was interested. It would be something different, and it paid reasonably well. I wrote my first article for them on August 26, 1974. I called it "The Falling Birthrate," and I talked about the changes the falling birthrate would involve in American society, especially with respect to the status of women. It appeared in the November 1974 issue of *American Way*, and additional articles continued at monthly intervals thereafter.

Three monthly columns were, however, too much, and I was tired of the "Please Explains" of *Science Digest*. There was a change in editor there, as Richard Dempewolff was let go. I suggested to the new ed-

itor that he might want to remold the magazine without my column,
and he seemed to agree. The January 1975 *Science Digest* therefore
carried my last column and, after 9½ years, that column came to an
end. It had lasted about as long as my *Hornbook* review column had
lasted. My *F & SF* column, however, now fifteen years old, was still
going strong.

27

Boys' Life was becoming a regular customer. They wanted a little
mystery story, and I wrote "Sarah Tops"[8] for them on August 26. It involved a young junior-high-school detective I grew instantly fond of,
and whom I knew I would use again if I could. The story appeared in
the February 1975 *Boys' Life*.

28

The thirty-second World Science Fiction convention was being
held in Washington and, on August 29, Janet and I took the train to
Washington in order to attend. It proved to be the largest World convention we ever attended—four thousand people.

The de Camps were there, with Sprague looking quite well.

On August 30, Harlan and I had a public duel of the kind we
often had to amuse the fans. This time we had a larger crowd than ever
and we stood on two separate platforms, answering questions and poking what we considered to be good-natured fun at each other. Harlan
was his usual salty self.

This time there was a Washington *Post* reporter in the audience,
and the duel was written up in most unflattering terms. Harlan was
horrified.

I said, "Forget it, Harlan. It was an in-joke for s.f. fans only and
the reporter just didn't understand."

Harlan would not be soothed. He said we must never do it again
and, of course, I said that if he didn't want to, we wouldn't.

The awards banquet on September 1 was not very successful. A
relatively new hand at it, Andy Offutt, was the toastmaster and the task
got away from him. Harlan didn't help with his comments from the audience.

We got home on September 2.

David was now well established in an apartment of his own in

8 See *The Key Word and Other Stories* (Walker, 1977).

Brighton, Massachusetts, and Robyn was about to start her college freshman year a second time—this time at Boston College.

29

Succeeding to the presidency had been Gerald Ford, an utterly undistinguished political wheelhorse who had been a U.S. representative at the time when Nixon had appointed him Vice President to replace Agnew.

Ford, on September 8, returned the compliment by pardoning Nixon without even eliciting an admission of guilt or regret. It was a miscarriage of justice on an absolutely cosmic scale. Furiously, I wrote a letter to Ford the next day, telling him that the act proved him unfit to be President.

40

Park Ten

1

On September 12, 1974, I began to put together the third of my books of recycled essays, *Asimov on Physics*.

2

For once the Dutch Treat Club had let me in for something uncomfortable.

Lowell Thomas was one of its oldest and most prestigious members, and I admired him tremendously—not for his politics, for he was far too conservative for me, but because, although he was well over eighty, he was sharp, vigorous, and hard-working. If I ever manage to grow old, it is my hope that I will be old in *that* way.

Consequently, when he came to me a year before to tell me that there would be a letter of invitation in the mail that he hoped I would accept, I thoughtlessly replied with an unqualified, "Certainly, Lowell."

The invitation came. It was from "the American Academy of Achievement" which, every year, put on a very lavish convention to which fifty "achievers" were invited and made much of, together with over a hundred high-school boys and girls who might be expected to be inspired by the achievers. I was invited as one of the achievers and would have been glad to go, if only because I had given my word to Lowell, were it not that the 1974 meeting was taking place in Salt Lake City.

What was I to do? There was no way I could get to Salt Lake City. I had to break my word and turn down the invitation with groveling embarrassment.

But now a year had passed and they were preparing the 1975 meeting and I was invited again. This time, the meeting was being held farther east than ever before (except for one meeting in Philadelphia in 1971.) The 1975 meeting was to be in Evansville, Indiana.

Ordinarily, I would have considered that far too distant for me also, but could I break my word a second time? I sighed and wrote a letter of acceptance in mid-September 1974. It meant that the following June I would have to drive westward nearly as far as the Mississippi River, something I viewed with the utmost apprehension—but I had said "Certainly, Lowell."

3

The Encyclopaedia Britannica had come out with its first brand-new edition in a generation. It had a ten-volume Micropedia, with numerous short entries that served as an index. There was also a nineteen-volume Macropedia, with long entries of selected subjects. I bought this new edition (and eventually gave the old one to Robyn as help with her schoolwork).

The new edition arrived on September 29, and I promptly found that the Micropedia included the item "Asimov, Isaac" which meant that I had made the Britannica while I was still alive. As a matter of fact, this had now become routine. Science fiction had become so respectable that any encyclopedia could now be expected to have entries on several of the better-known science-fiction writers. Usually I, myself, together with Arthur Clarke, Robert Heinlein, and Ray Bradbury were included.

4

Have You Seen These?, the little book I had done for the Boskone the year before, was not entirely satisfactory. It was a limited edition, and there would be no reprints, no paperbacks, no chance to get reasonable distribution.

On October 10, therefore, I suggested to Larry that I prepare a new story collection that would contain the eight stories of *Have You Seen These?* together with other stories of the period that I had not collected yet. It would serve as a third volume of literary biography to follow *Before the Golden Age* and *The Early Asimov*.

Larry was agreeable and it did not take long to put the book together. Since one of the stories contained was "Buy Jupiter," a title I loved, I called it *Buy Jupiter and Other Stories*. I had the complete manuscript at Doubleday by November 12, and, within a week, word reached me that Fawcett had bought the paperback rights.

5

Janet had been living in her apartment since the apartment house had been opened for occupancy in late 1968.

The six years had not been without flaws. There was an extraordinarily inefficient incinerator that routinely drenched us all in the smell of burning garbage; a central air-conditioning unit that didn't work nearly as often as it did; and, worst of all, such poor construction that any noise in any apartment could be heard in all neighboring apartments (with magnification, I think).

One could co-operate with neighbors, of course. Living right next to us was a theatrical writer and producer, Barton Behr, who had professional occasion to play the piano all night. Fortunately, he was a goodhearted person who made every effort to avoid bothering us and, on the whole, he succeeded. He even tried to cut down on his smoking when it turned out that the walls would allow the passage of cigarette smoke.

But then, over the Labor Day weekend of 1974, the people immediately above us (who had wall-to-wall carpeting and were very quiet) moved out and two young male denizens of hell moved in.

The wall-to-wall carpeting was ripped up and a large concert piano was moved in. One of the young men played Bach and other classics with consummate skill so that we had a periodic concert that sounded as loudly in our living room as his, except that he could turn it on and off to suit his convenience and we could not.

They also had a flute, which one of them practiced Sunday mornings and of which we missed not one note. They also had a complex hi-fi record player, which they played frequently, with the volume turned up. They were also weight lifters, and the weights bumped the floors periodically.

They were advanced enough to believe in high heels but not in carpets. Their bedroom, immediately over our bedroom, was a hive of activity at night, and every footstep cuddled its way into our ears.

Their bathrooms were active as well. They had frequent occasion to urinate, which they somehow managed to accomplish with all the sound effects of a horse standing over a puddle.

Nor did they believe in showers; they took baths instead. The water gurgled into the tub for fifteen minutes; then, as they luxuriously soaked, a body could clearly be heard frictioning against the tub; and finally the water gurgled out for fifteen minutes. Nothing so terrible about that, except that the young men generally felt the need for such a purifying bath at about 3:00 A.M.

The fact was that our apartment had become uninhabitable. We tried to reason with the young men; we tried to complain to the landlord; when both courses failed, we knew we would have to move. In October, we began our search.

We knew what we wanted. We wanted an apartment large enough to house both of us and both our offices. We could each work out of our apartment, and it seemed silly to be forced to separate daily, or for either of us to waste the time and discomfort of commuting. We also wanted an apartment on the top floor, since we were both determined to have no one over us ever again, and in an apartment house sufficiently well constructed to keep noise leakage to a reasonable minimum. We needed something in the neighborhood, for Janet wanted to be near Central Park, Lincoln Center, the Museum of Natural History, and the White Institute. Finally, it could not be a condominium, for the search quickly revealed that no condominium would allow Janet to practice in her apartment, unless the apartment were on the ground floor.

It wasn't going to be easy, but Janet scoured the neighborhood relentlessly; and if ever we felt ourselves weakening, the young men overhead would invariably supply us with new impetus.

6

Although the prospect of moving was a dismal one, life went on. On October 15, I wrote my twenty-first Black Widowers story, "Earthset and Evening Star,"[1] the gimmick of which rested upon the pronunciation of the name of a lunar crater. Fred Dannay rejected it on the ground that that was too esoteric for his readers. That very gimmick, however, made it a possible candidate for *F & SF*. I sent it off to Ed Ferman at once. He took it and it appeared in the August 1975 issue of that magazine.

Also on October 15, I had breakfast with Charles Renshaw, who was a prime example of how editors helped me infect the literary world.

I had first met him when he was working for the World Book Year Book. He then moved to Milwaukee, where he edited *National Wildlife* for some years. There he bought an occasional article from me, notably "What Do You Call a Platypus?,"[2] which appeared in the March–April 1972 issue of the magazine.

Then, he had moved again to Chicago, where he edited *Prism*, a magazine published by the American Medical Association, and in the new incarnation I sold him several articles again, including one on the rising average age of society, which I called "The Coming Age of Age"; it eventually appeared in the January 1975 issue of the magazine.

On the evening of October 14, Janet had asked me for Charlie

[1] See *More Tales of the Black Widowers.*
[2] See *Today and Tomorrow and—*

Renshaw's address so that she could send him an article she had written, an autobiographical reminiscence of her visit to Italy in 1948, when she fell badly ill and was treated by an unusual Italian doctor. She felt the story would be useful to medical students and to doctors and that *Prism* would be a good outlet for it.

"Don't bother mailing it," I said (rather astonished at the coincidence), "I'm having breakfast with Charlie tomorrow and I'll give him the manuscript."

This I did, and Charlie winced visibly when I handed it to him. I imagine he couldn't help but foresee the embarrassment of having to turn it down.

Time passed; Janet grew impatient; and finally when Charlie phoned me about something entirely different, I managed to ask him whether he had looked at that article yet. Embarrassed, he said he hadn't but he would that very day. The next day, he called again, full of enthusiasm, to tell me he was taking the article and writing a letter to Janet about it. It was clear from the sound of his voice that he was enormously relieved. He had never expected to like it.

I had not read the article myself and I was astonished at Charlie's enthusiasm. I asked Janet for a copy, read it, and was instantly full of enthusiasm myself. It was an absolutely delightful article.[3] Ever since then I have tried, very gently, to urge Janet to write more nonfiction, but I have had no luck. Her heart is in fiction.

7

On November 3, Janet's search for prospective apartments took her to Park Ten, an apartment house that was only five years old.

We discovered that there would be an apartment on the top floor available in four months. Its size and design were ideal. Each one of us could have two rooms for our respective offices and have them far enough apart to avoid our interfering with each other. The apartment was also on the thirty-third floor and offered a remarkable panoramic view of all of Central Park—and we began making plans to move.

(At this time, too, I began *Asimov's Guide to Food and Nutrition* for Basic Books.)

---

[3] *Prism*, alas, ceased publication before Janet's article could be published. Eventually, however, Janet managed to sell it a second time (this time without my intervention in any way) to *Medical Dimensions*, where it finally appeared in the May 1977 issue under the title "A Learning Experience."

8

November 17, 1974, was Rae Jeppson's seventy-eighth birthday. That was the birthday my mother had not managed to reach. We drove to New Rochelle and, along with Chaucy and Les, took her to lunch. She was as self-possessed and as mentally alert as ever, but was growing rather feeble.

9

On November 27, I passed a milestone when I wrote my two-hundredth *F & SF* essay. It was on the Martian surface as revealed by Mariner 9, and I called it "The Olympian Snows."[4] It appeared in the June 1975 issue of the magazine.

I had not missed an issue in the sixteen years and eight months since the series had begun, and I enjoyed it more with each passing year. So eager was I to do my monthly essay that my inability to hold back had me routinely sending them in two months ahead of deadline.

10

Three days later, on November 30, there was an even more important milestone, for Janet and I celebrated the first anniversary of our marriage. We went back to the same restaurant at which we had had our wedding dinner, and with us we took the Balks, our witnesses.

11

The New York *Times* had become an annoyance to me. I had gotten a larger percentage of rejections from the *Times* than from any other outlet but one[5] in thirty-five years. After they had rejected my article on the *Statendam* cruise two years before, I could hardly wait to have them ask me to do another article, so that I could turn them down and reverse the situation.

It was with glee, therefore, that I received a call from Gerry Walker in mid-November. I readied myself for the genial refusal—and he fooled me completely.

What he wanted was a science-fiction story. They even had the

[4] See *The Planet That Wasn't* (Doubleday, 1976).
[5] *Cosmopolitan* holds the record. They asked me for two articles, and rejected both.

theme. They wanted me to write a story dealing with human beings vs. machines.

I couldn't refuse that. Not to take the chance of getting science fiction into the New York *Times*, even if the chance were a small one, would be to betray the field. I had to agree, after I had quizzed Gerry rather thoroughly and made certain he really meant a science-fiction story.

I got to work on a story that dealt with a world run with unscrupulous efficiency by a giant computer, Multivac, and the efforts of a few free souls to liberate themselves from this its-for-your-own-good thralldom. One of them finally succeeded in subverting Multivac, and freedom was recaptured.

I finished it on December 6, 1974, and then couldn't sleep that night. I was dissatisfied with the story; something bothered me. And then I realized that the question was whether those who said they wanted freedom really wanted it.

The first thing in the morning, I rewrote the last two paragraphs to introduce a question mark and to leave the matter unresolved. Let each reader decide for himself whether he wants freedom or security if he must choose one or the other.

I sent it off on December 7, with a covering letter that said the last two paragraphs must not be fiddled with and waited for the inevitable rejection. It never came. The *Times* fooled me again by accepting the story, which they eventually named "The Life and Times of Multivac."[6]

Then, on December 9, I started *The Golden Door*, the fourth volume of my American history. It was to carry the story from the end of the Civil War to the end of World War I.

12

It was my turn (along with Lester, who had become my perennial partner in such things) to host the December meeting of the Trap Door Spiders. I busily counted the number of guests who arrived at the restaurant on December 13, 1974, for we had not used that particular restaurant before and I had guaranteed a minimum attendance of twelve.

When the twelfth guest arrived, I felt greatly relieved. But then, just as we were sitting down at the table, Lionel Casson (an archaeologist who spent half the year in Italy) burst in. He was the thirteenth man at the table and it was Friday the thirteenth.

6 See *The Bicentennial Man and Other Stories*.

Nothing happened as a result, naturally, but I did make up my mind to write a Black Widowers story based on that particular superstition. It was the twenty-second story of the series and I called it "Friday the Thirteenth."[7]

I wrote it on the last day of the year and in it I had a chance to discuss the calendar and its mechanics in some detail. Once again Fred Dannay rejected it as too esoteric, and once again I tried it on Ed Ferman with better luck. It appeared in the January 1976 issue of *F & SF*, and was the third Black Widowers story to appear in that magazine.

13

I had received a letter from a lawyer who represented Paul McCartney, who had once been a member of the Beatles singing group. On December 19, 1974, in consequence, I kept an appointment with McCartney.

McCartney wanted to do a fantasy, and he wanted me to write a story out of which a screenplay could be prepared. He had the basic idea for the fantasy, which involved two sets of musical groups: a real one, and a group of extraterrestrial imposters. The real one would be in pursuit of the imposters and would eventually defeat the imposters despite the fact that the latter had strange supernormal powers.

McCartney did not have any details on what it was the imposters were up to or how they could be stopped; he had only a snatch of dialog describing the moment when the real group realized they were being victimized by imposters.

I agreed to do a treatment preliminary to writing the story and did. In the treatment I accounted for everything; what the imposters were doing, and why, and how it was that the real group, with all the odds against them, could manage to win out. It was a suspenseful, realistic, and moving idea, and I took it in rather proudly.

I was paid for it, but McCartney didn't want it. He went back to his one scrap of dialog, out of which he apparently couldn't move, and wanted me to work with that. I bowed out politely and my career as a movie writer died a-borning—thank goodness.

14

Over Christmas, I wrote *How Did We Find Out About Atoms?* for Walker, the ninth in that series, and on December 29 I finally

[7] See *More Tales of the Black Widowers.*

finished *Eyes on the Universe,* having worked on it, on and off, for a year and a half.

15

I finished 1974 with eleven books published—less than in either of the two previous years, but a respectable number nevertheless. The eleven were:

148. *Asimov on Astronomy* (Doubleday)
149. *The Birth of the United States* (Houghton Mifflin)
150. *Have You Seen These?* (NESFA)
151. *Before the Golden Age* (Doubleday)
152. *Our World in Space* (New York Graphic)
153. *How Did We Find Out About Germs?* (Walker)
154. *Asimov's Annotated Paradise Lost* (Doubleday)
155. *Tales of the Black Widowers* (Doubleday)
156. *Earth: Our Crowded Spaceship* (John Day)
157. *Asimov on Chemistry* (Doubleday)
158. *How Did We Find Out About Vitamins?* (Walker)

16

On January 2, 1975, I was fifty-five years old and we celebrated by dining with the del Reys.

Another kind of birthday celebration came on January 5, when "The Life and Times of Multivac" ran in the magazine section of the New York *Times.* I was told that this was the first time in its history that the *Times* had run a piece of original fiction that they had directly commissioned.

Certainly no story I had ever written had had so large a public on a single day. For the following week, it seemed to me that everyone I talked to made a point of telling me he had read the story.

17

On January 7, I was at Channel 13, being interviewed, along with Gerard O'Neill, a physics professor at Princeton University. O'Neill had come out some months earlier with a detailed suggestion on the building of space settlements and had converted me to the enthusiastic support of such things. He was nearly my age, but was tall, slim, and looked much younger.

I was a little restless during the interview, for I had to get to the del Reys afterward and I was afraid that the natural delays inherent in television would make me late.

Once it was over I made my good-byes as brief as courtesy could manage, then dashed out into the street, hailed a taxi just passing, tumbled in, and gave Lester's address. The driver had seen me come tearing out of the Channel 13 building, and asked me what I was doing there.

"Being interviewed," I said, with businesslike conciseness.

"You an actor?"

"No. I'm a writer."

"I once wanted to be a writer," said the cabbie, "but I never got around to it."

"Just as well," I said, consolingly. "You can't make a living as a writer."

The taxi driver said argumentatively, "Isaac Asimov does."

I had no answer.

18

Another "Star Trek" convention began on January 10 at the Americana, and Robyn wanted to attend. She arrived with a friend the day before and was afraid that they would not be able to see much, considering the crowds that would attend. I told them to state her name in a good, clear voice and see what happened.

She got royal treatment; that's what happened.

The climax of the convention came on Sunday the twelfth, when William Shatner (Captain Kirk) spoke before a superenthusiastic audience of more than four thousand, who filled the seats and aisles to capacity. Shatner answered all questions with good humor and unpretentiousness and had everyone enthralled. When it was time to leave, he explained there was no way in which he could sign autographs for so huge a crowd and made ready to get off the stage.

At this point, the young man who had organized the convention whispered in my ear, "Quick. Get on the stage and hold the audience so that Shatner can get away."

I said, "They'll tear me limb from limb."

But he was physically pushing me onto the stage while one of his henchmen was busily announcing me.

I started talking—babbling, rather. I waited for a mad, furious rush to the stage on the part of disappointed "Star Trek" fanatics, but it didn't come. They seemed to be enjoying me, actually, and I was just beginning to relax and settle down when the organizer approached and whispered, "Shatner's safely away. Get off, so we can get on with the program." So I got off.

Talk about being used!

19

I took Janet and Robyn to a party at the Siglers' on the eleventh. (They were the organizers of the eclipse cruise.) Scott and Maria Carpenter were there, together with tons of Greek delicacies (Marcy was of Greek extraction), among which I wreaked havoc.

Phil Sigler was enthusiastically in favor of arranging a one-man Broadway show featuring me, and refused to listen to anything I could say against it. For a while, I thought Phil would manage to bring it off and that the day would come when I would find myself stepping out onto the stage of a theater, night after night, trying to hold an audience all by myself.

Fortunately, it never came to pass.

20

I had put together a collection of my little stories that had appeared in *Boys' Life* and elsewhere, intending it to serve as a juvenile. The longest of the stories was "The Heavenly Host," so I called the collection *The Heavenly Host and Other Stories* and presented them to Tom Aylesworth at Doubleday.

Tom liked the stories and I assumed that I had made another sale and entered it in my books as such. On January 14, however, I was rather thunderstruck when I received the manuscript back again. The Doubleday publishing board had turned it down.

It was only the third book that Doubleday had rejected out of the scores they had accepted (the other two rejections were *The Death Dealers* and *Fantastic Voyage*), and I had no reasonable complaint.

I took the collection to Walker & Company at once, since they had for a long time been asking me for any science-fiction book that Doubleday didn't want.

The trouble was that Walker didn't want a collection either, but, on reading the stories, they decided they *did* want "The Heavenly Host."

I said, "It's only thirty-seven-hundred words long."

"I know," said Beth. "Rewrite it and make it twice as long and we'll have a nice little children's Christmas book. Then we'll put out a collection later on."

I hate rewriting, but I also hate not selling a book, so I agreed to do as she wished.

21

On January 16, I took part in a day-long conference with a group of would-be promoters who were thinking of developing a science-cruise business. Also there were Carl Sagan and George Abell, another astronomer with a winning personality and with a two-tone beard to add to his charm.

The idea rose out of the very successful eclipse cruise of a year and a half before, and I was enthusiastic in a modified sort of way. I was willing to go on cruises, given ample warning so that I could adjust my schedule and provided I were not required to take airplanes or long overland trips to get to the ship.

We all had dinner together and I helped enliven it with limericks. Ever since the trip back from Great Britain I had been constructing them on occasion and I had half a dozen doozies written down. One of those I constructed on this occasion was:

> *A certain hard-working young hooker*
> *Was such an enchanting good-looker,*
> *There were fights 'mongst the fuzz*
> *Over whose turn it was*
> *To pinch 'er, and frisk 'er, and book 'er.*

The reaction was sufficiently favorable to cause the first dim sensation of possible publication of a limerick book to stir within me.

Nevertheless, the general success of the serious portion of the day's conference was limited, for the scheme never came to fruition.

22

More and more, I was writing my science-fiction stories for periodicals that were completely outside the science-fiction field as such. It was an indication of how respectable science fiction had become. The outsiders came to me much of the time because, through the years, I had somehow become the most visible of the science-fiction writers.

"The Life and Times of Multivac" in the New York *Times* was an example of this visibility, and one of the people who saw it was William Levinson, editor of *Physician's World*.

. In the same issue of the magazine section was an article entitled "Triage," dealing with a system of choosing whom to save and whom to allow to die when conditions do not allow of saving all. It occurred to Levinson that the subject, which was of interest to physicians, could be treated in particularly imaginative fashion through the medium of science fiction. Since my name was staring at him on the same Contents page, he approached me.

I was struck by the idea and agreed to try. I started the story, which I called "The Winnowing," on January 19. Levinson accepted the story.

On January 27, not long after "The Winnowing" had been successfully disposed of, Naomi Gordon appeared at the office again. She had been there months before in order to talk me into doing a story for her *Bicentennial Man* anthology, and now she was more urgent about it and more glowing about the tremendous plans she had for it.

She made it plain that she was not suggesting I write a science-fiction story set in the matrix of the Bicentennial year of 1976, but that I could deal with anything at all that might be suggested by the phrase "Bicentennial Man."

It was clear by the nature of things that the anthology would have to be published in 1976, and there was little time for delay. She had brought the contracts with her and offered to pay me in advance if I would sign on the spot. What with a fresh sale of "The Winnowing" spurring me on, I could not resist. I agreed to do a story for the anthology and signed the contract.

The deadline was April 1. That gave me two months, which I thought would be enough.

23

The AAAS was meeting in New York now and, on January 30, 1975, I gave a talk entitled "The Science-fiction Writer as Prophet" to an enthusiastic audience of three thousand attending the convention. I was told afterward that it was easily the best-attended and most enthusiastically received of any talk given during the convention.

Nevertheless, when, a few days later, the New York *Times* ran an overview of the convention, and specifically discussed the talks in terms of popularity and attendance, including the series of talks to which mine belonged, no mention was made of me at all. The *Times* might publish my science fiction, but they still prissily ignored a talk that referred to the field when the discussion was of science.

But then, early on the morning of Saturday, February 1, I attended a meeting of the National Organization of Non-Parents (NON). I had to give the keynote address to a group of less than a hundred attendees.

Presiding was the founder of the organization, Ellen Peck, an attractive young woman with a stunning figure and a natural penchant for wearing clothes that set it off. As I rose to speak, I smiled at Ellen with natural appreciation and referred to her as a "sexual tornado." Then, with mock caution, I added, "Of course, I don't know this myself, but her husband has assured me of it."

I went on, further, to loosen up the early-morning audience by reciting a limerick I had just constructed:

> *A young violinist named Biddle*
> *Played exceedingly well on the fiddle.*
> *Yet 'twixt women and art*
> *'Twas the girls won his heart*
> *Hands down—and hands up—and hands middle.*

I then delivered my short speech and departed amid a good round of applause.

After I left, however, some stern enthusiast in the audience rose to object to my "sexist remarks" and there was some discussion of that. And the New York *Times*, having failed to acknowledge the existence of the best talk given at the AAAS two days before, *did* manage to devote some space to this mighty imbroglio.

By now I had twenty-one limericks of my own construction in my collection. I had taken them to Sam Walker and told him that when I had a hundred I planned to try to get them published. Since he had done my *Sensuous Dirty Old Man*, I thought he might want to do my limerick book as well. He agreed to do it.

24

At this time, I also had ten Black Widowers stories toward my second collection, and only one of them had not been placed in a magazine. I needed two more, and I decided to write those two and to deliberately refrain from submitting them to any magazine. I would then have three previously unpublished stories in the second collection, as I had had in the first.

The first of this final pair was "The Unabridged"[8] (my twenty-third Black Widowers story), which I completed on February 3. As for the second, that had a somewhat complicated background.

Several of the Baker Street Irregulars were planning a collection of Sherlockian articles in honor of Julian Wolff, the leader of the organi-

---

[8] See *More Tales of the Black Widowers*.

zation. Banesh Hoffman asked me to write one. I felt impelled to do so because one of the requirements for membership in the BSI was the preparation of a piece of Sherlockiana, however trivial, and I had not done this.

My problem, though, was that I couldn't think of anything to write about. Banesh suggested that I write something about the evil Professor Moriarty's great treatise *Dynamics of an Asteroid*, something that (according to the sacred writings) contained mathematics so rarefied that hardly anyone could understand it.

That was right up my alley. Conan Doyle knew nothing about astronomy and had, I was sure, invented that title on a venture. Beginning with the title and the year in which it had supposedly appeared, and dealing with the astronomical situation as it then existed, I easily worked out what the treatise must have dealt with, given Moriarty's evil nature.

I called my Sherlockian article "Dynamics of an Asteroid" and it eventually appeared in a collection called *Beyond Baker Street*, a copy of which I received in May 1976.

Having finished "Dynamics of an Asteroid" on February 5, I immediately began another version of the same thing, nearly four times as long, which would be my twenty-fourth Black Widowers story. I called it "The Ultimate Crime,"[9] and now having twelve stories for my second collection, *More Tales of the Black Widowers*, I took it in to Doubleday on February 10.

At the same time I began a large book, *Alternate Sources of Energy*, for Houghton Mifflin.

And on February 19, 1975, Robyn was twenty years old and I no longer had teen-age children.

25

My limerick writing continued with amazing speed, and by Robyn's birthday I had my hundred. A hundred limericks do not take up much room, of course, so it was my intention to add a sizable Introduction and then place commentary after each limerick. In the commentary I discussed how I came to construct the limerick, alternate readings—anything I wished, actually.

The commentary occasionally involved Janet's role in criticizing or improving the limerick, and when Janet read what I had written, she said, "Oh my, I'll be driven out of town by my colleagues and family if this is published."

[9] See *More Tales of the Black Widowers*.

I said, hastily, "I'll eliminate all references to you, then."

"Don't you dare," said Janet at once.

Then, since I consistently referred to her as "my wife, the doctor" in the commentaries, I offered to dedicate the book to "my wife, the doctor," and she agreed to that, too.

On February 25, I took the manuscript to Walker, and it was decided to call it *Lecherous Limericks*.

26

Over in Boston, Alma Hill had died some weeks before. She had been the moving spirit behind the Boston chapter of the Interplanetary Exploration Society, fifteen years earlier.

Closer to home, Hans Stefan Santesson had died at the age of sixty-one. I remembered him best as the man who told me someone wanted to meet me and led me to a broadly smiling Janet Jeppson at the Mystery Writers' of America dinner back on May 1, 1959. I attended his funeral on February 26, 1975.

27

For years, Janet had been a faithful attendee of symphonic performances at the Philharmonic, and had been particularly fond of the oboeist, Harold Gomberg. She always came back from such performances burbling about what Harold had done and the way in which he looked at his reeds or scratched his head.

At a party at Lucy Jarvis's some months before I had met Margaret Gomberg, Harold's wife. I introduced myself and promptly told her of Janet's infatuation with her husband's oboe playing. It turned out that her husband enjoyed science fiction, so there was a reciprocal attraction between our families.

Margaret, an intelligent, no-nonsense woman, arranged a meeting, which was easy since we lived within walking distance of each other. On February 28, 1975, we had dinner with the Gombergs, and Janet met her idol. She found him as pleasant and as unpretentious as could be imagined and an interesting amateur artist as well. She eventually bought one of his paintings and put it up in our apartment.

28

On March 2, I finally began "The Bicentennial Man." It seemed to me that to avoid the actual 1976 Bicentennial, I would need another kind of bicentennial, and I chose to deal with a two-hundredth birthday. That would mean either a man with an elongated life span or a robot, and I chose a robot. Why, then, the "man" in the title? I decided to write about a robot who wanted to be a man and who attained that goal on the two-hundredth anniversary of its construction.

My vague original notion was to make it a somewhat humorous story, but once again, as in the case of *The Gods Themselves*, the thing got away from me. It was a seventy-five-hundred-word story that had been commissioned, but I had no way of stopping it before fifteen thousand words though I dug in my heels as hard as I could. For another, it turned into a moving story that had me almost in tears when I finished.[10]

I completed it on March 14, and mailed off one copy to Naomi Gordon, and another to Forrie Ackerman, who was working with her on the anthology. Both were enthusiastic.

29

Janet was discovering some of the woes of being a writer. Her book *The Second Experiment* had been published, and before long the British and French rights had been sold and Fawcett agreed to put out a paperback version.

On the other hand, there were some nasty reviews in some of the fan magazines, written by lower-echelon writers who apparently were chafed that Mrs. Isaac Asimov had managed to have a novel published. I had in no way helped her with either the writing of the book nor with the selling of it, but one reviewer in particular made it pretty plain that he believed I had put pressure on publishers to get Janet's novel into print.

This was ridiculous, first, because no such pressure had been applied, and second, because no such pressure would have been successful. If pressure from me could get my wife's book published, why could it not prevent some of my own books from being rejected?

I was dying to write a letter blasting the idiot, but I remembered my experience with Henry Bott twenty-two years before, and I knew it would be counterproductive.

Fortunately, Ben Bova, of his own accord, wrote a firm letter, pointing out that the novel had been submitted to him, that no pressure had been applied, that the novel had been rejected by him, and

10 See *The Bicentennial Man and Other Stories*.

that the Bova-Asimov friendship had continued without a ripple of unpleasantness despite that fact.

What bothered me most about the reviewer's snide accusation was that at Janet's express insistence, the book had been published under her maiden name with no mention anywhere of the identity of her husband so that there not even be the appearance of her trying to take advantage of the relationship.

30

Even as I was finishing "The Bicentennial Man," moving time arrived. Through the first half of March, our new apartment in Park Ten was being cleaned, painted, and refurbished. We kept moving things that the movers wouldn't handle—such as the avocado tree under which we had gotten married a year and a half before. Janet and Bart Behr, between them, moved the plant over the two-block separation of the apartments. We arranged for a telephone transfer and then, on March 18, 1975, the bulk of the moving was done professionally, and we arranged to sublet the remainder of our lease to our old apartment to Bart.

For a week I continued to work at the Cromwell and then, on March 25, my office was moved into Park Ten as well. I thus left the Cromwell after 4¾ years of occupancy.

With all its discomforts, my period at the Cromwell represented the only time in my life when I lived the equivalent of a bachelor existence, and when I had rooms of my own over which I was absolute master and total disposer. It was an odd feeling, which I rather liked.

Moving into Park Ten would have its conveniences—an office to which I did not have to travel, in which I could work all hours, one that could be kept clean and shipshape—but I was sure there would be times when I would miss the independence of the Cromwell.

31

I was in the Boston area on April 5 on speaking engagements, and I seized the opportunity to take Robyn to a large restaurant. We had to wait for a seat, but that didn't matter. I was delighted to be sitting next to Robyn, who was looking spectacular and who was finishing her freshman year in good health this time, whether we were at a table or not.

Then my name was called out over the loudspeaker system and I was led to my seat. In no time at all the hostess was at my table. My name had been heard and the cashier wanted a signature, while the hostess wanted one also for her daughter. I signed everything graciously, pleased to be able to show Robyn how famous her father was.

Then, as I noticed the hostess glancing curiously at my very young and very beautiful date, I thought I'd better allay any misapprehensions by saying, "And this is my daughter, Robyn."

The hostess went through the greetings, but when she left, Robyn said mischievously, "She didn't believe you, Dad."

32

On April 9, I finished the expansion of "The Heavenly Host," and it was ready to be delivered to Walker.

I also began *Animals of the Bible*, a juvenile for Doubleday that I had contracted for sixteen months earlier. The delay was, of course, occasioned by the artist. It had taken that long merely to get the preliminary sketches I could work from.

41
Murder at the ABA

1

John Bartholomew Tucker, a local talk-show host, had an idea for an adult-conversation panel, one in which panelists and guests would compete in the brilliance with which they would deal with off-the-cuff fantasies. He said he got the idea from a time when I was a guest of his and I had dealt brilliantly (he said) with a question, sprung upon me without warning, concerning whom I would invite to a dinner party if I had all the human beings who ever lived to choose from.

We taped a show on April 14, 1975 (just the audio portion, since the video would not contribute much), and I didn't think it went at all well. I did get a chance to meet Heywood Hale Broun, the sports commentator, who was a fellow panelist.

He had a mordant and biting wit that somehow didn't hurt—sparks of light that contained no heat. I was able to top him only once when he said, in rueful self-satire, "I look in the mirror and say: Where is that eager, handsome youth so determined to set the world on fire?"

"Here I am, Woody," I said at once.

The taping was intended to be a display to prospective sponsors and television networks, who were expected to fall over themselves to take the program. The expectations were not fulfilled.

2

I talked at the University of Maryland on April 16, and then went down to Washington for something more unusual. It came about thus:

For three years, Doubleday had joined with the Smithsonian Institution in sponsoring high-level talks on various aspects of exploration. I was slated to give the fourteenth talk in the series, one that was to be devoted to space exploration. Since these talks were published by Doubleday in collected form, it meant I would have to write the talk.

I had done this the previous January and had called it "The Moon as Threshold."[1] It was clear, though, that I couldn't read it, since it was

---

[1] See *The Beginning and the End* (Doubleday, 1977).

twelve thousand words long. It was my plan, however, to read only portions and to give summaries of the material between the portions.

On April 17, 1975, I appeared at the Smithsonian Institution for the purpose. There had been a posh dinner first, with everyone in formal dress, with a number of Doubleday people present, including Sam Vaughan and Larry Ashmead, with even a couple of congressmen present.

I was moderately uncomfortable at being surrounded by so glittering a throng, and not exactly delighted at having to deliver my talk in a tuxedo, an unprecedented and hampering situation for me.

I walked up to the podium, placed the manuscript before me, stared (rather daunted) at the impressive assemblage, shifted my gaze firmly to the air a few feet above the audience, and began to talk. As usual, the sound of my own voice had a tranquilizing effect, and I continued, with brisk animation, for an hour.

Afterward, Sam Vaughan said to me, "That was a pretty impressive trick you played on us, Isaac."

I was surprised. "What trick, Sam?"

"Come on, Isaac. Don't tell me you didn't do it on purpose. You put a thick sheaf of papers down on the podium, then rattled off your speech without glancing down at them once."

It was true. I had completely forgotten about reading *any* of my manuscript.

3

On April 22, I taped three segments of the "Today" show with Barbara Walters, for airing on three different mornings. Along with me were several others, including Gerard O'Neill, who had now become famous, thanks to his idea for space settlements, and Alvin Toffler, who had hit the jackpot with his book *Future Shock*.

What I remember most clearly about that show did not appear on television. While the cameras were being reloaded between the second and third segments, Barbara Walters kept prodding me about the number of my books. She asked me if I didn't have the impulse to do something other than write: if I didn't want to take vacations, go fishing, take long walks, sleep in the sun. Firmly I answered "No" to all these things. I was content to write.

In desperation, she finally said, "What if the doctors told you that you only had six months to live. What would you do then?"

I said, calmly, "Type faster!"

4

At the Nebula awards banquet on April 26, a new "Grand Masters award" was instituted, and the first recipient was, inevitably, Robert A. Heinlein.

Bob was there to accept it, of course. He was going on sixty-eight now, had suffered considerable bad health in recent years, and looked rickety, but one could still see clearly in his face the handsome young man I had first met a third of a century before.

5

On May 2, 1975, Robyn finished her freshman year at college at last, and I heaved a large sigh of relief.

A completion of lesser import came on May 8, when my two rooms at Park Ten were finally put in complete order.

Then, on May 20, I completed *Animals of the Bible*, having found it a short but not very enjoyable chore. I have yet to enjoy a collaboration.

I eased matters by promptly beginning a second book in my astronomy series for Chaucy: *Alpha Centauri: The Nearest Star*.

6

In Europe, someone had written a mystery about the Frankfurt Book Fair called *Murder at Frankfurt*. This inspired Larry Ashmead to wonder if a book entitled *Murder at the ABA* (that is, the American Booksellers Association) might not be written on this side of the Atlantic.

He automatically thought of me—he always does—and put it up to me earlier in the spring. I was attracted. I had written two dozen straight-mystery short stories and I felt I was ready to write a straight-mystery novel, with neither science nor science fiction in it.

I said, "Let me think about it, Larry," and then promptly forgot about it. About a month later, a contract arrived, and I stared at it in puzzlement for quite a while before I dimly remembered Larry's suggestion. Then I signed it.

As it happened, the ABA was meeting in New York to celebrate its seventy-fifth anniversary, and it was the first time in twenty-five years that it was meeting there. Larry said that this was my chance to attend the convention, without any need for traveling, and that I could, in this way, gather local color.

I said I had to attend anyway since I was slated for an autograph mission, but Larry said, firmly, "Attend all four days."

This introduced a slight complication. The convention was to be held over the Memorial Day weekend, and it opened on Sunday, May 25. On that day, however, I was scheduled to give a commencement address at the University of Connecticut. I couldn't very well get out of giving the address so, after some thought, I decided I would cheat and miss the opening day.

But then William Morris, secretary of the Dutch Treat Club, and a lexicographer with whom I had worked on the American Heritage Dictionary, phoned and asked me if I would be at the convention at 4:20 P.M. on Sunday to help him push a book.

Well, you can't let a pal down, so I calculated that if I left the university immediately after lunch and drove back briskly, I could make it with time to spare.

We drove back briskly indeed, but we were also caught in very unbrisk traffic jams on the Cross-Bronx Expressway, and by the time I got home, washed, shaved, changed, and made my way to the hotel by taxi, it was a very near squeak.

It was with great satisfaction that, despite everything, I walked into the rendezvous room at *precisely* 4:20 P.M.—only to be told by an unsympathetic publicity woman that the William Morris bit had just finished. I stared at my watch in concern and checked the time. It *was* 4:20 P.M.

What had happened was that Ellen Peck, the "sexual tornado" of the previous February, had been slated to push one of her books at the 4:00 P.M. slot and had come down in a peek-a-boo dress that had left too much latitude for peeking. She was persuaded to go back upstairs to change, and in order to keep the press from drifting away, Bill Morris was sent in twenty minutes early.

I was annoyed at this combination of events that had worked to make my hurried trip from the University of Connecticut meaningless, but since I was now at the convention I began to collect local color by attending a dinner party that very night.

The next day, Memorial Day, I heard Douglas Fairbanks, Jr., talk at lunch, was introduced to Anita Loos and Cathleen Nesbit, and participated in a Sense-vs.-Nonsense panel (not its official title, of course), with Walter Sullivan and Carl Sagan joining me on the "sense" side. For "nonsense," we had Uri Geller, who bends spoons, and Charles Berlitz, who talks about the Bermuda Triangle.

That night we were at a party given by Crowell, of which Abelard-Schuman and John Day were now divisions. All of this I observed carefully (I even made notes) so that I could include references to it in the eventual book.

On May 27, I devoted an hour to autographing books for Fawcett. Dan Rather, the newscaster, was signing books a small distance from me, and after the ceremonies were over we exchanged compliments.

Then on Wednesday, May 28, I had lunch with some pleasant editors from *The Saturday Evening Post,* including Mary Alice Simpson, and the convention was over. I had local color dripping out of my ears.

After it was all over, I went to see Larry Ashmead.

"Do you think you can write a mystery based on the convention?" he asked.

"I think so," I said. "I have a plot already."

"Good. We'll need it in time for the next convention."

"You'll have the manuscript in your hands long before next Memorial Day."

"Not the manuscript, Isaac. The complete book!"

I stared in horror. "Then when do you want the manuscript?"

"The end of August."

"But it's the beginning of June now."

"The beginning of August would be better."

I felt awful. I had never written a novel in three months except for *Fantastic Voyage,* and there I had had a screenplay to copy.

"I'll try," I said dubiously.

7

Meanwhile, there was disconcerting news concerning "The Winnowing," the science-fiction story I had sold to *Physicians' World* four months earlier. Bought and paid for, it was to be included in the June issue of the magazine and had even been set in type for the purpose when the magazine suspended publication.

What could I do? I took the story to Ben Bova on May 29, and he took it at once. It appeared, eventually, in the February 1976 *Analog.*[2]

8

Janet and I went to Connecticut on May 31, to spend the day with the Walter Sullivans. We had a remarkably good time, but what most

[2] See *The Bicentennial Man and Other Stories.*

marked the day was that I played a game of croquet for the first time in my life.

9

Lester del Rey celebrated his sixtieth birthday on June 2, 1975, and Judy-Lynn had the Asimovs and Bovas join them for a birthday dinner at which large lobsters were featured. It was the first lobster bash I had had since leaving Boston.

Judy-Lynn seized the opportunity to talk business.

"Asimov," she said, "I understand you wrote a science-fiction story for this cockamamy anthology about 'Bicentennial man.' How is it you don't do one for me?"

"Well, Judy-Lynn," I said, weakly, "the idea of the anthology interested me."

"How about my idea about a robot that had to choose between buying its own liberty and improving its body? I thought you said that was interesting."

My eyes widened. "Good Lord, Judy-Lynn, that's right, you did suggest that once. I'm afraid I incorporated something like that in the anthology story."

"*Again?*" she shrieked. "*Again* you're using my ideas for other people?[8] Let me see that story. Let me see it!"

I said, "What good will that do, Judy-Lynn? I've given it to Naomi Gordon."

"Don't you know anything, Asimov?" said Judy-Lynn. "That anthology isn't coming out. Write to her and you'll see."

So I gave Judy-Lynn a carbon of the story the next day and almost at once she telephoned me to say, "I did my best not to like it, Asimov, but I didn't manage. Get it back from that dame. I want it."

I wrote to Naomi Gordon, and Judy-Lynn was right. The anthology had fallen apart. Naomi had been plagued by ill health and marital problems. The other stories never came in or were unsuitable when they did. She returned "The Bicentennial Man" and I returned the sum she had advanced me. I felt terrible, for it had been a good idea, and poor Naomi sounded heartbroken.

Finally, in January 1976, "The Bicentennial Man" appeared in the anthology *Stellar-2* edited by Judy-Lynn.

[8] She was referring to "Feminine Intuition," which I had written six years before.

10

Janet's parents had, in their time, spent vacations at a huge, rambling resort, Mohonk Mountain House, set in a thoroughly isolated mountain spot near New Paltz, New York. They had thought it an idyllic wonderland.

A month before, on our way to Albany, where I was to give a talk, we passed New Paltz. Janet suddenly remembered, and since it was a beautiful day we turned off the highway and, on impulse, went to see what Mohonk Mountain House might be like.

We were thoroughly impressed. It was a holdover from a dying breed and it was like stepping back into the lavish days of an earlier age (with contemporary improvements). The countryside was delightful, and Janet had visions of a ramble in a pleasant wilderness. We arranged for a weekend there later on in the season, and on June 6, 1975, we drove there.

It was all that Janet expected. We walked endlessly, while she watched for birds through her opera glasses; we climbed to the top of a moderately tall hill; we canoed, visited gardens, danced, and, of course, ate like kings. It was just two days but they were terrific and we planned to return.

It was not a complete vacation, for there was *Murder at the ABA* to write. With its tight deadline, I dared not neglect it. I had started it on June 5, and while at Mohonk, I had to continue in pen-and-ink.

From the start, I made up my mind to stick as close to reality as I could. I began with the mad dash from the University of Connecticut and the failure to make a four-twenty appointment, even though arrival came at precisely four-twenty. I changed all the names, of course, and I didn't have myself as a protagonist, but someone else, whom I named Darius Just.

I modeled Just, physically, on Harlan Ellison, making him a good writer, highly intelligent, handy with his fists, attractive to women— and five feet, two inches tall. (Naturally, I had written to Harlan Ellison, who always insists he is five feet, five inches tall, to make sure he wouldn't mind. He sent me a letter giving full permission in the most generous possible way, so I eventually dedicated the book to him.)

I put myself into the book, too, under my own name. I had myself arrive at the convention in order to gather local color for a book to be called *Murder at the ABA*. I took care to describe myself exactly as I was, much as I had done in the case of Mortimer Stellar in "When No

Man Pursueth" (though to keep peace with Janet, I made myself a little less unlovable in this case).

Some of the events that actually took place at the convention I assigned to myself and some to Darius Just; and, of course, I invented everything that involved the murder and the detection. It sounds a little confusing, but I had myself (Isaac Asimov) in the *third* person, write the story for Darius Just (who was in the *first* person).

I even intended to have occasional footnotes in which Darius and I would quarrel over the interpretation of events and of his supposed description of me. I worried a bit about the propriety of this, but it was *fun*; I enjoyed it. And since I had less than three months to do the novel, I wasn't going to do anything that would spoil the fun. I needed the fun to keep me working.

11

On June 9, the John Bartholomew Tucker project came to life again. We were to make another test taping, but this time it was to be in a more elaborate studio. Heywood Hale Broun was there again, and this time so was William Rusher of *National Review*.

Rusher was one of the particularly articulate conservatives of the nation and I hated his politics—but I had to admit that he was a pleasant individual, quick-witted and genial. I got along with him very well.

12

I had lunch with James Fixx of *Horizon* on June 19 and we talked about possible articles I might do for the magazine. Fixx was intrigued by the wide variety of subjects my books dealt with and seemed particularly curious about my annotations. It seemed to him that they were odd books for a person like myself to have written.

"No," I said, "I like poetry—the old-fashioned kind with meter and rhyme."

"Could you annotate some poem for us?" he asked.

I reacted with considerable interest. Even while working on *Asimov's Annotated Paradise Lost*, I had been planning to do a book of annotations of poems that were based on historical events. Such poems would lend themselves to copious explanations of the historical references and that would give me great pleasure. My annotations were not big sellers, however, and I hung back from trying to stick Doubleday with another.

If I could do an annotation for *Horizon*, however, that might be a start. If it worked, I could do a series, and then offer Doubleday the collection. I told Fixx, rather jubilantly, that I would try.

13

Murder at the ABA was going very well. In three weeks I had written forty-five thousand words and was roughly half done with the first draft.

Even so, I maintained a social life, too. On June 20, Lester and I hosted a Trap Door Spiders meeting at a Chinese restaurant. We brought two guests. One was Mark Chartrand, who had succeeded Ken Franklin as director of the Hayden Planetarium. The other was the Amazing Randi, a clever magician and a rationalist, who was quite certain that Uri Geller was a fraud and who took every possible occasion to demonstrate the follies of those who took Geller seriously.

14

Now, at last, it was time to drive out to Evansville, Indiana, to fulfill my promise to Lowell Thomas and attend the meeting of the American Academy of Achievement. New York to Evansville was the longest automobile trip I had ever undertaken, even longer than the Boston-to-Detroit trip ten years before.

We left at noon on June 24, 1975, and, fortunately, the weather was beautiful. Janet, who had been looking forward to the trip with misgivings, found the slopes on either side of the road, all through Pennsylvania, covered by a purple sea of what we found out was crown vetch. She was ravished thereby. It was a small item to give her such pleasure, but then, she found pleasure in simple things—which made her completely delightful to live with.

By the evening of the twenty-fifth, we were in Cave City, Kentucky, and the next morning we toured Mammoth Cave, which was perfectly cool and comfortable despite the fact that it was hot and muggy above-ground. In midafternoon on the twenty-sixth we were in Evansville, having covered a little over a thousand miles in fifty hours.

Rather to our surprise we found ourselves enjoying the convention. From the standpoint of personal luxury, we certainly had no complaints. We were put up in a large and modern hotel, given comfortable rooms, and fed delightfully.

Then, too, we met a number of people we might not have met otherwise. There were Art Linkletter and Jim Nabors from show business; Colonel Sanders, who began his famous chicken business with his first

Social Security check; Jack LaLanne, a pint-sized physical marvel; Joe Gerard, the self-styled greatest salesman in the world, who had statistics to prove it; and many others.

On the evening of Saturday, June 28, we had the not entirely glorious pleasure of sitting through a banquet that actually lasted six full hours.

The fifty celebrities were seated around a vast U-shaped arrangement of tables, and some celebrities (notably Carl Sagan) showed up only for this banquet. We were seated in alphabetical order, with myself second from one end. The only person ahead of me was Nobel Laureate Carl D. Anderson, the discoverer of the positron. (He was quite deaf, and I don't think he heard much of what went on.)

On the other side of me was Rick Barry, a basketball player who, when he stood up, was about six feet, seven inches tall. Virtually all that height was due to the length of his thighbone and, as we sat side by side, I compared the length of his thigh to that of mine. After a while I had the distinct feeling that my femur had been chopped off midway and that I was deformed.

Louis Nizer, the well-known lawyer, gave the keynote address, and delivered a stirring description of what everyday life would be like seventy-five years hence. In accordance with the determinedly upbeat philosophy of the proceedings, he pictured a technological paradise, and did it very well without manuscript or notes.

I was a little taken aback, first because he invaded my turf, since the speech was pure science fiction. Second, Rick Barry turned to me in amazement and said, "Isn't it remarkable that he could speak that way without notes."

I'd been doing that for a quarter century, but I could only nod and say, hollowly, "Remarkable."

It was then the turn of each of the fifty celebrities to be lauded fulsomely, to walk up to the rostrum, receive a "golden plate," and utter a few words of thanks.

I was the second one up, and with the echo of Nizer's excellent address still softly reverberating, and Rick Barry's remark still rankling, I couldn't bring myself to confine my words to a mutter of thanks. I *had* to put on some display of my oratorical powers, even if only a brief one. I said:

"Mr. Nizer has given you an excellent picture of a wonderful future, and since I am a science-fiction writer, I can't help but envy the clarity and eloquence of his vision. However, we must remember that the various governments of Earth are, in these complex times of ours, the direct mediators of change and it is they who largely determine the nature, quantity, direction, and efficiency of change. We must also remember that most governments are in the hands of lawyers; certainly our own is. The question, then, is what may we expect of lawyers?

"And in that connection, there is the story of the physician, the architect, and the lawyer who once, over friendly drinks, were discussing the comparative ancientness of their respective professions.

"The physician said, 'On Adam's first day of existence, the Lord God put him into a deep sleep, removed a rib, and from it created a woman. Since that was undoubtedly a surgical operation, I claim that medicine is the world's oldest profession.'

"'Wait a moment,' said the architect. 'I must remind you that on the very first day of creation, six days at least before the removal of Adam's rib, the Lord God created heaven and earth out of chaos. Since that has to be considered a grand structural feat, I maintain that architecture must take pride of place.'

"'Ah yes,' purred the lawyer, 'but who do you think created the chaos?'"

And my heart was gladdened when the roar of laughter turned out to be the best of the evening. (Nizer was laughing, too, I was relieved to see.)

15

After breakfast on June 29, we left Evansville and deliberately chose a scenic route for our homeward journey. That night we were in the depths of West Virginia at a motor lodge high in the Appalachians.

After dinner, we wandered out on the grounds and managed to make our way to a rocky ledge (well fenced) and stared down into a gorge through which a river wound its way.

The cloudless sky was still bright, but the twilight was deepening; the vista was absolutely bursting with green; the river was a silver curve; and around the bend of a mountain there slowly came a long freight train dragged by four locomotives. It crawled its way precariously along the narrow space between mountain and river, with its busy chug-chug far enough away to sound like the panting of a giant anaconda.

After a long while, Janet said, in an awed whisper, "Isn't this amazing?"

"You bet," I said, briskly. "One hundred sixty-six cars! Longest freight train I ever saw."[4]

[4] It was on this day that Rod Serling died during open-heart surgery, at the age of fifty, less than a year after we had both received honorary degrees from Alfred.

16

On July 1 we were at Charlottesville, Virginia, where we steeped ourselves in Jeffersoniana at the University of Virginia and at Monticello. Janet was reading a biography of Jefferson at this time and was fascinated by every aspect of it.[5]

We were home on July 2, having been away for eight days and having had good weather throughout. Despite our initial misgivings and apprehensions, it had been a most successful trip.

17

The good weather didn't last. July came within a fraction of an inch of being the wettest in the New York Weather Bureau's records, and on July 7, during one of the many rains, we experienced a leak in the bathroom adjoining our bedroom. It was the first serious problem to arise in our apartment, and it rather diminished the joy I felt in completing the first draft of *Murder at the ABA* on July 9.

Robyn arrived on a visit on July 10. It was the first time she had seen our apartment at Park Ten and, unfortunately, considering the leak, it was not at its best.

Robyn left on July 13, and it was after that that both the rains and the leak reached their peak of intensity. We had to abandon the bedroom altogether, take the bed apart, lift up the carpet, and sleep for four nights on the couch in my section of the apartment.

It was not till July 22 that the management discovered and replaced the defective gasket in a pipe that could be reached only by breaking through the wall in the stairway leading up to our section of the roof.

Despite all this, however, I was racing ahead with final copy of *Murder at the ABA*.

18

On July 18, 1975, I visited Steve Spielberg, a movie director, at his room in the Sherry-Netherland. He had done *Jaws*, a phenomenally successful picture, and now he planned to do another, involving flying sau-

[5] When she finished the biography, she came to me in tears, saying, "Jefferson just died." I put my arms around her and said, "There, there, he's eighty-three years old and went quietly."

cers. He wanted me to work with him on it, but I didn't really want to. The visual media are not my bag, really.[6]

19

We left for our fourth summer visit to the Institute of Man and Science on July 27. As we drove along I told Janet that anything could give me an idea and promised I would have a highway plot for a Black Widowers story before we got to the institute. It wasn't five minutes before I noticed that the Exxon signs had the double "x" so designed as to resemble a tilted Cross of Lorraine, and that was all I needed.

While at the Institute I wrote my twenty-fifth Black Widowers story, thus doing the first one toward a possible third volume. I called it "The Cross of Lorraine" and based some of it on the June session of the Dutch Treat Club at which the Amazing Randi had impressed me with his impromptu tricks at the dinner table.

Fred Dannay took the story and it eventually appeared in the May 1976 EQMM.

The high point, professionally, of this particular seminar came on July 30, when Jay Forrester of MIT came in to argue his belief in the necessity of a world consisting of small, self-sufficient communities. My own view, stated rather forcefully, was that this was no novelty. It had been tried numerous times in world history and there were even names for it. It was called "feudalism" and "the Dark Ages."

The real high points, though, were not professional. We had a steady membership at these seminars now. The same people came year after year. They knew us and each other. It was a kind of intense reunion; there were parties each night; the meals were loving bedlam. Then when (after only four days) separation time came, there were sadness and withdrawal symptoms.

Janet always wept. She had become very fond, in particular, of a couple, Isidore and Annie Adler (he was a chemist at the University of Maryland), and she hated to say good-bye to them.

20

I finished Murder at the ABA on August 3. My diary notation for the day was:

"I just finished Murder at the ABA in exactly two months, al-

[6] He went on to do it without me and it became the phenomenally successful Close Encounters of the Third Kind. I have no regrets.

though I was off on trips for fifteen days all told, and I lost four more days writing three articles and a story—to say nothing of the anguish of two weeks of leaks."

I loved this particular book beyond any I had ever written—partly because it had been written so quickly and in so trouble-free a fashion, and partly because I liked the characters I had created, particularly Darius Just, Sarah Voskovek, and, of course, myself.

I took in the manuscript on August 4.

42
Three Books for Each Year

1

I had not forgotten my promise to James Fixx that I would annotate a poem for *Horizon*. He had sent me a possible list of poems, including Kipling's *If* and Stevenson's *My Shadow*, but I had my own candidate.

I wanted to annotate Kipling's *Recessional*, for it had a wealth of biblical references. Furthermore, it was written at the time of the very peak success of the British Empire—at Queen Victoria's Diamond Jubilee in 1897—yet it forecast the possible downfall of that Empire. Indeed, the downfall began two years later with the Boer War and continued to the complete disappearance of the Empire in half a century. There was therefore room for moralizing, too.

I began "The Annotated *Recessional*" on August 6 and had it in Fixx's hands two days later.

I was very proud of it and was certain that *Horizon* would be enraptured by it. How wrong I was, for it turned out I had been under a crucial misapprehension. Fixx had been under the impression that my annotations were humorous ones, and he expected my "The Annotated *Recessional*" to be a burlesque.

Not only was it serious, but also I wouldn't for a moment consider anything else, so they returned the manuscript and the project was dead.

2

On August 18, I received my advance copy of *Eyes on the Universe* from Houghton Mifflin. It had a statistical importance, for it was my 165th book and I was fifty-five years old. I had now reached the point where I had published three books for each year of my life.

And on August 20 (David's twenty-fourth birthday), I received my advance copy of *Lecherous Limericks*.

3

Casting a damper on the pleasure these books aroused was the sad news concerning Rae Jeppson's health. A medical examination had shown she had inoperable cancer and it looked as though her remaining life span could be measured only in months. Janet was plunged in grief.

It had been only two weeks before that that Rae had helped celebrate Janet's birthday. Rae had not seemed well then but we had no reason to think, at the time, that the feebleness was due to anything other than old age. Now it seemed she would never see another of her daughter's birthdays.

That was much on my mind on August 24, when Stanley and Ruth, along with Janet and I, visited the cemetery out on Long Island once again.

4

On August 27, I took in the manuscript of my twelfth collection of *F & SF* essays. I called it *The Planet That Wasn't*, from the title of one of the essays included.

Then two days later, on the twenty-ninth, I began a project that Beth Walker had been urging on me for many months. She had wanted a book on black holes. ("Think black holes," she kept saying every time she saw me.) I had agreed but it wasn't till now that a hole in my schedule had opened. I made use of the title that Beth herself had thought up: *The Collapsing Universe*.

Dick Winslow, for whom I had done *Life and Energy* at Doubleday fourteen years before, had been with Walker for quite some time now, and he was to be my editor for this one.

I did twenty-five thousand words of *The Collapsing Universe* in four days, before turning away in order to renew my depleted energies by doing some of *The Golden Door*.

I also gave some thought to "The Annotated *Recessional*," which *Horizon* had rejected. The intense pleasure I had experienced in doing it was not something I could lightly abandon.

It occurred to me that I had a contract and advance from Doubleday for *Asimov's Biographical Encyclopedia of War and Battle*, which had lain idle for two years now and which I did not honestly know when I could get to in the future. Once before, in connection with *Life and Energy*, I had revitalized dead contracts by doing an entirely new book under it. Why not again?

If Doubleday would agree to shift the War and Battle advance to a new book, *Familiar Poems, Annotated,* I could do that quickly and with the greatest of pleasure.

I could take in two annotated poems as samples. "The Annotated *Recessional*" I had already done, and on September 3, I annotated William Ernest Henley's *Invictus.* I then took them in to Larry, who was sympathetic, of course, but who had to consult the editorial board.

If I had been judicious I wouldn't have done another stroke of work on the book till I heard of Doubleday's decision, but I was caught. Although I did my best to work on *The Collapsing Universe* and *The Golden Door,* I found myself sneaking in bits of annotations. By the time I got the word, on September 16, that Doubleday had approved *Familiar Poems, Annotated,* and would do it on the War and Battle contract, I had completed the annotation of sixteen poems.

5

Unlikely markets were continuing to request science-fiction stories. *High Fidelity* magazine wanted a science-fiction story dealing with some aspect of sound in the future. On September 18, I wrote a story called "Marching In,"[1] on the use of music to treat mental disease. It appeared in the May 1976 issue of that magazine.

Bell Telephone magazine asked me to do a far-out story on communications, and on October 19, I did one called "Old-fashioned,"[2] which was, in a way, a deliberate reprise of my first published story, "Marooned Off Vesta" thirty-seven years before. "Old-fashioned" appeared in the January–February 1976 *Bell Telephone* magazine.

6

I was in Boston on October 9 to give a talk at Suffolk University, and I seized the occasion to call Robyn (who was a college sophomore now) and arrange to take her to dinner.

"Could you take a roommate, too, Dad?"

"Of course, Robyn," I said, expansively.

I drove out to Boston College and there was Robyn with *five* roommates. She had reserved a table for seven at a fancy steakhouse.

I recovered rapidly, however. After all, it meant I would be surrounded by no less than six lovely girls, each one of them twenty-one.

[1] See *The Bicentennial Man and Other Stories.*
[2] See *The Bicentennial Man and Other Stories.*

I couldn't resist a *little* kidding, though, "Girls," I said, as we crossed the parking lot toward the restaurant door, "feeding you all is going to be expensive, so I hope you will confine yourself to mixed green salads and, perhaps, grapefruit for dessert."

"*Dad*," said Robyn, scandalized, "don't say things like that. You'll *inhibit* them. They don't understand your sense of humor."

How could she say that? I hadn't been talking to the young women long, even while we were still back in the dormitory, before one of them interrupted my suave *double-entendres* and gushed, "Oh Dr. Asimov, you're *exactly* like Robyn's description of you." I can imagine what she must have described. My odd sense of humor, certainly.

Besides, they weren't inhibited. Those young girls, who were probably accustomed to eating squash seeds and marshmallows for dinner, one and all ordered shrimp cocktails, rib roasts, and pecan pie. It was like feeding survivors of a shipwreck who had been drifting for three weeks at sea.

7

Graham Chedd was an English science writer who was working in America for WGBH, the educational TV channel in Boston. He had film of James Watson, Francis Crick, and others that dealt with the discovery of the double-helix structure of DNA. Graham had written commentary for the film, and the whole was to air on "Nova," a highly esteemed science show.

He wanted *me* to recite the commentary, and to do it at Cold Spring Harbor, where there were important biological research laboratories, of which Watson himself was now head. Graham promised it would take no more than two days.

I drove there on October 14, and it did take two days—two days to recite not more than twenty minutes' worth of talk.

For the first time in my life I was an actor, reciting someone else's words. Of course, they kept saying they wanted me to give the information in my own words, using the written commentary as a guide, but they didn't really mean it. When I did it differently, they made me repeat.

What's more, they had a director who, even after I recited a passage letter-perfect, had me do it again in order to squeeze a different intonation or gesture out of me.

Then, even after I had done it absolutely correctly, I would have to repeat it because the Sun had gone behind a cloud midway and thrown off the camera—or, what was just as bad, the Sun had come out from behind a cloud.

Or else there were the sounds of hammering from a construction site nearby, or the sound of someone calling in the distance, or the sound of an automobile grating over the gravel in the nearby parking lot. It was almost impossible to keep the universe motionless and sound-less for forty-five seconds at a time.

And with every repetition of the same passage, it became more juiceless and insipid to me, more hateful to try to say.

And it was hot. The temperature soared into the eighties both days even though it was the middle of October. To maintain the proper air of scientific gravity that the show required, I had to wear a somber, long-sleeved shirt, with a four-in-hand tie, and a full business suit, while all around me were technicians and executives in sports shirts open at the neck.

I found the whole thing incredibly tedious, but in the end they had the show, and it has been shown over and over again on TV. I watched it on its first showing out of curiosity, but without pleasure.

8

After I had come back from Evansville four months before, I would have welcomed an end to long trips for a while, but on October 21, Janet and I took off for Dayton, Ohio.

The reason for that was that Joe Patrouch, who had written that excellent book about me and my science fiction, wanted me to speak at the University of Dayton where he taught, and I found myself unable to resist.

The talk took place on the evening of the twenty-second. Lennie Meisel, of my Navy Yard days, now lived in Dayton, so I met him at the talk, together with his sister, whom I recalled as an adolescent girl in Philadelphia.

The next day we drove eastward to Wooster, Ohio, where another science-fiction friend had wanted me. He was Tom Clareson, who edited a scholarly magazine, *Extrapolation*, which dealt primarily with science fiction, though at such a rarefied level that it rarely had occasion to mention me.

We reached home again on the twenty-fourth.

9

Shortly after I returned, I received a call from Larry Ashmead. "Are you sitting down, Isaac?" he asked.

That was always a dreadful question, portending doom. I said in alarm, "What's the matter, Larry?"

He said, "I've got good news, but I'm afraid it's bad news, in a way."

I didn't need any more. I may have my faults, but slowness of apprehension is not among them. "Oh my goodness," I said, "you're leaving Doubleday."

And he was. He had put off telling me until there was no way of hiding it anymore. I was the last person to be told, and no rumor of the change had reached me. I suppose no one dared be the one to tell me.

After he hung up, I remained in my chair, stricken, for a full hour, while Janet tiptoed around, wondering what was going to happen to me. After all, I hate losing *any* editor, but Larry wasn't just any editor.

From the time he was Dick Winslow's assistant and had dealt with *Life and Energy*, we had been working together for fourteen years, and in all that time there hadn't been one cross word between us, or a single failure to see eye to eye.

I went to Doubleday on October 27 to say good-bye. Larry knew that my primary loyalty was to Doubleday as a corporate entity, that my relationship with it antedated my friendship with him, and that not even for Larry could I leave it. He never asked me to.

Of course, I wasn't losing him altogether. He had taken a job with Simon and Schuster, and I could still see him regularly and, eventually, even do a book for him. That only cushioned the loss, however; it didn't cancel it.

I had to choose a new editor, though. By now, I had been with Doubleday for a quarter of a century and had published sixty-one books with them, so I could have picked my editor and chosen one as high in the echelons as I wished.

I didn't, though. I know my own eccentricities, and I felt it would be much safer to have someone who knew them also.

Cathleen Jordan had entered Doubleday as Larry's secretary, but she had quickly revealed enough ability to become an editor. She, rather than Larry, had handled the nuts and bolts of *Murder at the ABA*, and I had liked working with her.

I therefore asked if I might have Cathleen for my editor, and Doubleday was pleased at the choice. Oddly enough, Cathleen was,

too. My first book for her was my fourth recycling of my early essays—
Asimov on Numbers.

10

It was a difficult November. New York City was in a financial crisis and seemed on the edge of bankruptcy. I was laden down with New
York City bonds and had to face the possibility that if the city actually
went bankrupt, I would find myself semi-wiped out. Fortunately, the
city held on, even though it got no sympathy from the rest of the nation, and cruel sneers from many (including some from the Nixon-ap-
pointed and Nixon-pardoning President of the United States).

11

Fred Dannay had an idea for the *EQMM* issue that would be on
the newsstands at the time of the Bicentennial celebration. Why not
run three stories: a contemporary story dealing with the Bicentennial; a
historical story dealing with the 1876 Centennial; and a science-fiction
story dealing with the 2076 Tricentennial?

To handle the science fiction, he turned to me and I was
sufficiently intrigued by the notion to agree. I spent the first two weeks
of November writing "The Tercentenary Incident,"[3] and, on November 13, 1975, I took it in to the *EQMM* offices. It was a robot story and
rather stiff science fiction in which I had made no concessions for the
mystery audience. I was more than half afraid Fred Dannay would
reject it, but he didn't. He even paid me a bonus, and it appeared in
the August 1976 *EQMM.*

12

Meanwhile, I had not stopped writing limericks just because I had
published *Lecherous Limericks.* To be sure, the book was proving a disappointment, and I might well have abandoned the whole notion of
limericks as unremunerative—but I don't work for money alone.

Constructing limericks gave me pleasure, and before long I found I
had a hundred more. On November 13, therefore, I began to put together *More Lecherous Limericks.*

Neither I nor the Walkers had any real hopes it would do better
than the first book, but the Walkers were good-natured enough to go
along with me, and they told me, with what grace they could muster,

[3] See *The Bicentennial Man and Other Stories.*

that they would keep on putting out the books as long as I kept coming in with batches of a hundred.

13

Since we had had the bad news about Rae, Janet had been calling her every day and visiting her just about weekly. Rae held up remarkably well, however. Though she was failing, little by little, she remained sharp, cheerful, and was always a delight to be with.

On November 16, she celebrated her seventy-ninth birthday. We went to New Rochelle and took her to lunch, along with Chaucy, Les, and Leslie. Rae was with us all again at Chaucy's house on Thanksgiving.

14

For a long time, *Amazing Stories* had been the least regarded of the science-fiction magazines, but it was the first and the oldest. It was six years older than *Analog*, and had held on against all buffetings while dozens of other magazines had come and gone.

Now *Amazing* was going to celebrate fifty years of continuous publication and they planned to put out a special golden anniversary issue. I was asked to contribute a story and, of course, I agreed. I did not forget that it had been to *Amazing* that I had made my first sale.

On November 22, I wrote an eighteen-hundred-word story called "Birth of a Notion,"[4] which dealt specifically with Hugo Gernsback and the founding of *Amazing*. It was accepted and eventually appeared in the June 1976 issue of the magazine.

15

We had an anniversary, too. November 30, 1975, was our second wedding anniversary. Since it fell on a Sunday, we had the Balks to an elaborate buffet brunch at a restaurant just off Lincoln Center. We were an old married couple now, Janet and I.

16

On December 4, I gave a talk at Tufts University in the Boston area, and David came in to attend. He enjoyed it as much as he used to in the days when I lived in Newton. He had gained considerable

4 See *The Bicentennial Man and Other Stories.*

weight, however (much as I had done when I was his age), but I saw no reason why he should repeat my mistakes, and I spent some time urging him to reduce.

17

I had written enough science-fiction stories for another collection, and as soon as I returned from Boston I plunged into work. There was no question in my mind that, of the stories I was going to include, "The Bicentennial Man" was not only the longest, but was by far the strongest. I therefore called the collection, *The Bicentennial Man and Other Stories*.

On December 10, I took in the manuscript to Sharon Jarvis, the pretty young woman who had been editing Doubleday's science-fiction books since Diane Cleaver had left a couple of years earlier.

18

Caedmon Records was getting deeper into science fiction, and was persuading well-known names to read well-known science-fiction stories. They had bought the recording rights to the *Foundation Trilogy*, and on December 10 I went to their offices to hear William Shatner read the first section, which was to be marketed as *Foundation*.

And on December 13, I finally completed *The Golden Door*.

19

We left for Rae's house on December 24. We were to have the usual feast at Chaucy's, but it was Janet's plan to stay over and spend part of Christmas itself with her mother. Janet was certain it would be their last Christmas together.

While Janet and Rae were talking in the evening, I spent my time studying Rae's bookcases. I saw *Gone with the Wind* there, as I had seen it there every time I had looked. I had never read it; I would scorn to read it, certain as I was that it was a foolish book.

This time, simply out of curiosity, I opened it to look at the first page, for I had actually never even opened the book to look inside.

I read that first page, turned it automatically to read the second, and realized by the time I was on page five that I was *hooked*. I kept on reading (with shame and horror at my own fascination with it), waiting for a chance to break away, and never found one.

I went to bed late, under bitter protest, waited till Janet had fallen asleep, then crept out of bed and into the bathroom. I stayed up all night reading. I continued reading the next day and didn't stop till I was finished. It took me fifteen hours of nearly continuous reading to finish the book, and when I was done I was angry. I wanted *more!*

Nothing like that had happened to me with any book since I was a teen-ager.

20

I ended 1975 with eleven books published:

159. *Of Matters Great and Small* (Doubleday)
160. *The Solar System* (Follett)
161. *Our Federal Union* (Houghton Mifflin)
162. *How Did We Find Out About Comets?* (Walker)
163. *Science Past—Science Future* (Doubleday)
164. *Buy Jupiter and Other Stories* (Doubleday)
165. *Eyes on the Universe* (Houghton Mifflin)
166. *Lecherous Limericks* (Walker)
167. *The Heavenly Host* (Walker)
168. *The Ends of the Earth* (Weybright & Talley)
169. *How Did We Find Out About Energy?* (Walker)

21

On January 2, 1976, Janet and I celebrated my fifty-sixth birthday at a restaurant with Stan and Ruth and Lester and Judy-Lynn and a special birthday cake that Janet had quietly asked to have delivered to the table.

It was also time to start thinking of *The Hugo Winners, Volume III*, for which I took in the signed contract to Sharon Jarvis that very birthday. Only five years had passed since the second volume had appeared, but enough stories had accumulated to allow a third volume every bit as large as the second.

22

On January 3, Janet and I were at a party at the apartment of Eleanor Sullivan of *EQMM*. She lived in Stuyvesant Town, and her apartment was a precise duplicate of the one I had lived in twenty-eight years before. It was an exercise in nostalgia.

23

Alan R. Bechtold of Topeka, Kansas, had plunged into semiprofessional publishing. He wanted to put out little pamphlets containing an individual science-fiction story specially written for the series. It would appear under the imprint of Apocalypse Press and would consist of a strictly limited edition, with each copy signed by the author. It was to be sold only at science-fiction conventions.

He wanted a story from me and offered a price comparable to that paid by the science-fiction magazines. After the edition was sold out the story would be mine to do with as I pleased.

I was interested and agreed. On January 5, I began writing a story called *Good Taste*, which I set against a background of orbiting space settlements. As it turned out, I liked it very much. So did Bechtold, and the pamphlet eventually appeared (and I counted it among the number of my books).

Good Taste was the second in Bechtold's series. The first contained some very short items that were too recondite for my understanding. The third was to be a story by Harlan Ellison, but apparently it never showed up. Soon thereafter, Apocalypse Press came to an end, with my story not only second, but the last as well.

24

John Bartholomew Tucker was *still* after his adult-conversation show. Twice, he had taped the audio only; now he wanted to do video as well. On January 6, I went down to a television studio, where Broun and Rusher were also present, and once again we went through a question-and-answer session, trying to be as witty as possible. (I was asked what I would do if someone gave me a billion dollars. I said I would take it right over to the Internal Revenue Service and say, "Here! Now never bother me again!")

It was my notion that this was still only a demonstration piece designed to interest sponsors. Tucker, however, decided to allow the experimental run-through to appear on television later in the year, after an inexpert cutting that left us referring to statements that had been cut out. The program, called "Talking Heads," sank quietly and disappeared.

25

At the Baker Street Irregulars banquet on January 9, I received the honor of an investiture. This meant I was given a cognomen that consisted of some notable phrase that appeared somewhere in the sacred writings. Mine was "The Remarkable Worm," which represented one of the cases that Watson mentions but never wrote up. Whether it was thought to be particularly descriptive of me, no one said.

26

The New York branch of the Printers' Union has a banquet annually at a time near Benjamin Franklin's birthday (Franklin being the patron saint of American printers).

On that occasion, they always put out some small book containing Frankliniana, and for the occasion of the 1976 banquet, which was held on January 20, they put out a little collection of the Franklin pieces I had done for *The Saturday Evening Post*.

Janet and I were at the banquet,[5] and I received copies of the booklet, as did everyone else present.

The booklet was beautifully done, but it contained only three of the four stories, the first, second, and fourth. I do not know why they left out the third. They used the *Post*'s titles, of course, so that the booklet was entitled *"The Dream," "Benjamin's Dream," and "Benjamin's Bicentennial Blast."*

It was a private printing, not available for sale. On the other hand, the booklet contained three stories that had not been collected elsewhere and was longer than some of my children's books. After some hesitation, I numbered the booklet on my list of books. Later on in the year, though, when an even more beautiful little booklet was put out (with my permission) as a Christmas keepsake, and contained only "Benjamin's Bicentennial Blast," I drew the line and did not include it on my list of books.

27

In the first two months of 1976, there were three separate "Star Trek" conventions. I attended all three, or at least portions of them.

[5] Senator Jacob Javits and Mayor Abe Beame each made a cameo appearance and each sat in the seat next to mine.

The second was the most spectacular in some ways and, on January 23, as part of that second, I was on a panel with several writers, and we all tried to define science fiction.

Two of the other members of the panel were Harlan Ellison and Barry Malzberg. They (together with Robert Silverberg, who was not on the panel) had grown disillusioned with science fiction and were threatening to write no more of it. Harlan even argued that the name itself was mischievous and helped keep us all in a disregarded "ghetto." He wanted it called "speculative fiction."

Against this, I maintained the conservative view. I liked science fiction, I wanted to keep the name. I saw no reason why a science-fiction writer should feel he was in a ghetto. I pointed out that despite my thorough identification with science fiction, I could write anything else I wanted to write and be treated seriously.

Harlan retorted. "You're not a science-fiction writer. You're an Isaac Asimov."

I tried to return to the convention the next day, which was Saturday, but the organizers had sold two or three times as many tickets as they had room for people. On Saturday, all the ticket holders had shown up and there simply was no room for them.

I walked in, unsuspectingly, and found myself trapped in a mass of crystallized humanity (with children crying in disappointment and parents looking harassed and furious). I tried to get out and it took me half an hour to do so.

Meanwhile, Harlan Ellison, since he was in town for the convention, had agreed to attend a meeting that night and read a couple of stories. He had asked me to introduce him, and I was glad to do so and to listen to his reading thereafter. He's a terrific reader, simply marvelous. I was green with envy as I listened.

28

Seventeen wanted a science-fiction story with a Tricentennial motif. I agreed and, on January 27, 1976, began a story I called "To Tell at a Glance." It was a spy story with a background similar to that in "Good Taste."

It was eighty-three hundred words long and I thought it was very clever, but what I think scarcely counts. *Seventeen* wanted so thorough-going a revision that I preferred to consider it a rejection. I made some halfhearted efforts to find another home for it, failed, and retired it.

29

Apparently, the impromptu talk I had given on the QE2's "Cruise to Nowhere," two years before, had made it plain to the Cunard management that they could rely on me to amuse the passengers.

William North of Cunard, who had met me on that cruise, and who was a very pleasant, silver-haired, round-faced gentleman, asked me if I would go along on an eleven-day Caribbean cruise and give some talks in the process. "Absolutely," I said.

We boarded the ship on January 31, and it was almost inevitable, now, that I would proceed to write a Black Widowers story. I did this, now, almost every time I was away from my office for any length of time.

My idea for this one, my twenty-sixth, originated from the Trap Door Spiders dinner that Lester and I had cohosted on January 23. My accountant, Alex Zupnick, had been my guest, and he fascinated the membership with his information on tax accountancy. (That's something that hits home to everyone.) I called my story "The Family Man," and it eventually appeared in the November 1976 EQMM under the title of "A Case of Income-tax Fraud."

The QE2 stopped at any number of islands, but Janet and I refrained from going on any of the formal tours. It was our pleasure to wander about on our own in the immediate neighborhood of the point to which the ship, or a launch, took us. In this way we visited Martinique, Curaçao, and so on. On February 8, we were anchored off the port city of Caracas, Venezuela, and got off only long enough to feel the soil (or, rather, concrete) of South America under our feet. It was the first time either one of us had set foot on that continent.

The most exciting stop was Barbados, on February 6. The harbor was deep enough for the QE2 to come right up to shore, which meant we could get off the ship and onto shore without trusting ourselves to a motor launch (which suited me well).

I was slated to give a talk to the Astronomical Society on the island. Waiting for us onshore, therefore, was a handsome young Barbadian, with an automobile, who took us on a thorough tour of the island. This included a pleasant buffet luncheon at its fanciest hotel and a visit to a delightful botanical garden. It was the best day of the trip.

On the evening of February 10, we left the last island and headed for home. That meant two solid days onboard ship, and that was when the passengers had to be amused. I gave one talk on the eleventh, one on the twelfth, and early on the thirteenth we were home. Janet and I were quite literally the first ones off the ship.

30

In less than a week, it was going to be Robyn's twenty-first birthday. I hadn't been with her on a single one of her birthdays since she was fifteen, and I had made definite arrangements with her to come to New York so that we could celebrate her twenty-first in a big way.

I had had a small superstitious twinge that something might happen to me on the cruise that would prevent it, but nothing had, so I called her right away to assure her I was all right and to tell her how much I was looking forward to the birthday.

I rattled on at a great rate about the cruise and, particularly, about Barbados, when it finally dawned on me that she was not responding properly.

I stopped short. "Robyn," I said, "is something wrong?"

She burst into tears and, despite my entreaties, was unable to explain why she was crying for quite a while. I grew more and more panicky and finally she could choke it out. It was an agonizing story, but far from as bad as it might have been.

Robyn's classmates had been as anxious to celebrate her birthday as I was, so they had arranged a prebirthday party in her dormitory room on February 6—the very day I was so happy on Barbados.

It went well until some Boston College football players decided to crash the party.

Robyn advanced to ask them to leave. (She knows no fear—certainly not of boys, since as a beautiful girl she has always been accustomed to having boys grin ingratiatingly and do whatever they were told to do.)

Robyn, who is five feet, two inches tall, proceeded to get angry with the ringleader, who was six feet, three inches of brawn and who wore three-inch platform heels.

In the fracas that followed, Robyn was thrown to the ground and sprained her right knee so badly that she found herself unable to walk. An X ray, taken the next day, showed that nothing was broken, but she had torn a ligament and would have to stay on crutches for some weeks.

She was not fully mobile and she would not be able to come to New York—and that was why she was crying. For a full week she had been brooding over the necessity of telling me this and facing my disappointment.

What could I do? Disappointed I might be, but that was as nothing compared to my distress over what had happened. My impulse was to ask, in exasperation, why on Earth she had tried to fight with a football bruiser, but what good would that have done? I spent my time telling her that we would make up for it after her knee was better and to put it all down to misfortune and forget it.

Robyn had not been able to forget it, however. Laboring under a strong sense of injustice, she had brought charges against the football players before the college administration, and had applied to George Michaels for help.

Had I been reachable by phone and had she consulted me I would have advised against it. I could have told her that the football players, after all, like any of their brother anthropoids, were acting with only what rationality they possessed and were not deliberately trying to hurt her. And to expect the officials of Boston College to take action against football players, when football was the college's chief claim to academic excellence, was asking a lot of college nature.

But I had not been around to advise, and the hearing came up that very night of the thirteenth. The six-foot-three football player, balancing himself precariously on his hind legs, pointed to the five-foot-two girl on crutches whose room he had invaded uninvited, and pleaded self-defense.

The school, of course, did nothing. Robyn was infuriated by that and cast about for methods that would carry the matter higher, but now I was around to advise. I said, "Robyn, would you be satisfied if you got those boys expelled?"

"Yes," said she. "That's what I want."

"Then, consider. If they're expelled, the Boston College football team will probably lose games and the student body will consider it your fault and you'll be hounded out of the school. Do you think the Boston College students will care about your knee when a winning football team is at stake? Just let your knee get better and forget it."

Robyn might be as fiery about injustice as I am but she could understand that two and two are four, and she quieted down.

So when February 19 came, I had to celebrate Robyn's birthday at long distance.

Her birthday came, as it always did, during the Washington's birthday week, when schools in Boston invariably closed down and all the students scattered. One of Robyn's friends, Mary O'Conor, gave up her own vacation, however, and moved into Robyn's room to help take care of her for that week.

On Saturday, February 21, Janet and I drove to Boston and saw with our own eyes that Robyn was well, except for the knee, that she could indeed hobble about, and that she was not in worse condition than she said she was.

As the nearest we could come to a birthday celebration, we took her and Mary O'Conor (a very pretty and shy young woman) to the same steak house where I had fed Robyn and her five roommates nearly five months before (Mary had been one of them).

We stopped off to see Robyn the next day and then drove home.

31

But meanwhile, work continued. A deadline condemned me to produce a piece for *National Geographic*, one that dealt with an imaginary visit to a space settlement of the kind I had written about in "Good Taste" and "To Tell at a Glance."

I was a little nervous, since I had never written for the magazine before and since they were paying me $1.50 a word, a new high for me. I was anxious to be worth it and not certain I would be. I finished the article, which I called "A Visit to L-5," on Robyn's birthday.

Fortunately, *National Geographic* was happy with it and it appeared in their July 1976 issue under the title "The Next Frontier?"

43

Isaac Asimov's Science Fiction Magazine

1

I finished *Familiar Poems, Annotated* on February 26, 1976, and took it to Cathleen the next day. With that done, I traveled downtown to the offices of *EQMM* to hand in "The Family Man." Joel Davis, the publisher, asked to see me.

Joel is short, slim, good-looking, and always nattily dressed. He would see me occasionally when I was bringing in Black Widowers stories, usually when I was whooping it up with Eleanor and Connie.

Davis Publications, under his leadership, was doing well, and was expanding. He published more than a score of magazines but, to begin with, he had only a single fiction magazine, *Ellery Queen's Mystery Magazine*. When the competing *Alfred Hitchcock's Mystery Magazine* was failing, however, Davis bought it and converted it into a profitable enterprise once more. It was better for the field, he reasoned, to have two strong magazines than one, for with a larger market, writers would be encouraged and the story output would gain in quantity and quality.

He was looking for further areas of expansion, and one of his executives had taken his children to one of the "Star Trek" conventions just concluded. There the executive had been struck by the numbers and enthusiasm of the fans attending, and he suggested to Joel that a science-fiction magazine might do well.

Joel thought it might be a good idea, but if he was to have a third magazine he wanted it to incorporate a well-known name into its title, as *EQMM* and *AHMM* did. The one science-fiction writer he knew was myself—so it came about that on February 26 he suggested to me the founding of a magazine to be called *Isaac Asimov's Science Fiction Magazine*.

I pointed out the impediments. I had been writing a nonfiction column for *F & SF* for seventeen years and I would on no account give that up. Joel said it would not be necessary to. Since the column was nonfiction, I could keep that. He would only ask me not to publish fiction in competing magazines.

I said that the new magazine might hurt Ben Bova and Ed Ferman, who were particular friends of mine, but Joel said that another successful magazine would help the entire field.

I said that my name in the title would offend science-fiction fans and writers, who might interpret it as arrogance on my part. He said that was ridiculous.

I said I had no editorial expertise, no desire to be an editor, no time to be one. He said we would find an editor who would work along with me.

I said I would think about it.

I did. I asked both Ben Bova and Ed Ferman how they would react to a new successful magazine, and both told me it would help the field, using the same arguments that Joel had. I sounded out people on the use of my name in a magazine title, and no one, other than myself, seemed shocked.

Since I remained frightened of the project there seemed nothing to do but be quiet, refrain from pushing, and hope that Joel would forget about it.

2

Two young women, who had met me casually at one of the "Star Trek" conventions, happened to share the same birthday. It occurred to one of them that a good birthday present for the other would be a luncheon with myself as guest. I let myself be talked into it.

On March 5, 1976, therefore, I walked into a restaurant at noon and found them waiting for me and very relieved that I had not forgotten.

We had a very animated luncheon and I put myself out to be charming and amusing, since both of the young women were attractive and obviously pleased with me. Finally, since the girls had ordered a birthday cake, the waiter brought one with great éclat and put it in front of me, assuming naturally that it was my birthday and that my young granddaughters were helping me celebrate.

Whereupon I said, haughtily, "Waiter, place that cake in front of the girls. It is their birthday. I am the birthday present."

It was a pleasure to watch the waiter give the old-man-with-the-white-sideburns that look of sudden awed respect.

3

I was in Hershey, Pennsylvania, on March 12 to give a talk, and found the parking lot crowded. The teen-age boys who were acting as automobile ushers kept directing me farther and farther away from the lecture hall until I finally rebelled and drove my car back and parked it right at the front door.

A fifteen-year-old boy tried to tell me that I was forbidden to park there, but I snarled at him that I was the speaker, and he shriveled before my anger. He tried to explain that he was only following instructions, but I brushed past him angrily, without listening.

I then waited for speechtime and discovered that I would not be able to give it. I was feverish with remorse.

I said to Janet, "Wait here one minute," and dashed out to find the boy.

"Listen," I said, "I'm sorry. I should not have spoken roughly to you. You were doing your job and I was dead wrong. Please forgive me and I will move the car."

The boy looked surprised, but smiled and assured me it was all right and that my car could stay where it was and he would keep an eye on it. I went back inside feeling much better.

Yet never since have I been able to forget that moment when I was nasty to an innocent kid. How much better it would have been for me if I had parked at the edge of the parking lot and walked the distance in the cold to get to the entrance.

4

Finally, one month late, Robyn came to New York on March 17. She was greatly improved, but still used a cane. With her was Mary O'Conor, who had never before been in New York, and whom, in return for her loyal help to Robyn, I was determined to show a good time.

The next day, therefore (the first anniversary of our move into Park Ten), I took them to the top of the Empire State Building, something I had never before done, and arranged to have them take a bus tour of the city. That night Janet took them to a play at Lincoln Center. On the nineteenth, we let them roam the city on their own in the morning, and then took them to Radio City in the afternoon.

We kept up a steady drumbeat of museums, zoos, and elaborate meals. Janet even took Mary to St. Patrick's for Sunday-morning Mass. All through I kept stating firmly that it was a twenty-first birthday celebration, and by the time the girls left I had quite convinced myself that the month's delay didn't count.

Meanwhile, I worked on *How Did We Find Out About Nuclear Power?*, the tenth book in the series, and took it to Walker on March 24.

5

I talked at Georgetown University in Washington, D.C., on the evening of March 25. Izzie and Annie Adler (our pals at Rensselaerville) had dinner with us that night, and after the talk they took us on an automobile tour of Washington.

The next morning, Janet and I wandered through a neighborhood park. It was absolutely deserted and we had the delightful sensation of having unshackled ourselves, temporarily, from the world.

On the way to the train that was to take us to Baltimore, where I was to give another talk, the taxi driver toured us through the cherry-blossom district where the blossoms, as it happened, had come out early and, apparently, just for us. It was the pleasantest trip to Washington that either of us had ever had.

Yet something pleasanter took place shortly after I returned home. I received a letter from the president of Boston University, John R. Silber, a man whose dynamic personality makes him perhaps the most remarkable president the university has yet had. It went as follows:

Dear Dr. Asimov,

In the course of flying to Chicago on American Airlines recently, I read with pleasure and profit your interesting article in the March 1976 issue of *American Way*. I took some pride in thinking that you maintain a continuing relationship as an Associate Professor of Biochemistry at the Boston University School of Medicine.

I wonder if I might ask you to assist me in communicating to the public the quality and stature of our School of Medicine and our University by indicating, when it is appropriate, your affiliation with Boston University. You will appreciate that the reputation of an institution is only as good as the reputation of the its faculty and student body. I believe that your many loyal readers might find it instructive to know of your relationship with the University.

Your help will be greatly appreciated.

/s/ John R. Silber

On April 3, I answered, assuring him that I would co-operate to the full. And I rather luxuriated in the thought that this was my final and full vindication in that long-ago quarrel with Keefer, eighteen years before.

6

We were in a presidential election year and I, of course, favored the liberal Democrat who, this year, was Morris Udall. On April 6 I voted for him,[1] but I was quite certain that he wouldn't get the nomination. I was beginning to wonder if it might not be Jimmy Carter who would get it and labored to get myself to feel some enthusiasm for him.

7

Professor Dawson was going to be sixty-five on April 8, 1976, and that meant he would be retiring. On April 7, a cocktail party was being given in his honor, and Janet and I attended. She met him for the first time. He was thinner than he had been and his face was lined, but he was still my Professor Dawson.

Twenty-eight years had now passed since I had received my Ph.D. under him, and I had now been a "doctor" for just half my life.

8

I finished *Alpha Centauri* on April 13, but there was little cause for celebration that day.

I detected blood in the urine and thought at first I was having another kidney stone, but there was no pain, and the quantity of blood increased rapidly. I fled to Paul Esserman, who said there would have to be an examination to find the source of the blood, and that meant a cystoscopy.

For two days, I was uncomfortably aware that the cause could conceivably be cancer of the bladder. On April 15, I was cystoscoped at University Hospital and, having firmly refused general anesthesia, I didn't enjoy it at all.

However, there was absolutely no sign of cancer, and it seemed to be just a little prostatic bleeding of no great significance—just something that tends to become more likely with age. I was sent on my way with a pat on the shoulder and a supply of a sulfa drug to take to prevent the complications of infection.

As it happened, I was slated to be in Baltimore to attend a local science-fiction convention at which I was guest of honor. With my

[1] The next day, a young woman asked me who I voted for and I said, "Udall." She said, "But I wasn't running." I stared in puzzlement till I realized that "Udall" was pronounced "You, doll." I was quite chagrined at my slowness in comprehension.

clean bill of health, I went to Baltimore on the sixteenth, but my stay
there was considerably hampered by the fact that it took me a couple
of days to recover from the cystoscopy. I hadn't been so physically uncomfortable at a convention since the 1956 World Science Fiction convention in New York.

9

Joel Davis had by no means forgotten about *Isaac Asimov's Science Fiction Magazine*. All my objections had been met and it
remained to find an editor.

That would not be easy. We would have to find someone knowledgeable in the field of science fiction and with editorial experience, yet
someone who was not so well known that he would scorn to work on a
magazine bearing someone else's name. Furthermore, it would have to
be someone with my taste in science fiction so that we could work together harmoniously.

It occurred to me that George Scithers might be the man. He was
a science-fiction fan of long standing (I had met him seventeen years
before, when we had returned together from the Detroit convention of
1959), and he saw eye to eye with me. He had editorial experience,
since he ran a small publishing house called Owlswyck Press.

I consulted him on the matter, and on April 19 he said he would
like to try the job. I arranged to have him see Joel, and the result was
that George became editor of the magazine.

10

On April 25, 1976, I gave a talk at a temple in Syracuse, New
York, and in the course of the question-and-answer session afterward, I
had some harsh words to say about the Book of Deuteronomy. I don't
really think that had anything to do with what transpired afterward.

At the conclusion, I talked in the lobby to various people who had
been in the audience, and the lights were put out in the auditorium itself. Our coats were back there and Janet, fearing that I might hurt myself trying to get them in the dark, dashed back to run the errand herself.

On her way back, laden with coats, she managed to stumble over
some unguarded steps in the dark. She hurt one foot so badly she
couldn't stand.

Fortunately, Jay Kay Klein and his wife, Doris, were in the audience. With their help we got Janet to a nearby hospital, where they

X-rayed her foot, decided there were no breaks, and put her on crutches. (A later X ray in New York revealed that there was indeed a hairline fracture in one of the footbones, and she had to stay on crutches for six weeks.)

Syracuse was only the start of the lecture tour, and we had to drive out to Jamestown, New York, in the westernmost corner of the state, so that I might talk at Jamestown Community College.

That night I was suddenly struck by chills since I had, apparently, developed a drug reaction to the sulfa drug I was still taking. Had I told Janet I was having chills, she would have divined the cause and taken me off the pills. However, I dared not add to her troubles and, unaware of the cause, I continued to take the pills faithfully, and continued to get worse.

By the morning of the twenty-seventh, I knew I was feverish, but I had to get to Cornell for the third talk of the tour, and since Janet couldn't drive, I had to. I put a good face on it and tried to behave normally.

I managed to get to Cornell where, as bad luck would have it, they threw the book at me. There were three interviews, a cocktail party, a dinner, the talk, and then no less than two receptions, since Carl Sagan wanted to give one at his house, and the students wanted to give one on the campus, and neither would give in. I had to settle matters by agreeing to go to both.

On the morning of April 28, I drove back to New York, feeling worse than ever. We got back at 2:30 P.M. and I had just enough strength left to undress and fall into bed. Somehow I could no longer pretend that I was well, and I became semicomatose. I remember something poking at my mouth and found out later that it was a thermometer. The fever was high, of course, and a hobbling and panicky Janet managed to get me over to the hospital, where I was examined and where I was taken off the sulfa drug and put on Amphicillin.

The next day I was back to normal and got to work. In fact, I was well enough to drive to Boston on May 2 and then to Rhode Island, giving a talk in both places.

11

May 7, 1976, was the official publication date of *Murder at the ABA*, only eleven months after I had begun to write it. We had, indeed, achieved the goal of books by the next convention.

Doubleday wanted me to attend the convention as a way of promoting the book, but it was being held in Chicago, and with Janet on crutches and myself in the aftermath of two difficult trips, we just couldn't. It was disappointing all around.

12

Rae Jeppson was still alive but she was finally forced to admit that she could no longer run the house in which she had lived alone since her husband's death sixteen years before. Janet arranged to have full-time nurses in the house.

On May 9, 1976, which was Mother's Day, we took Rae to a restaurant for luncheon.[2] After lunch, we toured all the parts of the area that Rae loved—flower beds, lake shores, and so on. It was a gorgeous day and we let Rae call the shots, so that she filled her eyes with all the lovely sights of home that, we felt, she would never see again.

Then, when we could see she was tired, we took her back to the house, within which she was increasingly bedridden thereafter.

13

John Minahan had by now left *American Way* for what he felt was a better job on the West Coast. I had written twenty-one essays for him.

Taking over was his second in command, Diana Jones, a very sweet and pretty young woman, with whom I had no trouble. My essays went on with no perceptible jog.

14

As a result of the "Nova" program I had taped at Cold Spring Harbor the previous October, I had received an invitation to speak at the laboratories there.

The invitation had originally been for February, but I agreed only on condition that the talk be delayed till May so that it would be possible for Janet to do some nature sight-seeing.

Alas, when May came, Janet was on crutches, but we had to go

---

[2] Chaucy would not join us. She said it would be Rae's last Mother's Day and she should be with her daughter only. We pointed out that Chaucy had always behaved like a daughter to Rae, but Chaucy was adamant.

through with it, of course. We drove out to Cold Spring Harbor on May 15 and, crutches and all, Janet managed to negotiate Sagamore Hill and immerse herself in Theodore Roosevelt, whose home it had been. The next morning we visited an arboretum, which was gorgeous, and toured the laboratories under the guidance of James Watson.

It was all far better than we had a right to expect and, of course, it was all due to Janet, who gamely maneuvered her crutches and never allowed herself to grow sulky and self-pitying at the difficulty.

She was progressing, though, and the crutches were becoming less and less necessary. On May 22, she went to her mother's with me and, for the first time since the accident, she did the driving.

15

I let myself be persuaded to read some of my stories at the Brooklyn Museum on May 23 for a token fee. It was my first time reading, rather than speaking, and it had its pleasures, but I was dreadfully conscious of how far short of Harlan Ellison I fell as a reader.

16

It was college-commencement season. Over the Memorial Day weekend, I spoke at commencements at Drexel University and Ursinus College.

In Boston, David, who had taken a special course as a computer operator, had accepted a temporary job in the field to fill in for a hospitalized employee and had apparently given satisfaction.

As for Robyn, who had completely recovered from her knee injury, she had successfully completed her sophomore year as well.

Two more commencements came at Ramapo College on June 6 and at Kean College on June 10. It was the first time I had given four commencement addresses in a single season.

17

Janet was off the crutches now and walking just about normally. She did not come with me to the last two commencements, for she was now at Rae's bedside almost continually.

Meanwhile, I wrote a science-fiction story for an industrial firm that manufactured lasers. They wanted to publish it as a booklet that might serve as an interesting think-piece for its customers, and I called it "Think."

18

When I came back from Kean College on June 10, I found a message from Janet waiting for me. Her mother had died at 4 P.M.

Janet had been with her all that last day, sitting at her bedside for six hours. As Janet sensed the end approaching, she said, "I love you, Mother." Those were the last words Rae heard.

Rae stirred and whispered, "I love you, too," and those were the last words she spoke. A short while after, with Janet holding her hand, life peacefully ebbed away.

She died five months short of her eightieth birthday.

On June 15, we attended a memorial service for her. John and Maureen Jeppson had come in from California to attend. Janet and I sat in the first row and I kept my arm firmly around her while she wept quietly.

19

Rae's death meant there was the house to be disposed of. By Rae's will, it was Janet who inherited the house in which she had lived with her parents for years and that still held many of her youthful possessions.

I had thought, when I had first come to New York and gotten to know Rae, that if Janet ever inherited the house, she would want to move into it, and I was resigned to that.

As it turned out, however, Janet was not keen on suburban living and, now that we had found a satisfactory apartment, did not wish to leave Manhattan. (That suited me.) This meant, though, that she would have to face some months of disposing of its contents. Some she kept, some went to relatives and friends, but most went to various charitable organizations.

The one thing she did that she later bitterly regretted was to sell the grand piano at which she had sat and played uncounted times. There was just no room for it in our apartment and we got an upright piano instead. Once the deed was done, however, she found she could not reconcile herself to it and she found herself hating the upright as a poor and miserable substitute.

20

While Janet made a beginning at the long and formidable task of selling the house, I put together a third batch of limericks under the title of *Still More Lecherous Limericks*.

The matter of *Isaac Asimov's Science Fiction Magazine* (or *IASFM*, as I was beginning to think of it) was also progressing. On June 21 I spent the morning at Davis Publications having photographs taken of myself. It was Joel's plan to have my picture on the cover for issue after issue, as Alfred Hitchcock's was on his magazine. That did not strike me as a good idea, since I have strong opinions as to the limited nature of my visual appeal, but I was overridden.

21

For two years, Shell Oil had been running what it called the "Bicentennial Minute." Each evening there would be a one-minute presentation of something that had taken place two hundred years ago that day. And each day some other celebrity or semicelebrity would do the presenting.

Finally, after Shell had worked its way through 737 celebrities, they reached me as the 738th. On June 23, I taped a Bicentennial Minute for presentation on July 7 (the 738th Bicentennial Minute). It dealt with a bomb threat to Congress that was received on July 7, 1776—but was not carried through.

22

On the night of June 24, while Janet was in New Rochelle working on the house, I seized the opportunity to stay up late and do work on a manuscript to which I had been asked to write an Introduction. At about 1 A.M. I sniffed smoke.

I got out of bed, wandered through the apartment, and followed my nose to the door. I looked through the peephole and found the hall full of smoke.

For the first time in my life I was in a building that was on fire— and there I was, alone in an apartment on the thirty-third floor.

What had happened, apparently, was that there was an explosion and fire in an apartment on the twenty-ninth floor. The firemen had arrived eventually and by the time the smoke had penetrated my consciousness, the fire was under control. So well constructed was Park Ten that the fire had remained confined to the apartment in which it had originated.

Afraid that Janet might hear distorted news of the fire on the radio or in the newspapers, I called her on the morning of the twenty-fifth and told her the story in as humorous a fashion as I could.

It didn't help. She broke into tearful lamentations at the thought that I might have been fried in my bed, and no amount of my insistence that I had at no time been in even the slightest danger helped.

23

Scheduled for Bicentennial Day, July 4, 1976, was a parade of beautiful sailing ships ("tall ships") up the Hudson River. When Janet first heard of the plan the previous spring, she made reservations at a motel on the Hudson River so that she might watch the display.

We got into the motel room about noon, and with us were Stanley and Ruth, who had come to join us. The room we were in had windows angled southward so that we could see the ships coming northward from the harbor.

Immediately across the corridor was another room which was, through an incredible stroke of luck, empty, and the windows of which angled northward. A co-operative chambermaid left the door of the room open and Janet could watch the ships moving northward toward the George Washington bridge.

She kept dashing from room to room in a mad attempt to watch the ships coming and going simultaneously, while the television set remained on in both rooms so that she could see things at close quarters as well. Finally, even Janet had enough and, sated, all four of us left the motel for a jubilant dinner at an Italian restaurant.[3]

24

On July 9, we left for Rensselaerville for the fifth consecutive year. This time we arrived on a Friday, even though the program did not begin till Sunday. It meant we had two days entirely to ourselves, and that was delightful. We had a chance to visit with Hal Williams, who

[3] If anything more were needed to make the Bicentennial Day one of triumph, it was the news that came later that evening that Israel had organized a commando raid that had rescued a hundred or so hostages being held by terrorists in the Ugandan capital of Entebbe. The terrorists were killed and the airport was shot up. How I enjoyed the discomfiture of that bloody tyrant and comic-opera clown, Idi Amin of Uganda.

ran the institute and whom ordinarily we scarcely saw; to dine in relative privacy; and to ramble about freely by day and by night.

This time we had persuaded Ben and Barbara Bova to come. The program was to deal with space colonies, and the Bovas fit as though they had been manufactured for it. And, of course, Izzie and Annie Adler were present, also.

As was invariably the case, all went beautifully, and on the last morning, July 15, the festivities ended with Terri Rapoport (who had been an attendee two years before, but who now ran the show with intelligence and efficiency) presenting me with a plaque that, in essence, praised me for my suave way with women.

While Terri read from the plaque I slipped my arm around her waist. Since she was barely five feet tall, I misjudged and my hand ended on her right breast. There was laughter. I looked down in surprise and said, "Oh that's just the Asimov grip."

And from the audience, Ben Bova called out, "Is that anything like the swine flu?" I was wiped out again.[4]

I got back that evening to discover that advance copies of *The Bicentennial Man and Other Stories* had been received, and we then had dinner at Ruth Schoonmaker's. She lived in Park Ten also, and was a trustee of the White Institute. Tall, large, and hearty, she routinely took care of our apartment while we were gone, and we returned the compliment when she was gone.

25

While I had been in Rensselaerville, I wrote the first draft of my twenty-seventh Black Widowers story, "The Sports Page." I took it in to *EQMM* on July 19, and it appeared in the April 1977 issue of the magazine.

Meanwhile, I had to write a Christmas story for *Boys' Life*. On July 23, I wrote one called "The Thirteenth Day of Christmas,"[5] and I jubilantly thought it the cleverest children's detective story I had ever written. Robyn had arrived on a visit that day so I gave it to her to read and she agreed with me.

Unfortunately, and inexplicably, *Boys' Life* rejected it. That was perhaps because the story involved the Soviet legation to the UN and possible terrorist activity against them. *Boys' Life* may have felt it was too politically oriented.

[4] In the great world outside, the Democratic national convention nominated Jimmy Carter for President and Fritz Mondale for Vice President.
[5] See *The Key Word and Other Stories*.

In any case, I tried *EQMM* and I was rather astonished when it was taken. Perhaps the motif that made it unacceptable to *Boys' Life* was the very thing that made it right for *EQMM*. At any rate, the story appeared in the July 1977 *EQMM*.

26

Brad Darrach, a very pleasant and intelligent writer of about my age, came to interview me for *People* magazine. He explained that he planned to interview me periodically and to go places with me in an effort to get a rounded picture of me. For instance, Ben Bova and I were slated to go out to Long Island to do a TV bit about the movie *2001*, and Brad asked if he could go with us. Why not?

27

Janet turned fifty on August 6, 1976, and while the day wore on, festivities kept her mind off her age. Chaucy and Les Bennetts arrived and we had a good Chinese dinner. After dinner, Ruth Schoonmaker came up to join us.

The next day, though, Janet, conscious of her half century, and missing her mother badly, mourned her departed youth.

28

My magazine was approaching closer and closer. On August 8, I wrote an editorial for the first issue in my usual friendly and informal style, speaking directly to the reader. It struck the note I wanted to maintain and that I knew George would go along with. In fact, he wrote a set of directions to prospective writers, outlining what we wanted, in very much the same friendly style.

I began to feel good about the magazine.

29

Larry Ashmead had now been at Simon and Schuster for nine months and he suggested I do a book on the various ways in which the world might come to an end. By a peculiar coincidence I had just written an article on that very subject, which I called "A Choice of Catastrophes" (and which eventually appeared in the March 1977 *Popular Mechanics*).

I therefore said I would love to do a book on the subject for him, and Larry was delighted. He promptly set about putting the wheels in motion.

30

By August 20 (David's twenty-fifth birthday), Brad had enough material to feel he ought to get photographs. A woman photographer arrived and proceeded to take what seemed like hundreds of pictures.[6]

31

Earlier in the year, Janet had seen advertisements for an "astronomy cruise" to Bermuda. She wanted very much to go, and I had signed us up for it.

On August 21, 1976, we therefore boarded the *Statendam* (on which we had taken our very first cruise to see the Apollo 17 liftoff 3½ years before).

On August 22, we went on deck where Fred Hess, a planetarium expert, pointed out the star patterns visible to the naked eye. It was the first time I had ever had a chance to have the sky described by an expert. It was a beautiful mild night and the sky was more splendid than a planetarium dome could have been. Janet used her binoculars to look at the objects described, and the high point came when we saw the Andromeda Galaxy for the first time. If the cruise had ended at that point, we would have had our money's worth.

We arrived in Bermuda before sunrise on the twenty-third, and I was up on deck to see the sun lift above the horizon. The very first little bulge of light was apple-green, which meant I had seen the "green flash."

We remained four days at Bermuda, and it was delightful. (We had never been there before; the Caribbean cruise of the previous February, which had been slated to make its first stop there, had been unable to do so because of rough seas.)

The main activity was the observation period each night at a farm spot inland, where various people set up their telescopes and everyone took turns in looking.

---

[6] Meanwhile, Ford had narrowly defeated Ronald Reagan for the Republican nomination for the presidency. Senator Robert Dole was nominated for the vice presidency. Dole terrified me. He seemed to have the venom of Nixon and McCarthy.

That was not all. Peter Nelson (a middle-aged botanist with a heart of gold) took Janet and myself through the island's botanical gardens on the twenty-third with such a wealth of information for us that Janet might as well have been in the Garden of Eden, and the joy in her face made me glow.

We also took a tour in a glass-bottom boat, visited the aquarium and the zoo, wandered about the streets and shops of Hamilton, and in all ways enjoyed ourselves.

While we were doing this, I wrote my twenty-eighth Black Widowers tale, "The Second Best." Inspired by the presidential campaign, I had this one contain a puzzle involving presidential campaigns of the past. It didn't occur to me, unfortunately, that the story couldn't be published till after the campaign was over and that it would then be timely no longer.

Fred Dannay rejected it and I had to retire it for publication in what I hoped would eventually be a third Black Widowers collection.

We left Bermuda on the twenty-sixth and were in New York on the twenty-eighth. The cruise had been a complete success.

32

We bought a new car on September 8, and moved up in the world. Until then, I had owned only Plymouths and Fords; now I owned a Dodge. It was a smaller car than my most recent Ford, but I had headrests, leanback seats, and power windows for the first time.

What I also had was a mystery. Four days after I had obtained the car I went down into the garage to take it on an inaugural drive, and found it was completely and utterly dead. There was nothing to be done on a Sunday, but the next day, I managed to get it started from another car's battery, then took it cautiously down to the dealer's garage. I had it fiddled with and brought it back. By September 18, a Saturday this time, it was dead again.

I hit the ceiling with a thud that could be heard for miles and called my lawyer, Don Laventhal.

One thing about lawyers is that they stay cool. "You're a writer, Isaac," he said. "Compose a letter to the Chrysler people in Detroit. Then show it to the dealer."

I did so. It didn't take me long, and the letter breathed flame and fury. Fortunately, the dealer was open on Saturday. I took a taxi there, charged in, cornered the boss in his office, and read him the letter. It rather stirred him up.

He got a new battery, drove me down to the Park Ten garage, and (while wearing his business suit) replaced my battery. Then he started looking over the electrical attachments from headlights to taillights. He was nearly at the taillights, when he called out loudly, "Aha!!"

When the trunk opened, a light within automatically went on; when it closed, it automatically went out—except that in this particular car, it *didn't* go out. All the while the car sat in the garage, the lit interior of the trunk (invisibly lit, for the light could not be seen from outside) drained the battery.

"I will fix this," he said, "so the light will go out when you close the trunk."

"No," I said, "remove the bulb."

He did.

By September 22, with the car still alive, Janet and I made our first trip together in it. We went to Yale, where we had dinner and I gave a talk. We spent most of our time wondering if the car would be all right in the morning. It was. It had been cured.

33

While all this was going on, I finished *The Hugo Winners*, *Volume III* on September 10, and that night attended a Gilbert and Sullivan Society meeting, with Brad Darrach in attendance. That was the occasion on which I gave an impromptu speech (as William S. Gilbert) in a little amateur re-creation of an evening with Gilbert and Sullivan and their friends. I also recited a bab ballad with incredible brio and overacting while Brad's photographer took endless photographs.

On September 17, Lester and I cohosted a Trap Door Spiders dinner, at which Brad Darrach was my guest. He wanted to bring in the photographer, but she was a woman. I asked for a dispensation from the rest of the members, but Jean Le Corbeiller (a dryly humorous mathematician) objected, not on the ground that she was a woman but that she was a photographer. He objected to the publicity, so she didn't get in.

George Scithers was there, and an extraordinary change had come over him. Ordinarily, he was a quiet fellow who let others do the talking. This time, however, he was virtually manic with joy, and all he could talk about was *IASFM*. He had clearly thrown himself into the editor's job with all his heart and all his mind, and I was delighted. Clearly, I had chosen the right man.

34

On September 29, Brad Darrach came to see me one last time, with the photographer. The idea was to take a picture of me sitting on an armchair constructed of my books.

I objected. For one thing I thought it would be in poor taste. For another, I didn't want to pull my books out of the bookcase. They were carefully arranged in chronological order and would be troublesome to put back.

Brad persisted and finally beat me down. With very poor grace, I took out the books and piled them up about a hassock to make an imitation armchair, sat in it, and then put everything back.

35

On October 4, I completed *The Collapsing Universe* and took it in to Walker.

I immediately got started on another collection of science essays from miscellaneous sources, my fifth. I called this one *The Beginning and the End* after the most ambitious single essay it contained.

36

The presidential campaign featured debates between Carter and Ford, which I watched with my heart in my mouth. Carter, I thought, did worse than I had hoped, partly because he did not enunciate clearly. Ford, on the other hand, did much better than I had thought him capable of doing.

On October 15, I tried to watch the single debate between Mondale and Dole, the two vice-presidential candidates. Unfortunately, I was at the Trap Door Spiders at the time, and when I turned on the television set, Gilbert Cant (the prototype of the terrible-tempered Tom Trumbull of the Black Widowers) objected. Between my desire to see the debate, and the offense I took at Cant's tactless language, I stormed out of the place, went home, and watched it there.

I was glad I did. Dole's Nixonian viciousness must have turned off many voters, while Mondale's smooth gentlemanliness must have turned on an equal number. I thought, then, and had no reason to change my mind later, that it was that debate that held on to just enough Democratic votes to make the difference.

That same day, Janet finally sold the house in New Rochelle after having spent four months in the harassing details of cleaning it out and putting it into shape for sale.

44

Autobiography

1

The Carborundum Company wanted to give me an award for excellence, but I had to go to Niagara Falls to get it, and I had to be there on October 21.

By a curious coincidence, I was heading out to Western New York at that very time of year. It was the only trip I was making there in all of 1976, so that it was possible to do it. As it happened, however, the coincidence was entirely too good, and on October 21 I was committed to a talk at Alfred University. I explained that I could not be in two places at the same time.

The Carborundum people exploded. It had been Alfred University that had nominated me for the award, so how dare they hire me to talk on the evening of the award?

They called Alfred and in no time at all the Alfred talk was pushed forward two days. I could talk at Alfred on the nineteenth, at Brockford Community College on the twentieth, and be in Niagara Falls on the twenty-first.

To sweeten this extension of the trip, the Carborundum people insisted on sending a limousine for me that would take me everywhere, provide me with picnic lunches en route, and pay for all expenses. There was no way we could refuse the enveloping fog of corporate generosity.

On October 19, a limousine was waiting for us at 7:00 A.M., and over the next four days were indeed chauffeured everywhere. Going and coming, the car was laden with a food hamper that contained incredible delicacies in amounts that were at least five times what we could eat.

We were impressed by this royal treatment, but we could never relax with it. We were too old by far to take to such things. We missed the privacy and flexibility of being alone in our own car, and felt guilty of ingratitude because of it.

The luxury continued in Niagara Falls itself. We toured the Falls and the electric-generating plant. We had lunch in a revolving restaurant in a tower overlooking the Falls, and a fancy award dinner in a museum in Buffalo.

The award itself consisted of a modernistic bronze sculpture of something that looked like a woman's torso with a huge hole in the abdomen. Eventually, it was shipped to our apartment and, after some experimenting, we found a place for it in the living room. Oddly enough, I grew to like it.

We were home on October 22, and the next day I was finished with *The Beginning and the End.*

2

November 2 was Election Day. I voted the straight Democratic ticket at 8:30 A.M. and spent the rest of the day waiting. My side hadn't won a presidential election since 1964, and I wasn't at all sure we would win now. The polls said it would be razor-edge close, and it was.

It wasn't till 1:00 A.M. that I finally decided Carter would win, and even then I went to sleep not entirely confident there might not be a last-minute change with the final dribble of votes. Fortunately, there wasn't.

3

On November 12, I discovered that Mary K. would soon be leaving Houghton Mifflin. That was almost as great a shock as Larry's departure from Doubleday.

4

On November 15, we picked up the November 22, 1976, copy of *People* magazine, with Brad Darrach's article on me. I had already seen advertisements of it, including one on the back page of the New York *Times* in which I was shown seated on my armchair of books. And there it was in the article itself.

Another of the photographs showed me embracing Janet with my left arm encircling her neck and my right reaching down to her left buttock and squeezing it. I admit this was rather customary for me, but I had never thought this would be put on display before countless millions of strangers who might be leafing through the magazine. Fortunately, Janet didn't seem to mind.

The article itself was well written and good-natured. Such articles can easily eviscerate a subject in casual phrases here and there, but Brad had nothing but good things to say of me.

5

The Collapsing Universe seemed to be creating great interest, even in advance of publication. On November 19, Beth Walker called to tell me that the Literary Guild had picked up the book as an alternate selection for May 1977.

6

For once we did not go to Chaucy's for Thanksgiving. With great difficulty we prevailed upon her to let us take her out. After all, now that Rae were gone there was no reason she should feel compelled to prepare the feast for family reasons.

As it happened, Robyn was coming to visit us for Thanksgiving and she joined us, making it a party of five.

Robyn stayed till Sunday, and after she left I consoled myself by writing a small Valentine's Day science-fiction story, which *American Way* had requested of me. I called it "True Love." I took it in on November 29 and it appeared in the February 1977 issue of the magazine.

7

Janet and I went to Philadelphia on December 2 so that I could speak at the University of Pennsylvania that evening, and our hotel was across the street from Philadelphia General Hospital.

It was an exercise in nostalgia for Janet, for she had served a year's internship at the hospital in 1952–53, and now it was being phased out as a medical institution. On the morning of December 3, we walked over to the hospital, and Janet wandered somewhat disconsolately over its grounds. It was as though a year of her life were also being phased out.

She got into the building in which the room she lived in had been located and made her way up to its actual site. The area was now devoted to experimental animals.

"Well," said Janet, "it's gone up in the world."

8

On December 13, I finally finished *The Golden Door* after fully two years of on-and-off work. Naturally, with one book done, I had to

start another, and that was *Mars, the Red Planet*, the third in my astronomy series for Chaucy. I began it on December 14.

9

The first issue of *Isaac Asimov's Science Fiction Magazine* was
published on December 16, 1976. It began its life as a quarterly so that
the first issue was dated Spring 1977. On its cover was an incredibly
dignified photograph of myself, with dark jacket and four-in-hand tie.

Inside, we had two stories by John Varley (one under the pseudonym of Herb Boehm), whom I considered the very best writer to have
come into the field since Heinlein. Also included was an almost self-
contained portion of *Time Storm*, a forthcoming novel by Gordon
Dickson.

Charles Brown, the publisher of *Locus* (the science-fiction news-
magazine), contributed the first of a book-review column that was
planned for each issue, and Martin Gardner contributed the first of a
mathematical puzzle series.

As for myself, I contributed the editorial, and my story "Think!,"
which had appeared only in an advertising booklet previous to that.

As a way of celebrating, George Scithers brought Joel Davis as his
guest to a meeting of the Trap Door Spiders, which he was cohosting
on December 17. I was afraid Joel might find us too eccentric for com-
patibility, but Gilbert Cant engaged him in lively conversation so I
think our good publisher enjoyed himself.

10

I had, for a while, been exchanging letters with Martin Greenberg,
who was first at Florida International University and then at Michigan
State University, over the possibility of anthologizing some of my stories. The first time I received a letter from him, I responded by asking
cautiously if he were the Martin Greenberg who had once owned
Gnome Press.

When he answered in a very puzzled fashion that he was not, I
urged him to use his middle initial, at the very least, if he had one, if he
expected to deal fruitfully with the science-fiction world.[1] From then
on, he signed himself Martin H. Greenberg, and I invariably addressed
my letters to him, "Dear Marty the Other."

He and Joseph Olander (also of Florida International University)

[1] Lester del Rey suggested that he change his name altogether, but I thought that
was going too far.

had conceived the project of preparing an anthology of a hundred short-short science-fiction pieces (twice the number that Groff Conklin and I had anthologized fifteen years before), and they wanted me in on it. They would prepare Xerox copies of perhaps twice the necessary number; I would weed out the best and write blurbs and an overall Introduction.

In the end, I agreed. On December 21, I signed a contract with Doubleday for the book.

11

Having given up laboring over Thanksgiving, Chaucy could not be talked out of her Christmas feast. Rae, of course, was not there, and she was badly missed, but young Leslie made up the number by being accompanied by her fiancé, George, who had run for political office the month before (and had lost) and who was a very attractive man. Unfortunately, the engagement broke up eventually.

12

Actor José Ferrer visited us on December 30. Having heard of *Asimov's Guide to Shakespeare*, he arrived under the mistaken impression that I was a scholarly Shakespearean who could be useful to him in his work. I felt guilty at having to disappoint him and gave him a copy of the *Guide* as compensation.

13

The year 1976 saw twelve books published:

170. *"The Dream," "Benjamin's Dream," and "Benjamin's Bicentennial Blast"* (privately printed)
171. *Asimov on Physics* (Doubleday)
172. *Murder at the ABA* (Doubleday)
173. *How Did We Find Out About Atoms?* (Walker)
174. *Good Taste* (Apocalypse)
175. *The Planet That Wasn't* (Doubleday)
176. *The Bicentennial Man and Other Stories* (Doubleday)
177. *More Lecherous Limericks* (Walker)
178. *More Tales of the Black Widowers* (Doubleday)
179. *Alpha Centauri, the Nearest Star* (Lothrop, Lee & Shepard)

14

On January 2, 1977, I was fifty-seven years old, and for the first time since 1969 the del Reys were not part of the celebration. That had to be delayed but we had dinner with Chaucy, Les, and their son, Bruce.

15

Since the previous September I had been interviewed every Thursday afternoon for a program on the Canadian radio network. The topic was always some scientific point currently in the news, and there was generally another person being interviewed with me—he the particular specialist on that particular topic and I the perennial generalist.

I was very faithful about this and even interrupted my lunch in the revolving restaurant when I was out in Niagara Falls the previous October in order to be interviewed.

On Wednesday, January 5, however, hours were spent by the engineer of Park Ten on our refrigerator, which was giving us trouble, and I was sufficiently eroded by exasperation to give in to Janet's demand that I take a nap. I took the phone off the hook to avoid interruptions.

I awoke refreshed, went back to my typewriter, and put the phone back on the hook. It rang at once. I picked it up and a voice said reproachfully, "You bad boy! Where were you?"

It was the Canadian program. What I had forgotten was that on this particular week I was going to be in Philadelphia on Thursday to give a talk to IBM people there and simply would not be able to get to a telephone, so that the interview was being held on Wednesday instead.

It was incredibly humiliating to have forgotten an appointment and it was with difficulty that they could get me to stop apologizing. Fortunately, Lester del Rey agreed to stand in for me the next day and (of course) did a marvelous job.

Unfortunately, January 10 was our delayed birthday celebration with the del Reys, and Lester seized the opportunity to discuss the matter of having to pitch in for friends who were growing senile and could no longer be depended upon to fulfill their obligations.

I had no complaints, though. It took a long time for me to hear the end of it, but it would have taken a longer time for Lester to hear the end of it if the situation had been reversed.

16

I was slated to give still another talk in Philadelphia on the evening of January 16, and could, as a result, visit the local Philadelphia convention of "Philcon." There I met John Varley for the first time. He was young, handsome, and about six and a half feet tall. It seemed unfair for one person to have all those positive physical characteristics and to be so good a writer besides.

17

January 19, 1977, was the twenty-seventh anniversary of the publication of *Pebble in the Sky*, my first book. For eleven years I had been renewing the copyrights of my magazine stories, one by one, and now I had to face the first of the copyright renewals of my books.[2]

18

Murder Ink was a small bookstore on the Upper West Side, which had been established by Dilys Winn. It was devoted to the murder mystery, and by the time Dilys sold it to Carol Bremer, it had made itself a landmark.

Both young women were fertile with promotional notions, and one of them was to take mystery enthusiasts to Mohonk Mountain House for a weekend in January, one that was to be devoted to all sorts of mystery gimmicks and was to be called "Dead of Winter."

I was asked to come along as a speaker, and when we heard it was to be at Mohonk, we accepted at once. We were driven up to the resort on a no-smoking bus (itself a fine idea) on January 27.

Phyllis Whitney, a writer of Gothic novels, spoke charmingly the next day and I followed with a talk that dealt mainly with *Murder at the ABA*. There were also lectures on self-defense and on makeup.

At one point I was kidnaped at "gunpoint" by an extraordinarily beautiful young woman and taken to an unused lavatory where the rest of the group was to find me through deduction from planted clues—except that they never did. For one mad moment I thought the young

[2] The next day, Jimmy Carter was inaugurated the thirty-ninth President of the United States.

woman would stay with me in the lavatory, but the guarding was taken over by a couple of uninteresting young men.

Present at the festivities was Walter Gibson who, forty years before, had been "Maxwell Grant," the man who had written *The Shadow* novels from which my father had learned English. He was in his eighties now, still vigorous, and a delightful sleight-of-hand performer.

Bernie and Essie Fonoroff showed up unexpectedly. Bernie was wearing a beard and I would not have recognized him had Essie not been with him.

It was all delightful even down to the clothed life-sized plastic dummies scattered here and there to lend a sinister atmosphere,[3] and we went home on the thirtieth completely happy.

19

For a couple of years now, I had been hounding Doubleday to put out new printings of those of my science-fiction books that were no longer in hard-covers. (They were all in print in soft-covers, to be sure.)

Once Cathleen became my editor, I put it up to her and she said she would look into the matter. I left it at that, for I knew that Cathleen would do what she said she would do.

And she did. On February 3, Cathleen and I had lunch together and she told me that Doubleday planned to put my out-of-print books into uniform triple-volume editions. Two would be put out to begin with. One would contain *Earth Is Room Enough, The End of Eternity,* and *Pebble in the Sky,* and the other would contain *The Martian Way and Other Stories, The Currents of Space,* and *The Stars, Like Dust—.*

It was on this occasion that Cathleen and I talked about the possibility of an autobiography, as described in the introduction to *In Memory Yet Green.*

20

Ever since I had been working with Harry Walker, the schedule of my talks had been growing heavier. They had even invaded the winter season, which until then I had managed to keep fairly free of travel.

[3] The New York *Times* ran a photograph, a few days later, showing a panoramic view of the audience at one of the talks, with Janet and me in the front row and with one of the dummies on the other side of me. I was identified as "Isaac Asimov seated next to the dummy" and Janet pointed out that there was a certain ambiguity there but I assured her everyone would know which of my neighbors was the dummy.

I enjoyed the talks and sometimes the fringe activities as when, on February 10, I was taken to a farm while engaging in talks at IBM in East Fishkill and shown newborn lambs, allowed to pet a buffalo on the horn and, that night, even encouraged to look through a telescope in the snow so that I could see Saturn in all its beauty for the first time in my life.

But the traveling was tiresome and I found myself dragging. Janet began to get anxious, but I would not listen to any suggestion that I cut down on my engagements. It irritated me to be reminded that I might be subject to human limitations—especially as I grew older.

21

I was very fond of the TV situation comedy "Laverne and Shirley," and on February 15 there was a touching episode involving Shirley and her ne'er-do-well father. At least it touched me deeply, and when it was over I thought I would call Robyn, who was now in her junior year at Boston College.

She answered the phone and with a fine affectation of carelessness, I said, "Have you seen 'Laverne and Shirley,' Robyn?"

She said, "One moment, Dad." Then she called off to her room-mates, "Guys! My father wants to know if I watched 'Laverne and Shirley.'"

There followed wild laughter, and Robyn came back to the phone and said, "Yes I did, Dad."

I said, "Why all the laughter?"

"Well, Dad," said Robyn, "we were all watching and as they got drippier and drippier about fathers and daughters, and knowing that you always watch the show, I said, 'Oh God, my father is going to call me as soon as this is over.' And you did."

I suppose it *is* humorous to have a father who's so predictable.

22

Martin Harry Greenberg and Joseph Olander were editing a series of books on various science-fiction writers, each consisting of a dozen or so critical essays on their works. One of the first to be published was to be *Asimov*.

I received the manuscript of the collection on February 17, and read it with mounting astonishment. Some of the essays were fiendishly clever in interpreting my symbolism and intentions, but it was all news to me. However, I remembered Gotthard Gunther's remark to me con-cerning "Nightfall" a quarter-century before, and I was prepared to assume that the critics understood my fiction better than I did and that I had put in more than I knew.

I acceded to the publisher's request that I add an Epilog, and wrote "Asimov on Asimov," in which I pointed out why I couldn't possibly have inserted all the subtleties into my fiction that I was accused of having done. And then I refuted my own arguments and pointed out that I might have done so anyway.

Let the readers judge for themselves, I decided.

23

Robyn made up for the disappointment of the year before by arriving on February 19, 1977, to celebrate her twenty-second birthday with us. She remained with us till February 23, and on that day there was time for a concluding celebration, since Walker finally decided to do a collection of my juvenile detective stories involving my junior-high-school detective of "The Thirteenth Day of Christmas."

I only had four stories involving him and they needed five, so I had written one "The Key Word" especially for the book. Eventually, Walker decided to call it *The Key Word and Other Stories*.

On February 23, also, I finished *Mars, the Red Planet*.

24

On March 2, I put together my thirteenth collection of F & SF essays, which I called *Quasar, Quasar, Burning Bright*, after the title of one of the included essays.

25

George Scithers had suggested that I write a Black Widowers story for *IASFM*. It wasn't a bad idea. After all, I had written three that had appeared in F & SF, so why not one in my own magazine?

I needed something that would be suitable for a science-fiction magazine and, having just finished a book on Mars, I thought of a gimmick that would involve the appearance of the Martian sky. On March 8, then, I wrote my twenty-ninth Black Widowers story, "The Missing Item," which George liked and accepted.

26

About a month before, Cathleen and I had discussed the possibility of my writing my autobiography. On March 9, more on impulse than anything else, I began it, to see how it would go—and it went like an iceboat in a strong wind. In my father's year in Miami Beach, he had sent me a number of letters (at my request) concerning his early life, and these came in very handy indeed.

After racing through no less than fifty pages of manuscript, however, I found that I was still only three years old and just arriving in the United States. The notion dawned on me that it was going to be a long autobiography, and I began to worry about Doubleday's reaction.

27

On March 16, the second issue of *IASFM*, Summer 1977, was published. Again a photograph of myself was on the cover—a profile shot this time, in a sport shirt and bolo tie.

The issue contained two tiny stories of mine, each five hundred words long or less. One, "About Nothing," had appeared nearly two years earlier on a postcard published in Great Britain. A young man named George Hay had conceived the idea of "story postcards" in form analogous to the more common "picture postcards." I don't know how well he succeeded.

The second one, "Sure Thing," was written especially for the magazine.

Both were gag stories, ending in outrageous puns that I thought terribly clever. I must admit, however, that these things are matters of taste.

28

On the same day that the issue appeared, a writer named James Lincoln Collier interviewed me. I had thought that Brad Darrach's interview for *People* would represent a pinnacle for me, but Collier was interviewing me on behalf of *Readers' Digest*, which, in terms of circulation, had to be a notch higher.

29

I had been giving numerous talks to IBM groups, both in the Poughkeepsie and Philadelphia areas, all through the fall and winter, and had been doing well enough for IBM to want to pin me down to something more elaborate. I was therefore asked to come to Miami Beach.

My impulse was to refuse at once, but the World Science Fiction convention for 1977 was to be held in Miami Beach the following

Labor Day weekend, and I was actually anxious to go there if I could. It looked as though "The Bicentennial Man" might be nominated for the Hugo. If it were nominated and if it won, it would be my first award in the shorter fiction categories, and it would be nice to be there where it happened. Perhaps the trip for the IBM talk might test the practicality of going to Florida over the Labor Day weekend.

Then, too, it would offer us a chance to see the Everglades.

So I said yes, and at 10 A.M. on March 26, 1977, Janet and I boarded the train for the longest trip I had taken since my Army days thirty-one years before. We had a double room, which in some ways was more luxurious than a hotel room, since we had two bathrooms.

One discomfort was that we had to make our way to the dining car and back on four separate occasions. It meant scrabbling through six coaches filled with uncomfortable people, sprawling this way and that in an attempt to find some way of relaxing—crowded, smoky, smelly. I was altogether too conscious of our own luxurious accommodation and wondered if there might not be an uprising and if I might not be strung up on the nearest lamppost as a damned aristocrat.

We were at the Eden Roc Hotel in Miami Beach by 4 P.M. on March 27.

I gave my first talk on March 28. It wasn't a solo. Alvin Toffler was on the stage with me, and George Herman of CBS News introduced us. The whole program was done with IBM éclat, and was therefore elaborately introduced by a young magician who, in my eyes, stole the show.

That night I gave another talk to a group of journalists and, in between, I was interviewed by three different people. My time was, in fact, rather tightly occupied, and Janet and I grew rather upset at this. There we were in Miami Beach and yet we had scarcely a moment in which to relax.

Ben and Barbara Bova showed up on the evening of the twenty-eighth, for Ben was also represented by Harry Walker and Ben, too, at my recommendation, was sent down to Miami Beach. The IBM people weren't sorry, for he gave a terrific talk on the morning of the twenty-ninth. I was in the audience and loved it.

After the talk, I went out to Florida International University, where I met Joe Olander for the first time and gave a talk. In the evening I signed books at a Miami bookstore.

March 30 was our only day off, and that had been reserved for the Everglades. We were picked up by Daniel and Bettina Jackson, who were Olander's friends, and they spared nothing to show us a good time. They even brought along a "picnic lunch" which, for elaborateness and excellence, reminded me of the lunches Carborundum had supplied for us on our trip to and from Niagara Falls five months before.

The director of Everglades National Park came along with us, and for hours we toured it, filling ourselves with alligators, ravens, pelicans, mahogany trees, strangler figs, and so on. Janet, quite predictably, fell in love with the alligators and wanted to feed them, but the director told her that would spoil them and do them harm. However, when one alligator nosed up to shore when we were having lunch, he turned out to have one leg missing (bitten off in a fight, presumably), and Janet, in an agony of sympathy, insisted on feeding him some of her lunch.

Rather depressing was the carnage done by the cold snaps just ten weeks before. There had been snow in Miami in January for the first time in living memory, and temperatures had gotten down as low as 19° F in the Everglades. The tropical vegetation had no defense against freezing temperatures and there were huge patches of brown death.

We reached the southern tip of Florida and I got out of the car so that I might stare at the Gulf of Mexico—which I had never thought I would ever see.

On the thirty-first, I gave a second talk with Toffler and Herman, one that was, actually, a repeat of the first—but for a new batch of IBM people. Then, immediately after the talk, we were raced to the station and put on the train. We were home on the evening of April 1.

The trip back was more tedious than the trip there and I ended being a little dubious as to whether I could face the Miami run a second time come Labor Day.

30

There followed hard upon that the low point of my winter's heavy lecture schedule.

On April 6, I had to drive to Greenville, Pennsylvania, in the northwestern corner of the state, to talk at Thiel College. We drove much of the way through snow flurries, which did not accumulate and were no real danger, but represented a psychological hazard.

What was worse was that I came back from Florida with the beginnings of a cold that was degenerating into laryngitis, and the next day, April 7, I had to give two talks in Ohio, one at Youngstown State College and one at Cleveland State College, with informal talks, gracious luncheon and dinner chit-chat, and interviews interspersed. April 7 was virtually one solid session of talk on my part, with my voice slowly disappearing into a whispered trace and Janet almost beside herself with worry.

It was some satisfaction to me that in the three talks on the sixth and the seventh, I received three standing ovations, even though the final talk had to be carried out by whispering into a microphone.

Rather remorsefully, I tried to make things up to a very worried Janet by driving through Ashland, Pennsylvania, on the way home. It happened to be the little mining town in which Janet had been born a half century before. She had left it with her parents at the age of two, but she swore she remembered the main street.

31

We got home on the morning of April 9 and I promptly went to the Lunacon, New York's local annual science-fiction convention, where, at Janet's insistence, I wore a sign saying I had laryngitis so that people would not expect me to speak much.

Nevertheless, I did give a speech in a semiwhisper, talking about my autobiography and how I had discovered a published story of mine, "The Weapon," that I had thought no longer existed. It was in this way that I managed to get a copy of the magazine in which it appeared from Forrie Ackerman within a week.

At home I found a letter from Lloyd Roth—who had reached retirement age. I was, and am, rather grimly thankful that my own profession is such that nothing but death can retire me.

32

On April 14, I received a call from *Time*. They needed an essay on what life in the United States would be like if the energy supply failed, and (they said) the editorial staff had decided I was just the man to do it.

I said (rather cynically, perhaps), "If you decided I was your man, then what you need is not content, but speed. Right?"

A little embarrassed, the gentleman on the telephone said, "We need it tomorrow morning."

They had it the next morning, and three days later it appeared in the April 25, 1977, issue.

33

I just managed to get it done in time, for Janet and I were heading out to Mohonk Mountain House on April 15. Stanley and Ruth, at our recommendation, were coming, too, and the four of us spent an excellent weekend together. Of course, I gave a talk while there.

34

Fred and Babbie Whipple, whom I had first met in Boston twenty-eight years before, visited us unexpectedly and briefly on April 24. Fred, now seventy, was as slim and courtly as ever.

35

April 27 was the official publication date of *The Collapsing Universe*. Advance sales were very gratifying; Pocket Books had bought the paperback rights at a generous advance, and the Walkers, very pleased, hosted a publication party at the Hayden Planetarium, the most lavish shindig of the type in seven years.

36

Even better was the Mystery Writers' of America award banquet on April 29, which Janet and I attended together for the first time since we had met at one eighteen years before.

Best of all was the Nebula awards banquet on April 30. I was toast-master and I think I did a better job at it than I had ever done in my life. Cliff Simak was there and it was the first chance I had to meet my old friend since the Boston convention six years before.

Simak was given the Grand Masters award, and was the third to win it. The first had been Heinlein, of course, and the second had been Jack Williamson. All three were eminently deserving.

As for the Nebulas themselves, all else paled when I found I had been voted the Nebula for "The Bicentennial Man" as the best novelette of the year. I had hoped for it, but had not really dared expect it.

In the midst of my jubilation, I took a good look at the Nebula and found that my name on it had been spelled "Issac Asmimov"—both names wrong. Naturally, the SFWA offered to supply me with a new one, correctly spelled, but I refused. I said, rather dryly, that the misspelling made it more valuable and a better conversation piece.

37

Then came another long trip, one that was to take me down to Newport News, Virginia. We drove southward on May 1 and I kept assuring Janet that I *would* cut down on the long trips, but some were scheduled in the future, one even as late as April 1978, and those had to be fulfilled.

On the way back, on May 3, Janet and I stopped at Williamsburg, which we had last seen that famous snowy day seven years before, and we were home on May 4.

38

May 8 was Mother's Day, and for the first time, both Janet and I were motherless.[4] That Mother's Day I therefore spent in secular fashion at the New School for Social Research, where I took part in a panel on "Judaism and the Future." I had protested I knew nothing about Judaism, but the sponsors of the panel insisted and my talk was the only one that didn't mention Judaism.

I managed to get into a dispute with Elie Wiesel, who irritated me by saying he didn't trust scientists and engineers since so many of them had been involved in the Holocaust.

I maintained that a persecuted group did not automatically gain virtue by the fact that they were persecuted; that all human beings were potential persecutors given power; and that persecuted groups once they gained power often became persecutors. I mentioned Jews as having become persecutors under the Maccabees. Wiesel said, "It was the only time." I said, "It was their only chance."

[4] Mary Blugerman had, however, called me the day before. She was eighty-two years old now, but her voice was strong and she sounded as sharp as ever.

45

Coronary

1

On May 9, 1977, I was taking shirts to the dry cleaners at a distance of about three tenths of a mile from my apartment, and halfway there I became aware of a distinct discomfort just under my breastbone (the epigastric region) and a feeling as though I were short of breath. I stopped and the feeling passed. I started walking again, and it returned.

A chill of apprehension flooded me. I knew what it was. I had never felt the pain before but I had been waiting for it, in a way, for fifteen years.

My father had had angina pectoris at forty-two—and I had it now, at fifty-seven. My coronary arteries were clogging up. No wonder I had been feeling tired and aging through all the last half year when by the irony of circumstance my speaking schedule had been incredibly heavy.

What to do? Logically, I should make Paul Esserman my first port of call. If I told Janet of the pain, that would certainly happen. She would be on the phone in half a minute.

I might be wrong, though. It might be tension; it might be indigestion; it might be imagination. Why not wait, live normally, and observe the results? If the thing continued, I would see Esserman.

Besides, the next day I had to drive to Hartford to give a talk, and the day after that, Janet's institute was putting on their annual benefit show, of which I was the titular head, and after that there were other functions, other talks, to say nothing of my autobiography. I had no time for angina.

I carried on, therefore, and despite occasional discomfort, I could almost persuade myself that it was my imagination until May 13, 1977 (Friday the thirteenth, as it happened).

It was a busy day. Lunch with John Doherty of National Wildlife, followed by a party at Florence Freedman's (an elderly widow in the neighborhood, of whom Janet and I were very fond). Then I broke away to dash out to the monthly meeting of the Gilbert and Sullivan Society, and when that was over, I accompanied a group to the apartment of Jesse Shereff, president of the society. There I had sizable portions of a very rich and extraordinarily delicious cheesecake.

I then went home, but as I got into bed at midnight, I found that the discomfort that had been obtruding itself on my notice in the course of the day had become a severe cramp. I could not lie down, nor could I hide the fact from Janet. The pains in my epigastric region were acute.

Midnight it might be, but Janet, disregarding my panted protests, called Paul Esserman at his home. Paul said he would open his office the next day, even though it was Saturday, and I was to arrive at 11:30 A.M.

By morning, of course, the pains were gone and I felt only mildly hung over from a sleepless night, fears of angina, and the knowledge that I had to be speaking at Queensboro Library that afternoon.

Paul took an electrocardiogram and it proved to be normal. He said, "Now where was the pain last night?"

I pointed to the epigastric region and he said, "Angina is typically felt distinctly higher than that. Did you eat anything before going to bed?"

I mentioned the cheesecake.

He said, thoughtfully, "It could be gastroenteritis, a hiatus hernia, or gallstones. Don't eat anything after 6 P.M., stay away from rich, fatty foods, and we will arrange an X ray of the gall bladder."

So off I went to the Queensboro Public Library, knowing that whatever it was, I was going to have to reduce. Paul and Janet had been after me for years to do so, but now the pressure would be irresistible. The thirty pounds I had taken off thirteen years before were still off. I weighed 183 pounds on the day of the examination. I decided, morosely, that twenty more pounds would have to come off.

2

Meanwhile, it was commencement season again. On May 16, Janet and I drove to Haverford, Pennsylvania, so that I could give a commencement address at Haverford College, a Quaker-run school. On the morning of May 17, I attended a Quaker meeting for the first time in my life and found it rather unnerving. I just sat there until someone was moved to say a few words with no one else giving any sign of listening.

The commencement was held out of doors, and the president of the college asked me to speak for fifteen minutes. I announced at the start, with some braggadocio, that I would speak for fifteen minutes, and one faculty member promptly checked his watch. After the ceremony he told me I had spoken for fourteen minutes, thirty-two seconds, and he had not seen me look at a watch. How had I done it?

I said, "After speaking professionally for thirty years, I have a built-in stopwatch."

3

We drove to Philadelphia in the afternoon, and that night Janet, being hungry, suggested a late snack to be delivered by room service. I ordered a piece of cheesecake and it proved to be an unusually rich, fluffy, and delicious one.

I went to bed peacefully and woke at 1:30 A.M. of May 19, 1977, with an abdominal pain more excruciating than any I had experienced since my last bad kidney-stone attack eight years before. It was, again, in the epigastric region, higher than the kidney-stone pain, but otherwise like it.

Unable to lie, sit, or stand, I staggered back and forth for an hour while a white and frightened Janet watched. I wouldn't let her say anything. "Don't talk," I said, "just listen."

I then went on to explain, rather raggedly and incoherently, that if anything happened to me I didn't want weeping and wailing and whining. She was just to live her life normally because my will would take care of her and of my children, and I wanted her to know she had made me very happy in those years that I had been with her.

It didn't seem to reassure her.

Then at 3:00 A.M., the pain began to ebb away precisely as it would in my kidney-stone attacks, and I made motions with my hand as though I were leading an orchestra and indicating a softer and softer diminuendo. When it was gone, I got into bed and lay there on my back with all the relief of nonpain after agony.

"How do you feel, Isaac?" asked Janet.

"As though I'd died and gone to heaven," I said, and drifted off.

After I woke, there was a mild, continuing epigastric pain that made me feel poorly, but I followed my schedule. The show must go on. I attended a Planned Parenthood luncheon and, though I ate little, I gave my talk, which went well.

4

In the evening, Janet called Paul Esserman long-distance, told him what had happened, and put me on. He wanted me to describe exactly what happened, and seemed irritated when I told him I had once again eaten cheesecake.

"What was the pain like, Isaac?"

"Exactly like a kidney stone in the wrong place, Paul."

Paul said, "That's exactly how gallstones are described by people who have both. Janet says you've already made an appointment for a gall-bladder X ray. Till then, take it easy, rest, and for heaven's sake, stay away from rich food. A piece of cheesecake is just the thing to trigger gall-bladder contractions and cause the pain."

5

On May 19, we spent the morning sight-seeing while I countered Janet's repeated questions as to how I felt with a gaiety I did not exactly feel. In the evening I gave my third talk of the trip, this one to a group of cardiologists.

I was back in New York on May 20 and that night attended a Trap Door Spiders meeting at which I was far from my usual scintillating self. The deficiency was so marked that I had to explain, with considerable embarrassment, that I might be having a gallstone problem.

6

Janet was after me to go to Paul's for another examination, but I refused any appointment till the afternoon of May 25. I was lunching with Doubleday publisher Sam Vaughan and Ken McCormick, editor-in-chief emeritus, and as nearly as I can judge from universal reports, the best-loved man in publishing, and I wanted nothing to interfere with it. I was adamant, and Janet had to agree.

That meant I had time to give a talk (without fee) for Pauline Bloom, who, thirty-five years before, had introduced me to the Brooklyn Authors' Club, and for whom, thirty years before, I had given my first public talk. I warned her not to expect a free talk from me every thirty years, however.

The next day, the twenty-fifth, I had my lunch with Sam and Ken and we discussed the autobiography. I broke the news that it would be a long one and they took it calmly.

7

I left them in very good spirits and with ample time to get to Paul's for my appointment. The weather was pleasant, I felt good—why not walk, then, and test the angina business?

It was about a mile to Paul's office and I walked it briskly and jauntily, with scarcely any discomfort. Coming to his place, I ran up a flight of stairs and burst into his office. I was panting a bit and Paul's assistants wanted to know what was the matter.

I said, "Just testing. I walked a mile to get here and ran up the stairs. See, I feel fine."

Paul, who had emerged from his office in time to hear this, sputtered, "Who told you to test yourself? That's not the way to do it. *We'll* test you. Suppose you had had a cardiac arrest? Sit down and I'll be with you in a minute." I'd never seen him angry, and I don't think he had it in him to be angry, but he must have come as close to that emotion as he could at that time.

Janet walked in a moment later and I told her about the lunch and how I had tested myself. I was quite euphoric.

Paul then came to get me, strapped me down, attached the leads, and began taking another electrocardiogram.

The instrument had not been ticking for two seconds when he came back to me to make sure the leads were all making good contacts. One look at his face and I knew everything. Poor Paul had no poker face and I am not slow of comprehension.

"Uh-oh," I muttered.

Paul said nothing. He took the full EKG, then called in his partner, Howard Gorfinkel, showed him the strip, and said, "Any doubts?"

Howard said gravely, "None whatever." They then turned to face me and Paul said, "What you had on May 18 wasn't a matter of gallstones, Isaac. You had a coronary, even though the symptoms were entirely atypical."[1]

"Oh boy," I said. "How bad?"

"A mild one. We know it was a mild one from the fact that in the seven days since you've been carrying on like mad. If it hadn't been a mild one you would have died some time in this last week, probably as you ran up the stairs to my office."

"Well, I didn't, Paul. So let's forget it and I'll be a good boy and lose weight."

"We can't forget it. You're going into the hospital. Now."

"*Why?* I've been doing fine for a week, and I've got to give a commencement address at Johns Hopkins day after tomorrow. I can't let them down."

"You'll have to."

"But if I lived a week, I can live two days more."

[1] He was, of course, chagrined at having misdiagnosed the condition, especially as he knew that there wasn't a chance in Hades I'd ever let him forget it. He would say to me afterward, "Who told you to have the pain in the epigastric region?"

"What if you die on the speaker's platform?"

"It would be an honorable death."

That got Paul, Howard, and Janet all unaccountably furious, and I could see I had no choice in the matter.

Paul asked if I wanted to "go public" on the matter. I gathered that some people didn't like to admit they had a heart problem lest it affect their employability. I shrugged. "Sure I'll go public. I'll probably write articles about it."

I called up Harry Walker's and spoke to Carol Bruckner, the young woman who handles my speaking engagements (short, *zaftig*, intelligent, and with a ribald sense of humor) that I was being hijacked into the hospital and would have to cancel my talks till further notice. Then I called Cathleen to break the news to her and to assure her I would stay alive. And then I was forced into a taxi and taken away.

In the hospital, I was hooked up to an EKG machine, transfixed with an intravenous needle (in case of emergencies, they said), and filled full of Valium.

8

From then on, the procedure was much as it had been during my stay for the thyroidectomy five years before. I was constantly bothered by nurses, and every morning a goon squad of residents, interns, and fourth-year students would gather around me.

Naturally, I joked with them, and was suave with the young women among them, and when I finally made them laugh, I told them they were displaying heartless merriment over a suffering patient. That made them laugh even harder, and when the cardiologist, Dr. Kahn, arrived, I promptly accused them, one and all, of unethical behavior.

Kahn proved a pleasant person, so I went through some of my repertoire of doctor jokes during the intervals of his examination. I had to admit, though, that I didn't know any cardiology jokes.

"I know one," said Kahn, "which I'll tell you if you're not sensitive about your condition."

"Don't be silly," I said.

He said, "A fellow had a coronary like you, and was taken off sex, as you have been. He stayed in the hospital, as you are doing, then spent a period confined to his house, as you will be, and finally visited his doctor for an examination. The doctor was pleased with his progress, so the patient said, 'Well, doctor, can I have sex again?' The doctor considered carefully, then said, 'Well, all right—but only with your wife. I don't want you to get too excited.'"

I laughed heartily and added it to my repertoire.

Fun and games with the goon squad continued as a matter of course, and when some of them left because it was time for their rotation to other wards, they came to shake hands and say good-bye and how sorry they were to leave.

"I don't blame you," I said, "for being sorry. This seems like a fun ward."

Whereupon one of the women members, not recognizing irony, said, "Oh no, Dr. Asimov. This is a terribly depressing ward. Everyone is so downhearted and sad."

"I'm not," I said.

"Yes," said she, "and we don't understand it. We talk about it at breakfast."

(Of course, it helped me keep my spirits up when Janet came in every day to be with me, and Robyn came in on the twenty-seventh, and I was simply flooded with all kinds of well wishes.)

9

By May 28, the doctors were confident enough of my progress to take me out of the intensive-care unit and put me up in a private room. On the way out, I passed Ben Grauer, the veteran radio announcer. He had once interviewed me and, hearing I was in the unit, wanted to see me. They wheeled me over.

He had also had a coronary, a worse one than I had had, and he was lying in bed with an oxygen mask over his face. We talked for a few seconds and I was wheeled onward. Two and a half days later he was dead.

10

In my private room, I could have visitors at all hours, and they came in a steady stream: Stan and Ruth, Austin Olney, Don Laventhal and his partner, Bob Zicklin, Larry Ashmead, Cathleen Jordan, Sharon Jarvis, Chaucy and Les, Eleanor Sullivan, Jesse Shereff, Sam Moskowitz, and so on and so on.

Lester and Judy-Lynn came a couple of times and, of course, Ben Bova, who was substituting for me in several of the talks I had had to cancel[2] and who had actually, to my great indignation, tried to get them to send the checks to *me*. I had absolutely refused any such arrangement, of course.

[2] George Scithers substituted for a talk I had been scheduled to give at Brown University.

"How can you sit there, Ben," I said hotly, "in your Italian innocence and remorselessly activate my Jewish guilt by trying to refuse to accept the fees?"

"It's not Italian innocence," he said, "it's Italian superstition."

"What Italian superstition?"

"The one that says it's bad luck to profit through the misery of others."

"What are you talking about? The Mafia . . ."

"Oh well," said Ben, "it's different if you *cause* the misery."

11

Even though I wasn't hooked up to an EKG machine in my private room, I did wear little monitors that recorded my heart behavior somewhere—just in case. It meant I couldn't be *too* suave with the nurses or they'd come in to see what was wrong. And sometimes at night when I'd knock one of the leads loose as I turned in bed, an orderly would come in and manhandle me to fix it up again.

12

Paul Esserman had been worried that being in the hospital with nothing to do would drive me crazy. He consulted Janet, who said I had over a thousand pages of first draft of my autobiography that I could easily go over and revise.

"Good," said Paul. "Bring it in to him."

Then, just in case I might be nervous about having an irreplaceable manuscript taken out of the house, Janet arranged with Doubleday to have every page photocopied. Cathleen's secretary, Al Sarrantonio, took care of it personally and never let the manuscript out of his sight till it was done.

Janet then brought it in on May 27, and for the rest of my stay in the hospital, I went over the manuscript, correcting and revising to my heart's content.

Janet also brought in my mail and phone messages daily.

13

I let my beard grow while I was in the hospital and found, to my chagrin and embarrassment, that it was almost pure white. Toward the end of my stay I had the raffish look of Walter Huston in *Treasure of the Sierra Madre*.

There were some silly suggestions that I keep the beard, but I had it shaved off before leaving the hospital. White sideburns are enough.

14

I did have some fears that once people found out I had had a coronary, they might no longer be interested in asking me to do stories or articles for them, figuring I was as good as dead.

It didn't work that way. I received two orders from people who called the hospital itself to place their orders. Merrill Panitt of *TV Guide,* for instance, called me to express his condolences and then suggested that as long as I was in the hospital and had a TV set at my bed, I might as well watch some daytime television and write an article about it.

That I did, and it appeared in the October 1–7, 1977, issue of the magazine. (There was one article in which I discussed my coronary, as I had warned Paul I would.)

15

By June 8, I had finished the revision of the entire manuscript of the autobiography as far as I had gone, and after that I grew restless. Fortunately, I didn't have to remain restless long. On Friday, June 10, I left the hospital.

I was 176 pounds in weight when I got home, 7 pounds less than I weighed at the time of my first attack. I kept at my diet rigidly and by the end of July I had reached 163 and had lost 20 pounds.

16

I spent the next two weeks under house arrest. I went down to the lobby to get my mail now and then, and once, on June 15, when Robyn was leaving, after having driven to New York and stayed with us a couple of days, I actually stepped outside to watch her drive away. Except for that, the various walls of the apartment were my limit.

However, I kept working on my autobiography, on my *F & SF* essays (I didn't miss a beat there), and on other assignments.

17

The third issue of *IASFM,* Fall 1977, came out on June 16. Originally, Joel had only been prepared to subsidize three issues, but reports on the first issue were so heartening that George was going right on purchasing stories for additional issues.

The third issue had a letter column to which I added comments in reply to individual letters (another task), and it was clear from those letters that my face on each issue had outworn its welcome. I was smiling on the third issue, but it was a farewell smile. More conventional science-fiction covers were planned thereafter.

Inside the third issue, my story "Good Taste" was included.

18

Finally, on June 23, I visited Paul's office and had an electrocardiogram again, and it showed my heart was healing satisfactorily. Paul said I could resume my normal life with some discretion. I was to walk a lot, exercise, keep my weight down—and, most of all, not let myself get into a rat race of deadlines.

46

Recovery

1

On Monday, June 27, Robyn left for Europe. She was going to tour it for eight weeks with a school group and visit half a dozen countries. Mary O'Conor was to be with her.

On that same day, I finally went to Doubleday as my first business trip since the hospitalization. On July 3, we visited the Balks, and that was my first social call since the hospitalization.

I felt perfectly normal except that when I walked, especially after a meal, or under tension, I sometimes had mild epigastric distress. It meant, I suppose, that I was somewhat anginal, but not sufficiently so to prevent a normal life or to force me to take medication.

I decided, at this time, to stop work on the first draft of the autobiography and put what I had already done into final copy.

2

On July 8, we left the city for the first time since the hospitalization. It was to take care of a seminar at the Institute of Man and Science for the sixth year in a row. The strain would not be heavy, however. Everyone was careful to avoid loading me too heavily, and Janet accompanied me on constant walks.

This year, instead of one seminar, there were two in succession, the first to be chaired by Ben Bova and the second by me. Apparently, however, the splitup did not work out. The attendance shrank and the total of those attending both did not equal the number attending a single seminar in past years.

Terri Rapoport, who was leaving the institute to return to school, was quite depressed over this and, indeed, it did seem that the law of diminishing returns had set in. There was a serious question as to whether the sixth annual seminar ought not be the last.

While at the institute, I wrote my thirtieth Black Widowers story, "The Next Day." Fred Dannay accepted it and slated it for 1978 publication. I was now halfway toward a third Black Widowers collection.

3

Just before we left for home on July 14, we heard that there had been an all-night blackout in New York City, with riots and looting in many sections. For a while we hesitated, wondering if we ought not stay at a motel, since, if the power was off, we might arrive at Park Ten's lobby, but we could not get to the top floor.

A call to New York, however, proved that the power was back on at Park Ten, and we returned.

4

If we had had an unusually cold January, we now had an unusually hot July.

Fawcett Publications had raffled off a dinner with me on a Channel 13 auction, and I had postponed the original date because of the coronary and had finally settled on July 19. When that day came, the temperature outside went to 102.

Nevertheless the date was kept. It was at the beautiful and air-conditioned restaurant at the top of the World Trade Center (which we now visited for the first time), and we sat looking down upon the world as though we were in an airplane. To be sure, circumstance deprived us of much of a feeling of power. What if, in all this heat, the power should fail again? Would we be stranded in the skyscraper airplane?

Well, the couple who had bid the winning amount were each young, attractive, and intelligent, the food was good, and Greg Mowery of Fawcett publicity handled everything flawlessly. And the power remained firmly in place.

5

Three young women whom I had met at "Star Trek" conventions were anxious to take me to see Star Wars as a coronary-recovery present.[1] Janet, who was pointedly not included in the invitation, good-naturedly said I ought to go, and I set July 21 as the day.

Here my luck was even worse, however, for on July 21, the temperature went to 104, the second hottest day in the New York Weather Bureau's history. Nevertheless, we went. The theater was air condi-

---

[1] I had been invited to attend a preview, but that had been just before my hospitalization, and I hadn't felt well enough to go.

tioned, after all; I was surrounded by youthful pulchritude; and the movie was entertaining.

Afterward, we all had dinner at Sardi's, and except for my frustration at finding that the impecunious young women wouldn't allow me to pick up the tab for the evening, all went perfectly.

6

'On July 26, I obtained the August 1977 *Reader's Digest*, which had the Collier interview in it. It was entitled, "Asimov, the Human Writing Machine," and again, as in the case of the *People* interview, only kind things were said about me. In addition, *Reader's Digest* reprinted the *Time* essay I had written on a low-energy America.

While the glow of this still lingered, the Walkers asked me to drop by on July 29. *The Collapsing Universe* had done extremely well in every respect, and Sam and Beth Walker and Dick Winslow all joined me in a champagne toast on the balcony overlooking Fifth Avenue, while I was handed a check that was higher than any other check I had ever received that wasn't from Doubleday.

7

John and Maureen Jeppson arrived in New York on July 31, and with them were their children, Patti and Johnny. It was my first chance to meet the niece and nephew I had gained when I married Janet. They were attractive, pleasant youngsters, and I was delighted with them.

8

By August 3, I had five hundred pages of autobiography manuscript in final form, and since I was soon to be heading away on another trip, I wanted them out of the house. I took it in to Doubleday for safekeeping and handed in two boxes, one containing the original and one a carbon, to Cathleen.

"Guard them with your life, Cathleen," I said.

"Absolutely," she said. And at that very moment, whistles began to blow outside her office door. It was, we all thought, a fire drill.

I accompanied her down the stairs to the landing where we usually waited for the all-clear (I had been involved in fire drills before), but we were told to keep on walking. It was not a fire drill but a bomb scare (one of a whole group of them in midtown Manhattan on that day), and the building was being evacuated. I tried to go back for my manuscript, but nobody would let me.

Down and down we went. Cathleen made me stop every fifth floor and rest, although I didn't want to. Pat LoBrutto, a young man who had replaced Sharon Jarvis as science-fiction editor when the latter left for greener fields, helped Cathleen bully me.

I kept saying, "I don't want you two to hang around. Go on ahead. After all, if it's a real bomb and you linger with me you may be trapped in the rubble along with me."

They wouldn't trust me, however, to go through the ordeal properly and insisted on supervising my downward climb. It was forty-two stories altogether.

When we were finally out on the street, everyone else was there too, of course. It was Sam Vaughan's birthday and I said to him, "Sam, arranging this celebration of your birthday is nice, but you shouldn't have bothered. I've just brought in the first box of my autobiography, and now it's up there being looted."

"How much have you brought in?" he asked.

"Five hundred pages," I said.

"Then why worry? That's only the first two chapters, right?"

How's that for sympathy?

Meanwhile, Cathleen said firmly that I was to go straight to the doctor for an examination. Though the streets were a madhouse of policemen and emergency vehicles, she ran out and dragged back a taxi by the scruff of its neck. I had no choice but to go.

I caught Howard Gorfinkel at his lunch, and he ran the EKG while still chewing.

"Your EKG," he said, "looks better than last week's. Maybe you should walk down forty-two flights every day."

Never mind! Once was enough. My calf muscles were sore for three days, and everyone at Doubleday was limping. One young woman was on crutches for a while.

9

On August 6, 1977, Janet was fifty-one years old, and we were getting ready to board the QE2 again. What we were to do was to make the transatlantic crossing to Southampton, wait through the one-day layover, and then make the return trip. I was to give two talks each way.

As we were getting ready, Otto Penzler, one of the two greatest mystery buffs in the nation (his friend Chris Steinbrenner was the other, and we had met both at Mystery Writers' of America functions and at the "Dead of Winter" shindig a half year before), had come up with an idea. He wanted me to write a limerick (a clean one) for each of the fifty-six Sherlock Holmes short stories and four Sherlock Holmes novels in order of publication. He ran a small publishing firm, Mysterious Press, which would then put out the book in time for the next Baker Street Irregulars banquet.

I was delighted because it would be just the thing to keep me busy on the cruise and, to make it easier for me, Otto gave me a book that contained commentary on each of the sixty stories in order of publication. These could jog my memory as to the contents.

10

We got on the *QE2* on August 8 and I argued them into letting me have a typewriter so that I could type my limericks after I had constructed them. By the time we arrived in Southampton on the evening of August 13, I was better than half done with my limericks.

It had originally been our notion that we could stay on the *QE2* while it laid over at Southampton, but that proved impossible since the ship was literally shut down on that day.

At 9:00 A.M. on Sunday, August 14, therefore, we were at the Polygon Hotel in Southampton and were on our own.

It turned out well. We took a taxi to nearby Winchester and enjoyed the cathedral and saw the large statue of King Alfred (of which I had a small replica given me by Alfred University when I received my degree of Doctor of Letters six years before).

Then we went to Portsmouth, where we toured through Horatio Nelson's old flagship, the *Victory*, and were horrified at the low ceilings below-decks and, worse yet, at the tales of floggings. (Janet, of course, promptly fell in love with Nelson, who had been no taller than Harlan Ellison, apparently.)

Back to Southampton, then, where I underwent several interviews, took a nap, had an excellent dinner, and then went on a walk through neighborhood parks—clean, quiet, well-laid-out. On the whole, the twenty-four hours in England were the best part of the trip—something we had certainly not anticipated.

We were back on the *QE2* on the morning of the fifteenth, and the return trip was even pleasanter than the trip coming. Movie comedian Dom DeLuise was onboard ship and had the cabin right next to ours, though we didn't see much of each other. Lisa Drew, a Doubleday editor, gave two talks, which I attended and admired.

As for myself, I finished my sixty Sherlockian limericks on August 16, and was sorry that Conan Doyle had not written more Holmes stories.

We were home on August 20 (David's twenty-sixth birthday), and I promptly put all the limericks into final copy. Otto Penzler arrived the next day to pick them up. I wanted to call them *Polmes for Holmes* but Otto winced visibly at the suggestion and eventually insisted on *Asimov's Sherlockian Limericks*.

11

The fourth issue of *IASFM* had been published while I was off on the *QE2*. It was the Winter 1977 issue and was the first to have a traditional science-fiction scene on the cover, featuring an unearthly flying reptile. My face had not disappeared altogether, however. Small, but clear, it was in the "o" of "Asimov" in the title.

This issue contained "The Missing Item," my Black Widowers story.

12

A sadder note was struck by two deaths during my trip.

One was that of a Trap Door Spiders colleague, Edgar Lawrence, who had first invited me to the Baker Street Irregulars as his guest, and who had not survived to see my Sherlockian book, which had, in a way, become possible through my growing interest in such things through the BSI.

The other was that of Ray Palmer on August 15, 1977, at the age of sixty-seven. It had been Palmer who had sent me my first check for sixty-four dollars for "Marooned Off Vesta" thirty-nine years before. In all the time that had elapsed since, I had never met him face to face.

13

Robyn called me from London on the afternoon of August 22. She had completed her eight-week tour of Europe and had cathedrals and museums running out of her ears. Right now, she was dreadfully anxious to get back to the United States, but there was difficulty in getting a plane off the ground because of job actions at London's airport. She seemed quite good-humored about it.

She called me a second time in the evening, by which time she had been sitting up, quite uncomfortably, all night long at the airport—and there was still no sign of their plane. She was distinctly edgy and I did my best to soothe her.

At 8:15 A.M. on the twenty-third, she called a third time, and now she was hysterical. She wanted me to call the airport and "lean on them." I didn't see what good that could possibly do, but I had to give her the feeling she was doing something.

"Give me the number, Robyn," I said, "and I'll see what I can do."

She was halfway through her instructions when I heard a loud-speaker in the distance. Robyn called out excitedly, "That's my plane," and hung up.

At 6:15 P.M. she called from Kennedy Airport and at 11:00 P.M. she called from her dormitory room in Boston. She was home, and I heaved an enormous sigh of relief. I hadn't had to put my power to the test by calling London's airport and leaning on them. I did not have to destroy a young woman's faith in the omnipotence of good old Dad.

14

F. Marrott Sinex retired from his post as head of the Biochemistry Department at the med school on August 31, 1977, having served twenty years. Our initial unpleasantness was long forgotten.

Succeeding to the post and, therefore, my new boss in a way, was Carl Franzblau, whom I remembered as a young and capable instructor. I was pleased.

15

On August 30, I saw Jerome Agel, an entrepreneur who managed books for busy people who did not want to do all the work involved but who did not mind putting their name on as author.

What he wanted to do was to produce a book called *Isaac Asimov's Book of Facts*. The facts were to be culled by researchers who would use my books, among others, as sources.

I said that I would not consent to be listed as author of a book I did not prepare, but if the "fantastic facts" were sent to me and if I were allowed to accept, rewrite, and reject—and add some of my own —then I would be willing to have the book appear as "edited by Isaac Asimov."

We agreed on that.

16

On September 1, I took in the second batch of five hundred pages of final copy of my autobiography to Cathleen, and wondered wistfully what was happening in Miami Beach.

The thirty-fifth World Science Fiction convention was getting under way there and, considering my coronary, I had not thought it wise to repeat the arduous round-trip train journey.

But then, on September 4, Barbara Bova called from Miami to tell me that "The Bicentennial Man" had won the Hugo as best novelette of the year. It was the only story which, in 1977, took both the Nebula and the Hugo.

17

Larry Ashmead, having been at Simon and Schuster for twenty-two months, suddenly made another change and, as of September 1, 1977, became executive editor at Lippincott. He was working under Ed Burlingame now, who had edited my *Understanding Physics* and *The Universe*.

Apparently, though, Simon and Schuster did not want him to take my *A Choice of Catastrophes* along with him. Since I had refused to accept an advance until such time as I could give written notice that I had begun the book, I had the option of not doing it at all, if I couldn't do it for Larry.

18

My autobiography was taking virtually all my time. By early September I had been working on it for six months, leaving almost everything else to one side, except for various short pieces that had to be done.

On September 13, though, I desisted long enough to begin *How Did We Find Out About Earthquakes?*, my twelfth in the series for Walker. I delivered it on the twenty-sixth.

19

On September 16, Lester and I cohosted a Trap Door Spiders dinner, and Paul Esserman was my guest. Paul was very impressed with the

Spiders and they were equally impressed with him. Naturally, I introduced him as the man who had misdiagnosed my coronary, but everyone took that in good part, even (I was relieved to see) Paul.

20

On September 20, I undertook my first strictly-business speaking
engagement since my hospitalization. The arrangement was, however,
that I be taken there and back by limousine. It was also the first trip
out of the city alone since my hospitalization.

That evening I had dinner with the Bovas at Barbara's place in
West Hartford. (She maintained a house there while Ben had an apartment in Manhattan, and they more or less alternated weekends at the
two places.)

I gave my talk on the morning of September 21, my first *paid* talk
in four months, and I was relieved to find I could still do it.

21

On September 28 and 29 I made a swing through eastern Pennsylvania, speaking at Reading and at Chester. That went well, but we still
had occasional long trips to make—long trips that had been scheduled
prior to my coronary. One of them was for a talk at James Madison
University in Harrisonburg, Virginia, and Janet approached that one
with considerable trepidation.

We left on October 5, and got to Harrisonburg before noon on
the next day. There was no trouble at all, though Janet insisted on
doing most of the driving.

The trip back was excellent. We stopped off at the Luray Caverns,
which, nearly a decade before, I had visited with Gertrude and the children. After that it was back along the Skyline Drive. We were home
on the eighth, quite satisfied with the trip.

22

There was a voice from the past on October 10, when Charles D.
Hornig, who had bought such early stories of mine as "Ring Around
the Sun" and "Magnificent Possession," dropped by.

He had read *The Early Asimov*, in which I said I had never met
him, and he thought it was time to correct that. Rather embarrassed, I
explained that my closer readings of my diaries for the autobiography
had revealed that I had indeed met him once, thirty-eight years ago. I
agreed it was high time for a second meeting, though.

23

I discovered on October 11 that Diana Jones had resigned as editor of *American Way*. In her place was Walt Damtoft, a newcomer. Of the four employees of the magazine when I first started my articles three years before, only one, Priscilla Wilson, was left.

24

A third box of five hundred manuscript pages of final copy of my autobiography was taken in to Cathleen on October 19, and I swore to her that there would be only one more box.

25

Naturally, I had let John Ciardi know that I, too, was a published poet, having produced several volumes of verse. They were limericks, to be sure, but verse, nevertheless.

As I suspected, Ciardi had not been able to resist the challenge, and eventually I received Xerox copies of 144 limericks that he had constructed and was going to publish with W. W. Norton under the title *A Gross of Limericks*. Since his limericks were as lecherous as mine, the play on "gross" is obvious.

Ciardi suggested I might want to contribute another gross for the same book (the title would then be *Limericks: Too Gross*), and I was willing. About half a year earlier, in fact, I had begun to put together my fourth volume of limericks, but this had been overtaken and sent into suspended animation by my autobiography.

I pulled them out on October 20 and retyped them (without Introduction or commentaries), then added some I had intended for a fifth volume and constructed those that were still lacking. In doing so, I produced one of my all-time favorites as the 144th and last limerick of the group. I entitled it *John Ciardi and I* (I had titles for all mine, although Ciardi lacked titles for his), and this is how it went:

> *There is something about satyriasis*
> *That arouses psychiatrists' biases,*
> *But we're both of us pleased*
> *We're in this way diseased*
> *As the damsel who's waiting to try us is.*

I took in my batch of limericks to Eric Swenson of W. W. Norton on the twenty-fourth.

26

On October 31, Janet and I drove the car westward in leisurely fashion, and by the next day had reached Pittsburgh. (This was another precoronary engagement.)

On the morning of November 2, I spoke at a town hall meeting and experienced, to my surprise, a new low in introductions. I thought I had encountered all possible kinds of bad introductions, but I was wrong.

The woman introducing me began by directing latecomers to the front, where seats were still to be found. "There are seats in the front," she intoned over and over, waving her arms to show them. Then, having played the inappropriate role of usher, she began a routinely uninspired introduction.

At its conclusion, the audience broke into the conventional applause and the introducer *stepped on it*. She waved them quiet and began her broken-record repetition of "There are seats in the front. There are seats in the front."

I had to rise to a cold and silent audience, and my impulse was to render the introducer cold and silent by a prolonged and tight grip on her throat, but I controlled myself and went into my talk. It took me quite a while to warm up, and to warm the audience.

We then drove sixty miles eastward to a little town named Loretto, where I spoke at St. Catherine's College with much greater success. We were home on the evening of November 3.

27

The furor aroused by *Star Wars* was having a favorable effect on the prospects for movie science fiction generally. On November 4, I found that my book *The End of Eternity* had been optioned for the movies.

To balance that, however, *The Caves of Steel* option had been dropped after four years. I suspect that someone else will option it, with perhaps better results, in the future.

28

On November 9, Janet and I drove to the Concord Hotel, my first visit there since the time, eight years before, when I used it as the occasion to begin *Isaac Asimov's Treasury of Humor*. We had assigned to

us a rather unbelievable room designed in antique style, and there was a
pleasant dinner in which Janet sat next to Clifton Fadiman, who had
once been famous as the interlocutor of "Information Please."

The next morning I spoke to the New York State Reading Association and we drove home.

29

We were on the road again on November 11, however, and traveled to a western suburb of Philadelphia in order to help celebrate
Sprague de Camp's seventieth birthday (which was, in actual fact, not
due for two weeks). A number of the Spiders were there, including Lin
Carter and John Clark, and, although it was formal and I was compelled to wear a tuxedo, we had a good time.

Catherine was, of course, also approaching seventy, but it came as
no surprise to me that both she and Sprague were the least seventy-
looking seventy-year-olds anyone had ever seen.

30

David had visited New York with a friend, on impulse, and on November 19 dropped in on us without warning. He and I had dinner together. He had been experimenting with facial hair for years, and this
time he had a beard.

31

On November 24, Thanksgiving, Janet and I drove to Boston and
had a very successful dinner with Robyn at a restaurant near our motel.

My reason for being there was to attend a Mensa convention.
Gloria Saltzberg (who had first introduced me to Mensa fifteen years
before) was being honored on the twenty-fifth with a plaque as the
founder of the Boston area Mensa group, and I was to give it to her
with appropriate comments.

She was fifty years old now and, it seemed to me, not really in the
best of health, but she was very touched at the ceremony and I was very
pleased to have been able to take part in it.

Of course, Robyn joined us each day of my stay, and the climax of
that came on the twenty-sixth, when she and I went out to Quincy
Market, a new open-air emporium that had been established near Boston's new City Hall and that was full of *outré* stores and eating places.

That night, I watched three short "stag" films one of the Mensa group showed. They were the first such films I had ever seen, and in about three minutes I found my curiosity sated.

32

November 30 was our fourth wedding anniversary, and for the first time we were not able to celebrate it with the Balks, since Al was forced to be out of town on business. We had dinner with Bart Behr and his companion, Betty Batty, instead.

33

On December 2, Janet and I drove to Storrs, Connecticut, on the last of the precoronary engagements for the year. I spoke at the University of Connecticut and received a standing ovation.

34

On December 8, I took in more final copy of my autobiography, nearly three hundred pages of it, bringing the total to five hundred thousand words, though I feverishly explained that I was almost done.

Tom Sloane, who had edited *Asimov's Biographical Encyclopedia of Science and Technology*, had retired, and Cathleen had taken over that portion of my Doubleday output.

35

On December 13, I did something I generally try to avoid. I went to New York University to speak to a mystery writing class. I approached the task in a fever of uncertainty as to what I could possibly say, but it proved to be entirely question-and-answer and I was expected to talk only about myself (which, after all, as anyone reading this book can see, is my favorite topic). I ended up spending three enjoyable hours with the group.

36

For the first time I was to give a commencement address at some time other than in May or June. The University of Maryland holds a full commencement ceremony in December.

On December 18, Janet and I took the train to suburban Washington and there Izzy Adler met us. We had an excellent Chinese dinner with him and Annie, and the next morning, he drove us into Washington itself, where Janet and I spent several hours at the National Air and Space Museum.

Who would have thought, in 1938, when I began to sell science fiction, that in less than forty years I would be looking at exhibits of spacesuits and spaceships—*real* ones.

The most impressive thing, though, was a half-hour motion picture, *To Fly*, shown on a fifty-foot screen. It had views taken from the air, as though from a balloon, glider, or early airplane, that were so effective as to tie this acrophobe's intestines into knots.

On the evening of the nineteenth, I attended the commencement, delivered my talk, and got one more honorary Doctor of Science.

37

The fifth issue of *IASFM* had by now reached the stands. The magazine was now a bimonthly, and the fifth issue was dated January–February 1978. Joel was very elated at the progress of the magazine. Apparently, its sales and subscriptions were satisfactory, and he was talking of going on a monthly basis and of trying out a sister magazine aimed at younger readers.

On December 20, there was a reception at the Players' Club, hosted by Joel, for all the employees of Davis Publications. Janet and I were there, and I gave a short talk.

Afterward, Janet and I had dinner with the Davises and the Dannays.

38

Robyn arrived on December 24 to spend Christmas with us, and she and I went for a Christmas Eve walk around Central Park, down Fifth Avenue, and to Rockefeller Center to enjoy the unusual mildness of the day and to observe the Christmas hullabaloo.

On Christmas Day itself, the three of us drove to Chaucy's, where for the first time Robyn could join in the feast. Since Bruce and young Leslie were there, Robyn met them for the first time, too.

On the twenty-seventh, we had our belated anniversary dinner with the Balks, and it was the most elaborate one yet. Not only was Robyn there but the two Balk daughters, Laraine and Diane, as well. In addition, Al Balk's father, aged seventy-six, was there, and the most remarkable thing about him was that he was not an orphan. He had a mother (Al's grandmother) who was still alive and who had only a few months before she celebrated her hundredth birthday. We had a private room and it was a very happy dinner.

39

Robyn did not leave till the morning of the twenty-ninth, so that she was still in New York on the evening of the twenty-eighth, when Otto Penzler arrived with advance copies of *Asimov's Sherlockian Limericks*. This meant that 1977 ended with ten books published:

182. *The Collapsing Universe* (Walker)
183. *Asimov on Numbers* (Doubleday)
184. *How Did We Find Out About Outer Space?* (Walker)
185. *Still More Lecherous Limericks* (Walker)
186. *The Hugo Winners, Volume III* (Doubleday)
187. *The Beginning and the End* (Doubleday)
188. *Mars, the Red Planet* (Lothrop, Lee & Shepard)
189. *The Golden Door* (Houghton Mifflin)
190. *The Key Word and Other Mysteries* (Walker)
191. *Asimov's Sherlockian Limericks* (Mysterious)

The number of books published in 1977 was fewer than in any year since 1971, but that did not bother me, for my coronary year was ending on a high note. Not only had I survived, not only was I feeling well and entirely recovered, but also *I, Robot*, after having remained under movie option for eight years, was finally bought, and none other than Harlan Ellison had been engaged to do the screenplay.

And today, December 31, 1977, at 9:45 A.M., I have completed my autobiography.

except that—

Finishing a book is not quite the same as having it published.

In the first place, when I was done with the autobiography, it turned out to be 640,000 words long and Cathleen said it would have to be done in two volumes.

I said, with what I thought was unanswerable logic, "But, Cathleen, William Shirer's *Rise and Fall of the Third Reich* was 650,000 words long, according to my careful word count, and *that's* in one volume."

Cathleen said, patiently, "Now, Isaac!"

That's all she said, but two volumes it was. The first volume, *In Memory Yet Green*, with a title taken from the first phrase in the quatrain that appears at the start of each volume, took a little over a year to publish, and appeared on March 2, 1979. This second volume, which you are now holding, *In Joy Still Felt*, from the second phrase, also took a little over a year to do. Right now I am working on the galleys of that second volume and it is November 4, 1979.

It is my intention, if I live to the end of the century or thereabouts, to do a third and (I suppose) final volume to be called *The Scenes of Life*, from the third phrase of the quatrain. This will start with January 1, 1978, and continue.

However, the vicissitudes of life are uncertain, and I may not get the chance to do that third volume, so while I have you here, I suppose I might as well just say a few words about what has happened since December 31, 1977.

First, I'll bring the book count up to date.

In 1978, I had only seven books, the smallest number since 1970. The responsibility, of course, lay with this autobiography which consumed the time in which I might have written a number of ordinary-sized books. The seven are:

192. *One Hundred Science Fiction Short Short Stories* (Doubleday)
193. *Quasar, Quasar, Burning Bright* (Doubleday)
194. *How Did We Find Out About Earthquakes?* (Walker)
195. *Animals of the Bible* (Doubleday)
196. *Life and Time* (Doubleday)
197. *Limericks: Too Gross* (Norton)
198. *How Did We Find Out About Black Holes?* (Walker)

In 1979, book production was back to its usual pace (to my considerable relief) and in the first ten months of that year, eleven books were published. They are:

199. *Saturn and Beyond* (Lothrop, Lee & Shepard)
200. { *In Memory Yet Green* (Doubleday)
{ *Opus 200* (Houghton Mifflin)
202. *Isaac Asimov Presents the Great SF Stories, 1: 1939* (DAW)
203. *Extraterrestrial Civilizations* (Crown)
204. *How Did We Find Out About Our Human Roots?* (Walker)
205. *Isaac Asimov Presents the Great SF Stories, 2: 1940* (DAW)
206. *The Road to Infinity* (Doubleday)
207. *A Choice of Catastrophes* (Simon & Schuster)
208. *The Science Fictional Solar System* (Harper & Row)
209. *The Thirteen Crimes of Science Fiction* (Doubleday)

I can't be certain about the order of books between now and the publication of *In Joy Still Felt*, but here is my guess:

The catalog of books included at the end of *In Memory Yet Green* is repeated at the end of this book and is extended to include the fourteen books that have appeared since.

Notice that there is no book #201. Both Doubleday and Houghton Mifflin wanted my 200th book and there was no way I could disappoint either one. As soon as I finished my autobiography, I began *Opus 200* for Houghton Mifflin (which did for my second hundred books what *Opus 100* did for my first hundred).

I broke the news to each publisher as late in the game as I dared and assured each that the existence of two 200th books would amuse the public, and I was right. It was that, more than anything else, that got me some very nice attention in *Time*, in the New York *Times*, and in many other places.

Fortunately, both publishers decided to trust me in this. They arranged to publish the two books simultaneously and then co-sponsored a delightful joint-publication-day party. (And both books, thank goodness, did very nicely as far as sales were concerned.)

In other matters, I am glad that there are no tragedies to report.

Robyn completed her college work in May 1978, and at her commencement I cheered and yelled from the spectator stands. I couldn't help having the selfish thought that if she hadn't lost that freshman year at Windham because of her illness, she would have graduated in May 1977 and my coronary would have prevented me from attending.

After taking a year off, she enrolled in Boston University to do graduate work of a kind that will, in time, make a psychiatric social worker of her.

As for me—well, I overcame my dislike of travel long enough to make a trip to California in December 1978 (by train, both ways), and to Paris in September 1979 (by ship and train both ways).

Janet wrote an article on the trip to California and placed it with the New York *Times* without difficulty. It appeared under the headline "Crossing the Continent with a Man Who Won't Fly" and was very well received. People who recognized me in the street stopped *me* to tell me how much they liked *her* article. And her second science-fiction novel, *The Last Immortal*, is being published by Houghton Mifflin at just about the time this book is coming out.

One final note. In 1979, Boston University School of Medicine, of its own accord, and entirely without prompting from me, finally promoted me to the rank of full professor. After twenty-four years, I no longer need to include that tiresome word "Associate."

I am now *Professor of Biochemistry*.

TO BE CONTINUED EVENTUALLY

Catalog of Books
Isaac Asimov

Note: The numbers preceding the titles of books refer to the order in which they were published.

PART I—FICTION

A SCIENCE-FICTION NOVELS

1. *Pebble in the Sky* Doubleday, 1950
3. *The Stars, like Dust—* Doubleday, 1951
4. *Foundation* Gnome (Doubleday), 1951
5. *David Starr: Space Ranger* Doubleday, 1952
6. *Foundation and Empire* Gnome (Doubleday), 1952
7. *The Currents of Space* Doubleday, 1952
9. *Second Foundation* Gnome (Doubleday), 1951
10. *Lucky Starr and the Pirates of the Asteroids* Doubleday, 1953
11. *The Caves of Steel* Doubleday, 1954
12. *Lucky Starr and the Oceans of Venus* Doubleday, 1954
15. *The End of Eternity* Doubleday, 1955
17. *Lucky Starr and the Big Sun of Mercury* Doubleday, 1956
20. *The Naked Sun* Doubleday, 1957
21. *Lucky Starr and the Moons of Jupiter* Doubleday, 1957
26. *Lucky Starr and the Rings of Saturn* Doubleday, 1958
67. *Fantastic Voyage* Houghton Mifflin, 1966
121. *The Gods Themselves* Doubleday, 1972

B MYSTERY NOVELS

28. *The Death Dealers* Avon, 1958
172. *Murder at the ABA* Doubleday, 1976

C SCIENCE-FICTION SHORT STORIES AND SHORT-STORY COLLECTIONS

2. *I, Robot* Gnome (Doubleday), 1950
14. *The Martian Way and Other Stories* Doubleday, 1955

23. *Earth Is Room Enough* Doubleday, 1957
29. *Nine Tomorrows* Doubleday, 1959
60. *The Rest of the Robots* Doubleday, 1964
82. *Through a Glass, Clearly* New English Library, 1967
87. *Asimov's Mysteries* Doubleday, 1968
98. *Nightfall and Other Stories* Doubleday, 1969
113. *The Best New Thing** World Publishing, 1971
125. *The Early Asimov* Doubleday, 1972
146. *The Best of Isaac Asimov* Sphere, 1973
150. *Have You Seen These?* NESRAA, 1974
164. *Buy Jupiter and Other Stories* Doubleday, 1975
167. *The Heavenly Host* Walker, 1975
170. *"The Dream," "Benjamin's Dream," and "Benjamin's Bicen-tennial Blast"* Private print., 1976
174. *Good Taste* Apocalypse, 1976
176. *The Bicentennial Man and Other Stories* Doubleday, 1976

D   MYSTERY SHORT-STORY COLLECTIONS

155. *Tales of the Black Widowers* Doubleday, 1974
178. *More Tales of the Black Widowers* Doubleday, 1976
190. *The Key Word and Other Mysteries** Walker, 1977
212. *Casebook of the Black Widowers* Doubleday, 1980

E   SCIENCE-FICTION ANTHOLOGIES (EDITED BY ISAAC ASIMOV)

47. *The Hugo Winners* Doubleday, 1962
52. *Fifty Short Science-fiction Tales* (with Groff Conklin) Col-lier, 1963
76. *Tomorrow's Children* Doubleday, 1966
110. *Where Do We Go From Here?* Doubleday, 1971
115. *The Hugo Winners*, Volume II Doubleday, 1971
147. *Nebula Award Stories Eight* Harper, 1973
151. *Before the Golden Age* Doubleday, 1974
186. *The Hugo Winners*, Volume III Doubleday, 1977
192. *One Hundred Great Science-fiction Short-short Stories* (with Martin Harry Greenberg and Joseph D. Olander) Doubleday, 1978
202. *Isaac Asimov Presents the Great SF Stories, 1: 1939* (with Martin Harry Greenberg) DAW Books, 1979
205. *Isaac Asimov Presents the Great SF Stories, 2: 1940* (with Martin Harry Greenberg) DAW Books, 1979

208. *The Science Fictional Solar System* (with Martin Harry Greenberg and Charles G. Waugh) Harper & Row, 1979
209. *The Thirteen Crimes of Science Fiction* (with Martin Harry Greenberg and Charles G. Waugh) Doubleday, 1979
213. *Microcosmic Tales* (with Martin Harry Greenberg and Joseph D. Olander) Taplinger, 1980
214. *Isaac Asimov Presents the Great SF Stories, 3: 1941* (with Martin Harry Greenberg) DAW Books, 1980

PART II—NONFICTION

A GENERAL SCIENCE

31. *Words of Science* Houghton Mifflin, 1959
36. *Breakthroughs in Science** Houghton Mifflin, 1960
39. *The Intelligent Man's Guide to Science* Basic Books, 1960
61. *Asimov's Biographical Encyclopedia of Science and Technology* Doubleday, 1964
65. *The New Intelligent Man's Guide to Science* Basic Books, 1965
97. *Twentieth Century Discovery* Doubleday, 1969
102. *Great Ideas of Science** Houghton Mifflin, 1969
118. *Asimov's Biographical Encyclopedia of Science and Technology* (Revised Edition) Doubleday, 1972
120. *Asimov's Guide to Science* Basic Books, 1972
122. *More Words of Science* Houghton Mifflin, 1972
128. *Ginn Science Program—Intermediate Level A** Ginn, 1972
129. *Ginn Science Program—Intermediate Level C** Ginn, 1972
132. *Ginn Science Program—Intermediate Level B** Ginn, 1972
140. *Ginn Science Program—Advanced Level A* Ginn, 1973
141. *Ginn Science Program—Advanced Level B* Ginn, 1973
143. *Please Explain* Houghton Mifflin, 1973
207. *A Choice of Catastrophes* Simon & Schuster, 1979

B MATHEMATICS

32. *Realm of Numbers* Houghton Mifflin, 1959
35. *Realm of Measure* Houghton Mifflin, 1960
42. *Realm of Algebra* Houghton Mifflin, 1961
57. *Quick and Easy Math* Houghton Mifflin, 1964
66. *An Easy Introduction to the Slide Rule* Houghton Mifflin, 1965
142. *How Did We Find Out About Numbers?** Walker, 1973

C ASTRONOMY

D EARTH SCIENCES

E   CHEMISTRY AND BIOCHEMISTRY

    8. *Biochemistry and Human Metabolism* Williams & Wilkins, 1952

   13. *The Chemicals of Life* Abelard-Schuman, 1954

   18. *Chemistry and Human Health* McGraw-Hill, 1956

   22. *Building Blocks of the Universe* Abelard-Schuman, 1957

   25. *The World of Carbon* Abelard-Schuman, 1958

   27. *The World of Nitrogen* Abelard-Schuman, 1958

   43. *Life and Energy* Doubleday, 1962

   48. *The Search for the Elements* Basic Books, 1962

   50. *The Genetic Code* Orion Press, 1963

   62. *A Short History of Chemistry* Doubleday, 1965

   68. *The Noble Gases* Basic Books, 1966

   75. *The Genetic Effects of Radiation* (with Theodosius Dobzhansky) AEC, 1966

   95. *Photosynthesis* Basic Books, 1969

  158. *How Did We Find Out About Vitamins?** Walker, 1974

F   PHYSICS

   19. *Inside the Atom* Abelard-Schuman, 1956

   69. *Inside the Atom* (Revised Edition) Abelard-Schuman, 1966

   70. *The Neutrino* Doubleday, 1966

   72. *Understanding Physics*, Volume I Walker, 1966

   73. *Understanding Physics*, Volume II Walker, 1966

   74. *Understanding Physics*, Volume III Walker, 1966

  108. *Light** Follett, 1970

  123. *Electricity and Man* AEC, 1972

  131. *Worlds Within Worlds* AEC, 1972

  136. *How Did We Find Out About Electricity?** Walker, 1973

  169. *How Did We Find Out About Energy?** Walker, 1975

  173. *How Did We Find Out About Atoms?** Walker, 1976

  180. *How Did We Find Out About Nuclear Power?** Walker, 1976

G   BIOLOGY

   16. *Races and People* (with William C. Boyd) Abelard-Schuman, 1955

   33. *The Living River* Abelard-Schuman, 1960

   38. *The Wellsprings of Life* Abelard-Schuman, 1960

   51. *The Human Body* Houghton Mifflin, 1963

H   SCIENCE ESSAY COLLECTIONS

I   HISTORY

91. *The Near East* Houghton Mifflin, 1968
92. *The Dark Ages* Houghton Mifflin, 1968
94. *Words from History* Houghton Mifflin, 1968
96. *The Shaping of England* Houghton Mifflin, 1969
106. *Constantinople* Houghton Mifflin, 1970
116. *The Land of Canaan* Houghton Mifflin, 1971
126. *The Shaping of France* Houghton Mifflin, 1972
137. *The Shaping of North America* Houghton Mifflin, 1973
149. *The Birth of the United States* Houghton Mifflin, 1974
156. *Earth: Our Crowded Spaceship* John Day, 1974
161. *Our Federal Union* Houghton Mifflin, 1975
189. *The Golden Door* Houghton Mifflin, 1977

J THE BIBLE

44. *Words in Genesis* Houghton Mifflin, 1962
49. *Words from the Exodus* Houghton Mifflin, 1963
93. *Asimov's Guide to the Bible,* Volume I Doubleday, 1968
99. *Asimov's Guide to the Bible,* Volume II Doubleday, 1969
127. *The Story of Ruth* Doubleday, 1972
195. *Animals in the Bible** Doubleday, 1978

K LITERATURE

41. *Words from the Myths* Houghton Mifflin, 1961
104. *Asimov's Guide to Shakespeare,* Volume I Doubleday, 1970
105. *Asimov's Guide to Shakespeare,* Volume II Doubleday, 1970
130. *Asimov's Annotated Don Juan* Doubleday, 1972
154. *Asimov's Annotated Paradise Lost* Doubleday, 1974
181. *Familiar Poems, Annotated* Doubleday, 1977
191. *Asimov's Sherlockian Limericks* Mysterious Press, 1977

L HUMOR AND SATIRE

112. *The Sensuous Dirty Old Man* Walker, 1971
114. *Isaac Asimov's Treasury of Humor* Houghton Mifflin, 1971
166. *Lecherous Limericks* Walker, 1975
177. *More Lecherous Limericks* Walker, 1976
185. *Still More Lecherous Limericks* Walker, 1977
197. *Limericks: Too Gross* (with John Ciardi) Norton, 1978

M   MISCELLANEOUS

   100. *Opus 100* Houghton Mifflin, 1969
   200. *Opus 200* Houghton Mifflin, 1979**
   210. *Isaac Asimov's Book of Facts* Grosset & Dunlap, 1979

N   AUTOBIOGRAPHY

   200. *In Memory Yet Green* Doubleday, 1979**
   214. *In Joy Still Felt* Doubleday, 1980

* for children
** tie for 200th place

Title Index

*Italicized items are published books

Name Index